Offender Supervision

PI
ite
Yc
03

Offender Supervision

New directions in theory, research and practice

Edited by

Fergus McNeill, Peter Raynor and Chris Trotter

WILLAN
PUBLISHING

Published by

Willan Publishing
2 Park Square
Milton Park
Abingdon
Oxon
OX14 4RN

Published simultaneously in the USA and Canada by

Willan Publishing
270 Madison Avenue
New York
NY 10016

First published 2010

ISBN   978-1-84392-935-2 paperback
       978-1-84392-936-9 hardback

British Library Cataloguing-in-Publication Data

A catalogue record for this book is available from the British Library

Project managed by Deer Park Productions, Tavistock, Devon
Typeset by GCS, Leighton Buzzard, Bedfordshire
Printed and bound by T.J. International, Padstow, Cornwall

Mixed Sources
Product group from well-managed forests and other controlled sources
www.fsc.org Cert no. SGS-COC-2482
© 1996 Forest Stewardship Council

FSC

Contents

List of figures and tables ix
List of abbreviations xii
Acknowledgements xiv
Notes on contributors xv

1 Introduction: 'What's new and exciting?' 1
  Fergus McNeill, Peter Raynor and Chris Trotter

Part One: New directions in theory 17

2 Viewing offender assessment and rehabilitation
  through the lens of the risk-needs-responsivity model 19
  James Bonta and Don Andrews

3 The Good Lives Model of offender rehabilitation:
  basic assumptions, aetiological commitments,
  and practice implications 41
  Tony Ward

4 The desistance paradigm in correctional practice:
  from programmes to lives 65
  Shadd Maruna and Thomas P. LeBel

Part Two: Staff skills and effective offender supervision   89

5 Technology transfer: the importance of ongoing clinical
supervision in translating 'what works' to everyday
community supervision   91
Guy Bourgon, Jim Bonta, Tanya Rugge and Leticia Gutierrez

6 Skills and strategies in probation supervision:
the Jersey study   113
Peter Raynor, Pamela Ugwudike and Maurice Vanstone

7 Supervision skills in juvenile justice   130
Chris Trotter and Phillipa Evans

Part Three: Improving offender supervision   153

8 The role of risk, needs and strengths assessment in
improving the supervision of offenders   155
Hazel Kemshall

9 Managing chaos: implementing evidence-based practices
in correctional agencies   172
Faye S. Taxman and Judith Sachwald

10 Can structured programmes improve one-to-one
supervision?   193
Pauline Durrance, Nigel Hosking and Nancy Thorburn

11 Beyond supervision: judicial involvement in offender
managment   215
Gill McIvor

Part Four: Significant others and social networks   239

12 It's relational: integrating families into community
corrections   241
Carol Shapiro and Margaret DiZerega

13 Justice for all: family matters in offender supervision   257
Bas Vogelvang and Herman van Alphen

14 Working with families in criminal justice   282
    Chris Trotter

15 Collaborating with the community, trained volunteers
    and faith traditions: building social capital and
    making meaning to support desistance   301
    Tom O'Connor and Brad Bogue

Part Five: Offenders' compliance with supervision   323

16 Compliance with community penalties: the importance
    of interactional dynamics   325
    Pamela Ugwudike

17 Case management in corrections: evidence, issues
    and challenges   344
    Shelley Turner

18 The dynamics of compliance with offender supervision   367
    Gwen Robinson and Fergus McNeill

19 Exploring community service, understanding compliance   384
    Trish McCulloch

Part Six: Offender supervision in its contexts   407

20 The socio-political context of reforms in probation
    agencies: impact on adoption of evidence-based practices   409
    Faye Taxman, Craig Henderson and Jennifer Lerch

21 Revising the National Outcomes and Standards for
    criminal justice social work services in Scotland   430
    Tim Chapman

22 The purposes of supervision: practitioner and policy
    perspectives in England and Wales   451
    John Deering

23 Pre-sentence reports in England and Wales: changing
    discourses of need, risk and quality   471
    Loraine Gelsthorpe, Peter Raynor and Gwen Robinson

24 **Supervision in historical context: learning the lessons of (oral) history**   492
   Fegus McNeill

25 **Electronic monitoring: towards integration into offender management?**   509
   Mike Nellis

26 **Conclusion: where are we now?**   534
   Fergus McNeill, Peter Raynor and Chris Trotter

Index   *548*

Figures and tables

Figures

4.1	Recorded offender rates per 1,000 relevant population by age-year and sex, England and Wales, 2000	67
6.1	Possible and actual mean scores	125
6.2	Individual officer 6	126
6.3	Individual officer 4	126
6.4	Boxplot of total scores for six officers	126
9.1	Example of technology clusters in the adoption of evidence-based practices	179
9.2	Emotional intelligence in organisational change	187
12.1	An ecomap	248
13.1	How the four dimensions interact	267
14.1	General evaluation	294
14.2	Focus on the main problem	294
14.3	Has the service been beneficial?	295
14.4	Have goals been achieved?	296
15.1	The integrated model for implementing evidence-based policy and practices	305
15.2	Deficit mapping and low dream approach to our communities	311
15.3	Asset mapping and high dream approach to our communities	312
18.1	A typology of compliance	369
18.2	Bottoms' fourfold explanatory framework	370
18.3	Motivational postures of tax-payers	373

18.4   A dynamic model of compliance with community
       supervision   375
19.1   Four variants of compliant behaviour   387
20.1   Adoption of various EBPs by type of reform
       orientation   421
21.1   Levels of intervention   437

Tables

2.1   RNR principles of effective human service in justice
       and other contexts   21
2.2   The seven major risk/need factors along with some
       minor risk/need factors   27
2.3   Mean effect size (phi) by adherence to principles
       of risk, need and responsivity   31
2.4   Mean effect size (phi) by level of adherence to
       principles of risk, need and responsivity:
       residential and community   32
2.5   Comparative effectiveness for selected interventions   33
5.1   Skill/technique quality and discussion content
       variables for the experimental and control groups   104
5.2   Time elapsed since initial three-day training with skill
       and session content measures   105
5.3   Correlations of long-term officer skill and discussion
       content with participation in technology transfer
       processes   107
5.4   Long-term skill and discussion content comparisons   108
6.1   Sections and items in version 7C   124
7.1   Time spent using skills in interviews   139
7.2   Workers' use of role clarification skills   139
7.3   Client response to workers' use of role clarification
       skills   142
7.4   Workers' use of problem-solving skills   142
7.5   Client response to problem-solving skills   143
7.6   Criminogenic needs discussed during interviews   143
7.7   Client responses to issues discussed in interviews   144
7.8   Pro-social skills used in interviews   145
7.9   Client response to pro-social skills   146
7.10   Use of relationship skills by workers   147
7.11   Client response to relationship skills   147

7.12 Number of open and closed questions asked in each
       interview   148
7.13 Clients' estimates of the use of skills by their workers   149
9.1   Use of evidence-based practices by respondents   176
9.2   Importance of clinical and justice services relative to
       substance abuse treatment   181
9.3   Coefficients, standard errors, and pseudo z statistics
       for class correlates   184
10.1 Programme status of offenders referred to SSP   204
10.2 Programme status in relation to index offence   204
10.3 Reasons for non-completion of SSP   205
13.1 Generating responsiveness in multi-problem families:
       empowerment messages for probation workers   275
20.1 Use of evidence-based practices by respondents   418
20.2 Model fit criteria for one to five class models   420
20.3 Proportion of programmes reporting EBP use and
       proportions of most likely class membership for
       three class model   422
20.4 Coefficients, standard errors, and pseudo z statistics
       for correlates of latent class membership   423
21.1 Forms of capital and added value   436
21.2 National Outcomes and Standards: structure and
       content   447
23.1 Quality assurance guide   481
23.2 Do they mention risk?   483
23.3 How the offender is presented   484
23.4 Main focus of proposals   485

Abbreviations

ASAM	American Society of Addiction Medicine
ASPIRE	Assess – sentence plan – implement – review – evaluate
BIC	Bayesian information criterion
CCP	Core correctional practice skills
COSA	Circles of Support and Accountability
CPAI	Correctional Program Assessment Inventory
CREDOS	Collaboration of Researchers for the Effective Development of Offender Supervision
CS	Community service
DOC	Department of Corrections
DOM	Director of offender management
DTO	Detention and training order
DTTO	Drug treatment and testing order
EBP	Evidence-based practice
EM	Electronic monitoring
EMT	Electronic monitoring team
FDR	Fast delivery report
FFP	Functional family therapy
GLM	Good Lives Model
GLP	Good lives plan
GRIPP	Gain Respect Increase Personal Power
HDC	Home detention curfew
HMIP	Her Majesty's Inspectorate of Probation
IRT	Item response theory
IMSS	Intensive Monitoring and Support Services
ISSP	Intensive Supervision and Surveillance Programme

KPI	Key performance indicator
LCA	Latent class analysis
LS/CMI	Level of Service/Case Management Inventory
LSI-R	Level of Service Inventory – Revised
MAPPA	Multi-agency public protection arrangements
MST	Multi-system therapy
NCJTP	National Criminal Justice Treatment Practices
NOG	National Operations Group
NOMS	National Offender Management Service
NPS	National Probation Service
OASys	Offender Assessment System
OGRS	Offender Group Reconviction Scale
OMM	Offender management model
PSM	Pro-social modelling
PSR	Pre-sentence reports
R&R	Reasoning and rehabilitation
RNR	Risk-need-responsivity
ROM	Regional offender manager
RoSH	Risk of serious harm
SDR	Standard delivery report
SSP	Structured Supervision Programme
STICS	Strategic Training Initiative in Community Supervision

Acknowledgements

As we explain in the Introduction, this book is the product of a series of meetings of an international research network known as CREDOS (the Collaboration of Researchers for the Effective Development of Offender Supervision). Several bodies have been generous and helpful in providing funding for these meetings, including the Glasgow School of Social Work, Monash University, the Scottish Government and the University of Glasgow's Adam Smith Research Foundation. We are particularly indebted to the British Academy/ Association of Commonwealth Universities, who provided support for the preparation of this collection under their 2008–09 Grants for International Collaboration scheme.

CREDOS members who have attended our annual meetings since 2007 have enjoyed wonderful hospitality and excellent service from staff at the Monash University Centre in Prato, Italy (in 2007 and 2009) and at the University of Glasgow (in 2008). We want to express our thanks to all of those who worked 'behind the scenes' to make these meetings such a success.

Notes on contributors

Don Andrews is Professor Emeritus and Distinguished Research Professor in the Department of Psychology at the Carleton University Institute of Criminology and Criminal Justice. His interests include assessment, intervention, evaluation and theoretical issues in justice and other human service agencies. He is co-developer of several risk/need assessment instruments. *The Psychology of Criminal Conduct*, co-authored with James Bonta (5th edition, LexisNexis, 2010) was nominated for the Hindelang Award of the American Society of Criminology. He received the Margaret Mead Award for contributions to social justice and humanitarian advancement, the Career Contributions Award from CPA, and the Distinguished Senior Scholar Award ASC.

Bradford Bogue is a seasoned investigator, author and internationally recognised expert in probation case management practices. He has been the Primary Investigator (PI) for over 70 programme evaluations, workload analysis and outcome studies in community corrections and designed the Risk and Resiliency Check-Up assessment that RAND Corporation recently validated, along with numerous other innovations for the field (automated case plan applications, QA systems, etc.). He trained in 1992 as a Motivational Interview trainer and since then he has been training MI and exploring methods for MI, QA and implementing MI 'to scale' and in corrections. He was the lead author for a definitive book on case planning (*The Probation and Parole Treatment Planner*, Wiley, 2003) as well as the NIC position paper, 'The Principles of Effective Interventions', which serves as

NIC's current model for EBP in field supervision. Currently he is the PI in several national multisite projects related to EBP.

James Bonta received his PhD in Clinical Psychology from the University of Ottawa in 1979. Prior to graduating he worked with conduct-disordered children and their families, provided assessments of youths for juvenile courts, and acted as a consultant at a training school for youth. Upon graduating he became a psychologist at the Ottawa-Carleton Detention Centre, a maximum security remand centre for adults and young offenders, and later Chief Psychologist. During his 14 years at the Detention Centre he established the only full-time psychology department in a jail setting in Canada. In 1990 he joined Public Safety Canada and is presently Director of Corrections Research. Throughout his career he has held various academic appointments and professional posts and he was a member of the Editorial Advisory Boards for the Canadian Journal of Criminology and Criminal Justice and Behavior. He is also a Fellow of the Canadian Psychological Association and recipient of the Criminal Justice Section's Career Contribution Award for 2009. Dr Bonta has published extensively in the areas of risk assessment and offender rehabilitation. His latest publications include a book co-authored with D.A. Andrews entitled *The Psychology of Criminal Conduct* (5th edition, LexisNexis, 2010). He is also a co-author of *The Level of Service Inventory – Revised, The Level of Service Inventory/Case Management Inventory and The Level of Service/Risk Need Responsivity*. These offender risk-need classification instruments have been translated into five languages and are used by correctional systems throughout the world.

Guy Bourgon PhD is a clinical psychologist with 25 years' experience in correctional and criminal justice psychology. Presently a Senior Researcher at Public Safety Canada, he is the co-lead on the Strategic Training Initiative in Community Supervision, a risk-need-responsivity approach to offender supervision that includes probation officer training and clinical supervision. He has published articles on effective correctional treatment, risk assessment, and knowledge transfer to everyday practice. Dr Bourgon maintains a private practice, is an adjunct professor at Carleton University, and a member of the editorial board on *Criminal Justice and Behavior*.

Tim Chapman is a lecturer on the Masters in Restorative Practices programme at the University of Ulster. He spent 25 years working in the Probation Service in Northern Ireland. He played an active part in developing effective practice in the UK particularly through the publication of *Evidence Based Practice*, written jointly with Michael Hough and published by the Home Office. His 'Time to Grow' model for the supervision of young people has influenced youth justice practices especially in Scotland.

Dr John Deering is Senior Lecturer in Criminology and Criminal Justice at the University of Wales, Newport. He teaches undergraduate programmes in criminology, criminal justice and youth justice. Between 2006 and 2010 he was programme leader for the probation officer training BA degree in Wales. A former social worker and probation officer, his research interests include the attitudes and values of probation practitioners and trainees, as well as the changing nature of probation practice. He is a member of the Newport Centre for Criminal and Community Justice and the Welsh Centre for Crime and Social Justice.

Pauline Durrance is the Senior Research Officer for London Probation Trust. She is also a Visiting Lecturer at the University of Hertfordshire and formerly Research Fellow in Health Psychology at University College London. She has published articles on probation education and on programmes for women and black and minority ethnic offenders.

Phillipa Evans works as a Research Fellow with Monash University. She also holds the position of Juvenile Justice Counsellor in the Sex Offender Programme for New South Wales Department of Juvenile Justice. Her research interests include working with young people and skills and interventions utilised when working with offenders. She is currently completing her PhD examining effective methods of confrontation utilised when working with adolescent offenders.

Loraine Gelsthorpe is Professor of Criminology and Criminal Justice at the Institute of Criminology, University of Cambridge. She has published widely on issues relating to women, crime and criminal justice (most recently on sentencing, resettlement issues and 'what works' for women), community penalties (including the *Handbook of Probation*, Willan Publishing, 2007, edited with Rod Morgan), and youth justice. She first carried out research on pre-sentence reports in the late 1980s and early 1990s (with Peter Raynor) and has maintained a continuing interest in this area. As well as being a criminologist, Loraine is a UKCP registered psychoanalytical psychotherapist.

Leticia Gutierrez, MA (Candidate) is a second-year Master's student in the Forensic Psychology program at Carleton University and a Research Analyst in the Corrections Research Unit of the Department of Public Safety. Her areas of research include drug treatment courts, community supervision, aboriginal offenders and restorative justice. Currently, Leticia is assessing the role of therapeutic relationships in community supervision settings in Canada.

Craig Henderson is Associate Professor of Psychology at Sam Houston State University (SHSU) and Adjunct Research Assistant Professor of Epidemiology and Public Health at the University of Miami CTRADA. Dr Henderson received his PhD in Counseling Psychology from the University of North Texas in 2001, after which he joined the Center for Treatment Research on Adolescent Drug Abuse as a NIDA T-32 funded postdoctoral fellow. Dr Henderson completed his postdoctoral fellowship in 2003 and joined the faculty as Research Assistant Professor. While at the University of Miami, he served as investigator on five NIDA funded projects and directed an economic evaluation of adolescent drug abuse treatment and a randomized controlled trial for young substance abusing adolescents. Currently, he is the Principal Investigator of a randomized controlled trial comparing the Assertive Community Reinforcement Approach (ACRA) to services as usual for adolescents with drug problems under community supervision (CSAT Grant No. TI17817) and a National Institute on Drug Abuse (NIDA) grant examining gender and ethnic differences in 10 RCTs in which Multidimensional Family Therapy (MDFT) was tested against a variety of comparison treatments (R01 DA 029089) and has worked actively on three research protocols implemented in the NIDA collaborative Criminal Justice Drug Abuse Treatment Studies (CJDATS). He is an expert in state-of-the-art methodological approaches for data analysis, particularly RCT design and analysis, latent growth curve modeling, and general growth mixture modeling (GGMM). He has twice been awarded the Excellence in Teaching Award, once the Excellence in Research Award in the Department of Psychology and Philosophy, and once the Excellence in Research Award in the College of Humanities and Social Sciences at SHSU. He has also been the recipient of the College on Problems of Drug Dependence (CPDD) Early Career Investigator Award.

Nigel Hosking is a Senior Probation Officer with the London Probation Trust. He has a background in offending behaviour programmes, having worked as a practitioner delivering programmes, treatment manager, national trainer (for the Reasoning and Rehabilitation accredited programme) and programme manager. He is currently developing a one-to-one programme for offenders and has previously published an article on group dynamics in the *Journal of Psychiatry*.

Hazel Kemshall is currently Professor of Community and Criminal Justice at De Montfort University. She has research interests in risk assessment and management of offenders, effective work in multi-agency public protection, and implementing effective practice with high risk offenders. She has completed research for the Economic and Social Research Council, the Home Office, Ministry of Justice, the Scottish Government, and the Risk Management Authority. She both teaches and consults extensively on public protection and high risk offenders, including training for MAPPA chairs and panel members in England and Scotland. She has numerous publications on risk, including *Understanding Risk in Criminal Justice* (2003, Open University Press). She has completed three evaluations of multi-agency public protection panels for the Home Office (2001, 2005, 2007), and is currently researching polygraph use with sex offenders, and evaluating the public disclosure pilots. She is the lead author of the CD-Rom, *Risk of Harm Guidance and Training Resource* for NOMS PPU, and for the *Assessment and Management of Risk* CD-Rom in Scotland for the RMA. Her most recent book, *Understanding the Community Management of High Risk Offenders*, was published by the Open University in 2008.

Thomas P. LeBel is an Assistant Professor in the Department of Criminal Justice in the University of Wisconsin-Milwaukee's Helen Bader School of Social Welfare. In 2006 he received his PhD from the School of Criminal Justice at the University at Albany, State University of New York. Tom's scholarly work incorporates a 'strengths-based' perspective in regard to people currently or formerly incarcerated. He is the author or co-author of several articles and book chapters on prisoner reintegration, desistance from crime, prison reform, substance abuse treatment, and stigma. Tom has also served as a consultant, panellist and discussant for prisoner re-entry related projects sponsored by agencies such as the National Academy of Sciences Committee on Law and Justice and the Urban Institute.

Jennifer Lerch is a Research Associate for the Center of Advancing Correctional Excellence (ACE!) at George Mason University. Her current work focuses on organizational change which supports evidence-based practices in correctional settings. She is a doctoral student in the Department of Criminology, Law and Society. Jennifer received her BS in Political Science and Sociology from Shepherd University in Shepherdstown, West Virginia. She recieved her MA degree in Justice, Law, and Crime Policy at George Mason University.

Trish McCulloch is a Senior Lecturer in Social Work at the University of Dundee. Prior to joining the University in 2003, she worked as a social worker within youth and adult justice settings. Her publications have focused on various areas of criminal justice social work/probation practice, and include a particular focus on the social and community contexts of change. Trish is currently completing her doctorate and has recently undertaken an evaluative study in the area of community service (on which the chapter in this collection draws).

Gill McIvor is Professor of Criminology at the University of Stirling, Co-Director of the Scottish Centre for Crime and Justice Research (with responsibility for programme development) and visiting Professor at the Glasgow School of Social Work, University of Strathclyde. Her research interests include community sanctions, penal policy, women who offend and problem-solving courts. Her recent publications include two co-edited books: *Developments in Social Work with Offenders* (with Peter Raynor, Jessica Kingsley, 2007) and *What Works with Women Offenders* (with Rosemary Sheehan and Chris Trotter, Willan Publishing, 2007).

Fergus McNeill is Professor of Criminology and Social Work at the University of Glasgow. Prior to becoming an academic in 1998, Fergus worked for a number of years in residential drug rehabilitation and as a criminal justice social worker. His research interests and publications have addressed a range of criminal justice issues including sentencing, community sanctions, ex-offender reintegration and youth justice. His previous books include *Reducing Reoffending: Social Work and Community Justice in Scotland* (with Bill Whyte, Willan Publishing, 2007) and *Youth Offending and Youth Justice* (with Monica Barry, Jessica Kingsley, 2009).

Shadd Maruna is a Professor and Director of the Institute of Criminology and Criminal Justice at the School of Law, Queen's University Belfast. Previously, he has been a lecturer at the University of Cambridge and the State University of New York. His book *Making*

Good: How Ex-Convicts Reform and Rebuild Their Lives was named the 'Outstanding Contribution to Criminology' by the American Society of Criminology in 2001. His more recent books include *Fifty Key Thinkers in Criminology* (with Keith Hayward and Jayne Mooney, Routledge, 2009), *Rehabilitation: Beyond the Risk Paradigm* (with Tony Ward, Routledge, 2007), *The Effects of Imprisonment* (with Alison Liebling, Willan Publishing, 2005), and *After Crime and Punishment: Pathways to Ex-Offender Reintegration* (with Russ Immarigeon, Willan Publishing, 2004).

Mike Nellis is Professor of Criminal and Community Justice in the Glasgow School of Social Work, University of Strathclyde. He is a former social worker with young offenders and between 1990 and 2003 was closely involved in the training of probation officers at the University of Birmingham. He has written extensively on the changing nature of the probation service, the promotion of community penalties, the significance of electronic monitoring and the cultural politics of penal reform (including the educational use of prison movies and prisoners' autobiographies).

Tom O'Connor, PhD is a Research and Evaluation Manager with the Oregon Department of Corrections. Previously Tom led the Religious Services Unit in the department for nine years and worked extensively to train correctional staff and volunteers. Tom's research interests and publications focus on skill development among correctional staff and volunteers, increasing the fidelity of correctional agencies and programs to evidence-based and humane principles, organisational change, the role of spirituality in the desistance process, and the integration of religion and spirituality into effective correctional programming. Tom can be reached at: tom.p.oconnor@doc.state.or.us.

Peter Raynor is Professor of Criminology and Criminal Justice at Swansea University in Wales. A former probation officer and social work educator, he has been carrying out and publishing research on effective practice in probation services since the 1970s. His previous books include Social Work, Justice and Control (Blackwell, 1985); *Probation as an Alternative to Custody* (Avebury, 1988); *Effective Probation Practice* (with Smith and Vanstone, Macmillan, 1994); *Understanding Community Penalties* (with Vanstone, Open University Press, 2002); *Race and Probation* (with Lewis, Smith and Wardak, Willan Publishing, 2005); *Developments in Social Work with Offenders* (with Gill McIvor,

Jessica Kingsley, 2007) and *Rehabilitation, Crime and Justice* (with Gwen Robinson, Macmillan, 2009).

Gwen Robinson is Senior Lecturer in Criminal Justice at the School of Law, University of Sheffield. Her primary research interests are offender rehabilitation and management, community penalties, and restorative justice. Her publications include *Rehabilitation, Crime and Justice* (with Peter Raynor, Macmillan, 2009) and *Alternatives to Prison: Options for an Insecure Society* (with Tony Bottoms and Sue Rex, Willan Publishing, 2004).

Tanya Rugge has a BA in Law and a PhD in Psychology. Her doctoral dissertation examined the impacts of restorative justice processes on participants. She joined the Corrections Research team of Public Safety Canada in 1997 and is currently a Senior Research Officer. Over the past several years, she has interviewed numerous offenders and victims, conducted risk assessments, worked clinically with female offenders and conducted research on recidivism, high risk offenders, young offenders, aboriginal corrections, various pieces of criminal justice legislation, and evaluated several restorative justice programs as well as community supervision practices.

Judith Sachwald works as an independent consultant assisting state and local government agencies with leadership, organizational development and the implementation of evidence-based practice in offender management and organizational development. She spent the first 18 years of her career working for the State of Maryland in a variety of positions with a focus on elementary-secondary education, higher education and workforce development. In 1994, Judith was persuaded to apply her knowledge and experience to public safety and corrections. She worked for the Maryland Secretary of Public Safety and Correctional services for nearly six years and served as the Director of the Maryland Division of Parole and Probation for more than seven years. During her tenure as Director of Parole and Probation, she led and managed a community corrections agency with over 1,300 employees who provided supervision to approximately 70,000 individuals under probation, parole, mandatory supervision or home detention. She guided the development and implementation of a research-based approach to supervision which holds offenders accountable for their actions while assisting them in becoming law-abiding, responsible and productive members of the community. Under this new approach to supervision, offenders were 38 per cent less likely to be arrested or violate the rules of supervision. Ms. Sachwald cultivated organizational change by: requiring the Division's leaders to engage in critical thinking through timely analysis of data and its relationship to the Division's goals and objectives; engaging all employees in the change process; pursuing partnerships with other public agencies as well as non-profit service providers; providing employees with the technology and tools to perform their jobs; enriching opportunities for professional development; recognizing employees for their contributions through formal and informal means; and establishing a *What Works* committee to examine the ever-evolving body of research documenting evidence-based practices in community corrections and sharing their findings with other Division employees. She has received awards from the Maryland Crime Victims' Resource Center, the Middle Atlantic States Correctional Association, Alternative Directions, and the Maryland Chapter of the American Society for Public Administration.

Carol Shapiro has been an innovator in the field of criminal and social justice for over 30 years. Prior to joining Columbia University, Carol was the Founder and President of Family Justice, a non-profit organisation focused on tapping the strengths of families and their social networks to break cycles of victimisation and justice system involvement. She has devised and collaborated on numerous initiatives to more effectively address crime prevention, addiction, pre-release, re-entry, and a broad range of related issues. Much of her work centres on improving public safety and family well-being through the integration of a strengths-based, family-focused approach within the law enforcement, public health and public housing disciplines. Currently Carol is exploring new ways to scale innovation given new developments within technology and globalisation and continues to bring family-focused work to cross-disciplines. Carol serves as an advisor to many governmental and citizen-sector initiatives. She also provides technical assistance and consultation services to federal, state, and local governments and non-profit organisations in the US and abroad. Among her many awards and honours for social entrepreneurship, Carol is an Ashoka fellow and ambassador.

Faye S. Taxman, PhD is a University Professor in the Administration of Justice Department, Co-director of the Network for Justice Health, and Director of the Advancing Correctional Excellence at George Mason University. She is recognised for her work in the development of the seamless systems of care models that link the criminal justice with other service delivery systems as well as re-engineering probation and parole supervision services, and organisational change models. Her most recent work concerns the best strategies to advance the implementation of evidence-based practices in correctional, particularly probation, settings. Her work covers the breadth of the correctional system, from jails and prisons to community corrections and adult and juvenile offenders, including all types of interventions and system improvement factors. She has had numerous grants from the National Institute on Drug Abuse, National Institute of Justice, National Institute of Corrections, Office of National Drug Control Policy, and Bureau of Justice Assistance. She has active 'laboratories' with her nearly 20-year agreement with the Maryland Department of Public Safety and Correctional Services. She has published over 100 articles, including translational work such as *Tools of the Trade: A Guide to Incorporating Science into Practice*, a publication of the National Institute on Corrections which provides a guidebook to implementation of science-based concepts into practice. She is on the editorial boards of the *Journal of Experimental Criminology and Journal of Offender Rehabilitation*. She received the University of Cincinnati Award from the American Probation and Parole Association in 2002 for her contributions to the field. She is a Fellow of the Academy of Experimental Criminology and a member of the Correctional Services Accreditation Panel (CSAP) of England. In 2008, the American Society of Criminology's Division of Sentencing and Corrections recognised her as a Distinguished Scholar. She has a PhD from Rutgers University School of Criminal Justice and a BA from the University of Tulsa.

Nancy Thorburn worked as a Research Analyst for London Probation Trust in 2009. She has written reports on community payback and hate crime. She is now working in television and media.

Shelley Turner is employed by New South Wales (NSW) Juvenile Justice as the manager of the NSW Youth Drug and Alcohol Court Program's Joint Assessment and Review Team. She supervises a team of Juvenile Justice alcohol and other drug counsellors and officers and oversees an inter-agency team of senior practitioners. She has worked for Juvenile Justice agencies in both NSW and Victoria for the past decade in a variety of roles, including as a probation and parole officer, alcohol and other drug counsellor and clinical manager. Shelley is a social worker and is currently undertaking her PhD at Monash University, examining Juvenile Justice clients' understanding and experiences of case management.

Chris Trotter, PhD is Associate Professor in Social Work at Monash University and convenor of the Monash Criminal Justice Research Consortium. He worked for many years as a probation officer and a manager in community corrections prior to his appointment to Monash. He has published widely and is well known for his work on the effective supervision of offenders. The supervision model developed in his research has been implemented in many corrections services around the world. His book *Working with Involuntary Clients*, now in its second edition (Sage, 2006), has sold widely and has been published in multiple languages.

Pamela Ugwudike is Lecturer in Criminology at the University of Swansea. She trained as a lawyer and completed her PhD in Criminology and Criminal Justice at Swansea. Her research interests include drawing on theoretical insights and empirical evidence underpinning effective practices to explore the effectiveness of offender management policy and practice, evaluating policy provisions and practices in the field of offender management in order to assess the impact of implementation processes on outcomes, exploring the correlates and dynamics of compliance with legal authorities. She is currently working with Professor Peter Raynor on a research project examining the impact of supervision skills on the outcome of community penalties. Her future research objectives include developing insights into the interface between contemporary policy developments and responses to offenders with specific demographic attributes, particularly offenders from ethnic minority groups.

Herman van Alphen is an organisational psychologist; he works as a lecturer at the Academy for Social Work at Avans University (Den Bosch, The Netherlands), and as researcher for the Expertise Centre for Safety Policy and Criminal Justice of Avans University. He has worked for 15 years with offenders, as probation worker and penitentiary worker, and seven years as senior advisor at the Ministry of Justice. Currently, he is involved in research into oral probation history, the desistance processes of women and ethnic minorities, and the role of family processes in risk asessment and offender supervision.

Maurice Vanstone is Emeritus Professor of Criminology and Criminal Justice in the Centre for Criminal Justice and Criminology at the University of Wales, Swansea. The author of numerous articles, chapters and books, he has had experience of practice, training and research on community sentences over a 30-year period, and has been a regular contributor to teaching and research. He is the author of *Supervising Offenders in the Community: A History of Probation Theory and Practice* (second edition, Ashgate, 2007) and co-editor (with Philip Priestley) of *Offenders or Citizens? Readings in Rehabilitation* (Willan Publishing, 2010).

Bas Vogelvang is a developmental psychologist and pedagogue; he works as Professor of Probation Services and Safety Policy at the Expertise Center for Safety Policy and Criminal Justice of Avans University (Den Bosch, The Netherlands), and as expert consultant in the field of Administration of Justice at the Van Montfoort Research and Development Group (Woerden, The Netherlands). He developed the risk assessment instrument 'RISc' for the Dutch probation services, numerous offender behaviour treatment programmes that have been accredited by the Dutch Ministry of Justice, and is currently introducing, together with Dutch probation services, Circles of Support and Accountability in the Netherlands (a re-entry public protection arrangement for released high risk sex offenders). Bas Vogelvang is a member of the scientific board of the Dutch probation services and numerous advisory commissions of research projects instigated by the Dutch Ministry of Justice.

Tony Ward, PhD, DipClinPsyc, is currently Professor of Clinical Psychology and Head of School at Victoria University of Wellington, New Zealand. He has taught both clinical and forensic psychology in the past at the universities of Canterbury and Melbourne, and was director of the Kia Marama special treatment unit for sex offenders. His research interests include desistance and reintegration processes, cognition in offenders, and ethical issues in forensic psychology. He has over 270 academic publications and his recent books include *Rehabilitation: Beyond the Risk Paradigm* (with Shadd Maruna, Routledge, 2007), *Morals, Rights and Practice in the Human Services* (with Marie Connolly, Jessica Kingsley, 2008), and *Desistance from Sexual Offending: Alternatives to Throwing Away the Keys* (with Richard Laws, Guilford Press, 2010).

Chapter 1

Introduction: 'What's new and exciting?'

Fergus McNeill, Peter Raynor and Chris Trotter

The story of this book

The origins of this collection lie in the development of an international network of researchers interested in one way or another in 'offender supervision'. The initial idea to establish such a network was Chris Trotter's. During the European Society of Criminology's Annual Conference in 2006 in Tübingen in Germany, Chris discussed the idea with Peter Raynor and Fergus McNeill. The initial discussions centred on a common concern; although the 'what works?' movement in probation (or correctional) research had achieved a great deal, new impetus seemed to us to be necessary to allow the effectiveness agenda to develop beyond its historical emphasis on the principles of effective programmes. Reflecting our different backgrounds, interests and experiences – both in practice and in research – we saw broader questions and issues arising both from effectiveness research itself (for example, about the role of workers' practice skills, styles and approaches, and about the organisational contexts of interventions) and from research on desistance from offending and how it can be best supported (for example, about the significance of personal and professional relationships in the process, and about the importance of developing social capital).

In order to explore the potential for developing such a network, we contacted as many probation or corrections researchers as we could and organised a day seminar at the Monash University Centre in Prato, Tuscany on 13 September 2007. Those who attended the seminar included very eminent and well-established scholars, doctoral researchers and others early in their careers, and researchers and analysts within private and governmental institutions as well as more traditional academic settings. Importantly, several of the attendees worked across the research/practice divide. Those present included Loretta Allen-Weinstein (New South Wales Juvenile Justice, Australia); Jill Annison (University of Plymouth, UK); Jim Bonta (Public Safety Canada); John Deering (University of Wales at Newport); Philippa Evans (Monash University/NSW Juvenile Justice, Australia); Liz Fabiano (T3 Associates, Canada); Loraine Gelsthorpe (Cambridge University, UK); Nigel Hosking (London Probation Area, UK); Gill McIvor (then at the University of Lancaster, UK); Trish McCulloch (University of Dundee, UK); Fergus McNeill (University of Glasgow, UK); Margaret Malloch (University of Stirling, UK); Helen Miles (Swansea University/Jersey Probation Service); Dave Morran (University of Stirling, UK); Briege Nugent (then at the University of Edinburgh, UK); Frank Porporino (T3 Associates, Canada); Peter Raynor (Swansea University, UK); Colin Roberts (University of Oxford, UK); Jenny Roberts (formerly Chief Probation Officer, Hereford and Worcester, UK); Gwen Robinson (University of Sheffield, UK); Shelley Turner (Monash University/NSW Juvenile Justice, Australia); Chris Trotter (Monash University, Australia); Pamela Ugwudike (Swansea University, UK); and Bill Whyte (University of Edinburgh, UK).

Several of these initial participants have contributed to this volume, and the first versions of some of the chapters herein were discussed at that first meeting. Importantly, however, the group also used that first meeting to discuss and agree their shared agenda. Settling on the acronym CREDOS (Collaboration of Researchers for the Effective Development of Offender Supervision), the founding members agreed on the following statement of objectives and principles:

CREDOS is an international network of researchers, and policy and practice partners in research, who share a common interest in the effective development of offender supervision. We believe that this interest requires us to engage in high quality, collaborative and comparative research and scholarship exploring:

- How best to measure effectiveness in offender supervision.
- The nature and features of effective offender supervision.
- The characteristics, styles and practices of effective offender supervisors.

- The qualities and features of effective relationships between offenders and those that work with them.
- The social, political, cultural, organisational and professional contexts of effective offender supervision and how these contexts impact upon it.

In pursuing this agenda, CREDOS is committed to:

- Pursuing our research agenda through a diverse range of research methods, recognising that methodological pluralism is necessary to yield the insights required to move policy and practice forward.

- Undertaking collaborative and comparative research wherever possible, so that lessons can be learned about what works in specific national and local contexts and about whether and to what extent there are practices in and approaches to offender supervision that work across diverse contexts.

- Exploring issues of diversity among offenders in relation to effective supervision.

- Working to engage offenders and their families in the research process, recognising the value and importance of their insights into effective practice and what works for them.

Since its inception, CREDOS has convened annual meetings (in Glasgow in 2008, in Prato in 2009 and Melbourne in 2010) in order to progress these objectives, principally by enabling its members to engage in ongoing discussion about their work and, where possible, to encourage them to work together. The network also allows for electronic communication about ongoing relevant research – theoretical and empirical (more of which below). Importantly, CREDOS is an inclusive network – open to any and all researchers with an active interest in these issues – and one that is keen to maintain or establish close and mutually respectful engagements with policy and practice in any and all jurisdictions. Since our inaugural 2007 meeting, the network has expanded to include about 40 members from Australasia, Europe and North America – and we hope to reach out beyond these three continents in the near future. We recognise the need to address the over-representation of anglophone jurisdictions in our network; an over-representation that reflects our own identities and networks but deprives us of access to extensive bodies of research and experience – and other ways of understanding and constructing the issues and practices that concern us.

This collection is essentially the product of the first three CREDOS annual meetings (most particularly the third meeting in Prato in 2009 which was generously supported by a small grant from the British Academy/Association of Commonwealth Universities), though it has been seasoned and supplemented by contributions from scholars who for one reason or another did not attend these meetings. Reviewing the contents of the collection, it is encouraging to recognise the extent to which CREDOS has already begun to achieve its objectives – and how much it has stayed true to its principles. All of the chapters of this book address the network's original objectives. Moreover, the methodological diversity reflected in the collection is in keeping with the principles we established. Perhaps partly because of our anglophone bias, it might be said that we have failed in one area: despite our expressed commitment to address issues of diversity, they are tackled in a somewhat partial and piecemeal fashion in this collection – clearly, this is something that we should seek to remedy as our work moves forward.

A problem with the book's title

Rightly in our view, some members of CREDOS have questioned the merits of entitling this book *Offender Supervision*. As will quickly become apparent to readers, all of the contributors to this collection are committed not just to the belief that human beings can change but also to the pursuit of evidence about how, why and when we change, and about how positive change can be best supported. Does it make sense therefore to collude with uses of language that arguably serve to confirm and cement precisely those identities and behaviours that we are concerned with changing? If we want people to leave offending behind, why do we insist on labelling or defining them as offenders; why do we define our core interest as *offender* supervision?

One principled answer to this challenge is that the term 'offender supervision' at least serves to remind us that those people supervised by probation, parole, correctional or criminal justice social work services are rarely undergoing supervision by choice; 'offenders' are in most circumstances 'involuntary clients' of human services (Trotter 2006). They are being supervised because they have offended. Researchers and practitioners do well to remember this for two main reasons. First, such recognition serves to balance the proper aspirations of offender supervisors to serve and to support their 'clients' with recognition of their obligations to supervise also in the interests of the broader community, preserving its safety. Second, and equally important, the offending and only the offending is what justifies the intrusion of involuntary supervision, its inevitable deprivations of liberty and privacy and the other 'pains' (intended, incidental and obiter) that it entails (Durnescu 2009; Raynor 1978, 1985). Although the aspirations of offender supervisors for those people being supervised are and should be much broader than the mere cessation of their offending – and may include enhancing their lives in all sorts of ways – supervisors should *encourage* but have no right to *require* more than the cessation of offending. If the European history of criminal justice under totalitarian regimes has taught us to appreciate the proper limits of the State's right to compel change in the individual, then the North American history of criminal justice under the influence of too unrestrained a version of the 'rehabilitative ideal' (American Friends Services Committee 1971) perhaps teaches us a parallel lesson.

More pragmatically, we have called the book *Offender Supervision* in an attempt to escape at least some of the vagaries and variations of terminology across jurisdictions. In some countries the business of supervising offenders in the community lies firmly within social work; in others it is a function of probation and/or parole agencies; in others the relevant organisations are defined as (community) correctional services; in one jurisdiction the business has become known as 'offender management'. For some, the term supervision may invoke surveillance and discipline (*pace* Foucault) rather than rehabilitation, but the latter term is also ambiguous, contested and problematic (see Raynor and Robinson 2009). That said, both supervision and rehabilitation seem better terms than mere 'management', particularly when set in the context of contemporary critiques of changes in penal systems that are seen as representing the emergence of an 'actuarial regime' (Feeley and Simon 1992, 1994) or a 'culture of control' (Garland 2001); both critiques suggest that the dominant concern has become the management of risks rather than the promotion of positive change.

None of these arguments satisfactorily addresses the problem of negative labelling in the book's title, but perhaps this brief acknowledgement of our own discomfort serves to provide some useful qualification and clarification of what the title is and is not intended to convey.

'What's new and exciting?'

So what is this book all about? Towards the end of January 2010, while this collection was in preparation, Don Andrews emailed some colleagues a message entitled: 'What's new and exciting?' His request was as follows:

> **Don Andrews:** Hello everyone. I agreed to do a paper for James McGuire for a special edition of *Legal and Criminological Psychology* on non-programmatic factors and treatment outcome. I can't find anything new but for Jim's training project (STICS [see Chapter 5]) and a few others noted below. Have I just been out of it for too long and hence I am too far removed from the action? HELP! Is there anything new in the correctional treatment/crime prevention area? I am not asking you to do my job. I just can't find much post-2006. Am I simply missing some great new stuff? ...

Jim Bonta forwarded Don's message to the CREDOS network. Over the course of the ensuing weeks, there was a series of responses from CREDOS members. In the first response, as well as directing Don to a recent literature review commissioned by the Scottish Government (McNeill 2009), one of us offered the following suggestion:

> **Fergus McNeill**: Aside from the importance of developing debates about the implications of desistance research for 'correctional' practice, I'm inclined to think that the main emerging area relates to the interfaces between the effectiveness literature (specifically your work on CCPs [core correctional practices – see Chapter 2]) and the literature on the importance of legitimacy in other CJ areas (you'll probably know Tom Tyler's work in this area?). It seems to me that we need to think a bit harder about the moral qualities of organisations, of practitioners and of interventions, since I think there is now pretty strong evidence that offenders (like everyone else) assess and respond to certain moral qualities of those that have authority over them.

> **Don Andrews**: ... As you might expect, I am pleased to see your references to core practices. I know that Chris Trotter has developed some of the ideas into a model of social work practice with reluctant clients. Now you too make reference to core practices in your model of offender supervision. The

motivational and desistance pieces should prove very valuable. Needless to say, I am very pleased ... [but] I don't understand the programming versus supervision issue that you refer to in relation to RNR [the risk-needs-responsivity model – see Chapter 2]. Do you think that RNR only applies to formal treatment programmes? It applies to human services, social services and clinical services and the supervision of offenders. I think it also applies to crime prevention services outside of corrections. Indeed, we can use the same principles in analyses of the impact of family, school, neighborhood etc. on future criminal activity. Looking forward to the book and seeing what everyone is up to. You have created a very interesting group ... .

Fergus McNeill: ... In terms of the programmes/supervision issue, maybe I haven't been clear enough in terms of separating the theory or model from the way it was implemented – over here at least. You probably know this story, but my take on it is that your work (essentially RNR) got mixed up with public sector reforms in the UK (more specifically England and Wales) which were focused on saving costs and reducing the power of the professions – all part of the managerialisation and mechanisation of human services. The result was that ... assessment and intervention systems ... were superficially based on RNR but ... lacked sensitivity to the complexities of offenders' lives and neglected the need for professional reflexivity and ingenuity in individualising the generalised messages from research (and in applying the tools and programmes sensitively). To put it crudely and probably exaggerating a little ... the significance of the 'human' in human services (and their social and organisational contexts) somehow got lost. Accreditation systems belatedly tried to correct this (by insisting on recognition of the wider context, the links to supervision and social supports), but of course by their nature they too placed all the emphasis on programmes.

I guess that sometimes, in discussing RNR, I (like many others) may mix up the model as designed [with] the model as applied! That said, I do think that the desistance perspective (basically forefronting the change process and how we understand and support it, ahead of thinking about interventions [see Chapter 4]) and the GLM [the Good Lives Model, see Chapter 3] do add something new and move the debates on – but these approaches are just as vulnerable to misappropriation and misuse. For example, I have to work quite hard when presenting desistance material to prevent practitioners from taking away the message that they 'just' need to have good relationships with offenders and to offer a bit of practical help.

Shadd Maruna: What an interesting question [What's new and exciting?]. I'd like to echo Fergus's points and throw in a couple of plugs for books that are forthcoming ... Both books are in the sex offender treatment field, but to be honest (because of the investment in that area of treatment and the resources at their disposal) they are really streets ahead of the rest of us in many regards, and I would say that 95 per cent of the arguments in the two books apply fully to rehabilitation work with ordinary prisoners as well (whatever ordinary is).

The first book is all about the importance of non-programmatic factors (therapeutic alliance, relationships, etc.) and makes a strong case for the significance of these factors over the content of actual programming. It is (ironically) the work of four Canadian authors (W. L. Marshall, G. A. Serran, L. E. Marshall and M. D. O'Brien), all eminent [practitioners and scholars], and is exceedingly well researched. Currently titled *The Treatment of Sexual Offenders: A Positive Approach*, it is forthcoming in a book series I am editing for APA Books (American Psychological Association) called 'Psychology, Crime and Justice' ...

The other forthcoming book is by Laws and Ward (I believe coming out with Guilford) ... It is an application of the desistance literature and desistance framework to the question of sex offender treatment, is equally well-written and researched, and likewise looks beyond programmes to recovery/change process more broadly. I have a feeling that the publication of both of these books at once will herald a real turning point in the way therapists think about sex offender treatment (actually, both books make the case that this 'positive approach' is already the zeitgeist and they are just reporting from the front lines) ... So, it does seem there is a real interest in that field for thinking about desistance.

In addition, I would second Fergus's point about legitimacy research (e.g. Gwen Robinson's fantastic work) which I think is definitely making major waves and also add the increasingly voluminous literatures on 're-entry' and restorative justice, both of which are now getting more sophisticated about process factors and dynamics. Oh, that reminds me of another unpublished book – this time with Oxford – Catherine Appleton's *Life after*

Life Imprisonment – a mixed method (qual-quant) desistance book with definite implications for practice. She interviewed a large sample of lifers released from UK prisons and looks at what factors predicted recall to prison versus success. No surprise, she finds more support for relationship factors with supervisor, legitimacy issues, therapeutic alliance issues, etc.

All three books will likely be out in late 2010, but now you CREDOS folks will (as always) be ahead of the curve …

Faye Taxman: I want to offer another perspective that elaborates on Fergus's comments. Probation, particularly in the US, [was] left out of the RNR movement until very recently (last five years) mainly since the focus on CBT and interventions suggested that it is all in the 'therapy'. The use of tools such as risk and needs assessment also seemed to get lost in the shuffle between NEW tools instead of looking at the adequacy of existing tools … Probation continued to be marginalised with little emphasis on how the probation officer's role could be enhanced in light of the RNR model. While there are pockets of 'brilliance', the supervision field itself is still struggling with [its] identity. And, part of that struggle is the classic goal clarification between monitoring offenders and facilitating behavioural change.

A few of us have tried to focus on the role of the probation officer to improve the environmental context of probation. An overemphasis on standards of conduct (conditions, expectations, etc.) without both a humanistic perspective on the process of the human condition and human change and a theory of probation officer role in this brave new world has resulted in more revocations, and more attention to the failure of the offender to change. Probation systems are subject to much socio-political pressure to define their goals in the criminal justice system context, and in doing so are often pushed into more of a law enforcement role. In the US this has been exaggerated by probation assuming law enforcement functions (carrying guns, etc.) – generally not out of a desire to be law enforcement but to achieve the same civil service benefits as law enforcement (i.e. retirement systems, health insurance, etc.).

While the RNR model is clearly applicable … it was also coupled with trying to demonstrate that the context of probation services needs to be altered. There is some movement in the US to do this but there is general resistance since it is unclear whether the vision is for probation to become part of the desistance process. That is the larger question right now.

Frank Porporino: To add my two cents, I think what we may be missing is the broader cultural and political forces that keep pushing the CJS (and other systems) towards quicker fix solutions ... I certainly don't think that RNR ever set out to feed into the hands of the managerialists, technocrats, and mechanised pragmatists ... but unfortunately I agree that's what happened. When only superficially understood, RNR seemed to offer a tidy little framework ... assess, sort and then treat ... a kind of medical triage model for what works. The breadth and nuances of RNR were never really appreciated ... and even if they were ... they were dismissed as just adding unrealistic 'messiness' to the formula. Of course the 'treat' part of the formula quickly became the exclusive territory of CBT programmes ... nice, packaged solutions that could be easily marketed by consultants ... and easily marketed by government officials as the new 'evidence-based' means to reduce reoffending. Rod Morgan in the UK coined the term 'programme fetishism' ... bemoaning the narrow focus on accredited programmes ... even when the accreditation panel itself was trying to champion a more individualised and continuous case-management driven approach.

The bottom line for this old timer is how can an ethical, committed, professional, human-service case-work orientation be brought back into the field. I really don't care if parole and probation officers are influenced by RNR, CBT, GNR, desistance, or MI. If they understood any of these frameworks well they would do a great job; if they understood them *all* well they would do a fantastic job. Programmes were never intended to substitute for sensitive and attuned case work ... and RNR was never intended to mechanise that process!

Ralph Serin: From my vantage it has always been the case that agencies (and politicians) will most often seek simple solutions to complex issues. The easier something is to 'count' the better it must be, although it would be nice to think that validity trumps reliability. In Don's initial comments he refers to human service delivery. For me this is preferable to RNR (which has been unnecessarily slandered, in some cases likely out of ignorance in that it is far more refined and elegant than is initially apparent) because it is more inclusive. It also implies there is a change process. Ironically, corrections has somehow assumed that the sole responsibility for change is that of the offender, and perhaps his family (Ward and others are clear exceptions to this bias). Thus corrections has missed the opportunity to be partners in this change process; in the case of probation/parole officers, they indeed can and should be agents of change. It is not lost on [me] that the very staff skills/competencies that Don, Jen Skeem and others have noted are important to be effective in offender programming and supervision (fair, empathic, authoritative but not authoritarian) also insulate corrections staff from burnout and lead to improved correctional outcomes. Hence, following his human service model is good for staff (and their families), the agency, AND offenders. BUT, yes it does require sustained effort.

My students and I have been somewhat active in conducting offender-based research. Sadly, access to data even through collaboration is a major challenge ... Our desistance work operationalises constructs that Maruna and others have highlighted as important in the process of desistance. We see our work as transitional, a kind of bridge between the R/N focus of crime acquisition and eventual crime desistance. Since the factors that predict entry and exit from crime are different, we have been trying to develop a constellation of measures that reflect indices or moderators of this transition (agency, positive and negative expectancies of crime and desistance, etc.). We have preliminary but exciting findings. We have also recently been doing work on offender competencies to also inform our understanding of offender change. Most recently we have reviewed literature that confirmed our suspicion that current measures of intra-individual change (pre-post measures in programming) have weak predictive validity – in short there are alarmingly few studies linking change to outcome, few agreed upon measures, and few published studies with predictive validity. This reaffirms our view that new measures/constructs/models of offender change are required to complement the stellar work done by Don, Jim and Paul G ...

Bottom line – there needs to be a social or moral compass that guides correctional staff to be agents of change. This will lead to safer prisons and safer communities.

Peter Raynor: I agree, Frank has this exactly right. One of the problems has been that in England and Wales 'programmes' has meant manualised group programmes, when in other places it can mean any structured and purposeful work with offenders.

So in England and Wales we have seen a neglect of 'what works' issues in individual supervision and offender management, as if these were just administrative processes to route people into 'interventions'. Part of the reason for this was that the Home Office and later the Ministry of Justice have wanted to 'package' interventions in such a way that they could be put out to tender for provision by private sector and/or voluntary organisations, and it is difficult to do this with core probation tasks. This is one reason why some of us are now looking at the impact of skills in individual supervision ... It is also quite clear that the best methods to help offenders are not likely to produce the best results unless they are used in a system that prefers rehabilitation to punishment, and in organisations that value the skills and abilities of practitioners ...

I also read with interest the comments on RNR. It seems to me it is right to see this group of ideas and methods in a broad rather than narrow way. In particular I think the idea that it only deals with deficits ignores the fact that in actual work with offenders based on this or any other effective model, it is difficult or even impossible to engage effectively without an optimistic and hopeful approach, which in turn requires some emphasis on strengths and positives. Some of the differences between RNR and Good Lives models seem to be much more evident in theory than in good practice.

We include this sample of the relevant exchanges here (with the permission of those involved) partly to illustrate the value of the CREDOS network in allowing for precisely this sort of near-instant dialogue across disciplines, continents and perspectives. Such exchanges matter a great deal. This is partly because there have been highly significant policy and practice transfers across these boundaries, but it appears that, not for the first time, many important nuances about the meaning of research evidence have been lost in translation (Jones and Newburn 2007). In a different sense, the exchanges underline the significance of this collection – addressing as it does many of the major themes raised in the discussion. In one sense, it is CREDOS itself that is new and exciting, but more exciting still is the dialogue that it has enabled, only some of which is reflected in this book.

The structure of the book

This collection is organised in six parts. The three chapters in the first part play an important role in setting the scene for what follows. Bonta and Andrews provide a brief and up-to-date account of their influential and important risk-need-responsivity model of offender supervision; Tony Ward presents the more recently developed Good Lives Model; and Shadd Maruna and Thomas LeBel outline the importance of desistance research for debates about offender supervision. We strongly recommend that readers begin here, if only because so many of the subsequent chapters make reference to the ideas and concepts outlined in these three critical chapters.

Part Two describes the three closely related empirical studies that have formed the bedrock of CREDOS's meetings and discussions since 2007. Bourgon and his colleagues outline the Straight Thinking in Corrections Study (STICS); Raynor and his colleagues describe their Jersey study; Chris Trotter and Phillipa Evans discuss their study of Juvenile Justice in New South Wales. All three studies are concerned with the role of staff skills in the effectiveness of offender supervision.

Part Three examines a broader range of issues related to improving offender supervision. Hazel Kemshall examines the crucial role of risk, needs and strengths assessment in improving supervision; Faye Taxman and Judith Sachwald show how the organisation and culture of criminal justice agencies can help or hinder the adoption of effective practices; Pauline Durrance, Nigel Hosking and Nancy Thorburn examine the implementation of a structured approach to one-to-one supervision in London; and Gill McIvor examines the pros and cons of judicial involvement in offender supervision and its potential contribution to improving outcomes.

In Part Four, three quite different but complementary chapters, by Carol Shapiro and Margaret DiZerega, by Bas Vogelvang and Herman van Alphen, and by Chris Trotter, examine the significance for and role of families in offender supervision. Tom O'Connor and Brad Bogue retain the focus on less formal sources of support, but examine in particular the roles of the community, of volunteers and of faith groups.

Part Five of the collection tackles the vexed and increasingly important issue of compliance with supervision. Pamela Ugwudike presents findings from an empirical study which reveals the significance of interactional dynamics in supporting compliance. Shelley Turner looks more broadly at case management issues, interrogating both the conceptual basis of and the empirical evidence about case management in correctional contexts. Gwen Robinson and Fergus McNeill provide a theoretical model that aims to outline and account for the dynamics of compliance with supervision. Trish McCulloch draws on similar theoretical resources, and on the findings of her Scottish study, to consider compliance with community service in particular.

The last section of the book looks to the broader political and historical contexts of offender supervision. The chapters by Faye Taxman, Craig Henderson and Jennifer Lerch, by Tim Chapman and by John Deering, address key questions about the relationships between the contested goals of offender supervision, its methods and practices and its evidence base. Though they deal with different jurisdictions and use different methodologies and approaches, they reach interestingly congruent conclusions. The chapters by Loraine Gelsthorpe, Peter Raynor and Gwen Robinson and by Fergus McNeill both offer historical analyses of the changing nature of offender supervision. Whereas McNeill's oral history examines the lived experience of probation at a particular time and place – and its long-term effects – Gelsthorpe and her colleagues use pre-sentence reports from different eras to examine the changing discursive constructions of offenders since the 1960s. Finally, Mike Nellis painstakingly examines the lessons that emerge from the development of electronic monitoring in the UK, analysing the prospects for its integration within other forms of offender management.

For fear of prejudicing the reader's own interpretation, we say nothing more here about what conclusions might be drawn within these chapters or about how we assess the significance of their diverse but recurring themes. That task we leave for the Conclusion. Suffice it to say that we hope you enjoy reading these important contributions as much as we have enjoyed hearing, reading and editing them.

References

American Friends Services Committee (1971) *Struggle for Justice.* New York: Hill and Wang.

Durnescu, I. (2009) 'The pains of probation: effective practice and human rights', paper presented at the 9th Annual Conference of the European Society of Criminology, University of Ljubljana, 9–12 September 2009.

Feeley, M. and Simon, J. (1992) 'The new penology: notes on the emerging strategy of corrections and its implications', *Criminology*, 30: 449–74.

Feeley, M. and Simon, J. (1994) 'Actuarial justice: the emerging new criminal law', in D. Nelken, (ed.) *The Futures of Criminology*. London: Sage.

Garland, D. (2001) *The Culture of Control*. Oxford: Clarendon Press.

Jones, T. and Newburn, T. (2007) *Policy Transfer and Criminal Justice*. Maidenhead: Open University Press.

McNeill, F. (2009) *Towards Effective Practice in Offender Supervision*. Glasgow: Scottish Centre for Crime and Justice Research. Available at: www.sccjr.ac.uk/documents/McNeil_Towards.pdf.

Raynor, P. (1978) 'Compulsory persuasion: a problem for correctional social work', *British Journal of Social Work*, 8 (4): 411–24.

Raynor, P. (1985) *Social Work, Justice and Control*. Oxford: Blackwell.

Raynor, P. and Robinson, G. (2009) *Rehabilitation, Crime and Justice*. 2nd edn. Basingstoke: Palgrave Macmillan.

Trotter, C. (2006) *Work with Involuntary Clients*, 2nd edn. London: Sage.

Part One

New Directions in Theory

Chapter 2

Viewing offender assessment and rehabilitation through the lens of the risk-need-responsivity model[1]

James Bonta and Don Andrews

Introduction

The risk-need-responsivity (RNR) model is perhaps the most influential model used to guide the assessment and treatment of offenders (Blanchette and Brown 2006; Ward *et al.* 2007). First formalised in 1990 by Andrews, Bonta and Hoge, the RNR model has been elaborated upon and contextualised within a general personality and cognitive social learning perspective of criminal conduct (Andrews and Bonta 2010). Since 1990, a number of principles have been added to the original principles of risk, need and responsivity. These additional principles describe, for example, the importance of staff establishing collaborative and respectful working relationships with clients and correctional agencies and managers providing policies and leadership that facilitate and enable effective interventions (Andrews 2001; Andrews and Bonta 2010; Andrews and Dowden 2007).

This chapter summarises the RNR model and describes how the model has influenced the development of offender assessment instruments and rehabilitation programmes. In so doing, we show that the criminal behaviour of offenders can be predicted in a reliable, practical and useful manner. We also demonstrate that rehabilitation programmes can produce significant reductions in recidivism when these programmes are in adherence with the RNR model.

The RNR model

The RNR model is shown in Table 2.1. The overarching principles, 1 through 4, describe the values, goals and theoretical bases to the RNR model. The core principles, however, are found in principles 5 through 11. The risk principle (principle 5) states that intensive rehabilitative services should be offered to moderate and high risk cases while low risk cases receive minimal rehabilitation services. Low risk cases have low probabilities of recidivism in the absence of services and reductions in recidivism rates are found among moderate and high risk cases. Some clinicians may prefer to treat the YAVIS client (young, attractive, verbal, intelligent and successful; Schofield 1964) but the low risk client is exactly the client who does not respond well to intensive rehabilitation services. You do not want to increase association with high risk others or risk disruption of existing strengths in the domains of cognition, family and school/work.

The need principle (principle 6 in Table 2.1) makes a distinction between criminogenic and non-criminogenic needs. Offenders have many needs but not all of them are functionally related to their criminal behaviour. For example, increasing an offender's self-esteem without regard to pro-criminal attitudes may result in a self-confident criminal (Wormith 1984). Criminogenic needs are dynamic risk factors and serve as the intermediate targets (between overarching objectives and case specific factors) in rehabilitation programming, bridging changes within a specific treatment to changes in future recidivism. Of course, higher risk offenders will have more criminogenic needs requiring a breadth of services (principle 7).

Principle 8, general responsivity, speaks to the influence strategies of choice, namely, cognitive social learning practices. Presently, some are suggesting that quality of relationship and therapeutic alliance are more important than cognitive behavioural intervention factors (Ahn and Wampold 2001; Wampold 2007). The general responsivity principle does not deny the importance of the therapeutic relationship but does say that structured, cognitive behavioural intervention is an important component of effective correctional treatment.

Principle 9, specific responsivity, individualises treatment according to strengths, ability, motivation, personality and bio-social characteristics such as gender, ethnicity and age. The principle invites treatment planners to build on strengths and consider removal of any

Table 2.1 RNR principles of effective human service in justice and other contexts

Overarching principles
1 *Respect for the person*: Pursue the ethical, legal, just, moral, humane, decent, professional, cost-effective and otherwise normative implementation of RNR.
2 *Psychological theory*: Base program on an empirically solid psychological theory (a general personality and cognitive social learning approach is recommended).
3 *Introduce human service*: Do not rely on deterrence, restoration or other principles of justice.
4 *Enhancement of crime prevention services*: The reduction of criminal victimisation is viewed as a legitimate objective of service agencies within and outside of justice.

Risk-need-responsivity
5 *Risk*: Match intensity of rehabilitative service with risk level of cases. Work with moderate and high risk cases. Keep low risk cases away from higher risk cases.
6 *Need*: Target criminogenic needs predominately. The theoretically and empirically most appealing targets are the central eight (see Table 2.2).
7 *Breadth/multimodal*: Target a number of the criminogenic needs of higher risk cases.
8 *General responsivity*: Employ social learning and cognitive behavioural strategies.
9 *Specific responsivity*: Match the mode, strategies and styles of service with the learning styles, motivations, readiness to change, stages of change, abilities, strengths, personality and bio-demographics of individual offenders.
10 *Strengths*: Assess strengths to enhance prediction and scope of specific responsivity.
11 *Professional discretion*: Deviate from the RNR principles for specified reasons (e.g. functional analysis suggests personal distress is a risk factor for *this* person).

Structured assessment
12 *Assessments of strengths and risk-need-specific responsivity factors*: Employ structured and validated assessment instruments.
13 *Integrated assessment and intervention*: Every planned intervention and contact should be informed by the assessments.

Program delivery
14 *Dosage*: Engage higher risk cases and minimise their drop-out from RNR programmes.

15 *Core correctional staff practices*: Effectiveness of interventions is enhanced when delivered by staff with high-quality relationship skills in combination with structuring skills. Quality relationships are characterised as respectful, caring, enthusiastic, collaborative and valuing of personal autonomy. Structuring practices include pro-social modelling, effective reinforcement and disapproval, skill building, problem-solving, effective use of authority, advocacy/brokerage, cognitive restructuring and motivational interviewing.

Organisational concerns

16 *Community-based*: Community-based services are preferred but, if the setting is residential or institutional, the RNR principles still apply.

17 *Management*: Promote the selection, training and clinical supervision of staff according to RNR and introduce monitoring, feedback and adjustment systems. Build systems and cultures supportive of effective practice and continuity of care.

---

barriers to full participation in service, issues particularly important to minority cultural groups (Vasquez 2007) and women (Belknap 2007). The matching of treatment to client characteristics is one of the hallmarks of all psychological treatments (Barlow 2004; Kazdin 2008). Principle 10 introduces strengths with their potential in sharpening the prediction of anti-social outcomes as well as specific responsivity factors (that is, building on the strengths of the case).

Our, some would say over-zealous, efforts to bring these core principles to the attention of the field of corrections have been at the cost of neglecting some other important principles. Lately, we have been trying to correct some misperceptions of the RNR model and once again, we remind the reader of the importance of the other RNR principles. Among the overarching principles, Principle 1 stresses the values underlying intervention while Principle 2 underscores the importance of a theory of the criminal behaviour of individuals. Principle 3 highlights the role of human service within a justice context. This principle takes the position that relying on punishment to control recidivism will be unsuccessful. Indeed, narrative and meta-analytic reviews of the imprisonment literature consistently show that incarceration does not lead to reductions in recidivism beyond the period of incapacitation (Doob and Webster 2003; Smith *et al.* 2002; Villettaz *et al.* 2006; Von Hirsch *et al.* 1999). Principle 4 extends the model beyond criminal justice agencies and encourages non-justice agencies (such as health, social services, schools, youth and family services) to become involved in efforts to reduce crime and victimisation.

Principles 12 and 13 have been introduced because, in practice, we find many agencies fail to conduct validated risk/need assessments (or if conducted, they fail to actually treat differentially in accordance with the results of the assessment; Andrews 2006; Bonta *et al.* 2008). Principle 14, somewhat related to the risk principle, emphasises the need for agencies to make an active effort to engage higher risk clients in treatment. Many programmes often exclude such offenders, labelling them as 'unmotivated' or 'psychopathic and unable to change'.

Principle 15, within the 'Program delivery' set, is of extraordinary significance. Andrews (1980) has been stressing staff practices since the 1970s but considerations of staffing continue to be limited in correctional and forensic settings where a 'caring' relationship is best paired with 'fairness' in the exercise of authority (Skeem *et al.* 2007). Core correctional practices within RNR directly reflect two specific sets of skills, namely relationship and structuring skills (for example, prosocial modelling, contingent application of rewards and punishment, behavioural rehearsal of new skills). Finally, we complete the RNR model with a recognition that the effective delivery of services will vary by the context of service delivery. Service delivery in the community is preferred over custody-based services (Principle 16) and Principle 17 highlights the responsibility of management for effective human service delivery.

The 17 principles outlined in Table 2.1 are more than a compilation of required elements for effective rehabilitation. The principles are derived from a general personality and cognitive social learning perspective of criminal conduct (Andrews and Bonta 2010). Note that the RNR model is not constrained by the justice and deterrence models that are so prevalent today. Rather, the principles are based on psychological theory and evidence as to the major risk/need factors, the most effective techniques to influence behavioural change and the organisation and staff characteristics to support changes in the behaviour of offenders. Justice and deterrence models simply do not, or perhaps cannot, speak to these relevant factors.

A brief history of risk assessment

For much of the first half of the twentieth century, the assessment of offender risk was guided by one's professional training and experience. The assessment of risk was a matter of professional judgement. Beginning in the 1970s, there was a growing recognition that the assessment of risk needed to depend more upon actuarial, evidence-based science and less on professional judgement. Research reviews repeatedly showed that actuarial-based instruments performed better than clinical or professional judgement when making predictions of human behaviour (Ægisdóttier *et al.* 2006; Andrews *et al.* 2006; Grove *et al.* 2000). The superiority of actuarial prediction has been extended to such diverse offender groups as mentally disordered offenders (Bonta *et al.* 1998) and sex offenders (Hanson 2009; Hanson and Morton-Bourgon 2009). As a consequence of the predictive superiority of actuarial-based risk assessments, more and more correctional jurisdictions adopted this type of assessment for classifying offenders and assigning differential supervision practices.

The period between 1970 and 1980 saw a movement from what Bonta (1996) called first-generation assessment (professional judgements of risk) to second-generation assessment (actuarial-based assessment of risk). Although second-generation risk assessment instruments predict relatively well, they have two major shortcomings. First, these instruments are atheoretical. The items that create these instruments are chosen simply because they are easily available and show an association with recidivism. The items are not chosen because they are theoretically relevant. Thus, the majority of the items are criminal history items – the type of information that correctional systems are quite efficient at collecting and distributing.

The second weakness is that most items are of a historical nature (for example history of drug abuse). Criminal history and past behaviour are static, immutable risk factors. This is a major shortcoming because second-generation risk assessments are unable to account for offenders changing for the better. Rather, the possibilities are (a) an individual's risk level does not change (if one scored positive for a history of drug abuse that risk factor will always remain no matter if he/she has learned to abstain from drugs), or (b) an individual's risk increases (new offences are committed and criminal history scores increase). There is little possibility for diminished risk (to be fair, some of the second-generation instruments do have dynamic items; however, they represent a minority of items in second-generation risk scales).

Recognising the limitations of second-generation risk assessment, assessment instruments that included dynamic risk factors were developed in the late 1970s and early 1980s (Bonta and Wormith 2007). Criminal history items remained an important feature of these third-generation risk assessment instruments, as they should. However, in addition to static factors, dynamic items investigating the offender's current and ever-changing situation were introduced. Questions were asked about present employment (after all, one can lose a job or find a job), criminal friends (one can make new friends and lose old friends), and family relationships (supportive or unsupportive). The third-generation risk instruments were referred to as 'risk-need' instruments and a few of these were theoretically based (such as the Level of Service Inventory–Revised: LSI-R; Andrews and Bonta 1995).

Third-generation risk-need instruments were sensitive to changes in an offender's circumstances and also provided correctional staff with information as to what needs should be targeted in their interventions. For example, there is now evidence that changes in LSI-R scores are associated with changes in recidivism (Andrews and Robinson 1984; Arnold 2007; Motiuk et al. 1990; Raynor 2007; Raynor et al. 2000). Evidence of dynamic validity – that is, changes in risk scores signalling changes in the likelihood of committing a new offence – is immensely important for correctional programmes and the staff charged with managing offender risk. These risk-need instruments offer a way of monitoring the effectiveness, or ineffectiveness, of programmes and supervision strategies. Furthermore, because dynamic risk factors (substance abuse, employment, companions) are embedded in third-generation instruments, correctional staff can be guided in directing intervention to these dynamic risk factors. Successfully addressing these dynamic risk factors would contribute to an offender's reduction in risk (Bonta 2002).

To complete the story of offender risk scale development, the last few years have seen the introduction of fourth-generation assessment instruments. These new instruments integrate systematic intervention and monitoring with the assessment of a broader range of offender risk-need factors heretofore not measured and other personal factors important to treatment (Andrews et al. 2006). An example of a fourth-generation risk assessment instrument is the Level of Service/Case Management Inventory (LS/CMI; Andrews et al. 2004).

What is notable in this history is that third- and fourth-generation assessment instruments would not have been possible without the RNR model of offender assessment and rehabilitation.

Risk-need-responsivity model and offender risk assessment

The risk principle hypothesises that offender recidivism can be reduced if the level of treatment services provided to the offender is proportional to the offender's risk to reoffend. The principle has two parts to it: (1) an assessment of risk to reoffend and (2) the appropriate level of treatment. We will reserve our discussion of offender treatment for later but here we focus on the offender's risk to reoffend.

As we reviewed earlier, criminal behaviour can be predicted in a reliable manner beyond any specialised training and experience (the actuarial versus professional judgement debate). If one of our correctional goals is to reduce offender recidivism then we need to ensure that we have a reliable way of differentiating low risk offenders from higher risk offenders in order to provide the appropriate level of treatment. Today, we have the assessment technology to make distinctions among offenders according to their differential probabilities of reoffending (Campbell *et al.* 2009).

The need principle calls for the targets of correctional treatment to be *criminogenic needs*. Criminogenic needs are dynamic risk factors that are directly linked to criminal behaviour. Offenders have many needs deserving of treatment but not all of these needs are associated with their criminal behaviour. These criminogenic needs are subsumed under the major predictors of criminal behaviour referred to as the 'central eight' risk/needs factors (Andrews and Bonta 2010; Andrews *et al.* 2006).

Table 2.2 presents an overview of the major risk/need factors along with some less promising targets for interventions (that is, non-criminogenic needs) and suggestions for assessment and treatment. The seven major risk/need factors are part of the central eight (criminal history completes the list but it is a static risk factor). These seven criminogenic needs are worth assessing and targeting in interventions. To further illustrate the distinction between the two types of needs let us examine pro-criminal attitudes that are labelled criminogenic. Shifting attitudes through treatment from the pro-criminal to the pro-social will lead to less criminal behaviour and more pro-social behaviour (what you think influences how you behave). However, increasing self-esteem without changes in pro-criminal attitudes runs the risk of resulting in confident criminals while decreasing self-esteem may lead to miserable criminals. Note that criminal behaviour may or may not change as a function of self-esteem.

Table 2.2 The seven major risk/need factors along with some minor risk/need factors

Risk/need factor	Indicators	Intervention goals
Major factors		
Anti-social personality pattern	Impulsive, adventurous, pleasure-seeking, aggressive and irritable	Build self-management skills, teach anger management
Pro-criminal attitudes	Rationalisations for crime, negative attitudes towards the law	Counter rationalisations with pro-social attitudes; build up a pro-social identity
Social supports for crime	Criminal friends, isolation from pro-social others	Replace pro-criminal friends and associates with pro-social friends and associates
Substance abuse	Abuse of alcohol and/or drugs	Reduce substance abuse, enhance alternatives to substance use
Family/marital relationships	Inappropriate parental monitoring and disciplining, poor family relationships	Teach parenting skills, enhance warmth and caring
School/work	Poor performance, low levels of satisfaction	Enhance work/study skills, nurture inter-personal relation-ships within the context of work and school

| Pro-social recreational activities | Lack of involvement in pro-social recreational/leisure activities | Encourage participation in pro-social recreational activities, teach pro-social hobbies and sports |

Non-criminogenic minor needs

Self-esteem	Poor feelings of self-esteem, self-worth
Vague feelings of personal distress	Anxious, feeling blue
Major mental disorder	Schizophrenia, manic depression
Physical health	Physical deformity, nutrient deficiency

In terms of offender assessment, the need principle requires the assessment of criminogenic needs/dynamic risk factors. As we have already pointed out, third- and fourth-generation risk instruments do just that.

Third, we have the responsivity principle. Most often, general responsivity is considered within the context of treatment and refers to the fact that cognitive social learning interventions are the most effective way to teach people new behaviours. However, specific responsivity calls for treatment interventions to consider personal strengths and socio-biological personality factors. This is where assessment of such factors becomes important as treatment should then be tailored to these factors.

In the assessment for effective rehabilitation, psychological characteristics that may affect the delivery of services (for example, mental disorder, anxiety, intelligence), socio-economic factors (poverty, culture) and biological variables (race, gender) all play a role. Some of these factors influence how an offender learns new behaviour (such as a concrete thinking style) while others are barriers to addressing criminogenic needs and must be addressed early in intervention (for example, psychotic symptoms). Offender assessment should involve a sampling of these responsivity factors (the LS/CMI, fourth-generation assessment instrument actually has a separate section on responsivity).

Before we draw this section to an end, we would like to make a very important point that is sometimes lost among risk assessment researchers. Good offender assessment is more than making decisions on level of risk. If one only cared about differentiating low risk from high risk offenders so that the high risk offender can be controlled through incapacitation or strict monitoring then second generation risk scales are up to the task. However, in our view this is short-sighted as it largely ignores the fundamental human condition of change. At the same time it has the potential of violating our sense of fairness. People are always changing their behaviours as a consequence of environmental demands and through their own deliberate, autonomous, self-directed change. By adhering to the need and responsivity principles through the assessment of criminogenic needs and responsivity factors we acknowledge that change is an important aspect of life and behavioural change can be facilitated by the appropriate intervention. As we will see in the next section, assessments of risk, criminogenic needs and responsivity all figure largely in effective offender treatment.

Offender rehabilitation

Brief history of offender rehabilitation

For a long time there has been evidence that some interventions can reduce recidivism. In 1954, Kirby found four studies evaluating correctional counselling. The studies compared offenders receiving treatment to offenders who had no treatment. He found that three of the studies demonstrated lower recidivism rates for the offenders who received treatment. Subsequent reviews continued to unearth more and even more controlled evaluations of correctional treatment and these reviews found that, in approximately 50 to 60 per cent of the studies, treatment was effective (Bailey 1966; Logan 1972).

Throughout the 1950s and 1960s, rehabilitation was seen as a promising approach to reducing recidivism. Although earlier reviews found that treatment does not 'work' in half of the studies, the bottle was seen as half full. That changed as a consequence of a report by Robert Martinson and his colleagues (Lipton *et al.* 1975; Martinson 1974). Martinson's group reviewed over 230 evaluations of offender 'treatment' (we place quotation marks around the word as a very liberal definition of what constituted treatment was used). They found, like the reviewers before them, that approximately 50 to 60 per cent of studies supported the effectiveness of treatment. However, this time the conclusion was, 'nothing works'.

The 'nothing works' movement seized criminal justice, particularly in the United States. If offenders could not be rehabilitated then what was society to do with the problem of crime? Many answered that punishment or deterrence could reduce criminal behaviour. Thus began the 'get tough' movement. However, after 30 years of experimentation with getting tough, not only have prison and probation populations skyrocketed but the weight of the evidence is that deterrence has had hardly any impact on offender recidivism and in some situations, actually increased recidivism (see Chapter 13 of Andrews and Bonta 2010; Pogarsky and Piquero 2003; Pratt and Cullen 2005; Smith *et al.* 2002; Villettaz *et al.* 2006; Von Hirsch *et al.* 1999).

The one good thing that came out of the 'nothing works' ideology was that researchers became more rigorous in their evaluations of treatment and some researchers developed a theoretical model to explain why some interventions were effective and others were not (see Andrews *et al.* 1990).

The RNR model and offender rehabilitation

Recall that the risk principle has two components. The first part emphasises the importance of reliably predicting criminal behaviour, and thus the need for evidence-based risk-need instruments. The second component highlights the need to properly match the level of service to the offender's risk level. That is, as risk level increases then the amount of treatment needed to reduce recidivism also increases. To the reader, this may appear to be common sense – higher risk offenders have more criminogenic needs than lower risk offenders and therefore more intervention is required to address these needs. However, in everyday practice there is a tremendous pressure to focus resources on lower risk offenders. After all, low risk offenders are more cooperative and motivated to comply with treatment demands than high risk offenders.

Inappropriate matching of treatment intensity with offender risk level can lead to wasted treatment resources and in some situations actually make matters worse. Note in the first row of Table 2.3 that treatment services provided to high risk offenders show a higher effect size (phi) compared to treatment provided to low risk offenders. In 374 tests of the risk principle, treatment delivered to

Table 2.3 Mean effect size (phi) by adherence to principles of risk, need and responsivity (k)

	Adherence to principle	
Principle	No	Yes
Risk: services delivered to higher-risk cases	.03 (96)	.10 (278)
Criminogenic needs:		
Criminogenic needs targeted	−.01 (205)	.19 (169)
General responsivity:		
Social Learning/Cognitive		
behavioural strategies	.04 (297)	.23 (77)

Note: k = number of tests.

high risk offenders was associated with an average 10 percentage point difference in recidivism (Andrews and Bonta 2006).

Table 2.3 also demonstrates that providing treatment to low risk offenders is associated with a very mild effect (about a 3 per cent reduction in recidivism). There are, however, a few studies that show that *intensive* services to low risk offenders may actually increase criminal behaviour. For example, Bonta, Wallace-Capretta and Rooney (2000) found that low risk offenders who received minimal levels of treatment had a recidivism rate of 15 per cent and low risk offenders who received intensive levels of services had more than double the recidivism rate (32 per cent). In the same study, the high risk offenders who did not receive any intensive treatment services had a recidivism rate of 51 per cent but the high risk offenders who received intensive services had almost half the recidivism rate (32 per cent). The risk principle calls for intensive treatment services to be reserved for the higher risk offender.

Can we achieve reductions in recidivism beyond 10 per cent by limiting ourselves to the risk principle? What happens when we include the need and responsivity principles? Based on tests of the need principle, successfully addressing criminogenic needs is associated with an average 19 per cent difference in recidivism (row 2 of Table 2.3; Andrews and Bonta 2006). Treatments that focus on non-criminogenic needs are associated with a slight increase in recidivism (about 1 per cent). If we examine only adherence to the general responsivity principle we find, on average, a 23 per cent difference in recidivism

Table 2.4 Mean effect size (phi) by adherence to principles of risk, need and responsivity: residential and community

	Phi	
Level of adherence	Residential	Community
Adherence to one principle	.01	.03
Adherence to two principles	.12	.22
Full adherence	.17	.35
Across settings:		
Full adherence		.28

Source: Andrews and Bonta (2006).

(see row 3 of Table 2.3). Finally, what happens when offender treatment programmes put all three principles into action? Table 2.4 shows the remarkable accumulating effectiveness of treatment when there is increased adherence to the risk-need-responsivity principles.

Treatment interventions that do not adhere to any of the three principles (that is, they target the non-criminogenic needs of low risk offenders using non-cognitive behavioural techniques) are actually criminogenic! This situation is particularly exacerbated when the treatment is given in residential/custodial settings (we presume because the offender cannot escape from the well-intentioned but poorly designed treatment). However, if a treatment intervention begins to adhere to one of the principles we start to see reductions in recidivism and when all three principles are evident in a rehabilitation programme then we see average recidivism differences between the treated and non-treated offenders of 17 per cent when delivered in residential/custodial settings and 35 per cent when delivered in community settings. Treatment can work in residential and custodial settings but effectiveness is maximised when the treatment is in a community setting.

To have 17 and 35 per cent point differences in recidivism may not seem like much. Some may ask why the figures are not higher. Why not 40 or 50 or even 100 per cent? Besides answering that a complete reduction in recidivism or a 'total cure' is an unrealistic goal, let us examine the 17–35 per cent success rate in relation to other widely acceptable success rates. As presented in Table 2.5, offender treatment programmes that adhere to the principles of risk,

Table 2.5 Comparative effectiveness for selected interventions

Intervention	Target	Success rates
Criminal justice		
Police clearance rates	Break and enter	0.16
	Auto theft	0.12
Offender treatment (RNR)	Recidivism	0.29
Medical interventions		
Aspirin	Cardiac event	0.03
Chemotherapy	Breast cancer	0.11
Bypass surgery	Cardiac event	0.15

Sources: Andrews and Bonta (2010); Fedorowycz (2004); Lipsey and Wilson (1993).

need and responsivity measure up quite well to the police's ability to clear a crime and even some common medical interventions.

Generality of the RNR model

The general personality and cognitive social learning (GPCSL) perspective of criminal behaviour (Andrews and Bonta 2010) fundamentally reflects a personality predisposition and the learning of criminal behaviour governed by the expectations an individual holds and the actual consequences to his or her behaviour. Behaviour that is rewarded or that the individual expects will be rewarded is likely to occur and behaviour that is punished or is expected to be punished is unlikely to occur.

Criminal behaviour is likely when the rewards and costs for crime outweigh the rewards and costs for pro-social behaviour. Rewards and costs can be delivered by others (family, friends, teachers, employers and co-workers), they can be produced from within (such as feelings of pride and shame) and sometimes they arise automatically from the behaviour itself (a feeling of relaxation after ingesting a drug, or the feeling of excitement when breaking into a house). The accumulation of rewards for crime and the costs for pro-social behaviour can tip the balance towards criminal conduct.

The GPCSL perspective underlies the RNR model of offender assessment and rehabilitation. When we conduct risk assessments we are essentially sampling the rewards and costs associated with criminal conduct. Does the individual have criminal friends? If so, then we know that the individual likely receives rewards and encouragement for criminal behaviour. Does the individual like his or her job and the people with whom they work? If so, then we know that rewards are available for pro-social behaviour. We can go further and dissect GPCSL in order to construct the links to RNR.

1 General personality. With respect to criminal behaviour, we refer specifically to an anti-social personality pattern. Anti-social personality pattern is not limited to the psychiatric diagnostic category of anti-social personality disorder or the forensic label of psychopathy. It is more comprehensive and captures the history of generalised rule violation and trouble, some of the personality factors that function as criminogenic needs (impulsivity, self-centredness) and responsivity factors (need for excitement, shallow affect).

2 Cognitive. The cognitive aspect of the theory includes deliberate self-conscious and automatic self-regulation and points to the importance of pro-criminal attitudes, values and beliefs as causes to criminal behaviour.

3 Social learning. This part of GPCSL highlights the importance of learning within the social contexts of friends, family, school, work and leisure. Assessments of the rewards and costs for criminal and pro-social behaviour within these social contexts, along with automatic rewards and costs associated with some behaviours (for example, drug use), provide a comprehensive survey of criminogenic needs and strengths. As we have already said, an assessment of the 'Central Eight' (Andrews and Bonta 2010; Andrews et al. 2006) then lays the foundation for effective intervention by directing services to those risk factors linked to criminal behaviour.

The GPCSL perspective, at the broadest level, is a general understanding of human behaviour that takes into account personality, cognitions and the social context of learning. Thus, the GPCSL perspective and the subsumed RNR model are expected to be relevant across a range of offenders. For the most part, and with some minor exceptions, the evidence suggests that the RNR model of assessment and treatment can be applied to women offenders (Blanchette and Brown 2006; Dowden and Andrews 1999a), mentally disordered offenders (Andrews, Dowden and Rettinger 2001; Bonta et al. 1998), the extremely poor and those without financial problems (Andrews et al. 2001), young offenders (Dowden and Andrews 1999b), sex offenders (Hanson et al. 2009; Lovins et al. 2009) and Aboriginal offenders (Rugge 2006). The RNR model is robust indeed.

Summary and conclusions

During the past 20 years there has been tremendous progress in our ability to reliably differentiate offenders in terms of risk and to assist offenders with becoming more pro-social. Many of these positive developments have been greatly influenced by the formulation of the RNR model. This is not to say that other approaches to risk assessment and treatment have not made important contributions. There are, for example, many valid second generation risk instruments that have been developed from a non-theoretical perspective using highly sophisticated psychometric methods (Campbell *et al.* 2009). However, very few of these risk instruments contribute to planning for effective intervention. The RNR model has not only contributed to the development of offender risk-need instruments that predict as well as the atheoretical, actuarial instruments, but also provides information useful for offender treatment.

We do not mean to paint a rosy picture where all offenders can be perfectly assessed and successfully treated. We do not think that prediction will ever be perfect and that each and every offender can be treated to never offend again. Human behaviour is far too complex for our assessment instruments and treatment programmes. We also recognise that some may object to our emphasis on criminogenic needs at the expense of non-criminogenic needs that may be particularly important to an individual's happiness. The RNR model, however, does *not* exclude attention to personal levels of distress. As we have stated before (Bonta and Andrews 2003), achieving personal satisfaction for offenders involves attention to both types of needs. Nevertheless, by attending to criminogenic needs we achieve practical improvements in the prediction and treatment of offenders. When offenders can move away from a criminal lifestyle that often brings anguish and misery to themselves, their loved ones and others towards a pro-social lifestyle, it is not only the public that gains but also the offender and those around him or her.

The greatest challenge is transferring the RNR model into 'real world' settings. It is one thing for scientists to demonstrate that a risk instrument or a treatment programme can work; it is a very different matter to make it work in correctional agencies with a diverse workforce in terms of education, values and experience, conflicting criminal justice policies, and management practices that are not conducive to selecting and training staff in effective assessment techniques. We know that with time the assessments completed by staff become less accurate due to errors and there is a general drift in the integrity of assessments (Bonta *et al.* 2001; Lowenkamp *et al.* 2004). What we do not know enough of is how to maintain the assessment expertise of staff over extended periods of time.

We also know that when treatment programmes that have demonstrated reduced recidivism in controlled experiments are rolled out on a larger scale, their effectiveness is significantly diminished (Lipsey 1999). Andrews and Bonta (2010) reported that the effectiveness of treatment delivered in the real world is about half of the effect of the experimental, demonstration programme. Despite this sobering finding we are also learning what is necessary to enhance the delivery of effective treatment services.

Given the research to date, in order to provide the best assessments and interventions, correctional agencies need to:

- Embrace a general vision that it is in the best interest for all to provide cognitive behavioural services to offenders.
- Select, properly train and supervise staff in the use of RNR assessments and the delivery of services that adhere to RNR.
- Provide policies and organisational supports for the RNR model.

Agencies that are able to achieve this level of commitment show significant reductions in recidivism, compared to agencies that fail to adhere to the risk-need-responsivity principles (Andrews and Dowden 2005; Lowenkamp *et al.* 2004, 2006). Obviously, there is still much work to do but the RNR gives us a roadmap of what must be done.

Note

1 The opinions expressed in this report are those of the authors and do not necessarily represent the views of Public Safety Canada.

References

Ægisdóttier, S., White, M. J., Spengler, P. M. *et al.* (2006) 'The meta-analysis of clinical judgment project: fifty-six years of accumulated research on clinical versus statistical prediction' *Counseling Psychologist*, 34: 341–82.
Ahn, H. and Wampold, B.E. (2001) 'Where oh where are the specific ingredients? A meta-analysis of component studies in counseling and psychotherapy', *Journal of Counseling Psychology*, 48: 251–7.

Andrews, D.A. (1980) 'Experimental investigations of the principles of differential association through deliberate manipulation of the structure of service systems', *American Sociological Review,* 45: 448–62.

Andrews, D.A. (2001) 'Principles of effective correctional programs', in L.L. Motiuk and R.C. Serin (eds) *Compendium 2000 on Effective Correctional Programming.* Ottawa: Correctional Services of Canada.

Andrews, D.A. (2006) 'Enhancing adherence to risk-need-responsivity: making quality a matter of policy', *Criminology and Public Policy,* 5: 595–602.

Andrews, D.A. and Bonta, J. (1995) *The Level of Service Inventory – Revised.* Toronto: Multi-Health Systems.

Andrews, D.A. and Bonta, J. (2006) *The Psychology of Criminal Conduct,* 4th edn. Newark, NJ: LexisNexis.

Andrews, D.A. and Bonta, J. (2010) *The Psychology of Criminal Conduct,* 5th edn. Newark, NJ: LexisNexis.

Andrews, D.A. and Dowden, C. (2005) 'Managing correctional treatment for reduced recidivism: a meta-analytic review of program integrity', *Legal and Criminological Psychology,* 10: 173–87.

Andrews, D.A. and Dowden, C. (2007) 'The risk-need-responsivity model of assessment and human service in prevention and corrections: rehabilitative jurisprudence', *Canadian Journal of Criminology and Criminal Justice,* 49: 439–64.

Andrews, D.A. and Robinson, D. (1984) *The Level of Supervision Inventory: Second Report.* Toronto: Ontario Ministry of Correctional Services.

Andrews, D.A., Bonta, J. and Hoge, R.D. (1990) 'Classification for effective rehabilitation: Rediscovering psychology', *Criminal Justice and Behavior,* 17: 19–52.

Andrews, D.A., Bonta, J. and Wormith, S.J. (2004) *The Level of Service/Case Management Inventory (LS/CMI).* Toronto: Multi-Health Systems.

Andrews, D.A., Bonta, J. and Wormith, S.J. (2006) 'The recent past and near future of risk and/or need assessment', *Crime and Delinquency,* 52: 7–27.

Andrews, D.A., Dowden, C. and Rettinger, J.L. (2001) 'Special populations within corrections', in J.A. Winterdyk (ed.) *Corrections in Canada: Social Reactions to Crime.* Toronto: Prentice-Hall.

Andrews, D.A., Zinger, I., Hoge, R.D., Bonta, J., Gendreau, P. and Cullen, F.T. (1990) 'Does correctional treatment work? A psychologically informed meta-analysis', *Criminology,* 28: 369–404.

Arnold, T. (2007) 'Dynamic changes in the Level of Service Inventory–Revised (LSI-R) and the effects on prediction accuracy', unpublished Master's dissertation, St Cloud University, St Cloud, Minnesota.

Bailey, W.C. (1966) 'Correctional outcome: an evaluation of 100 reports', *Journal of Criminal Law, Criminology and Police Science,* 57: 153–60.

Barlow, D.H. (2004) 'Psychological treatments', *American Psychologist,* 59: 869–78.

Belknap, J. (2007) *The Invisible Woman: Gender, Crime and Justice* 3rd edn. Belmont, CA: Wadsworth.

Blanchette, K. and Brown, S. L. (2006) *The Assessment and Treatment of Women Offenders: An Integrative Perspective*. Chichester: John Wiley.

Bonta, J. (1996) 'Risk-needs assessment and treatment', in A.T. Harland (ed.) *Choosing Correctional Options that Work: Defining the Demand and Evaluating the Supply*. Thousand Oaks, CA: Sage.

Bonta, J. (2002) 'Offender risk assessment: guidelines for selection and use', *Criminal Justice and Behavior*, 29: 355–79.

Bonta, J. and Andrews, D.A. (2003) 'A commentary on Ward and Stewart's model of human needs', *Psychology, Crime, and Law*, 9: 215–18.

Bonta, J. and Wormith, S.J. (2007) 'Risk and need assessment', in G. McIvor and P. Raynor (eds), *Developments in Social Work with Offenders*. Philadelphia, PA: Jessica Kingsley.

Bonta, J., Bogue, B., Crowley, M. and Motiuk, L. (2001) 'Implementing offender classification systems: lessons learned', in G.A. Bernfeld, D.P. Farrington and A.W. Leschied (eds) *Offender Rehabilitation in Practice: Implementing and Evaluating Effective Programs*. Chichester: John Wiley.

Bonta, J., Law, M. and Hanson, R.K. (1998) 'The prediction of criminal and violent recidivism among mentally disordered offenders: a meta-analysis', *Psychological Bulletin*, 123: 123–42.

Bonta, J., Rugge, T., Scott, T.-L., Bourgon, G. and Yessine, A. (2008) 'Exploring the black box of community supervision', *Journal of Offender Rehabilitation*, 47: 248–70.

Bonta, J., Wallace-Capretta, S. and Rooney, R. (2000) 'A quasi-experimental evaluation of an intensive rehabilitation supervision program', *Criminal Justice and Behavior*, 27: 312–29.

Campbell, M.A., French, S. and Gendreau, P. (2009) 'The prediction of violence in adult offenders: a meta-analytic comparison of instruments and methods of assessment', *Criminal Justice and Behavior*, 36: 567–90.

Doob, A.M. and Webster, C.M. (2003) 'Sentence severity and crime: accepting the null hypothesis', in M. Tonry (ed.) *Crime and Justice: A Review of Research*, Vol. 30. Chicago: University of Chicago Press.

Dowden, C. and Andrews, D.A. (1999a) 'What works for female offenders: a meta-analytic review', *Crime and Delinquency*, 45: 438–52.

Dowden, C. and Andrews, D.A. (1999b) 'What works in young offender treatment: a meta-analysis', *Forum on Corrections Research*, 11: 21–4.

Fedorowycz, O. (2004) 'Breaking and entering in Canada – 2002', *Jursitat*, 24, Ottawa: Canadian Centre for Justice Statistics.

Grove, W.M., Zald, D.H., Lebow, B.S., Snitz, B.E. and Nelson, C. (2000) 'Clinical versus mechanical prediction: a meta-analysis', *Psychological Assessment*, 12: 19–30.

Hanson, R.K. (2009) 'The psychological assessment of risk for crime and violence', *Canadian Psychology*, 50 (3): 172–82.

Hanson, R.K. and Morton-Bourgon, K. (2009) 'The accuracy of recidivism risk for sexual offenders: a meta-analysis of 118 prediction studies', *Psychological Assessment*, 21: 1–21.

Hanson, R.K., Bourgon, G., Helmus, L. and Hodgson, S. (2009) 'The principles of effective correctional treatment also apply to sexual offenders', *Criminal Justice and Behavior*, 36: 865–91.

Kazdin, A.E. (2008) 'Evidence-based treatment and practice: new opportunities to bridge clinical research and practice, enhance the knowledge base, and improve patient care', *American Psychologist*, 63: 146–59.

Kirby, B.C. (1954) 'Measuring effects of treatment of criminals and delinquents', *Sociology and Social Research*, 38: 368–74.

Lipsey, M.W. (1999) 'Can rehabilitative programs reduce the recidivism of juvenile offenders? An inquiry into the effectiveness of practical programs', *Virginia Journal of Social Policy and the Law*, 6: 611–41.

Lipsey, M.W. and Wilson, D.B. (1993) 'The efficacy of psychological, educational, and behavioural treatment: confirmation from meta-analysis', *American Psychologist*, 48: 1181–209.

Lipton, D., Martinson, R. and Wilks, J. (1975) *The Effectiveness of Correctional Treatment: A Survey of Treatment Evaluation Studies*. New York: Praeger.

Logan, C.H. (1972) 'Evaluation research in crime and delinquency: a reappraisal', *Journal of Criminal Law, Criminology and Police Science*, 63: 378–87.

Lovins, B., Lowenkamp, C.T. and Latessa, E.J. (2009) 'Applying the risk principle to sex offenders: can treatment make some sex offenders worse?', *The Prison Journal*, 89: 344–57.

Lowenkamp, C.T., Latessa, E.J. and Holsinger, A.M. (2004) 'Empirical evidence on the importance of training and experience in using the Level of Service Inventory–Revised', *Topics in Community Corrections*, 49–53.

Lowenkamp, C.T., Latessa, E.J. and Smith, P. (2006) 'Does correctional program quality really matter? The impact of adhering to the principles of effective intervention', *Criminology and Public Policy*, 5: 575–94.

Martinson, R. (1974) 'What works? – Questions and answers about prison reform', *The Public Interest*, 35: 22–54.

Motiuk, L.L., Bonta, J. and Andrews, D.A. (1990) 'Dynamic predictive criterion validity in offender assessment', paper presented at the Canadian Psychological Association Annual Convention, Ottawa, June.

Pogarsky, G. and Piquero, A. (2003) 'Can punishment encourage offending? Investigating the "resetting" effect', *Journal of Research in Crime and Delinquency*, 40: 95–120.

Pratt, T.C. and Cullen, F.T. (2005) 'Assessing macro-level predictors and theories of crime: a meta-analysis', in M. Tonry (ed.) *Crime and Justice: A Review of Research*, Vol. 32. Chicago, IL: University of Chicago Press.

Raynor, P. (2007) 'Risk and need assessment in British probation: the contribution of the LSI-R', *Psychology, Crime, and Law*, 13: 125–38.

Raynor, P., Kynch, J., Roberts, C. and Merrington, S. (2000) *Risk and Need Assessment in Probation Services: An Evaluation*, Home Office Research Study 211. London: Home Office.

Rugge, T. (2006) *Risk Assessment of Male Aboriginal Offenders: A 2006 Perspective*, User Report 2006–01. Ottawa, Ontario: Public Safety Canada.

Schofield, W. (1964) *Psychotherapy: The Purchase of Friendship*. Englewood Cliffs, NJ: Prentice-Hall.

Skeem, J.L., Louden, J.E., Polaschek, D. and Camp, J. (2007) 'Assessing relationship quality in mandated community treatment: blending care with control', *Psychological Assessment*, 19: 397–410.

Smith, P., Goggin, C. and Gendreau, P. (2002) *The Effects of Prison Sentences and Intermediate Sanctions on Recidivism: General Effects and Individual Differences*, User Report 2002-01. Ottawa, Ontario: Public Safety Canada.

Vasquez, M. J. T. (2007) 'Cultural difference and the therapeutic alliance: an evidence-based analysis', *American Psychologist*, 62: 878–85.

Villettaz, P., Killias, M. and Zoder, I. (2006) *The Effects of Custodial vs. Noncustodial Sentences on Re-offending: A Systematic Review of the State of the Knowledge*, Report to the Swiss National Science Foundation and the Campbell Collaboration Crime and Justice Group. Institute of Criminology and Criminal Law, University of Lausanne, Switzerland.

Von Hirsch, A., Bottoms, A.E., Burney, E. and Wikström, P.-O. (1999) *Criminal Deterrence and Sentencing Severity: An Analysis of Recent Research*. Oxford: Hart.

Wampold, B.E. (2007) 'Psychotherapy: the humanistic (and effective) treatment', *American Psychologist*, 62: 857–73.

Ward, T., Mesler, J. and Yates, P. (2007) 'Reconstructing the risk-need-responsivity model: a theoretical elaboration and evaluation', *Aggression and Violent Behavior*, 12: 208–8.

Wormith, J.S. (1984) 'Attitude and behavior changes of correctional clientele: a three year follow-up', *Criminology*, 22: 595–618.

Chapter 3

The Good Lives Model of offender rehabilitation: basic assumptions, aetiological commitments, and practice implications

Tony Ward

Introduction

The Good Lives Model (GLM) of offender rehabilitation is a strength-based approach by virtue of its responsiveness to offenders' core aspirations and interests, and its aim of providing them with the internal and external resources to live rewarding and offence-free lives. It is closely aligned with positive psychology (Linley and Joseph 2004) because of its stress on promoting offender well-being and its overall constructive orientation to correctional interventions, although it was developed independently of this perspective. The core idea at the heart of the GLM is that of *practical reasoning*. Practical reasoning involves judgements concerning the worthiness of an individual's goals and how best to achieve them through coordinated action. The concept of practical reasoning is distinguished from theoretical reasoning by the fact that it is concerned to guide *action* rather than specify norms for forming and evaluating beliefs. Audi (2006) has captured the difference between the two types of reasoning well: 'Practical reasons might be said to be reasons *for acting*; theoretical reasons might be described as *reasons for believing*' (2006: 1). Correctional programmes involve both types of reasoning but in my view the emphasis ought ultimately to be on practical reasoning because of its close connection with individuals' goals and subsequent actions. Ultimately, the aim of intervening with offenders is to encourage them to act differently and any changes in their cognitive and emotional processes are arguably only useful insofar as they result in socially acceptable outcomes (Ward and Nee 2009).

However, the focus on practical reasoning and offenders' status as agents has deeper scientific and normative roots than simply utilitarian considerations. From an explanatory viewpoint, research evidence and theories point to a conceptualisation of human beings as practical decision-makers who have the following properties: they are physically embodied organisms who formulate plans and intentionally modify themselves and engineer their environments in order to increase their chances of achieving their goals. The environment confronting human beings typically includes social, cultural, biological and physical materials that provide the resources necessary to implement their plans successfully. Thus, from the viewpoint of the GLM, the overall purpose of correctional rehabilitation ought to be to help offenders acquire the core competencies for undertaking valued activities such as being intimate, managing stress and so on, and to be able to effectively coordinate their goals and adjust them depending on the prevailing contingencies of the world.

From a normative perspective, the GLM is agency-centred because it is founded on the ethical concepts of human dignity and human rights. In a previous paper I have argued that human dignity is ultimately grounded in the capacity of human beings to act in pursuit of their own freely chosen goals in ways that reflect their status as human agents (Ward 2009). Furthermore, in order to be able to successfully function as agents, human beings require certain freedom and well-being 'goods', such as freedom of movement, freedom of conscience, problem-solving abilities, adequate physical and mental health, and sufficient knowledge of themselves and the outside world. Human rights function as protective capsules that ensure that the resources required for people to make their own decisions are available and they are not unjustifiably restricted from living lives they freely choose. While I appreciate that offenders face legitimate restrictions on their freedom of movement and some of their other rights, their access to the majority of the core freedom and well-being goods should be guaranteed by virtue of the fact that they are human beings and as such are protected by human rights norms.

Once it is accepted that it is ethically obligatory to acknowledge the agency status of offenders, and that engaging them as fellow members of the moral community is the right way to relate to them, it follows that treatment and rehabilitation programmes ought to be mindful of this requirement. Furthermore, the scientific evidence from cognitive science, evolutionary research, motivation, social and clinical psychology also indicates the remarkable abilities of human beings to actively control aspects of themselves and their environments in goal-enhancing ways (Clark 2008; Gibbs 2006; Johnson 2007; Robbins and Aydede 2009). Interestingly, the ethical obligation to acknowledge the agency of offenders and the scientific evidence underlining this feature of human beings converge in the GLM's stress on promoting offenders' goals alongside reducing their ability to harm other people.

In the rest of this chapter I outline the fundamental assumptions of the GLM concerning the most appropriate ways to effectively rehabilitate or reintegrate offenders. My intention is to provide a reasonably detailed summary of the GLM as well as reformulate it slightly in accordance with a stronger agency orientation than evident in previous descriptions (see Laws and Ward, in press). First, I briefly discuss the structure of a rehabilitation theory and its relationship to punishment. Second, I outline the core assumptions, aetiological commitments and practice implications of the GLM. Third, I examine the relationships between the GLM and desistance theory and research. I have chosen desistance theory because of its focus on the factors associated with offenders' ability to cease offending and to maintain this state of desistance. There has been some exciting recent work by theorists such as McNeill (2006) and Maruna (2001) that has sought to make connections between research on criminal careers and desistance, and offender rehabilitation (see also Maruna and LeBel, this volume). I think that the GLM can add to this work and provide a theoretically robust conduit between desistance research and correctional practice (see Laws and Ward, in press).

The Good Lives Model of offender rehabilitation

In this chapter I assume the validity of distinguishing between two distinct, overlapping normative frameworks evident in the criminal justice system, that are often conflated (Ward and Langlands 2009): a response to crime (punishment) and rehabilitation initiatives that follow this response. Each of these two normative frameworks revolves around a core set of values, ethical in the former (relating to the coordination of competing interests) and prudential in the latter (relating to self-interests and well-being). The aim of a just response to crime is to arrive at a solution that balances the harm inflicted on offenders in response to the damage they have done, with their interests and those of the rest of the community. Theories of punishment are designed to provide a justification of the structure of penalties arrived at that is reasonable and not arbitrary. The aim of rehabilitation is to assist offenders to re-enter society and ultimately to become productive and accepted citizens; a critical piece of the rehabilitation puzzle is to enable offenders to live fulfilling and happy lives. Although punishment and rehabilitation are underpinned by contrasting sets of values (ethical versus prudential) each is also subject to the influence of both types of values. When administering punishment it is important to take offenders' welfare into account and when working therapeutically it is imperative to ensure that any intervention plans are ethically acceptable. Although the two frameworks are overlapping, generally speaking they remain distinct criminal justice perspectives with their own cluster of practices (Ward and Salmon 2009). This is an important issue because if punishment and rehabilitation practices are conflated then it is easy to focus on risk management concerns at the expense of offenders' well-being and search for meaning and fulfilment. It is easy to do this because risk management within the criminal justice arena is about public protection and typically involves imposing considerable burdens upon offenders, burdens that can plausibly be construed as aspects of punishment (Glaser 2003). From a desistance perspective, rehabilitation is as much about promoting social reintegration and a sense of meaning as it is about risk containment. Therefore, it makes sense to distinguish between the two frameworks and it is also more consistent with the ethical approach rooted in equal dignity assumed in this chapter.

I propose that rehabilitation theories are composed of three levels of ideas: (1) a set of general assumptions concerning the ethical values guiding rehabilitation, the nature of human beings, conception of risk, and the aims and purpose of rehabilitation practice; (2) a set of general aetiological (causal) assumptions that account for the onset and maintenance of offending; and (3) the practice implications of both of the above. In my view, it is helpful to think of the three levels as ordered in terms of their degree of abstractness, with the general aims and values providing a conceptual foundation for the subsequent levels (aetiology and practice). Each level of the GLM is discussed in greater detail below.

The Good Lives Model was formulated as an alternative approach to correctional treatment that has the conceptual resources to integrate aspects of treatment not well addressed by the risk-need-responsivity (RNR) model (Andrews and Bonta 2007, see also Bonta and Andrews this volume), such as the formation of a therapeutic alliance, agency concerns, and motivating individuals to commit themselves to treatment and ongoing desistance from offending (Ward *et al.* 2007; Ward and Maruna 2007; Ward and Stewart 2003). The GLM has been most extensively applied to rehabilitation work with sex offenders and therefore the assessment process and interventions consistent with the GLM have been developed in the most detail with this particular population. It important to note, however, that the GLM is a general rehabilitation theory which is relevant for a wide range of problems, including other types of criminal behaviour, and is not restricted to use with sex offenders. It has recently been applied to individuals convicted of violent, non-sex-related crimes (Langlands *et al.* 2009; Whitehead *et al.* 2007), young offenders (Robertson 2008), offenders with a personality disorder (Brookes 2008), substance dependent offenders (Blud 2007), indigenous offenders (Spivakovsky 2008), and individuals with medical disabilities (Siegert *et al.* 2007).

Principles, aims, and values of the GLM

Embodiment, plasticity, and cognitive extension

The first major set of theoretical assumptions of the GLM revolves around recent research and theory in cognitive science relating to the nature of human agency. More specifically, this research suggests that: (a) human agents' physical embodiment has a profound impact on their cognitive functioning and interface with the world; (b) human agents are characterised by plasticity of cognitive functioning; and (c) human agents have cognitive systems that incorporate both internal and external components (Ward, in press). The above claims converge in a picture of organisms who are (naturally) designed to act in pursuit of biological, psychological and social goals (Clark 2008). I will briefly discuss each of these assumptions in turn.

The claim that human beings are embodied is based on a unified conception of the mind and body and a rejection of dualism. That is, mental properties are thought to be causally dependent upon the body and their form determined in part by the experience of physical embodiment (Johnson 2007; Ward and Nee 2009). Furthermore, the body also plays an important part in altering the environment in ways that facilitate problem clarification and effective action. It is the interface between inner and outer resources that makes it possible for individuals to bring about goal-directed changes in the environment and ultimately within themselves.

The dependence of goal-directed action and psychological functioning upon the body creates a source of vulnerability for human agents and underlines the need to ensure that threats to physical integrity are effectively managed. The provision of adequate food and water, safe and hygienic environments, freedom from physical danger, and accommodation are necessary ingredients of a good life. Typically (in this stage of evolution!) this means that individuals need educational and vocational skills to be able to work in order to pay for these essential materials. The fact of being physically vulnerable agents points to our ultimate interdependence and reliance on each other for access to vital goods or at least to the means of providing them for ourselves. Offenders as embodied human agents require the materials needed to protect their physical integrity and subsequent ability to act in pursuit of their goals.

The second assumption concerning the nature of human beings and their capacity for agency trades on the view that they are cognitively versatile animals who are able to quickly adapt to novel situations and acquire new cognitive repertoires and tools with relative ease (Clark 2008). Human beings' sense of self is derived from the ability to effectively change the world and themselves in accordance with their personal commitments (Clark 2008; Korsgaard 2009). From a rehabilitation standpoint, the 'soft' nature of human agency reminds correctional practitioners that enhancing offenders' abilities to achieve better life plans is likely to alter their sense of themselves in ways that are socially beneficial as well as personally fulfilling (Ward, in press).

The third agency-related assumption builds on the fact of human beings' cognitive plasticity and claims that external cognitive resources such as language, computers, other minds, and social and cultural institutions under some circumstances can be viewed as part of people's (extended) minds. In other words, people are not cognitively limited by the biological boundaries of skin and skull and are able to intentionally incorporate internal and external elements when engaged in cognitive tasks. I do not have the space to fully explain this complex and novel idea but point out that it is logically connected to the previous two assumptions (see Ward, in press). It is because human beings are physically embodied that they are able to use tools of various kinds to change themselves and their world. Furthermore, it is their cognitive plasticity and soft agency (agency that is capable of modification and extension using a variety of cognitive and physical tools) that enables people to actively incorporate internal and external cognitive resources when engaged in problem-solving activities. The implications of this assumption for offender rehabilitation is that it makes sense to focus our efforts on what matters to people and to realise that external social and cognitive resources may well be actively recruited in offenders' problem-solving routines and strategies. If offenders are quarantined in environments that only contain others like them and few pro-social models, the chances are that their beliefs, values, and actions will continue to be anti-social in nature.

Primary human goods

The above set of three presuppositions of the GLM centred on human embodiment and agency are the most fundamental ones and the following assumptions are really derived from them. The biological nature of human beings and the supervening of psychological properties on physical processes and structures means that in order for individuals to function effectively their basic needs have to be met (Deci and Ryan 2000). Furthermore, the biological and psychological evidence suggests that all people, including offenders, are naturally inclined to seek certain goals, or what we have called *primary human goods* (for example, relatedness, creativity, physical health and mastery – see Laws and Ward, in press; Ward and Maruna 2007; Ward and Stewart 2003).

In essence, primary goods are states of affairs, states of mind, personal characteristics, activities, or experiences that are sought for their own sake and are likely to increase psychological well-being if achieved (Kekes 1989; Ward and Stewart, 2003). In addition to these primary goods, *instrumental* or secondary goods provide particular ways (the means) of achieving primary goods: for example, certain types of work or relationships. For instance, it is possible to secure the primary good of relatedness by the way of romantic, parental or personal relationships. The notion of instrumental goods or means is particularly important when it comes to applying the GLM to offending behaviour as it is assumed that a major reason individuals commit offences is that they are seeking primary goods in socially and often personally destructive ways.

The psychological, social, biological and anthropological research evidence provides support for the existence of at least ten groups of primary human goods (see Aspinwall and Staudinger 2003; Deci and Ryan 2000; Emmons 1999, 2003; Linley and Joseph 2004; Nussbaum 2006; Ward and Maruna, 2007), including the following:

1 *Life*: The primary good of life incorporates physical needs and factors that are important for healthy living and physical functioning, such as food, water, a physically healthy body, and so on.

2 *Knowledge*: This primary good is based on the notion that human beings are inherently curious and possess the desire to understand aspects of themselves, their natural environments, and other people.

3 *Excellence in play and work*: This primary good refers to the desire to engage in leisure or fun activities for their own sake and to strive for mastery at work-related and leisure or recreational activities.

4 *Autonomy*: The primary good of autonomy refers to the desire to formulate one's own goals and to seek ways to realise these through actions and activities of one's choice without facing undue interference from others (moderated by cultural and social norms).

5 *Inner peace*: The primary good of inner peace refers to emotional self-regulation and the ability to achieve a state of dynamic emotional equilibrium and competence.

6 *Relatedness*: The good of relatedness refers to the natural desire of human beings to establish warm, affectionate bonds with other people. It is noted that these relationships range from intimate, romantic relationships to close family relationships to platonic relationships and friendships.

7 *Community*: The primary good of community refers to the desire human beings have to belong to social groups and to feel connected to groups that reflect their interests, concerns and values.

8 *Spirituality*: The primary good of spirituality refers to the desire to discover and attain a sense of meaning and purpose in life.

9 *Happiness*: The primary good of happiness refers to a hedonic (pleasure) state or the overall experience of being content and satisfied with one's life, and includes the sub-good of sexual pleasure.

10 *Creativity*: The primary good of creativity refers to the desire for novelty and innovation in one's life, the experience of doing things differently, or engaging in a specific activity that results in an artistic output or other novel or creative product.

Recent research indicates that the goods of agency, relatedness, inner peace (emotional regulation) and happiness are particularly relevant for sexual offenders and are also directly implicated in their offending (Yates *et al.* 2009). An especially significant characteristic of the GLM is that the goods are plural rather than singular, and therefore a fulfilling life will most probably require access to all the primary goods even though individuals can legitimately vary in the way they value or rank them, or even constitute them. This means that there are multiple sources of motivation and that each has their origin in the evolved nature of human beings.

Values and practical identities

The plural nature of the goods sought is likely to result in their differential weightings or endorsement by individuals. While all the primary goods need to be present to some degree (that is, meet a threshold requirement) if persons are to achieve good lives, there could be significant differences in the experiences, objects and activities they consider most important. According to Korsgaard (1996), conceptions of practical identity provide 'a description under which you value yourself and find your life worth living and your actions to be worth undertaking' (1996: 101). Thus individuals' sense of identity emerges from their basic value commitments, the goods they pursue in search of better lives. Interestingly, Korsgaard argues that when there are conflicts between different practical identities, people have to work hard to establish some degree of unity in their lives; she suggests that a way of assisting this process is by focusing on our common humanity and our (shared) inherent dignity. The existence of a number of practical identities also means that each of us will draw from a variety of distinct value sources when faced with decisions about how best to act (Korsgaard 2009). For example, a person may value being a father, psychologist, scientist, citizen, and member of a political party, and each of these practical identities will exert some normative pressure on his actions and life. At times the aims and subsequent actions arising from the value commitments of each of these practical identities conflict. The relevance of variation in value endorsements is that if offenders' sense of themselves and what really matters depends upon the things they most value, then correctional practitioners ought to identify what primary goods are most heavily endorsed and, in particular, how they are expressed in offenders' lives (Archer 2000; Emmons 2003; Clark 2007).

Because of the fact that human beings are thinking animals, there is a reflective gap between the experience of a desire to act in pursuit of a natural good or incentive, and actually doing so (Korsgaard 2009). This reflective gap allows individuals space to critically evaluate desires and to decide whether or not they are worthy of fulfilment; whether they are really of value. Arguably, problematic actions such as offending partly arise from individuals making faulty judgements and reveal a lack of forethought or knowledge concerning the relevant facts and the real value of the proposed actions. Thus, the process of rehabilitation requires not just the targeting of isolated 'factors', but also the holistic reconstruction of the 'self.'

Goods and risks

According to the GLM, correctional interventions should aim to (a) promote offenders' aspirations and plans for better lives, as well as (b) manage/reduce their risk to the community. This assumption has both normative and pragmatic strands to it. Normatively, the assertion that interventions should promote well-being alongside reducing risk reflects the ethical foundation of the GLM in human rights theory and practices (Law and Ward, in press). Pragmatically, it is assumed that because criminogenic needs and human needs are causally related (see below), the promotion of adaptive approach goals should also reduce dynamic risk factors. *Approach* goals are representations of situations or states that a person is seeking to achieve (such as a relationship or a job) while *avoidance* goals represent undesired states or situations (such as conflict or imprisonment). Thus a major aim of correctional reintegration work is to help individuals to construct a life plan that has the basic primary goods, and ways of effectively securing them, built into it and does not involve inflicting harm on others.

Ecological selves

As discussed above, according to the GLM people are multifaceted beings, comprising a variety of interconnected biological, social, cultural and psychological systems, and are interdependent to a significant degree. What this entails is that complex animals such as human beings can only flourish within a community that provides emotional support, material resources, education and even the means of survival. The complexity of human functioning means that an adequate explanation of something as important as crime will require multiple levels of analysis and theoretical perspectives. In particular, the interdependency of human behaviour points to the necessity of adopting an ecological framework.

The fact that human beings are interdependent and that, therefore, a satisfactory understanding of behaviour will always involve an appreciation of the contexts in which they exist, has important implications for therapists when designing reintegration programmes. Thus, according to the GLM, any assessment and intervention should take into account the match between the characteristics of the individual and the likely environment where he or she will be functioning. Rather than viewing the offender as essentially a self-contained deviancy machine (or bearer of risk – see below), and therefore viewing treatment as being designed to restore or repair or, more frequently, to manage the offender's faulty system, the aim is to locate him or her within a social network. Treatment consistent with the GLM is viewed as furnishing individuals with some of the agency scaffolding and resources required to establish important social bonds and to engage meaningfully with the world.

The nature of risk

Because people are conceptualised to be constituted from, and to be embedded within, complex systems, risk is viewed as multifaceted rather than purely individualistic (Denny 2005; Ward and Maruna 2007). In my view, risk is best considered in contextual terms rather than conceptualised purely as constituted by individual deviancy. Thus it is to be expected that an adequate risk management plan would need to take into account individuals' particular lifestyles and environments. Even those dynamic risk factors that can be said to be located 'inside' individuals (for example, impulsivity or aggressiveness) are only meaningful in their specific, cultural and situational contexts.

The trouble with psychometric approaches to risk assessment and management is that they have a tendency to identify risk primarily in terms of individuals' deviancy and to view offenders as essentially bearers of risk (Ward and Maruna 2007; Ward and Stewart 2003). By 'bearers of risk' we mean that in some sense risk is seen as inhering within individual offenders, and to a lesser extent their environments. A difficulty with such a static conceptualisation is that it fails to appreciate how risk can be created by correctional interventions and policies that effectively isolate offenders, such as community notification or geographical restrictions (Vess 2009).

The nature of intervention

Finally, according to the GLM, an intervention plan should be explicitly constructed in the form of a good lives conceptualisation. In other words, it should take into account the individual's strengths, primary goods and relevant environments, and specify exactly what competencies and resources are required to achieve these goods. An important aspect of this process is respecting the individual's capacity to make certain decisions him or herself, and in this sense accepting his or her status as an autonomous individual. This is in direct contrast to previous recommended practice in the treatment of offending behaviours, where therapists were cautioned not to allow offenders to participate in decision-making (see Salter 1988). Using the GLM, each individual's preference for certain primary goods should be noted and translated into his or her daily routine (for example, the kind of works, education and further training, and types of relationships should be identified and selected to achieve primary goods).

Aetiological assumptions of the GLM

As stated earlier, the aetiological component of a rehabilitation theory flows logically from a theory's basic assumptions, is general in nature, and functions to give correctional workers a cognitive map or general overview of the broad causes of criminal or anti-social behaviour.

According to the GLM, goals are usefully construed as primary human goods translated into more concrete forms, and as such are typically the objects of intentions and actions. Goals are the ultimate and intermediate ends of any actions and collectively give shape to people's lives insofar as they create a structure of daily activities that represent what is of fundamental importance to them. In terms of practical identities, goals are thematically linked to concrete identities and the various roles and tasks they imply. For example, as a psychologist a person has responsibility for the assessment and treatment of psychological disorders. Each of these domains of professional practice is linked to actions, guided by particular goals, such as conducting an interview competently, interpreting psychological tests, or assisting an individual to overcome his or her fears of intimacy. Alternatively, the practical identity of being someone's romantic partner generates a variety of tasks such as providing emotional support, spending time together, and (for some) maintaining a household. In other words, goals are typically clustered together under specific descriptions; these descriptions are ultimately anchored in practical identities (Emmons 1999; Korsgaard 2009).

According to the GLM there may be a number of distinct problems within the various domains of human functioning that can result in offending behaviour: emotional regulation difficulties, social difficulties, offence-supportive beliefs, empathy problems, and problem-solving deficits. Yet, such individuals' general underlying personal motivations/goals are rarely inherently bad. Instead, it is the means used to achieve these goods that are deviant. The value of this understanding is that it helps to focus practitioners' attention on primary goods, the ultimate underlying motivating factors, and away from an exclusive focus on the psychosocial difficulties with which individual clients are struggling. That is, there are likely to be distortions in the internal and external conditions required to achieve the primary goods in socially acceptable and personally satisfying ways. The GLM guided analysis goes beyond deficit-based aetiological theories (theories that focus on what individuals lack) by encouraging clinicians to think clearly about just what it is that the person is seeking when committing the offence. This information has direct intervention implications and can provide a powerful way of motivating individuals to engage in therapy; the aim is to help them to secure human goods that are important to them, but to do so in ways that are socially acceptable and also more personally satisfying. The latter point is especially important, as most criminal causal factors involve self-defeating attempts to seek personally valued goals and consequences. The GLM can explain why this is so and provide practitioners with a clear understanding of where the problems reside in an individual's life plan.

From the perspective of the GLM, there are two primary routes to the onset of offending, each reflecting individuals' agency: direct and indirect (Ward and Gannon 2006; Ward and Maruna 2007). The direct pathway is implicated when offending is a primary focus of the (typically implicit) cluster of goals and strategies associated with an individual's life plan. This means that the individual intentionally seeks certain types of goods directly through criminal activity. For example, an individual may lack the relevant competencies and understanding to obtain the good of intimacy with an adult, and furthermore may live in an environment where there are few realistic opportunities for establishing such relationships. Thus, the actions constituting offending are a means to the achievement of a fundamental good.

The indirect route to offending occurs when the pursuit of a good or set of goods creates a ripple effect in the person's personal circumstances and these unanticipated effects increase the pressure to offend. For example, conflict between the goods of relatedness and autonomy might cause the break-up of a valued relationship and subsequent feelings of loneliness and distress. The use of alcohol to alleviate the emotional turmoil could lead to loss of control in specific circumstances and this might increase the risk of offending. These indirect or ripple effects are particularly evident when two practical identities a person is invested in conflict, and cause him or her uncertainty about how best to act. An example of this conflict of identities is when an offender values his role as both a worker and a husband. The two identities can on occasions clash and in some circumstances the pressure to work longer hours in order to get a job done might interfere with his responsibilities as a partner.

From the standpoint of the GLM, criminogenic needs are conceptualised as *internal* or *external obstacles* that frustrate and block the acquisition of primary human goods. I suggest that there are four major types of difficulties often evident in individuals' life plans. In my view these types of problems are overlapping but conceptually distinct. It is also important to note that the real problem resides in the secondary goods rather than the primary ones. In other words, it is the activities or strategies used to obtain certain primary goods that create problems, not the primary goods themselves (that is, primary goods are sought by all humans).

First, an individual who has problems with the *means* he uses to secure goods may be using inappropriate strategies to achieve the necessary primary goods needed for a good life. Second, an individual's life plan might also suffer from a lack of *scope* with a number of important goods left out of his or her plan for living. Third, some people may also have *conflict* (and a lack of coherence) among the goods being sought and their associated practical identities and therefore experience acute psychological stress and unhappiness (Emmons 1999). Fourth, a final problem is when a person lacks the *capabilities* (knowledge or skills) to form or effectively implement a life plan in the environment in which he lives, or to adjust his or her goals to changing circumstances (for example, impulsive decision-making). The problem of capability deficits has both internal and external dimensions. The internal dimension refers to factors such as skill deficits while the external dimension points to a lack of environmental opportunities, resources and supports.

In summary, the aetiological commitments of the GLM are general in form and stem from a view of human beings as creatures capable of reflective agency; usually acting under the conceptual constraints of a range of practical identities. That is, I propose that human beings are goal-seeking, culturally embedded animals who utilise a range of strategies to secure important goods from their environments when occupying personally valued social or cultural roles (such as partners, workers, citizens, playmates, artists, helpers). When the internal or external conditions necessary to achieve valued outcomes associated with practical identities are incomplete or absent, individuals tend to become frustrated and may engage in criminal or anti-social behaviour. These aetiological commitments serve to orient probation or correctional workers and require supplementation from specific theories to supply more fine-grained explanations of criminal and anti-social behaviour and particular types of offences.

Implications of the GLM for practice

A GLM-oriented treatment programme seeks to tailor an intervention plan around an offender's core values and associated practical identities. The good lives plan unfolds from this value centre and incorporates all of the various goods required to function as a reflective and effective agent within specific environments. Where possible, local communities and resources are recruited and the objective is to assist in the building of a better life rather than simply try to contain risk. For example, an individual's intervention plan could be based on his desires to learn a trade (perhaps become a mechanic) and establish a romantic relationship. The skills required to become a mechanic, such as mechanical knowledge of engines, effective work habits, at least a reasonable degree of social and communication skills, affective and self-control competencies, may reduce risk while consolidating the offender within a social network. Access to workmates and hobbies that cohere with his interests might further open up opportunities to meet potential partners who are law-abiding and supportive. The result of such a plan will hopefully be a life that is fulfilling, meaningful, ethically acceptable and socially productive (Burnett 2002; Maruna 2001).

I now briefly describe each of the five phases of a GLM rehabilitation framework (for more detail on GLM-oriented treatment see Laws and Ward, in press; Ward *et al.* 2007; Ward and Maruna, 2007; Ward and Stewart, 2003).

The *first phase*, when intervening with offenders from the standpoint of the GLM, involves the detection of the social, psychological and material phenomena implicated in individuals' offending. This requires a careful analysis of offenders' level of risk, their living circumstances, physical and social problems and psychological capabilities around the time of their offending and stretching into their past as well. Offenders are likely to have multiple problems such as poverty, substance abuse, lack of accommodation, high levels of impulsiveness and aggressive behaviour, and so on.

In the *second phase* of the GLM, the function of offending (what the individual expected to achieve *via* his or her offending) is established through the identification of primary goods that are directly or indirectly linked to the criminal actions. In addition, the identification of the overarching good or value, around which the other goods are oriented, should also be ascertained. This step requires that practitioners identify the practical identities endorsed by offenders and clarify how they are causally related to their offending actions. It is anticipated that the core goods (such as mastery, or caring) will be translated into more concrete values and tasks that directly connect with the offender's general life circumstances and their offence-related actions.

In the *third phase* of the GLM rehabilitation process, the selection of the practical identities and their overarching good(s) or value(s) is undertaken and made a focus of a plan. As discussed earlier, frequently practical identities are aligned with the primary goods and in a sense simply flesh out the abstractness of the good in question. In effect, practical identities and their goals, strategies and practices provide the detail needed to effectively work with an offender. For example, an individual might nominate knowledge and relatedness as the two most important goods and decide that going to university and establishing an intimate relationship are means to these ends.

In the *fourth phase*, a greater level of detail is added to the above developing plan and the selection of secondary goods or values that specify how the primary goods will be translated into ways of living and functioning is undertaken. In this step, identification of the contexts or environments in which the person is likely to be living while in the community during or following intervention is conducted. For example, the practical identity of being a university student (and partner in a relationship) is now examined with respect to a possible environment and the educational, social, psychological and material resources required to make this possible are noted. The GLM is a regulatory and pragmatic model so it is imperative that the probable environments a person will be living in are identified and their potential to provide the required resources to realise the good lives plan ascertained.

In the *fifth phase*, the practitioner constructs a detailed intervention plan for the offender based on the above considerations and information. The plan will be holistic, specify the internal and external conditions required to successfully implement it (revolving around offenders' core values and their associated practical identities) and the various tasks for correctional practitioners will be carefully detailed. Dynamic risk factors or criminogenic needs are indirectly targeted when cognitive behavioural techniques and social interventions are utilised in the acquisition of offender competencies. Thus, taking into account the kind of life that would be fulfilling and meaningful to the individual (primary goods, secondary goods, and their relationship to ways of living and possible environments) the evaluator notes the capabilities or competencies the individual requires in order to have a reasonable chance of applying the plan. Practical steps are then taken to organise the various actors involved and to put the good lives plan into action. The offender is consulted in all the various phases and in a robust sense he or she drives the content of the plan, if not its form. Furthermore, the practitioner seeks to balance the ethical entitlements of the offender with those of victims and members of the community.

The GLM and desistance

In their recent book on desistance theory and the GLM, Laws and Ward (in press) discuss the meaning of 'desistance' and its relevance for sex offender treatment. They state:

> We are all familiar with the word 'desist'. Its formal dictionary definition is 'to cease or stop doing something' (Encarta World English Dictionary 1999, p. 489). We are probably most familiar with the usage of the word in an order to 'cease and desist', to cease (stop) doing something and to desist (refrain) from doing it again. It is the state of stopping and staying stopped that we refer to as 'desistance'.

Research work on natural and assisted desistance goes back well over 60 years and is an extremely valuable resource for practitioners because of its strong data base and array of theoretical resources.

We do not have the space to discuss these important criminological theories in any depth here but will briefly consider their relationship to the GLM (for a book-length discussion see Laws and Ward, in press); a relationship that I believe adds to the theoretical coherence of the GLM and also speaks to its ability to guide interventions with offenders that go well beyond the confines of formal treatment programmes.

It is possible to identify three strands in desistance theory: those that stress the importance of maturation, agency and social relationships (McNeill *et al.* 2005; Maruna 2001). Theorists have sometimes contrasted objective desistance factors (a job, or marriage) (Glueck and Glueck 1968; Giordano *et al.* 2007; Laub and Sampson 2003) with a subjective sense of meaning, arguing for the primacy of one over the other (Bottoms *et al.* 2004; Weaver and McNeill 2010). More recent theoretical work has emphasised the interaction between all three sets of desistance factors and the fact that it is in the interfaces between these variables that desistance exerts its effect (McNeill *et al.* 2005; McNeill 2009).

According to the GLM, offenders' core values enable them to capitalise on, or create, objective events that reflect their practical identity. There is no separation: people constitute themselves through actions that necessarily involve opportunities and objective events. Because of its stress on the importance of the past in fashioning practical identities and the associated socialisation and acculturation processes, the GLM also has a strong developmental focus without adopting a fatalistic tone. There is arguably a red thread that runs through offenders' lives from the past to the future, linking core values, life plans, identity, and ultimately meaning. Furthermore, the GLM's stress on agency and the importance of reflectiveness is entirely consistent with desistance theorists' emphasis on 'turning points' (Laub and Sampson 2003) or critical events that create a sense of crisis in offenders and ultimately prompt them to re-evaluate their lives and reconstruct their identities. Identity reconstruction (Maruna 2001) works through the location of the primary goods (see below) that are most important to offenders and analysis of alternative ways to seek them. Practical identities are constituted by practices and ways of acting in the world and inevitably involve norms that regulate specific actions, dress, habits and so on. What I am saying is that the process of constructing new narrative identities, or redemptive scripts (Maruna 2001), can be unpacked in terms consistent with the GLM's basic assumptions about agency and identity. The flexibility of human beings, and their natural press to seek certain outcomes and to view their lives as meaningful and unified, is likely to contribute to self-refection following crises or turning points. It goes without saying that adequate self-control is a consequence of possessing the capabilities needed to be a reflective and effective agent, and correspondingly, a lack of self-control will be reflected in problematic ways of seeking primary goods (Gottfredson and Hirschi 1990).

I argue that the GLM has the conceptual resources to incorporate desistance ideas by virtue of its stress on agency, interdependency and development. In other words, there is natural resonance between desistance theory and the GLM because of their overlapping theoretical ideas and broad way of conceptualising the relationship between human beings and their social world. In fact, in my view the GLM has some desistance concepts built into it, but they are underdeveloped. While I accept that there are distinct theories of desistance, each with varying emphasis on the types of factors thought to be causally related to cessation from further offending, there is relative agreement that any account of desistance needs to address developmental, special and agency variables. There appears to be an overlapping consensus among desistance theorists that the truth of why individuals permanently refrain from further offending lies in the interaction between social encounters and opportunities, and psychological capacities (skills, reflectiveness, agency, for example). It is not enough to be presented with social capital such as a job or a promise of an intimate relationship. Without an individual feeling that such opportunities are worthy of his or her investment, they are unlikely to taken up.

There are reasonable grounds for concluding that rehabilitation programmes for offenders are effective in reducing recidivism rates (Laws and Ward, in press; Bonta and Andrews, this volume). What is not so evident, however, is *how* they actually generate change. A virtue of the GLM's focus on practical reasoning and its assumption that crime can be understood as involving inappropriate ways of seeking primary goods is that programmes can be viewed as focused and powerful ways of strengthening or instilling the core conditions of agency. The claim is that all people are naturally inclined to need and seek certain primary goods using a range of strategies that are socially and culturally acquired. Sometimes, however, the use of ineffective or counterproductive cognitive and behavioural strategies arising from impoverished or flawed good lives plans can result in personally frustrating and/or socially unacceptable actions. By participating in well-structured intervention programmes such individuals are more likely to be able to engineer, or take advantage of, 'natural' desistance opportunities and processes in the future (by 'natural' I mean opportunities that occur outside of the therapeutic orbit).

Some individuals require more scaffolding than others in acquiring the capacities necessary to construct and put into action a plan for living that is adaptive and meaningful. Sometimes a greater need for professional input is a legacy of offenders living in particularly impoverished social environments with minimal social capital and sometimes it is because they possess few psychological resources of their own. In either of these situations rehabilitation programmes can be helpful; the former setting out to instil psychological skills and the latter concentrating on creating social opportunities and supports. All human beings require help from other people to acquire and utilise the psychological capabilities and social resources necessary to realise their aspirations, whether this involves completing job training, participating in social activities, or remaining crime-free. Exactly what kind of help is needed or likely to be most useful will be a function of their personal characteristics and situation. If what I have proposed makes sense then it follows that a model such as the GLM is ideally placed to integrate desistance ideas while still advocating for the utility of 'treatment' programmes for *some* offenders. What rehabilitation options are offered to offenders should depend on their specific needs and capacities (psychological or 'human' capital) in conjunction with their social circumstances, networks and opportunities (social capital). It may be that following a period of intensive (community) social support and vocational skills training a person with a criminal history will be able to satisfactorily cope with the day-to-day demands of living an offence-free life. Alternatively, a person needing more ongoing specialist interventions because of major social and self-regulation skills deficits may require participation in a variety of treatment programmes to help him to translate his personal goals and interests into tangible benefits. From a rehabilitation viewpoint, the key point is that the level and duration of support needed by individuals ought to be based around their capacity to act in service of their goals in ways that are ethically permissible and meaningful.

As a strength-based perspective the GLM is committed to using cognitive and behavioural treatment techniques to establish competencies that will aid an individual to put into action, and maintain, a good lives plan (GLP) that he has endorsed and helped to formulate. Thus skill acquisition is always in the service of building social and psychological resources and never solely focused on risk or problem reduction. The practice relationship ought to be collaborative and founded on mutual respect. Furthermore, because the purpose of intervention is to strengthen, repair or create the capacity for agency in ways that balance offenders' and members of the community's interests, it follows that any GLP will address risk concerns. Given the desistance and ecological orientation of the GLM, re-entry and reintegration are at the forefront of probation and correctional practitioners' minds from the beginning of the assessment process. The GLP developed for an individual will be individually tailored, cohesive and holistic in nature, seek to provide a conduit between aspects of his past and future, and also integrate the various primary goods.

Conclusions

The GLM has the theoretical resources, range, depth and flexibility to provide guidance for practitioners working both within and outside offender programmes. It can easily accommodate good lives plans (GLPs) that are centred upon employment training or the creation of social relationships and community support structures. And its utility in clinical settings is increasingly accepted (McGrath *et al.* 2009; Ward and Maruna 2007) and has been the thrust of most research and clinical attention in the last five years. The GLM can guide treatment, re-entry and reintegration initiatives because of its primary emphasis on agency and its role in supporting the pursuit of good lives. Risk reduction and containment are crucial pieces of the rehabilitation puzzle but in my view should always be embedded within intervention plans that offer people a chance at a more fulfilling life as well as a less harmful one.

References

Andrews, D.A. and Bonta, J. (2007) *The Psychology of Criminal Conduct* 4th edn. Cincinnati: Anderson.
Archer, M. S. (2000) *Being Human: The Problem of Agency*. Cambridge: Cambridge University Press.
Aspinwall, L.G. and Staudinger, U.M. (eds) (2003) *A Psychology of Human Strengths: Fundamental Questions and Future Directions for a Positive Psychology*. Washington, DC: American Psychological Association.
Audi, R. (2006) *Practical Reasoning and Ethical Decision*. Oxford: Routledge.

Blud, L. (2007) 'Young men, alcohol, and violence: a poisonous relationship', paper presented at the Unhooked Thinking Conference, Bath, UK.

Bottoms, A., Shapland, J., Costello, A., Holmes, D. and Muir, G. (2004). 'Towards desistance: theoretical underpinnings for an empirical study', *Howard Journal of Criminal Justice*, 43: 368–89.

Brookes, M. (2008) 'Working with personality disordered offenders in a therapeutic community setting at HMP Grendon', paper given at the British Psychological Society Division of Forensic Psychology Annual Conference, Edinburgh.

Burnett, R. (2002) *The Dynamics of Recidivism*. Oxford: University of Oxford Centre for Criminological Research.

Clark, A. (2007) 'Soft selves and ecological control', in D. Spurrett, D. Ross, H. Kincaid and I. Stephens (eds) *Distributed Cognition and the Will*. Cambridge, MA: MIT Press.

Clark, A. (2008) *Supersizing the Mind: Embodiment, Action, and Cognitive Extension*. New York: Oxford University Press.

Deci, E.L. and Ryan, R.M. (2000) 'The "what" and "why" of goal pursuits: human needs and the self-determination of behavior', *Psychological Inquiry*, 11: 227–68.

Denny, D. (2005) *Risk and Society*. London: Sage.

Emmons, R.A. (1999) The psychology of ultimate concerns. New York: Guilford Press.

Emmons, R.A. (2003) 'Personal goals, life meaning, and virtue: wellsprings of a positive life', in C.L.M. Keyes and J. Haidt (eds) *Flourishing: Positive Psychology and the Life Well-lived*. Washington, DC: American Psychological Association.

Gibbs, R.W. (2006) *Embodiment and Cognitive Science*. New York: Cambridge University Press.

Giordano, P.C., Schroeder, R.D. and Cernkovich, S.A. (2007) 'Emotions and crime over the life course: A neo-Median perspective on criminal continuity and change', *American Journal of Sociology*, 112: 1603–61.

Glaser, B. (2003) 'Therapeutic jurisprudence: an ethical paradigm for therapists in sex offender treatment programs', *Western Criminology Review*, 4: 143–54.

Glueck, S. and Glueck, E. (1968) *Delinquents and Nondelinquents in Perspective*. Cambridge, MA: Harvard University Press.

Gottfredson, M.R. and Hirschi, T. (1990) *A General Theory of Crime*. Stanford, CA: Stanford University Press.

Johnson, M. (2007) *The Meaning of the Body: Aesthetics of Human Understanding*. Chicago: University of Chicago Press.

Kekes, J. (1989) *Moral Tradition and Individuality*. Princeton, NJ: Princeton University Press.

Korsgaard, C.M. (1996) *The Sources of Normativity*. Cambridge: Cambridge University Press.

Korsgaard, C.M. (2009) *Self-constitution: Agency, Identity, and Integrity*. New York: Oxford University Press.

Langlands, R., Ward, T. and Gilchrist, E. (2009) 'Applying the Good Lives Model to male perpetrators of domestic violence', in P. Lehmann and C. Simmons (eds) *Strengths Based Batterer Intervention: A New Paradigm in Ending Domestic Violence*. New York: Springer.

Laub, J.H. and Sampson, R.J. (2003) *Shared Beginnings, Divergent Lives: Delinquent Boys to Age 70*. Cambridge, MA: Harvard University Press.

Laws, D.R. and Ward, T. (in press) *People Like Us: Desistance from Crime and Paths to the Good Life*. New York: Guilford Press.

Linley, P.A. and Joseph, S. (2004) 'Applied positive psychology: a new perspective for professional practice', in P. A. Linley and S. Joseph (eds) *Positive Psychology in Practice*. New Jersey: Wiley.

McGrath, R.J., Cumming, G.F. and Burchard, B.L. (2009) 'The safer society 2009 North American survey: current practices and emerging trends in sexual abuser management', presented at the 28th Annual Research and Treatment Conference of the Association for the Treatment of Sexual Abusers, Dallas, Texas.

McNeill, F. (2006) 'A desistance paradigm for offender management', *Criminology and Criminal Justice*, 6: 39–62.

McNeill, F. (2009) 'What works and what's just?', *European Journal of Probation*, 1: 21–40.

McNeill, F., Batchelor, S., Burnett, R. and Knox, J. (2005) '21st century social work', *Reducing Re-offending: Key Practice Skills*. Edinburgh: Scottish Executive.

Maruna, S. (2001) *Making Good: How Ex-convicts Reform and Rebuild their Lives*. Washington, DC: American Psychological Association.

Nussbaum, M. (2006) *Frontiers of Justice: Disability, Nationality, Species-membership*. Cambridge: Belknap Press.

Robertson, D. (2008) 'Indigenisation and developmental adaptation of the Good Lives Model', unpublished manuscript.

Robbins, P. and Aydede, M. (eds) (2009) *The Cambridge Handbook of Situated Cognition*. New York: Cambridge University Press.

Salter, A.C. (1988) *Treating Child Sex Offenders and Their Victims: A Practical Guide*. Newbury Park, CA: Sage.

Siegert, R., Ward, T., Levack, W. and McPherson, K. (2007) 'A Good Lives Model of clinical and community rehabilitation', *Disability and Rehabilitation*, 29: 1604–15.

Spivakovsky, C. (2008) 'Approaching responsivity: the Victorian Department of Justice and indigenous offenders', *Flinders Journal of Law Reform*, 10: 649-62.

Vess, J. (2009) 'Fear and loathing in public policy: Ethical issues in laws for sex offenders', *Aggression and Violent Behavior*, 14: 264–72.

Ward, T. (2009) 'Dignity and human rights in correctional practice', *European Journal of Probation*, 1: 110–23.

Ward, T. (in press) Extending the mind into the world: a new theory of cognitive distortions. *Journal of Sexual Aggression*.

Ward, T. and Gannon, T. (2006) Rehabilitation, etiology, and self-regulation: the Good Lives Model of sexual offender treatment', *Aggression and Violent Behavior*, 11: 77–94.

Ward, T. and Langlands, R. (2009) 'Repairing the rupture: restorative justice and offender rehabilitation', *Aggression and Violent Behavior*, 14: 205–14.

Ward, T. and Maruna, S. (2007) *Rehabilitation: Beyond the Risk Paradigm*. London: Routledge.

Ward, T. and Nee, C. (2009) 'Surfaces and depths: evaluating the theoretical assumptions of the cognitive skills programmes', *Psychology, Crime and Law*, 15: 165–82.

Ward, T. and Salmon, K. (2009) 'The ethics of punishment: correctional practice implications', *Aggression and Violent Behavior*, 14: 239–47.

Ward, T. and Stewart, C. (2003) 'Criminogenic needs and human needs: a theoretical model', *Psychology, Crime and Law*, 9: 125–43.

Ward, T., Mann, R. and Gannon, T. (2007) 'The good lives model of offender rehabilitation: clinical implications', *Aggression and Violent Behavior*, 12: 87–107.

Weaver, B. and McNeill, F. (2010) 'Travelling hopefully: desistance research and probation practice', in F. Cowe, J. Deering and J. Pakes (eds) *What Else Works? Creative Work with Offenders and Other Socially Excluded People*. Cullompton: Willan Publishing.

Whitehead, P., Ward, T. and Collie, R. (2007) 'Time for a change: applying the Good Lives Model of rehabilitation to a high-risk violent offender', *International Journal of Offender Therapy and Comparative Criminology*, 51: 578–98.

Yates, P.M., Simons, D., Kingston, D. and Tyler, C. (2009) 'The self regulation and good lives models of sexual offender treatment: a comprehensive analysis of relationship to risk, treatment progress, and clinical application', presented at the 28th Annual Research and Treatment Conference of the Association for the Treatment of Sexual Abusers, Dallas, Texas.

Chapter 4

The desistance paradigm in correctional practice: from programmes to lives

Shadd Maruna and Thomas P. LeBel

Introduction

Interventions for reducing reoffending are frequently criticised for not being based upon a foundation of empirical evidence (see Latessa *et al.* 2002). As a response, over the past three decades, there has been a sustained international movement, sometimes known as the 'what works' movement, to promote 'evidence-based' best practices in criminal justice. In some ways, the present moment may be the pinnacle of this 'what works' movement internationally. For instance, at a recent National Institute of Justice Annual Conference, US President Barack Obama's Attorney General Eric Holder warmed many academic hearts in the room when he said:

> Let me be clear: this administration shares your belief in the power of evidence-based research to help address some of our nation's most significant challenges. President Obama has renewed our nation's commitment to rely on science in the development of public policy. He understands, as I do, that sound judgement derives from solid evidence. (Austin 2009)

However, evidence-based practice has been the buzzword in the United Kingdom at least since the emergence of New Labour in 1997, and there are some indications that the welcome for effectiveness research has worn somewhat thin. Most infamously, New Labour's crime advisor (or crime 'czar') Louise Casey has been heard to remark, 'If No. 10 says bloody "evidence-based policy" to me one more time, I'll deck them' (Bowcott 2005).

In this chapter, we describe an emerging way of thinking about evidence-based practice, sometimes referred to as the 'desistance paradigm' (McNeill 2006; Porporino 2010); this approach focuses less on evaluation evidence of '*what* works', and instead draws from criminological research on '*how* change works'. We begin by outlining what we see as the key features of this paradigm and contrast it to the traditional correctional paradigm. Next, we provide one possible illustration (out of many) of what the desistance paradigm might look like in practice. Like the 'what works' evaluation literature (and indeed any body of scientific research), the research on desistance from crime is a dynamic and contested literature. For the purposes of this chapter, we have therefore chosen to focus on only one strand of the desistance work – not coincidentally the one that our own research has contributed to – for illustrative purposes. In the final section, we outline the policy implications of this particular strand of the desistance literature in order to demonstrate how one application of the desistance paradigm might actually take shape in practice.

The promise of a desistance paradigm

What works in reducing crime? There are two ways to answer this. One common strategy is to review the evaluation evidence (in particular randomised control trials) of programmes designed to target criminality. Yet this is not the only type of evidence that might help answer this question.

Take the following example. In a recent article with the provocative title 'Why crime went away', the American news weekly *Time Magazine* tries to grapple with the sharp drop in the rates of murder and violent crime in the United States over the past 20 years (Von Drehle 2010). The article begins by quoting a number of police chiefs who, of course, claim that all the credit goes to police chiefs, but then surveys academic criminologists who instead point to the changing age demographics of American society. It is well known, for instance, that crime waves are associated with large numbers of young people in a population; most famously, the coming of age of the 'baby boomer' generation in the 1960s and 1970s corresponded with a huge increase in crime. With the baby boom generation approaching retirement, however – and even their children approaching middle age! – the current American age profile has shifted discernibly. Whereas the median age for Americans at the peak of the crime wave that began in the 1960s was 32 years old, by 2010 the median age of Americans had risen to over 36 years old. Criminologists see this correlation as far more than a coincidence. The *Time Magazine* article concludes: 'Violence is typically a young man's vice; it has been said that the most effective crime-fighting tool is a 30th birthday' (Von Drehle 2010: 24).

In other words, maturation is more powerful than any 'programme' designed by the police, prison service or others to reduce crime. This argument is certainly supported by considerable evidence. For most individuals, participation in 'street crimes' like burglary, robbery and drug sales (the types of offences of most concern to criminologists) generally begins in the early teenage years, peaks rapidly in late adolescence or young adulthood, and dissipates before the person reaches 30 years of age (see Figure 4.1).

Official conviction statistics, like those represented graphically in Figure 4.1, are not easy to interpret and might be skewed by any number of factors (older offenders may be better at avoiding apprehension than young people, young offenders might die early or spend long periods incarcerated, and so forth). However, longitudinal

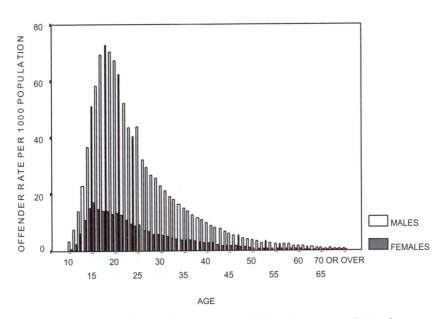

Figure 4.1 Recorded offender rates per 1,000 relevant population by age-year and sex, England and Wales, 2000.
Source: Bottoms et al. (2004).

cohort studies such as the Cambridge Study in Delinquent Development (CSDD) consistently confirm that the primary reason that relatively few street crimes are committed by older persons is that they have desisted from these behaviours. Farrington (1992), for instance, found that for the CSDD sample, self-reported criminal behaviour peaks at around age 17 or 18 and decreases sharply as the young adults progress through their twenties.

For precisely this reason, policy researchers like Dan A. Lewis (1990) have called for a shift from thinking about 'programmes' to thinking about 'lives'. Lewis points out that almost all of the research evidence suggests that 'programmes' have a remarkably minor impact on life outcomes like going to prison, and yet policy researchers devote all of our time to evaluating them. Lewis instead suggests that we turn our lens to human lives in their full biographical and historical context to better understand why and how programmes work for some individuals and why (most often) they fail.

This shift of lenses has become a core element of the desistance paradigm and one of the major contrasts to the correctional or 'medical model' of change (see Bazemore and Stinchcomb 2004). McNeill (2006: 46), for instance, explains this 'desistance paradigm' thus: 'Put simply, the implication is that offender management services need to think of themselves less as providers of correctional treatment (that belongs to the expert) and more as supporters of desistance processes (that belong to the desister).' Likewise, Porporino (2010: 80) writes: 'The desistance paradigm suggests that we might be better off if we allowed offenders to guide us …, listened to what they think might best fit their individual struggles out of crime, rather than continue to insist that our solutions are their salvation.'

The desistance paradigm starts by asking what is empirically known about why some individuals persist in criminal behaviour over time and others desist from criminal behaviour. Then, it seeks to determine how interventions can support or accelerate approximations of these 'organically' occurring processes (see Farrall 2004; Halsey 2006; Harris 2005; Lewis 2005; Maguire and Raynor 2006; Maruna et al. 2004; McNeill 2003; Raynor and Robinson 2005; Rex 1999; Robinson 2008; Robinson and Crow 2009; Rumgay 2004; Ward and Maruna 2007). This idea has animated desistance researchers at least since Sheldon and Eleanor Glueck (1937: 205), who wondered: 'Can educators, psychologists, correctional workers, and others devise means of "forcing the plant", as it were, so that benign maturation will occur earlier than it seems to at present?' Of course, criminal justice interventions can work the other way as well, impeding rather than accelerating the normative forces of maturation. Indeed, arguably, the majority of criminal justice interventions (especially imprisonment) can be said to work against normal forces of maturation rather than with them (see Liebling and Maruna 2005).

Traditionally, questions of process – or the dynamics of change – have been ignored in the effectiveness literature or kept inside what is called the 'black box' of treatment research (see Pawson and Tilley 1997; Maruna 2001; Farrall 2002). 'What works' literature typically begins with a review of the evaluation research on existing international (mostly North American) programmes, and advocates the importation of those models that have been demonstrably successful into other jurisdictions. Yet, disappointing evaluation results of rehabilitative interventions in England and Wales (see Harper and Chitty 2004) have led many in corrections to focus less on the importation of models that have been successful elsewhere ('what works') and instead to focus on issues of implementation, delivery and effective practice ('how change works') (see especially Maguire 2004; Raynor 2003). This has opened a door at least temporarily to desistance research in the United Kingdom and elsewhere and generated considerable interest in the topic internationally (Serin and Lloyd 2009).

The precise nature of what the desistance paradigm actually entails remains somewhat undefined and the theoretical models are only in the earliest stages of development. Nonetheless, some consistent themes have started to emerge in these efforts to define the paradigm. Several observers (see, for example, McNeill 2006; Raynor and Robinson 2005) have compared the desistance framework to the 'non-treatment paradigm' first developed by Bottoms and McWilliams (1979). Writing at the height of the 'nothing works' backlash against treatment, Bottoms and McWillams argued for a shift in thinking in probation away from 'treatment' models towards 'help' models, away from 'diagnosis' and towards 'shared assessment', and away from 'client needs' towards 'collaborative defined tasks'. McNeill (2006) and other advocates of the desistance paradigm have updated this list with the benefit of two decades of desistance research.

Farrall (2004) distinguishes 'desistance-focused' perspectives from 'offending-related' approaches on the basis that whereas the latter concentrates on targeting or correcting offender deficits, the former seeks to promote those things thought to be associated with desistance (such as strong social bonds, pro-social involvements and social capital). Although 'subtle', this distinction is crucial, as desistance from crime may be associated with completely different factors from those that predispose a person to crime in the first place (Harris 2005). For instance, although much research demonstrates that convicted persons 'think differently' from non-offenders, there is much less evidence that changing these thinking patterns is associated with desistance from crime, nor does such knowledge provide guidance as to how ex-offenders should think differently (Maruna 2001).

> Offenders might begin offending, in part at least, because of their impulsivity, failure to attend to consequences, preference for anti-social associates, unstructured lifestyles and emerging pro-criminal sentiments … and so on. But it doesn't follow that a reversal in these anti-social personality traits, behaviours and attitudes is what is key in moving offenders into desistance, or even in maintaining it. (Porporino 2010: 69)

Others have argued for a shift from 'deficit-based' interventions (focusing on risk factors and 'needs' as defined by the experts) to 'strengths-based' approaches that seek to promote 'good lives' as defined by the person him or herself (Burnett and Maruna 2006; Ward and Maruna 2007). Bazemore (1996: 48) argues that with its 'singular focus on the psychological needs and social deficits of the offender', traditional correctional interventions characterise prisoners and probationers as 'objects of remedial services or therapeutic interventions'. Desistance-focused interventions instead would seek to empower individuals to achieve the sorts of attachments, roles and life situations that appear to be empirically associated with successful social engagement upon release (Farrall 2004; Ward and Brown 2004). Many have drawn parallels here to community reintegration efforts (Petersilia 2003; Travis 2005), restorative justice (Bazemore and Maruna 2009), and 'rights-based rehabilitation' (Rotman 1990), where any 'treatment' provided is primarily intended to counter the harmful side-effects of imprisonment.

All of these differences make the desistance paradigm distinct from traditional approaches to rehabilitation. Indeed, these differences may be the most apparent where they matter the most: from the perspective of prisoners and probationers themselves. Drawing on her extensive work with prisoners in Pennsylvania, Harris (2005) argues: 'Many people who are currently or were formerly in prison embrace the self-change, empowerment, and desistance perspective.' At the same time, however, 'They hold negative attitudes toward the concept of rehabilitation and correctional treatment programs.'

In general, the distaste for such programs is linked to a sense that these interventions involve things being 'done to' or 'prescribed for' passive recipients who are characterized as deficient, ineffectual, misguided, untrustworthy, possibly dangerous, and almost certain to get into trouble again. Although people who have been incarcerated often believe that some staff members or other outside parties and some types of programs can be helpful, their effectiveness stems from the potential they offer for empowering participants rather than trying to compel them to change. Most argue, 'No one else can rehabilitate you. You rehabilitate yourself.' If there is distaste for correctional treatment programs among people under correctional supervision, there is even stronger antipathy toward interventions tailored to actuarial risk assessments. (Harris 2005: 318)

Although the preferences of criminal justice clients are not typically viewed as being highly relevant to policy-makers, it needs to be emphasised that if members of this target population do not engage with or commit themselves to an intervention, the 'treatment' is unlikely to succeed. Indeed, the drop-out/retention rates for most rehabilitative interventions are abysmal and the true level of engagement among even those who do attend regularly is often minimal to say the least (see Maruna *et al.* 2009). Programme completion has been a consistent problem in the implementation of treatment programmes throughout the UK (McMurran and McCulloch 2007). Attrition rates range from 10 per cent for some prison-based CBT trials (see Cann *et al.* 2003) to over 65 per cent for some community-based CBT interventions (see Steele and Van Arendsen 2001; Hollin *et al.* 2004). The Crime Reduction Programme's pathfinder evaluation of the Enhanced Thinking Skills (ETS) programme, for instance, found that of the 4,089 individuals allocated to the programme, only 1,311 went on to complete the entire course, resulting in a completion rate of 32.1 per cent (Palmer *et al.* 2007: 255). These high drop-out rates make it difficult to accurately assess the success of the programme, and more worryingly suggest a lack of engagement among probationers and prisoners (see McMurran and McCulloch 2007).

The desistance paradigm – based as it is on the experiences of successfully reformed ex-offenders themselves – takes the views and voices of correctional clients very seriously and assigns the issue of 'motivation' a central role in understanding the change process (see Farrall 2004; McMurran and Ward 2004). As desistance is understood as an agentic process in this framework, any rehabilitation option offered to prisoners and probationers needs to make sense to clients themselves and be clearly relevant to the possibility of their living better lives (Miller and Rollnick 2002; Prochaska and Levesque 2002; Trotter 1999). This is not always the case in the traditional correctional paradigm. Porporino (2010: 63) writes:

> In this exuberant momentum towards a directed and prescriptive *change-the-offender* agenda in corrections ... we may have blinded ourselves to other ways of approaching the challenge ... We may have narrowed in on too few approaches, too prematurely, and with too much uncertainty about the real process of change that offenders move through.

In sum, the desistance paradigm holds that the search for 'what works' should not begin with existing expert models of crime reduction, but rather should begin with an understanding of the organic or normative processes that seem to impact offending patterns over the life course. That is, if turning 30 is the 'most effective crime-fighting tool' (Von Drehle 2010), then we should seek to learn as much as we can about that process and see if we can model these dynamics in our own interventions. Questions remain, however, about what such a desistance paradigm may look like in practice. It is easy to critique existing practices; it is far more difficult (and dangerous) to put forward an alternative. In the following section, we try to do just that by sketching out one possible 'desistance-focused' intervention.

A labelling model for desistance-based practice

There is no single 'desistance theory' any more than there can be said to be a single theory of crime or of poverty. As with any area of social scientific study, the literature on desistance from crime is dynamic with numerous theoretical strands competing and combining to explain the phenomenon at hand (see, for example, Sampson and Laub 1993; Warr 1998; Giordano *et al.* 2002). Below we focus on one particular theoretical explanation of both persistence in, and desistance from, criminal behaviour. We make no pretence at neutrality here: this area of desistance theory happens to be one typically associated with the two authors of this chapter (see Maruna 2001; Maruna *et al.* 2009). However, this framework is also useful because it builds directly upon previous research on desistance by others and seeks to complement rather than compete with these theoretical frameworks.

A labelling perspective on persistence

Among the best-developed frameworks for understanding persistence in offending over time is Terrie Moffitt's (1993) highly influential theory of life-course persistent and adolescence-limited criminality. At the heart of her theory are bio-psychosocial factors such as subclinical neuropsychological difficulties involving attention deficits, impulsivity and low self-control, but also problems with verbal and 'executive' functions, leading to frustration in efforts to communicate. According to Moffitt's theory, these difficulties are primarily caused by heredity and disruption in the development of the foetal brain (due to maternal alcohol/drug use). Such factors are largely outside of the purview of rehabilitative interventions (although not prevention work).

However, Moffitt also argues that these neurological factors interact with social-environmental factors, and these social factors are more dynamic and subject to manipulation. In particular, Moffitt (1993; see also Caspi and Moffitt 1995) describes three types of person-environment interactions thought to be implicated in the persistence of criminality over the life course:

- reactive interactions
- proactive interactions
- evocative interactions.

Reactive interactions involve the socio-cognitive interpretations that life-course persistent offenders typically make about the social world around them. Based on their personality traits, such individuals often interpret the same stimuli differently or pick up different cues from the social environment than their peers. The best example of this is the 'hostile attribution bias' identified by Kenneth Dodge (1993). Dodge found that aggressive young people are more likely than others to attribute hostile intentions to apparently ambiguous social interactions (for example, the stare of a stranger or an accidental collision between two pedestrians).

In *proactive interactions* individuals with certain characteristics will seek out situations that are compatible with their dispositions. This involves self-selection into occupations and peer networks that support and help to sustain certain personality traits, as well as assortative mating whereby life partners are chosen among those who are most receptive to a person's faults. By selecting these environments, individuals provide themselves with fewer deterrents to change their ways.

Finally, *evocative interactions* include the reactions that certain individuals evoke from the social environment that ironically and unintentionally help to maintain and escalate the individual's pattern of anti-social behaviour. Criminality has long been understood as a 'transaction' by interactionists (see Lemert 1951; Toch 1997): an individual does something, others react to it, and these reactions, themselves, often lead to further criminality. In what Patterson (1993) refers to as 'coercive cycles', laboratory-based research has demonstrated that certain young people can literally evoke 'poor parenting' behaviours from adults (that is, precisely the 'wrong' sort of modelling behaviours to encourage the young person to desist).

In summary, Moffitt (1993) argues that individuals can become 'ensnared by the consequences of antisocial behaviour'. She describes offending as having both 'contemporary' and 'cumulative consequences' across the life course. In the latter, behaviours at one stage in the human development process (such as failure to pay attention in primary school) can have lasting, cumulative consequences at later stages (such as frustration and disadvantage in secondary school), which leads down a slippery slope towards life-course persistent criminality (skipping school, followed by early drop-out, leading to poor work opportunities, which in turn can encourage involvement in offending, which can lead to a criminal record, which can further reduce work opportunities, leading to personal frustration – in a vicious, repeating cycle). In other words, the fact that past behaviour is the best predictor of future behaviour does not necessarily mean that some individuals are permanently or somehow 'naturally' deviant. The continuity in criminal behaviour over time may instead be accounted for through predictable environmental interactions or 'cumulative disadvantages' enhanced by criminal engagement itself. Offenders, although certainly disadvantaged in many ways, may be perfectly capable of leading non-criminal lives were it not for this social-environmental cycle of cumulative continuity.

This is, of course, the key premise behind the idea of labelling theory in criminology, described by Sampson and Laub (1997) as the only truly longitudinal or life-course theory in the classic criminology canon. Indeed, labelling theory has found its greatest empirical support from the best-developed longitudinal research following cohorts of offenders over long periods (see, for example, Farrington 1977). Life-course criminologists like Sampson and Laub (1997) and Braithwaite (1989), therefore, have argued convincingly in favour of resuscitating labelling theory – which had suffered unfair criticism in the 1980s (see Paternoster and Iovanni 1989; Petrunik 1980) – in the cause of understanding such criminal persistence. Sampson and Laub (1997) argue that persistent offending may not necessarily be attributable to permanent traits of individuals, but could also be explained by a process of 'cumulative continuity' whereby future opportunities to lead a conventional life are 'knifed off' as a consequence of choices made in adolescence. They argue that deviant behaviour might be seen as a kind of 'chimera' (Patterson 1993), 'mortgaging one's future' (Nagin and Paternoster 1991) by blocking opportunities for achieving success in employment, education, and even in marriage. Braithwaite (1989) argues that when society's reaction to deviants is to stigmatise, segregate and exclude, such persons are left with limited opportunity for achieving self-respect and affiliation in the mainstream – but are welcomed among subcultural groups of similarly stigmatised outcasts. Hence, the vicious circle of persistent offending.

This developmental version of labelling theory has received considerable empirical support in recent years (see, for example, Bernburg and Krohn 2003; Bernburg et al. 2006; Taxman and Piquero 1998; Fagan et al. 2003; Hagan and Palloni 1990). In a study of 95,919 men and women who were either adjudicated or had adjudication withheld, Chiricos and colleagues (2007) found that those who were formally labelled were significantly more likely to recidivate within two years than those who were not. Interestingly, Bernburg and colleagues (2006) found that the process worked in much the same way as theorised by Braithwaite: intervention by the juvenile justice system predicted involvement with deviant gangs, which then led to increased offending. LeBel and colleagues (2008) also found that individual perceptions of being stigmatised are an important mediating mechanism in the return to criminality. Research participants in the LeBel study who reported feeling stigmatised and socially excluded during a prison-based interview were more likely to be reconvicted and reimprisoned in a ten-year follow-up study, even after controlling for the number of social problems the individual experienced after release. In the sample, only two out of the 40 (5 per cent) participants who felt that they were stigmatised as ex-prisoners were not reconvicted of a crime, versus 24 per cent (21/86) of participants who did not perceive stigma against them.

In short, desisting from crime is a difficult process, especially for those who are deeply entrenched in criminal networks and living in disadvantaged circumstances. Successfully changing one's life in such circumstances requires a tremendous amount of self-belief, and this is made highly difficult, if not impossible, when those around a person believe the person will fail. Interviews with long-term, persistent offenders suggest that many of these individuals develop a sense of hopelessness and despair, believing that all legitimate opportunities have been blocked for them (see Maruna 2001).

A labelling perspective on desistance

How, then, is it possible for long-term persistent offenders, caught up in these cycles, to desist from criminal behaviour? We argue (see Maruna 2001; Maruna *et al.* 2009) that desistance may be best facilitated when the desisting person's change in behaviour is recognised by others and reflected back to him in a 'delabelling process' (Trice and Roman 1970).

In our work we draw upon Rosenthal's so-called 'Pygmalion effects', from educational psychology, to argue that the *high* expectations of others can lead to greater self-belief (and subsequent performance) in individuals (Rosenthal and Jacobson 1992). Here, the term Pygmalion derives from the Greek myth of the sculptor who falls in love with his statue, bringing it to life, and the subsequent George Bernard Shaw drama about a peasant girl transformed into a society lady. In *Pygmalion in the Classroom*, Rosenthal and Jacobson (1992) describe Pygmalion effects as the influence of teachers' beliefs about a student's abilities on the student's self-beliefs and subsequent performance in the classroom. When teachers were made to believe that their students could achieve great things, the students began to believe this, and their outcomes confirmed this optimism (see also McNatt 2000).

We argue that personal transformation (or 'recovery' in the highly related arena of addiction treatment) also contains a looking-glass element. People start to believe that they can successfully change their lives when those around them start to believe they can. In other words, rehabilitation (or recovery) is a construct that is negotiated through interaction between an individual and significant others (Shover 1996: 144). Not only must a person accept conventional society in order to go straight, but conventional society must accept that this person has changed as well. Meisenhelder (1977: 329), for instance, uncovered what he calls a 'certification' stage of desistance, whereby 'some recognized member(s) of the conventional community must publicly announce and certify that the offender has changed and that he is now to be considered essentially noncriminal' (Meisenhelder 1977, 329). This 'status elevation ceremony' served 'publicly and formally to announce, sell and spread the fact of the Actor's new kind of being' (Lofland 1969: 227), and effectively worked to counter the stigma of the person's criminal record. According to Makkai and Braithwaite (1993: 74), such recognition of efforts to reform can have 'cognitive effects on individuals through nurturing law-abiding identities, building cognitive commitments to try harder, encouraging individuals who face adversity not to give up ... and nurturing belief in oneself'.

There is scattered support for these sorts of Pygmalion effects in the behavioural reform process. Maruna (2001), for example, found evidence of what he calls 'redemption rituals' in the life stories of successfully desisting ex-convicts. As with the 'degradation ceremony' (Garfinkel 1956) through which wrongdoers are stigmatised, these de-labelling ceremonies are directed not at specific acts, but to the whole character of the person in question (Braithwaite and Braithwaite 2001: 16). Although this research is retrospective in nature, it is supported by some experimental work inside and outside the laboratory. In one ingenious real-world experiment, for example, Leake and King (1977) informed treatment professionals that they had developed a scientific test to determine who among a group of patients were most likely to be successful in recovering from alcoholism. In reality, no such test had been developed. The patients identified as 'most likely to succeed' were picked purely at random. Still, the clients who were assigned this optimistic prophecy turned out to be far more likely to give up drinking than members of the control group. Apparently, they believed in their own ability to achieve sobriety because the professionals around them seemed to believe it as well (see also Miller 1998).

Outside of criminological research, of course, hundreds of different studies have found confirmation for the idea that one person's expectations for the behaviour of another can actually impact on the other person's behaviour. Meta-analyses of studies conducted both inside and outside the research laboratory suggest an average effect size or correlation (r) of over .30 in studies of interpersonal expectancy effects (Rosenthal 2002; Kierein and Gold 2000). In the most famous example, Rosenthal and Jacobson (1992) found that teacher expectancies of student performance were strongly predictive of student performance on standardised tests, and that manipulating these educator biases and beliefs could lead to substantial improvements in student outcomes (see also Miller et al. 1975). A nursing home study demonstrated that raising caretakers' expectations for residents' health outcomes led to a significant reduction in levels of depression among residents (Learman et al. 1990). Similar Pygmalion effects and expectancy-linked outcomes have been found in courtroom studies, business schools, and numerous different workplaces (for example, Babad *et al.* 1982; Eden 1984; McNatt 2000; Reynolds 2007; see Rosenthal 2002, for a review).

Whether the same processes could be called into play in the rehabilitation process remains an open question. Performance on standardised tests or even in a factory setting is far different from criminal recidivism, as the latter is arguably impacted by a wider variety of influences. At the same time, criminal behaviour may involve a greater element of choice or agency than is involved in exam performance (Laub and Sampson 2003). It might be, then, that Pygmalion processes could be more influential in criminology than in education.

Implications of the pro-social labelling perspective for policy

If this argument around the importance of labelling to criminal persistence and desistance is supported in future research (and this remains an 'if'), then what policy implications would such evidence have for work with probationers and prisoners? First and most obviously, if stigma and labelling influence the longevity and persistence of criminal behaviour over time, as the research increasingly suggests, then policy efforts should seek to avoid such 'collateral damage' (Travis 2005), removing barriers to full participation in society whenever possible.

Where criminal sanctions have already created stigma and applied labels, perhaps the strongest form of symbolic de-labelling an offender could receive from the state is the chance to officially wipe the slate clean and move on from the stigma of one's criminal record. Research on desistance from crime refers to such a process as 'knifing off' one's criminal past whereby individuals sever themselves from past selves and personal entanglements by moving to a new location and starting a new life (Laub and Sampson 2003; Maruna and Roy 2007). The past cannot be taken away, of course, and nothing can undo the harm that has been done. Convictions, on the other hand, are merely labels given by the state in the name of punishment, and equally these can be taken away or sealed in the name of reintegration, along with a restoration of the full civil rights, liberties and duties that all of us share (Uggen *et al.* 2004). Such rewards provide an opportunity for qualified individuals with criminal records to demonstrate that they have paid their debt to society and earned the right to have statutory bars to jobs or other services lifted, as well as to have civil rights and public benefits reinstated (Choo 2007).

There are numerous examples of such systems of sealing and expungement of criminal records internationally, notably including the Rehabilitation of Offenders Act 1974 in the United Kingdom. However, almost all of these opportunities, including the UK Act, are only available to individuals who have already been successful in desisting from crime for long periods of time (typically five or more years). In Canada, former prisoners are eligible to apply for formal 'pardons' after remaining crime-free over a specified waiting period. Although almost all applicants are successful, only a tiny fraction of ex-offenders actually apply. Ruddell and Winfree (2006) estimate the take-up at less than 5 per cent of those convicted between 1996 and 2002. In the United States, 'certificates of good conduct' or 'certificates of rehabilitation' can be issued by state authorities (such as prisoner review boards) to law-abiding ex-prisoners, but these are currently used very sparingly and by only a handful of US states (Love and Frazier 2006; Samuels and Mukamal 2004).

The research on labelling and criminal careers would suggest that, to be useful, such opportunities might be made available earlier in the desistance process. Ex-prisoners, for example, might be allowed to 'earn' a pardon or 'certificate of rehabilitation' through doing volunteer work or making other efforts to make amends for what they have done (Maruna and LeBel 2003). One advantage of this would be that individuals could earn a pardon after only a short time in the community or even during one's period of incarceration in some instances. Another advantage would be that this would make the rehabilitation process 'active' rather than 'passive'. That is, one would have to 'do something' to earn the right to be rehabilitated, rather than simply wait for the passage of time (for instance, the usual five to seven years of crime-free behaviour that is currently required to prove one's reform).

The award of such certificates or pardons may provide an ideal opportunity to mimic or orchestrate the sorts of organic rituals of reintegration observed in studies of desistance (see Leong 2006; Maruna 2001). Indeed, this research suggests that de-labelling might be most potent when coming from 'on high', particularly official sources like treatment professionals or teachers, rather than from family members or friends – where such acceptance can be taken for granted (Wexler 2001). Moreover, if the de-labelling were to be endorsed and supported by the same social control establishment involved in the 'status degradation' process of conviction and sentencing (judges or peer juries), this public redemption might carry considerable social and psychological weight for participants and observers (see Maruna and LeBel 2003; Travis 2005, for development of this idea).

The idea that such positive acknowledgement can be crucial to the consolidation of a non-criminal identity is a theory that is shared, at least implicitly, by many ex-prisoner professionals who now work to support other ex-prisoners. The following quotes are from ex-prisoner staff at a large New York-based halfway house and job training programme:

> **Counselor 1:** My philosophy is pretty simple: Show them that you believe in them, and they believe in themselves.
> **Counselor 2:** I had a client who said to me I have 30 days clean. He has never had that in his life. That is tremendous, because he's not in our housing, we're not monitoring him. He walks almost 2 miles to come here to the clinic on his own. You understand what I'm saying to you? That's a step. With that individual I would say to him 'congratulations'. We would clap and we would be happy. To this point he has achieved a milestone. It's like achieving his [high school diploma], gee whiz. That's how important it is to the guy. And (we have to) acknowledge that. (Maruna *et al.* 2009)

The role of significant others (including, perhaps especially, authority figures) in recognising efforts at reform and 'certifying' desistance through ritual, pro-social labelling and formal recognition is one possible policy implication of this strand of the desistance literature.

Last words: the irony of the desistance paradigm

There is something ironic and possibly dangerous about the notion of a desistance paradigm for rehabilitation work. After all, the study of desistance emerged as a sort of antithesis of rehabilitation. Rehabilitation was seen as a top-down, medical model whereby professionals sought to change or 'correct' individuals, whereas desistance was framed as a more naturalistic process that took place without any official intervention. Ex-prisoners who give up crime were said to experience either rehabilitation or else spontaneous desistance, as if these were very different processes.

These assumptions have been challenged in recent desistance research (see especially Maruna et al. 2004). Although it is true that ex-prisoners typically adhere to the notion that 'You rehabilitate yourself', very few desisting former offenders would take full credit for their own life turnarounds. Most will typically credit family, friends, and even some professionals with being extremely helpful along the way (Maruna 2001). The real lesson of desistance research, therefore, is not that ex-offenders should be left alone to 'get on with' the business of self-change. The process of desistance takes far too long and leaves too many victims in its wake. The lesson of desistance research is that correctional interventions should recognise this 'natural' (or at least normative) process of reform and design interventions that can enhance or complement these spontaneous efforts (Farrall 2002; McNeill 2006; Raynor and Robinson 2005).

Increasingly, then, the desistance paradigm understands re-habilitation as a relational process best achieved in the context of relationships with others (Bazemore 1996). In fact, the interest in desistance research has corresponded very closely with a revival of interest in 'relational rehabilitation' (Raynor and Robinson 2005). Some advocate that rehabilitation work itself should be devolved by the state on to families and communities, in a process akin to that of justice reinvestment (Tucker and Cadora 2003). In an essay titled 'Who owns resettlement?', for instance, Maruna (2006) argues that reintegration belongs to communities and ex-prisoners and has been 'stolen' away by the state.

At the same time, desistance research is increasingly coming to the attention of the state, and policy-makers have found several implications of the research to be useful in efforts to reduce crime. The theoretical strand of desistance research reviewed above has many implications for what the state can do wrong in terms of stigmatising and labelling individuals if it wants to reduce reoffending. At the same time, the labelling literature also suggests specific policies that might reduce reoffending through de-labelling as well. This research is not as prescriptive as the 'what works' evidence, but may be just as important in the formulation of effective practice in crime reduction.

References

Austin, J. (2009) 'The limits of prison based treatment', *Victims and Offenders*, 4: 311–20.

Babad, E., Inbar, J. and Rosenthal, R. (1982) 'Pygmalion, Galatea, and the Golem: Investigations of biased and unbiased teachers', *Journal of Education Psychology*, 74: 459–74.

Bazemore, G. (1996) 'Three paradigms for juvenile justice', in J. Hudson and B. Galaway (eds) *Restorative Justice: International Perspectives.* Monsey, NY: Criminal Justice Press.

Bazemore, G. and Maruna, S. (2009) 'Restorative justice in the reentry context: building new theory and expanding the evidence base', *Victims and Offenders*, 4: 375–84.

Bazemore, G. and Stinchcomb, J. (2004) 'A civic engagement model of re-entry: involving community through service and restorative justice', *Federal Probation*, 68 (2): 14–24.

Bernburg, J.G. and Krohn, M.D. (2003) 'Labeling, life chances and adult crime: the direct and indirect effects of official intervention in adolescence on crime in early adulthood', *Criminology*, 41: 1287–318.

Bernburg, J.G., Krohn, M.D. and Rivera, C.J. (2006) 'Official labeling, criminal embeddedness, and subsequent delinquency: a longitudinal test of labeling theory', *Journal of Research in Crime and Delinquency*, 43: 67–88.

Bottoms, A. and McWilliams W. (1979) 'A non-treatment paradigm for probation practice', *British Journal of Social Work*, 9 (2): 160–201.

Bottoms, A., Costello, A., Holmes, D., Muir, G. and Shapland, J. (2004) 'Towards desistance: theoretical underpinnings for an empirical study', *Howard Journal of Criminal Justice*, 43 (4): 368–89.

Bowcott, O. (2005) 'The Guardian profile: Louise Casey', *The Guardian*, 9 September. Online at: www.guardian.co.uk/politics/2005/sep/09/ukcrime.prisonsandprobation (accessed 18 June 2009).

Braithwaite, J. (1989) *Crime, Shame and Reintegration*. Cambridge: Cambridge University Press.

Braithwaite, J. and Braithwaite, V. (2001) 'Part one', in E. Ahmed, N. Harris, J. Braithwaite and V. Braithwaite (eds) *Shame Management Through Reintegration*. Cambridge: Cambridge University Press.

Burnett, R. and Maruna, S. (2006) 'The kindness of prisoners: strength-based resettlement in theory and in action', *Criminology and Criminal Justice*, 6: 83–106.

Cann, J., Falshaw, L., Nugent, F. and Friendship, C. (2003) *Understanding What Works: Accredited Cognitive Skills Programmes for Adult Men and Young Offenders*. London: Home Offiice.

Caspi, A. and Moffitt, T.E. (1995) 'The continuity of maladaptive behavior: from description to understanding in the study of antisocial behaviour', in D. Cicchetti and D.J. Cohen (eds) *Developmental Psychopathology, Vol. 2: Risk, Disorder and Adaptation*. New York: Wiley.

Chiricos, T., Barrick, K. and Bales, W. (2007) 'The labelling of convicted felons and its consequences for recidivism', *Criminology*, 45 (3): 547–81.

Choo, K. (2007) 'Run-on sentences: ABA, others focus on easing the added punishments for those convicted of crimes', *ABA Journal*, January, p.38.

Dodge, K.A. (1993) 'Social cognitive mechanisms in the development of conduct disorder and depression', *Annual Review of Psychology*, 44: 559–84.

Eden, D. (1984) 'Self-fulfilling prophecy as a management tool: harnessing Pygmalion', *Academy of Management Review*, 9 (1): 64–73.

Fagan, J.A., Kupchick, A. and Liberman, A. (2003) *Be Careful What You Wish For: The Comparative Impacts of Juvenile Versus Criminal Court Sanctions on*

Recidivism among Adolescent Felony Offenders. New York: Columbia Law School Public Law and Legal Theory Working Group.

Farrall, S. (2002) *Rethinking What Works with Offenders.* Cullompton: Willan Publishing.

Farrall, S. (2004) 'Social capital and offender reintegration: making probation desistance focused', in S. Maruna and R. Immarigeon (eds) *After Crime and Punishment: Pathways to Offender Reintegration.* Cullompton: Willan Publishing.

Farrington, D.P. (1977) 'The effects of public labelling', *British Journal of Criminology,* 17: 112–25.

Farrington, D.P. (1992) 'Explaining the beginning, progress, and ending of antisocial behavior from birth to adulthood', in J. McCord (ed.) *Advances in Criminological Theory, Vol. 3: Facts, Frameworks, and Forecasts.* New Brunswick, NJ: Transaction.

Garfinkel, H. (1956) 'Conditions of successful degradation ceremonies', *American Journal of Sociology,* 61: 420–4.

Giordano, P.C., Cernkovich, S.A. and Rudolph, J.L. (2002) 'Gender, crime and desistance: toward a theory of cognitive transformation', *American Journal of Sociology,* 107: 990–1064.

Glueck, S. and Glueck, E. (1937) *Later Criminal Careers.* New York: Kraus.

Hagan, J. and Palloni, A. (1990) 'The social reproduction of a criminal class in working class London', *American Journal of Sociology,* 96: 265–99.

Halsey, M. (2006) 'Negotiating conditional release: juvenile narratives of repeat incarceration', *Punishment and Society,* 8: 147–81.

Harper, G. and Chitty, C. (eds) (2004) *The Impact of Corrections on Re-offending: A Review of 'What Works',* Home Office Research Study 291. London: Home Office. Online at: www.homeoffice.gov.uk/rds/pdfs04/hors291.pdf.

Harris, M.K. (2005) 'In search of common ground: the importance of theoretical orientations in criminology and criminal justice', *Criminology and Public Policy,* 4: 311–28.

Hollin, C.R., Palmer, E.J., McGuire, J., Hounsome, J., Hatcher, R., Bilby, C. and Clark, C. (2004) *Pathfinder Programmes in the Probation Service: A Retrospective Analysis.* London: Research Development and Statistics Directorate, Home Office.

Kierein, N.M. and Gold, M.A. (2000) 'Pygmalion in work organizations: a meta-analysis', *Journal of Organizational Behavior,* 21: 913–28.

Latessa. E.J., Cullen, F.T. and Gendreau, P. (2002) 'Beyond correctional quackery: professionalism and the possibility of effective treatment', *Federal Probation,* 66, September: 43–9.

Laub, J. and Sampson, R.J. (2003) *Shared Beginnings, Divergent Lives.* Cambridge, MA: Harvard.

Leake, G.J. and King, A.S. (1977) 'Effect of counselor expectations on alcoholic recovery', *Alcohol Health and Research World,* 1 (3): 16–22.

Learman, L.A., Avrorn, J., Everitt, D.E. and Rosenthal, R. (1990) 'Pygmalion in the nursing home: the effects of caregiver expectations on patient outcomes', *Journal of the American Geriatrics Society,* 38: 797–803.

LeBel, T.P., Burnett, R., Maruna, S. and Bushway, S. (2008) 'The "chicken and egg" of subjective and social factors in desistance from crime', *European Journal of Criminology*, 5(2): 130–58.

Lemert, E.M. (1951) *Social Pathology: Systematic Approaches to the Study of Sociopathic Behavior*. New York: McGraw-Hill.

Leong (2006). *Felon Reenfranchisement: Political Implications and Potential for Individual Rehabilitative Benefits*. Stanford, CA: California Sentencing and Corrections Policy Series, Stanford Criminal Justice Center Working Papers.

Lewis, D.A. (1990) 'From programs to lives: a comment', *American Journal of Community Psychology*, 18: 923–6.

Lewis, S. (2005) 'Rehabilitation: Headline or footnote in the new penal policy?', *Probation Journal*, 52 (2): 119–36.

Liebling, A. and Maruna, S. (eds) (2005) *The Effects of Imprisonment*. Cullompton: Willan Publishing.

Lofland, J. (1969) *Deviance and Identity*. Englewood Cliffs, NJ: Prentice-Hall.

Love, M.C. and Frazier, A. (2006) 'Certificates of rehabilitation and other forms of relief from the collateral consequences of conviction: a survey of state laws', in ABA Commission on Effective Criminal Sanctions (ed.) *Second Chances in the Criminal Justice System: Alternatives to Incarceration and Reentry Strategies*. Washington, DC: American Bar Association.

Maguire, M. (2004) 'The Crime Reduction Programme in England and Wales: reflections on the vision and the reality', *Criminology and Criminal Justice*, 4 (3): 213–37.

Maguire, M. and Raynor, P. (2006) 'How the resettlement of prisoners promotes desistance from crime: or does it?', *Criminology and Criminal Justice*, 6: 19–38.

Makkai, T. and Braithwaite, J. (1993) 'Praise, pride and corporate compliance', *International Journal of the Sociology of Law*, 21: 73–91.

Maruna, S. (2001) *Making Good: How Ex-convicts Reform and Rebuild their Lives*. Washington, DC: American Psychological Association.

Maruna, S. (2006) 'Who owns resettlement? towards restorative re-integration', *British Journal of Community Justice*, 4(2): 23–33.

Maruna, S. and LeBel, T.P. (2003) 'Welcome home? Examining the reentry court concept from a strengths-based perspective', *Western Criminology Review*, 4 (2): 91–107.

Maruna, S. and Roy, K. (2007) 'Amputation or reconstruction? notes on "knifing off" and desistance from crime', *Journal of Contemporary Criminal Justice*, 23: 104–24.

Maruna, S., Immarigeon, R. and LeBel, T. (2004) 'Ex-offender reintegration: theory and practice', in S. Maruna and R. Immarigeon (eds) *After Crime and Punishment: Pathways to Ex-Offender Reintegration*. Cullompton: Willan Publishing.

Maruna, S., LeBel, T., Naples, M. and Mitchell, N. (2009) 'Looking-glass identity transformation: Pygmalion and Golem in the rehabilitation process', in B. Veysey, J. Christian and D.J. Martinez (eds) *How Offenders Transform Their Lives*. Cullompton: Willan Publishing.

McMurran, M. and McCulloch, A. (2007) 'Why don't offenders complete treatment? Prisoners' reasons for non-completion of a cognitive skills programme', *Psychology, Crime and Law*, 13(4): 345–54.

McMurran, M. and Ward, T. (2004) 'Motivating offenders to change in therapy: an organizing framework', *Legal and Criminological Psychology*, 9: 295–311.

McNatt, D.B. (2000) 'Ancient Pygmalion joins contemporary management: a meta-analysis of the result', *Journal of Applied Psychology*, 85(2): 314–22.

McNeill, F. (2003) 'Desistance-focused probation practice', in W.H. Chui and M. Nellis (eds) *Moving Probation Forward*. Harlow: Pearson Longman.

McNeill, F. (2006) 'A desistance paradigm for offender management', *Criminology and Criminal Justice*, 6: 39–62.

Meisenhelder, T. (1977) 'An exploratory study of exiting from criminal careers', *Criminology*, 15: 319–34.

Miller, R.L., Brickman, P. and Bolen, D. (1975) 'Attribution versus persuasion as a means of modifying behavior', *Journal of Personality and Social Psychology*, 31: 430–41.

Miller, W.R. (1998) 'Why do people change addictive behavior?', *Addiction*, 93: 163–72.

Miller, W.R. and Rollnick, S. (2002) *Motivational Interviewing: Preparing People for Change*. New York: Guilford Press.

Moffitt, T.E. (1993) 'Adolescence-limited and life-course-persistent antisocial behavior: a developmental taxonomy', *Psychological Review*, 100 (4): 674–701.

Nagin, D.S. and Paternoster, R. (1991) 'On the relationship of past and future participation in delinquency', *Criminology*, 29: 163–90.

Palmer, E. J., McGuire, J., Hounsome, J.C., Hatcher, R.M., Bilby, C.A.L. and Hollin, C.R. (2007) 'Offending behaviour programmes in the community: the effects on reconviction of three programmes with adult male offenders', *Legal and Criminological Psychology*, 12: 251–64.

Paternoster, R. and Iovanni, L. (1989) 'The labeling perspective and delinquency: an elaboration of the theory and an assessment of the evidence', *Justice Quarterly*, 6: 359–94.

Patterson, G.R. (1993) 'Orderly change in a stable world: the antisocial trait as chimera', *Journal of Consulting and Clinical Psychology*, 61: 911–19.

Pawson, R. and Tilley, N. (1997) *Realistic Evaluation*. London: Sage.

Petersilia, J. (2003) *When Prisoners Come Home: Parole and Prisoner Reentry*. Oxford: Oxford University Press.

Petrunik, M. (1980) 'The rise and fall of "labelling theory": the construction and destruction of a sociological strawman', *Canadian Journal of Sociology*, 5: 213–33.

Porporino, F. (2010) 'Bringing sense and sensitivity to corrections: from programmes to "fix" offenders to services to support desistance', in

J. Brayford, F. Cowe and J. Deering (eds) *What Else Works? Creative Work with Offenders*. Cullompton: Willan Publishing.

Prochaska, J.O. and Levesque, D.A. (2002) 'Enhancing motivation of offenders at each stage of change and phase of therapy', in M. McMurran (ed.) *Motivating Offenders to Change: A Guide to Enhancing Engagement in Therapy*. Chichester: John Wiley.

Raynor, P. (2003) 'Evidence-based probation and its critics', *Probation Journal*, 50: 334–45.

Raynor, P. and Robinson, G. (2005) *Rehabilitation, Crime and Justice*. Basingstoke: Palgrave.

Rex, S. (1999) 'Desistance from offending: Experiences of probation', *Howard Journal*, 38: 366–83.

Reynolds, D.R. (2007) 'Restraining Golem and harnessing Pygmalion in the classroom: a laboratory study of managerial expectations and task design', *Academy of Management Learning and Education*, 6 (4): 475–83.

Robinson, G. (2008) 'Late-modern rehabilitation: the evolution of a penal strategy', *Punishment and Society*, 10 (4): 429–45.

Robinson, G. and Crow, I (2009) *Offender Rehabilitation: Theory, Research and Practice*. London: Sage.

Rosenthal, R. (2002) 'Covert communication in classrooms, clinics, courtrooms, and cubicles', *American Psychologist*, 57: 839–49.

Rosenthal, R. and Jacobson, L. (1992) *Pygmalion in the Classroom*, expanded edn. New York: Irvington.

Rotman, E. (1990) *Beyond Punishment: A New View of the Rehabilitation of Criminal Offenders*. Westport, CT: Greenwood Press.

Ruddell, R. and Winfree Jr. T. (2006) 'Setting aside criminal convictions in Canada: a successful approach to offender reintegration', *Prison Journal*, 86: 452–69.

Rumgay, J. (2004) 'Scripts for safer survival: pathways out of female crime', *Howard Journal of Criminal Justice*, 43: 405–19.

Sampson, R.J. and Laub, J. (1993) *Crime in the Making: Pathways and Turning Points through Life*. Cambridge, MA: Harvard University Press.

Sampson, R.J. and Laub, J. (1997) 'A life-course theory of cumulative disadvantage and the stability of delinquency', in T.P. Thornberry (ed.) *Advances in Criminological Theory, Vol. 6: Developmental Theories of Crime and Delinquency*. New Brunswick, NJ: Transaction.

Samuels, P. and Mukamal, D. (2004) *After Prison: Roadblocks to Reentry*. New York: Legal Action Center.

Serin, R. and Lloyd, D. (2009) 'Examining the process of offender change: the transition to crime desistance', *Psychology, Crime and Law*, 15(4): 347–64.

Shover, N. (1996) *Great Pretenders: Pursuits and Careers of Persistent Thieves*. Boulder, CO: Westview Press.

Steele, R. and Van Arendsen, J. (2001) 'Reconviction of offenders on Think First: a twelve month follow up of offenders expected to complete Think First between Sep 2000 and Sep 2001', unpublished report from

Merseyside Probation Area Research and Information Services, National Probation Service.

Taxman, F.S. and Piquero, A. (1998) 'On preventing drunk driving recidivism: an examination of rehabilitation and punishment approaches', *Journal of Criminal Justice*, 26: 129–43.

Toch, H. (1997) *Corrections: A Humanistic Approach*. Guilderland, NY: Harrow and Heston.

Travis, J. (2005) *But They All Come Back: Facing the Challenges of Prisoner Reentry*. New York: Urban Institute.

Trice, H.M. and Roman, P.M. (1970) 'Delabeling, relabeling and Alcoholics Anonymous', *Social Problems*, 17: 538–46.

Trotter C. (1999) *Working with Involuntary Clients: A Guide to Practice*. Sydney. Allen and Unwin.

Tucker, S. and Cadora, E. (2003) *Justice Reinvestment*. New York: Open Society Institute.

Uggen, C., Manza, J. and Behrens, A. (2004) 'Less than the average citizen: stigma, role transition and the civic reintegration of convicted felons', in S. Maruna and R. Immarigeon (eds) *After Crime and Punishment: Pathways to Offender Reintegration*. Cullompton: Willan Publishing.

Von Drehle, D. (2010) 'Why crime went away. The murder rate in America is at an all-time low. Will the recession reverse that?', *Time Magazine*, 22 February, 22–5.

Ward, T. and Brown, M. (2004) 'The good lives model and conceptual issues in offender rehabilitation', *Psychology, Crime, and Law*, 10: 243–57.

Ward, T. and Maruna, S. (2007) *Rehabilitation: Beyond the Risk Paradigm*. London: Routledge.

Warr, M. (1998) 'Life-course transitions and desistance from crime', *Criminology*, 36: 183–215.

Wexler, D.B. (2001) 'Robes and rehabilitation: how judges can help offenders "make good"', *Court Review*, 38: 18–23.

Part Two

Staff skills and effective offender supervision

Chapter 5

Technology transfer: the importance of ongoing clinical supervision in translating 'what works' to everyday community supervision[1]

Guy Bourgon, James Bonta, Tanya Rugge and Leticia Gutierrez

As we enter into the twenty-first century, there is a growing demand in community corrections to implement evidence-based practices to reduce reoffending. After decades of get-tough policies and practices, probation and parole agencies have shown an interest in using the 'what works' body of research to enhance risk-reducing community supervision efforts. The 'what works' literature provides the principles of risk, need and responsivity (RNR) as guides for organisations attempting to design and implement effective community supervision (Andrews and Bonta 2006; see also Bonta and Andrews, this volume). However, the transfer of this body of knowledge to the field *via* the generation and implementation of evidence-based policies, practices and programmes has been difficult. Often referred to as the process of 'technology transfer', there is now a growing body of literature indicating that the effectiveness of these efforts diminishes when 'what works' knowledge is translated from well-controlled research projects to the 'real world' of everyday corrections (Andrews and Bonta 2006). The present challenge for researchers is to pay particular attention to the behaviour of those who are attempting to use the technology and provide answers to the following questions: What methods were used to transfer the technology to those in the field? Do such transfer processes result in staff using the new technology as it was intended to be used (that is quality use)? What factors are related to enhanced quality? Answers to such questions could provide invaluable information to those seeking to bring knowledge of 'what works' into community corrections.

The present chapter examines specific implementation or technology transfer processes to probation officers supervising offenders in the community. The Strategic Training Initiative in Community Supervision (STICS) project developed, implemented and evaluated an RNR-based model of community supervision. Specific emphasis was placed on evaluating the technology transfer processes of training and ongoing clinical supervision of the skills and techniques used by probation officers during supervision sessions with clients. It is hoped that the results of this study will assist agencies to more effectively implement 'what works' knowledge in the real world of community corrections.

The challenge of technology transfer

Transferring 'what works' to the real world is arguably one of the biggest challenges facing corrections today. It is critical for researchers and practitioners alike to demonstrate not only 'what works' but also 'how to make it work' (Andrews 2006; Cullen 2002). Correctional jurisdictions relying on the 'what works' evidence continue to invest considerable resources into using this body of knowledge to develop policies, practices and services. With these efforts comes the expectation of benefits to correctional systems, offenders and the community, through reduced reoffending. With increased emphasis on accountability it must be shown that these investments are worthwhile.

Although there are many different factors affecting the implementation of scientific knowledge to practice, technology transfer consists of two basic components (for an extensive review see Fixsen *et al.* 2005). One component is the 'technology' (that is the empirically-based practice, service or product an organisation uses to achieve a desired goal) and the second component is the 'transfer' of this 'technology' to the organisation and its staff (the processes employed to develop, enhance and maintain appropriate and quality use of the 'technology'). In corrections, the 'technology' of interest is the 'what works' body of knowledge and its corresponding principles of effective correctional treatment. The goal is reducing recidivism. The *caveat*, of course, is the 'transfer' process in which an organisation and its staff learn and become competent in the use of the skills, strategies and techniques. Success in this 'transfer' process, described as high fidelity, quality implementation, or programme integrity, refers to the degree to which staff and/or an agency use the 'technology' as it was designed and intended in day-to-day practice.

To date, an abundance of 'what works' research provides guidance as to what is the best technology to achieve reduced reoffending (Andrews and Bonta 2006). The RNR principles and their relationship to correctional treatment are well documented and described in an earlier chapter (see Bonta and Andrews, this volume). Technologies that adhere to these principles are related to greater reductions of reoffending across a wide range of offenders (Andrews and Bonta 2006; Bonta et al. 1998; Dowden and Andrews 1999, 2000; 2003; Gutierrez and Bourgon 2009; Hanson et al. 2009). Although these results demonstrate that adherence to RNR is a necessary condition for effective services, it is not a sufficient condition to guarantee success.

As more and more efforts are made to implement evidence-based programmes and services in situations beyond demonstration projects and well-controlled experiments, it has become apparent that the effectiveness of this technology in the real world of everyday corrections is mediated by the implementation processes. There are two general threats to the integrity of real world implementation: ineffective 'technology' and poor or inadequate 'transfer'. One threat to effective technology transfer is when the technology is flawed to begin with or is changed in sufficient ways to alter its congruence with empirical literature. The results of the Project Greenlight re-entry programme are an excellent example of how this threat resulted in iatrogenic effects of a 'what works'-based re-entry programme (Wilson and Davis 2006).

Project Greenlight provided offenders with intensive transitional services immediately prior to release. The eight-week programme targeted cognitive skills and pro-criminal attitudes, substance abuse, employment and housing, in addition to enhancing the offenders' links to community services. Designed to adhere to the RNR principles, the programme's two critical foundations or technology were the Reasoning and Rehabilitation programme (R&R) developed by Ross and Fabiano (1991) and the transtheoretical stages-of-change (McConnaughy et al. 1983). With expectations high for this evidence-based programme to reduce recidivism, the evaluation showed that the programme actually had iatrogenic effects for programme participants.

Rhine, Mawhorr and Parks' (2006) commentary on Project Greenlight and its surprising results described how the original technology was altered and ultimately deviated from empirically derived 'what works' principles due to various systemic and organisational pressures. These accommodations compromised the therapeutic integrity of the programme and services delivered. Even more troublesome was Marlowe's (2006) observation that the technology itself was flawed to begin with. Marlowe's review of the research literature of the R&R programme and stages of change suggests that, at best, these two technologies have very weak empirical support. He suggested that regardless of the quality of the transfer processes, Project Greenlight was doomed from the beginning as it employed unproven and unreliable technology to effect offender re-entry.

The second major threat to the technology transfer is the transfer processes themselves. This includes training efforts (staff training and workshops, clinical supervision, coaching and feedback) and supports (organisational climate, leadership, and administrative and financial supports). The technology transfer processes employed, particularly with human service interventions, are critical to ensure that staff learn and use the new technology appropriately.

Staff training

Numerous authors have discussed the necessity for adequate staff training and ongoing clinical supervision to ensure quality technology transfer (Armstrong 2003; Hubbard and Latessa 2004; Landenberger and Lipsey 2005). Taxman (2008) has examined organisational supports and climates and their relationships to successful implementation of evidence-based practices. Her research regarding implementation and changing the correctional environment described some of the various technology transfer processes used in Maryland (such as staff development seminars, booster sessions, supervisor training), but did not directly evaluate its impact on staff behaviour. Rather, her work showed that a RNR-based model of community supervision implemented with a variety of technology transfer processes can lead to some positive client outcomes.

Perhaps the most commonly used technology transfer process is brief didactic training provided in seminars or workshops (Sholomskas *et al.* 2005). Such workshops often provide descriptions and evidence supporting the technology with exercises (for example role-plays) to facilitate trainees' learning and enhance skills. Less common is the addition of other transfer processes such as ongoing clinical supervision through feedback and case supervision. Such practices are typical in clinical efficacy trials to ensure standardisation and maximum levels of quality (Crits-Christoph *et al.* 1998).

Apart from the addiction field, there are few empirical studies that have examined the overall effectiveness of workshops and ongoing clinical supervision processes to create, maintain, and/or enhance the skills and techniques targeted (Backer *et al.* 1995). A recent systematic review (Walters *et al.* 2005) of 17 studies examined the effectiveness of various transfer processes on staff skills. These authors found that although workshop training typically improves trainees' knowledge, confidence and attitudes regarding the technology and techniques, evidence suggests that there is only minor skill improvement immediately following training. When training consists only of workshops, such minor improvements are not maintained over longer periods of time. The authors concluded that additional transfer processes, such as ongoing supervision, consultation and feedback, are necessary for long-term skills benefits.

Not surprisingly, there is almost a complete absence of evaluations of training efforts for probation officers. The sole exception is the work conducted by Chris Trotter (1996, 2006) who provided a five-day 'pro-social approach' training workshop to officers. He found that the four-year recidivism rate of the 97 clients for 12 trained officers was lower than the rate for the 273 clients of the 18 untrained officers (53.8 per cent *vs* 64.0 per cent). Although Trotter's work suggests that training officers can pay dividends, his work does not address the relative merits of various technology transfer processes to enhance officer skills and quality of interventions.

In an effort to address this gap in our knowledge regarding the effectiveness of technology transfer processes, this chapter describes the Strategic Training Initiative in Community Supervision (STICS) project and evaluates the technology transfer processes that were used to implement an empirically derived model of community supervision. The focus is to examine the relationship between the technology transfer processes and the quality of probation officers' skills exhibited with their clients. The following three questions are addressed:

1 Overall, did the transfer processes of STICS enhance the quality of officers' skills and techniques as well as improve the content of their discussions with their clients?
2 What happens to the quality of officers' skills and techniques and the content of their discussions with clients over time?
3 What is the relationship between enhanced usage of the various technology transfer processes and long-term quality of officers' skills, techniques and content of their discussions with clients?

Strategic Training Initiative in Community Supervision (STICS)

The goals of the STICS project were to design a model of community supervision that was consistent with the RNR principles, put together a means to implement the model into everyday practice, and create an evaluation strategy that would provide valuable technology transfer information for community supervision. STICS supervision targets pro-criminal attitudes (the need principle) for medium and high risk offenders (the risk principle). The responsivity principle is concerned with how officers target and facilitate change. Recognising that community supervisors need the knowledge, skills and structures to deliver services in a way that is responsive to the client's learning styles, STICS provided specific transfer processes. These included a three-day training workshop, monthly clinical supervision meetings, a refresher course, and specific feedback on audiotaped officer–client supervision sessions. In essence, STICS attempted to strike a balance between facilitating pro-social change and monitoring compliance (for further details see Bourgon *et al.* 2009).

The probation officers

Eighty probation officers from three Canadian provinces (British Columbia, Saskatchewan and Prince Edward Island) volunteered to participate in the project. These three provinces met all of the necessary prerequisites, which included the use of a validated risk-needs assessment instrument, policies congruent with the RNR principles (for example higher-risk cases receive higher levels of service), and managerial support for the technology transfer of STICS. Managerial support included top-down verbal commitments to support probation officers' participation in all aspect of STICS and all managers of the officers involved in STICS were required to attend the three-day training.

The probation officers were randomly assigned either to STICS training or to a control group. We used a 60:40 assignment ratio, over-sampling experimental officers in order to have sufficient power for planned analyses. In total, 51 officers were assigned to the experimental group and 29 officers were assigned to the control group.

Overall, the majority of probation officers were female (67.5 per cent) with an average age of 38.9 years ($SD = 10.4$) and an average of 10.3 years' experience ($SD = 8.6$). All probation officers had a university degree, most with specialisations in the social sciences (such as psychology, criminology or social work). No significant differences were found between officers assigned to the experimental (STICS training) and the control (no training) group on demographic variables.

Despite recruiting volunteers and having implementation structures in place to minimise attrition, 28 probation officers (18 experimental, ten control) did not recruit any clients for the study after training. The drop-outs fell into two main groups. The first group consisted of 18 officers (11 experimental, seven control) who did not participate because they felt that they could not meet the demands of the extra work required by the project. The second group of ten officers (seven experimental, three control) did not recruit clients for benign reasons (for example, transferred to new jobs, on maternity leave). Comparisons of the officers who continued with the project and those who dropped out showed no significant differences on demographic characteristics. In order to verify that officer attrition did not adversely affect the equality of the two groups, statistical comparisons between the participating officers in the experimental group (n = 33) and the participating officers in the control group (n = 19) were conducted. No significant between-group differences were found.

The clients

Clients were considered to be recruited and participating in the project once they provided consent, the intake session was recorded, and the audiotape submitted. The intake session had to be recorded within three months of commencing community supervision. The 52 participating probation officers recruited a total of 143 clients, with 100 clients supervised by 33 STICS officers and 43 clients supervised by 19 control group officers. Although each STICS probation officer recruited, on average, more clients (M = 3.03, SD = 1.70, MDN = 3) than each control group officer (M = 2.26, SD = 1.63, MDN = 1), this difference was not significant ($t(50)$ = 1.588; p = .119).

The majority of clients were male (86.0 per cent), Caucasian (69.9 per cent), and with an average age of 34.5 years (SD = 10.9; range from 18 to 63 years). About half were employed (39.2 per cent full-time and 10.5 per cent part-time) and three clients were going to school full-time (2.1 per cent). Slightly over half (57.3 per cent) were sentenced for a violent offence (for example, armed robbery, assault, sexual offences). A custodial component was included in the sentence for 40.6 per cent of the clients. The length of the community supervision order averaged 15.7 (SD = 7.1) months. No significant differences were noted between clients supervised by STICS officers and the clients supervised by the control group officers.

Although we asked officers to recruit two medium and four high risk clients, there were a couple of participating probation officers who supervised only low and medium risk clients. As a result, 55.2 per cent (n = 79) of our sample consisted of high risk clients, 39.9 per cent (n = 57) were medium risk clients, and the remaining 4.9 per cent (n = 7) were low risk. No significant differences on risk levels were found between the two groups.

Control group

Officers assigned to the control group were brought together for a half-day seminar where they were provided with an overview of the 'what works' literature, the research requirements, and the importance of random assignment. By providing an overview of the offender rehabilitation literature, we raised the possibility that probation officers may be encouraged to engage in some core correctional practices if they were not doing so already. In addition, the research team held bi-monthly teleconferences with the control group to answer their questions about the research and to reiterate their importance in the evaluation. The control group was promised the three-day training at the end of the evaluation in the event of favourable research results.

Experimental group: technology transfer processes

Initial training
The transfer process began with a three-day workshop conducted in small groups (maximum of 16), facilitated by two trainers who developed and created the STICS training package and manual. At its core, STICS training provided officers with a coherent and comprehensive cognitive behavioural model of behaviour. Throughout training, workshop facilitators demonstrated how this cognitive behavioural model was applicable to the behaviour of their clients as well as their own behaviour.

The initial training focused on 'why' officers should change their behaviour when working with clients, 'what' skills and techniques are desirable, and, most importantly, 'how' to use and develop these skills and techniques to facilitate a client's pro-social attitudinal and behavioural change. The 'why' was addressed by providing research evidence in support of the cognitive behavioural model, the officer skills and techniques taught, and the various structuring skills and framework of STICS. 'What' the officers learned included a specific cognitive behavioural model, a set of structuring and relationship skills, as well as session and supervision structures to follow in order to facilitate pro-social cognitive and behavioural change in their clients.

Training emphasised 'how' to use this new technology of RNR-based skills, techniques and concepts. This was accomplished in three distinct ways. One was by keeping the model, language and skills simple, concrete, and relevant to both the probation officers and to their clients. The second way was *via* the trainers modelling the concepts, skills and techniques being taught throughout the training. The third method was ensuring that the exercises during training were practical, addressed client examples, and focused on identifying and facilitating change to pro-criminal thoughts and behaviours. In an effort to maximise the officers' learning of the 'what' and the 'how' to apply this technology to their everyday work, the training followed an additive approach where each subsequent component built upon the previous skill or intervention that had been taught. STICS training acknowledged and attempted to address realistic challenges presented in community supervision (for example, unmotivated high risk clients and communities with minimal resources).

Monthly meetings

Following the initial training, probation officers met monthly in small groups to discuss their use of STICS concepts and skills. Each group consisted of between three and twelve trained officers working in the same office or in the same geographical region. Each group had a 'champion' whose role was to coordinate meetings (the scheduling and location), disseminate information among the group members, and liaise with the trainers. Monthly meetings were either face to face with other group members or *via* teleconference. At least one trainer was always present *via* teleconference to provide the clinical supervision. Clinical supervision typically consisted of reviewing short samples of audiotaped sessions between officers and clients and completing various relevant exercises. The major focus was on skill development, maintenance and application of STICS.

Initially, there were six different groups holding monthly meetings. However, during the approximately two years of the project, these six groups eventually became four due to dwindling numbers. On average, officers attended 11.2 meetings ($SD = 5.4$) with a range of one to twenty monthly meetings attended during the course of the project. As we were interested in the effects of monthly meetings on officer behaviour, we examined officer attendance at these meetings prior to his/her last audiotape submission. We found that attendance averaged 5.3 (SD = 2.9, MDN = 6) meetings with a range of none to ten meetings during the period of submitting data.

In addition to attendance, the officers' participation in these meetings was rated by one of the trainers approximately one year following training. Ratings were made on a three-point (1 to 3) Likert scale; from *poor* participation (attended half or fewer of scheduled meetings; did not participate in discussions), to *average* participation (attended half to three-quarters of meetings, provided some input and engaged in discussions), to *excellent* participation (attended almost all meetings, active participation in discussions, offered audiotapes or exercises to group). With an average rating of 2.1 (SD = 0.77), eight officers were rated as having poor participation, fourteen officers as average, and eleven officers as excellent.

Feedback

All trained officers were encouraged to submit audiotapes specifically for the purpose of receiving individual clinical feedback. When requested, a trainer listened to the audiotape and provided detailed feedback (in almost all cases this was written, but for two cases the feedback was oral). The feedback focused on the officers' use of STICS concepts, skills and techniques, with an emphasis on rewarding and encouraging their use. In addition, feedback also provided officers with alternative STICS strategies that could be employed with the clients.

A total of 20 of the 33 experimental officers submitted an audiotaped session and received formal clinical feedback. Of these 20 officers, twelve officers received formal feedback on a single audiotape, six officers received feedback on two audiotapes, one officer received feedback on three audiotapes, and one officer received feedback on six audiotapes.

Refresher course

To further enhance skill maintenance and development, STICS provided a one-day refresher course facilitated by one of the trainers approximately one year after the initial three-day training. In this refresher course, STICS concepts, skills and techniques were reviewed; attendees engaged in additional interactive exercises, reviewed small samples of audiotaped officer–client sessions, and discussed their difficulties with applying STICS with ongoing cases. In total, 20 of the 33 officers attended the refresher course.

Officer behaviour and technology transfer measurement

A critical question to technology transfer efforts is evaluating their effects on the recipients of the technology. In the case of STICS, the technology transfer processes (STICS training, monthly meetings, feedback and refresher course) were our attempt to alter the behaviour of the probation officers during their sessions with the clients they supervise, which in turn, we hoped, would have positive effects on the clients' behaviour. The focus here was on the transfer processes of STICS to impact and maintain change in the officers' supervision behaviour, and having them intervene according to the RNR principles. Consequently, the following describes the details of assessing the officers' behaviour and their participation in the various technology transfer processes.

Assessment of officer behaviour

Audiotapes have been widely used to evaluate the effectiveness of training (Walters *et al.* 2005), the fidelity of treatment interventions (Ball *et al.* 2007; Barber *et al.* 1997; Gondolf 2008) and monitoring supervision provided by probation officers (Bogue *et al.* 2007; Bonta *et al.* 2008). Audiotapes have the advantage of being relatively unobtrusive and non-threatening compared to videotapes or observers sitting in on sessions.

In the STICS project, officers were asked to audiotape three sessions for each client recruited for the study (the first soon after intake, then after three months and after six months of supervision). The 33 experimental officers submitted 220 audiotapes on 100 clients (56 high risk, 40 medium risk and four low risk clients) and the 19 control group officers submitted 75 audiotapes on 43 clients (23 high risk, 17 medium risk and three low risk clients). The length of the sessions on average was comparable between groups, with an average of 26¾ minutes for the experimental group and an average of just over 24½ minutes for the control group.

Following a detailed coding manual (available upon request from the authors), trained raters, in teams of two, evaluated the presence and quality of skills and techniques as well as the content of the discussions between the officer and his/her client. The quality of skills and intervention techniques were based on the coding of 24 items rated between 0 and 7, with higher scores representing higher quality. These items were grouped *a priori* into five key intervention/ skill quality constructs, comprising: (a) *structuring skills*, which assessed the level of structure of the session; (b) *relationship skills*, which assessed skills related to building a collaborative working relationship; (c) *behavioural techniques*, which assessed the quality of behavioural intervention skills; and (d) *cognitive techniques*, which assessed the quality of cognitive intervention techniques. These four constructs were also then combined into (e) a *global RNR skills* score. Skill quality scores for each officer were calculated by summing the respective item in each session and averaging across all audiotapes the officer submitted.

In addition to these five skill quality measures, the content of the officer–client discussions was also coded from the audiotapes. Discussion content was assessed by coding each five-minute session segment for the presence or absence of specific topics of discussions. Discussion topics included each specific criminogenic need identified for that particular client as assessed by the intake risk/need assessment (such as pro-criminal attitudes, anti-social personality, peers, family/marital, employment/education, substance abuse, leisure/recreation), non-criminogenic needs (for example self-esteem, depression, criminogenic needs assessed as not relevant for that offender), and conditions of probation (conditions, community service hours, restitution). Using these frequency counts, five discussion content measures were calculated for each session and average scores were aggregated for each officer across all audiotapes the officer submitted. Two variables focused on the discussion of pro-criminal attitudes: (a) the mean percentage of sessions in which the officer and his/her client discussed pro-criminal attitudes (*Per cent sessions: pro-criminal attitudes*); and (b) the mean proportion of the session during which the officer and his/her client discussed pro-criminal attitudes (*Session ratio: pro-criminal attitudes*). The third variable was the mean proportion of the session during which the officer and his/her client discussed the identified criminogenic needs (*Session ratio: criminogenic needs*). The last two discussion content variables were (a) the mean proportion of the session during which the officer and client discussed non-criminogenic needs (*Session ratio: non-criminogenic needs*); and (b) the mean proportion of the session during which the officer and his/her client discussed the conditions of probation (*Session ratio: probation*).

Assessment of participation in technology transfer processes

The following three items were created to assess each officer's overall participation in the ongoing transfer processes: *Monthly meetings;*

Feedback; and *Refresher course*. The first item, participation in *monthly meetings*, assessed the officer's use of monthly meetings by combining attendance and participation ratings. Using a median split of monthly meeting attendance, officers were awarded 1 point for low attendance (five or fewer meetings) or 2 points for high attendance (six or more meetings). This was multiplied by the participation ratings and the resulting product (ranging from 1 to 6) was dichotomised using a median split. An officer's *monthly meeting* score was 1 (attendance-participation products of 3 or fewer; n = 18) or 2 (attendance-participation products of 4 or more; n = 15).

The second item, *Feedback*, assessed the amount of formal feedback on audiotapes the officer requested and received. Officers were awarded 2 points when they received feedback on two or more audiotapes (n = 8), 1 point when they received feedback on one audiotape (n = 12), and no points if they did not receive any feedback (n = 13). The third item, *Refresher course*, provided officers with 1 point if they attended the refresher course while still submitting data (n = 12) and no points if they did not attend the refresher course or attended only after they had completed submitting data, as the refresher course would have no impact on the data they had already submitted (n = 21).

Finally, a global *Ongoing supervision* participation score was calculated by summing the three items described above. The *Ongoing supervision* participation score ranged from 1 to 5 with a mean of 2.7 (SD = 1.5) and a median of 2.0. A total of ten officers had a score of 1, seven had a score of 2, six had a score of 3, four had a score of 4, and six had a score of 5. For certain analyses, experimental officers were split into one of two groups based on the *Ongoing supervision* score. Officers with scores of 3 or less were categorised as the *low participation* group, and officers with scores of 4 or more were categorised as the *high participation* group.

Results

Question 1: Overall, did the transfer processes of STICS enhance the quality of the officers' skills and techniques as well as improve the content of their discussions with their clients?

We anticipated that the experimental group would demonstrate significantly better skills and that their discussions with clients would significantly focus on topics in line with the need principle (that is, more discussions on criminogenic needs and pro-criminal attitudes in particular, and fewer discussions on non-criminogenic needs and conditions of probation). Mean skill quality scores and discussion content variables for the experimental and control group are presented in Table 5.1. Between-group comparisons found the experimental group to be significantly better on all measures ($p < .05$) except on *behavioural techniques* ($p = .064$), which approached significance.

Overall, the STICS transfer processes resulted in enhancing the officers' RNR-based skills and improved the content of their discussions with clients. The results show that the technology transfer processes utilised in this project resulted in improved officer skills and enhanced the focus of supervision sessions to targeting criminogenic needs in general and pro-criminal attitudes specifically.

Question 2: What happens to the quality of officers' skills and techniques and the content of their discussions with clients over time?

Table 5.1 Skill/technique quality and discussion content variables for the experimental group and control groups

	Experimental group	Control group
	M (SD)	M (SD)
Skill/technique quality		
Structuring skills*	13.07 (5.59)	8.92 (3.69)
Relationship skills*	13.61 (2.64)	11.56 (2.21)
Behavioural techniques	10.23 (3.02)	8.67 (2.54)
Cognitive techniques*	1.58 (2.21)	0.01 (0.03)
Global RNR skills*	38.49 (11.38)	29.16 (7.27)
Discussion content variables		
Per cent sessions: pro-criminal attitudes*	34.5 (27.6)	2.4 (7.4)
Session ratio: pro-criminal attitudes*	.107 (.094)	.007 (.026)
Session ratio: criminogenic needs*	.581 (.166)	.424 (.269)
Session ratio: non-criminogenic needs*	.334 (.154)	.490 (.223)
Session ratio: probation*	.119 (.094)	.268 (.261)

*$p < .05$
Notes: Experimental group $n = 33$. Control group $n = 19$.

One technology transfer concern raised in the literature was that short-term benefits of training disappear over time, with no benefits observed six months later (Walters *et al.* 2005). Was this also the case with STICS? To answer this question, we assessed changes in officer behaviour over time. Skills and discussion content of each session of the 33 officers in the experimental group were correlated with the time elapsed since the initial three-day training to the recording of that session (see Table 5.2).

Results indicated that *relationship skills, behavioural techniques,* and *global RNR skills* were significantly and negatively related with time elapsed since initial training. *Structuring skills* was also negatively related but did not reach significance ($p = .06$). These results indicate that even though additional ongoing supports were provided, some of the skills targeted in training showed deterioration over time. Only *cognitive techniques* showed no relationship to time elapsed since training.

In comparison, none of the discussion content variables were significantly related with time. Only the *session ratio on non-criminogenic needs* approached significance ($p = .06$). This negative relationship ($r = -.13$), contrary to the findings of skill deterioration, indicated that for the trained officers, discussions on non-criminogenic needs reduced over time.

Question 3: What is the relationship between enhanced usage of the various technology transfer processes and long-term quality of officers' skills, techniques, and content of their discussions with clients?

Table 5.2 Time elapsed since initial three-day training with skill and session content measures.

Skill/technique quality	r	Discussion content	r
Structuring skills	−.13	Per cent sessions: pro-criminal attitudes	.07
Relationship skills	−.28*	Session ratio: pro-criminal attitudes	.10
Behavioural techniques	−.15*	Session ratio: criminogenic needs	.02
Cognitive techniques	.02	Session ratio: noncriminogenic needs	−.13
Global RNR skills	−.17*	Session ratio: probation	−.10

*$p < .05$
Notes: Time elapsed ranges from 1 to 585 days. 220 audiotapes recorded by 33 probation officers.

This question addresses the issue that typical technology transfer efforts fail to result in lasting, long-term gains to staff skills and behaviour. With the implementation of monthly meetings, feedback and a refresher course, we wanted to examine if there was a relationship between participation in these processes and long-term skills and behaviour. To assess the officers' long-term skills and content of discussions, we examined only those sessions that were recorded at least nine months after the initial three-day training (typically, the first audiotaped session occurred months after training, considering the requirements around recruiting a client to the project and completing the risk-needs assessment). Long-term officer behaviour was evaluated on 76 of the 220 audiotapes submitted by 23 of the 33 experimental officers (ten officers submitted all of their data within nine months of training). These sessions were recorded between 272 and 585 days after the initial three-day training, with a mean elapsed time of approximately one year (M = 356 days; SD = 77 days). Following the same strategy in previous analyses, skill level and content discussion variables for each officer were calculated by aggregating all audiotapes that the officer recorded 270 days or longer post-training. In this manner, we could assess officers' behaviour after the bulk of the ongoing clinical supervision was provided.

Our expectation was that higher participation in the technology transfer process would be related to higher quality of officer skills and discussions with the clients. First, the three ongoing supervision items and the *global ongoing supervision* measure were correlated to the officers' long-term skill and discussion content measures (see Table 5.3). Of particular note, *cognitive techniques* showed significant positive correlation to participation in all of the technology transfer process indices. In addition, *structuring skills, behavioural techniques,* and *global RNR skills* demonstrated a similar but not significant pattern. That is, greater participation in the technology transfer processes was associated with higher skill scores. Only *relationship skills* did not follow this pattern; rather, this skill appeared to have a minimal and negative association with participation in the technology transfer processes.

In terms of discussion content, a similar pattern emerged showing higher participation correlated to higher quality discussions. Specifically, greater participation in the technology transfer processes was related to increased discussions on pro-criminal attitudes (more sessions and higher session ratio) and less time discussing non-criminogenic needs. Although not significant, the *session ratio on criminogenic needs* showed the same pattern. Overall, these results

Table 5.3 Correlations of long-term officer skill and discussion content with participation in technology transfer processes.

	Monthly meeting	Feedback	Refresher	On-going super-vision
	R	r	R	R
Skill				
Structuring skills	.23	.16	.25	.24
Relationship skills	−.05	−.10	.05	−.06
Behavioural techniques	.13	.27	.11	.22
Cognitive techniques	.37*	.40*	.42**	.46**
Global RNR skills	.24	.24	.28	.30
Session content				
Per cent sessions: pro-criminal attitudes	.23	.44**	.24	.39*
Session ratio: pro-criminal attitudes	.21	.36*	.28	.35*
Session ratio: criminogenic needs	.24	.22	.31	.29
Session ratio: non-criminogenic needs	−.45 **	−.48**	−.17	−.46**
Session ratio: probation	−.17	−.16	−.05	−.16

*$p < .10$. **$p < .05$.
Note: $n = 23$.

suggest that greater participation in the ongoing clinical supervision process was associated with enhanced skills and more appropriate discussions approximately one year after training.

The final analysis examined three groups to further explore participation in the transfer processes and long-term officer skill and discussion content. First, experimental officers were divided into two groups. Experimental officers with *overall ongoing supervision* scores of 4 or higher were grouped together and designated as *high participation* ($n = 10$) in the technology transfer process. Experimental officers with scores of 3 or less were grouped into the *low participation* ($n = 13$) group. The long-term skills and content discussion variables of these two groups were compared to the overall scores (assessed from all submitted sessions) of the control group ($n = 19$; see Table 5.4).

The ANOVA results revealed significant between-group differences on *cognitive techniques* ($F(2,39) = 14.91$; $p < .001$); *global RNR skills* ($F(2,39) = 4.71$; $p = .015$); *percentage of sessions on pro-criminal attitudes* ($F(2,39) = 16.08$; $p < .001$), *session ratio on pro-criminal attitudes* ($F(2,39)$

Table 5.4 Long-term skill and discussion content comparisons.

Skills	Experimental group Assessed 270+ days post-training		Control group
	High participation	Low participation	
	M (SD)	M (SD)	M (SD)
Structuring skills	14.39 (6.57)	10.03 (7.31)	8.92 (3.69)
Relationship skills	12.16 (1.92)	12.55 (1.55)	11.56 (2.21)
Behavioural techniques	10.42 (1.99)	8.92 (2.88)	8.67 (2.54)
Cognitive techniques*	3.73 (3.50)[1]	0.69 (1.04)[1]	0.01 (0.03)[2]
Global RNR skills*	40.70 (12.11)[1]	32.19 (10.69)[1]	29.16 (7.27)[2]
Session content			
Per cent sessions:			
pro-criminal attitudes*	.597 (.346)[1]	.298 (.353)[2]	.024 (.074)[3]
Session ratio:			
pro-criminal attitudes*	.231 (.189)[1]	.105 (.132)[2]	.007 (.026)[3]
Session ratio:			
criminogenic needs*	.644 (.181)[1]	.594 (.249)[1,2]	.424 (.269)[2]
Session ratio:			
non-criminogenic needs*	.187 (.111)[1]	.371 (.325)[1,2]	.490 (.223)[2]
Session ratio:			
probation*	.068 (.054)[1]	.127 (.155)[1,2]	.268 (.261)[2]

*ANOVA $p < .05$.
Notes: High technology transfer participation $n = 10$. Low technology transfer participation $n = 13$. Control group $n = 19$. [1,2,3]indicate groups significant different $p < .05$.

$= 11.92$; $p < .001$); *session ratio on criminogenic needs* ($F(2,39) = 3.31$; $p = .047$); *session ratio on non-criminogenic needs* ($F(2,39) = 5.179$, $p = .010$); and *session ratio on probation* ($F(2,39) = 3.897$; $p = .029$). For *structuring skills*, the ANOVA results ($F(2,39) = 3.081$; $p = .057$) approached significance. *Post-hoc* analyses found the high participation group was significantly superior to the control group on each of these measures; and in general, the skills and discussion content scores of the low participation group were more similar to the control group than to the high participation group.

Overall, these results indicate that higher levels of participation in the various technology transfer processes were associated with enhanced 'quality' of cognitive techniques and all of the measures of the content of officer–client discussions. It is noteworthy that in all of the officers' skills, with the exception of *relationship skills*, the high participation group were ranked highest among the three groups. Although the low participation group had slightly higher skills scores than the control group, this low participation group more closely resembled the skill levels found in the control group than what was found for the high participation group.

Implications

Taken as a whole, the technology transfer processes employed by STICS had the desired effect on probation officers' skills and the content of the discussions during supervision with their clients. In line with the recent meta-analysis of Walters *et al.* (2005), our results also showed that only some skills targeted in training deteriorated over time even though there were additional ongoing supports. However, the variation in officer participation in the monthly meetings, refresher course, and obtaining formal feedback appeared to mediate officer behaviour one year after training. Specifically, more participation in the additional technology transfer processes was associated with higher quality of officer–client discussion content and higher quality cognitive techniques, a key skill targeted by STICS. In general, officers who actively used the ongoing STICS supervision and supports engaged in significantly higher quality behaviours than officers in the control group. The quality of the skills and discussions of officers who minimally used these added technology transfer strategies closely resembled what was found in the control group.

For those community corrections agencies and probation officers interested in bringing 'what works' knowledge to community supervision, the results of the present study provide some guidance on how to achieve higher quality implementation. For probation officers, the present study illustrates that to change how you supervise your clients requires time, effort, and the practice of new skills and techniques with appropriate clinical supervision and supports. Without ongoing clinical supervision and supports, any gains in employing RNR-based technologies from participating in training workshops are likely to dissipate over time. Just like substance abusers trying to maintain sobriety without ongoing supports, relapse is likely. For agencies, these results provide empirical evidence that ongoing clinical supervision and supports are critical to bring about sustainable and long-term change in officer behaviour. In fact, additional technology transfer processes beyond workshop training appear to be crucial, particularly for the development of more complex intervention skills and high quality officer–client discussion content. It is recognised that additional transfer processes, such as formal feedback on sessions and monthly clinical supervision and skills development meetings, do not come without a cost. Commitments to quality will require correctional agencies to re-examine financial and human resources and limitations.

Finally, we encourage the field to pay closer attention to the behaviour of those who are trying to apply the 'what works' knowledge. To better identify how to make it work, practitioners, managers and researchers must collaboratively examine how 'what works' is brought to the field and evaluate the impact that the various implementation processes have on everyday interactions with offenders. Such a knowledge exchange between front-line staff, management and researchers regarding officer skills and behaviour and their link to the behaviour and attitudes of clients can potentially help the field to identify concrete and practical 'what works' practices.

Note

1 The opinions expressed in this chapter are those of the authors and do not necessarily represent the views of Public Safety Canada.

References

Andrews, D.A. (2006) 'Enhancing adherence to risk-need-responsivity: making quality a matter of policy', *Criminology and Public Policy*, 5: 595–602.

Andrews, D.A. and Bonta, J. (2006) *The Psychology of Criminal Conduct*, 4th edn. Newark, NJ: LexisNexis.

Armstrong, T.A. (2003) 'The effects of moral reconation therapy on the recidivism of youthful offenders', *Criminal Justice and Behaviour*, 32: 3–25.

Backer, T.E., David, S.L. and Saucy, G. (1995) *Reviewing the Behavioural Science Knowledge Base on Technology Transfer*. Rockville, MA: National Institute on Drug Abuse.

Ball, S.A., Martino, S., Nich, C., Frankforter, T.L., Van Horn, D., Crits-Christoph, P., Woody, G.E., Obert, J.L., Farentinos, C. and Carroll, K.M. (2007) 'Site matters: multisite randomized trial of motivational enhancement therapy in community drug abuse clinics', *Journal of Consulting and Clinical Psychology*, 75: 556–67.

Barber, J.P., Krakauer, I., Calvo, N., Badgio, P.C. and Faude, J. (1997) 'Measuring adherence and competence of dynamic therapists in the treatment of cocaine dependence', *Journal of Psychotherapy Practice and Research*, 6: 12–24.

Bogue, B., Pampel, F. and Vanderbilt, R. (2007) *Evaluation of Alternative Sanction Programs, Connecticut Probation and Related Services*, Report to the Connecticut Judicial Branch. Wethersfield, CT: Court Support Services Division.

Bonta, J., Law, M. and Hanson, R.K. (1998) 'The prediction of criminal and violent recidivism among mentally disordered offenders: a meta-analysis', *Psychological Bulletin*, 123: 123–42.

Bonta, J., Rugge, T., Scott, T., Bourgon, G. and Yessine, A. (2008) 'Exploring the black box of community supervision', *Journal of Offender Rehabilitation*, 47: 248–70.

Bourgon, G., Bonta, J., Rugge, T., Scott, T. and Yessine, A. (2009) *Translating 'What Works' into Sustainable Everyday Practice: Program Design, Implementation and Evaluation*. Ottawa: Public Safety Canada.

Crits-Christoph, P., Siqueland, L., Chittams, J., Barber, J.P., Beck, A.T., Frank, A. Luborsky, L, Mark, D, Mercer, D., Majavitis, L.M., and Woody, G. (1998) 'Training in cognitive, supportive-expressive, and drug counselling therapies for cocaine dependence', *Journal of Consulting and Clinical Psychology*, 66: 484–92.

Cullen, F.T. (2002) 'Rehabilitation and treatment programs', in J.Q. Wilson and J. Petersilia (eds), *Crime and Public Policy*. 2nd edn. San Francisco: ICS Press.

Dowden, C. and Andrews, D.A. (1999) 'What works for female offenders: a meta-analytic review', *Crime and Delinquency*, 45: 438–52.

Dowden, C. and Andrews, D.A. (2000) 'Effective correctional treatment and violent reoffending: a meta-analysis', *Canadian Journal of Criminology*, 449–67.

Dowden, C. and Andrews, D.A. (2003) 'Does family interventions work for delinquents? Results of a meta-analysis', *Canadian Journal of Criminology and Criminal Justice*, 327–42.

Fixsen, D.L., Naoom, S.F., Blasé, K.A., Friedman, R.M. and Wallace, F. (2005) *Implementation Research: A Synthesis of the Literature*. Tampa, FL: Louis de la Parte Florida Mental Health Institute.

Gondolf, E.W. (2008) 'Program completion in specialized batterer counseling for African-American men', *Journal of Interpersonal Violence*, 23: 94–116.

Gutierrez, L. and Bourgon, G. (2009) *Drug Treatment Courts: A Quantitative Review of Study and Treatment Quality*. User Report 2009–04. Ottawa: Public Safety Canada.

Hanson, R.K., Bourgon, G., Helmus, L. and Hodgson, S. (2009) 'The principles of effective correctional treatment also apply to sexual offenders', *Criminal Justice and Behavior*, 36: 865–91.

Hubbard, D.J. and Latessa, E.J. (2004) *Evaluation of Cognitive-behavioural Programs for Offenders: A Look at the Outcome and Responsivity in Five Treatment Programs*. Cincinnati, OH: University of Cincinnati. Online at www.uc.edu/ccjr/Reports/ProjectReports/CogEvaluationFINAL_REPORT.pdf (accessed 16 November 2009).

Landenberger, N.A. and Lipsey, M (2005) 'The positive effects of cognitive-behavioural programs for offenders: a meta-analysis of factors associated with effective treatment', *Journal of Experimental Criminology*, 1: 451–76.

Marlowe, D.B. (2006) 'When "what works" never did: dodging the "scarlet M" in correctional rehabilitation', *Criminology and Public Policy*, 5: 339–46.

McConnaughy, E.A., Prochaska, J.A. and Velicer, W.F. (1983) 'Stages of change in psychotherapy: measurement and sample profiles', *Psychotherapy: Theory, Research and Practice*, 20: 368–75.

Rhine, E.E., Mawhorr, T.L. and Parks, E.C. (2006) 'Implementation: the bane of effective correctional programs', *Criminology and Public Policy*, 5: 347–58.

Ross, R. and Fabiano, E. (1991) *Reasoning and Rehabilitation: A Handbook for Teaching Cognitive Skills*. Ottawa: T3 Associates.

Sholomskas, D.E., Syracuse-Siewert, G., Rounsaville B.J., Ball, S.A., Nuro, K.F., and Carroll, K.M. (2005) 'We don't train in vain: a dissemination trial of three strategies of training clinicians in cognitive-behavioral therapy', *Journal of Consulting and Clinical Psychology*, 73: 106–15.

Taxman, F.S. (2008) 'No illusions: offender and organizational change in Maryland's proactive community supervision efforts', *Criminology and Public Policy*, 7: 275–302.

Trotter, C. (1996) 'The impact of different supervision practices in community corrections: cause for optimism', *Australian and New Zealand Journal of Criminology*, 29: 1–18.

Trotter, C. (2006) *Working with Involuntary Clients: A Guide to Practice*, 2nd edn. Thousand Oaks, CA: Sage.

Walters, S.T., Matson, S.A., Baer, J.S. and Ziedonis, D.M. (2005) 'Effectiveness of workshop training for psychosocial addiction treatments: a systematic review', *Journal of Substance Abuse Treatment*, 29: 283–93.

Wilson, J.A. and Davis, R.C. (2006) 'Good intentions meet hard realities: an evaluation of the Project Greenlight Reentry Program', *Criminology and Public Policy*, 5: 303–38.

Chapter 6

Skills and strategies in probation supervision: the Jersey study[1]

Peter Raynor, Pamela Ugwudike and Maurice Vanstone

During the process of observing practitioners at work, whether in one-to-one interviews or group-based programmes, the fact that some are more effective than others in communicating, engaging, enthusing and motivating is as easily recognisable as an elephant would be if it walked into the interview room. That recognition, however, begs two pressing questions: the first concerns the actual elements of that effectiveness, and the second the relationship between that effectiveness and success in promoting desistance from offending. Responding to the second question is relatively straightforward (though not simple), involving as it does the application of well-tested evaluation methods; engaging with the first is altogether more difficult. Although the performance of the effective practitioner is not magical but rather made up of observable behaviours and actions (see, for example, Andrews and Kiessling 1980), identifying them is a challenging task for any observer. This might explain in part why implementation was ignored for so long in corrections literature (Gendreau *et al.* 1999), and in particular why there is a need for more research that endeavours to clarify what particular characteristics of practice are effective in helping to change behaviour (Dowden and Andrews 2004).

Recognition of the importance of the relationship between the probation officer and the probationer is age-old[2] and in their seminal work on the effectiveness of counselling Truax and Carkhuff (1967: 117) argued, following Carl Rogers, that the person 'who is better able to communicate warmth, genuineness, and accurate empathy is more effective in interpersonal relationships no matter what the goal of intervention'. Since then research has expanded our knowledge of what such communication entails. Ross and Fabiano (1985), criticised by some for precipitating rigid, handbook-driven programmes, have stated as clearly as they could (for those prepared to read their work) that the quality of the practitioner is a basic determinant of the effectiveness of programmes of help; and they provided a checklist to illustrate what they meant by quality – the ability to motivate, enthuse and empathise; the capacity to model effective reasoning and problem-solving; sensitivity to discrepancies and distortions; creativity, and the ability to share their bag full of socio-cognitive skills. Dowden and Andrews (2004) have highlighted openness, warmth, enthusiasm, respect and likeability as fundamental; and Antonowicz and Ross (1994: 99) have added some of the key skills to go on top – 'modeling, graduated practice, rehearsal, role-playing, reinforcement, or cognitive restructuring'.

It would be a mistake, however, to think that we have this all wrapped up (we have identified the perfect practitioner, so let's train them and get the crime rates down!): uncertainties remain. For example, Truax and Carkhuff (1967: 95) themselves identified research that rated elements of practitioners' characteristics differently – warmth most important and empathy least; and Trotter (1990: 17) showed that 'probationers of high empathy officers committed slightly more offences than probationers of low empathy officers', and that those officers who were pro-social in their approach were effective even when the level of their empathy was low. So we are not dealing with certainties, and the knowledge base needs extending: indeed, it is important to remember that practice 'even when intended to be facilitative or helpful, can be *for better or for worse*' (Truax and Carkhuff 1967: 143, italics in the original), and that is one of the motivations for our research. If our respect for probationers is genuine, then it is as important to identify non-effective practice as it is practice that works.

Our research interest in the effectiveness of probation officers is older than at least two of us care to remember (Raynor 1988; Raynor and Vanstone 1984), and what we are endeavouring to do with the cooperation and help of both practitioners and managers in Jersey is to contribute to the addition of another layer of knowledge to the effectiveness canon. So in this chapter we are not concerned with elephants, but instead we attempt to focus on the efforts of practitioners in the helping process in order to clarify the components of good and bad practice and develop a framework for evaluating the relationship between that practice and future reconviction. The setting for the study is in some ways unusual: the Channel Island of Jersey is in effect a self-governing microstate with its own criminal justice system and legislation. The small Jersey Probation Service, comprising about 14 probation officers plus support staff, has a long-standing commitment to the effective use of social work methods in the supervision of offenders, and the current study is a continuation of a partnership in research on effective practice that goes back to 1996 (Raynor and Miles 2007) – an example of the 'critical culture' in action (Vanstone 2010). Without this background we suspect it would be difficult to carry out such potentially sensitive research. In this chapter we describe our methodology, and in particular the rationale for developing the observation instrument, the process of designing and applying it, the limitations associated with our particular observation technique, and some early findings from the interviews observed so far. Almost all the probation staff participating in the study are employed as probation officers: the study also includes a community service specialist and a substance misuse specialist, but all are involved in similar roles in relation to the interviewing of offenders. For convenience all are referred to in this paper as 'officers' or 'practitioners'.

Methodology of the study

In recent years, the communication and helping skills referred to above have been conceptualised as the 'core correctional practice skills' (CCPs) required for implementing the cognitive, behavioural and social learning models of intervention that have been shown to reduce recidivism (see also McGuire 2007). Studies including large-scale meta-analysis point to the role of the CCPs in enhancing the effectiveness of programmes and reducing recidivism (Dowden and Andrews 2004), and accordingly an observation instrument – designed to facilitate an assessment of the use of the CCPs and constructed also on the basis of empirically driven indicators of effective practice skills originally identified in the research referred to earlier in this chapter – was used to analyse the skills of probation officers during routine supervision of probationers and the implementation of a one-to-one programme. Specifically, the broad range of CCPs demands that practitioners possess a combination of interpersonal and intellectual abilities that pertain to (Andrews and Kiessling 1980):

- the effective use of authority
- pro-social modelling skills
- problem-solving techniques
- making adequate referrals
- effective communication skills.

The instrument assesses context as well as the skills deployed, and the research suggests that skills are best applied within an interview context that maximises the chances of the probationer's active involvement. Such a context is created by an effectively structured interview, which clearly summarises the themes that were discussed in the previous interview, sets out the objectives of the interview, encourages disclosure, provides feedback to the client, schedules the next interview and sets tasks for the interim (Taxman *et al.* 2004: 42, 43). Moreover, the relevant literature suggests that the actual setting of the supervision interview can impact on outcomes through the limits it places on levels of disclosure, and that an appropriate setting is one that ensures a degree of privacy with limited distractions and also ensures that the distance between both parties is not so wide that it is alienating or so close that it restricts freedom of movement (Egan 1994).

Before moving on to evaluate our methodology and describe the process of designing the instrument, it is important for us to clarify how we have understood and engaged with the five categories of the CCPs listed above. The first, effective use of authority, involves the clarification of roles and responsibilities (Trotter 2006), and the avoidance of negative responses such as arguing, blaming, criticising (Dowden and Andrews 2004) and 'interpersonal domination', confrontational enforcement or abuse (Andrews and Bonta 2003: 305). Motivational interviewing skills that are considered relevant to the effective use of authority – as well as to effective practice in general – are incorporated in the instrument: they include empathy, reflective and open-style questions intended to encourage the client to reflect on and re-evaluate their position. When developing the section of the instrument that addresses the legitimate use of authority, we drew on the insights provided by the literature on motivational interviewing (Miller and Rollnick 2002) and pro-social modelling techniques (Trotter 2006) and also on studies that highlight the link between the perceived legitimacy of authority and compliance. Studies show that the ability to demonstrate respect to the recipient of authority, and also the effort to incorporate in decision-making the views and concerns of the client, may enhance the perception that the quality of treatment received is fair and may encourage trust in the motives of the representatives of authority (Tyler 2003: 294). Perceived fair treatment and trust in the motives of the representatives of authority are mutually reinforcing concepts that have been empirically linked to perceived procedural justice, which is an important antecedent of the perceived legitimacy of authority (Tyler 1990). Studies have found links between the perceived legitimacy of authority and compliance during interactions with the police (Tyler 1990) or with prison officers (Cooke 1989).

Closely related to the effective use of authority are pro-social modelling skills, and the instrument assesses the use of pro-social modelling techniques (see generally Trotter 2006) that are characterised by the demonstration of pro-social behaviour, the use of disapproval to challenge anti-social behaviour, thinking or comments, and the use of rewards to reinforce pro-social behaviour. As Andrews and Bonta (2003: 312) explain, anti-social expressions are 'the specific attitudes, values, beliefs, rationalisations and techniques of neutralisation that imply the criminal conduct is acceptable'. The emphasis of the approach is on positive reinforcements because they 'have staying power while punishments are easily forgotten, especially once the threat of them is lifted', and 'behaviours are learned only when they are rewarded' (Taxman et al. 2004: 13, 58). Directing the reward or challenge at the target behaviour is necessary as this communicates to the client the link between the challenge and the behaviour, and disapproval and rewards should be 'swift, certain and predictable' (Taxman et al. 2004: 63): moreover, the probationer should be informed 'immediately of the reasons for approval' or disapproval (Andrews and Bonta 2003: 305). Each of these elements should be contained within structured processes that aim to encourage the client to re-evaluate their anti-social comments, attitudes or thought processes and replace these with pro-social thought patterns (cognitive restructuring). Indeed, the importance of this is indicated by the fact that an additional section focused on identifying some basic cognitive restructuring techniques was introduced in 2008 after studying the use of cognitive restructuring items in the Correctional Program Assessment Inventory (Gendreau and Andrews 2001).

The third component of CCPs, problem-solving skills, if applied effectively must involve the collaborative identification of problems, goals and possible solutions. Furthermore, the problem-solving process may involve the fourth component, the business of making appropriate referrals to relevant service providers or performing other acts of advocacy on behalf of the probationer (Dowden and Andrews 2004: 205). The final component, good interpersonal skills, is pivotal to success (Dowden and Andrews 2004: 205), and some go as far as to say that good interpersonal communication is the key to effective supervision 'far outweighing the effects of intervening factors such as the interview environment, or the gender, race or age of staff and offenders' (Taxman *et al.* 2004: 42). So the practitioner should be skilled in developing an enthusiastic dialogue and should employ mainly open questions that encourage disclosure, and the active contribution of the client to the interview. Importantly, the practitioner should also possess a disposition that is genuine, humorous, empathic, respectful and indicative of a commitment to help the client and optimism about the possibility of change (Dowden and Andrews 2004: 205). It is argued that demonstrating a belief in the individual's capacity to change can affect self-perception and encourage desistance (Farrall and Calverley 2005). The instrument, therefore, incorporates multiple indicator items for assessing the use of interpersonal skills – the skills that are also relevant for the effective use of pro-social modelling and motivational interviewing techniques.

While not specifically listed by Andrews and Kiessling 1980, it could be argued that motivational interviewing is implicitly a part of CCPs in so far as it is 'a directive client-centred counselling approach for initiating behaviour change by helping clients to resolve ambivalence' (Miller 1996: 835). This is an essential element of effective supervision because it is concerned with the impact of the practitioner's behaviour on the learner's 'motivation for and participation' in change (Emmons and Rollnick 2001: 68), and there appears to be more substantial empirical support for the efficacy of motivational interviewing techniques when applied within therapeutic healthcare settings (Emmons and Rollnick 2001: 70). Moreover, there is growing evidence that these techniques can be usefully applied within the contexts of criminal justice interventions (Miller and Rollnick 2002) although the need for reinforcements after the duration of the intervention has been emphasised (Emmons and Rollnick 2001). The instrument assesses the use of motivational interviewing skills using a multiple indicator item that was constructed with due reference to the four basic principles of motivational interviewing set out by Miller and Rollnick (2002: 218): expressing empathy, developing discrepancy, rolling with resistance, and supporting self-efficacy. Respectively these techniques are demonstrated through an empathic approach and reflective listening skills, inviting the client to consider the possible discrepancies between their current state and their desired state, avoiding arguments by using reflective comments and questions to encourage the client to re-evaluate their thinking rather than challenging resistance, and also acknowledging the client's ability to contribute effectively to the change process.

Additional motivational interviewing skills assessed by the instrument include the practitioner's effort to adapt to the client's level of motivation (also relevant to ensuring responsivity; see Bonta and Andrews, this volume) and to elicit self-motivating comments from the client. The instrument seeks to assess not simply the technical application of the motivational interviewing technique but also the style of delivery – the quality of the interactions between both parties. Reinforcing the findings of previous studies, Miller and Rollnick (2002: 22) observe that good interpersonal skills provide the basis for the effective use of most of the CCPs: 'motivation for change can not only be influenced by but in a very real sense arises from an interpersonal context'. Therefore, the instrument assesses whether the practitioners develop a rapport with the client, maintain interpersonal contact and develop a client-centred orientation that encourages the client to personally resolve the ambivalence inhibiting change, with the assistance, rather than dominance, of the practitioner.

Apart from verbal communication skills, the instrument also assesses non-verbal communication and applies the SOLER test developed by Egan (1994). SOLER is an acronym for 'squarely' facing the client, 'open' posture, 'leaning' forward, 'eye' contact and 'relaxed'. As the test implies, the seating arrangements should be such that the practitioner squarely faces the client, displays an open posture, which may be indicated by uncrossed arms and legs, slightly leans forward, intermittently maintains adequate levels of eye contact and displays a relaxed disposition. In sum, SOLER assesses the degree to which the practitioner can be said to be physically attentive to the client.

Each item on the instrument has been constructed on the basis of the relevant theoretical and empirical literature to assess the use of the CCPs during the delivery of accredited programmes and during routine supervision, and it is designed to support an assessment of the overall relationship between practitioners and their clients. It has been observed that effective practitioners are those who are able to develop 'high quality relationships' with their clients (Andrews and Bonta 2003: 313).

Evaluating the methodology

There are several limitations associated with observational techniques in social research. There are threats to reliability, which can be exacerbated where the instrument is applied by multiple raters. We have tried to limit these threats by clearly delineating each item contained in the instrument in order to reduce observer bias and enhance consistency. In addition, all interviews have been observed and rated by the same person, although assisted by one or two others during inter-rater reliability exercises. The end product of these processes has been the current version (Version 7C).

With observational methods there can also be problems posed by reactive effects whereby research participants adjust their behaviour and project atypical forms of behaviour. It is difficult to imagine what atypical behaviour the officers and their clients might display during recorded sessions. Indeed, it seems rather unlikely that interactions between both parties would become contrived because a session is being recorded. It is theoretically possible that the fact that an interview is being recorded for observation could focus an officer's mind on the conscious deployment of skills, but we do not get the impression of such artificial performances from the recordings we have seen. Nevertheless, the instrument is designed to assess the use of a specific skill set. The problems posed by the possibility of contrived and other atypical behaviours can be overcome by observing the participants over a period of time (each officer is observed through at least four interviews, and ideally ten) so that a skills profile can be constructed for each participating officer. Another potential limitation is the generalisability of the study's findings – the sample was drawn from a non-random sample of probation officers (that is, those who volunteered, constituting a majority but not all of the Jersey probation officers) and the probationers they supervise (those participating in the interviews that supervisors happened to record). However, the exploratory nature of the current study does not require the observed interviews to be fully representative of all interviews carried out by Jersey probation staff, but only to be broadly representative of the work of particular officers. Wider application of our observation checklist would ideally need to be supported by testing in larger samples.

The structured observation technique also has several obvious advantages. There is the opportunity to generate data on behaviour based on the observation of actual behaviour rather than written records or unreliable recollections. Observational methods are particularly useful where the subject matter of the research may be considered sensitive, as can be the case where practitioners believe their practices are the subject of official or other scrutiny. Further, observational methods have the advantage of strong validity given that they provide the opportunity to observe behaviour directly. Key aspects of effective supervision skills that are not readily amenable to other research methods can be observed, including body language, reflective listening, demonstrating empathy, maintaining eye contact and other elements of non-verbal communication.

Designing and using the instrument

There were, of course, a number of different ways in which previous knowledge and experience could be applied to the development of a checklist or instrument to structure and standardise the observation process, and we tried a number of different ways. The fact that the version eventually chosen for use is called version 7C gives a clue to the long and complicated development process. It was clear from the start that we needed a checklist that captured a range of skills, captured differences in the skill sets used in different interviews, and was simple enough to be used without long training or years of experience, so that the study could be carried out by a team with varying levels of exposure to probation work. We were also aware of instruments in use in other studies discussed at CREDOS meetings (see Bourgon *et al.* and Trotter, this volume). Two of the team had experience of training probation officers and social workers in interviewing skills using techniques that included structured observation and feedback (Raynor and Vanstone 1984), and one also had experience of designing and applying instruments used specifically to check for programme integrity (Raynor and Vanstone 1996; Vanstone 2008). The third member of the team had carried out a detailed study of techniques used by probation officers to promote compliance with supervision requirements, and was familiar with the way officers typically worked (Ugwudike 2008). We were also interested in developing something that could be widely understood, and could in principle be used for feedback to officers carrying out the interviews. It also needed to be suitable for use with video recordings rather than other forms of record. A possible long-term goal was, and remains, the development of a staff development or training aid to promote effective one-to-one work in probation.

The main method for developing and refining the instrument was highly pragmatic: as each draft reached a stage that looked capable of application, all three researchers would apply it to the same three interviews and generate independent ratings, then meet to discuss them, exploring differences and putting forward possibilities for improvement. An early version was tried on a larger number of tapes, and discussed both with probation staff in Jersey and with CREDOS members at the 2008 Glasgow meeting. Both these discussions introduced important new elements: in particular, the CREDOS discussion pointed to the importance of assessing 'structuring' skills, which were under-represented in the early versions. We also believed it was important to convey the right tone and purpose. The officers taking part in the study were all volunteers, and the study involved them in extra work videotaping their interviews onto MiniDV cassettes, which were then copied onto DVDs in Swansea. It also asked them to take the risk of exposing their work to others, and to a form of assessment that was not normally part of their job.

We felt that it was important to distinguish the study very carefully from any management or staff development processes: this was important, and had the full support of managers, after an early misapprehension about possible use of the tapes by managers almost led to staff withdrawing from the project. We also believed that we should not over-sell the evidence-based nature of our instrument before the evidence was collected, nor should we risk appearing dismissive of the probation officers' own opinions and skills, especially as many of them were clearly well informed and highly skilled, and we have adopted a number of their suggestions. Participation in the study needed to be nurtured and maintained: it is a large project for a small staff group, requiring many months to collect a reasonable number of interviews, and it is quite easy for officers to forget about it, or to assume it is over when they have heard nothing about it for a while. Four officers so far have taken up the offer of private feedback on their interviewing based on our observation of their tapes, and we think that this has probably helped to maintain interest in the project.

At the time of writing, version 7C of our instrument (the Jersey Supervision Interview Checklist) is firmly established in the methodology of the project, and we are two-thirds of the way towards our target of 100 tapes. The study is not complete and we do not attempt to draw any final conclusions in this chapter: the focus is on what we have learned so far about the performance of the checklist and about the skills shown in the tapes we have seen.

Version 7C differs from earlier versions in the range of skills included, and in the deliberate use of a non-judgemental tone in the preamble and instructions contained in the checklist: the emphasis is on a descriptive identification of skills used in interviews rather than on whether officers are good at their jobs. For example, the instructions now say:

> The checklist identifies a number of different things which might happen in an interview, or which the officer might do. Not all of them will be appropriate in a particular interview, and there is no assumption that an interview which does not contain them all is necessarily a bad interview. The aim is to develop an overall picture of the range of practices, methods and skills used by officers in a range of interviews.

In addition, after experimenting with three- and four-point scales for the assessment of each item we have eventually come down in favour of a simple tick to indicate the use of a skill, adding up ticks to see how far a particular set or package of skills is represented in the interview. This has proved much more popular with people observing and rating interviews than earlier, more complicated versions, and we do not think much useful information is lost as a result of simplifying, provided that enough relevant items are available. We cannot, of course, claim to have achieved the impossible goal of capturing every subtlety of interaction between probation officers and the people they supervise, and we were not attempting to do this. Instead we were trying to design a simple way to capture the major components of effective interviewing as identified so far in the available research literature, which is itself, like all research, provisional.

In addition to generating a quantified database of skills used in interviews, the study also involves collecting data on offenders' progress, in order to see if there is any relationship between the use of a wide range of appropriate skills by officers and progress made by offenders. Repeated risk-need assessments are carried out to a high standard in Jersey and used as a measure of progress. Previous research has shown that these are reliably related to differences in reoffending (Raynor 2007), and we plan to examine the progress of offenders supervised by officers in the study, including a reconviction study if enough data is available. Consequently we are not publishing version 7C here, as we do not want to encourage its premature use to assess interviewing before it is shown to be related to outcomes for offenders, but the long-term intention is to make it available for wider use and to use it in other studies. In the meantime this chapter gives a basic description of what version 7C covers and some findings about interviews so far, based on those officers who have already submitted several tapes for analysis and were included in the first 50 to be rated on the new instrument.

One reason for undertaking several redesigns of the instrument was that early versions tended to produce similar scores, and high scores, over a number of different interviews by different officers. We suspected that they were not picking up enough differences: our impression was that the Jersey service was lucky to have a number of skilled and experienced officers, but that they should not all be producing similar skill profiles on the instrument. The introduction of more structuring skills was intended to help with this problem, and so in this interim analysis we were particularly interested in whether officers would now score differently from each other. In addition we were interested to see whether officers used a similar skill set across a range of interviews, so that their scores would tend to cluster, or whether all officers would tend to produce a wide spread of scores. What follows mainly addresses these questions. Version 7C includes sections addressing several different types of skill, and Table 6.1 summarises these, including the number of items on the checklist that address them. The fact that different skill types contain different numbers of items does not represent any judgement about weighting, but simply the number of criteria found convenient for observers in identifying skills. The table also shows which sections are new for version 7C, following the decision to include more 'structuring' skills.

Table 6.1 Sections and items in version 7C.

Section of checklist	Number of items in section	Abbreviation used in figures
Set-up	4	S
Non-verbal communication	5	N
Verbal communication	10	V
Use of authority	5	A
Motivational interviewing	9	M
Pro-social modelling*	5	P
Problem-solving*	10	S
Cognitive restructuring*	7	C
Overall interview structure	8	O

*newly introduced sections for version 7C.

Figure 6.1 compares the mean ratings of the six officers on each of the nine skill types with the maximum possible scoring available on the checklist. This shows that most officers routinely meet most or all of the criteria for use of some types of skill, particularly in the set-up of interviews, quality of communication, use of authority (mainly relationship skills) and in pro-social modelling (in which all the officers have been trained), but with larger differences evident in other structuring skills – motivational interviewing, problem-solving and cognitive restructuring. However, the picture changes somewhat when we consider individual officer profiles. Figures 6.2 and 6.3 show the pattern of skills used in interviews by two of the officers, and it appears that the officer who generally scored highest in the group did so across the full range of skills, while the lower-scoring officer tends to score lower on use of structuring skills than on others. This was a general pattern in the group: lower scores were concentrated among the newer 'structuring' items in the checklist. Officers were also fairly consistent in the skills they used across a range of interviews: Figure 6.4 shows a boxplot of scores for each officer showing the median, the interquartile range and the extremes, with just one 'outlier' interview that was untypical of that officer's work. Officers' scores tend to cluster closely around their personal median, with some showing a very high degree of consistency.

Clearly these are very preliminary and limited findings at this stage. There is much more work to be done as the study proceeds, particularly when information about the progress of offenders is added, and this chapter reports simply a preliminary exploration of early data. There are also many interviews and several officers to be added to the analysis as their number of videotaped interviews

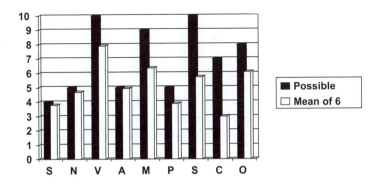

Figure 6.1 Possible and actual mean scores.

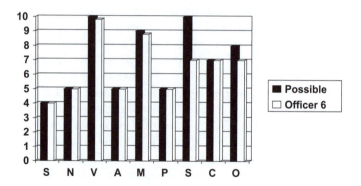

Figure 6.2   Individual officer 6.

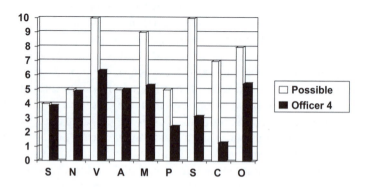

Figure 6.3   Individual officer 4.

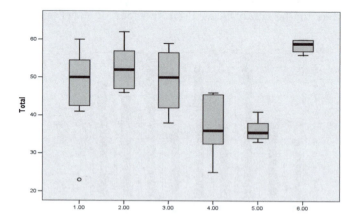

Figure 6.4   Boxplot of total scores for six officers.

reaches the level where analysis becomes worthwhile. However, it is now possible to propose some tentative answers to questions raised earlier in the chapter. It appears that version 7C does now show substantial differences from officer to officer, and that these differences are fairly consistent across a number of interviews. Greater differences are evident in 'structuring' skills rather than 'relationship' skills. This may reflect the social work training received by most Jersey probation officers, which is likely to have concentrated more on the skills needed to establish and maintain a relationship. The next step is to extend these measurements to a larger group, and to see if they are related to any other measures of the impact of probation officers' work. However, our experience of this study so far does suggest a potentially useful contribution to the development of effective probation practice. Until now the technique of evidence-based analysis of videotaped probation work has been applied mainly to the delivery of accredited group programmes: this study shows that it is feasible to use it in the context of one-to-one interviews, which have not so far been seen as a priority in the development of 'what works' in England and Wales. Now that concerns are being expressed about the quality of probation officers' engagement with offenders and the possible impact of more negative and punitive attitudes (see Gelsthorpe, Raynor and Robinson, this volume), attention to the individual interview is clearly overdue. We hope that the systematic recognition of personal skills can help to empower individual practitioners and to legitimate a skilled, mindful and value-based approach to the one-to-one contact that used to be seen as the core of the probation officer's work.

Notes

1 We are grateful to the Jersey Probation Service for supporting this study; to all the probation officers and their interviewees who have allowed themselves to be recorded and observed; and to Brian Heath, Helen Miles and Barbara Machon for invaluable assistance in the study.
2 Le Mesurier (1935) in the first probation handbook uses a quote about 'the power to release the true personality of the person we are trying to help' (p.60).

References

Andrews, D.A. and Bonta, J. (2003) *The Psychology of Criminal Conduct.* Cincinnati: Anderson.

Andrews, D.A. and Kiessling, J.J. (1980) 'Program structure and effective correctional practices: a summary of the CaVic research', in R.R. Ross and P. Gendreau (eds) *Effective Correctional Treatment.* Toronto: Butterworth.

Antonowicz, D. and Ross, R. (1994) 'Essential components of successful rehabilitation programs for offenders', *International Journal of Offender Therapy and Comparative Criminology,* 38: 97–104.

Cooke, D.J. (1989) 'Containing violent prisoners: an analysis of the Barlinnie Special Unit', *British Journal of Criminology,* 29: 129–43.

Dowden, C. and Andrews, D.A. (2004) 'The importance of staff practice in delivering effective correctional treatment: a meta-analytic review of core correctional practice', *International Journal of Offender Therapy and Comparative Criminology,* 48(2): 203–14.

Egan, G. (1994) *The Skilled Helper: A Problem Management Approach to Helping.* Pacific Grove, CA: Brooks/Cole Publishing Company.

Emmons, K.M. and Rollnick, S. (2001) 'Motivational interviewing in healthcare settings: opportunities and limitations', *American Journal of Preventive Medicine,* 20: 68–74.

Farrall, S. and Calverley, A. (2005) *Understanding Desistance from Crime.* Buckingham: Open University Press.

Gendreau, P. and Andrews, D.A. (2001) *The Correctional Program Assessment Inventory (CPAI) 2000.* St John: University of New Brunswick.

Gendreau, P., Goggin, C. and Smith, P. (1999) 'The forgotten issue in effective correctional treatment: programme implementation', *International Journal of Offender Therapy and Comparative Criminology,* 43 (2): 180–7.

Le Mesurier, L. (1935) *A Handbook of Probation.* London: National Association of Probation Officers.

McGuire, J. (2007) 'Programmes for probationers', in G. McIvor and P. Raynor (eds) *Developments in Social Work with Offenders.* London: Jessica Kingsley.

Miller, W.R. (1996) 'Motivational interviewing: research, practice and puzzles', *Addictive Behaviours,* 21: 835–42.

Miller, W.R. and Rollnick, S. (2002) *Motivational Interviewing: Preparing People for Change.* New York: Guilford Press.

Raynor, P. (1988) *Probation as an Alternative to Custody.* Aldershot: Ashgate.

Raynor, P. (2007) 'Risk and need assessment in British probation: the contribution of LSI-R', *Psychology, Crime and Law,* 13 (2): 125–38.

Raynor, P. and Miles, H. (2007) 'Evidence-based probation in a microstate: the British Channel Island of Jersey', *European Journal of Criminology,* 4 (3): 299–313.

Raynor, P. and Vanstone, M. (1984) 'Putting practice into theory', *Issues in Social Work Education,* 4 (2): 86–93.

Raynor, P. and Vanstone, M. (1996) 'Reasoning and rehabilitation in Britain: the results of the Straight Thinking On Probation (STOP) programme', *International Journal of Offender Therapy and Comparative Criminology*, 40 (4): 279–91.

Ross, R.R. and Fabiano E.A. (1985) *Time to Think: A Cognitive Model of Delinquency Prevention and Offender Rehabilitation.* Johnson City, TN: Institute of Social Sciences and Arts.

Taxman, F.S., Shepardson, E. S. and Bryne, J. M. (2004) *Tools of the Trade: A Guide to Incorporating Science into Practice.* National Institute of Corrections US Department of Justice and Maryland Department of Public Safety and Correctional Services.

Trotter, C. (1990) '"Probation can work": a research study using volunteers', *Australian Social Work*, 43 (2): 13–18.

Trotter, C. (2006) *Working with Involuntary Clients: A Guide to Practice*, 2nd edn. London/Thousand Oaks, CA: Sage.

Truax, C.B. and Carkhuff, R.R. (1967) *Towards Effective Counselling and Psychotherapy.* Chicago: Aldine.

Tyler, T.R. (1990) *Why People Obey the Law.* New Haven, CT: Yale University Press.

Tyler, T.R. (2003) 'Procedural justice, legitimacy and the effective rule of law', *Crime and Justice*, 30: 283–357.

Ugwudike, P. (2008) 'Developing an effective mechanism for encouraging compliance with offender supervision', PhD thesis, Swansea University.

Vanstone, M. (2008) 'Maintaining programme integrity: the *FOR ... A Change* programme and the resettlement of ex-prisoners', *International Journal of Offender Therapy and Comparative Criminology*, online.

Vanstone, M. (2010) 'Creative work: an historical perspective', in F. Cowe, J. Brayford and J. Deering (eds). *What Else Works.* Cullompton: Willan Publishing.

Chapter 7

Supervision skills in juvenile justice

Chris Trotter and Phillipa Evans

This chapter focuses on supervision skills used by probation officers. It provides a summary of the research about the relationship between supervision skills and effectiveness. It then reports on a study in the department of youth justice in New South Wales, Australia which involved the observation of interviews between probation officers and their clients, the identification of the skills that were used in those interviews and the responses by clients to the use of those skills.

Effective supervision

There is a growing literature, much of which is summarised in this volume, that suggests that the way in which offenders are supervised or treated makes a difference to recidivism (for example, Gendreau 1996; Andrews 2001; Raynor 2003; McNeill 2003; Farrington and Welsh 2005; McIvor 2005; Trotter 2006; McNeill and Whyte 2007). The argument presented in the literature is not that correctional interventions always work but that appropriate forms of intervention can be effective. In a review of meta-analysis of treatment effectiveness Andrews and Bonta argue that appropriate treatment led to reductions of recidivism of 'a little more than 50 percent from that found in comparison conditions' (2006: 329).

Much of the research on the effectiveness of correctional interventions, has, however, been undertaken on specific interventions, for example: cognitive behavioural programmes or drug treatment programmes. Less attention has been paid to the routine supervision of offenders on probation, parole or other community-based orders, despite the number of offenders placed under supervision in those programmes. Nevertheless the research suggests that certain practices are effective in the supervision of offenders across a range of settings including routine supervision in community corrections and juvenile justice. These practices or skills are outlined below.

Pro-social modelling and reinforcement

Pro-social modelling and reinforcement has been shown to be effective in a number of studies and it is included as one of the key components of effective practice identified in reviews of correctional interventions (Gendreau 1996; Raynor 2003; McNeill 2003; Andrews and Bonta 2006; Trotter 2006).

Some studies have also shown the effectiveness of pro-social modelling and reinforcement in community corrections. A Canadian study (Andrews *et al.* 1979) found that probation officers who scored high on a scale of pro-social disposition (measured by the California Personality Inventory Socialisation Scale) and who also had high levels of empathy, had clients with recidivism rates 50 per cent lower than those of other probationers. The socialisation scale measures the extent to which people have pro-social or pro-criminal attitudes. Those higher on the scale were inclined to model pro-social behaviours, to focus on the pro-social behaviours of their clients and to appropriately challenge the pro-criminal comments of their clients.

Following on from these studies, two studies in corrections (Trotter 1990, 1996), one with juvenile offenders, and another with adult offenders each found that probation officers and community corrections officers who scored high on the socialisation scale had clients with lower reoffending rates compared to those who scored low on the scale. Again the differences were up to 50 per cent.

Further support for pro-social approaches is evident in more recent studies in child protection (see Trotter 2004) which have found, for example, that outcomes were better (outcomes included client satisfaction, worker satisfaction and time to case closure) when clients reported that their worker showed basic pro-social modelling skills: 'The worker did what they said they would do. The worker challenged me when I made excuses for offending and other anti-social behaviour. The worker encouraged me when I said non-criminal and positive things. The worker was punctual.'

A study of women offenders under supervision in the community also found that women did better in terms of client satisfaction and reduced reoffending if they reported that their workers were reliable, friendly and focused on the their clients' pro-social comments and actions (Trotter and Sheehan 2005).

Problem-solving

Effective interventions in corrections address the issues which have led offenders to become offenders. The literature reviews and meta-analyses often refer to the concept of criminogenic needs. Criminogenic needs are those needs or problems that are related to offending, but are possible to change, such as: employment, family relationships, drug use, peer group associations, housing, finances, or pro-criminal attitudes (Gendreau *et al.* 1996, Andrews and Bonta 2006).

A number of studies also suggest that working collaboratively with offenders and focusing on the issues or problems that the offenders themselves identify leads to lower recidivism (Trotter 1996, 2006; McNeill and Whyte 2007). The general counselling literature is replete with research studies that point to the importance of working with the client's view of his or her problems (see, for example, Hepworth *et al.* 2010 for more detail on this issue) and it appears that effective work in supervision of offenders also involves a collaborative approach, which helps the client to acknowledge their offence-related problems.

There is also support for problem-solving approaches whereby workers canvass a wide range of client issues, reach agreement on problems to be addressed, set goals and develop strategies to achieve those goals (Trotter 2006; Andrews and Bonta 2006).

Role clarification

Much of the work with offenders involves what Ronald Rooney (1992) and Jones and Alcabes (1993) refer to as client socialisation, or what others have referred to as role clarification (for example, Trotter 2006). One aspect of role clarification involves helping the client to accept that the worker can help with the client's problems even though the worker has a social control role.

Other aspects of role clarification involve exploring the client's expectations, helping the client to understand what is negotiable and what isn't, the limits of confidentiality and the nature of the worker's authority and helping the client to understand that the worker has both a helping and a social control role (Shulman 1991; Videka Sherman 1988, Trotter 2006).

Relationship

This concept of role clarification ties into the importance of the worker relationship skills, which Dowden and Andrews (2004) suggest is one of the elements of core correctional practice. Relationship skills are also referred to in other reviews (see Gendreau 1996). Relationship skills may be defined as including openness and honesty, empathy, optimism, capacity to understand and articulate the client's feelings, appropriate self-disclosure and humour (Trotter 2006).

The importance of relationship skills in the supervision of offenders has, however, been questioned. Two Australian studies and a Canadian study found that probation officer empathy levels, for example, did not relate to reoffending rates (Trotter 1990, 1996, Andrews *et al.* 1979). Andrews and his colleagues (1979) found that high empathy workers only did better with their clients if they made use of other skills. It does appear that while worker relationship skills are important in offender supervision they may only be valuable if they are combined with other effective practice skills such as pro-social modelling and problem-solving.

Other factors

Outlined above is a summary of skills that relate to positive outcomes in routine supervision of offenders on probation or other community-based orders. There are a number of other practices that the research suggests are related to positive outcomes for corrections interventions in general. These include the need to focus on medium to high risk offenders – a core skill that is referred to many times in this volume. Multi-modal approaches, which rely on a range of intervention methods, may be more effective than those that rely on only one method (Andrews and Bonta 2006). There is support for work with families of young offenders (see Trotter, this volume) and for matching workers and clients according to learning style and personality (Gendreau *et al.* 1996; Chui and Nellis 2003). Research support also exists for the use of relapse prevention techniques (identifying and avoiding precursors to offending), particularly when used in combination with the effective practice principles outlined above (Dowden *et al.* 2003). There is evidence in favour of cognitive behavioural programmes (Andrews and Bonta 2006), which address among other things the pro-criminal attitudes of offenders. These programmes are usually targeted towards groups of offenders rather than individuals; nevertheless, cognitive behavioural techniques may be used in routine supervision in probation and parole – in fact, pro-social modelling and reinforcement could be described as a cognitive behavioural technique.

Application of the effective practice principles

It is clear, therefore, that some things work better in the supervision of offenders than others. To summarise, effective workers model and reinforce pro-social attitudes and carefully challenge pro-criminal attitudes; help clients with offence-related problems (criminogenic needs) using a collaborative approach; reach agreement with their clients on the problems to be addressed, and goals and strategies to achieve them; and help their clients understand their purpose and role, particularly their dual helping/authority role. We know less about the extent to which these skills are used in practice and how clients respond to the way the skills are used in practice.

Evidence suggests that some workers tend not to use effective practice skills in work with offenders. Andrews and Dowden (2005) refer to the concept of therapeutic integrity. In other words, programmes or interventions should be delivered in a manner that is consistent with the way in which they were intended, if they are to be successful. Andrews and Dowden undertook a meta-analysis of therapeutic integrity in correctional treatment. The results from 273 studies suggest that where interventions were not implemented as planned, treatment effectiveness was subsequently compromised. An Australian study involving observations of 30 interviews between child protection workers and their clients also found low levels of use of skills such as empathy, goal-setting and challenging clients. Often, however, workers and clients felt that the skills were being used. Clients felt understood, for example, even though there were few identifiable examples of reflective listening or empathy in the interviews (Trotter 2002, 2004).

There have been few studies analysing interviews in probation settings. However, James Bonta and colleagues (2004) undertook an examination of audiotaped interviews between 62 probation officers and their clients. They also found that probation officers did not generally make use of practices that research suggests are effective, but focused more on complying with probation conditions. They reported little attention to criminogenic needs such as anti-social attitudes, or to pro-social modelling, for example.

To sum up: a lot of time and energy has been devoted to research on effective practices in corrections but less to routine supervision of offenders, even though large numbers of offenders receive supervision on probation and other community-based orders. In fact, most serious offenders who are involved in criminal justice systems around the world at some stage spend time under community supervision. The more knowledge we have about what goes on in supervision sessions in community corrections the more capacity we have to influence what goes on and in turn influence reoffending rates among the offenders involved. The study reported on in this chapter is unique in its focus on research officers personally observing and examining probation supervision sessions.

Methodology

Aim of the study

The study reported on in this chapter aims to identify the extent to which the effective practice skills referred to in the literature are used in interviews between probation officers and clients working in juvenile justice in New South Wales. It also considers how clients respond to the use of those skills. This study involves examining the relationship between compliance with the order, recidivism and the use of the skills by workers. The study also includes a qualitative analysis of the interviews in an attempt to identify the way individual probation officers use particular skills and the use of skills that may not have been identified in previous research. These aspects of the study will, however, be the focus of future publications and are not reported on in this chapter.

Sample

A total of 137 worker/client interviews were observed between 2006 and 2009. The interviews were conducted by juvenile justice counsellors or juvenile justice officers. Juvenile justice counsellors have relevant tertiary qualifications and have a counselling or problem-solving role, whereas juvenile justice officers are expected to focus more on compliance and practical issues.

The data collection was completed in two phases. In the first phase, which was funded jointly by the Faculty of Primary Health Care, Monash University and by NSW Juvenile Justice, 39 observations were conducted. The second phase was funded by the Australian Criminology Research Council with support from NSW Juvenile Justice. The two phases had similar aims; however, the second phase included interviews with workers and clients, in addition to the observation of 98 interviews.

Consistent with ethics requirements, the project was dependent on workers and clients volunteering to participate and on workers facilitating the observations by the research officer. It was initially intended to observe 200 supervision sessions including 50 juvenile justice workers and the next four clients allocated to them following the date data collection commenced. Unfortunately participation fell short of this, due to several key factors including the reluctance of some staff to be involved, clients often not presenting for scheduled supervision sessions, and the considerable distances involved in travelling to interviews in rural and outback areas. Ultimately, as stated earlier, 137 interviews were observed.

Observations

Observations of supervision sessions were undertaken in the first three months of the young person's legal order, with a second observation occurring where possible after six months. The second observations often did not occur, however, due to a number of extraneous factors including the reallocation of clients to other workers, clients relocating, and staffing movements including leave, promotions and turnover. The interviews took place in a number of venues including the juvenile justice offices, in the client's home, in other community settings, or on two occasions in the worker's car. In the first phase of the project, and the initial stages of the second phase, interviews were manually recorded with as much detail as possible. Permission was then sought from the University and Juvenile Justice ethics committees to audiotape the interviews, and subsequent interviews were audiotaped. Non-verbal cues elicited by both the worker and the client were recorded by the research officer.

An Aboriginal research officer undertook 16 of the observations. A high proportion of the clients in juvenile justice in NSW are Aboriginal and it was felt that an Aboriginal research officer might identify particular practices or interactions that might help to identify culturally appropriate approaches to supervision.

Coding of observations

A coding manual was developed following consultation with investigators on similar research projects conducted by Peter Raynor and colleagues in Jersey (UK) and by James Bonta, Guy Bourgon and colleagues in Canada (see chapters in this volume). The manual aims as far as possible to assist in the accuracy and reliability of the estimates of the extent to which the skills were used in the interviews.

At the time of writing the coding was being undertaken. Thirty transcripts had been coded, in most cases by the research officer who observed the interview. Eight of the transcripts of the interviews were also second-coded by another research officer familiar with the literature and trained in the content of the training manual. There was a high level of consistency in the coding. The coding manual itself was also updated during this process with additional questions being added on use of cognitive behavioural skills, risk assessment and the nature of the strategies used to address client issues.

Interviews with workers and clients

In the second phase of the project data were also collected through interviews with clients and workers directly following the observed supervision session. The use of triangulation, in other words 'using several methods to explore the same phenomenon' (Davies 2007: 34) is a common method of helping to establish the credibility or trustworthiness of data in both quantitative and qualitative research.

Following each interview that was observed, the research officer sought information from the client about aspects of the interview that the client found most helpful and believed would contribute to increased compliance and reduced reoffending. Similarly the workers were interviewed following the worker/client supervision session in order to gather information about what the worker felt worked best in the interviews in terms of engaging clients and ultimately helping to reduce reoffending. Questions were also asked of the worker and client about the general nature of their supervision sessions to get a sense of the extent to which the observed interview is typical of what routinely occurs in supervision.

Limitations

The results presented below must be considered in the light of the limitations of the study. First, each of the interviews observed followed an expression of interest by a worker in being involved in the project. Those who volunteered represent only a proportion of the total number of juvenile justice workers in NSW Youth Justice and may not be representative of all workers in the system. Second, the results presented here are based on only 30 of the 137 interviews that have been observed and only 15 of the client interviews. The small numbers may have skewed the results. Coding the transcripts is an imperfect science. While there was considerable consistency in the coding, the judgements of the coders may have also influenced some of the results. Further, what occurred in one interview may be different from what occurs in another – there are clear limitations in only observing one interview.

On the other hand there were reasonably high rates of inter-rater reliability, with the coders rarely scoring more than one point apart. Also there was some degree of consistency in relation to the skills observed in the interviews and the views of the clients regarding what went on in the interview. To take one example, in relation to problem-solving there was a correlation of .496 on the time spent on needs analysis recorded by the research officers and the total number of problems discussed as reported by the client.

The limitations of the study itself and of this preliminary report on the findings are acknowledged. Nevertheless the results outlined below do provide some insights into the way in which a sample of probation officers in NSW juvenile justice carry out their work and the way in which their clients respond.

Results

The following results are based on 30 coded transcripts: 17 coded by the research officer/observer and 13 coded by a trained research officer. Eight transcripts were cross-coded by the two research officers to establish inter-rater reliability.

The average time for a supervision session was 32 minutes; however, there was considerable variation between different interviews, with the shortest being six minutes and the longest 64 minutes. Female staff had longer interviews than male staff, with female staff averaging 37 minutes and male staff averaging 25 minutes. The clients had an average age of 16, with the youngest being 14 and the oldest 19. The young people were either on probation, parole, suspended sentence or a supervised bond.

General use of skills

The observer rated the extent to which workers used the skills during the interview. This was rated on a five-point scale, dependent on whether the skill was:

1 not present at all
2 infrequently present (at least one example present through entire duration of the interview)
3 occasionally present (several examples are present during the interview)
4 numerous examples of this being present during the interview
5 present (worker is clearly using this skill deliberately with the client throughout the entire interview).

As shown in Table 7.1, role clarification was only occasionally present in the interviews whereas there were numerous examples of the worker conducting needs analysis. The workers made some use of pro-social modelling skills.

Role clarification

The observer rated on a five-point scale the extent to which the various aspects of role clarification were used. As shown in Table 7.2, the workers occasionally discussed the conditions of the order, how the

Table 7.1 Time spent using skills in interviews.

	Mean on 5-point scale
Time spent discussing role clarification	2.80
Time spent conducting needs analysis	4.24
Time spent conducting problem-solving	3.26
Time spent discussing strategies	3.53
Time spent using pro-social modelling	3.65

Table 7.2 Workers' use of role clarification skills.

	Mean on 5-point scale
Spoke about conditions of order	3.33
Nature/authority of the worker	2.06
Time worker has for client	1.83
How the worker can help	3.13
Restrictions of organisation	1.43
Purpose of worker's interventions	3.03
Dual role helper/investigator	1.86
Negotiable/non-negotiable areas	1.80
Confidentiality	1.50

worker can help the client (for example, by making referrals to other agencies or counselling the client) and the purpose of the worker's intervention. There were infrequent examples in the supervision sessions of the nature of the worker's authority (for example, what happens if a client misses an appointment), the worker's dual role as a helper and investigator (for example, the worker explaining the difference between being a helper/counsellor and their mandated position to the court) and to the negotiable and non-negotiable areas of probation (for example, the time and day of the appointment may be negotiable whereas the frequency of supervision may not be negotiable), and the time the worker has for the client. There was little if any reference to the other role clarification skills of helping the client to understand the extent to which the interviews are confidential, or the nature/role of the worker in relation to their organisation.

In the transcripts analysed, role clarification was generally raised in the context of discussing the young person's legal order, highlighting the reason for the supervision order and the repercussions of failure to comply with those conditions. Outlined below is an excerpt from one of the supervision sessions:

Worker: You are on a Good Behaviour Bond, so as part of the supervision on your order you will need to see me at least once a month. You will also need to do counselling because your order requires that. But I am the alcohol and other drug counsellor, so we can make that part of your supervision process.

Young person: That sounds good.

Worker: We will be doing a case plan to start off with. So to begin with we will start off by seeing each other once a fortnight, but that is something we can negotiate.

Young person: OK.

Worker: I now want to explain what my role is to you. I am responsible to make sure you do attend appointments and also to provide counselling. My job is to help you stay out of trouble. As we talk and discuss the issues we might find ways to do that to suit you. We will arrange ways to help you to get in and I can come and see you. I also have another role – I am here to support you but if you don't attend I need to let the court know. Also if you tell me about specific offences I need to report this to police.

Young person: No, that is your job.

Worker: Have you got any problems with this?

Young person: No.

In this excerpt the worker was rated high for discussing conditions of the order, the dual role of the worker and the purpose of the worker intervention. She provides a specific timeframe for which supervision will occur. She emphasises her role as one that is going to assist the young person get through her court order; however, she outlines the limitations to her role and emphasises her obligations to both the court and the police. The young person appears to both understand and accept this explanation.

The observers then rated the extent to which the client was engaged by the skill used by the worker. The scoring of 1–5 represents the degree to which the client was engaged when the worker used a particular skill. This is captured by the client's immediate response to the skill used by the worker.

1 Client non-responsive, looking away, monosyllabic responses.
2 Client partially engaged in conversation, occasional eye contact but responses still limited.
3 Client is occasionally engaged in the conversation and is responsive to a proportion of what the worker is saying.
4 Client appears engaged in session although may appear distracted or disinterested at times.
5 Client is taking notice, listening, responding to the worker, actively learning.

As shown in Table 7.3, clients were most likely to be engaged with the worker when the worker discussed issues of confidentiality even though this was infrequently discussed by the workers. Similarly they were at least occasionally engaged when the worker talked about the conditions of the order, the restrictions of the organisation and negotiable and non-negotiable areas.

Problem-solving

Table 7.4 shows that when workers used problem-solving techniques to address client issues they focused predominantly on exploring problems with clients. They occasionally focused on problem survey

Table 7.3 Client response to workers' use of role clarification skills.

	Mean on 5-point scale
Spoke about conditions of order	3.70
Nature/authority of the worker	3.09
Time worker has for client	2.85
Helping orientation of worker	3.04
Restrictions of organisation	3.50
Purpose of worker's interventions	3.04
Dual role helper/investigator	2.54
Negotiable/non-negotiable areas	3.50
Confidentiality	4.25

Table 7.4 Worker's use of problem-solving skills.

	Mean on 5-point scale
Problem survey	2.90
Problem ranking	2.20
Problem exploration	4.06
Setting goals	2.40
Developing contract	1.26
Developing strategies	2.80

whereby the worker and the young person talked about a range of problems the young person might be facing from the young person's perspective. They also occasionally focused on developing strategies or courses of action that may be taken and evaluating which steps are the most likely to succeed. This includes formal or informal cognitive behavioural strategies aimed at helping clients change their way of thinking about crime. They made less use of goals and contracts or problem ranking (deciding which problems are most appropriate to work on).

As shown in Table 7.5, although contracts were used infrequently the clients responded positively when they were used. Similarly the clients were engaged in the process of problem exploration and at least partially engaged when the workers surveyed problems and developed strategies.

Table 7.5 Client response to problem-solving skills.

	Mean on 5-point scale
Problem survey	3.77
Problem ranking	3.33
Problem exploration	3.92
Setting goals	3.60
Developing contract	4.50
Developing strategies	3.65

Table 7.6 Criminogenic needs discussed during interviews.

	Mean on 5-point scale
Accommodation	2.46
Employment/education	4.23
Substance abuse	2.83
Attitude	2.63
Family/relationships	3.26
Financial	2.16
Emotional stability	1.93
Anti-social peers	2.89
Social/recreation	2.16
Health	1.50
Anger management	2.90
Offences	2.80

The criminogenic needs most commonly identified in interviews revolved around employment and education issues, with family and relationships the next most commonly identified. Drug use, peers, anger and offences were also discussed occasionally. These results are similar to Bonta *et al.* (2004), who examined criminogenic needs among 66 youth under probation supervision in Canada. The needs identified in that study were, in order: family (identified in 95 per cent of cases), peers, academic/vocational, substance abuse and accommodation.

There were minimal differences in the extent to which the clients were engaged in discussions about the various issues. They were at least partially engaged in discussions about each of the issues shown in Table 7.7.

Table 7.7   Client responses to issues discussed in interviews.

	Mean on 5-point scale
Accommodation	3.31
Employment/education	3.77
Substance abuse	3.31
Attitude	3.33
Family/relationships	3.77
Financial	3.41
Emotional	3.44
Anti-social peers	3.47
Social/recreation	3.63
Anger management	3.37
Offences	3.90

The following excerpt includes elements of problem survey and problem exploration. It is not, however, done in a collaborative way and does not involve problem exploration, or working together on goals or strategies to achieve them.

Worker: So what are you interested in? Sounds like you are not that interested in fencing?

Young person: Nah.

Worker: So we work with a programme with Mission. A worker from there just works with JJ clients.

Young person: Yeah, I have done Mission before. Employment skills.

Worker: So would you be interested in looking at your employment?

Young person: Nah, not really, it would interrupt with work.

Worker: But you are not working and it is important that you are in either education or employment.

Young person: I will just do work for the dole through Centrelink.

Worker: You don't want to be on Centrelink for the rest of your life, do you? It is probably better to go out and get your own job and not have to rely on Centrelink. You are very fortunate to have a job waiting for you.

Young person:	Which one?
Worker:	Fencing.
Young person:	It's alright – better than working with bricks.
Worker:	Cause you have done that before. So what about in the next fortnight you can give your boss a call.
Young person:	I have a cold.
Worker:	Hopefully you will get better so and be able to give your boss a call.
Young person:	For sure.

Pro-social modelling and reinforcement

There were numerous examples of identifying pro-social actions and comments by clients and of the worker providing rewards through praise or other methods for pro-social actions and comments. There were fewer examples of pro-social modelling (for example, expressing views about the value of pro-social pursuits) and few examples of challenging clients' pro-social actions or comments. This has similarities with the Bonta *et al.* (2004) study, which found high levels of prompting and encouragement in interviews, high levels of pro-social reinforcement, and low levels of challenging pro-criminal actions and comments. They also found low levels of pro-social modelling (see Table 7.8).

Table 7.8 Pro-social skills used in interviews.

	Mean on 5-point scale
Identifying pro-social actions	3.9667
Rewarding pro-social actions	3.8000
Challenging pro-criminal actions	2.3667
Modelling desirable behaviours	3.2667

The following interview excerpt shows an example of pro-social re-inforcement:

Young person:	I am doing the Ark programme and may have trouble with getting in here on certain days.
Worker:	We can work around that.

Young person:	Tiffany said the programme is good.
Worker:	Tiffany spoke with me too and we can work around this. The programme teaches you skills.
Young person:	Cooking.
Worker:	Do you know at this stage when you start?
Young person:	I go on Wednesday at 2.30 to meet the chef and from then I say when I want to start.
Worker:	It's all happening for you. You are doing really well. Things are going your way since you got out of custody.
Young person:	Yes.
Worker:	You've made a lot of changes.

This segment was rated high for pro-social reinforcement because the observer felt that the worker provided flexibility with the appointments because the young person was engaging in programmes. The young person responds positively to this praise and agrees with the positive changes she has made since leaving custody.

The clients were engaged when workers identified and rewarded pro-social actions by clients. They were less engaged, as shown in Table 7.9, when the workers challenged their pro-criminal actions or expressions.

Relationship

The workers were, in the judgement of the observers, open and honest, non-blaming, enthusiastic and friendly. They also were often engaging. They made less use of skills of challenging rationalisations, reflection of feelings and paraphrasing of client comments, and of humour. They rarely if ever used aggressive or judgemental confrontations. Bonta *et*

Table 7.9 Client response to pro-social skills.

	Mean on 5-point scale
Identifying pro-social actions	3.86
Rewarding pro-social actions	4.15
Challenging pro-criminal actions	3.35
Modelling desirable behaviours	3.50

al. (2004) examined some of these variables in their Canadian study. They found that openness was evident in 54 per cent of interviews observed (for adults and youth), whereas enthusiasm was present in only 27 per cent of interviews. Empathy increased and enthusiasm decreased in subsequent interviews (see Table 7.10).

The clients responded positively when the workers used self-disclosure, although they did not use it often. There was only one instance when the worker used judgemental confrontation, in the judgement of the observer, and the client responded well in this instance. Generally the clients were engaged to some extent when the workers used relationship skills, as shown in Table 7.11.

Table 7.10 Use of relationship skills by workers.

	Mean on 5-point scale
Open and honest	4.58
Challenge rationalisations	3.44
Non-blaming	4.20
Enthusiastic	4.40
Self-disclosure	2.06
Humour	3.26
Engagement	3.90
Friendly	4.52
Paraphrasing	3.10
Reflection of feelings	3.06
Aggressive judgemental confrontation	1.06
Judgemental confrontation	1.20

Table 7.11 Client response to relationship skills.

	Mean on 5-point scale
Open and honest	3.88
Challenge rationalisations	3.73
Non-blaming	3.56
Enthusiastic	3.71
Self-disclosure	4.40
Humour	3.59
Engagement	3.75
Friendly	3.88
Paraphrasing	3.61
Reflection of feelings	3.75
Aggressive judgemental confrontation	2.00
Judgemental confrontation	4.00

Another relationship skill is the ability to ask open rather than closed questions. Many of the workers did not utilise open-ended questions (see Table 7.12). They would tend to ask questions such as 'Do you get on with your mother?' rather than 'Can you tell me about your mother?' Clients were more engaged, however, when workers asked open questions. There was a strong correlation ($r =$ .372) between the use of open questions and the extent to which the clients were engaged in the interview.

Table 7.12 Number of open and closed questions asked in each interview.

	Mean number
Open questions asked	22.40
Closed questions asked	26.14

The following excerpt provides an example of a series of closed questions utilised by a worker:

Worker:	How's things going there?
Young person:	OK.
Worker:	Things getting better?
Young person:	Yeah.
Worker:	Cause last time we met you were not able to go to your mum's, what changed?
Young person:	Not much, got sick of Grandma.
Worker:	Is Grandma cool with it?
Young person:	Yeah.
Worker:	Any major blues?
Young person:	Not yet.
Worker:	Yeah, do you think you can avoid it.
Young person:	Yeah.
Worker:	Cause that's how you got into trouble last time.
Young person:	Yeah.

It appears that the worker is aware that the young person may be at risk of engaging in criminal behaviour or jeopardising his accommodation. However, the questions utilised do not elicit or facilitate any further conversation regarding this issue.

The client's perspective

After each interview was completed, in the second phase of the study the research officer/observer conducted an interview with the client in order to gain another perspective on the extent to which the skills were used in the probation interview. Only 15 client interviews had been coded at the time of writing. As shown in Table 7.13, the questions to clients were framed differently from those used in the coding process so they would be meaningful to clients. Nevertheless they confirm the coders' estimates of high use of some relationship skills, the use of praise, the incidence of problem exploration and the less frequent use of goal-setting and developing strategies or solutions. Overall, the interviews analysed to date suggest that the clients feel very positively about the probation experience, with clients saying that they like their probation officer and that their probation officer helps them to find ways of not getting into trouble

Table 7.13 Clients' estimates of the use of skills by their workers.

	Mean on 5-point scale
Did you discuss goals during that session?	1.57
Did your worker praise you if you said good or positive things?	4.46
Did your worker ask about worries/concerns you have at the moment?	3.08
Do you understand your worker's authority?	4.59
Does your worker do what they say they will do?	4.85
Is your worker friendly?	4.88
Do you like your worker?	4.47
Does your worker understand your problems?	4.76
Does your worker help you find ways of not getting into trouble again?	4.57
Did you discuss confidentiality in this interview?	3.15
Has confidentiality been discussed in other sessions?	4.85
Did you discuss possible solutions to your concerns?	2.00

again. There was limited discussion about confidentiality; however, this appears to have often been addressed in previous interviews. The client comments also highlight that even though a skill is not evident in one interview it may have been evident in others.

Discussion

The ratings of the observers of the 30 supervision sessions indicate that juvenile justice workers in the sample make at least some use of the effective practice skills referred to in the introduction to this chapter. There are numerous examples in the interviews of the workers conducting needs analysis in particular. On the other hand, role clarification skills were less evident. Workers focused a lot on problem exploration, a process that engaged their clients. They rarely used contracts, although on the few occasions that they did the clients were particularly engaged. The criminogenic needs most commonly identified and discussed were employment/education, family issues, anger management, peers, and substance abuse, in that order. The clients were partially engaged in these discussions regardless of the particular issue. There were numerous examples of identifying and reinforcing pro-social actions and comments but fewer of challenging clients' pro-criminal comments and actions. Workers were friendly, non-blaming and enthusiastic but made only occasional use of paraphrasing, and reflection. Clients were at least partially engaged by the relationship skills used by workers.

These results are, in many aspects, consistent with the only recent similar study that the authors have been able to locate – Bonta *et al.* (2004), undertaken in Canada with adult and youth probationers. Like this Australian study, the Canadian study found family, school/ work and peers to be frequently identified criminogenic needs. They found that workers were strong on pro-social reinforcement and on at least some relationship skills, and found few examples of challenging pro-criminal actions and comments.

The research officer/observer interviews with the clients are important to this study because they help to address some of the limitations of the study in as much as they provide another view about what was happening in the supervision sessions. To some degree they confirm the findings of the interview analysis particularly in terms of the workers' focus on pro-social reinforcement, problem exploration and relationship skills, and the limited focus on goals and strategies. The results do suggest, however, that from the client's perspective what they receive is helpful often when the skills do not appear to be used. Further, while a skill may not be evident in an interview it may have been present in earlier interviews.

This raises the question of what should be expected of a probation interview. Previous research suggests that when the skills are present the outcomes are better. However, the extent to which skills should be used is difficult to determine. If clients have an understanding of the role of the probation officer and confidentiality issues after years in the criminal justice system, for example, is it necessary to raise it again? It is anticipated that these and other questions can be addressed once the complete data is analysed.

References

Andrews, D.A. (2001) 'Effective practice: future directions', in D. Andrews, C. Hollin, P. Raynor, C. Trotter and B. Armstrong (eds) *Sustaining Effectiveness in Working with Offenders*. Cardiff: Cognitive Centre Foundation.

Andrews, D.A. and Bonta, J. (2006) *The Psychology of Criminal Conduct*. Cincinnati: Anderson Publishing.

Andrews, D. and Dowden, C. (2005) 'Managing correctional treatment for reduced recidivism: a meta-analytic review of programme integrity', *Legal and Criminological Psychology*, 10 (2): 173–87.

Andrews, D.A., Keissling, J.J., Russell, R.J. and Grant, B.A. (1979) *Volunteers and the One-to-One Supervision of Adult Probationers*. Toronto: Ontario Ministry of Correctional Services.

Bonta, J., Rugge, T., Sedo, B. and Coles, R. (2004) *Case Management in Manitoba Probation*. Ottawa: Public Safety Canada.

Chui, W.H. and Nellis, M. (eds) (2003) *Moving Probation Forward: Evidence, Arguments and Practice*. Harlow: Pearson Longman.

Davies, M. (2007) *Doing a Successful Research Project*. New York: Palgrave Macmillan.

Dowden. C. and Andrews, D.A. (2004) 'The importance of staff practice in delivering effective correctional treatment: a meta-analytic review of the literature', *International Journal of Offender Therapy and Comparative Criminology*, 48 (2): 203–14.

Dowden, C., Antonowicz, D. and Andrews, D. (2003) 'The effectiveness of relapse prevention with offenders: a meta-analysis', *International Journal of Offender Therapy and Comparative Criminology*, 47 (5): 516–28.

Farrington, D.P. and Welsh, B. (2005) 'Randomized experiments in criminology: what have we learned in the last two decades?', *Journal of Experimental Criminology*, 1 (1): 9–38.

Gendreau, P. (1996) 'The principles of effective intervention with offenders', in A.T. Harland (ed.) *Choosing Correctional Options that Work*. Newbury Park, CA: Sage.

Gendreau, P., Little, T. and Goggin, C. (1996) 'A meta-analysis of the predictors of adult recidivism: What Works!', *Criminology*, 34: 575-607.

Hepworth, D.H., Rooney, R.R. and Larson, J.A. (2002) *Direct Social Work Practice*. Pacific Grove, CA: Brooks Cole.

Jones, J.A. and Alcabes, A. (1993) *Client Socialisation: The Achilles Heel of the Helping Professions*. Westport, CT: Auburn House.

McIvor, G. (2005) 'Addressing youth crime: prevention, diversion and effective intervention', in M. Mellon, J., McGee and B. Whyte (eds) *Meeting Needs, Addressing Deeds: Working with Young People who Offend*, Glasgow: NCH Scotland.

McNeill, F. (2003) 'Desistance focused probation practice', in W.H. Chui and M. Nellis (eds) *Moving Probation Forward: Evidence, Arguments and Practice.* Harlow: Pearson Longman.

McNeill, F. and Whyte, B. (2007) *Reducing Reoffending: Social Work and Community Justice in Scotland.* Cullompton: Willan Publishing.

Raynor, P. (2003) 'Research in probation: from nothing works to what works', in W.H. Chui and M. Nellis (eds) *Moving Probation Forward: Evidence, Arguments and Practice.* Harlow: Pearson Longman.

Rooney, R. (1992) *Strategies for Work with Involuntary Clients.* New York: Columbia University Press.

Shulman, L. (1991) *Interactional Social Work Practice: Toward an Empirical Theory.* Itasca, IL: F.E. Peacock.

Trotter, C. (1990) 'Probation can work: a research study using volunteers', *Australian Journal of Social Work*, 43 (2): 13–18.

Trotter, C. (1996) 'The impact of different supervision practices in community corrections', *Australian and New Zealand Journal of Criminology*, 29 (1): 29–46.

Trotter, C. (2002) 'Worker style and client outcome in child protection', *Child Abuse Review*, 11: 38–50.

Trotter, C. (2004) *Helping Abused Children and their Families.* Sydney: Allen and Unwin: London.

Trotter, C. (2006) *Working with Involuntary Clients.* Sydney: Allen and Unwin.

Trotter, C. and Sheehan, R. (2005) 'Women's access to welfare after prison', paper presented to 'What Works with Women Offenders' Conference, Monash University, Prato, Italy.

Videka Sherman, L. (1988) 'Meta-analysis of research on social work practice in mental health', *Social Work*, 33 (4): 323–38.

Part Three

Improving offender supervision

Chapter 8

The role of risk, needs and strengths assessment in improving the supervision of offenders[1]

Hazel Kemshall

The growing penal policy focus on risk and public protection across the major Anglophone jurisdictions from the 1990s onwards saw increased attention to formal assessment in order to improve the targeting of scarce resources according to risk, and to improve the effectiveness of interventions (see Bonta and Andrews, this volume). By drawing on practice in the English and Welsh probation service as the primary exemplar, this chapter reviews the role of risk, needs and strengths in the assessment and supervision of offenders, outlining key developments from the early domination of the risk-need-responsivity model to the more recent impact of the 'Good Lives Model'.

From the early 1990s to the present day probation practice in England and Wales (under significant central policy direction) has striven to 'close the gap' between assessment and intervention, and to ground supervision practice in an evidence-based approach (see Burnett *et al.* 2007). A key element in this more structured approach to supervision has been the use of formal assessment tools to focus supervision on the 'right stuff'. These tools have been subject to almost constant refinement and development, with some commentators arguing that we are now on the 'fourth generation' of risk-needs tools (Bonta and Wormith 2007; Kemshall 2003; Bonta and Andrews, this volume). To some extent, the history of assessment tool development can also be understood as a journey from objectifying, actuarially based risk tools producing aggregated probability scores of the risk of reoffending (for example, the OGRS)[2], to more recent structured professional judgement tools comprising risks, needs and strengths, producing assessments that are both more individualised and holistic, and in some cases concerned with the risk of harm as well as the risk of reoffending (see Hanson *et al.* 2007).

It is also the history of extensive debate about the extent to which risk has replaced need as the key rationale for probation interventions, and the extent to which rehabilitation has been superseded by risk management (see Kemshall 2003, chapter 4 for a full review; Robinson 1999, 2003). This chapter explores the contribution risk, needs and strengths assessment has made to changes in supervision practice with offenders.

The meshing of risk and needs in assessment

There can be little doubt that risk and public protection have transformed the work and character of the probation service; the extent to which the discourse of need and rehabilitation has been replaced by risk and actuarially based assessments continues to be much debated (Robinson 2003). While the contention that the probation service in England and Wales (and in other anglophone jurisdictions) has been totally reconfigured by risk may be overstated (see Kemshall 2008, for example, and for key differences in Scotland see McNeill *et al.* 2005[3]); the welfarism of 'advise, assist and befriend' has indeed been superseded by an economic rationality of crime management and a risk-driven agenda in which 'rehabilitation' is increasingly inscribed in a framework of risk rather than a framework of welfare (Garland 2001: 176). This is evidenced by the use of risk assessment to 'tier' offenders according to the level of supervision intensity and type of intervention required (currently four tiers in England and Wales: NOMS 2005a, 2005b, 2006; NPS 2005a), and to target offenders for cognitive behavioural treatment programmes. A broader bifurcation can be discerned, with a legislative, policy and practice separation of 'dangerous offenders' for special measures. In this sense, risk assessment has a dual function, the identification of high risk (or 'dangerous') offenders for community monitoring, surveillance and intensive supervision usually under the multi-agency public protection arrangements (MAPPA); and the channelling of other offenders to tiered responses based largely on the risk of reoffending. In this sense, risk is both a rationing and a targeting mechanism within an economic discourse of probation practice (Garland 1997), and has a number of functions ranging from efficient targeting of offenders for interventions, and the efficient targeting of costly multi-agency resources at the problematic few. Within the assessment and regulation of the problematic few, there are also gradations, ranging from low to high risk of serious harm (Home Office 2007, chapter 8), hence risk assessment, even for harm, is concerned with creating a 'ladder of risk' to justify the efficient and equitable distribution of scarce intervention and supervision resources.

This concern to assess and manage both the risk of harm and the risk of reoffending, coupled with a growing penal policy focus on public protection throughout the 1990s, resulted in a 'new rehabilitationism' driven by 'risk classifications' (Rotman 1990; Kemshall 2003: 99). This was epitomised by the strange linguistic hybrid of 'criminogenic need' in which offender needs were legitimised and addressed only in so far as they contribute to offending (Aubrey and Hough 1997; see also Chapman and Hough 1998). Risk assessment tools began to focus extensively on criminogenic needs and these came to form the basis of ASSET, for use with young offenders, and OASys for adult offenders (Home Office 2007; Youth Justice Board 2005). Such tools also represent an ideological hybrid between the world of welfare needs and the world of risk, although this hybridisation has not always made the tools more acceptable to staff (Kemshall 2003).

While some commentators see the new rehabilitationism as a potential vehicle of compatibility between risk and need and between risk management and rehabilitation (Robinson 2002), empirical studies, particularly in the UK context although not exclusively so, have demonstrated that the new rehabilitationism does not necessarily translate purely into the operational reality of front-line practice (Kemshall and Maguire 2003). Risk classifications, for example, are still subject to the residual autonomy and discretion of probation officers (Kemshall *et al.* 2002) and criminogenic risk/need tools are not always used with integrity (Beaumont *et al.* 2001). While risk classifications and subsequent targeting are driven by the principle of eligibility (the offender meets the risk score), probation officers are also concerned with issues of suitability (is the offender suitable for the programme, willing and motivated?), and with viability (can the offender get there, does it fit with their lifestyle?) (Kemshall *et al.* 2002). In essence, staff struggle to balance individualised assessments against the aggregated assessments from risk scores. While targeting may mean tiering and rationing on the basis of risk thresholds for policy-makers and senior managers, for practitioners it means directing the offender to the most appropriate intervention (Kemshall 2003: 100; Kemshall *et al.* 2002). Hence risk and targeting can be understood and operationalised differently. This can make the operation of case management systems based on 'risk bands' very difficult to achieve. This is particularly acute now that the offender tiering bands have been linked to workload management within the English and Welsh probation service, with points allocated to cases depending on tiering, and linked to grades of staff who provide the supervision. (The impact of resource pressure on tiering and case management responses is discussed below.)

Within England and Wales, the National Offender Management Service (NOMS) has created four tiers for case management, with greater intensity of input as the tiers increase. In brief, these are: tier 1: punish; tier 2: help; tier 3: change; tier 4: control (NOMS 2005a; NPS 2005a). However, Burnett, Baker and Roberts (2007: 222) remind us that the 'tiers are not mutually exclusive, but are layered one on the other, so that each involves the interventions of all lower levels as well as those specified at its own level'.

Lower tiered cases are almost exclusively managed by probation service officers. In the English and Welsh context these are staff who receive less pay and training than probation officers, and whose input is targeted at less risky cases, with probation officers deployed as 'offender managers' to cases requiring more intensive interventions or presenting greater risk. Assessment is seen as key to this NOMS case management model (NPS 2005a; NOMS 2005a), with a cyclical process dubbed ASPIRE as a core feature: assess–sentence–plan–implement–review–evaluate (see Burnett *et al.* 2007 for a full discussion). However, mis-assessments of risk and hence mis-tiering have been implicated in Serious Further Offence reviews. These are conducted in England and Wales by Her Majesty's Inspectorate of Probation where an offender on probation or parole supervision, or subject to a community sentence under probation service management, commits a further serious offence against the person.[4] The most notable recent review is that of Damien Hanson and Elliot White following the murder of John Monckton (HMIP 2006a). The review concluded that Hanson was mis-assessed as medium risk prior to release, thus seriously weakening the subsequent case management response and the level of scrutiny and control Hanson was subject to.

Impact on the supervision of offenders

However, policies can be significantly mediated, resisted and ignored by staff (Kemshall 1998, 2008). As Ericson puts it, there will be 'variation across institutions and contexts in how risk is conceived, understood, manipulated and managed' (2007: 965). There is potential for a gap between the vast architecture of risk (assessment tools, policies, procedures, systems, registers) and whether and how they impact upon the daily life of practitioners and offenders.

The key question is whether assessments grounded in risk/needs have actually impacted on the everyday decisions and practices of practitioners. In particular, has supervision practice changed and benefited from the introduction of risk/needs assessment? The period from 1997 and the introduction of the term 'criminogenic need' by Aubrey and Hough (1997) to 2009 has seen unprecedented pressure on the probation service to adopt and use risk assessment tools and also to improve supervision practice. Much of this pressure arose out of high profile case management failures, particularly around risk (the most notable cases being Hanson and White, and Anthony Rice; HMIP 2006a, 2006b); but also from financial and economic pressures to manage offenders more efficiently and effectively (Kemshall 2003). The merging of the prisons and probation service into the National Offender Management Service (NOMS) and the growing list of key performance indicators (KPIs) added to the focus on efficient and effective 'end-to-end offender management'. During this period the National Probation Service (NPS) and latterly NOMS increasingly adopted the language of business risks – targets, attention to audit, operational and reputational risks, risk registers and so forth.

Impact upon supervision practice

In this climate, and against the backdrop of severe criticism from the Home Secretary on the day following the Hanson and White serious further incident (HMIP 2006a), reputational risk also became a significant policy and management issue (Kemshall 2008). Certainly there has been major momentum for change. As Farrow, Kelly and Wilkinson put it: 'The relative simplicity of the original police court missionary's role has given way to more complex and complicated responses to crime' (2007: 7). One impact upon supervision practice has been the transformation of the worker–offender relationship into one characterised by a shift 'towards technical skill and management of people through a process' (Farrow et al. 2007: 13). This resulted in a technicist approach to supervision with both practitioners and offenders enmeshed in a vast architecture of risk literally boxing them into programmes, particular methods based on cognitive behavioural treatments, and a sense that 'one size fits all' (Kemshall et al. 2004;

Farrow *et al.* 2007). This was reinforced by a managerialist approach to criminal justice as a whole, and a growing distrust of practitioners seen as having a vested interest in staying the same. As Burnett and Roberts (2004) put it, there was a growing suspicion by central policy-makers (and politicians) that one-to-one practice meant ineffective practice and the exercise of inappropriate professional discretion. In this climate 'the relationship' didn't just fall off the agenda, it was discredited.

Paralleling this, there continued to be confusion for practitioners and local managers between risk of harm and risk of reoffending, a confusion not helped by the use of the term 'criminogenic need', resulting in an unhelpful elision of risk and need factors that served to confuse practitioners completing assessments and led to imprecision in the use of key terms central to assessment and offender management (Kemshall 2003; McGuire 2004). In addition, risk-based interventions were critiqued on the grounds that their 'universality' did not take account of diversity (Shaw and Hannah-Moffat 2004), and that needs were transmuted into risks (Hannah-Moffat 2005), reinforcing an unhelpful pathology of offending and increasing the 'responsibilisation of offenders' (see Kemshall 2002 for a full discussion).

Improvements in risk assessment tools, including the development of what Bonta and Wormith have called 'fourth generation' tools, have taken place (2007), with the most notable being the Level of Service/Case Management Inventory (LS/CMI) – a Canadian-based tool that is currently under evaluation in Scotland. While the predictive validity of the LS/CMI is presented as the same as for its predecessor, the Level of Service Inventory (LSI), the primary aims of the LS/CMI are to enhance the integration of assessment and case management, and to include specific risk/need criteria in order to refine individual assessments (Bonta and Wormith 2007). To some extent, risk prediction has taken second place to the development of a case management tool and the strengthening of assessment techniques to enhance the matching of offenders to interventions.

As part of these developments, criminogenic need was transformed into dynamic risk factor (Andrews *et al.* 2006; Bonta and Wormith 2007), with a clearer message provided to NOMS staff in *The Risk of Harm Guidance and Training Resource* (Kemshall *et al.* 2006) and in case management guidance (NPS 2005a, 2005b).

These changes in probation practice within the English and Welsh service also took place in a climate of diminishing resources. The Chief Inspector of Probation in England and Wales has noted the significant impact of low resources and diminished capacity in the adequate supervision of offenders. He refers to the 'Long Squeeze' – a situation over a period of time where resources have not kept pace with rising workload, with increasing public and political expectations of what can be delivered. While a simple causal relationship cannot necessarily be drawn between quantity and quality in the workload (HMIP 2007), the Effective Supervision Inspections found that less than 60 per cent of cases had a satisfactory risk of harm assessment carried out (similar to the findings of Kemshall *et al.* 2005 on MAPPA cases), although interventions were satisfactory in around 80 per cent of cases (HMIP 2005). This measure largely related to the frequency of contact and the frequency of home visiting.

Rediscovering the worker–offender relationship

One result of the dominance of evidence-based correctional practice has been the dilution of the offender–worker relationship (Farrow *et al.* 2007), perhaps unkindly characterised by Robinson (2005) as a 'pass the parcel' approach to the offender. The NOMS offender management model has been much critiqued as a fragmented and depersonalised approach (see Burnett *et al.* 2007). NOMS, for example, describes the offender management model as involving 'different people from different agencies, doing different things with the same offender, at different stages of the sentence' (NOMS 2005a: 13). The 'hub' of this OM model is the offender manager, providing a 'thread of continuity, binding issue-specific interventions into a coherent whole' (NOMS 2005a: 13).

However, a number of difficulties have already been identified in the OM model, specifically difficulties in responding to escalating risk; the separation of the case management and supervisor roles in a high number of cases; difficulties in maintaining continuity of service and 'pro-social messages' (see Burnett *et al.* 2007); and difficulties in engaging positively with offenders over the long term. The latter has been seen as critical by Her Majesty's Inspector of Probation (Bridges 2005). Offender perception surveys highlight that offenders value the 'continuity of the relationship' and high quality relationships with a nominated supervisor (Dominey *et al.* 2005; PA Consultancy and MORI 2005).

More recent work and practice attention to the worker–offender relationship have been supported by meta-analytic reviews in mental health that have shown the importance of empathy, warmth, respect and dignity in achieving positive outcomes (Lambert and Ogles 2004); and significant work in Scotland on social work skills with offenders has stressed their critical importance to assessment and case management (McNeill *et al.* 2005; see also McNeill 2009a, 2009b for a full review). Parallel work on offender perceptions of assessment and supervision (including high risk offenders) has complemented these studies. Offenders cite a range of important factors to assessment, including the knowledge, skill and competence of the assessor; the time taken to 'get to know them'; the level of their inclusion in the assessment; whether they were given sufficient credit for change; and whether negative factors were balanced with positive ones (Attrill and Liell 2007: 201). In a similar study, Wood and Kemshall (2007: 8–15) found that offenders value accuracy, fairness, clear explanations of assessments, and positive supervisory relationships characterised by 'strong relationships between police, probation and offenders' where a more positive construction of the offender as someone who 'can and will change behaviour in most cases' was the prevailing assumption. The supervision practices that were most effective reflect those characterised as 'pro-social modelling' (Trotter 1999, 2000, 2007 for a full discussion, and Trotter, this volume). Staff adopting this approach in their work with sex offenders felt that it was 'playing a key role in the prevention of further offending' (Wood and Kemshall 2007: 8).

This focus on pro-social supervisory techniques and greater emphasis on the quality of the worker–offender relationship has also stimulated increased research and practice attention to a more holistic and constructive way of conceptualising and engaging with offenders, focusing less on individual offender deficits and more on the personal, interpersonal and social contexts required to enable offenders to live and sustain a 'good life' (McCulloch and Kelly 2007: 15; see also McAlinden 2005, 2006; Ward and Marshall 2004). This approach has led to alternative approaches to assessment and interventions rooted in restorative justice and the 'good lives' model (McAlinden 2005, 2006; Ward and Marshall 2004). Proponents of this approach have also critiqued the risk-need-responsivity model, on the grounds that it does not sufficiently 'consider a broader range of human needs', and 'the role of identity and agency in offending means that it ultimately pays insufficient attention to core therapeutic and intervention tasks (e.g. treatment alliance, motivational issues)' (Ward and Maruna 2007: 105).

The following section considers the implications of the 'Good Lives Model' for assessment and offender supervision.

Developing strengths: the potential contribution of GLM

The Good Lives Model (see Ward, this volume) is essentially a strengths-based approach which 'focuses on promoting individuals' important personal goals, while reducing and managing their risk for future offending' (Whitehead *et al.* 2007: 579). In brief:

> It takes seriously offenders' personal preferences and values – that is, the things that matter most to them in the world. It draws upon these primary goods to motivate individuals to live better lives; and ... therapists seek to provide offenders with the competencies (internal conditions) and opportunities (external conditions) to implement treatment plans based on these primary goods. (Whitehead *et al.* 2007: 580)

GLM works with the offender to reframe approach goals and the means to achieve them positively and legitimately, and assists the offender in reconstructing a new identity that can action personal goals legally (Whitehead *et al.* 2007; see also Kemshall 2008: 94–7, 134–5; see McNeill 2009a, 2009b for a full review). The implications for assessment and supervisory practice are potentially wide-ranging. In terms of assessment, GLM requires a more transparent and collaborative approach to assessment, with offenders directly engaged and included in the assessment process (a component valued by the offenders in the studies conducted by Attrill and Liell (2007) and Wood and Kemshall (2007); see also Mann and Shingler 2004). In addition, GLM assessments emphasise the offender's 'strengths and life achievements' including the offender's priorities, goals and aspirations for life (Ward and Maruna 2007: 131–2). However, Ward and Maruna acknowledge that the latter do not lend themselves to formal lists and risk assessment tools, but rather require extended, face-to-face interviews that guide the offender through a journey of self-exploration (2007: 132). Such assessments form the basis of a rehabilitation plan that provides the offender with a legitimate route for the achievement of life goals and provides 'goods' they value (Ward and Maruna 2007: 134). Relevant interventions are seen as likely to enhance motivation and compliance.

However, GLM has been critiqued on a number of grounds, not least that it is culturally and context specific, developed from work with indigenous peoples, and lacks transferability. It has to be combined with a risk management approach, but a therapeutic focus on needs may obscure attention to risks, and the tensions between promoting the 'primary goods' of the offender and protecting the public may be hard to reconcile (McNeill 2009a, 2009b). The model also has limited efficacy with people with psychopathic personalities who display limited empathy and remorse (Whitehead *et al.* 2007; Hemphill and Hart 2002). In addition, it is difficult to establish in a multi-modal approach the impact achieved by GLM over and above more traditional risk management methods. Finally, comparison of GLM and more traditional risk management strategies are still lacking (see Bonta and Andrews 2003 for a full review). While Ward and Maruna outline a number of instances of the use of GLM in programmes with a range of offenders across a number of anglophone jurisdictions, they acknowledge that there is a lack of 'direct, compelling research evidence for GLM-inspired programs' (2007: 170).

GLM has, however, made a number of important contributions to assessment and supervision practice with offenders, in particular the emphasis on a more holistic view of offenders, and a rebalancing of strengths and risks. GLM also emphasises engagement and motivation as key processes of change, and promotes rehabilitation plans that focus on social inclusion and reintegration as key mechanisms for the prevention of offending, including sexual offending (Ward *et al.* 2009). For example, in the arena of domestic violence, safety plans for women and children have gained from the reinforcement and monitoring of key family/network members as well as professionals (Morris and Gelsthorpe 2000), and from the censure such significant others can place on abusive behaviour. The support and modelling of men who are 'anti-violence' has also been critical (Braithwaite and Daly 1994), exemplified by probation programmes for violent and abusive men facilitated by male role models (see, for example, the CHANGE programme in Scotland; Morran 1996).

Supervision practice under GLM has prioritised the role and importance of the 'therapeutic alliance' between worker and offender in promoting change (Marshall *et al.* 2003), and a re-legitimisation of non-criminogenic needs such as attention to self-esteem (Mann *et al.* 2004). Drawing on the work of Maruna (2001), GLM has also focused on identity formation, in particular the construction of non-offending identities and the promotion of the 'agentic self' – a person capable of making changes and of constructing a non-offending lifestyle if given the skills and competences to do so. A further useful area has been the increased attention to approach rather than avoidance goals; that is, positively framed goals on change rather than avoidance goals to 'avoid offending situations', or 'avoid risky behaviours'. A key example might be to encourage violent offenders to 'rehearse at least two ways of managing my temper when provoked' rather than to 'avoid getting into fights' (see Kemshall *et al.* 2006).

GLM's attention to strengths and rehabilitation (rather than punishment and control) can be placed within the broader focus on restorative approaches. In brief, commentators critical of retributive and punitive justice have argued that restorative approaches can apply to serious crimes as they promote genuine engagement with offenders and assist the process of change; they hold offenders accountable for their actions; and victims and communities are empowered by becoming part of the solution(s) (see McAlinden 2005 for a review). Restorative approaches to offenders have their roots in Braithwaite's restorative justice (2002), and while there is some debate about terminology and conceptual definitions (for example, with restorative and integrative approaches being seen as interchangeable by some commentators), McAlinden has helpfully stated: 'general principles of providing restitution to victims and communities, promoting offender reintegration and repairing relationships between victims, offenders and communities are well understood' (2006: 206).

Restorative approaches to sexual and violent offending have been largely restricted to the arena of intimate family violence, reflecting that around 80 per cent of sexual offending occurs within families or personal networks (Grubin 1998; Gelles 1997), and that most violence towards women by men occurs within family settings (Morris and Gelsthorpe 2000). However, Newell (2007) has reviewed the use of restorative justice practice in work with prisoners including 'randomised controlled trials testing the effects of restorative justice in cases where offenders had been remanded in custody awaiting sentence for serious burglary and robbery offences, and for offenders actually serving sentences for violent crime' (2007: 234). The project is presented positively in terms of reducing prison violence and bullying (see Edgar and Newell 2006 for a full discussion) and has the potential to assist prisoners with handling conflict pro-socially on release, particularly through the use of approach goals. Restorative approaches also have positive benefits for victims who suffer less post-traumatic stress and re-victimisation (Daly 2006), with UK and international work demonstrating that nearly 90 per cent of victims take up the restorative justice process and that only 4 per cent who do so fear re-victimisation (Strang *et al.* 1999: 20).

This is strong evidence that victims as well as offenders benefit from restorative approaches.

Conclusion

The risk-need-responsivity model and the cognitive behavioural interventions that have stemmed from it have dominated correctional practice in most anglophone jurisdictions. However, this approach has been subject to increasing critique (see Ward and Maruna 2007).

Supervision and intervention strategies that promote pro-social modelling and 'strengths' are now seen as effective mechanisms for reducing risk and promoting offender integration into communities safely (Kemshall 2008: 130–3). Offenders themselves view such interventions as helpful, effective and legitimate, and compliance is often enhanced by such approaches (Wood and Kemshall 2007), particularly if the 'therapeutic alliance' is strengthened. While further evaluations are required, particularly of the Good Lives Model, the promotion of more holistic interventions emphasising strengths rather than risk, and integration over punishment is to be welcomed. As McNeill puts it: 'To achieve safer communities we need better integrated citizens' (2009a: 22).

Notes

1 Some of the material presented here on GLM is adapted from Kemshall (2008) and is reproduced with the kind permission of the Open University Press.
2 The Offender Group Reconviction Score (Home Office 1996). See also Copas and Marshall (1998).
3 The position in Scotland is currently subject to change. See McIvor and McNeill (2007).
4 See HMIP, *Risk of Harm to others*, online at: www.justice.gov.uk/inspectorates/hmi-probation/risk-of-harm-to-others.htm (accessed 4 January 2010).

References

Andrews, D., Bonta, J. and Wormith, S. J. (2006) 'The recent past and near future of risk and/or need assessment', *Crime and Delinquency*, 52 (1): 7–27.
Attrill, G. and Liell, G. (2007) 'Offenders' views on risk assessment', in N. Padfield (ed.) *Who to Release? Parole, Fairness and Criminal Justice.* Cullompton: Willan Publishing.

Aubrey, R. and Hough, M. (1997) *Assessing Offenders' Needs: Assessment Scales for the Probation Service*, Home Office Research Study 166. London: Home Office.

Beaumont, B., Caddick, B. and Hare-Duke, H. (2001) *Meeting Offenders' Needs: A Summary Report on the Meeting Assessed Needs Evaluation*, Report for the National Probation Service, Nottinghamshire Area. Nottingham: Home Office.

Bonta, J. and Andrews, D.A. (2003) 'A commentary on Ward and Stewart's model of human needs', *Psychology, Crime and Law*, 9: 215–18.

Bonta, J. and Wormith, S. (2007) 'Risk and need assessment', in: G. McIvor and P. Raynor (eds) *Developments in Social Work with Offenders*, Research Highlights 48. London: Jessica Kingsley.

Braithwaite, J. (2002) *Restorative Justice and Response to Regulation*. Oxford: Oxford University Press.

Braithwaite, J. and Daly, K. (1994) 'Masculinities and communitarian control', in T. Newburn and E. Stanko (eds) *Just Boys Doing Business*. London: Routledge.

Bridges, A. (2005) *The Long Haul: Improving Effectiveness in the Criminal Justice System*. Foreword in HMI Probation 2004/2005 Annual Report. London: HMIP.

Burnett, R. and Roberts, C. (2004) (eds) *What Works in Probation and Youth Justice: Developing Evidence-Based Practice*. Cullompton: Willan Publishing.

Burnett, R., Baker, K. and Roberts, C. (2007) 'Assessment, supervision and intervention: fundamental practice in probation', in L. Gelsthorpe and R. Morgan (eds) *Handbook of Probation*. Cullompton: Willan Publishing.

Chapman, T. and Hough, M. (1998) *Evidence Based Practice: A Guide to Effective Practice*. London: HMIP.

Copas, J. and Marshall, P. (1998) 'The Offender Group Reconviction Scale: the statistical reconviction score for use by probation officers', *Journal of the Royal Statistical Society*, Series C, 47: 159–71.

Daly, K. (2006) 'Restorative justice and sexual assault: an archival study of court and conference cases', *British Journal of Criminology*, 46: 334–56.

Dominey, D., Knight, V. and Kemshall, H. (2005) 'The perception of the participant on accredited programmes in the probation service', *VISTA*, 10 (2): 72–80.

Edgar, K. and Newell, T. (2006) *Restorative Justice in Prisons – A Guide to Making It Happen*. Winchester: Waterside Press.

Ericson, R. (2007) *Crime in an Insecure World*. Cambridge: Polity Press.

Farrow, K., Kelly, G. and Wilkinson, B. (2007) *Offenders in Focus: Risk, Responsivity and Diversity*. Bristol: Policy Press.

Garland, D. (1997) 'Governmentality and the problem of crime: Foucault, criminology and sociology', *Theoretical Criminology*, 1 (2): 173–214.

Garland, D. (2001) *The Culture of Crime Control: Crime and Social Order in Contemporary Society*. Oxford: Clarendon Press.

Gelles, R. J. (1997) *Intimate Violence in Families*. London: Sage.

Grubin, D. (1998) *Sex Offending Against Children: Understanding the Risk*. London: Home Office.

Hannah-Moffat, K. (2005) 'Criminogenic needs and the transformative risk subject: hybridizations of risk/need in penality', *Punishment and Society*, 7 (1): 29–51.

Hanson, R.K., Harris, A., Scott, T.-L. and Helmus, L. *Assessing the Risk of Sexual Offenders on Community Supervision: The Dynamic Supervision Project*. Ottawa: Public Safety Canada. Online at: www.publicsafety.gc.ca/res/cor/rep/fl/crp2007-05-en.pdf (accessed 2 November 2009).

Hemphill, J.F. and Hart, S.D. (2002) 'Motivating the unmotivated: psychopathy, treatment, and change', in M. McMurran (ed.) *Motivating the Offender to Change: A Guide to Enhancing Engagement in Therapy*. Chichester: John Wiley.

HMIP (2005) *Managing Sex Offenders in the Community: A Joint Inspection on Sex Offenders*. London: Home Office.

HMIP (2006a) *An Independent Review of a Serious Further Offence Case: Damien Hanson and Elliot White*. London: HMIP. Online at: www.justice.gov.uk/inspectorates/hmi-probation/docs/hansonandwhitereview-rps.pdf (accessed 4 January 2010).

HMIP (2006b) *An Independent Review of a Serious Further Offence Case: Anthony Rice*. London: HMIP.

HMIP (2007) *Effective Supervision Inspection of the National Probation Service for England and Wales*. London: HMIP.

Home Office (1996) *Guidance for the Probation Service on the Offender Group Reconviction Scale*. London: Home Office.

Home Office (2007) *OASys Handbook*. London: Home Office.

Kemshall, H. (1998) *Risk in Probation Practice*. Aldershot: Ashgate.

Kemshall, H. (2003) *Understanding Risk in Criminal Justice*. Open University/McGraw-Hill.

Kemshall, H. (2008) *Understanding the Community Management of High Risk Offenders*. Open University/McGraw-Hill.

Kemshall, H. and Maguire, M. (2003) 'Sex offenders, risk penality and the problem of disclosure to the public', in A. Matravers (ed.) *Sex Offenders in the Community: Managing and Reducing the Risks*. Cullompton: Willan Publishing.

Kemshall, H., Canton, R. and Dominey, J. (2002) *The Effective Management of Programme Attrition. Report for the NPS*. London: National Probation Service and Leicester: De Montfort University.

Kemshall, H., Holt, P., Bailey, R. and Boswell, G. (2004) 'Beyond programmes: organisational and cultural issues in the implementation of "What Works", in G. Mair (ed.) *What Matters in Probation*. Cullompton: Willan Publishing.

Kemshall, H., Mackenzie, G., Miller, J. and Wilkinson, B. (2006) *The Risk of Harm Guidance and Training Resource* (CD-ROM). London: NOMS and Leicester: DeMontfort University.

Kemshall, H., Mackenzie, G., Wood, J., Bailey, R. and Yates, J. (2005) *Strengthening Multi-Agency Public Protection Arrangements (MAPPAs)*. Home Office Development and Practice Report, 45. London: Home Office.

Lambert, M.K. and Ogles, B.M. (2004) 'The efficacy and effectiveness of psychotherapy', in M.J. Lambert (ed.) *Bergin and Garfield's Handbook of Psychotherapy and Behaviour Change*, 5th edn. New York: Wiley.

Mann, R.E. and Shingler, J. (2006) 'Collaboration in clinical work with sexual offenders: treatment and risk assessment', in: W.L. Marshall, Y.M. Fernandez, L. E. Marshall and G. E. Serran (eds) *Sexual Offender Treatment: Controversial Issues*. Chichester: John Wiley.

Mann, R.E., Webster, S.D., Schofield, C. and Marshall, W.L. (2004) 'Approach versus avoidance goals in relapse prevention with sexual offenders', *Sexual Abuse: A Journal of Research and Treatment*, 16: 65–76.

Marshall, W., Serran, G., Fernandez, Y., Mann, R. and Thornton, D. (2003) 'Therapist characteristics in the treatment of sexual offenders: tentative data on their relationship with indices of behaviour change', *Journal of Sexual Aggression*, 9 (1): 25–30.

Maruna, S. (2001) *Making Good: How Ex-Convicts Reform and Rebuild their Lives*. Washington DC: American Psychological Association.

McAlinden, A. (2005) 'The use of "shame" with sexual offenders', *British Journal of Criminology*, 45 (3): 373–94.

McAlinden, A. (2006) 'Managing risk: from regulation to reintegration of sexual offenders', *Criminology and Criminal Justice*, 6 (2): 197–218.

McCulloch, T. and Kelly, L. (2007) 'Working with sex offenders in context: which way forward?', *Probation Journal*, 54 (1): 7–21.

McGuire, J. (2004) *Understanding Psychology and Crime: Perspectives on Theory and Action*. Maidenhead: Open University Press/McGraw-Hill Education.

McIvor, G. and McNeill, F. (2007) 'Developments in probation in Scotland', in G. McIvor and P. Raynor (eds) *Developments in Social Work with Offenders*. London: Jessica Kingsley.

McNeill, F. (2009a) 'What works and what's just?', *European Journal of Probation*, 1 (1): 21–40.

McNeill, F. (2009b) *Towards Effective Practice in Offender Supervision*, Report 01/09. Scottish Centre for Crime and Justice Research.

McNeill, F., Batchelor, S., Burnett, R. and Knox, J. (2005) *21st Century Social Work Reducing Reoffending: Key Skills*. Edinburgh: Scottish Executive.

Morran, D. (1996) 'Working in the "Change" programme: probation-based groupwork with male domestic violence offenders', in: T. Newburn and G. Mair (eds) *Working with Men*. Lyme Regis: Russell House Publishing.

Morris, A. and Gelsthorpe, L. (2000) 'Re-visioning men's violence against female partners', *Howard Journal*, 39 (4): 412–28.

Newell, T. (2007) 'Face to face with violence and its effects', *Probation Journal*, 54 (3): 227–38.

NOMS (2005a) *The NOMS Offender Management Model, Version 1*. London: Home Office.

NOMS (2005b) *Restructuring Probation to Reduce Re-Offending*. London: Home Office.

NOMS (2006) *The NOMS Offender Management Model*. London: Home Office.

NPS (2005a) *National Standards (2005) and the National Offender Management Model: Application of Tiering Framework*, Probation Circular, 65/2005. London: Home Office.

NPS (2005b) *Offender Assessment System (OASys) Quality Management Plan*, Probation Circular 48/2005. London: Home Office.

PA Consultancy and MORI (2005) *Action Research Study of the Implementation of the National Offender Management Model in the North West Pathfinder*, Home Office Online Report 32/05. Online at: www.noms.homeoffice.gov.uk/downloads/Action_research_study_NOMS_Model_NW_Pathfinder.pdf (accessed 30 October 2009).

Robinson, G. (1999) 'Risk management and rehabilitation in the probation service: collision and collusion', *Howard Journal*, 38 (4): 421–33.

Robinson, G. (2002) 'A rationality of risk in the Probation Service: its evolution and contemporary profile', *Punishment and Society*, 4 (1): 5–25.

Robinson, G. (2003) 'Technicality and indeterminacy in probation practice: a case study', *British Journal of Social Work*, 33 (5): 593–610.

Robinson, G. (2005) 'What works in offender management?', *Howard Journal*, 44 (3): 307–18.

Rotman, E. (1990) *Beyond Punishment: A New View of the Rehabilitation of Offenders*. Westport, CT: Greenwood Press.

Shaw, M. and Hannah-Moffat, K. (2004) 'How cognitive skills forgot about gender and diversity', in: G. Mair (ed.) *What Matters in Probation*. Cullompton: Willan Publishing.

Strang, H., Barnes, G.C., Braithwaite, J. and Sherman, L. (1999) *Experiments in Restorative Policing: A Progress Report on the Canberra Reintegrative Shaming Experiments (RISE)*. Canberra: Australian National University.

Trotter, C. (1999) *Working with Involuntary Clients: A Guide to Practice*. London: Sage.

Trotter, C. (2000) 'Social work education, pro-social modelling and effective probation practice', *Probation Journal*, 47: 256–61.

Trotter, C. (2007) 'Pro-social modelling', in G. McIvor and P. Raynor (eds) *Developments in Social Work with Offenders*, Research Highlights 48. London: Jessica Kingsley.

Ward, T., Collie, R. M. and Bourke, P. (2009) 'Models of offender rehabilitation: the good lives model and the risk-need-responsivity model', in: A. Beech, L. Craig and K. Browne (eds) *Assessment and Treatment of Sex Offenders: A Handbook*. Chichester: Wiley-Blackwell.

Ward, T. and Marshall, W.L. (2004) 'Good lives, aetiology and the rehabilitation of sex offenders: a bridging theory', *Journal of Sexual Aggression*, 10 (2): 153–70.

Ward, T. and Maruna, S. (2007) *Rehabilitation*. London: Routledge.

Whitehead, P.R., Ward, T. and Collie, R.M. (2007) 'Time for a change: applying the good lives model of rehabilitation to a high-risk offender', *International Journal of Offender Therapy and Comparative Criminology*, 51 (5): 578–98.

Wood, J. and Kemshall, H. (with Maguire, M., Hudson, K. and Mackenzie, G.) (2007) *The Operation and Experience of Multi-Agency Public Protection Arrangements (MAPPA)*, online report 12/07. London: Home Office, Research and Statistics Department. Online at: www.homeoffice.gov.uk/rds/pubintro1.html.

Youth Justice Board (2005) *Risk and Protective Factors*. London: Youth Justice Board.

Chapter 9

Managing the chaos: implementing evidence-based practices in correctional agencies

Faye S. Taxman and Judith Sachwald

'If I have seen further it is by standing on the shoulders of Giants.'

Sir Isaac Newton, 5 February 1676

The transformation of an agency in terms of adopting evidence-based practices must be customised to take place within the context of that organisation and its external and internal environment. Senior executives are required to lead the transformation process, and there is much debate as to the knowledge and skills used to change an organisation. Of course, the nature of the change – whether a small adjustment, an introduction of new technology (either hardware or software), or a major re-engineering or overhaul – affects the change process. But, as pointed out by Rogers (2003), diffusion processes have similar features regardless of the size and scope of the innovation. To a large extent, innovations must meet the test of being perceived as adding value, not so complex that they can not be translated into operational components, something that can tried, and observable or 'felt' by those involved. This is a tall order in that the innovation must be acceptable within the organisation, which means that the internal social networks of the organisation and communications are needed to reinforce the utility and advantages of the innovation. Essentially, three Cs define the innovation process – consistency, constant, and chaos – in that the transformation process requires attention to these factors to facilitate the change process and to orchestrate a commitment to continue forward even when challenges occur.

Over the past several decades in the United States and elsewhere, the criminal justice system has focused on a punishment orientation that reflects societal attitudes towards the best ways to deter criminal conduct in society (see Garland 2001). The evidence-based practices literature, evolving from Canadian researchers (see Bonta and Andrews, this volume), illustrated how using research findings can alter the processing of offenders to achieve the desired outcomes of reduced recidivism. While counter to the focus on punishment, the 'what works' framework provides the wherewithal and technology to advance broader principles that align to a correctional environment. This alignment improves the fit between the research findings and the daily practice of supervising offenders in the community or administering prisons and jails. In many ways the demands placed on the adoption of science into practice under the 'what works' framework is demanding for many correctional agencies. The evidence-based practices (EBPs) generally focus on the whole business process, not just one particular practice. In terms of corrections, this means that the focus is on both offender processing and offender change strategy. Consider the risk-need-responsivity core components: the offender must be assessed for risk for recidivism, assessed for a myriad criminogenic needs, and then assigned to programmes, services, or controls that are appropriate for the risk-needs of the offender. All of these activities require steps where decisions are contingent on the risk-needs assessment(s) as well as having the appropriate programmes/services in place to be responsive to the findings of the risk-needs assessment. As discussed in Friedmann, Taxman and Henderson (2007), few correctional agencies have such processes in place. Of the 15 identified evidence-based practices, the average community correctional agency has implemented approximately five of these practices. For example, the use of a risk assessment tool, a recommended practice, is used by 30 per cent of the surveyed community correctional agencies.

The question is, what are the factors that affect the adoption of evidence-based practices in community correctional agencies? This basic question can be found in a survey of the field in the US that examines the EBPs in place as well as the organisational factors that affect the adoption of said EBPs. Included in this survey are questions pertaining to the characteristics of the leaders (such as personal belief in rehabilitation, educational attainment, leadership style, use of team processes, orientation of reforms) and organisations (performance-driven culture, proportion of clinical staff, networking with external agencies, and so on) that influence the adoption of

EBPs (see Taxman *et al.* 2007). The following provides an overview of major findings from the survey across a spectrum of studies. The focus is on identifying the key patterns and traits that affect the adoption of EBPs. We then discuss the implications of these findings of the ways in which leaders can manage the diffusion of EBPs in their correctional agencies.

Methodology

This chapter summarises the wealth of information derived from analysis of the National Criminal Justice Treatment Practices (NCJTP) survey that was conducted in the US in 2004–05. The survey captured information on administrative practices in these settings and their use of evidence-based practices (see Taxman *et al.* 2007 for a detailed description of the survey). As reported in another chapter on the socio-political context of reforms in probation agencies (see Taxman, Henderson and Lerch, this volume), the survey is based on a sampling frame for the community correctional agencies that included selecting counties (census driven statistical areas of jurisdictions) and then surveying all agencies that operate within those 72 jurisdictions. The second stage was a census of all probation and parole agencies, prisons/jails, and community-based treatment programmes in these counties. A paper and pencil survey was conducted, with a response rate of 67 per cent (Taxman *et al.* 2007).

Defining evidence-based practices

A number of articles have been published from data from this survey. The survey included a consensus-driven approach to define evidence-based practices. The justification for these EBPs is provided in Taxman *et al.* (this volume) using this survey data:

1 Use of a standardised risk assessment tool.

2 Use of substance abuse assessment procedures (such as DSM-IV) and treatment matching (similar to the ASAM or other patient matching criteria).

3 Use of motivational techniques to engage and retain clients in treatment (such as motivational interviewing, engagement).

4 Use of therapeutic community, cognitive behavioural or other standardised treatment orientations which have been found to be

effective for offender populations (see Andrews and Bonta 1998; NIDA 2000).

5 A comprehensive approach to treatment and ancillary needs through comprehensive treatment services.

6 Practices to address co-occurring disorders through specialised screening and treatment.

7 Use of family therapies or multi-systemic family interventions.

8 Treatment programmes that are 90 days or more in duration.

9 Integration of multiple systems to optimise care and outcomes (see Fletcher *et al.* 2009).

10 Continuing care or aftercare to expand duration of treatment.

11 Use of drug testing.

12 Use of graduated sanctions for addressing non-compliance.

13 Use of contingency management or incentives to encourage progress.

14 Qualified staff.

15 Assessment of treatment outcomes.

16 Use of medications to treat substance abuse.

17 Use of detoxification programmes.

18 HIV/AIDS testing.

These were used to create a linear scale to indicate which of the evidence-based practices the supervision (or corrections agency) had adopted. Other measures were used to indicate which ones were fully implemented in the setting.

Results

What factors predict the adoption of EBPs in probation and parole settings in the US?

As shown in Table 9.1, there is tremendous variation in the adoption of evidence-based practices across the spectrum of community correctional agencies, with the mean agency adopting five on this list

Table 9.1 Use of evidence-based practices by respondents.

	n	%
Engagement techniques	255	39
Use of standardised substance abuse assessment tool	379	59
Use of standardised risk assessment tool	100	23
Comprehensive services	446	69
Co-occurring disorders	298	46
Continuing care	230	36
Family involvement	250	39
Systems integration	343	53
Graduated sanctions	138	32
Incentives	283	66
90-day duration	190	44
Drug testing	182	42
Treatment orientation	67	16
Qualified staff	148	68
Assessment of treatment outcomes	126	58
Medications used to treat substance abuse	65	15
Detoxification program	70	16
HIV/AIDS testing	214	50

Note: $n = 647$.
Source: Taxman *et al.* (this volume).

of evidence-based practices. A series of linear regression models were conducted to examine adoption in community correctional agencies (see Friedmann *et al.* 2007) that revealed the following variables were statistically important to adoption: community correctional agencies were more likely to adopt than institutional based correctional agencies ($\beta = -.57, p < .01$); administrator has a background in human services ($\beta = .20, p < .01$); administrator knowledgeable about EBPs ($\beta = .14, p < .02$); agency had a performance achievement culture ($\beta = .15, p < .05$); administrators perceive that they provide adequate training and staff development resources ($\beta = .16, p < .05$); administrators perceive that they have adequate internal support ($\beta = .22; p < .01$); and administrators support rehabilitation ($\beta = .16; p < .05$). Combining these factors in a multivariate model resulted in explaining 42 per cent of the variability in EBP adoption in correctional settings.

The analyses also established that the following factors were insignificant to the adoption of EBPs, which is equally important as recognising those factors that contribute to the adoption of EBPs. Size of the correctional population served does not matter as to whether organisations pursue the adoption of EBPs. Commonly held beliefs about organisations did not turn out to be important in the adoption of EBPs in these settings, such as the perception of available funding, physical resources, available staffing, or resources. That is, administrators who adopted EBPs were just as likely to have scarce resources as those who did not adopt, and their perceptions of these factors did not influence the decisions to invest in EBPs in their settings. Knowledge and commitment appear to be the stronger factors that influence the adoption of evidence-based practices.

What factors affect the likelihood of implementing and using EBPs in correctional settings?

Friedmann *et al.* (2007) looked at the issue of adoption – that is, whether the agency indicated that they had in place the mechanism. But, adoption is just the first step, when the real issue is implementation or the degree to which the innovation is used in the organisation (in the recent implementation science literature this is often referred to as uptake or penetration). Using another statistical technique, item response theory (IRT) (specifically Rasch modelling), Henderson, Taxman and Young (2008) examined the extent to which settings are using evidence-based practices and which EBPs are most commonly used. Given that the prior results found substantial variability in the types and numbers of EBPs adopted, the Rasch model was used to examine the clustering of practices in adult agencies. This allows us to explore how the adoption of one EBP may affect the adoption of other EBPs (defined as technology clusters by Rogers 2003) which can be used in implementation strategy to springboard or facilitate adoption of multiple EBPs consecutively.

For the purposes of this chapter, we do not describe the Rasch modelling technique but we do want to explain the rationale for using this strategy (see Henderson *et al.* 2008 for a discussion of this). Rasch (1960) modelling was used to construct a continuous indicator of the issues of interest. The technique has a number of advantages. First, Rasch-scaled survey items are measured on a true interval scale in that the number of EBPs used are the same over the entirety of the measure. As a result, Rasch-derived measures are considered sample-independent and are more likely to generalise to other similar populations. Second, through this technique a standard error of measurement for each EBP independent is derived. Each is independent of other items that improve the overall accuracy of the assessment of EBP use across settings and program populations. Finally, since the NCJTP survey involved two types of respondents – correctional administrators and treatment directors – the statistical model allows us to link the responses from each type of administrator to better address missing data and to integrate the perspectives of correctional administrators and treatment directors.

Consistent with the Friedmann *et al.* (2007) findings, organisational structure and leadership correlated with EBPs use ($F[7, 263] = 6.63$, $p < .001$, $R^2 = .15$). State level prisons use more EBPs than county-based correctional facilities (that is, jails and probation/parole offices combined; $\beta = -.18$, $t = -3.13$, $p = .002$). Facilities whose administrators reported greater knowledge of EBPs ($\beta = .24$, $t = 4.09$, $p < .001$) and education or experience in human services ($\beta = .21$, $t = 3.64$, $p < .001$) were more likely to use EBPs. Organisational culture and climate variables were related to EBP use ($F[6, 292] = 4.99$, $p < .001$, $R^2 = .09$), with performance achievement culture ($\beta = .15$, $t = 2.05$, $p = .041$) and climates more conducive to learning ($\beta = .25$, $t = 2.82$, $p = .005$) associated with more adoption and implementation.

Regarding the issues related to implementation (that is, the tendency to use the EBPs wholesale instead of for a small segment of the population), it appears that these are factors that are important to the utilisation of the practice and these factors are different from those that affect the decision to adopt. The perception of training and resources correlated with EBP use ($F[7, 466] = 9.62$, $p < .001$, $R^2 = .13$), especially training ($\beta = .20$, $t = 3.85$, $p < .001$), resources ($\beta = -.46$, $t = -3.45$, $p = .001$), physical facilities ($\beta = .43$, $t = 3.34$, $p = .001$), and internal support ($\beta = .22$, $t = 4.46$, $p < .001$). Administrator attitudes were related to EBP use ($F[5, 378] = 7.88$, $p < .001$, $R^2 = .09$), with attitudes favourable to rehabilitation ($\beta = .17$, $t = 3.20$, $p = .001$) and attitudes emphasising less punishment ($\beta = -.18$, $t = -3.36$, $p = .001$) associated with greater use. Finally, integration or working relationships with treatment agencies was related to EBP use ($F[3, 171] = 18.07$, $p < .001$, $R^2 = .26$) with stronger relationships with both criminal justice ($\beta = .24$, $t = 2.79$, $p = .006$) and non-criminal justice agencies correlated with more use of EBPs ($\beta = .31$, $t = 3.54$, $p = .001$).

The bubble chart (Figure 9.1), a typical output from Rasch modelling. It illustrates how adoption and use are affected by the nature of the EBPs. Certain practices are generally found together. These figures

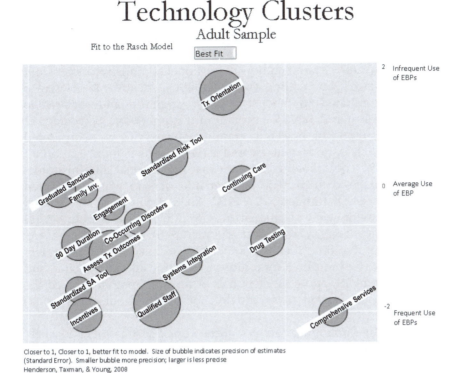

Figure 9.1 Example of technology clusters in the adoption of evidence-based practices.

Source: Henderson *et al.* (2008).

indicate a cascading effect for certain EBPs, where use of one EBP may facilitate the use of others. For example, the use of motivational engagement techniques, assessment of treatment outcomes, and a planned 90-day duration of treatment have approximately equal difficulty levels but they seem to cluster together. It suggests that agencies that examine outcomes of offenders from their treatment programmes are also more likely to be involved in techniques that engage the offender in treatment. And, these agencies are more likely to have treatment services that are longer in duration (at least 90 days).

How do correctional administrators handle the competing values of providing treatment and other educational and vocational services?

Correctional administrators, and correctional programmes themselves, must operate in multifaceted domains to serve the various purposes of sentencing, and this generally creates contradictions in the organisational goals and culture. The administrators are charged with the responsibility of addressing the punishment *vs* rehabilitation cultures that often clash when difficult decisions are made. Henderson and Taxman (2009) examined how correctional administrators consider the importance of providing substance abuse treatment services to offenders compared to other typical programmes and services in correctional systems. Table 9.2 provides the number and percentage of respondents reporting how important a given service was considered to be: much less important (scored as 1) to much more important (scored as 5). The following services that correctional administrators are often required to provide or refer offenders to were considered educational/GED training, (2) HIV/AIDS treatment, (3) mental health counselling, (4) vocational training, (5) life skills training, (6) transitional housing, (7) work assignment, (8) community service, (9) criminal thinking therapy, and (10) job placement. With few exceptions (for example, community service, transitional housing, and work assignment), approximately half of the administrators rated the programmes and services as equally important as substance abuse treatment.

The relative ambiguity about substance abuse treatment is likely due to the inherent tension involved in resolving goals, as well as the lack of specificity of the correctional administrators about the importance of any one type of intervention. This lack of specificity means that the administrator is less likely to commit their organisation to any specific programming, which illustrates less organisational commitment than would be desired in the efforts to implement EBPs that focus on addressing substance use disorders, which are prevalent among the offender population. That is, if administrators are ambivalent about a specific type of programming, it means that they are less likely to be willing to commit to that style of reform. For example, administrators who are ambivalent about substance abuse treatment programming are less likely to also support criminal thinking therapies, mental health counselling or other interventions. It appears that these administrators are more likely to follow trends in the field without committing the organisation to an investment in one specific programming. And, for reforms that involve multiple steps, often with conflicting and contradictory support, this means that the reform is less likely to be sustained over time.

As shown in Table 9.3, administrators in the *high substance abuse treatment importance* class (using latent class models) reported that their facilities were using more EBPs than those in the *moderate low*

Table 9.2 Importance of clinical and justice services relative to substance abuse treatment.

	N	%
Education/GED training		
Much less important	12	1.2
Somewhat less important	53	12.3
Same importance	199	46.3
Somewhat more important	91	21.2
Much more important	70	16.3
HIV/AIDS treatment		
Much less important	27	6.3
Somewhat less important	84	19.5
Same importance	217	50.5
Somewhat more important	59	13.7
Much more important	35	8.1
Mental health counselling		
Much less important	2	.5
Somewhat less important	27	6.3
Same importance	226	52.6
Somewhat more important	111	25.8
Much more important	61	14.2
Vocational training		
Much less important	16	3.7
Somewhat less important	114	26.5
Same importance	188	43.7
Somewhat more important	72	16.7
Much more important	31	7.2
Life skills training		
Much less important	17	4.0
Somewhat less important	87	20.2
Same importance	220	51.2
Somewhat more important	65	15.1
Much more important	37	8.6
Transitional housing		
Much less important	44	10.2
Somewhat less important	127	29.5
Same importance	171	39.8

	N	%
Somewhat more important	57	13.3
Much more important	18	4.2
Work assignment		
Much less important	73	17.0
Somewhat less important	164	38.1
Same importance	131	30.5
Somewhat more important	37	8.6
Much more important	10	2.3
Community service		
Much less important	97	22.6
Somewhat less important	162	37.7
Same importance	119	27.7
Somewhat more important	27	6.3
Much more important	13	3.0
Criminal thinking therapy		
Much less important	41	9.5
Somewhat less important	84	19.5
Same importance	199	46.3
Somewhat more important	62	14.4
Much more important	29	6.7
Job placement		
Much less important	28	6.5
Somewhat less important	109	25.3
Same importance	173	40.2
Somewhat more important	72	16.7
Much more important	38	8.8
Facility type		
Adult	289	67.2
Juvenile	141	32.8
State prison	255	59.3
County jail or probation/parole	175	40.7
	N	%
Region of United States		
South	164	38.1
West	113	26.3
Northeast	81	18.8
Midwest	72	16.7

Table 9.2 (continued)

	N	%
EBP use (*M, SD*)	−0.45	1.02
Punishment attitudes (*M, SD*)	4.54	0.49
Rehabilitation attitudes (*M, SD*)	2.46	0.87

Source: Henderson and Taxman (2009).

substance abuse treatment importance class (*pseudo z* = 2.01, *p* < .05). Administrators in the *high substance abuse treatment importance* class were also more likely to work in correctional programmes operating in jails and probation and parole offices (*pseudo z* = 2.09, *p* < .05) than administrators in the *moderate low substance abuse treatment importance* class.[1]

Administrators in the *equal importance* class (ambivalent) reported that their facilities used marginally more EBPs than those in the *moderate low substance abuse treatment importance* class (*pseudo z* = 1.79, *p* < .10). The ambivalent administrators are more likely to be in southern regions (*pseudo z* = −2.33, *p* < .05). Relative to administrators in the high substance abuse treatment importance class, administrators in this ambivalent group reported more favourable attitudes towards offender rehabilitation (*pseudo z* = 2.95, *p* < .01), which illustrates that they are seeking socially desirable behaviours. Favourable attitudes towards offender rehabilitation were also marginally higher in the *equal importance* than the *moderate low substance abuse treatment importance* class (*pseudo z* = 1.83, *p* < .10).

What type of reform strategy advances the use of EBPs in correctional settings?

In another chapter in this book (see Chapter 20) Taxman, Henderson and Lerch report on the style of reform that facilitates the adoption of EBP. We discuss three reform strategies: (1) a focus on treatment and treatment programming; (2) an emphasis on offender accountability and treatment intertwined with accountability; and (3) no particular philosophy. Administrators seeking a style of reform that focuses on clinical interventions – advancing more treatments and treatment processes within the setting – are more likely to adopt EBPs than those who focus on reforms that focus on holding the offender accountable or no particular focus. This emphasis on accountability seems to accentuate the efforts to use controls that often do not complement treatment services. The results found that agencies that adhere to a criminal justice reform strategy are less likely to adopt evidence-based practices.

Table 9.3 Coefficients, standard errors, and pseudo z statistics for class correlates.

Variable	Coefficient	Standard error	*Pseudo* z value
Class 1 (moderate) vs Class 2 (high)			
EBP use	0.43	0.21	2.01*
Rehabilitation attitudes	−0.28	0.41	−0.67
Punishment/deterrence attitudes	−0.21	0.24	−0.88
Adult or juvenile facility	0.07	0.39	0.18
State vs county facility	0.80	0.38	2.09*
Southern, Midwestern and Northeastern states vs Western states	−0.60	0.43	−1.39
Southern, Western and Northeastern states vs Midwestern states	0.85	0.66	1.28
Southern, Western and Midwestern states vs Northeastern states	0.39	0.49	0.80
Class 1 (moderate) vs Class 3 (low)			
EBP use	0.13	0.26	0.50
Rehabilitation attitudes	1.01	0.66	1.55
Punishment/deterrence attitudes	0.32	0.37	0.87
Adult or juvenile facility	0.54	0.53	1.02
State vs county facility	0.24	0.51	0.47
Southern, Midwestern and Northeastern states vs Western states	−1.23	0.67	−1.85
Southern, Western and Northeastern states vs Midwestern states	−0.76	0.82	−0.93
Southern, Western and Midwestern states vs Northeastern states	−1.11	0.77	−1.44
Class 1 (moderate) vs Class 4 (equal importance)			
EBP use	0.44	0.25	1.79
Rehabilitation attitudes	0.80	0.44	1.83
Punishment/deterrence attitudes	0.07	0.24	0.28
Adult or juvenile facility	−0.03	0.41	−0.07
State vs county facility	0.49	0.40	1.23
Southern, Midwestern and Northeastern states vs Western states	−1.11	0.48	−2.33*
Southern, Western and Northeastern states vs Midwestern states	−0.48	0.86	−0.56
Southern, Western and Midwestern states vs Northeastern states	−0.67	0.52	−1.28

Variable	Coefficient	Standard error	*Pseudo* z value
Class 2 (high) vs Class 3 (low)			
EBP use	−0.30	0.21	−1.43
Rehabilitation attitudes	1.29	0.68	1.90
Punishment/deterrence attitudes	0.53	0.40	1.33
Adult or juvenile facility	0.48	0.49	0.97
State vs county facility	−0.56	0.48	−1.16
Southern, Midwestern and Northeastern states vs Western states	−0.63	0.63	−1.00
Southern, Western and Northeastern states vs Midwestern states	−1.61	0.64	−2.53*
Southern, Western and Midwestern states vs Northeastern states	−1.50	0.66	−2.29*
Class 2 (high) vs Class 4 (equal importance)			
EBP use	0.02	0.19	0.08
Rehabilitation attitudes	1.07	0.37	2.95**
Punishment/deterrence attitudes	0.28	0.20	1.37
Adult or juvenile facility	−0.10	0.37	−0.27
State vs county facility	−0.31	0.38	−0.80
Southern, Midwestern and Northeastern states vs Western states	−0.51	0.47	−1.09
Southern, Western and Northeastern states vs Midwestern states	−1.32	0.51	−2.58**
Southern, Western and Midwestern states vs Northeastern states	−1.06	0.42	−2.49**
Class 3 (low) vs Class 4 (equal importance)			
EBP use	0.32	0.22	1.44
Rehabilitation attitudes	−0.21	0.63	−0.33
Punishment/deterrence attitudes	−0.25	0.35	−0.72
Adult or juvenile facility	−0.58	0.47	−1.21
State vs county facility	0.25	0.46	0.55
Southern, Midwestern and Northeastern states vs Western states	0.12	0.57	0.21
Southern, Western and Northeastern states vs Midwestern states	0.28	0.71	0.40
Southern, Western and Midwestern states vs Northeastern states	0.44	0.68	0.65

Notes: Class 1 = moderate substance abuse treatment importance; Class 2 = high substance abuse treatment importance; Class 3 = very low substance abuse treatment; Class 4 = equal importance.
*p < .050 **p < .01.
Source: Henderson and Taxman (2009).

Discussion: consistency, constancy and chaos

The research findings above reveal that the type of leader affects the adoption or implementation of EBPs. But it appears that leaders can be either transformational (have a vision) or transactional (provide a good role model); both can have an impact if they have a positive attitude towards adoption of evidence-based practice (Aarons 2006). And, even the most charismatic and committed leaders can fail at EBP adoption without attention to the social networks within their organisations and the attention to the issues related to the diffusion of innovations.

Across the various studies, we have learned that the decision to adopt is more likely to occur when administrators have a background in human services and have knowledge of evidence-based practices. The study findings reveal that the administrators who are spearheading reforms also must have a belief in rehabilitation concepts as well as a commitment to providing treatment services. That is, the findings demonstrate that the style of leadership may not be as important as the emphasis on the 'message' successful in the adoption and implementation process. Administrators thus control the message about the importance of the EBPs framework through the decisions that they make. Being consistent about the message of the value of EBPs, working through the difficult chaos related to the change processes within a punishment focused culture, being constant about the need to be focused on outcomes and outputs, and appear to be facilitative drivers to uptake of EBPs in these settings. As indicated by Rogers (2003), the message is important, as well as engaging the organisation (employees at all levels and external stakeholders) in the design, decisions, implementation and refinement process. The implementation journey should involve all members of the organisation with the goal of re-engineering the operational processes. The effective transition to EBP should be considered a team sport. To this end, it is important to consider the lessons that experts in management and change processes offer. William Bridges asserts that there are three phases employees experience in the innovation diffusion process (see Figure 9.2): (1) ending, losing, letting go; (2) the neutral zone; and (3) the new beginning. The names implicitly describe the feelings experienced during each phase.

This model helps consider some of the options of avoiding the chaos and tensions that occur within the periods of diffusion and uptake. It may start with throwing out the policy manual but must continue by helping to develop the organisation to be responsive and to embrace the components of EBPs. This includes the focus on quality over process – the notion that quality components are implicit in EBPs. As previously discussed, an important part of the RNR model is not just using the risk and need assessment tools but how the tools are

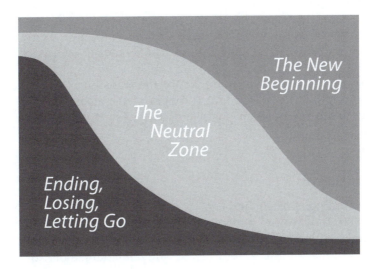

Figure 9.2 Emotional intelligence in organisational change.

1 Letting go of the old ways and the old identity people had. This first phase is an ending, and the time when you need to help people to deal with their losses.
2 Going through an in-between time when the old is gone but the new isn't fully operational. We call this time the 'neutral zone': it's when the critical psychological realignments and repatternings take place.
3 Coming out of the transition and making a new beginning. This is when people develop the new identity, experience the new energy, and discover the new sense of purpose that make the change begin to work.

used with offenders. Research confirms the importance of building rapport between offenders and professional workers as an important component to offender change, and to effectively use risk and need assessment tools there is a need to focus on the working relationship with the offender (Taxman and Ainsworth 2009).

Drawing on the work of Kouzes and Posner (2007) and Patterson *et al.* (2008) we propose a five-step methodology for guiding the transition journey to full usage of evidence-based principles and practices for internal operations and supervision and treatment protocols. These features are designed to ensure that the message is consistent and constant, and that the chaos can be reduced through clear messaging:

Vision and mission embrace EBP and all employees know how their duties and responsibilities contribute to achieving the vision and mission.
Abolish duties that do not advance the transition to EBP.
Learning culture is standard throughout the agency.
Illuminate progress on goals and objectives inside and outside the agency.
Data drives mid-course adjustments to policy and practice.

Vision and mission

Study findings clearly indicate that the values of the correctional administrator are important in the adoption of EBPs. Formal vision and mission statements need to be aligned to the new innovations, but also reflect these values. These are the main tools to advance the adoption of EBPs since they provide visible signs that the organisation is moving forward. To ensure maximum buy-in and speedy implementation, a broad cross-section of employees should be involved in revisiting and refining the vision or mission of the organisation to incorporate the EBPs. The employees workgroup also should consider how the refined vision, mission and values statements require redefinition of duties and responsibilities of core functions.

Abolish duties that do not advance the transition to EBP

A major component of reducing chaos is to abolish the work that is unrelated to the core processes of the EBPs. A process to reduce unnecessary work offers an important and positive message to the organisation. It concentrates energy around implementation of the core EBP components and illustrates that the organisation is genuinely committed to the key components associated with EBPs. This step includes an examination of how resources are committed to evidence-based policy and practice and redirects resources from policies and practices that contradict or interfere with EBP implementation. Organisations also should ensure that their EBP implementation plan identifies regular intervals for reviewing current practice and identifying duties that are not advancing EBP.

A related component is the need to communicate with external stakeholders (law enforcement agencies, the courts, parole boards, treatment and other service providers) to ensure that they stand by the efforts to advance EBPs in the community corrections agencies as well as the other criminal justice agencies. Since criminal justice agencies are intended to function as system, changes made by one agency affect the entire system's effectiveness.

Learning culture is standard throughout agency

One feature identified by the Rasch model was that the implementation of EBPs requires the creation of a learning culture, where the goal is to foster a risk-taking environment through the engagement of the organisation in a desire to seek knowledge and then apply the information to the operations. Bridges (2003) presents a model to consider how to support employees through all three stages of the transition process. By adopting the philosophy of 'learning for a living', this will create the opportunity to implement EBP as practitioners and researches learn more about effective interventions. A key component of creating a learning culture is for the organisation to be focused on professional development. That is, the emphasis should be placed on creating a culture where decision-making is diffused through the organisation and the employees recognise themselves as professionals.

Professional development extends the concept of training to include skill development and decision-making. The emphasis should be on a process that involves learning, practice, reinforcement, coaching, and mentoring with feedback. This process will ensure that employees develop the professional judgement to be decision-makers (Burke and Hutchins 2007). This intuition is only developed through a reinforcement of the importance of the EBPs.

Illuminate progress on goals and objectives inside and outside the agency

A major focus of organisational commitment is transparency, where the benchmarks and progress are clearly articulated and publicised inside the agency, with stakeholders and the general public. All data should be open to the public to ensure that the focus is on achieving the specified performance. This provides a public statement supporting the advancement of the EBPs. Leaders should take note that the agency's professional development efforts may need to include data interpretation as well as coaching from supervisors until field employees become accustomed to using data tools.

Data drives mid-course adjustments to policy and practice

The EBP model focuses on fine-tuning the organisation and its processes consistent with science. Compstat (Burrell and Gelb 2007) and other efforts have shown that regularly focusing on and discussing data (drug test results, employment, contacts met, or other conditions that indicate positive outcomes from offenders) can influence the performance of an organisation; in fact this data is useful to make incremental and significant alterations to the business process. By providing data it improves the knowledge of the organisation about key processes, besides providing the key tools to improve performance. The organisation can shift to certain goals and objectives that are consistent with the EBP goals. Data can reinforce the importance of organisational processes being innovative in their networks to pilot new processes that demonstrate consistency in EBPs.

Leadership can manage the chaos associated with the myriad demands of adopting EBPs throughout an organisation. As shown through the studies described in this chapter, correctional administrators are the key to sustaining the forward motion of the reinvention process. For each challenge, the commitment to EBP is tested as the organisation and employees make the journey to the EBP way of doing business.

Conclusion

The 'what works' framework has provided an opportunity to integrate science into practice. The messages and methods that administrators use are important to reinforce the 'why are we doing this' concerns that typically exist in change processes. Chaos occurs in this 'why' since there is hesitancy within the organisation and across external partners as to the value of using EBPs. And, there is a greater concern that the journey will be worthwhile. Administrators need to believe that the path that they are taking is important – and the decisions that they make will provide visible evidence to others as to their commitment. Being mindful of this journey will ensure that the EBP mindset is 'made to stick'.

Acknowledgements

Original funding from this study came from Grant U01 DA016213-01 (Action Research to Advance Drug Treatment in the CJS) which includes funding from the Bureau of Justice Assistance, Center for Substance Abuse Treatment, Center for Disease Control and Prevention, and National Institute on Alcohol Abuse and Alcholism. The contents are solely the responsibility of the authors and do not necessarily represent the official views of NIH/NIDA or other federal government agencies.

Note

1 We conducted the analyses separating jails and probation and parole departments using dummy coding procedures with prisons as the reference group, but the results were not statistically significant.

References

Aarons, G.A. (2006) 'Transformational and transactional leadership: association with attitudes toward evidence-based practice', *Psychiatric Services*, 57 (8): 1162–9. PubMed PMID: 16870968; PubMed Central PMCID: PMC1876730.

Andrews, D.A. and Bonta, J. (1998) *The Psychology of Criminal Conduct*, 2nd edn. Cincinatti, OH: Anderson.

Bridges, W. (2003) *Managing Transitions: Making the Most of Change*, 2nd edn. Boston: Nicholas Brealey Publishing.

Burke, L.A. and Hutchins, H.H. (2007) 'Training transfer: an integrative literature review', *Human Resource Development Review*, 6: 263–96. doi: 10.1177/1534484307303035.

Burrell, W. and Gelb, A. (2007) *You Get What You Measure: Compstat for Community Corrections*. Philadelphia: Pew Charitable Trusts, Public Safety Performance. Online at: www.pewtrusts.org/uploadedFiles/wwwpewtrustsorg/Reports/sentencing_and_corrections/corrections-measurement.pdf.

Fletcher, B.W., Lehman, W.E., Wexler, H.K., Melnick, G., Taxman, F.S. and Young, D.W. (2009) 'Measuring collaboration and integration activities in criminal justice and substance abuse treatment agencies', *Drug and Alcohol Dependence*, 103 (Suppl. 1): S54–S64 (doi: http://dx.doi.org/10.1016/j.drugalcdep.2009.01.001).

Friedmann, P.D., Taxman, F.S. and Henderson, C.E. (2007) 'Evidence-based treatment practices for drug-involved adults in the criminal justice system', *Journal of Substance Abuse Treatment*, 32(3): 267–77.

Garland, D. (2001) *The Culture of Control: Crime and Social Order in Contemporary Society*. Chicago: University of Chicago Press.

Henderson, C. and Taxman, F.S. (2009) 'Competing values among criminal justice administrators: the importance of substance abuse treatment', *Drug and Alcohol Dependence*, 103 (Suppl. 1): S7–S16.

Henderson, C.E., Taxman, F.S. and Young, D.W. (2008) 'A Rasch model analysis of evidence-based treatment practices used in the criminal justice system', *Drug and Alcohol Dependence*, 93 (1–2): 163-75. Epub 2007 Oct 29. PubMed PMID: 18029116; PubMed Central PMCID: PMC2293644.

Kouzes, J. and Posner, B. (2007) *The Leadership Challenge*, 4th edn. San Francisco: Jossey-Bass.

National Institute on Drug Abuse (NIDA) (2000) *Principles of Drug Addiction Treatment: A Research Based Guide*. (NIH Publication No. 99-4180). Rockville, MD: National Institute of Health.

Patterson, K., Grenny, J., Maxfield, D., McMillan, R. and Switzer, A. (2008). *Influencer.* New York: McGraw-Hill.

Rasch, G. (1960) *Probabilistic Models for Some Intelligence and Attainment Tests*. Danish Institute for Educational Research.

Rogers, E.M. (2003) *Diffusion of Innovations*, 5th edn. New York: Free Press.

Taxman, F.S., Young, D., Wiersma, B., Mitchell, S. and Rhodes, A.G. (2007) 'The national criminal justice treatment practices survey: multilevel survey methods and procedures', *Journal of Substance Abuse Treatment*, 32 (3): 225–38.

Taxman, F.S. and Ainsworth, S. (2009) 'Correctional milieu: the key to quality outcomes', *Victims and Offenders*, 4 (4): 334–40.

Chapter 10

Can structured programmes improve one-to-one supervision?

Pauline Durrance, Nigel Hosking and Nancy Thorburn

In their major study of community supervision, 'Exploring the black box of community supervision', Bonta and colleagues found that although 'cognitive behavioural methods appear to have been most effective in bringing about change in offenders', there was limited evidence of them being used in supervision (Bonta *et al.* 2008). Bonta's 'black box' reflects the intrinsic difficulties in probing into what actually goes on within the relatively private world of one-to-one supervision and the barriers that these raise to its evaluation. In order to make an assessment of whether something is or is not successful one has to be able to form a cogent picture of what that something is.

Referring to Losel's finding that multi-modal, skills-oriented interventions result in larger effects, Burnett (2004) makes the point that these approaches could equally be incorporated within a group-work context or carried out on a one-to-one basis. However, the route taken in England and Wales since the introduction of accredited programmes in 2000 has been to deliver this type of work within a group-work setting. As accredited group-work programmes became embedded, there was a parallel shift away from probation officers – or offender managers as they were now known – carrying out offence-focused work during one-to-one supervision. Offender managers were now expected to assume a brokering role, referring offenders to programme tutors and an army of partnership workers to do the kind of work that they had previously carried out themselves. Unsurprisingly this left some staff feeling relatively deskilled.

However, the growing evidence from the desistance research (for example, Rex 1999; Farrall and Calverley 2005; Ward and Maruna 2007) has reasserted the crucial role played by the offender manager in developing a relationship with the offender, incorporating traditional social work values of warmth, empathy, optimism, loyalty and trust. The notion of 'case work' and the 'therapeutic alliance' is, therefore, re-emerging.

This chapter, through providing an account of the introduction of the Structured Supervision Programme (SSP) within London Probation, sets out to explore the merits of using a structured approach within a one-to-one setting. Three key features usually associated with group-work programmes were here employed within the context of a one-to-one intervention, these being structure (provided through a broadly cognitive behavioural approach), training (in the use of programme material), and the subsequent treatment management of practice. Relying heavily on the reactions of staff and offenders to working with the programme, it will seek to capture the issues that have emerged as SSP beds down into practice.

History of the SSP

SSP was originally developed by two senior probation officers seconded from London Probation to the Romanian probation service as part of a European twinning project. Romanian managers had felt that staff might benefit from the guidance that a structured one-to-one programme could provide. Probation officers' feedback following the initial pilot was so positive that the service decided to roll out the programme across the whole country. On returning to the UK the relevance of the Romanian experience became apparent. Offender managers, concerned about the large number of individuals with no programme requirement, or on licences so short they could not engage with programme work, were requesting a structured one-to-one approach to help focus supervision.

Whereas in an earlier era the content of training and induction into practice should have ensured that staff felt able to work confidently with offenders on a one-to-one basis, this was not necessarily true for staff recruited more recently or who had taken different training routes into the service. The need for an intervention like SSP appeared to be clear-cut with the impetus coming from front-line staff rather than management.

Given that many promising approaches flounder due to issues relating to implementation, it was fortunate that the identified need for SSP coincided with a local initiative running at the time within the London Borough of Southwark. The Model Borough constituted an attempt by probation staff within one London borough to think through the range of initiatives that would need to be available if an effective service were to be provided to the broad range of offenders being supervised within this inner London borough. SSP was adopted as one of the Model Borough projects. As in Romania, positive feedback from both staff and offenders led to a decision to extend the pilot to a number of other London boroughs. Again, this new pilot was timely as it coincided with the government allocating additional funding to probation areas to spend on projects that might contribute to reducing the short-term prison population. The roll-out of SSP beyond Southwark was one of the beneficiaries of this larger project. While, arguably, this could have happened without the initiative, these extra resources made it possible to recruit a dedicated custodian of the programme, someone with time to think through and resolve implementation issues. As one of the authors of the programme, he also had a pre-established interest in ensuring its success.

Theoretical approach

In common with most group-work programmes, SSP draws from a broad range of cognitive behavioural theories that have been expounded at length elsewhere (Andrews 1995; Bonta and Andrews, this volume). These stress the interdependence of perceptions, thoughts, feelings and behaviours and argue that through changing thoughts it may be possible to exert some impact on feelings and behaviours. Offending is seen as learned behaviour which is influenced by personal and social factors. The work of Ellis (1962), Bandura (1975) and others has, therefore, been drawn together to inform techniques by which offenders can be helped to look critically at their perceptions, expectations and beliefs about how the world is and how it should be. Working on the assumption that recidivist offenders are likely to lack certain cognitive skills and/or have developed inappropriate ways of behaving, addressing these constitutes a central focus of SSP.

Encouraging offenders to develop new approaches to problem-solving and helping them reflect on habitual ways of relating to others have also been drawn into the mix. Two studies suggest that desistance is likely to be related to the way offenders think about their problems as well as their social situations. Zamble and Quinsey (1997) in a study of ex-prisoners in Canada showed that whether they reoffended or not depended to some extent on their state of mind and level of optimism about their ability to deal effectively with the problems they encountered. Maruna's (2001) study of offenders in Liverpool shows that whether people see themselves as in control of their lives, and therefore responsible for what happens to them, or as victims of circumstance, tends to be related to the likelihood of reoffending. In other words, repeat offenders often don't recognise themselves as being responsible for their circumstances, whereas offenders who desist tend to be able to develop strategies for addressing their problems without offending (Vanstone 2007).

Where SSP may stray from most group-work approaches, however, is in drawing more fully on attachment theory with its acknowledgement of the deep-seated roots of much maladaptive behaviour. In her recent paper, Ansbro (2008) refocuses attention on the relevance of attachment theory to offending. Though this relevance has rarely been denied, more recently it has struggled to make itself felt within the content of structured interventions.

> Many of our clients are not being wilfully obtuse when they seem oblivious to others' situations, whether it is their own partner or the victim of the robbery. Developments of the self reflective capacity with the assistance of a Probation worker offering a taste of a secure base, add to, and complement, a cognitive behavioural understanding of empathy. (Ansbro 2008: 239)

Arguably, the potential for offering 'a taste of a secure base' should be easier to achieve within a one-to-one rather than a group-work context. SSP programme material aims to foster this, with early exercises focusing on exploring the offender's own personal history. These provide a clear message that the focus of attention will be on them and their experience and that these experiences constitute acceptable material to discuss within supervision. It is by no means obvious whether offenders are always aware of where the parameters of what can be discussed within supervision lie.

SSP also draws upon the Good Lives Model (GLM) developed by Ward and Maruna (2007). The GLM describes a strengths-based approach to rehabilitation, the aim being to enhance an individual's capacity to live a meaningful, constructive and happy life free from further criminal actions. The GLM assumes that offenders share the same inclinations and basic needs as other people and are naturally predisposed to seek certain goals or aspects of a 'good life', such as creativity, physical health and mastery. Criminal actions are thought to occur when individuals lack the internal and external resources to attain their goals in pro-social ways.

Ward and Maruna (2007) suggest that if individuals are to desist from offending, they should be helped to develop the knowledge, skills and resources they, like anyone, would need in order to live a 'good life' that reflects their own preferences, interest and values. It is assumed that because criminogenic needs and human needs are causally related, the promotion of these goals should also reduce dynamic risk factors. Thus, a major aim of correctional reintegration work is to help individuals construct a life plan that can help them to achieve these goals without inflicting harm on others. The GLM is interwoven throughout the whole of SSP with the prospect of defining and working out ways to realise goals being used as the motivation for changing to a lifestyle that does not include offending.

Content of SSP

As we have already seen, SSP is a one-to-one programme that offender managers can use to structure supervision sessions, usually in cases where there is no group-work programme requirement. It is anticipated that the 12 SSP sessions, each taking approximately one hour, will be undertaken at the start of the order, when the expectation is that offenders will be seen weekly. The aim is to help offenders alter their behaviour by acquiring new skills and to change or 'reframe' the accompanying thoughts, attitudes and beliefs that may sabotage their attempts to achieve pro-social personal goals.

The 12 sessions are contained within five modules, the content of each one building upon the previous ones. The approach, therefore, is very much one of structured 'building blocks' rather than a collection of pick-and-mix exercises.

Module One is essentially motivational and comprises two sessions. The first is centred round an autobiographical exercise, which provides both a personal history and an opportunity for the offender manager and offender to establish a working relationship. Further exercises explore attitudes and beliefs and link these to thoughts, feelings and behaviours. The second session focuses on explaining the motivational cycle and getting participants to locate themselves on it. Participants are then encouraged to set realistic and measurable goals. Thoughts, feelings and behaviour are then considered in relation to their offence.

Module Two focuses on problem-solving and assertive communication. Given that these are core skills that will underpin most offenders' attempts to move on, they are spread over four sessions. In order to make these sessions as meaningful as possible, staff are encouraged to refer to issues arising from the offender's assessment and current problems. The content is based on well-established and familiar approaches to problem-solving, commencing with problem awareness and continuing with early recognition, distinguishing fact from opinion, generating alternative solutions, consequential thinking and perspective taking.

With building blocks in place, the two sessions that make up Module Three revisit the participant's goals and the cycle of change. This time the focus is on self-talk and how unhelpful thoughts can be changed to provide a more positive self-narrative. Worksheets are used to explore the idea in the abstract, before focusing on the participant's own thinking.

Though perspective-taking is implicit throughout SSP, the session covered in Module Four specifically focuses on victim awareness and empathy. Participants are encouraged to think about their own experience as victims before going on to think of who were the direct and indirect victims of their offences and what the likely effects may have been.

The remaining three sessions make up Module Five and focus on planning to avoid relapse, signposting to community resources and thinking through what the participant needs to achieve after the end of the programme. The concepts of lapse and relapse are introduced and individuals encouraged to think about what factors in their lives might serve as triggers. The final session revisits goals and the motivational cycle and together the participant and offender manager work out what any future supervision sessions might include.

It is anticipated that SSP practice will evolve as new ideas emerging from the research literature become incorporated into practice. Already a further, gender-specific programme, has been produced with material reworked to reflect a more female perspective and with sessions focusing on budgeting, emotions and relationships added. SSP for Women has been designed to address concerns that cognitive behavioural programmes, by underplaying social factors, tend to be relatively insensitive to the needs of women (Rex 2002). As Baroness

Corston observes 'relationship problems feature strongly in women's pathways to crime' (Corston 2007: 6) and 'coercion by men can form a route into criminal activity for some women'. In order to be responsive to the needs of women, therefore, programmes need to address these issues.

In much the same way as group-work programmes, SSP is contained within a manual that contains accompanying worksheets. A theory manual, guidance notes, information leaflets, homework and assignments building up to nationally-validated and employer-recognised awards were all features common to other programme work. In the context of group-work programmes, structure has sometimes been equated with inflexibility, the need to follow a programme of work limiting the extent to which staff feel able to respond to the needs of particular individuals. A central question any evaluation of SSP would need to answer would be whether undertaking the work on a one-to-one basis could help circumvent some of these perceived limitations. Crucially, does structure in one-to-one supervision facilitate the building of good relationships between offender managers and offenders or detract from it?

Supporting programme delivery

From the very beginning, the developers of SSP acknowledged that merely providing programme materials would not be sufficient to engage offenders if certain skills were not present in the staff delivering them. The NOMS offender management model states that programmes based upon 'what works' principles are most effective when the staff delivering them deploy a set of behaviours that researchers have labelled 'core correctional practices'. Dowden and Andrews (2004) identify the required five behaviour clusters as being the firm, fair and clear use of authority; the modelling of pro-social and anti-criminal attitudes, cognitions and behaviours; the teaching of concrete problem-solving skills; the use of community resources; and the formation of and working through, warm, open and enthusiastic relationships.

Thinking through ways in which these could be developed was, therefore, essential to the introduction of SSP. A first step was to specify that to be eligible for training, staff should have previously passed the core curriculum training and been trained in motivational interviewing. Ongoing support was provided through action learning sets, fora within which offender managers delivering SSP could meet and get to know each other, discuss practical issues and share knowledge.

A further means of support and development work came about through transplanting the concept of treatment management commonly practised in group-work settings to one-to-one work. Treatment management fulfils two main functions. First, it seeks to ensure that staff members are carrying out the programme work as envisaged by the developers. This usually involves video-recording programme sessions, reviewing these recordings against a checklist, and feeding back learning points to staff. This connects to its second function, that of developing the skills staff use when delivering the programme material. Treatment management, therefore, holds real potential for ongoing training, recognising and building on strengths and identifying instances where coaching might be necessary.

Inevitably, treatment management of one-to-one work raises challenges that may be less problematic in the case of group-work programmes. Sessions are more diffuse in terms of when and where they take place than group-work sessions, making the installation of video equipment common to group-work programmes impractical. SSP addressed these issues by using voice-recording equipment, which appears to work remarkably well, intonation allowing treatment managers to gain a good impression of the interaction between staff and offenders (see also Raynor *et al.* this volume).

This scenario of a treatment-managed, structured one-to-one approach, therefore, offered a rare opportunity to look inside Bonta and colleagues' 'black box' of supervision. The structure of the programme provides information on what should be happening within the private world of supervision with monitoring being addressed through treatment management.

Evaluation of SSP

As part of the process of introducing SSP into London Probation, the developers commissioned the London Probation research department to carry out an initial, limited evaluation. Evaluating work that is still developing can be problematic. Commissioners understandably want to know whether the work is effective. Yet to answer questions around effectiveness it is necessary to build up a critical mass of cases. This will only be achieved if enough staff can be encouraged to work with the new material. It also has to be accepted that at this early developmental stage it may be necessary to make changes both to the programme itself and the processes surrounding it. A full evaluation carried out at an early stage may, therefore, reflect a situation that has already moved on.

It was agreed between the programme manager and the research department, therefore, that an initial evaluation would focus on collating information on referrals, starts and completion rates, the completion rates being used as an indicator of offender engagement. This was to be augmented by interviews with staff and offenders working with SSP, including those who had been trained but not yet started working with the programme material. These interviews would focus on their experiences of the programme material, how they felt it compared to other approaches to supervision and issues they felt would need to be addressed if the new initiative were to bed down into practice. It was acknowledged that the best way to 'grow' SSP into the critical mass of cases needed to support a full evaluation would be to determine whether those already involved felt that there were real benefits to be had from working with the programme and to feed this back to other practitioners in the organisation on an ongoing basis.

Targeting of SSP

The SSP targeting criteria provided to staff were relatively broad. Some reflected the purpose and content of the programme (the inclusion of offenders with no accredited programme requirement and offenders having an established pattern of offending); others related to risk. The risk-need-responsivity principle, which has guided much probation work in recent years, states that the intensity of interventions should reflect the level of risk posed by an individual, that they should target relevant crime-related needs and be delivered in a way that has meaning for the offender (Ward and Maruna 2007). In line with this, high risk of harm offenders were excluded, as were those convicted for domestic violence and sexual offences. Offenders with medium to high risk of reoffending scores were included. However, offender managers could also include individuals who fell below the specified level of risk if they could demonstrate that they had problems that would be addressed by the programme material (lifestyle and associates; attitudes; thinking and behaviour; emotional well-being; and relationships).

We accept that this approach to targeting could lead to practice deviating from the risk-need-responsivity principle by including offenders who would be regarded as at low risk of reoffending. Research has suggested that relatively intensive interventions can lead to an escalation in reoffending in low risk offenders (Andrews and Dowden 2006). However, SSP, by adopting a 'strengths-based' forward-looking approach, may minimise the risks of converting the low risk individual into a confirmed offender, which their offending behaviour to date may not justify. Further evaluation could explore this in more detail. It also has to be remembered that the offenders undertaking SSP are subject to court orders that include a supervision element. The intention is to maximise the impact of this requirement.

Getting offenders onto the programme

Prior experience has suggested that attendance at training events does not always translate into subsequent changes in practice. In order to try and avert this possibility, a condition of attendance at the training was that each member of staff trained would be allocated two offenders with whom they could work using SSP material. Despite this stipulation and the existence of many suitable candidates, three months after training the 79 offenders engaged with SSP was considerably less than might have been expected, given that 116 staff had been trained.

The relatively low number of offenders allocated to SSP gave rise to concern, especially given the broad selection criteria and the availability of treatment managers to advise on the suitability of cases. It soon became apparent that the likelihood of an offender manager starting to use SSP diminished dramatically with the time elapsed since training. One treatment manager noted a 'build-up of resistance' and 'general scepticism', sometimes explained in terms of the difficulties of managing high caseloads. What is interesting, however, is that these same offender managers reported having found the training very useful and using some elements of it with offenders who had not been allocated to the intervention.

Confidence levels appeared to constitute another reason for not working with SSP material after training. Some offender managers admitted to an initial lack of confidence, though this dissipated as they progressed with the programme. This would suggest that being encouraged to deliver the programme soon after training might be crucial to embedding the material into everyday practice. Interestingly, it was noted that completion rates tended to be higher if the offender was introduced to SSP as early as possible in the order, preferably signing the contract at their first appointment.

In other instances, as confidence and satisfaction with the programme material grew, some staff members began to take the initiative and identify suitable candidates from among their caseloads, looking to their managers to endorse decisions rather than waiting for them to allocate cases. One trainee probation officer, recognising the potential in the SSP approach, had started using it with nine offenders ranging across offence types and ages. Her personal enthusiasm and her offenders' positive response spoke volumes.

Issues around allocation, however, remain. As senior probation officers are central to the allocation process, understanding any potential reservations they might have about SSP work is crucial. Although training events had not targeted seniors, many had heard about SSP through information leaflets, meetings with treatment managers and presentations at a variety of management meetings. Seniors' reticence appeared to be linked to the high caseloads carried by many offender managers: would their staff have the time to commit to an hour-long intervention over a protracted number of weeks? The expectation that SSP should be carried out in its entirety, that it was not a 'pick-and-choose' exercise, added to these reservations. Interestingly one manager felt that the allocation criteria should be broader, identifying 'a lot of people who would benefit, however, the criteria don't work. We should make SSP available to everyone.' It would appear that some offender managers concurred, as many reported using elements of SSP with offenders who they were supervising but who were not officially allocated to the programme.

Take-up of the programme

The good news, however, was that of those 79 offenders who had been identified, most were either still working with the programme material, had completed the work, or were waiting to begin. SSP was being used successfully across a broad range of offenders: male and female, different ages and ethnicities. One in five offenders referred was female, approximately twice as many as would appear in the remainder of the caseload. This is not surprising as it was always anticipated that the flexibility of SSP would make it particularly suitable for women, many of whom have commitments that make it difficult to attend group-work programmes. As Table 10.1 suggests, however, these problems may not be entirely solved as more women

Table 10.1 Programme status of offenders referred to SSP.

	Total referred	Not yet started	Ongoing	Completed	Failed to complete
Females	16	25%	50%	13%	13%
Males	63	10%	46%	19%	25%

have yet to start SSP. The sample size available at the time of writing, however, can provide only very tentative indications.

The age range of offenders referred to SSP spanned from 18 to over 60 although almost half were aged between 21 and 30. Half the participants identified themselves as White British, a quarter as Black, and Asian offenders were relatively under-represented.

Given the strong focus on managing risk, it is important to note that approximately a third of the offenders identified as suitable for SSP had been convicted of violent offences or offences against the person; theft and handling, driving and drug offences also figured largely (see Table 10.2).

With the same *caveats* about sample size making it inappropriate to draw conclusions, take-up of the programme in relation to offence type is interesting. This suggests that offenders convicted of violent offences may be more likely to engage with SSP than those convicted of theft-related offences. It may be that the issues surrounding the type of instrumental offending suggested by theft-related offences are less well addressed by SSP than those underlying violent offending. A fuller evaluation using a larger sample would be necessary to determine whether this pattern is sustained.

Table 10.2 Programme status in relation to index offence.

	Total referred	Not yet started	Ongoing	Completed	Failed to complete
Offences against the person/violence	27	15%	41%	26%	19%
Theft and handling	21	19%	38%	10%	33%
Drug offences	8	13%	63%	25%	0%
Driving offences	10	10%	70%	10%	10%
Other	13	0%	62%	15%	20%
Total	79	13%	49%	18%	20%

Looking at the reasons underlying why 18 offenders did not complete showed that, in many cases, these were not directly related to programme material (see Table 10.3).

It would appear that issues around referring offenders with substance misuse problems or who have an insufficient command of English to SSP need to be clarified if offenders are not to be set up to fail. The situation of offenders with literacy problems is less clear. While work with some offenders had stopped due to literacy problems, one member of staff had found ways to adapt the programme material to make it more accessible. Using charts to make information more visual or completing 'homework' together within the session itself helped ensure that the work could continue.

The experiences of staff and participants

In order to understand how SSP was being received by staff and offenders it was necessary to move beyond looking at completion rates and explore both staff and offenders' experiences of working with the programme. A number of themes emerged.

One-to-one format

Offenders appeared to react well to the one-to-one format of SSP, the structure keeping both offender manager and offender on track while leaving sufficient flexibility to match the pace of sessions to the offender's ability to grasp and apply key concepts. Some staff dealt with the inevitable issues that arose in their supervisees' lives by delaying sessions. With experience, however, others were recognising the potential of using these issues to personalise the programme material. Most offender managers seemed to find it possible to

Table 10.3 Reasons for non-completion of SSP.

Reason	Number
Language and literacy issues	3
Order expired	5
Moved away from the area	1
Reoffended/breached the order	4
Not motivated to complete SSP	2
Unsuitability due to substance misuse	3

complete most if not all sessions within the hour as intended. With experience, the amount of time taken could be reduced still further. Although this might encourage seniors concerned about staff workload to allocate more offenders to SSP, it is possible that cutting down the time spent working with offenders could jeopardise effectiveness. Further research is needed to confirm this possibility.

Staff felt that the programme material persuaded some offenders to open up more than would have been likely in either a group-work setting or in other approaches to supervision. This increased willingness to disclose information was particularly noticeable when staff had supervised the same offender prior to the introduction of SSP:

> The Personal History Questionnaire brought up a lot of emotions for the offender as she started to talk about her childhood which was upsetting for her. Even though I had supervised this offender on a previous order, I was not aware of the issues which were raised by the questionnaire. (Offender manager)

Offenders with a previous history of probation intervention reported this too, with one stating that he was grateful to have the opportunity to 'air my thoughts and opinions' rather than 'just supervision'. Instead of ascribing this willingness to disclose and explore potentially sensitive issues to either the one-to-one format or the programme material, it would appear that the two are working together. Whereas structured programmes have sometimes been represented as being inflexible to the needs of individuals, in this case it appears that it is the nature of the exercise that is encouraging offenders to disclose sensitive material.

Reactions to programme content

Reaction to the programme material itself was generally good, with the exception of one session which focused on the distinction between fact and opinion. Staff found this session relatively difficult to deliver and some offenders struggled to grasp the concepts. This highlights the need to review the trainers' guidance notes for this session. Offender managers were particularly enthusiastic about the first session's Personal History Questionnaire. Though the nature of the questions sometimes made this exercise 'a little uncomfortable' it proved to be excellent in engaging offenders. This reaction on the part of both offenders and offender managers is interesting and raises questions about whether more target-led approaches to supervision have moved the focus of attention away from the offender's unique experience both past and current to such a degree that some staff no longer feel at ease taking personal histories.

A further issue relating to the programme content stemmed from the fit between the material and targeting criteria. Given that SSP is designed for those with a pattern of general offending, some of the examples and exercises in the manual, understandably, refer to this. This led to some first-time offenders, referred because of needs profiles, feeling that SSP had not been designed for them even though much of the material was relevant.

> I'm not a repeat offender so it was not always relevant. Everything is there, but sometimes too much. I'd recommend it to people who are repeat offenders; I'm not. (SSP participant)

There may be a danger in allowing offenders to feel that some material isn't relevant as this could lead them to distance themselves from the need to address very pertinent issues. Developing a version with examples that do not allude to patterns of offending is being considered. This would seem preferable to excluding first-time offenders from work that could be instrumental in deflecting them from further offending.

At the other end of the spectrum were offenders with previous experience of probation. Reactions varied, with some participants enjoying having previous relevant knowledge and others becoming frustrated and demotivated at having to go over familiar material. As in the case of all probation work, keeping offenders motivated is crucial. A commitment to undertaking SSP at the time of sentence was liable to dissipate as sessions actually started. This reluctance, however, could be short-lived as offenders began to realise the relevance of the programme material:

> Initially, although this offender agreed to engage with SSP, he was very reluctant ... But as we progressed, he slowly began to engage with the sessions and he became more interested in completing the exercises and homework. (Offender manager)

Impact on offenders

Offenders tended to be very enthusiastic about the programme. Even those who felt that they did not really fit within the target group, for example because they were not repeat offenders, said that they would recommend it to others.

> I wouldn't recommend getting on Probation but it's been great. The education, training and employment should go beyond Probation for anyone. (SSP participant)

One offender who had been particularly struck by the material stated that it 'will open your eyes'. The feedback from offenders swings, therefore, between detached acknowledgement and personal enthusiasm for the programme.

Inevitably, not all offenders agreed that SSP was a positive experience, but dissenting voices were few and usually involved offenders who expected the probation service to solve very practical problems. This accentuates the importance of ensuring that participants understand what attendance on SSP can reasonably deliver while recognising that some offenders, whatever they are told, will expect a panacea for their problems.

The majority of comments revealed positive outcomes from SSP, with 13 of the 16 offenders interviewed being able to explain the nature of the impact. These ranged from a generalised effect on everyday life, to specific benefits relating to employment and qualifications, rehabilitation from substance misuse or improved personal relationships. Interestingly, one of the three offenders who felt the impact of SSP had been minimal attributed his lack of progress to his 'situation [being] the problem, not the programme'. Unfortunately a lack of detail in the feedback means the particulars of his 'situation' remain unclear.

Recognising the importance of setting goals appeared to play an important role in helping the offenders move towards addressing their needs. A number described practical achievements which they attributed, at least in part, to this. These included improving their prospects of employment or completing courses and qualifications or, in one case, embarking on a new business venture. Given that 40 per cent of the offenders who had either completed or were still on SSP were known to be unemployed, it is not surprising that qualifications and employment-focused benefits were so often raised at interview.

A number of offender managers attributed positive outcomes to changes in participants' thinking. As one offender manager put it:

> [The offender] does think more consequentially. He is also able to generate options effectively which would suggest that his risk of reoffending is not as high as before. (Offender manager)

Recognising triggers appeared particularly important and could impact on avoiding relapse into drug use and subsequent reoffending:

> SSP helped the offender to think and helped him to address/stop his drug misuse which is a trigger for his offending. (Offender manager)

Both offender managers and offenders described how different facets of the programme were used to avoid lapses into old patterns of behaving, often spontaneously referring to techniques learned on SSP. Several reported experiencing a sense of pride and achievement on realising that they had arrived at the maintenance stage in the cycle of change, accompanied by a desire not to return to what one offender deemed 'square one'. Such accounts accentuate the importance of providing offenders with ways of conceptualising their own behavioural patterns.

In addition to reviewing their past in the preliminary sessions, SSP also invites offenders to consider their aims for the future. One offender found that it was the juxtaposition between the two that was illuminating:

> The Time Line made me think about the future, which made me reflect on the past. The clash of these needs to build [something] positive. (SSP participant)

This illustrates how, given the right circumstances, offenders can be encouraged to seek a coherent view of how different aspects of their lives, past, present and into the future, might fit together. As one member of staff recounts, helping offenders unravel how their different experiences have brought them to their current position holds out the hope of a new, reconstituted future:

> I think it reduces the risk as it unpicks it, it unpicks them so they get a good understanding of why they have offended. I had one guy who was on his second stalking offence and it really helped him understand his offending. (Offender manager)

Discussing aims for the future also helped offender managers identify skills that still required development. Some of these were relatively focused: education and training, accommodation needs and those related to substance misuse; others were more diffuse: assertiveness, problem-solving and the setting of personal goals. Discussions around these issues with offenders were used to send a message that this work was only the start of a trajectory and that skills imparted by SSP would need to be built upon if permanent change were to be achieved. The prospect of achieving their own goals hopefully provides the motivating force. Ward and Maruna (2007) argue persuasively that offenders have for far too long been seen as passive recipients of 'interventions'. As one staff member reminds us:

> They all want to be involved in something. It might be that they aren't doing much in their life and the programme involves doing something just for them. (Offender manager)

What does SSP add to supervision?

What, then, does SSP as a structured programme add to supervision? Does it add anything? Returning to Bonta's 'black box', the only possible answer is that we cannot say; quite simply, there is too little information about what happens elsewhere within supervisory relationships to support a judgement. Equally, it is too early to argue for the success of SSP in terms of an eventual impact upon subsequent offending. What we can say is that almost without exception, staff and offenders have perceived their involvement with the programme as a meaningful experience that has facilitated the exploration of pertinent issues. Not only do the majority of offenders appear to engage with the programme but the benefits have been extended as staff use elements of the work with other offenders.

Concerns that the structured nature of SSP might limit its responsivity to the needs of specific individuals appear to be unfounded. On the contrary, some of the earlier exercises seem to actively encourage participants to disclose the kind of personal information that not only helps inform offender managers' understanding of their offenders but also contributes to the formation of nurturing relationships. This concurs with Dahlen and Johnson's (2010) conclusion that cognitive behavioural and humanistic approaches can be combined to rehabilitate offenders.

Most reservations voiced in interviews focused on whether or not staff would be able to devote sufficient time to carrying it through. The principal stumbling block, therefore, would appear to relate to resources rather than the programme itself.

While reactions to SSP are overwhelmingly positive, to date the numbers undertaking it have been relatively low. This leads to problems with demonstrating its effectiveness because a robust evaluation would require a larger sample of offenders and, preferably, a broader range of staff working with the programme material. The solution to a very similar situation in the case of accredited programmes was to set targets in an attempt to increase numbers. The same may well be true here as this would set clear expectations to the different levels of management, with the message filtering down *via* those allocating cases to front-line staff.

Two comments, one from a member of staff – 'Isn't this what we should be doing?' – and another from an offender – 'This is better than supervision' – reflect the general thrust of this chapter: that SSP represents a valuable addition to the range of probation techniques and that it should be more widely available. However, these quotes also raise interesting questions around what the nature of supervision should be and what probation managers expect their staff to be doing within the relatively private world of one-to-one supervision. The concept of 'a supervision requirement' introduced under the 2003 Criminal Justice Act suggests something considerably different from the brokering role assigned to offender managers within the offender management model. We would suggest that the format of SSP would provide an excellent starting point for discussions around what the content of supervision could or should be.

Arguably SSP gives us the best of both worlds. It reintroduces the concept of case-work into supervision, with all the advantages of a focus on the individual, their concerns and aspirations, without losing the rigour of the structured approach characteristic of group-work programmes. Ansbro's 'secure base' provides the safe environment within which offenders are allowed to explore their offending, what has led up to it, how they might move on and provide some understanding of how it relates to the rest of their lives. We also have to think of the more subliminal messages conveyed within this relationship. Implicit when an offender manager goes out of their way to help are messages around worthiness – you are worthy of assistance. Worthiness, in turn, is related to value; when others value you, you start to value yourself. To return again to Ansbro (2008), it may be difficult to be 'self-reflective' when you fear that there is little in the self to value.

The hope is that by getting offenders to value themselves more they will come to feel confident enough to make their own decisions and take advantage not only of those opportunities offered by probation interventions but also those arising within local communities. This may mean that SSP work could also improve compliance with other probation requirements as offenders come to see these as opportunities that may contribute to achieving desired goals rather than hurdles to negotiate. Surely this is what many offenders hope for when they walk through probation's door. Understandably, within probation there is much discussion about how best to motivate offenders to engage with interventions and complete their orders. Our experience of SSP however, bears out the findings of Rex (2002) and Farrall and Calverley (2005) and, more recently, Ward and Maruna's (2007) findings that many offenders are actively looking for assistance with finding direction in their lives, will welcome an intervention that they perceive as responding to their own concerns, and will feel let down if this is not forthcoming.

But if offenders need support to become confident, so do staff. Arguably the support and constructive criticism provided by treatment managers constitutes a form of ongoing training which has raised staff's performance and contributed to the positive experience reported by most offenders. Miller and Mount (2001) concluded that one-off training events need to be augmented by ongoing scrutiny and support if staff are to become proficient in new ways of working. Were an SSP approach to be widespread it is likely that this support, currently provided by treatment managers, would have to be absorbed into more routine staff supervision structures. This, in turn, raises questions about the function of staff supervision and the amount of time that should be devoted to discussions of clinical practice.

Empowering offenders to solve their own problems is not sufficient. We also have to be mindful of the content of those solutions. Factors underlying negative behaviours need to be examined in order to provide an understanding, as without this it can be difficult for the offender to move on or the offender manager to know how best to assist with this process. Our belief is that SSP provides the framework within which the offender and offender manager can together work through issues emanating from the past, consider their impact and plan how to build a more productive future.

What is clear, however, is that this would involve resources, staff with the time to carry out the work in its entirety and managers with the time to foster new skills. Should a robust evaluation of this work demonstrate it to be effective, the question is whether the resources necessary to maximise its impact would be made available. To put this another way, to what extent are we committed to changing the thinking and behaviour of offenders during supervision? Or are we content to simply manage them?

References

Andrews, D.A. (1995) 'The psychology of criminal conduct and effective treatment', in M. Maguire (ed.) *What Works: Reducing Reoffending: Guidelines for Research and Practice.* Chichester: John Wiley.

Andrews, D.A. and Dowden, C. (2006) 'Risk principles of case classification in correctional treatment', *International Journal of Offender Therapy and Comparative Criminology,* 50: 88–100.

Ansbro, M. (2008) 'Using attachment theory with offenders', *Probation Journal,* 55 (3): 231–44.

Bandura, A. (1975) *Social Learning and Personality Development.* New Jersey: Holt, Rinehart and Winston.

Bonta, J., Rugge, T., Scott, T., Bourgon, G. and Yessine, A.K. (2008) 'Exploring the black box of community supervision', *Journal of Offender Rehabilitation,* 47 (3): 248–70.

Burnett, R. (2004) 'One-to-one ways of promoting desistance: in search of an evidence base', in R. Burnett and C. Roberts (eds) *What Works in Probation and Youth Justice: Developing Evidence-Based Practice.* Cullompton: Willan Publishing.

Corston, J. (2007) *The Corston Report: A Review of Women with Particular Vulnerabilities in the Criminal Justice System.* London: Home Office.

Dahlen, K. and Johnson, R. (2010) 'The humanism is in the details: an insider's account of humanistic modifications to a cognitive-behavioural treatment program in a maximum-security prison', *Prison Journal* 90 (1): 115–35.

Dowden, C. and Andrews, D.A. (2004) 'The importance of staff practices in delivering effective correctional treatment: a meta-analysis of core correctional practices', *International Journal of Offender Therapy and Comparative Criminology,* 48: 203–14.

Ellis, A.T. (1962) *Reason and Emotion in Psychotherapy.* New York: Lyle Stuart.

Farrall, S. and Calverley, A. (2005) *Understanding Desistance from Crime.* Berkshire: Open University Press.

Maruna, S. (2001) *Making Good: How Ex-convicts Reform and Rebuild their Lives.* Washington, DC: American Psychological Association.

Miller, W.R. and Mount, K.A. (2001) 'A small study of training in motivational interviewing: does one workshop change clinician and client behaviour?', *Behavioural and Cognitive Psychotherapy,* 29: 457–71.

Rex, S. (1999) 'Desistance from offending: experiences of probation', *Howard Journal of Criminal Justice,* 38: 366–83.

Rex, S. (2002) 'Beyond cognitive-behaviouralism? Reflections on the effectiveness of literature', in A. Bottoms, L. Gelsthorpe and S. Rex (eds) *Community Penalties: Change and Challenges.* Cullompton: Willan Publishing.

Vanstone, M. (2007) 'The resettlement of prisoners in England and Wales: learning from history and research', in G. McIvor and P. Raynor, (eds) *Developments in Social Work with Offenders*. Research Highlights in Social Work Series. London: Jessica Kingsley.

Ward, T. and Maruna, S. (2007) *Rehabilitation*. Abingdon: Routledge.

Zamble, E. and Quinsey, V. (1997) *The Criminal Recidivism Process*. Cambridge: Cambridge University Press.

Chapter 11

Beyond supervision: judicial involvement in offender management

Gill McIvor

Anyone new to drug court would be astonished by its informality, where the center stage is fully accorded to the judge ... Drug court offers a different approach, with the judge becoming more than a stylistic figure. He or she will frequently engage in a dialogue with the offender ... These inclusive personal contacts can produce affection and loyalty from some offenders; they will often say, with admiration, that no other judge has ever bothered to discuss with them the details of their personal lives. (Bean 2002: 236)

Introduction

The task of supervising and managing offenders subject to court orders in the community has traditionally fallen to probation officers or social workers, with sentencers having a limited role once an order has been made. Since the introduction of the first drug courts in the USA more than 20 years ago, there has been a growing interest internationally in the capacity of 'problem-solving courts' to help bring about and support changes in offenders' circumstances and behaviour. A distinctive feature of problem-solving courts is the active involvement of the sentencing judge in reviewing the progress of offenders subject to community supervision and adapting the content of supervision accordingly. Empirical studies of drug courts suggest that the role of the sentencing judge may have a positive impact upon offenders' compliance and behaviour, with this being attributed to enhanced perceptions of procedural justice and, as a consequence, heightened judicial legitimacy (McIvor 2009). However, despite recent legislative and policy developments in the UK that allow for a greater role for sentencers in offender management, judicial involvement of this type has also attracted criticism on both legal and professional/therapeutic grounds. This chapter therefore considers the advantages and disadvantages of an enhanced role for sentencers in the management of offenders subject to community sanctions and the implications for their contribution to effective offender supervision.

The emergence of specialist courts and therapeutic jurisprudence

The concept and practice of sentencer involvement in offender management has its roots in drug courts and other problem-solving courts, which were first introduced in the United States and are now established across a number of jurisdictions (including the UK, Canada, Australia, Norway, Ireland and New Zealand: see Nolan 2009 for a comparative analysis). Drug courts were established initially in the United States in the late 1980s, initiated by sentencers who were frustrated at the limited range and effectiveness of existing criminal justice measures for dealing with drug-related crime. The impetus for the establishment of drug courts in North America came from a growing acknowledgement of the link between drug misuse and crime along with increasing evidence of the efficacy of drug treatment, including treatment that is compelled rather than undertaken on a voluntary basis (see Hough 1996; Gebelein 2000; and more recently McSweeney *et al.* 2007). Operationally, drug courts vary across jurisdictions, but all are designed to reduce drug use and related offending by combining drug treatment with ongoing supervision and court-based review.

An important impact of the drug court 'movement' was the impetus that these courts provided to the development of other forms of specialist, problem-solving courts. These include domestic abuse courts, mental health courts, disability courts (for offenders with learning difficulties or 'cognitive disabilities'), community courts (which adopt a community-focused problem-solving approach to local crime) and re-entry courts (which aim to support the resettlement of prisoners in the community after a prison sentence). In problem-solving courts judges adopt a different role through the active reviewing of offenders' progress and court-based dialogue where 'the empathic connection between the judge and client is a central focus of the courtroom drama' (Nolan 2001: 99). According to Bakht (2004: 32), in problem-solving courts 'the judicial role has been transformed from a detached, neutral arbiter to the central figure in a team', reflecting what Nolan (2001: 93) refers to as the emergence of the 'romantic judge' (see also Boldt and Singer 2006) who is characterised by 'judicial boldness, energy and compassion'. While Maruna and LeBel (2003: 100) observe that 'rewarding positive achievements rather than punishing violations is an unusual role for the courts', Saum and Gray (2008) point out that offenders also take on a new role through the requirement that they become active participants in the problem-solving process.

Drug courts – and other problem-solving courts – represent an approach to criminal justice processing that has been termed 'therapeutic jurisprudence' (Wexler and Winick 1992) and refers to the capacity of legal processes and procedures (including the actions and approaches of criminal justice professionals) to have therapeutic or anti-therapeutic outcomes. Therapeutic jurisprudence emerged in the USA in relation to mental health law in the 1980s with mental health courts founded specifically on therapeutic jurisprudence principles. It was subsequently 'adopted' as a justifying principle by drug courts (Casey and Rottman 2000) which represented its first systematic and widespread use in the USA (Hora and Schma 1998). Under traditional court models, rehabilitation may be an aim of criminal justice processing but within a model of therapeutic jurisprudence it is intrinsic to the process. A key question for therapeutic jurisprudence is 'whether the law's antitherapeutic consequences can be reduced, and its therapeutic consequences enhanced, without subordinating due process and other justice values' (Wexler and Winick 1996: xvii).

The concept of therapeutic jurisprudence has been embraced to varying degrees by legal professionals in different jurisdictions. As Nolan (2009) notes, support for the approach is particularly strong among problem-solving courts in North America, and also in Australia where, for example, magistrates in Western Australia unanimously resolved to apply the principles of therapeutic jurisprudence in their courts (King and Wager 2005). In the UK, by contrast, judges in problem-solving courts would not necessarily describe their practice as being influenced directly by principles of therapeutic jurisprudence (Nolan 2009), though it is clear that the concept has underpinned judicial involvement in offender management at least implicitly. As one Scottish drug court sheriff commented, review hearings represented the point where the 'the legal side of things melds with the non-legal, sort of therapeutic side of things'. As 'the process which joins the two together', reviews could be conceptualised as 'the nexus between the two aspects of the approach' (McIvor 2009: 38).

Writing from an Australian perspective, King and Wager (2005: 32) describe the role of the judge in a therapeutic jurisprudential approach as 'motivating rather than intimidating. It is emphasising the standing and authority of the judge or magistrate rather than the judge or magistrate's power to impose sanctions.' However, in the context of problem-solving courts, the judge will also sanction offenders, which may ultimately result in a short period of time in prison. According to Burns and Peyrot (2003), the interactions that take place in drug courts can be construed as a form of 'tough love' in which the threat of incarceration is held over the offender by the 'therapist-judge' (2003: 418). In a similar vein, the 'carrot and stick' approach that characterises judicial supervision was described by a Scottish drug court sheriff as a 'Sword of Damocles' (Eley *et al.* 2002b: 54). Maruna and LeBel (2003), in their discussion of re-entry courts in the USA, question whether punitive and therapeutic approaches can be easily reconciled. As they observe, 'the history of crime control in the 20th Century suggests that when both tools (the therapeutic and the punitive) are available, the latter will almost always win out or at least undermine the former' (2003: 96).

Casey and Rottman (2000) have argued that the rights perspective has dominated the administration and provision of justice in North America and that this may have contributed to a growing schism between the courts and the public. They suggest that therapeutic jurisprudence may help to bridge the gap between the 'rights' perspective (which focuses on justice, equality and legal decision-making and which represents a masculine ideal of justice) and the 'care' perspective (which reflects a feminine model of compassion and responsiveness to needs).

Therapeutic jurisprudence has, however, been acknowledged even by its proponents to lack precise definition and to be 'time-consuming, interdisciplinary, and inexact' (Casey and Rottman 2000: 454). This 'vagueness' or lack of theoretical coherence of which therapeutic jurisprudence has been accused (Mackenzie 2008) has been said to result in difficulties in measuring its operation in practice, with the result that relatively little is known about how particular practices affect individuals and how the characteristics of individuals themselves modify or shape the problem-solving process (Casey and Rottman 2000). Therapeutic jurisprudence can therefore be more appropriately conceived of as a set of organising principles (McIvor 2009) or an 'interpretive lens' (Nolan 2001: 186).

Developments in the UK

In the UK, sentencers have traditionally had limited involvement with community orders once they have been imposed unless the order is breached and the offender is brought back to court. Provision for sentencers to periodically review community orders was first introduced by the 1998 Crime and Disorder Act in the context of drug treatment and testing orders (DTTOs). DTTOs, which drew upon the US drug court model, included provision for sentencers to take an active role in reviewing the progress of offenders on orders by bringing them back to court on a regular basis (or, alternatively, scrutinising progress through paper-based reviews).

DTTO schemes were introduced in England in 1998 in three pilot sites (Turnbull *et al.* 2000), and in 1999 and 2000 respectively in two Scottish pilot sites (Eley *et al.* 2002a). The English pilots varied in terms of how successfully they had been implemented. With respect to judicial review, practice was variable across the pilot sites in terms of both frequency and the degree of judicial continuity across successive reviews (Turnbull *et al.* 2000). In the Scottish pilots, despite some differences across the two sites in terms of how reviews were conducted (in Fife the provision for in-chamber reviews was interpreted literally by sheriffs who usually conducted face-to-face reviews with offenders in chambers), the review process was believed on the whole to work well, with continuity of sentencer being achieved in most cases and offenders reporting that reviews helped to keep them 'on their toes' (Eley *et al.* 2002a).

DTTOs were not, however, without their critics. For example, although DTTOs were informed by the drug court model that had evolved in the USA, Bean (2002) described them as 'watered down' versions of drug courts because they did not allow for the development of the coordinated multi-professional team approach – with the judge as 'team leader' – that characterised drug courts in other jurisdictions. In a similar vein, Turnbull *et al.* (2000: 5) observed in that 'the role of US sentencers in drug courts approximates far more to that of "case manager". This, coupled with a sentencing ideology that emphasises reward as well as punishment, distinguishes drug courts from the DTTO pilot sites.'

Two years into the DTTO pilot, the Scottish Executive rolled out DTTOs nationally and established pilot drug courts at the DTTO pilot sites in Glasgow and Fife. The Scottish drug courts shared many features in common with those in other jurisdictions, including integration of substance misuse treatment with criminal justice processing; the use of a non-adversarial approach; early identification of eligible participants with rapid access to treatment; a coordinated approach by sentencers, prosecution, defence and treatment providers to secure compliance by participants; ongoing judicial review of participants' progress; and partnerships with other relevant agencies to provide ongoing support for participants (McIvor *et al.* 2006a). They targeted repeat offenders whose offending was directly related to their dependence on or propensity to use drugs and who were at immediate risk of a custodial sentence. They were located within the sheriff summary courts, presided over by two sheriffs in Glasgow and one in Fife, whose role in review hearings was to motivate, encourage and sanction the offender depending upon progress made. As McIvor (2009) notes, the dialogues that took place in the context of drug court reviews were viewed as a key feature of the drug court process by professionals and offenders alike.

A significant element of the Scottish drug courts which has not been replicated in other specialist/problem-solving courts in Scotland – the youth courts (McIvor *et al.* 2006b) and domestic abuse court (Reid-Howie Associates 2007) – or in the dedicated drug courts subsequently introduced in England and Wales (Matrix Knowledge Group 2008) was the provision for relatively informal pre-review meetings which enabled multi-professional discussion of offenders' progress. These meetings were valued by sheriffs for providing a rounded picture of each participant and their progress, furnishing them with up-to-date information about offenders from the professionals involved in their supervision. The information gleaned at the pre-review meetings was important in helping sheriffs to decide 'which buttons to push' in their subsequent dialogue with participants: whether there were particular achievements to acknowledge or, conversely, whether there were setbacks that should be commented upon in court (McIvor 2009).

In England and Wales, DTTOs were rolled out nationally then subsequently replaced, in 2005, by community orders and suspended sentence orders with drug treatment requirements. Pilot dedicated drug courts (DDCs) were introduced in 2005 in London and Leeds (though the latter had had a drug court model in operation since 2001), with further pilot sites announced by the Secretary of State for Justice in March 2008. In 2003 the government announced its intention to pilot a community justice centre in north Liverpool and a second in Salford. The community justice centres were based on the Red Hook Community Court in Brooklyn, New York, which was established in June 2000 to offer a coordinated, problem-solving response to local problems of crime and disorder. The North Liverpool Community Justice Centre was presided over by a single judge while the Salford Community Justice Initiative operated with a rotating bench of magistrates. In addition to dealing with offenders appearing for sentence and subject to community orders, the North Liverpool Community Justice Centre also aimed to support the resettlement of prisoners in the community after their sentences, in a manner akin to re-entry courts in the USA (Maruna and LeBel 2003). Proposals for the development of a community justice centre and community court in Scotland (with the role of the judge being purportedly 'central' to the operation of the proposed court) were announced by the Justice Minister in March 2007 but subsequently withdrawn in May 2009 in light of the anticipated capital costs.

The potential for wider judicial involvement in offender management in England and Wales was heralded by the Halliday Report (Home Office 2001), which proposed that sentencers should have the option of undertaking periodic reviews of offenders subject to community supervision. Section 178 of the Criminal Justice Act 2003 subsequently introduced the option for courts to review offenders' progress on community orders. This power was made available in the first instance to the community justice centres in north Liverpool and Salford before being extended to a second tranche of 11 community justice centres that were introduced in England and Wales in 2007. Not all orders made in North Liverpool Community Justice Centre had Section 178 conditions attached to them, though the majority of those made by magistrates in the Salford Community Justice Initiative did (Brown and Payne 2007). Mair *et al.* (2008) found that sentencers had mixed attitudes towards the review power for community orders. Some magistrates expressed concern about the significant resource implications for the courts and probation service and some thought the practice would overlap with the probation service's responsibility for dealing with compliance. Others, however, believed that the power to review community orders would facilitate and strengthen enforcement and engender greater public confidence in orders.

The Green Paper 'Engaging Communities in Criminal Justice', published in April 2009, contained proposals to roll out problem-solving principles to all magistrates courts in England and Wales and to encourage courts to make greater uses of the section 178 powers to review community orders 'in order to enable the judiciary to build relationships with offenders, acting as a source of encouragement, praise and reprimand as appropriate' (Criminal Justice System 2009: 32), and with a particular emphasis on how they might be used intensively in specific locations to address persistent local crime problems and anti-social behaviour. The consultation paper also sought views on whether the power to review community orders should be extended to those under 18 years of age (Criminal Justice System 2009).

Proposals also exist in Scotland to make judicial review a more regular and central feature of community-based offender management. The 2007 review of community penalties by the Scottish Government contained proposals to extend the power of judicial review from DTTOs and probation to all community penalties, with these powers thought to be particularly useful 'in ensuring compliance during the early stages of a community penalty, when the offender is most likely to reoffend and may be struggling to establish a routine' (Scottish Government 2007: 27). Broadly similar proposals were put forward by the Scottish Prisons Commission (2008) which recommended the establishment of 'progress courts' presided over by particular judges with responsibility for this specialised task (Scottish Prisons Commission 2008). The Scottish Government, in response, rejected the need for separate progress courts (Scottish Government 2008) but instead introduced legislation, in the Criminal Justice and Licensing (Scotland) Bill, to enable sentencers to set review hearings – taking the form of 'informal discussions between the judge and the offender' (Scottish Government 2008: 14) – in the context of a proposed new community sentence (the Community Payback Order) which would replace the existing community service, probation and supervised attendance orders (Scottish Government 2008). Formal responses by both the judiciary and social work professionals to the proposals for legislated periodic review have been generally positive, while stressing the importance of effective targeting to ensure the best use of staff and court time and highlighting the need for further detailed guidance to maximise consistency in the operation of reviews across the country (Scottish Parliament 2009).

In different jurisdictions, therefore, provisions are being introduced to give sentencers a greater say in the active management of community orders. Advocates for increased judicial involvement in offender management have pointed to its potential to provide 'better' justice by improving judicial decision-making, promoting procedural justice, enhancing compliance and achieving improved outcomes. However, this enhanced role for sentencers has also attracted criticisms, including the risk that it may lead to an erosion of due process and concern that it both widens the net of social control in an invidious way and enables judges to engage in 'therapeutic' practices for which they have not been professionally trained. These purported benefits and disadvantages are now considered in turn.

Benefits of judicial involvement

Improving court processes

Ongoing judicial involvement in problem-solving courts is aimed at improving both compliance and client outcomes through the use of legal practices and processes that are more likely to achieve therapeutic or rehabilitative aims (Nolan 2009). King and Wager (2005) argue that problem-solving approaches can promote rehabilitation through addressing the underlying problems that contribute to offending. However, Makkai (2002) has suggested that the most significant change brought about by drug courts has been the linking of treatment directly with the judge whereby 'the notion of an impartial arbitrator is replaced with a caring, but authoritarian, guardian' (Payne 2005: 74). Similarly, the increased courtroom interaction with defendants was viewed by professionals associated with the Salford Community Justice Initiative as one of the most innovative changes to have taken place (Brown and Payne 2007) while a professional associated with the pilot drug courts in Scotland described sentencer involvement in dialogue with offenders as 'a major step forward in legal history' (McIvor 2009: 40).

In the Salford Community Justice Initiative, although some stakeholders expressed reservation about magistrates engaging in dialogue with offenders, the process was recognised as furnishing the magistrate with more information about the defendant, thereby improving sentencing decisions (Brown and Payne 2007). Magistrates themselves were very positive about the review process, which enabled them to respond quickly to a lack of progress or compliance or, if appropriate, to encourage and praise offenders when their progress was good (Brown and Payne 2007). Saum et al. (2002) found that most drug court participants in their US study believed that the judge was influential in facilitating their progress through the appropriate use of warnings and praise. In the Red Hook Community Court, perceived helpfulness and objectivity of the judge, being treated with respect and the quality of courtroom communication were the most important predictors of defendants' perceptions of procedural fairness (Frazer 2006).

In attempting to enhance offenders' compliance, judges operating within a therapeutic jurisprudence framework may also utilise the 'theatre' of the court (Nolan 2001) to reinforce their influence and persuasion over clients by arranging the court calendar so as to maximise the impact of communication from the bench upon those awaiting their reviews. This practice (involving, for example, reviews being undertaken first with those appearing from custody to serve as a warning to others of the consequences of non-compliance) was reported to be widespread in US drug courts (Nolan 2001). In Scotland, too, drug court sheriffs recounted how they would 'choreograph' the review hearings to amplify the message conveyed to the court (McIvor 2009), a practice that was facilitated by the multidisciplinary pre-review meetings that were convened to discuss the progress of participants who were due to appear in court.

Achieving improved compliance and outcomes

A review of specialist courts commissioned by the then Department of Constitutional Affairs for England and Wales concluded that judicial monitoring of offenders was related to their success (Plotnikoff and Woolfson 2005). Evidence that sentencers may have a key role to play in determining court outcomes derives principally from drug court research. For example a long-term study of a drug court in Oregon found that recidivism rates differed widely among judges, with reductions of recidivism varying from 4 per cent to 42 per cent (Finigan et al. 2007). Although Sanford and Arrigo (2005) found no consistent evidence that the *frequency* of judicial reviews was associated with improved drug court outcomes, Marlowe et al. (2004, 2005) found that more frequent reviews resulted in improved outcomes for *higher risk* offenders.

Belenko (2001) found that judicial interaction and monitoring were believed by participants to be an important element of drug court programmes while Cooper et al. (1997) reported that offenders regarded judicial supervision and encouragement to be critical in achieving success. Senjo and Leip (2000) found that supportive comments offered by sentencers during review hearings had a significant effect on drug court programme completion and that offenders were particularly responsive to the use of positive reinforcement as opposed to the more traditional use of punishment. This is consistent with Maruna and LeBel's (2003) assertion that strengths-based approaches are more effective than coerced obedience in engaging offenders and promoting intrinsic motivation to change.

As Brown and Payne (2007: 29) note in their evaluation of the Salford Community Justice Initiative, a key assumption is that 'the continuity of magistrates should create a greater sense of personal accountability on the part of the offender, leading to improved compliance with sentence requirements'. Prior to the introduction of the Salford pilot, offenders sometimes reported a sense of injustice at being dealt with by different magistrates on successive court appearances (Brown and Payne 2007). There is, indeed, emerging evidence that consistency or continuity of sentencers is linked to drug court success. For example, Goldkamp (2004) found that higher levels of contact with the same judge resulted in lower levels of recidivism, while the process evaluation of the dedicated drug courts in England found that continuity of sentencer across court appearances was associated with enhanced compliance with court hearings, lower levels of positive drug tests for heroin, an increased rate of completion and a reduced frequency of reconviction (Matrix Knowledge Group 2008). In the North Liverpool Community Justice Centre offenders reacted positively to reviews and 'increased engagement with the proceedings and the continuity provided by the single judge model ... served to increase offenders' accountability to the court' (McKenna 2007: 32). Offenders who were subject to review requirements reported fewer issues in completing their sentence and there was some evidence that their completion rates were higher than those of comparison cases dealt with in another court (McKenna 2007).

The significance of continuity and consistency has also been highlighted by Holt (2000) in relation to effective case management in probation, providing a basis for the development of positive working relationships between client and worker and making the experience of supervision integrated and coherent. However, achieving consistency and continuity across review hearings has presented practical difficulties in magistrates courts in England and Wales, which operate with a rotating three-magistrate bench. This problem was noted by Turnbull *et al.* (2000) in the evaluation of the pilot DTTOs and in the process evaluation of the dedicated drug courts (Matrix Knowledge Group 2008). And although professionals associated with the Salford Community Justice Initiative reported a good level of continuity across hearings, this could not be quantified

(Brown and Payne 2007). As a possible solution the 2009 Green Paper 'Engaging Communities in Criminal Justice' proposes that continuity, which can 'have a powerful effect', might be achieved by having at least one magistrate continuously involved throughout the case review process (Criminal Justice System 2009: 30).

Wexler (2001) has suggested that judicial involvement in specialist courts can promote rehabilitation by contributing to the 'desistance narratives' (Maruna 2001) that help to facilitate and sustain desistance from crime. McIvor (2009) has argued that the exchanges that take place between sentencers and offenders in drug court can enhance procedural justice (Tyler 1990), which confers greater legitimacy upon judges, promotes normative as opposed to constraint-based or instrumental compliance (Bottoms 2001) and increases the responsiveness of participants to exhortations that they should change. Support for such an argument can be found in Gottfredson *et al.*'s (2007) finding that judicial review directly reduced drug use and indirectly reduced criminal behaviour by increasing participants' perceptions of procedural fairness. By contrast, King and Wager (2005) have suggested that court processes that are insensitive to the needs and circumstances of defendants can result in disrespect for and lack of compliance with court orders.

Further evidence that perceptions of procedural fairness are more important than outcomes comes from the evaluation of the Red Hook Community Court. Red Hook defendants' perceptions of fairness did not vary according to the outcome of their case, whereas in the traditional comparison court defendants expressed more favourable views of the judge if their case was dismissed (Frazer 2006), lending some support to Winick and Wexler's (2003: 17) suggestion that 'relationships and processes are more important than the substance of therapies and sanctions'.

Accommodating diversity

It has also been suggested that practices characterised as therapeutic jurisprudence – including the regular judicial review of offenders' progress – may render court processes less discriminatory and more capable of responding appropriately to diverse groups of offenders. For instance, experience in Western Australia suggests that aboriginal people tend to respond positively to the opportunity for dialogue in court (King and Wager 2005) while the Red Hook evaluation suggested that defendant satisfaction with court processes varied less according to race and socio-economic status than it did in a traditional court (Frazer 2006).

There is also some evidence that women may be particularly responsive to judicial interaction in a problem-solving court setting. For example, Johnson *et al.* (2000) found that women were more likely than men to state that regular court hearings helped them to remain drug-free, while Saum and Gray (2008) found that women were more likely than men to be satisfied with their interactions with the judge. In comparison with men, women were more likely to value praise from judges and to believe that judges had given them an opportunity to relate their side of the story, had been fair to them, had treated them fairly and had treated them with respect. Saum and Gray suggest that women may be better able than men to utilise judicial interaction to their advantage because they are able to develop meaningful connections with judges, to communicate their needs and to respond to the judges' requests. Being better able to express themselves in court may be both personally fulfilling for women and may facilitate aspects of the drug court process. Saum and Gray argue that a 'care perspective' operates in drug court and that 'this more feminine model of justice appears particularly beneficial to the women who encompass it' (2008: 115). This chimes with the broader suggestion that through advocating different criminal justice responses to different types of offences, therapeutic jurisprudence and the problem-solving approach it underpins represent a more effective response to offending (Casey and Rottman 2000).

Enhancing sentencers' job satisfaction

A final argument that has been advanced in favour of greater judicial involvement in offender management is that it enhances judges' job satisfaction by enabling them to see successes as well as failures and to 'believe that they are for the first time really making a difference in people's lives' (Nolan 2001: 109). This enhanced sense of satisfaction – which has been highlighted by prominent judicial proponents of therapeutic jurisprudence (for example, Hora and Schma 1998; Hora *et al.* 1999) – may help to explain judges' enthusiasm for problem-solving approaches, especially where their discretion has been increasingly constrained by developments such as sentencing guidelines and they are increasingly perceived by the public as 'out of touch' (Nolan 2001).

Arguments against judicial involvement

Revival of the rehabilitative ideal and new forms of surveillance

Critics of therapeutic jurisprudence have expressed concern that it reflects a return to the 'rehabilitative ideal' in which the offender is pathologised and punishment is justified as a means of 'curing' or 'reforming' the offender (Rosenthal 2002) to produce, in the drug court context, 'self-governing citizens, free of the burden of drugs and crime' (Took 2005: 35). The rehabilitative justification for punishment has been criticised on the grounds that it variously promotes indeterminancy, results in loss of civil liberties by criminalising anti-social behaviour, is potentially 'soft' on crime and may result in differential sentencing that is unjustified and arbitrary (Rosenthal 2002). With respect to judicial engagement with offenders, Boldt (1998: 1262–3) expresses particular concern reading the potential for excessive and unwarranted judicial expression arguing: 'In gross terms the informality, and immediacy of the judge's relationship with the defendant confers a potentially ungovernable discretion similar to that which so riled critics of the rehabilitative ideal nearly thirty years ago.'

Bean (2002) has also pointed out that, despite the apparent informality that characterises dialogues between judges and offenders in drug courts, the judge ultimately sets the parameters, decides when they have been exceeded and determines the sanction that is imposed. In many respects, he suggests, drug courts (and problem-solving courts more generally) are at risk of reproducing earlier rehabilitative practices that were subject to much criticism and debate. In particular, drug courts – and the revised judicial role they support – may represent a return to an era of discretionary justice characterised by the central importance and powerfulness of the judge. In this respect, he argues, enhanced judicial involvement may be perceived as 'sometimes getting dangerously close to a system that offers scope for accusations of bias and favoritism' (2002: 249). Mackenzie (2008: 516) goes further in suggesting that drug courts represent 'state-imposed therapeutic coercion driven by officials who fear their traditional sources of legitimation have lost their effect'.

Nolan (2001) has argued that problem-solving courts encapsulate a *new* form of rehabilitation in which private issues are open to judicial exploration and oversight and which makes possible the expansion of judicial authority. Judicial involvement in offender supervision and management has been criticised as representing a new, and deeper, form of *surveillance* as a consequence of the information about offenders gained by judges and the discretion that they are able to exercise when sentencing them, responding to lack of compliance and deciding what is in their best interests (Burns and Peyrot 2003). The 'net result', according to Burns and Peyrot (2003: 434) is 'the expansion of the state's supervision, monitoring and control over offenders' lives because they are being "rehabilitated"'.

The transparency that is often claimed to arise from the court-based reviews of offenders' progress raises a further concern with respect to the airing of sensitive issues in open court. In the Scottish DTTO pilots, this issue was dealt with in Glasgow through the clearing of the court if sensitive topics were discussed, though this was not always welcomed by offenders who were concerned about how this would be publicly interpreted (Eley *et al.* 2002a). In the pilot drug courts, by contrast, the discussion of participants' circumstances at pre-review meetings provided an opportunity for sensitive issues relevant to the offender's progress to be brought to the sheriff's attention confidentially and in private, thereby preventing the need to make reference to them in open court (McIvor *et al.* 2006b).

Blurring of professional boundaries and competences

Judges in problem-solving court settings have been variously referred to as assuming the role of social worker (Saum and Gray 2008), probation officer (Hoffman 2000), case manager (Turnbull *et al.* 2000) and therapist (Bean 2002). The apparent blurring of professional boundaries that may occur when judges step beyond their traditional role has attracted criticism on the grounds that it may result in judges 'overstepping the mark' and making decisions that they are not professionally trained or competent to make. Hoffman (2000: 1530), for example, suggests that in drug courts the 'crowned chief probation officer is by definition an amateur' while Bean (2002) questions the therapeutic value of the dialogue between judges and offenders because the nature and extent of contacts with the offender fall far short of what would be considered necessary in most therapeutic relationships.

Saum and Gray (2008) have suggested that judges in problem-solving courts operate from what might be better described as a 'social worker' perspective, developing close relationships with their clients over time as they meet to discuss and monitor progress. However, the Law Reform Commission for Western Australia (2009) suggests that taking a problem-solving approach does not mean that sentencers are acting as 'social workers': 'Although therapeutic aims are encouraged, judicial officers in court intervention programs continue to perform judicial functions – they remain bound to apply the law and ensure that the legal rights of participants are protected' (2009: 31).

This is an important observation and highlights the need for appropriate safeguards to protect offenders' rights, particularly given the centrality of the judge in the problem-solving court process (Bean 2002). As Bean observes (2002: 248), 'drug courts have been designed for judges with high levels of imagination, insight, and moral integrity; there are few controls and few formal constraints … What then of an overly enthusiastic judge, a sadistic judge or an incompetent judge?' Judicial decision-making in a problem-solving context needs to be informed by the information and advice provided by other professionals who have day-to-day responsibility for the supervision of the offender, rather than the judge assuming and usurping these other professionals' roles. In other words, while the dialogue that takes place between judges and offenders may be aimed at achieving 'therapeutic' outcomes, the advice upon which it is based should be professionally grounded and for this reason the judge him/herself cannot be considered to be a 'therapist' in the technical sense of the term.

However, the observation that 'drug court judges spend much of their time doing things that could and should be done by probation officers' (Hoffman 2000: 1529) had led to accusations that judicial involvement in offender management represents a doubling-up of effort. In the Salford Community Justice Initiative, for example, some professionals thought that reviews were overused by magistrates and often amounted to an unnecessary duplication of monitoring (Brown and Payne 2007). This concern did not extend, though, to the North Liverpool Community Justice Centre where the judge tended to convene reviews only where there were concerns about an offender's ability to comply with an order (McKenna 2007).

By contrast, the Law Reform Commission of Western Australia (2009) raises an interesting question of equality: if judicial monitoring is of benefit to offenders, should it not be available to *all* offenders and not just those who are dealt with in problem-solving courts? In the UK, legislated provision exists in England and Wales and is planned in Scotland for periodic judicial review to form a component of any community order where the sentencer believes that this would be of benefit in encouraging compliance with an order. The *option* of judicial review of any community orders appears to offer a workable compromise between the danger of duplication of effort and the need for equal access to justice, allowing for review hearings to be convened if it is considered in the best interests of the offender for this to happen. *Requiring* that all community orders are subject to judicial review has a number of attendant risks. For example, not all sentencers will possess the inclination or the skills to engage in a meaningful way with offenders so as to encourage and support them during their orders and it is unclear to what extent and how easily these skills can be acquired. In the Salford Community Justice Initiative, for example, although magistrates received training in how to engage with offenders, the part-time nature of their role meant that it took some time to gain adequate experience of adopting a problem-solving approach (Brown and Payne 2007).

In Scotland, the approach to reviewing orders in the drug courts and youth courts was markedly different, illustrating how the nature and quality of judge–offender dialogues is context-specific. Drug court reviews were generally encouraging and motivating and participants regarded dialogue and building a rapport with the sheriff as a central feature of the review process (McIvor *et al.* 2006a). As one drug court sheriff commented, 'it is possible to a considerable degree to form an impression of the individual and it is even possible to build up a relationship with that individual which is meaningful in the context of the court' (O'Grady 2003: 65). In the youth courts, by contrast, there tended in most cases to be limited exchange between the young person and the sheriff during reviews. Judicial dialogue was generally brief with an emphasis on the consequences of non-compliance or normative judgements about the kind of person the young person should strive to become (McIvor *et al.* 2004). Young people spoke rarely and appeared awkward when doing so, while sheriffs, though broadly supportive of reviews, stressed that the purpose was *not* to establish a relationship or build rapport (Popham *et al.* 2005; Barnsdale *et al.* 2006). These qualitative differences in review procedures are likely to reflect in part the age of the offenders concerned, but they are also likely to reflect the fact that sheriffs in the drug courts had volunteered to take on that role while *all* sheriffs in the courts hosting them were expected to preside over the youth courts on a rotational basis. The risk is that *requiring* sentencers to take on a role with which they do not feel comfortable may at best do more harm than good (for example, by engaging with offenders in ways that reinforce the authority of the court in a negative way and promote instrumental as opposed to normative compliance) and at worst may result in resistance to the use of community orders (and an increased use of imprisonment instead).

Erosion of due process

Nolan (2001) observes how in drug courts judges may alter their courtroom practices to convey compassion and understanding of their clients – for example, not wearing judicial robes, addressing clients by their first names and hugging clients – but questions whether under these circumstances a level of judicial impartiality and consistency in sentencing is valued and maintained. Particular concerns relate to the individualised nature of sanctions imposed in the event of non-compliance and the possibility that detailed information gleaned through open dialogue with offenders may be used against them in a future court case or when resentencing an offender in the event of an order being breached (Nolan 2001).

Casey and Rottman have argued that adherence to due process requirements without attention to defendants' needs and relationships may lead to 'legally relevant but ineffective decisions' (2000: 447). However, Mackenzie adopts a more cynical position, suggesting that problem-solving court practices reflect 'a retreat from the prison of procedural justice to justice with a happy face' (2008: 522) while Hoffman (2000: 1534) contends that: 'It is time, especially for judges, to resist the lemming-like dash toward a society in which bedrock legal principles that have served us for generations are sacrificed for the immediate gratification of the latest political fad.'

Alert to concerns such as these, the Law Commission for Western Australia (2009), in a consultation on court intervention programmes, highlights the importance of procedural safeguards being in place and legal rights not being prejudiced to achieve court intervention goals. Proponents of therapeutic jurisprudence themselves acknowledge the need for practice to be subsumed under principles of rights and justice and for therapeutic jurisprudence only to be applied once the law has been administered fairly, impartially and with regard to due process (Nolan 2001). For example, King and Wager (2005) argue that judicial case management can be carried out in such a way that it does not compromise traditional values of judging because therapeutic jurisprudence represents a *practice* reform rather than *legal* reform (Casey and Rottman 2000), while Rosenthal (2002) observes that the goal of therapeutic jurisprudence is not to eclipse or ignore other judicial considerations but to ensure that they are placed in a proper context. In this regard, Nolan (2009) highlights the Scottish drug court pilots as an example of therapeutic jurisprudence (even if not explicitly acknowledged as such by the sheriffs themselves) which operates within a clear set of procedural safeguards, suggesting that the adoption of a problem-solving approach that includes active judicial oversight of court orders need not necessarily conflict with other legal and judicial concerns.

Conclusions

The enhanced role that sentencers are adopting with respect to the supervision of offenders on court orders represents an important shift in judicial practice. However, if judicial oversight of offenders aims to promote both procedural justice and improved outcomes for offenders, the preceding discussion suggests that a number of considerations should apply. For example, not all sentencers will have the necessary skills or inclination to successfully undertake this wider role and it is important that those who do so do it on a voluntary basis with the necessary training and support. It is also critical that sentencers are facilitated to reach decisions based upon the advice of other relevant professionals, without stepping into professional terrain and taking on responsibilities for which they are not qualified. This requires that professional roles and responsibilities are clearly defined and appropriate procedural safeguards are in place to ensure that offenders' rights are not infringed. Finally, given the apparent significance of offenders having contact with the same judge throughout the course of an order, arrangements should be made to ensure judicial continuity over successive reviews. This will to enable sentencers to better get to know the offenders they are dealing with, establish rapport with them and communicate and reinforce consistent messages from the court.

Despite widespread enthusiasm for an increasingly active role in the monitoring of offenders' progress among judges who have embraced problem-solving court practices, others have sounded a cautionary note regarding adverse consequences that may arise, including the risks of increased surveillance into areas of private life that were hitherto beyond the gaze of the state, threats to due process arising from the knowledge that is gained and the engagement of judges in practices that extend beyond their professional competence and expertise. Yet there is evidence that through engaging offenders in regular dialogue about their progress and circumstances, judges can improve offenders' compliance with court orders and play an active role in supporting their efforts to change. On balance, therefore, the increased involvement of judges in offender management may have something to contribute to the supervision of offenders in the community, so long as the practices involved avoid flouting long-standing values that have traditionally underpinned the administration of justice in criminal law.

References

Bakht, N. (2004) *Problem Solving Courts as Agents of Change*. Ontario: National Judicial Institute. Online at: www.iadtc.law.ecu.edu.au/pdfs/Problem%20Solving%20Courts%20Paper%20final%20ppr.pdf (accessed 23 December 2009).

Barnsdale, L., MacRae, R., McIvor, G., Brown, A., Eley, S., Malloch, M., Murray, C., Murray, L., Piacentini, L., Popham, F. and Walters, R. (2006) *Evaluation of the Airdrie Sheriff Youth Court Pilot*. Edinburgh: Scottish Executive Social Research.

Bean, P. (2002) 'Drug courts, the judge, and the rehabilitative ideal', in J. L. Nolan Jr (ed). *Drug Courts: In Theory and in Practice*. New York: Aldine de Gruyter.

Belenko, S. (2001) *Research on Drug Courts: A Critical Review 2000 Update*. New York: National Center on Addiction and Substance Abuse at Columbia University.

Boldt, R.C. (1998) 'Rehabilitative punishment and the drug treatment court movement', *Washington University Law Quarterly*, 76: 1205–306.

Boldt, R. and Singer, J. (2006) 'Juristocracy in the trenches: problem-solving judges and therapeutic jurisprudence in drug treatment courts and unified family courts', *Maryland Law Review*, 65: 82–99.

Bottoms, A.E. (2001) 'Compliance and community penalties', in A. Bottoms, L. Gelsthorpe and S. Rex (eds) *Community Penalties: Change and Challenges*. Cullompton: Willan Publishing.

Brown, R. and Payne, S. (2007) *Process Evaluation of the Salford Community Justice Initiative*. London: Ministry of Justice.

Burns, S.L. and Peyrot, M. (2003) 'Tough love: nurturing and coercing responsibility and recovery in California drug courts', *Social Problems*, 50 3: 416–38.

Casey, P. and Rottman, D.B. (2000) 'Therapeutic jurisprudence in the courts', *Behavioral Sciences and the Law*, 18: 445–57.

Cooper, C.C., Bartlett, S.R., Shaw, M.A. and Yang, K.K. (1997) *1997 Drug Court Survey Report, Volume IV: Participant Perspectives*. Washington, DC: US Department of Justice.

Criminal Justice System (2009) *Engaging Communities in Criminal Justice*, Cm 7583. London: The Stationery Office.

Eley, S., Gallop, K., McIvor, G., Morgan, K. and Yates, R. (2002a) *Drug Treatment and Testing Orders: Evaluation of the Scottish Pilots*. Edinburgh: Scottish Executive Social Research.

Eley, S., Malloch, M., McIvor, G., Yates, R. and Brown, A. (2002b) *Glasgow's Pilot Drug Court in Action: The First Six Months*. Edinburgh: Scottish Executive Social Research.

Finigan, M.W., Carey, S.M. and Cox, A. (2007) *The Impact of a Mature Drug Court Over 10 Years of Operation: Recidivism and Costs*. Portland, OR: NPC Research.

Frazer, M.S. (2006) *The Impact of the Community Court Model on Defendant Perceptions of Fairness: A Case Study of the Red Hook Community Justice Center*. New York: Center for Court Innovation.

Gebelein, R.S. (2000) *The Rebirth of Rehabilitation: Promise and Perils of Drug Courts, Sentencing and Corrections: Issues for the 21st Century*. Washington DC: NIJ.

Goldkamp, J.S. (2004) *'Judicial 'hands on' in drug courts: moving from whether to how drug courts work'*, paper presented at the 1st Key Issues Conference of the International Societies of Criminology, Paris.

Gottfredson, D.C., Kearley, B.W., Najaka, S.S. and Rocha, C.M. (2007) 'How drug treatment courts work: an analysis of mediators', *Journal of Research in Crime and Delinquency*, 44 (1): 3–35.

Hoffman, M.B. (2000) 'The drug court scandal', *North Carolina Law Review*, 78: 1437–534.

Holt, P. (2000) *Case Management: Context for Supervision*, Community and Criminal Justice Monograph 2. Leicester: De Montfort University.

Home Office (2001) *Making Punishments Work: Report of a Review of the Sentencing Framework for England and Wales* (The Halliday Report). London: Home Office.

Hora, P.F. and Schma, W.G. (1998) 'Drug treatment courts: therapeutic jurisprudence in practice', *Judicature*, 82 (1): 9–12.

Hora, P.F., Schma, W.G. and Rosenthal, J.T.A. (1999) 'Therapeutic jurisprudence and the drug treatment court movement: revolutionizing the criminal justice system's response to drug abuse and crime in America', *Notre Dame Law Review*, 74: 439–538.

Hough, M. (1996) *Drug Misuse and the Criminal Justice System: A Review of the Literature*. London: Home Office.

Johnson, S., Shaffer, D.K. and Latessa, E.J. (2000) 'A comparison of male and female drug court participants', *Corrections Compendium*, 25 (6): 1–9.

King, M. and Wager, J. (2005) 'Therapeutic jurisprudence and problem-solving case management', *Journal of Judicial Administration*, 15: 28–36.

Law Reform Commission of Western Australia (2009) *Court Interventions Programs: Final Report*. Perth, WA: Law Reform Commission of Western Australia.

Mackenzie. R. (2008) 'Feeling good: the ethopolitics of pleasure, psychoactive substance use and public health and criminal justice governance: therapeutic jurisprudence and the drug courts in the USA', *Social and Legal Studies*, 17 (4): 513–33.

Mair, G., Cross, N. and Taylor, S. (2008) *The Community Order and the Suspended Sentence Order: The Views and Attitudes of Sentencers*. London: Centre for Crime and Justice Studies.

Makkai, T. (2002) 'The emergence of drug treatment courts in Australia', *Substance Use and Misuse*, 37: 1567–94.

Marlowe, D.B., Festinger, D.S. and Lee, P.A. (2004) 'The judge is a key component of drug court', *Drug Court Review*, 4 (2): 1–34.

Maruna, S. (2001) *Making Good: How Ex-inmates Reform and Rebuild their Lives*. Washington, DC: American Psychological Association.

Maruna, S. and LeBel, T.P. (2003) 'Welcome home? Examining the "reentry court" concept from a strengths-based perspective', *Western Criminology Review*, 4 (2): 91–107.

Matrix Knowledge Group (2008) *Dedicated Drug Court Pilots: A Process Report*. London: Ministry of Justice.

McIvor, G. (2009) 'Therapeutic jurisprudence and procedural justice in Scottish drug courts', *Criminology and Criminal Justice*, 9 (1): 29–49.

McIvor, G., Barnsdale, L., Malloch, M., Eley, S. and Yates, R. (2006a) *The Operation and Effectiveness of the Scottish Drug Court Pilots*. Edinburgh: Scottish Executive Social Research.

McIvor, G., Barnsdale, L., MacRae, R., Dunlop, S., Brown, A., Eley, S., Malloch, M., Murray, C., Murray, L., Piacentini, L., Popham, F. and Walters, R. (2006b) *Evaluation of the Airdrie and Hamilton Youth Court Pilots*. Edinburgh: Scottish Executive Social Research.

McIvor, G., Brown, A., Eley, S., Malloch, M., Murray, C., Piacentini, L. and Walters, R. (2004) *The Hamilton Sheriff Youth Court Pilot: The First Six Months*. Edinburgh: Scottish Executive Social Research.

McKenna, K. (2007) *Evaluation of the North Liverpool Community Justice Centre*. London: Ministry of Justice.

McSweeney, T., Stevens, A., Hunt, N. and Turnbull, P. (2007) 'Twisting arms or a helping hand? Assessing the impact of "coerced" and comparable "voluntary" drug treatment options', *British Journal of Criminology*, 47 (3): 470–90.

Nolan, J.L. Jr (2001) *Reinventing Justice: The American Drug Court Movement*. Princeton, NJ: Princeton University Press.

Nolan, J.L. Jr (2009) *Legal Accents, Legal Borrowing: The International Problem-solving Court Movement*. Princeton, NJ: Princeton University Press.

O'Grady, M. (2003) 'Drug courts – the Scottish experience', *Scottish Journal of Criminal Justice Studies*, 9: 55–68.

Payne, J. (2005) *Final Report on the North Queensland Drug Court*. Canberra, ACT: Australian Institute of Criminology.

Plotnikoff, J. and Woolfson, R. (2005) *Review of the Effectiveness of Specialist Courts in Other Jurisdictions*. London: Department of Constitutional Affairs.

Popham, F., McIvor, G., Brown, A, Eley, S., Malloch, M., Piacentini, L. and Walters, R. (2005) *Evaluation of the Hamilton Sheriff Youth Court*. Edinburgh: Scottish Executive Social Research.

Reid-Howie Associates (2007) *Evaluation of the Pilot Domestic Abuse Court.* Edinburgh: Scottish Executive Justice Department.

Rosenthal, J.T.A. (2002) 'Therapeutic jurisprudence and drug treatment courts: integrating law and science', in J.L. Nolan Jr (ed.) *Drug Courts: In Theory and in Practice.* New York: Aldine de Gruyter.

Sanford, J.S. and Arrigo, B.A. (2005) 'Lifting the cover on drug courts: evaluation findings and policy concerns' , *International Journal of Offender Therapy and Comparative Criminology,* 49 (3): 239–59.

Saum, C.A. and Gray, A.R. (2008) 'Facilitating change for women? Exploring the role of therapeutic jurisprudence in drug court', in T. Anderson (ed.) *Neither Villain Nor Victim: Empowerment and Agency Among Women Substance Abusers.* New Brunswick, NJ: Rutgers University Press.

Saum, C., Scarpitti, F.R., Butzin, C.A., Perez, V.W., Jennings, D. and Gray, A.R. (2002) 'Drug court participants' satisfaction with treatment and the court experience', *Drug Court Review,* 4 (1): 39–82.

Scottish Government (2007) *Reforming and Revitalising: Report of the Review of Community Penalties.* Edinburgh: Scottish Government.

Scottish Government (2008) *Protecting Scotland's Communities: Fair, Fast and Flexible Justice.* Edinburgh: Scottish Government.

Scottish Parliament (2009) *Justice Committee Inquiry – Criminal Justice and Licensing (Scotland) Bill: Written submissions received.* Online at: www.scottish.parliament.uk/s3/committees/justice/inquiries/CriminalJusticeandLicensing/ju-criminaljustice-evid.htm (accessed 6 January 2010).

Scottish Prisons Commission (2008) *Scotland's Choice: Report of the Scottish Prisons Commission.* Edinburgh: Scottish Prisons Commission.

Senjo, S. and Leip, L.A. (2001) 'Testing therapeutic jurisprudence theory: an empirical assessment of the drug court process', *Western Criminology Review,* 3 (1). Online at: wer.sonoma.edu/v3n1/senjo.html (accessed November 2009).

Took, G. (2005) 'Therapeutic jurisprudence and the drug courts: hybrid justice and its implications for modern penality', *Internet Journal of Criminology.* Online at: www.internetjournalofcriminology.com/Glenn%20Took%20-%20Therapeutic%20Jurisprudence.pdf (accessed 6 January 2010).

Turnbull, P.J., McSweeney, T., Webster, R., Edmunds, M. and Hough, M. (2000) *Drug Treatment and Testing Orders: Final Evaluation Report,* Home Office Research Study 212. London: Home Office.

Tyler, T.R. (1990) *Why People Obey the Law.* New Haven, CT: Yale University Press.

Wexler, D.B (2001) 'Robes and rehabilitation: how judges can help offenders "make good"', *Court Review,* Spring: 18–23.

Wexler, D.B. and Winick, B.J. (1992) 'The potential of therapeutic jurisprudence: a new approach to psychology and the law', in J.R.P. Ogloff (ed.) *The Law and Psychology: The Broadening of the Discipline.* Durham, NC: Carolina Academic Press.

Wexler, D.B. and Winick, B.J. (1996) 'Introduction', in D.B. Wexler and B.J. Winick (eds) *Law in a Therapeutic Key: Developments in Therapeutic Jurisprudence*. Durham, NC: Carolina Academic Press.

Winick, B.J. and Wexler, D.B. (eds) (2003) *Judging in a Therapeutic Key*. Durham, NC: Carolina Academic Press.

Part Four

Significant others and social networks

Chapter 12

It's relational: integrating family into community corrections

Carol Shapiro and Margaret diZerega

Introduction

Families entwined in the justice system and their extended social networks are a natural, though underutilised, resource for community corrections. These families – defined broadly to include both traditional and elected members such as godparents, mentors, and clergy – are complex, facing serious issues and challenges, yet also possessing strengths and resources that probation and parole agencies can leverage to support successful community supervision. Who is there 24 hours a day and instantly recognises signs of distress? Who knows best the person under supervision? And who will be there long after supervision ends? By working with the families and the community supports of individuals on probation and parole, officers can capitalise on existing formal and informal resources to realise several benefits, not the least being reduction of technical violations and desistance from crime. Family engagement is a necessary component of any community corrections strategy that aims to interrupt cycles of juvenile and criminal justice involvement, improve family well-being, and promote public safety.

This chapter introduces readers to an innovative and practical family-focused approach that was piloted in one New York City neighbourhood in partnership with probation and parole staff, and has since been applied in several states. The authors highlight research that supports strength-based, family-focused approaches and successful practices, and offer concrete examples of how community corrections staff can integrate tools and methods into existing supervision practices. The research and examples provided underscore the value of leveraging strengths, instead of focusing on deficits and pathology, both as individual officers and as an organisation. There is not only one way of adopting or applying a strength-based, family-focused approach; it is the authors' hope that the readers will be inspired to reflect, experiment, and tailor the tools and methods presented to best enhance your current practice.

Families as context

People under probation or parole supervision and their families are disproportionately affected, often across generations, by poverty, violence, mental illness, substance abuse, chronic illnesses, including HIV/AIDS, and a host of co-occurring disorders (Travis and Petersilia 2001; Rose and Clear 1998). Discovering this family context provides community corrections officers with a fuller, more accurate picture of the lives of the individuals they supervise.

It is not uncommon to hear about the concentrations of people under community supervision residing in particular neighbourhoods and the challenges that this can pose for community corrections officers and families alike. Many re-entry efforts are informed by neighbourhood maps that reveal where local resources could be targeted (Swartz and Cadora 2001, cited in Travis 2005: 283). For example, community corrections officers may shift their caseload so that it is geographically specific and make more time for home visits. Or police officers, in concert with probation and parole, may elect to focus on certain neighbourhoods and to understand the networks at play. While the neighbourhood concentration of people involved in the justice system can seem daunting, it can also provide an opportunity for concentrating resources, and working community-wide to tap the often positive and supportive connections people have to their neighbours.

Using a broad definition of family can help identify the most significant people in an individual's life.[1] A family, broadly defined, includes friends, neighbours, faith-based organisations and other members in a person's social network, as well as immediate and extended blood relatives. This inclusive definition takes into consideration that a range of people play pivotal roles in the lives of supervisees and often share in their successes and their struggles.

Families and social networks as resources for community corrections

Despite the challenges outlined above, many community corrections professionals have found that with proper support, even fragile families can provide crucial resources. These resources include stable housing, symptom or problem monitoring, medication management, crisis intervention, connections to employment opportunities or treatment programmes, and a source of feedback to probation and parole officers. This feedback can be instrumental to officers in making appropriate decisions to ensure that supervision mandates are followed without overusing periods of incarceration as a sanction. Families and social networks are a natural system for early crisis intervention; family members see the symptoms or early indicators when a loved one with a drug addiction is relapsing or at risk of relapse. They see changes in behaviour and other signs if someone is no longer taking medication for mental illness or another serious condition. As research has demonstrated, family relationships can be a significant influence in preventing relapse among parolees dealing with addiction (Slaght 1999). By serving as an early warning system of approaching problems, families can assist community corrections officers in balancing their obligations to guard the public safety without expending public funds.

A large body of research shows that by serving as sources of motivation and support, family members can help decrease recidivism among their loved ones in addition to helping each other deal with drug use and other challenges (Visher *et al.* 2004; La Vigne *et al.* 2004; Visher *et al.* 2006; Brooks *et al.* 2005; La Vigne and Kachnowski 2005; Bobbitt and Nelson 2004; Nelson *et al.* 1999; Center for Substance Abuse Treatment 2004). In studying probationers, Farrall and Calverley examined the connection between reuniting people with their families and avoiding activities that could lead to new crimes. They found that families play two roles: 'families of formation appeared to have acted as a motivating influence on probationers' desire to desist, whilst families of origin appear to have offered an avenue of support in achieving this change' (Farrall and Calverley 2006: 23).

The impact of this family motivation and support on treatment and community supervision adherence can be impressive: during six months of family case management at La Bodega de la Familia – a demonstration project of the Vera Institute of Justice from which the national nonprofit Family Justice grew – arrest rates among drug users were 11 per cent, in contrast to 21 per cent in a comparison group. Among families, 80 per cent resolved social service needs and 90 per cent resolved medical service needs (Sullivan *et al*. 2002).

The literature on desistance elucidates how the motivation, encouragement and emotional support families and social networks provide acts to increase public safety. Community members, including neighbours and employees of social service agencies, can play a key role in offering someone recently released from prison a new perspective on their capabilities to meet goals and comply with supervision mandates. As Maruna (2001: 96) describes, 'At first, the individual had no belief in himself or herself, but someone else (often a partner or a social organization) "believed in" the person and made the ex-offender realize they did in fact have personal value.' The process of seeing oneself differently and more favourably can facilitate a new path to desistance for someone who has been incarcerated or otherwise entangled in the criminal justice system. Parents, children, siblings, godparents, friends, neighbours, and community and faith leaders: these are the people who can help individuals see their possibilities and keep them invested.

One way in which family and community networks provide avenues of support is by serving as conduits of information and distributors of resources through and among their members. This information can be vital for individuals on community supervision to overcome key challenges of re-entry. Take, for example, the challenge of finding a job. Economists have argued that employment is positively correlated with connections to relatives, friends and acquaintances because people in social networks transmit job information to their contacts. Unemployed individuals, including formerly incarcerated individuals, very frequently learn of job opportunities through social networks (Calvó-Armengol and Jackson 2004). Family, friends and other network contacts can help distribute information and point the way towards existing resources. When agencies and professionals tap family members and equip them with the tools they need to support one another, they can decrease reliance on government and costly social service agencies.

Engaging families as partners in problem-solving and supervision monitoring, community corrections officers can access long-term connections that outlast government interventions or treatment. When someone finishes parole, loses touch with their case manager, or stops going for check-ups at a local clinic, family members remain in that individual's life. Even during treatment or supervision, family members are available to one another day or night, after offices close and programmes end; with support, they can play a unique, 24-hour role in preventing crime.

Network ties can be strengthened in many ways, including through corrections and community corrections staff. For prison staff and probation and parole officers, the challenge is to develop new approaches that recognise, reinforce and capitalise on family and social support networks. Tapping the resources of social networks requires treating families with respect, recognising their strengths, and acknowledging their power to make decisions and maximise their resources. When families feel comfortable reaching out to probation and parole officers, they can work as a team to prevent escalation of the harm, or violations of supervision orders.

Applying a family-focused approach to community supervision

When community corrections officers or agents become aware of the important family influences that may affect the success of reintegration, the possibility of new alliances can be formed within the family, community and service providers. Indeed, the individual returning home can serve as a conduit for prevention or intervention for the whole family, opening up opportunities for disrupting the harmful cycles of involvement with the justice system. Understanding the multiple players in a supervisee's environment is essential for probation and parole officers when encouraging self-sufficiency and preventing relapse. Given the multiple and intersecting challenges often faced by people under supervision and their families, it is important to identify and draw on available resources without ignoring challenges other family members are facing that may impact a supervisee's ability to adhere to mandates. A 2005 study of La Bodega de la Familia (discussed earlier as an effective family case management programme) demonstrated the prevalence of criminal justice involvement, substance abuse and HIV/AIDS co-occurring among families:

> Of the 62 families (with a total of 592 individuals) 82% had at least one other member besides the index case with a history of substance use, 62% had two or more, and 40% had three or more; 72% had one other member with a history of criminal justice involvement, 45% had two or more, 24% had three or more. At least one member had HIV/AIDS in 49% of the families, 16% had two or more, 10% had three or more. Of the 105 family members who reported a history of criminal justice involvement, 88% had a history of substance use. (Barreras *et al.* 2005: 162)

During the re-entry transition, probation and parole officers interact consistently with people under community supervision and have access to a range of resources and services useful to support parolees, probationers and their families as they deal with these complicated issues of mental illness, drug use and addiction, child support and family violence.

Recognising informal social controls and stressors, such as influences by the family, peers or the broader community, corrections professionals can better design case plans to meet the needs of the individual. The stressors to family members living with someone under probation or parole, on an electronic monitoring device, or waiting for someone to return home who is incarcerated can affect the entire family system, impair the mutual exchange of quality support within a family, and weaken the physical and mental health of other family members. For example, a family member with mental illness who is having difficulty complying with her medication regimen may make it difficult for someone under supervision to comply with supervision requirements. High stress can lead to missed appointments as well as affect overall stability. Family members can support one another in meeting the commitments associated with community supervision and in acquiring medication, counselling, access to self-help groups, and a range of other available formal and informal supports. The needs of the individual, their family, and the community can be comprehensively met during incarceration and reintegration (Pattillo, *et al.* 2004).

Although some probation or parole officers may never meet the families of people under community supervision, asking the right questions can still clarify the context of how social networks and families affect a person's success under community supervision. Who do you help and who helps you? If things were to change in your life, who would be the first to notice? These types of questions might reveal hidden resources and responsibilities, such as a sister who can help with childcare, transportation, or financial support; an uncle or pastor who could lend computer skills, help fill out an application, or know a small-business owner who can offer a job; or a supervisee who is responsible for checking in to make sure his grandmother is taking her medication. Questions about family can also unearth stressors that could lead to supervision violations; for example, information that a recently released daughter who has not followed through with employment counselling repeatedly fights with her mother with whom she is living.

A family-focused approach can be employed by institutional parole agents who are assisting people to prepare for re-entry, as well as agents working in the field. Some prison-based re-entry workers have used email, teleconferencing, and video conferencing to enable better preparation for resettlement at home. The growing use of technology helps families interact more frequently and often enables family members to participate in the case planning process (Pattillo et al. 2004). The Singapore Prison System encourages incarcerated individuals to stay in contact with family through 'tele-visits' when families cannot visit in person (Singapore Prison Service 2008). The Scottish Prison System invites families to participate in annual case conferencing meetings and employs family contact development officers to help loved ones maintain connections during incarceration. In addition to helping address substance use of people who are incarcerated, the officers also address substance use within the family (Stöver and Weilandt 2007). When officers and families work together to draw on a family's social network of support, their interaction demonstrates respect for a family's culture and dynamics and helps gather information on the kinds of specific supports necessary for success while under community supervision. Cultivating collaboration, respect and trust with people under community supervision and their families can reset their relationship with government, and help a family stabilise and improve their well-being.

Family mapping

Individuals leaving prison and jail often return to families coping with multiple issues and consequently are involved in multiple governmental systems. The 'ecomap', a family mapping tool, depicts government agencies and private organisations involved in the lives of the participant and family. A local state school attended by a child, a community-based agency providing preventive services, a health clinic, a drug treatment programme, or a peer support group at a local ministry could all feature prominently in an ecomap. The ecomap provides a visual representation of the family in this institutional environment, highlighting conflict between services and the need for coordination. However, an ecomap can also identify valuable resources outside the family – potential sources of support that may be tapped in new ways. Ecomaps can display significant nurturing or conflicted connections between the family and the world (Hartman and Laird 1983). An ecomap resembles a diagram of a solar system, with the family as the sun in the centre, and other important people and institutions depicted as circles around the centre – planets orbiting the sun (see Figure 12.1).

The ecomap can be constructed in the early stages of community supervision during a home visit when more than one family member is present, during office visits, or even during re-entry planning. The ecomap is used to draw out existing resources, prevent duplication of services, and help justice-involved individuals think creatively to identify places, people and organisations they had not previously considered resources. Although only one person may be under supervision, the pooled resources of the family should be gathered when creating the ecomap. It should reflect the resources of the primary support system, along with those of the person under supervision. The ecomap is a dynamic, flexible tool that the community supervision agent and the family can regularly reference and update.

The connections among family members and the resources in their ecological system can be elicited by asking open-ended questions. 'Think about an average week in your life. What appointments do you keep?' 'What do you do on a Saturday afternoon?' 'Who picks

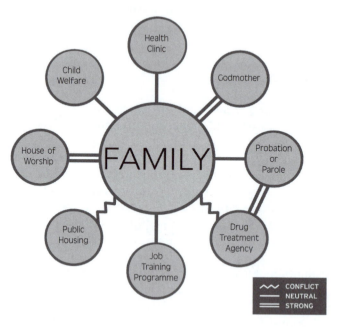

Figure 12.1 An ecomap.

your children up from school?' 'Who asks you for help?' These are all questions that can begin a conversation about the family's resources. As each new resource is mentioned, the parole officer, a designated family member, or the person under supervision writes the information in one of the circles surrounding the family. As a resource is recorded, the parole officer asks questions about the family's relationship to that resource. For example, if the person under supervision talks about wanting to get a referral to a health clinic or a substance abuse treatment programme, the parole officer can ask, 'What health clinics in the neighbourhood have your family members frequented? Have they found those clinics helpful? Who might be able to tell you more about the clinic and how to schedule an appointment?'

As information about the nature of the family's relationship with the resource is disclosed, a line is drawn from the centre circle to the outer circle containing the information about the treatment programme. The pattern of the line (strong, neutral, conflict) indicates the type of relationship between the family and the resource. If a family member recently started counselling, the relationship line should indicate the strength of the relationship with the counsellor. Questions the probation or parole officer can ask to assess the quality of the relationship might include: 'Can you tell me a little about your relationship with your counsellor?' or 'In what ways has your counsellor been helpful?' This enquiry allows the family, the person under community justice supervision, and the probation or parole officer to assess the nature of the relationship together.

Families should be actively engaged in the assessment of their institutional networks; community supervision officers can use the following questions to promote participation and to explore family-system relationships:

- What is the relationship with a particular system?
- What is positive about the relationship? What is challenging about the relationship?
- Which relationships would the family like to keep in its life? Why?
- Which connections would the family like to change? Why?

Exploring the involved systems and the quality of the relationships to those systems allows the parole officer to assess the resources in use and those not being accessed but potentially available to the family. This process also helps to prioritise intervention and determine areas in need of immediate attention.

249

Seeing a graphic depiction of their networks can be a revelatory experience for families. For the first time, they may recognise all of the people, agencies and entities in their lives. Many of the systems with which they are involved may not be systems they would typically choose (such as child welfare, parole, probation, drug treatment). The goal is for the individual or family to see their ecomap change over time, so that the systems with which they are involved are increasingly systems of their own choosing.

Case study: Oklahoma Department of Corrections

In Oklahoma, Family Justice spurred the Department of Corrections (DOC) to integrate families and social networks throughout its Oklahoma City operations; the DOC is interested in enhancing its work similarly throughout the state. Since forging this partnership in 2004, the DOC has incorporated training on a strength-based, family-focused approach into new staff orientation and has reinforced the message through brochures for families, in senior staff meetings, and with the Board of Corrections.

Through its partnership with the American Probation and Parole Association, Family Justice provided training and technical assistance to community supervision officers in Oklahoma City. Those officers now routinely use family-mapping tools; staff members invite families into meetings because they know what a vital resource social support can be in helping people complete supervision successfully. As part of the initial assessment, probation agents now ask about capable guardians: supportive individuals the person under supervision can rely on during the course of supervision. Now that local facilities are using the Relational Inquiry Tool – an engagement tool Family Justice developed for corrections case managers to learn about prisoners' strengths and social support (DiZerega and Shapiro 2007) – staff will have the added benefit of drawing on information from the tool when discussing social support with people under community supervision.

Integrating the family-focused approach at the agency level

Choosing to integrate a family-focused approach into community corrections practice is a catalytic step towards effecting organisational change and broadening the types of outcomes an agency can measure. In certain agencies, this choice can lead to a broader change effort while in others it can be the focal point of a reform movement. While organisational and policy changes can be a benefit to workplace safety, morale and diversity of opportunity, their implementation will require follow-up. Introducing change to an organisation's structure alters the climate and the culture of the workplace for its employees (Schneider, *et al.* 1996). Such change can be successfully managed by exercising clear communication and encouraging learning among staff at all levels throughout the organisation (Mohrman *et al.* 2003). Introducing change in community corrections and correctional settings can be particularly challenging because of the long-standing history of the environment, the priority placed on safety and security, and staff tenure. Thus, it is essential to have a vision that is fully supported by those who will make efforts to engage staff, whether an individual is a supervisor, parole officer or administrator.

A cultural change is most effective when approached with more than a traditional top-down effort (Hubbell and Abbott 2006). A strength-based and family-focused approach may shift a perceived balance from the law enforcement component of community corrections towards a social service orientation. This is likely to generate intense reactions and must be carefully managed. Community corrections agencies can take several key steps to guide organisational cultural shifts, and support, rather than enforce, the use of a strength-based, family-focused approach (Mullins and Toner 2008):

- Assess and challenge, when necessary, staff assumptions about their own roles in engaging and working with families.

- Examine policies and procedures to assess whether they may inhibit (even inadvertently) the application of a family-focused approach.

- Review, revise, or create new forms to gather information about social support providers for people under community supervision.

- Develop a system of graduated responses for addressing non-compliance and providing incentives for positive behaviour.

- Provide training for staff on the tools and methods of a strength-based, family-focused approach.

- Develop a plan for assessing staff and agency performance and outcomes related to implementing the approach.

Successful implementation of a strength-based, family-focused approach requires training and technical assistance specifically adapted to the needs of the department or agency. Perhaps most importantly, a democratic and encompassing decision-making process is necessary for the site-specific use of the approach; this allows for a diversity of roles, experiences and opinions. The authors recommend the creation of a work group comprising front-line staff, mid-level managers and senior-level supervisors. Staff selected for the work group, by representing a range of opinions and perspectives, will be able to select the key focus areas, raise and address implementation challenges, and serve to guide their peers through this change process.

In addition to using supportive methods in planning, probation and parole agents must receive strength-based supervision as they learn to use new tools. Managers and supervisors must make a serious commitment to apply a strength-based approach to interactions with their staff and with one another. By modelling strength-based values and skills in interactions with staff, supervisors can help community corrections officers develop and use these values and skills in their work with participants. Creating an environment where identifying and building on strengths and motivation are commonplace will deepen staff understanding and experience of a strength-based approach. Strategies for incorporating strength-based supervision include using open-ended questions when discussing cases; helping staff identify and talk about their strengths; and talking with staff about their reactions to their work. Importantly, commitment by managers in everyday practice will reduce any stigma associated with integrating this new approach.

Understanding officers' emotional response to the people they work with is key to positively affecting their interventions with people under community supervision. Self-awareness is critical to effective case management; officers must recognise that they have different reactions to different people based on their own values, beliefs, judgements and prejudices. An officer's choice to explore or avoid particular areas of content may be directly related to personal comfort or discomfort with the material. The choice and phrasing of questions may reveal to supervisees the officer's enthusiasm or judgement. For example, an officer who has personal experience with substance abuse, either first-hand or with a family member, may be over-sympathetic to a participant struggling with the same challenge, or angry and upset with their behaviour. To keep those feelings in check, officers must be willing to explore their own feelings while working with an individual. It is important for officers to be able to recognise whether emotional reactions result from a supervisee's behaviour, or if such reactions are projections based on the officer's own personal or familial history. Continued success in applying a new way of looking at individuals under community supervision will require both explicit and implicit guidance from those in supervisory roles.

Case study: a multi-agency collaboration

In San Francisco, the juvenile and adult probation departments are collaborating on an innovative initiative of the Mayor's Office to bring a strength-based, family-focused approach to the Bayview-Hunters Point area. The neighbourhood was selected as an area for innovation after maps revealed that many of its residents are involved in numerous government systems including juvenile and adult probation, child welfare and public housing. Like every family, those that find themselves navigating multiple systems also possess natural strengths and resources. The San Francisco initiative, with technical assistance and training from Family Justice, is working to tap this social capital to improve neighbourhood safety, ease the burden on families, reduce their involvement in government systems, and increase family well-being.

The multi-agency group leading the initiative includes Adult Probation, Juvenile Probation, the Human Services Agency, the Unified School District, the Department of Public Health, and several community-based programmes providing mandated and supportive services to residents of Bayview-Hunters Point. The initiative will closely mirror San Francisco's Children's System of Care (CSOC), a strength-based, family-driven approach that uses a collaborative model in working with families. Underlying CSOC is the idea of exercising family voice and choice to leverage the natural supports of social networks and communities. CSOC puts this principle into action by assisting families in addressing their needs and government mandates to achieve their goals. Current plans call for a neutral facilitator to lead a process that includes family-driven meetings. Family members will invite government or community-based partners to guide them as they formulate a plan to resolve the challenges they face. This family action plan will be based on the strengths and resources of each family, broadly defined, and will include formal and informal supports.

The San Francisco initiative offers a glimpse into the ways community corrections can fully integrate a family-focused approach – thinking not only beyond the individual to include the family, but going a step further by integrating the other systems in which the family is involved. What aspects of a family-focused approach could be applied in your agency tomorrow? Some may be specific things you can try within supervision meetings while others may have a larger impact on your colleagues. Whatever you select, there is too much knowledge about the impact of justice involvement on families, and the potential for family members to be tapped as a resource, not to try something new.

Conclusion

A family-focused approach to community supervision not only helps actualise the goals of community corrections to increase compliance with supervision requirements and improve public safety, but also builds on these successes to address social issues and injustices. As Donald Evans in *Corrections Today* states:

> [Community corrections] cannot be viewed as solely working with the individual, but rather ... should also be concerned about correcting injustices, social problems and advocating for improved social environments that foster pro-social behavior. Community corrections involves both holding the offender accountable for his or her actions and speaking to the responsibility and accountability of communities in preventing crime. (Evans 2004: 6)

A tough economy, coupled with growing caseloads for community corrections officers, underscores the perfect opportunity to tap a natural, cost-effective and underutilised resource: the family. Best of all, by shifting away from deficits and pathology-oriented supervision, we reinforce the value of line staff and mid-level managers' expertise to model this enhancement. There is no better time for managers and their staff to experiment with the integration of strength and family-focused tools and methods. As the pressure mounts for this field of practice to achieve long-term, sustainable public safety, community corrections must seek cost-effective and long-term allies. Families are often the first victims and may be a part of the problem, but they are certainly a key ingredient for the solution.

Note

1 Throughout this chapter, the term family is defined broadly. Family includes traditional and non-traditional members, which may mean friends, significant others, clergy, co-workers, or other important people in one's social network.

References

Barreras, R., Drucker, E. and Rosenthal, D. (2005) 'The concentration of substance use, criminal justice involvement, and HIV/AIDS in the families of drug offenders', *Journal of Urban Health*, 82 (1).

Bobbitt, M. and Nelson, M. (2004) *The Front Line: Building Programs that Recognize Families' Role in Reentry*. New York: Vera Institute of Justice.

Brooks, L.E., Solomon, A.L., Keegan, S., Kohl, R. and Lahue, L. (2005) *Prisoner Reentry in Massachusetts*. Washington, DC: Urban Institute.

Calvó-Armengol, A. and Jackson, M.O. (2004) 'The effects of social networks on employment and inequality', *American Economic Review*, 94 (3): 426–7.

Center for Substance Abuse Treatment (2004) *Selected Research Outcomes for Family Approaches to Substance Abuse Treatment*. Rockville: Substance Abuse and Mental Health Services Administration.

DiZerega, M. and Shapiro, C. (2007) 'Asking about family can enhance reentry', *Corrections Today*.

Evans, D. (2004) 'Why community corrections matters', *Corrections Today*.

Farrall, S. and Calverley, A. (2006) *Understanding Desistance from Crime: Emerging Theoretical Directions in Resettlement and Rehabilitation*. Maidenhead: Open University Press.

Hartman, A. and Laird, J. (1983) *Family-Centered Social Work Practice*. New York: The Free Press.

Hubbell, L. and Abbott, S. (2006) 'Cultural change in a maximum security prison', *Public Manager*, 35 (2): 29–33.

La Vigne, N.G. and Brazzell, D. (2008) *Mapping Community Data on Children of Prisoners: strategies and insights*. Washington, DC: Urban Institute.

La Vigne, N.G. and Kachnowski. V. (2005) *Texas Prisoners' Reflections on Returning Home*. Washington, DC: Urban Institute.

La Vigne, N.G., Visher, C. and Castro, J. (2004). *Chicago Prisoners' Experiences Returning Home*. Washington, DC: Urban Institute.

Maruna, S. (2001) *Making Good: How Ex-convicts Reform and Rebuild their Lives*. Washington, DC: American Psychological Association.

Mohrman, S.A., Tenkasi, R.V. and Mohrman, A.M. (2003) 'The role of networks in fundamental organizational change', *Journal of Applied Behavioral Science*, 39 (3): 301–23.

Morenoff, J.D. and Sampson, R.J. (1997) 'Violent crime and the spatial dynamics of neighborhood transition: Chicago 1970–1990', *Social Forces*, 76 (1): 31–64.

Mullins, T. and Toner. C. (2008) *Implementing the Family Support Approach for Community Supervision*. Lexington: American Probation and Parole Association/New York: Family Justice.

Nelson, M., Deess, P. and Allen, C. (1999) *The First Month Out: Post-incarceration Experiences in New York City*. New York: Vera Institute of Justice.

Pattillo, M., Weiman, D. and Western, B. (eds) (2004) *Imprisoning America: The Social Effects of Mass Incarceration*. New York: Russell Sage Foundation.

Rose, D.R. and Clear, T.R. (1998) 'Incarceration, social capital, and crime: implications for social disorganization theory', *Criminology*, 36 (3): 441–79.

Schneider, B., Brief, A.P. and Guzzo, R. (1996) 'Creating a climate and culture for sustainable organizational change', *Organizational Dynamics*, 24: 7–19.

Singapore Prison Service (2008) *New Visit Centres Increase Convenience for Inmates to Maintain Family Ties*. Online at: www.prisons.gov.sg/press/27052008.html (accessed 5 November 2009).

Slaght, E. (1999) 'Family and offender treatment focusing on the family in the treatment of substance abusing criminal offenders', *Journal of Drug Education* 29 (1): 53–62.

Stöver, H. and Weilandt, C. (2007) 'Drug use and drug services in prisons', in L. Møller, H. Stöver, R. Jürgens, A. Gatherer and H. Nikogosian (eds) *Health in Prisons: A WHO Guide to the Essentials in Prison Health*. World Health Organization. Online at: www.icpa.ca/tools/download/582/WHO_Prison_Health_Guide.pdf (accessed 4 November 2009).

Sullivan, E., Mino, M. Nelson, K. and Pope, J. (2002) *Families as a Resource in Recovery from Drug Abuse: an evaluation of La Bodega de la Familia*. New York: Vera Institute of Justice.

Travis, J. (2005) *But They All Come Back: Facing the Challenges of Prisoner Reentry*. Washington, DC: Urban Institute Press.

Travis, J. and Petersilia, J. (2001) 'Reentry reconsidered: a new look at an old question', *Crime and Delinquency*, 47 (3): 291–313.

Visher, C., Baer, D. and Naser, R. (2006) *Ohio Prisoners' Reflections on Returning Home*. Washington, DC: Urban Institute.

Visher, C., La Vigne, N.G. and Travis, J. (2004) *Returning Home: Understanding the Challenges of Prisoner Reentry*. Washington, DC: Urban Institute.

Chapter 13

Justice for all: family matters in offender supervision

Bas Vogelvang and Herman van Alphen

Introduction

When considering the role of the client's nuclear and extended family in offender supervision, some preliminary remarks are necessary. First, no probation client is limited to his role as 'offender' only. Although the justice system and the current offender supervision methods based on the Psychology of Criminal Conduct ('what works'; see Bonta and Andrews, this volume) focus on the probation client's role as offender while intervening in his life, it is clear that this role is temporary and that it stands in the broader context of the offender's role as a child of his parents, and often as a sibling, partner, parent and extended family member. Roles involve a set of practical and developmental tasks, linked with expectations and responsibilities. Living up to these is highly correlated with acceptance of and reciprocity with others, both in the family system of the probation client and in the justice system. The duration and importance of family roles, however, go beyond the time-limited role as probation client, and are of crucial importance for his individual development and attainment of personal goals. Family lasts a lifetime.

Second, from a juridical point of view, the justice system (offender supervision included) and the nuclear and extended family have no relationship with each other (except in connection with intra-familial offences). Cooperation of family members in offender supervision can never be forced by law. Family and probation officers always work together on a voluntary basis.

Our third point follows from this and is the main theme of this chapter. How can the best of both worlds be combined: the potential of family roles for human development and the strengths of offender supervision (combined with behavioural interventions and additional care) to promote and reinforce a lifestyle without crime? Which diagnostic frameworks are available for assessment of family matters within a judicial framework? Which supervision strategies and intervention techniques in this domain are known to be best practices for probation officers and partner organisations, or have even been proven effective?

In our attempt to answer this question in this chapter, we will first present some evidence about the prevalence of family problems and strengths in the Dutch probation population, and their relationships with crime and recidivism. Then, following a synopsis of the knowledge base regarding working with families in the context of offender supervision, we will look into the current practices of Dutch probation officers when working with family systems. Based on a comparison of the knowledge base and current practices, we present a family-focused framework for diagnosis and treatment planning, following the insights of the family therapist Boszormenyi-Nagy. We conclude this chapter with a set of recommendations.

The knowledge base: the role of the family in delinquency and desistance[1]

Offenders and family problems

Marital and family problems are prevalent in a substantial part of the offender population. Based on a survey of 2,797 RISc assessments,[2] it appeared that 55.9 per cent of the offenders with a moderate to high risk of reconviction were diagnosed as having moderate to severe problems with marital and family relations (Van der Knaap et al. 2007). With low risk cases included, the prevalence appears to be 44 per cent (Bambacht and Van Deursen 2009). Investigating the predictive validity of the RISc, Van der Knaap and Alberda (2009) report that marital and family problems are highly prevalent in the probation population, but do not seem to be related to recidivism. Domestic violence, however, proved to be the exception: ranging from low to high risk offenders, domestic violence significantly contributed to the prediction of violent recidivism (Van der Knaap and Alberda 2009). If families themselves are not supported, they can be drawn into what could be described as 'prison culture' and become consumed by the issues facing their loved one in prison and isolating themselves further from their communities (thereby weakening the communities as well). Families are indeed at risk of being seen as the 'forgotten victims' of the criminal justice system (Matthews 1989).

It is worth mentioning, however, that numerous reports show a mix of both positive and negative aspects of family and partner relationships, and probably 30 to 50 per cent of all offenders experience *only* positive relationships or at most limited problems in this domain. Families and partners can provide advice and guidance to offenders and are often the first people to point out to the offender the negative consequences of engaging in criminal activity. They can encourage a sense of responsibility and persuade offenders to accept help from other agencies including offender supervision. Farrall concludes that the extended family often is of crucial importance for the offender, offering them housing and helping them find a job after leaving prison (see La Vigne *et al.* 2009). Therefore, it may be presumed that the impact of interventions might be increased if families and partners were more involved in discussions between agencies and the offender (Garland *et al.* 2001).

Within the offender supervision (and broader criminology) literature, family and partner relations are often conceptualised as aspects of *social capital* (McNeill 2002; Maruna and Toch 2003), pointed out by many researchers as some of the most important factors in both criminal careers and desistance processes (for example, Farrall 2000; Gendreau *et al.* 1996). McNeill (2009a) distinguishes bonding, linking and bridging social capital. Bonding capital relates to strong and (emotionally) expressive ties with others in similar social circumstances, such as family members, intimate partners, neighbours and friends. Several studies show us that stable family and partner relationship ties are indeed key factors in the effective reduction of reoffending (Ohlin 1954; Glaser 1964; Holt and Miller 1972).

The workings of bonding capital are, however, complex. Offender maturity appears to be a mediating variable: reviewing the literature has led Claessens (2006) to conclude that having a stable relationship significantly affects the desistance process of male offenders only over the age of 25. Bonding social capital can be criminogenic as well, with well-known examples of 'delinquent' or criminal families, gangs and racist groups. Within these social ties, pro-social behaviour is certainly present (emotional and material support are available), but they are often accompanied by violent forms of control and intimidation.

Finally, it is worth mentioning that *non*-criminogenic social capital need not always lead to success or well-being. Particularly emotionally enmeshed families or religious sects can be demanding and oppressive, leading to excessive feelings of obligation and loyalty that can hold back an individual in his efforts to outgrow or leave his social group or milieu (Boeck *et al.* 2006).

The above examples tend to imply a one-way linear effect of the social context (sender) on the offender (receiver). A fundamental assumption of the human development perspective, however, is its bi-directional nature; the developing individual influences his social context, thereby influencing his own development in a reciprocal manner (Bronfenbrenner 1979, 1988, 1992, 2005). Thus we should see the 'desister' as someone who will actively seek, select and reinforce people and opportunities that assist him or her in his or her efforts to keep away from criminal behaviour. According to Farrall, circular causality of desistance is visible in the fact that, when such supports or opportunities are available, their successful use appears to depend on the motivation and skills of the offender. Farrall and Calverley (2006) state that the effort to keep a job, a living space, or a good relationship, combined with the (fear of) possible loss of good reputation or respect, together form the offender's share in the desistance process.

Application of the knowledge base in Dutch offender supervision

The mission statement of probation services in most European countries focuses on individual responsibility of the offender and offender supervision as a means to make for a safer society (Van Kalmthout and Durnescu 2008; Poort 2008). For example, in spite of the high prevalence of crime-related marital and family problems and the huge protective potential of these relationships, intervention techniques for family work and system intervention are very scarce in probation supervision. The one important exception to this is the growing attention to domestic violence within the probation services. For all other family matters, however, the new official Dutch supervision method recommends 'systemic work', which is restricted to just one page (Poort 2009; RN/LJ&R/SVG 2009). Partners and family members in the assessment phase are often limited to having an informant role (Bambacht and Van Deursen 2009). Family members, interviewed by these researchers, expressed a need for clear agreements about their involvement. Concrete interventions or strategies for family work are not described, and as a consequence it is down to the probation officer to design, use and evaluate these, using their practice-based resources (Vogelvang 2009).

Additional file-research by Bambacht and Van Deursen revealed a gap between the identification of family-related problems and the rate of actually formulated goals and interventions to tackle these problems. In just 37 per cent of all cases with a high need in this domain, goals were formulated in the supervision plan. Additional analysis revealed that in only 31 per cent of all files, positive remarks were made about the marital or family system, leading to goals and/ or interventions in only 47 per cent of these cases (15 per cent in all). The authors conclude that treatment planning by probation workers is highly individual and mostly problem-oriented; families are rarely seen as a positive resource in the change process. And although their formal/judicial mandate and task allows them to engage in family work, the probation services currently offer no training to improve these skills.

To conclude, the potential strengths of marital and family relations are probably not fully appreciated in offender supervision. We find the discrepancy between the frequency and severity of observed family-related problems and strengths on the one hand, and the lack of available training and actual applied interventions on the other, quite alarming. Robinson and Raynor (2006) define offender supervision as a relational process, stating that reintegration takes place in the context of relationships and interactions with significant others. It follows that not only individual and situational needs must be addressed, but also the social ties of the offender with these significant others and society as a whole. In the remainder of this chapter, we present a theoretical basis and framework for family- and desistance-focused practice in offender supervision.

The contextual perspective

Desistance and reciprocity

According to Farrall (2004), finding, achieving or being offered something that is of great personal importance and relevance is crucial for probation clients to re-evaluate their life, to start a desistance process and to persevere in it. It must be something that 'fits you and hits you' (Vogelvang 2008), and opens the door for developing an identity that no longer relies on criminal behaviour to validate itself. Within the context of the family as a source of bonding social capital, the above also implies that the family (or at least one or more members) is (still) prepared and willing to give something to the probation client, and that the probation client is at least willing to accept it. This exchange transcends a businesslike transaction, because family members are not bound by contract to do these things. When offered something, and then being able to accept it and work with it, the probation client experiences feelings of self-respect and (a possibly overwhelming) obligation to (finally) make things work. This is the symbolic value of getting a job, a living space, or a parenting role, of having a family member who is willing to monitor your risk behaviour, of being allowed to visit your children: the probation client is still part of the family dynamics of giving and taking, redemption and forgiveness, loyalty and merit. The probation client is still in a position to influence these dynamics by receiving with gratitude and giving back, and is allowed to make good, to repair past mistakes. The probation client is included in what the family-therapist Boszormenyi-Nagy refers to as the dynamics of relational ethics (Boszormenyi-Nagy and Spark 1973; Boszormenyi-Nagy *et al.* 1991; Le Goff 2001).

Relational ethics

In Boszormenyi-Nagy's view, the most fundamental but often neglected aspect in (extended) family systems is *relational ethics*, the justice in the family system as subjectively perceived by all its members (Boszormenyi-Nagy and Spark 1973). Relational ethics are at the core of family life. To give an example:

Probation officer: Did your children help you when you were in prison?

Father: They hardly did. I felt lonesome.

Child: But Dad, how can you say that! We visited you every weekend!

A relationship is perceived as fair or righteous when the participants in this relationship are experienced as reliable persons. Someone who unfairly treats a family member is not reliable or trustworthy. The extent to which a person is judged to be a reliable person depends on the trust he has rightfully gained through his actions (such as weekend visits). To trust someone else means, in Boszormenyi-Nagy's view, being willing to be dependent on somebody we presume to be reliable because of his or her actions. The whole system of perceived family justice relies on real-world actions of giving and taking. Verbal declarations and cognitive intentions are not enough to gain trust.

The dynamics of giving and taking within family systems are fuelled by two sources: *loyalty* and *merit*.

The first and most basic factor is loyalty. Family loyalty is defined as an indelible duty or obligation to give (for instance, to protect and raise your child), as well as the duty to take (for instance, to accept the gratitude of your child or partner), within blood ties or kin relationships. It is very important to mention that showing loyalty is not the same thing as being reliable. In being loyal to one person one can be seen as utterly unreliable by another person. Marital problems, for instance, can arise out of conflicts between indestructible family loyalty and still feeble spousal loyalty. As an example, being a horrible person to your wife, your child or an outside victim can, at the same time, be an act of loyalty to your own father. The individual counterpart of loyalty is entitlement; that is, the individual conviction to have the right to give and to take. Boszormenyi-Nagy points out that its perverse form, destructive entitlement, is a crucial contributing factor to child abuse, domestic violence and crime. Within the more psychological 'what works' tradition, destructive entitlement can be filed under anti-social attitudes.

The second factor fuelling family justice is merit. The Dutch family therapists Van den Eerenbeemt and Oele define relationships as 'opportunities to give and receive' (1987). Within family relationships, a person can define himself (as a partner, parent, child), and validate himself (as being a good or bad partner, parent or child). Positive validation of these roles leads to accumulation of merit. 'One who gives shall receive.' In other words, a man committing a crime (maybe fuelled by destructive entitlement) and being sent to prison can be perceived as invalidating his role as partner and father, leading to loss of merit, as well as an increased entitlement of his partner and children to expect restorative actions from him. Only when he really performs these restorative actions (and not just states the intention to 'do better') will he be viewed as a reliable person again.

A very complicating, and sometimes quite moving, aspect is the built-in asymmetry in parent–child relationships; children feel an obligation to show existential loyalty to their parents at all costs. Parents are entitled to expect their child's loyalty because they gave life to their child, even when they have been very unreliable and lost all their merit. For children (including as adults), being able to show loyalty to their parents is of extreme importance for personal development. Parents who deny, or not wholeheartedly accept, this deny their child the accumulation of merit; they lose merit themselves in the process, and thus can contribute to the development of destructive entitlement and, ultimately, of criminal tendencies in their child. In this sense, a criminal act is a statement of unreliability. The criminal act is motivated by the destructive right to be unreliable and serves to still show loyalty to an unresponsive or unavailable parent. Fortunately, existential loyalty also implies that restorative actions of parents within families are often encouraged and welcomed by their children (though this is something that can be exploited as well, such as by giving the child excessive presents or making enticing promises). The complex dynamics in relational ethics can place probation workers in difficult and ambivalent situations, because discussing (the apparent lack of) parental responsibilities or restorative actions can be a threat to the child's loyalty (causing split loyalty in the child).

In Boszormenyi-Nagy's view, loyalty is the most basic of the two, but it is merit that counts. Only merit makes a person reliable and trustworthy. Only a person with merit can be forgiven, and thus become entitled once again to ask or to take in a non-destructive manner. Merit is kept on a family balance sheet. When nothing is returned or given back, de-merit stays on the sheet, even in cases in which retribution/ restoration is no longer possible.

Accompanying the two factors fuelling perceived justice within the family system is a third factor, *multilateral bias*, balancing the giving and taking of all family members and thereby ensuring the reliability of the family system as a whole. This bias implies that every family member takes into account the rights and interests of all other family members.

A systems framework for offender supervision

The four dimensions

Criminal acts, detention and offender supervision can interfere with the possibilities for family members to express loyalty and entitlement in a positive way and thus be reliable persons. The same can be said of many other factors, such as economic deprivation or psychopathology. In essence, all factors hindering or promoting a healthy balancing of merit within the family system can be said to be possible hindrances to or facilitators of the individual desistance process. Boszormenyi-Nagy has categorised these possible factors in four dimensions, which we believe could also function as a comprehensive systems framework for offender supervision.

Facts, life events and circumstances: Nagy refers to these as more or less static factors, such as age, gender, handicaps, talents and strengths, and life events. Within the justice domain, we can also observe things that cannot be undone: criminal acts, having been a victim, being arrested and sentenced, being incarcerated, and being under offender supervision. Destructive and restorative actions that have been undertaken also count as facts.

Individual psychology: Skills, emotions and cognitions, motivations. The focus of the justice system as well as offender supervision based on psychological insights is primarily on the individual dimension. The desistance approach can be considered as a combination of an individual and systems approach.

Systemic characteristics of the nuclear and extended family: Systems theory defines systems as a set of consistently interacting elements, whereby the elements are mutually interdependent, and the relationships among elements are highly patterned, such that changes in one element affect the status of all others (Kuhn 1974). Starting in the 1960s, psychologists and anthropologists have applied this theory to family life, relating individual problem behaviour to its context: that is, the human relations in which all humans participate and develop (Vandereycken and Van Deth 2004; Nabuurs 2007). Changing one part of the system will lead to changes in other parts; an individual being arrested, or a probation client receiving treatment, for instance, will result in changes in behaviour patterns of other family members. In family systems theory, a distinction between characteristics of process and structure is helpful. Regarding process, observation of family life will reveal patterns in communication between family members (often named transactions or feedback), in adaptation patterns (family responses to life events and developmental stages of individuals), and in cohesion patterns (the degree of overt emotional togetherness). On a structural level, family observation reveals characteristics that both regulate process and are a product of process: subsystems with roles, tasks and responsibilities (spouses, children, the extended family), all separated by their subsystem boundaries – displaying a degree of permeability (for example, do the children interfere in the married life of their parents?). For optimal functioning of a family system, giving sense and purpose to its members, Houweling and Visser (2006) formulate the following conditions: the system allows both common, shared goals and individual goals to be strived for, the energy needed to make the system work is available and used efficiently, the structure is kept flexible in order to adapt, and communication with the outside world (of the family) is as open as possible.

It is evident that interference of the justice system as a result of criminal behaviour is a very stressful event that can influence the family system in both positive and negative ways. On top of the justice intervention itself, families often have to adapt to stigma, isolation, increased economic hardship, health issues and also loss and separation issues. The additional stress can be overwhelming. This is especially the case when adaptation and cohesion processes within the family system were already problematic before the justice system intervened, and the family was already dealing with complicated issues such as mental illness, drug use and addiction, child support and family violence. Outside events, such as offender supervision being imposed on the probation client, can easily overstretch the family's ability to keep its fragile balance. It is by no means an exaggeration to say that these events are experienced as a huge challenge and can trigger a family crisis or intensify an already chronic family crisis. This leads to more extreme forms of reaction, pushing the family towards a (perhaps even more) dysfunctional system. At such a moment, we can observe opposite reactions (Olson *et al.* 1979, Olson 1993): adaptation is either too fast and chaotic, not following any plans or rules, or it is too rigid and slow. The overt emotional exchange around the justice intervention (cohesion) is disengaged, (exchange of emotions between family members is lacking), leading to loneliness within the family and a clash of individual goals, or it is too intense and enmeshed, leading to overdependence, conflicts, a lack of individual space. It is clear that probation officers must have access to a range of resources and services geared towards supporting probation clients and their families.

Relational ethics: As described earlier, relational ethics refer to norms and values in family life. Giving and receiving can be reinforced, but also hampered or made impossible by facts, life events, circumstances, individual psychology and systems characteristics. Based on this mix, the fourth dimension develops a dynamic of its own, well kept on a balance sheet of merit and entitlement.

The above described four dimensions interact with each other, as depicted in Figure 13.1.

Applying the framework

When applying a family-focused approach, it depends on the probation officer's mandate and available time, whether he will work with only the probation client or the entire family system. In either case, desistance as a process depends more on the structural support a family is willing and able to give to the probation client than on the time-limited and incidental support of the probation officer. Therefore, during both assessment and supervision stages, it is crucial that probation workers assist families directly or indirectly in strengthening their own supportive social networks, and prevent family systems from developing long-term dependencies on governmental/non-profit institutions.

Family-focused assessment

Employing a range of tools – such as ecomaps, strength-based risk and needs assessments, pre-sentence investigation reports, and others – can help probation officers recognise, tap into and coordinate community resources while helping the family system.

We advise probation workers to focus on the adaptation process (systems dimension) first, and engage the family around urgent

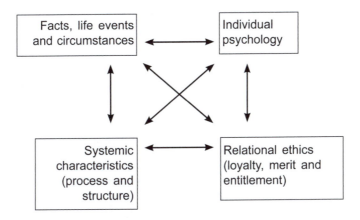

Figure 13.1 How the four dimensions interact.

themes. This approach involves an assessment of practical material needs and available or lacking resources to meet these needs. Closely related to these are recent facts, life events and circumstances that stem from the justice intervention and the additional stress ('slipstream') the family experiences. Ecomaps, which diagram (the quality of) the formal and informal resources available to families, are very helpful for probation officers to recognise existing, but less obvious sources of community support. They systematise contact information about various community resources, assess the relationships that families have with these resources (and how they change over time), and guide goal-setting and compliance with probation clients (POPS 2007).

When working with probation clients and/or their family members, probation officers can consider the following (from Family Justice, n.d.):

1 Whom do they consider 'family'? Do they include people other than blood relatives?

2 If time prevents you from engaging the probation client's family, what type of questions can be asked to draw on the social networks of probation clients?

3 How can engaging a mother of a probation client coming home from prison help with keeping both of them employed?

4 How can supportive social networks help probation clients manage their medications or arrive at their jobs on time?

5 What are the resources, strengths and challenges in these broadly defined families?

6 What are their relationships to their communities? Are there formal and informal resources that can be tapped into support them in managing their health, their lives, and meeting supervision mandates?

7 When a probation client relapses into drug or alcohol abuse, or other risk behaviour, who would be the first to notice?

8 How does recognising the presence of mental illness, drug use and addiction, family violence, housing concerns and other issues among your probation clients shape your interaction with them? Are there ways that they can better navigate the multiple governmental systems with which they are involved?

It usually takes more time for probation clients and their family members to assess other family dimensions. Discussing the impact of psychology issues on the family and cohesion and relational ethics with outsiders is more difficult. Probation workers have to deal with (a mixture of) three emotions: rage and sadness from the past, fear of the future, and an often unattended craving for care and intimacy (Vogelvang 1996). There is a reasonable chance that probation workers experience feelings of futility themselves. Probation workers are not family therapists, but they do need to assess the major characteristics of these issues and communicate to the probation client or family members that they have observed them, as well as encourage them to also discuss these matters among themselves. When they are left unmentioned, the probation officer more or less rewards the family system for escaping difficult discussions and sticking to practical matters only. It will leave sources for the desistance process untapped.

How can this problem be efficiently tackled? The dimension of 'facts' can function again as a starting point, because the criminal act(s), the justice intervention (ranging from arrest to detention, to the current supervision order), and even the presence of the probation officer himself are facts that cannot be denied or undone, and thus have impact on the other three dimensions. The probation worker can respectfully make remarks to open up a discussion about these dimensions, such as: 'A father who has committed a crime can feel ashamed to face his family.' 'Sometimes, circumstances make it very difficult or impossible for you to set things straight, and you must come to terms with that.' 'In order to be able to provide for your family, you need their support too.'

Based on the reactions to these openings, the probation worker and the family must decide which themes warrant forms of guidance or therapy that transcend the mandate or competence of the probation worker. A referral to individual social work or family therapy will then be part of the supervision plan.

Family-focused supervision

When engaging the family system in order to improve personal development of the offender, probation workers restricting their interventions to the socio-economic level face the risk of increasing the family's dependency, a process sometimes referred to as *dilution* of family systems (Colapinto 1995). As mentioned before, many families suffer from individual shortages in coping abilities, and from chaotic and or rigid adaptation patterns at the level of the systemic dimension. Addressing only socio-economic needs, probation workers will then be at risk of feeling overwhelmed or confused. On the level of emotional communication, many families suffer from dysfunctional patterns, either being much too close and lacking individual space (enmeshment), or living apart together, not sharing feelings or even rejecting each other (disengagement). Projection of these patterns onto the relationship with the probation worker – who is then rejected or 'smothered' as well – is not uncommon. To improve the stage for working with cohesion themes and expressing loyalty and entitlement, the family system as a whole must be addressed differently and carefully. Because family members feel powerless to make major changes, the main task of probation workers is to empower the family. To achieve this, they can take the following three steps (see Vogelvang 1996, 2001).

At first, the probation worker makes clear to the family members that they are *in control* of communication and cooperation, by means of (a) reaching out and (b) overtly accepting their perspectives on the situation as important reference points. These interventions are necessary to engage the family in a long-term working alliance. Second, the probation worker explains to the family members that they are *capable of change*, by means of redefining problems, their causes and solutions, in workable, manageable bits, that can be tackled by the family and with professional help. This message has to be realistic, based on facts. Therefore, the probation worker needs to engage family members in their initial efforts to improve practical, material and economic needs (the adaptation process), by assigning small tasks and working together as much as possible. By doing this, it is possible to gather evidence of being capable of change that the family members cannot deny. This activates the family and restores hope, making the family system now *responsive*. Third, the probation worker can respond to family system dynamics in a responsive family context. (This strategy is elaborated in the Appendix.)

The fundamental notion in the wraparound model of care is that long-term changes are possible only when interventions are combined in a plan that has been designed by a team composed of the family itself, assisted by informal contacts with the family (relatives, neighbours, friends) and professionals (Hermanns 2009; Eber 2003). The family group conference is a well-known method to achieve such a plan (McGarrell and Kroovand Hipple, 2007; Mutter *et al.* 2008). All relevant domains must be included in it: housing/resettlement, family matters, child development and rearing, cognitions, behaviour and emotions, education and work, finances and budgeting, immigration and other legal matters, social networks, safety and medical care. This implies that the probation officer must negotiate to make sure that activities related to both short-term and long-term supervision goals for the probation client are included in the plan, based on their criminogenic needs and responsivity. The intensity and duration of these activities depend on risk of reconviction and risk of harm. After designing and agreeing upon the plan, all activities are coordinated by both the case manager (probation worker) and the family. Ideally, the process starts during detention and continues until all goals are met. The wraparound model was initially developed in the 1980s as a means for maintaining youth with the most serious emotional and behavioural problems in their home and community. The model is now evidence-based and cost effective (Carney and Buttell 2003). The model restores the capacity of family members to have control over their lives and to be capable of change, but unfortunately its application on a large scale is still absent, due to prevailing discontinuities in the process and corresponding lack of coordination. It could be argued that these roadblocks actually disempower families. Worth mentioning in this context is the offender supervision method of the Israeli Prisoner Rehabilitation Authority (Hoffman 1998). Israeli probation workers are mandated by law to work with the family system as a whole. The PRA involves the complete extended family in the probation client's rehabilitation, starting in the detention phase. Family members are involved on a voluntary basis. The position and active role of children in the supervision process is given special attention. Volunteer academic students act as their mentors and role models, and this appears to reinforce the probation clients' desistance process as well.

Of course, family support has particular value during periods of imprisonment, in preparation for release and in the resettlement process. Contact throughout the custodial period can help alleviate the 'pain of imprisonment' for some prisoners and as such can potentially reduce or at least identify the risk of self-harm for some prisoners. Findings from Woolf (1991) and the HMCIP (1999), both cited in POPS (2007), recognised family ties as important to the stability of prison regimes and for the well-being of prisoners. Preparation for release for both prisoners and their family members is an important area for development. The experience of imprisonment can cause untold damage to offenders and their families, and for those who have managed to maintain family relationships during this period, release can be seen as another anxious time. Even when it has been identified that some families are in a position to be supportive, they typically receive little or no assistance in their role in resettlement. Prisoners are also unprepared for life upon release; for many, problems appear when they return to their families and realise that relationships have changed considerably (Noble 1995). The probation officer should advocate that, to assist the resettlement process for prisoners and their families, there needs to be an active resettlement programme within prisons that would include family relationships. In order to participate in this, families have to be supported and empowered to take on this role. The 'continuum of care' or 'wraparound care' model for the offender would also include, where appropriate, the involvement of families (Hermanns 2009; De Graaf and Veldhuizen 2009).

Taking a position of multilateral bias is essential for social professionals, and probation workers are no exception. This position implies that the probation worker advocates the rights and interests of all family members, and does not look for easy compromises. When forgetting or denying these rights and interests, the worker will lose merit and be confronted by a whole family feeling entitled to throw him or her out! Whenever possible, the probation worker must accept invitations of the probation client or other family members to at least listen to, or maybe discuss, matters of trust and reliability. In discussions, the probation worker could investigate with family members possible ways to actively invest in (the restoration) of reliable relationships. The ecomap, or genogram, visualising their relationships, can be a helpful tool, because it can make probation clients and their family members less dependent on verbal communication only, pointing out maybe forgotten but possibly helpful resources, and showing them to all persons involved. In family therapy, more complex work involves the exoneration of the probation client by his partner or children. Sometimes referred to as forgiving, exoneration means that the probation client is ethically purified by his loved ones. His partner or children publicly denounce both their 'revenge' (destructive entitlement) and the client's duty to pay back because of his unreliable actions. The victims put an end to this. Exoneration can start as soon as the partner or children have found an acceptable explanation for the probation client's attitude and behaviour, and the probation client is willing to accept the fact that the resulting sadness and anger of his partner or child are justified. Exoneration takes time, acceptance and trust, but will lead to a new ethical balance in the family.

Conclusion

Family-focused offender supervision can reach families when they most need it. The stress of seeing a family member begin probation – or incarceration – can affect the entire family system, impair the mutual exchange of support within a family, and weaken the physical and mental health of other family members.

A family-focused approach to offender supervision both builds upon and helps actualise the goals of community corrections to increase compliance with supervision mandates and improve public safety. In turn, families can see their social networks strengthened, their communities stabilised, and their health restored – effectively breaking cycles of addiction, relapse and incarceration. Cultivating collaboration, respect and trust with probation client's families can recast their interaction with government agencies.

To fully make use of this potential, we advocate the following: the current societal focus on risks and individual responsibility, behaviour change, and the 'use' of offender supervision (and imprisonment) primarily as a means to increase public safety, elicits a focus on criminogenic risks within the family and tends to weaken the attention for positive aspects (McNeill 2009b). This imbalance is counter-productive for the probation client and their family. It needs to be changed into structural risk assessment instruments, probation methods/interventions and case management, training and worker supervision (Mullins and Toner 2008). The desistance process of probation clients will thrive when family-focused assessment and guidance develop into an integrated part of probation work.

Appendix

Working with family dynamics in offender supervision.

1a Reaching out. Families with probation clients are usually referred to social services when they are in the middle of a crisis or important transition. Dell (1982) pointed out convincingly that asking for assistance at these moments can also be regarded as a strategy to regain family balance (homeostasis) by temporarily letting outsiders in. As soon as the actual crisis is over, the social service representative is asked to leave again, sometimes kindly, sometimes bluntly. Solving only the presented crisis, the social service is first enmeshed in the family system, and consequently disengaged by it. In this way, family members experience repeated, self-inflicted abandonment, and only temporary relief. Conscious of this pitfall, the probation worker must try to engage the family in a working relationship in a respectful and persistent way. This means visiting the family at home, offering concrete material services, and never letting the family down. By a more intensive and concentrated approach, compared with more traditional services, the probation worker shows the family it is worth his utmost effort.

1b Siding. The probation worker explicitly validates the perception of *all* family members of the problems and dilemmas they face (multilateral bias). Siding with family members during family visits and even in individual contacts with the probation client alone serves as a strategy to find and validate these perceptions. Siding also means that the family decides whether the probation worker is allowed to enter the home, and decides for which problems assistance is needed. This strategy is referred to by Weitzmann (1985) as 'engaging the family around the symptom'. Symptoms, such as delinquent behaviour, are often being used as defences against facing painful intra- or inter-generational family issues. In the initial stage of supervision, symptom behaviour is very important, as the family is willing to 'give' the probation worker these symptoms as working themes.

2 Redefining incongruence. Whenever possible, probation workers explicitly conclude that different perceptions of family members are in effect congruent, when redefined in terms of deficits in communication and/or cooperation skills. Empowering the family in terms of Olson's circumplex model of family functioning means that probation workers redefine dysfunctional aspects in terms of the opposite, functional aspect. Enmeshment is redefined as a skills deficit in terms of individuality. Disengagement is redefined as skills deficit in terms of mutuality. Chaotic adaptation is redefined as skills deficit in terms of structured adaptation, and rigid adaptation is redefined as skills deficit in terms of flexible adaptation. The rationale of this is that by giving the family control over their acquisition of these skills, responsivity is being generated. The 'redefinition table' (see Table 13.1) comprises two sets of strategic messages and their encodings: messages from the family, conveying a lack of possibilities or unwillingness to be responsive, and possible reactions from probation workers, conveying the opposite message, while leaving family members in control.

Table 13.1 Generating responsiveness in multi-problem families: empowerment messages for probation workers.

Family member messages	Probation worker responses
Emotional enmeshment *Message*: Be with us. Without you, we will cease to be. Do not confront us with our problems. *Encodings*: (a) Can you make/do … for us? (b) Let's blame the outside world. (c) Let's blame our most problematic family member/ scapegoat. (d) Don't you agree nothing's going wrong, actually?	**Emotional individuality** *Message*: You are in control. I will validate the perception each of you has of the situation, even if they may differ. But in terms of skills, they are congruent. So don't be afraid, you can safely remain together as a family, there will be no collapse. *Encodings*: (a) I will, but stay with me while I try to help. (b) Let's talk about ways to get rid of its influence. (c) I am not here to judge. Let's ask the most problematic family member/scapegoat if he is happy with his situation. If not, let's talk about ways to help him get rid of his behaviour. (d) Yes, except from these messages coming in from outside (the system). We cannot ignore them. We have to do something to prove these messages wrong, or there will be another crisis.
Emotional disengagement *Message*: We'll manage. We take care of our own business and we don't want you around. *Encodings*: (a) Being absent. (b) Being silent, not talking about fears and disappointments. (c) Disqualify the worker: 'It didn't help. You're worth nothing either.'	**Emotional mutuality** *Message*: You are in control. You decide what to do, in order to avoid stagnation, new crises, or state intervention. *Encodings*: (a) I miss the one being absent. His opinion or contribution might be crucial. (b) You don't need to talk. Please tell me if I push too hard or ask too much.

Table 13.1 continues overleaf

Table 13.1 continued

Family member messages	Probation worker responses
(d) Filthy/dangerous/dark/noisy living circumstances: 'We will scare you out.' (e) Crazy, restless, verbally abusive behaviour: 'We will scare you out.'	(c) Exactly, why trust me? Please tell me what your solution is. (d) I am feeling uncomfortable. Anyone else? (e) I am not running away. I offer concrete services until this is over.

Adaptation chaos
Message: We are helpless. We cannot cope. We are being overwhelmed.

Encodings:
(a) 'It's just one big mess.'
(b) Independent over-activity by different family members.

Adaptation structure
Message: You are in control. Every one of you can contribute in order to adapt.

Encodings:
(a) Setting priorities. Contracting family members for different, concrete and feasible tasks. Transfer of effective old strategies.
(b) Asking other family members to assist and join efforts. Dividing tasks. Contracting.

Adaptation rigidity
Message: Only this solution works, and nothing else ever did or ever will.

Encodings:
(a) Apathy ('Apparently, your solution doesn't trigger our system').
(b) Using the same solutions/rules again and again ('Don't be too complicated, please. We will only try this, until it works, as it always did').

Adaptation flexibility
Message: For every (new) situation, a fresh approach is needed. Old strategies serve as very useful learning material.

Encodings:
a) Increasing tension by prescribing *no change* and predicting future dependency ('You and me will have to learn to live with this').
(b) Shake up the system:
(1) continuous change of training and discussion situations (place, time, duration, attendants);
(2) differentiation of family members' needs; and (3) sorting out useful and ineffective (aspects of) old strategies together.

Source: Vogelvang (1996).

3 Working with responsiveness. Every time, as soon as responsiveness has been generated (that is, family members express a willingness to take action and work together), the probation worker activates the family to formulate treatment goals. If needed, the family worker again gives material, practical aid, but also starts parent education, individual counselling, family sessions/'boards', and/or behaviour modification. In most cases, parents will ask for material help, or ask probation workers to 'fix' the person the family has identified as the origin and/or carrier of problems. In both cases, the parents seek solutions in letting persons or situations be repaired by others, without playing any role in this. The family worker introduces these roles. Giving material help, such as housing, repairs, clothing or food, requires the family to prioritise their needs. This 'not only teaches them a skill but also conveys the message that they are capable, strong, and best know their own needs' (Kaplan 1986: 30). The probation worker redefines 'fixing the identified patient' in terms of a deficit of skills of family members on the level of communication and/or cooperation. Skills that can be acquired in small, feasible steps, hereby again giving family members control.

Notes

1 Desistance is defined here as the failure of criminal behaviour to occur during an extended period of time, associated with (1) a convinced (interiorised) and active (behavioural) investment of the desister in his social and material context to reach personal and interpersonal goals by pro-social means and to avoid or reject anti-social means, and (2) a continuous validation by the social context of the desister of both his conviction and actual efforts to both reach these goals and to eliminate a criminal lifestyle (Vogelvang 2009; see also Maruna, this volume)
2 RISc: the Dutch probation services' structured risk assessment tool (Vinke *et al.* 2004). The RISc is the Dutch version of the Offender Assessment System applied in England and Wales (OASys 2002).

References

Bambacht, G. and Van Deursen, C. (2009) *Verwanten als veiligheidspartner.* Den Bosch: Avans Hogeschool Academie voor Sociale Studies/Social Work/Lectoraat Reclassering en Veiligheidsbeleid.

Boeck, T., Fleming, J. and Kemshall, H. (2006) 'The context of risk decisions: does social capital make a difference?', *Forum: Qualitative Social Research*, 7 (1): Art.17.

Boeck, T., Fleming, J. and Kemshall, H. (2006) 'The context of risk decisions: does social capital make a difference?', *Forum: Qualitative Social Research*, 7 (1): Art.17.

Boszormenyi-Nagy, I. and Spark, G.M. (1973) *Invisible Loyalties: Reciprocity in Intergenerational Family Therapy*. New York: Harper and Row.

Boszormenyi-Nagy, I., Grunebaum, J. and Ulrich, D. (1991) 'Contextual therapy', in A. Gurman and D. Kniskern (eds) *Handbook of Family Therapy*, Vol. 2. New York: Brunner/Mazel.

Bronfenbrenner, U. (1979) *The Ecology of Human Development: Experiments by Nature and Design*. Cambridge, MA: Harvard University Press.

Bronfenbrenner, U. (1988) 'Interacting systems in human development: research paradigms: present and future', in N. Boler, A. Caspi, G. Downey and M. Moorehouse (eds) *Persons in Context: Developmental Processes*. New York: Cambridge University Press.

Bronfenbrenner, U. (1992) 'Ecological systems theory', in R. Vasta (ed.) *Six Theories of Child Development: Revised Formulations and Current Issues*. London: Jessica Kingsley.

Bronfenbrenner, U. (2005) 'The bioecological theory of human deveopment', in N.J. Smelser and P.B. Baltes (eds) *International Encyclopedia of the Social and Behavioral Sciences*, Vol. 10. New York: Elsevier.

Carney, M.M. and Buttell, F. (2003) 'Reducing juvenile recidivism: evaluating the wraparound services', *Research on Social Work Practice*, 13: 551–68.

Claessens, K. (2006) *Het stopzetten van een delinquente carriere: Desistance* (Doctoraalscriptie). Leuven: Katholieke Universiteit Leuven/Faculteit Rechtsgeleerdheid.

Colapinto, J.A. (1995) 'Dilution of family process in social services: implications for treatment of neglectful families', *Family Process*, 34 (3): 59–74.

De Graaf, G. and Veldhuizen, S. (2009) *Deskundig verwant; Verwanten als veiligheidspartners*. Den Bosch: Avans Hogeschool Academie voor Sociale Studies/Social Work/Lectoraat Reclassering en Veiligheidsbeleid.

Dell, P.F. (1982) 'Beyond homeostasis: toward a concept of coherence', *Family Process*, 21: 21–41.

Eber, L. (2003) *The Art and Science of Wraparound*. Bloomington, IN: Forum on Education at Indiana University.

Family Justice (n.d.) *Tapping Social Networks: A Resource for Probation and Parole Officers to Improve Supervision*. New York: Family Justice (www. familyjustice.org).

Farrall, S. (2000) 'Introduction', in S. Farrall (ed.) *The Termination of Criminal Careers*. Aldershot: Ashgate.

Farrall, S. (2004) 'Social capital and offender reintegration: making probation desistance focused', in S. Maruna and R. Immarigeon (eds) *After Crime and Punishment: Pathways to Offender Reintegration*. Cullompton: Willan Publishing.

Farrall, S. and Calverley, A. (2006) *Understanding Desistance from Crime: Theoretical Directions in Resettlement and Rehabilitation*. Cullompton: Willan Publishing.

Garland, C., Pettigrew, N. and Saunders, T. (2001) *Reintegrating Ex-prisoners and Reducing Re-Offending*. BMRB report to the Social Exclusion Unit, August 2001.

Gendreau, P., Little, T. and Goggin, C. (1996) 'A meta-analysis of the predictors of adult offender recidivism: what works!', *Criminology*, 34 (4): 575–608.

Glaser, D. (1964) *The Effectiveness of a Prison and Parole System*. Indianapolis: Bobbs-Merrill.

Hermanns, J. (2009) 'Continuïteit en discontinuïteit in het leven van mensen met crimineel gedrag', in J. Hermanns and A. Menger (eds) *Walk the Line. Over continuïteit en professionalisering in het reclasseringswerk. Openbare les Maart 2009*. Utrecht/Amsterdam: Hogeschool Utrecht, Kenniscentrum Sociale Innovatie/SWP.

Hoffman, A. (1998) 'Programs for the families', in A. Hoffman (ed.) *The Prisoner Rehabilitation Authority Philosophy and Programs*. Jerusalem: State of Israel Prisoner Rehabilitation Authority.

Holt, N. and Miller, D. (1972) *Explorations in Inmate-Family Relationships*, Research Report 46. Sacramento, CA: California Department of Corrections.

Houweling, O. and Visser, K. (2006) *Sociale agogiek – Systeemgerichte beleidsontwikkeling*. Assen: Koninklijke van Gorcum.

Kuhn, A. (1974) *The Logic of Social Systems*. San Francisco: Jossey-Bass.

La Vigne, N.G., Schollenberger, T.L. and Debus, S.A. (2009) *One Year Out: Tracking the Experiences of Male Prisoners Returning to Houston, Texas*. Washington, DC: Urban Institute.

Le Goff, J.F. (2001) 'Boszormenyi-Nagy and contextual therapy: an overview', *Australian and New Zealand Journal of Family Therapy*, 22 (3): 147–57.

Maruna, S. and Toch, H. (2003) *Making Good: How Ex-convicts Reform and Rebuild their Lives*. Washington, DC: American Psychological Association.

Matthews, J. (1989) 'Forgotten victims', in R. Light (ed.) *Prisoners' Families*. Bristol: Bristol and Bath Centre for Criminal Justice.

McGarrell, E.F. and Kroovand Hipple, N. (2007) 'Family group conferencing and re-offending among first-time juvenile offenders: the Indianapolis experiment', *Justice Quarterly*, 2: 221–46.

McNeill, F. (2002) *Beyond 'What Works': How and Why Do People Stop Offending?*, CJSW Briefing Paper 5. Glasgow: Scottish Centre for Crime and Justice Research.

McNeill, F. (2009a) *Towards Effective Practice in Offender Supervision*. Glasgow: Scottish Centre for Crime and Justice Research. Online at: www.sccjr. ac.uk/documents/McNeil_Towards.pdf.

McNeill, F. (2009b) 'What works and what's just?', *European Journal of Probation*, 1 (1): 21–40.

Mullins, T.G. and Toner, C. (2008) *Implementing the Family Support Approach for Community Supervision*. New York: Family Justice.

Mutter, R., Shemmings, D., Dugmore, P. and Hyare, M. (2008) 'Family group conferences in youth justice', *Health and Social Care in the Community*, 16 (3): 262–70.

Nabuurs, M. (2007) *Basisboek systeemgericht werken*. Baarn: HB Uitgevers.
Noble, C. (1995) *Prisoners' Families: The Everyday Reality*. Ipswich: Ormiston Children and Families Trust.
Offender Assessment System (OASys) (2002) *User Manual*. London: Crown Copyright.
Ohlin, L. (1954) 'The stability and viability of parole experience tables', PhD dissertation. University of Chicago.
Olson, D.H. (1993) 'Circumplex model of marital and family systems: assessing family functioning', in F. Walsh (ed.) *Normative Family Processes*, 2nd edn. New York: Guilford Press.
Olson, D.H., Sprenkle, D.H. and Russell C.S. (1979) 'Circumplex model of marital and family systems, I: Cohesion and adaptability dimensions, family types, and clinical applications', *Family Process*, 18: 3–28.
Poort, R. (2008) *Fundamenten voor toezicht. Over de grondslagen voor de ontwikkeling van reclasseringstoezicht*. Utrecht: Reclassering Nederland.
Poort, R. (2009) *Begeleiding in toezicht*. Notitie voor de directies van de drie reclasseringsorganisaties. Reclassering Nederland.
POPS (Partners of Prisoners and Families Suport Groups)(2007) *Families ... A Critical Time for Change*. Manchester: POPS.
Robinson, G. and Raynor, P. (2006) 'The future of rehabilitation: what role for the probation service?', *Probation Journal*, 53.
RN/LJ&R/SVG (Reclassering Nederland/Leger des Heils Jeugdzorg en Reclassering/Stichting Verslavingsreclassering GGZ-Nederland) (2009) *Ontwerp Toezicht*. Utrecht/Amersfoort: interne publicatie reclasseringsorganisaties.
Van den Eerenbeemt, E. and Oele, B. (1987) 'De contextuele therapie: verdiende vrijheid', in *Handboek Gezinstherapie*. Deventer: van Loghum Slaterus.
Van der Knaap, L. and Alberda, D.L. (2009) *De predictieve validiteit van de Recidive Inschattingsschalen (RISc)*. Den Haag: WODC.
Van der Knaap, L., Weijters, G. and Bogaerts, S. (2007) *Criminogene problemen onder daders die in aanmerking komen voor gedragsinterventies. Cahier 2007-7*. Den Haag: WODC.
Van Kalmthout, A.M. and Durnescu, I. (2008) 'European Probation Service Systems: a comparative overview', in A.M. van Kalmthout and I. Durnescu (eds) *Probation in Europe*. Nijmegen: Wolf Legal Publishers.
Vandereycken, W., Deth, R. van (2004) *Psychiatrie, van diagnose tot behandeling*. Houten/Antwerpen: Bohn Stafleu van Loghum.
Vinke, A., Vogelvang, B.O., Erftemeijer, L. and Veldkamp, E. (2004) *Handleiding RISc: Recidive Inschatting Schalen. Gebruikersversie 1.0*. Woerden/Utrecht: Adviesbureau Van Montfoort/Stichting Reclassering Nederland.
Vogelvang, B.O. (1996) 'Improving communication, cooperation and responsiveness in multi-problem families', in H.J. Schulze (ed.) *Who Cares*. London: Wiley and Sons.

Vogelvang, B.O. (2001): *Betrokken Instanties: vraaggericht samenwerken in de geïndiceerde jeugdzorg*. Rotterdam/Alphen a/d Rijn: St Jeugdzorg Rotterdam Zuid-Holland Zuid/Horizon.

Vogelvang, B.O. (2008) *Put your Trust in What Works*. Lezing PSW, Helvoirt, November.

Vogelvang, B.O (2009) *Een sterk verhaal. Over de invloed van reclasseringswerkers op het stoppen met criminaliteit na detentie*. Lectorale rede, in verkorte vorm uitgesproken tijdens het congres 'Perspectieven voor jongvolwassenen na detentie; successen vanuit beleid, wetenschap en praktijk', Avans Hogeschool, 10 November. Den Bosch: Avans Hogeschool/Expertisecentrum Veiligheid.

Weitzmann, J. (1985) 'Engaging the severely dysfunctional family in treatment: basic considerations', *Family Process*, 24: 473–85.

Chapter 14

Working with families in criminal justice

Chris Trotter

Introduction

This chapter is about working with the families of offenders. It is focused particularly on the work that might be done by probation and parole officers (or others who work with offenders in the community) with young offenders and their families. It is also relevant to work with adult offenders. The chapter addresses the general relationships between 'family dysfunction' and criminality and between family dysfunction and reoffending. The literature on the effectiveness of working with the families of offenders is then discussed along with the general principles of effective work with offenders. One particular approach to working with families, collaborative family problem-solving, is then introduced and reference is made to evaluation studies on the model.

Families and criminality

There seems little doubt that family relationships are a factor in the development of delinquent and criminal behaviour. The relationship between family and criminal activity can be explained through a number of criminological theories including learning theory, labelling theory and social control theory. Children and young people may be socialised into pro-social or criminal behaviour by a process of reinforcement and through the models to whom they are exposed (Burke 2005).

There is also considerable research support for the importance of family in the development of pro-social and pro-criminal behaviours. Longitudinal studies have shown relationships between family dysfunction and criminality (Turner *et al.* 2007). Studies have shown that exposure to violence in the home is related to subsequent criminality – both direct violence and violence among other family members witnessed by children (Hayne *et al.* 2009). Other studies have shown that inadequate family support, family problems and family disruption among young people contribute to pathways into offending for women and male offenders (Salisbury and Van Voorhis 2009; Wareham *et al.* 2009).

The relationships between adult criminal behaviour and quality of parent/child relationships have also been shown to exist independently of other factors such as race, age, education level, employment, neighbourhood and peers (Ganem and Agnew 2007). There is also evidence of criminality within families enduring across as many as three generations (Putkonen *et al.* 2007).

Andrews and Bonta (2003) refer to family relationships as a risk factor for delinquency and refer to 'emotional neglect – lack of attachment to others and poor monitoring and supervision – learning of aggressive disruptive behaviour and failure to acquire anti-criminal verbalisations' as being related to further offending (2003: 223). Earlier work by Loeber and Stouthamer-Loeber (1986) pointed to family dysfunction as the strongest predicator of delinquency.

Families and reoffending

There is also evidence that family relationships are a factor not just in the development of offending but in reoffending. This applies to both family of origin, where young offenders may be living with families, and to relationships between adult offenders and their partners or children. Families are thus a key factor included in risk of re-offending prediction instruments for adults and young people. For example, the Global Risk Assessment Device (Gavazzi *et al.* 2008), the Level of Service Inventory – Revised and the Youth Level of Service Inventory (YLSI) (Andrews and Bonta 2003) all highlight the importance of family. The YLSI analysis of risk factors places it alongside prior offences, substance abuse, peer relations, education and employment, and personality type as major correlates of reoffending.

Bonta and colleagues (2008) found family issues to be the most commonly identified criminogenic need emerging from a sample of risk assessments of adult offenders placed on probation in Canada. It was identified more often than drug use, for example. It was also identified frequently for young offenders although not as often as substance abuse. For both young and adult offenders family issues were discussed in probation supervision (analysed through tapes of interviews) more than any other issue. An earlier study (Trotter 1994) found that 45 per cent of 380 adult community corrections clients surveyed reported that family was an issue for them, whether the issue applied to family of origin or partners and children.

Interventions with families can be effective

It is clear, therefore, that families are a factor in the development of criminality and an ongoing factor in the lives of offenders. There is also evidence that working with the families of young offenders can lead to reduced recidivism. A meta-analysis by Woolfenden, Williams and Peat (2002) examined eight randomised control trials looking at whether family and parenting interventions benefit children and adolescents with conduct disorder and delinquency. They found that family and parenting interventions significantly reduced the time spent by juveniles in institutions and the intervention led to a significant reduction in the risk of a juvenile delinquent being rearrested.

Farrington and Welsh (2003) undertook a meta-analysis of the effectiveness of 40 family-based crime prevention programmes. They concluded that the family-based programmes were related to reduced delinquency and anti-social behaviour by children. They found that the most effective types of programmes used behavioural parent training, home visiting, day care/preschool, home/community and multi-systematic therapy programmes.

A meta-analysis by Latimer (2001), on the other hand, found that although family intervention appears to be effective, when the methodology of the studies is examined critically the benefits disappear. Dowden and Andrews (2003) acknowledge Latimer's findings but found in their meta-analysis of the effectiveness of 38 family interventions that these interventions were effective when based on effective practice principles; that is, when they complied with the principles of risk, need and responsivity (see Bonta and Andrews, this volume). In other words, the more effective interventions focused on medium to high risk offenders rather than low risk, the interventions focused on factors related to the offending behaviour – in particular, 'family affection/communication and monitoring/supervision' –

and they were based on cognitive behavioural and social learning approaches, including 'modelling, graduated practice, rehearsal, role playing, reinforcement, resource provision, and detailed verbal guidance and explanations' (Dowden and Andrews 2003: 2).

There are a number of specific intervention models that have also proved to be successful in reducing recidivism among offenders. Multi-systemic therapy (MST) involves the provision of intensive resources to families and includes problem-solving, among a number of other interventions (Sexton and Alexander 2002; Perkins-Dock 2001).

Functional family therapy (FFT) is, like MST, used in a number of corrections departments around the world. It is a short-term systems behavioural model for working with young offenders and their families, usually over 12 home-based sessions (Washington State 2002). A search of criminal justice abstracts includes four references to the model, each of which indicates it reduces recidivism. Notably, one evaluation, undertaken by Washington State (2002), using a waiting list control group ($n = 323$), found that while those receiving FFT from competent therapists (204) had lower recidivism, those receiving FFT from those with lower levels of competence had higher recidivism. Family work, like other interventions in criminal justice, needs to be based on effective practice principles and those principles need to be applied in practice by competent staff.

Principles of effective work with offenders

The view that some family-based interventions are more effective than others is supported by the general research in relation to the effectiveness of correctional interventions. There has been an abundance of research on what works and what doesn't in offender supervision, moving from the view held in the 1970s that 'nothing works' to a more recent view that correctional interventions are effective if they comply with certain principles. Many studies and numerous meta-analyses (summarised in Trotter 2006) point to certain approaches by corrections workers that are consistently related to reduced offending. These include clarity of role and purpose by the worker, modelling by the worker of pro-social values, and the reinforcement of pro-social actions and comments by clients, and working collaboratively on problems particularly those that relate to the offending behaviour. Other approaches that have support in the research include a positive worker/client relationship, the use of humour, realistic optimism, case management skills, focus on high risk clients, and working with families. There is also support for corrections interventions based on cognitive behavioural principles.

Collaborative family problem-solving

In this chapter I am focusing on a model known as 'collaborative family problem-solving'. I am focusing on this model for several reasons. It is based on and incorporates each of the 'what works' principles referred to above. It can be learned relatively quickly and can be applied by staff members who are not expert family therapists. It can be seen as an additional skill in the repertoire of correctional workers that builds on the practice skills they are likely to have learned in preparatory courses. It is a user-friendly model that is accessible and understandable for corrections clients and their families.

The model may be used by those who work directly with offenders in the community, for example probation and parole officers, community corrections officers, correctional psychologists or correctional social workers. It may also be used by professional staff in prisons and youth residential centres to help offenders work with family issues or to help them to prepare for release.

The model is an adaptation of problem-solving models that have been around for many years. In fact, Helen Harris Perlman (1957) developed her social work problem-solving model more than 50 years ago. The collaborative family problem-solving model discussed in this chapter has its beginnings in publications by Epstein and Bishop (1981) and William Reid (1985). The model presented here, however, has been further developed, taking into account the principles of effective practice referred to above and the comments from workers and families who have made use of the model. It also focuses on the particular issues that relate to the offending behaviour of the clients, and incorporates the principles of pro-social modelling and reinforcement (Trotter 2006).

The model

The model as it was initially developed involved eight steps: (1) role clarification, (2) problem survey, (3) problem ranking, (4) detailed problem exploration, (5) setting goals, (6) developing a contract, (7) setting strategies and (8) ongoing review. In order to make the model more accessible to clients the following terminology can also be used:

1 Set ground rules.
2 Identify issues you would like to change.
3 Decide what to work on first.
4 Explore the issue in more detail.
5 Set goals – what do we want to achieve?
6 Do a contract – write out the ground rules, issues and goals and make sure everyone agrees with them.
7 Work out ways of achieving the goals.
8 Review how we are going.

Outlined below is a brief description of the model. More detail is provided in Trotter (2006, chapter 7).

Preparation

Prior to beginning the work with the family group (the client plus one or more family members) the worker discusses with the client and the family members the nature of the family work and what is expected of them in the process. These discussions can then be followed up in the first session. Preparing the family members for the sessions can be very important in gaining the cooperation of the family from the beginning.

Home-based model

Family counselling sessions may be held in the worker's office or in the family's home. Home-based sessions have advantages and the students and professionals who participated in my research studies have undertaken most of the sessions in the family home. Certainly it seems that family members are more likely to participate when this occurs.

Co-counselling

It is common in family therapy and in using this model for two workers to work with the family. The aim in using two workers or co-counsellors is both educational and supportive. It also addresses some of the safety issues related to home visiting.

There is potential for difficulties in the co-counselling role particularly if one counsellor is not making an equal contribution or perhaps the family is warming to one worker rather than the other. Each worker should see it as their role to ensure that the person they are working with is comfortable with their role as co-counsellor. Workers should be empathic and positive towards each other in the same way as they should be empathic and positive towards family members.

The method used with this model is one that is often used in family mediation. That is, one worker leads the discussion on a particular issue, free from interruptions from the other counsellor. At the completion of a segment the second worker who has been taking notes summarises the position of each of the family members or summarises the content of the previous discussion. A whiteboard may be used if one is available or alternatively the summaries can be written on sheets of paper. The roles are then reversed.

Pro-social modelling

Pro-social modelling is one of the core practices that relate to positive outcomes in criminal justice work and the use of pro-social modelling skills is an integral part of the collaborative family problem-solving model. These skills are outlined in some detail in Trotter (2006). To summarise briefly, pro-social modelling involves modelling pro-social values (for example, reliability, punctuality), identifying pro-social comments and actions in clients and client family members (for example, valuing non-criminal pursuits), reinforcing those comments and actions (for example, by praise, file notes) and subtly challenging pro-criminal comments and actions (for example, 'Can you explain why you say that the victim asked for it?'). Pro-social modelling works best when the numbers of instances of reinforcement for pro-social comments and actions clearly outweighs the challenging of pro-criminal comments and actions.

The model

I Set the ground rules

Initially the worker reviews with the family members what is involved in the sessions, including the way they will be conducted and how the model works. Copies of the family problem structure might be taken by the worker to the family home, if that is where the sessions are to take place, or displayed in the worker's office.

The aim then is to generate discussion about how the sessions will be conducted. Some of the issues that should be discussed include those relating to confidentiality: who will know about what goes on in the sessions? Will the information be discussed with others? What if disclosures are made about child abuse or further offences? Can information from the sessions be included in court reports? Other issues might include: Can individual family members have discussions with the counsellor between sessions and will these discussions be confidential? Is the counsellor neutral or acting on behalf of the young person who is the primary client? Will the worker do follow-up tasks between sessions, for example, speaking to schoolteachers? Will the sessions be held in the family home or in the office or at some other venue? Is participation voluntary? Is the TV to be turned off? Can anyone leave at any time? What happens if one family member is abusive towards another, or if people try to talk over each other?

The worker then writes down the guidelines for conducting the sessions so that all family members can see them. This results in a number of written guidelines or ground rules and might include, for example: sessions will be for 45 minutes once a week; abusive language will not be accepted; the TV and phones will be turned off; family members may leave the session temporarily if they are feeling distressed; the content of sessions will not be discussed with anyone outside of the sessions; and all family members will be invited to all sessions.

2 Identify issues you would like to change (problem survey)

Each family member is then asked to describe issues that are of concern to them, or things they would like to change. The worker prompts the family members so that a full picture of the issues is presented (how are things at school, who are your friends, do you have enough money?). The worker then lists the problems of each family member on a whiteboard or on paper.

The workers encourage family members to express problems in non-blaming terms. For example, the worker might reframe problems for the client. A 12-year-old boy might say that his biggest problem is his sister – 'she goes out whenever she likes and teases me all the time'. This might be reframed in terms of, for example: 'It upsets me that my mother does not have fair rules about what my sister is allowed to do and what I am allowed to do. I feel like they are ganging up on me.'

The worker then tries to identify common family problems. For example, concern about different expectations for family members might be a common issue. Failure to listen to each other might also be a common concern.

3 Decide what to work on first (problem ranking)

The next stage of the process involves attempting to reach agreement with the family members as to which problems are to be worked on in the short and longer term.

In making a decision about which problems to address, a number of factors should be taken into account. It is vital that: the problem or problems to be worked on are the clients' problems; all or most family members should agree that they are important; if family members have different problems it may be necessary to work on one problem for each family member involved; achievable problems should be addressed first. It might be best, for example, to start with a problem with pocket money rather than a problem with a parent who is not involved in the counselling and has no interest in the family. It is better to deal with problems where there are resources available to help; for example, if the family has a problem with lack of adequate housing then it is much easier to deal with this if there is a possibility of getting better housing. If one family member is subject to a formal mandate or authority it may be appropriate to start with formal requirements; for example, if a child is to be expelled from school unless certain things occur or if a young person is required to undertake certain actions as part of a court order, then this should take precedence. If the family or any family members are facing an immediate crisis this, of course, may need to be dealt with immediately; for example, if the family is homeless this might have to take immediate priority.

Finally, consistent with the literature on criminogenic needs (Andrews and Bonta 2003), the model focuses on practical issues or problems that relate to the client's offending. The focus should be on issues such as housing, employment, drug use, peer group, rather than intra-psychic issues such as self-esteem, anxiety or depression.

4 Explore the issue in more detail.

The next stage involves a detailed exploration of the problem with the family in order to get a clear picture of the nature and degree of the problem and about what has been done to address it previously. It is important that this is done thoroughly so that realistic strategies to address the problem can be developed. Questions that the family members should address include: What is the history of the problem? When does it occur? How did it begin? What has the family done to address the problem previously? Have these things helped or hindered? What is the client getting out of it? Are there occasions when the problem is not present?

5 What do we want to achieve? Setting goals

The next step involves setting goals – clear and specific goals that are agreed on by the worker and the clients and are directly related to the problems. For example: 'For Amy and Mrs L to reach agreement on whether Amy should continue to see her boyfriend and if so how often and where she should see him. This goal to be achieved by week 7.'

Some examples of goals that have been set by workers who have used the model include: developing communication between a father and son when all communication had ceased; coming to an agreement between a mother and daughter regarding the amount of freedom the young person should be allowed; and reuniting a young person, who had been living away from home, with her family.

6 Contract

The worker and the family then develop a contract. The contract should summarise the agreement between the family members about the ground rules, problems to be addressed, goals to be pursued and conditions of the agreement.

7 Work out ways of achieving the goals – strategies/tasks

Strategies or tasks are then developed by the worker and family members to address the goals. Strategies or tasks might be carried out in the counselling session, such as role play, teaching listening skills, helping family members to acknowledge what other family members are saying, brainstorming solutions or expressing problems in a non-blaming way. Strategies may also be carried out at home, for example engaging in mutually enjoyable activities, spending specified time together, a mother visiting a school, or a child coming home early in return for the mother giving more pocket money. The worker might also have tasks, perhaps undertaking to approach social security.

8 Review how we are going

The final step in the problem-solving process relates to ongoing review. While the steps in the model are straightforward, families do not tend to organise their problems with problem-solving processes in mind. The aim is to try to use the structure to provide a framework for the intervention but not to be tied to it in a way that creates inflexibility. It is important to regularly revise what has been done and where the family is in relation to the steps in the model. Often the steps will be conducted in a different order; for example, it may be necessary, after some weeks, to go back to the original problem survey as new problems emerge.

Application and evaluation of the model

The collaborative family problem-solving model has been used by probation and parole officers, youth justice workers, youth workers, students, school counsellors and others during the past 15 years. Many probation staff in the UK and in Australia have received training in the model. Three small-scale evaluations have been undertaken on the effectiveness of the model.

During 1992 and 1993, 24 final-year social work students (12 in each year) undertook an option in family problem-solving. In the first semester they were offered eight two-hour classes in the model. This involved some instruction and some experiential work (role plays). None of the students had prior experience in a family counselling role.

The students worked in pairs with twelve families, either in the family home or a local family centre which provided the referrals to the students. The families had a range of problems. Some of the primary clients were young offenders on referral from either juvenile justice or child protection. Presenting problems included young people running away from home, offending, truancy and violence towards other family members. In several cases more severe problems emerged as the counselling sessions progressed and there were a number of instances of domestic violence and child abuse including child sexual abuse. These instances were referred to the appropriate agencies. In each case the family members completed evaluation sheets at the conclusion of the counselling.

The second project evaluation involved VicSafe, an arm of the Victorian government, which funded a series of training courses in the model in 1995 and 1996 with a view to considering its effectiveness with a group of community-based welfare professionals. Forty-eight people were offered training in family counselling. Those involved responded to an invitation from the Monash University Office of Continuing Education to participate in a two-day training course, with two follow-up half-days. About 50 per cent of the participants were from schools, mostly student counsellors or pupil welfare coordinators. Six were police officers from Melbourne Community Policing Squads and the remainder were youth, family or other welfare workers from places such as the Wesley Mission and the Salvation Army.

Few people in the group had specific qualifications or training in working with families. Similarly, few had experience in family counselling. Participants were recruited into the course for the purposes of undertaking an introductory course in family counselling with some practical follow-up. The group was characterised, therefore, by its limited experience in family counselling.

The participants were asked to provide evaluation material from the families they worked with and five participants did so. The number of evaluations provided was small and represented only a proportion of the interventions that were offered. Issues of confidentiality and client and organisational consent to release information provided part of the explanation for this.

The five client families had a range of problems. In one family, for example, a young person suffering from depression was in conflict with her mother. Another involved a 14-year-old who was living in foster care and sought help from a youth worker to achieve some reconciliation with his parents.

The third project undertaken during 2007 and 2008 involved offering family interventions to families following referral to the GRIPP program (Gain Respect Increase Personal Power) from the Dandenong Children's Court. Cases were adjourned pending young people's involvement in family counselling and other programmes. Evaluations from six client families were provided by the workers in the GRIPP programme.

In total, 31 evaluation sheets were completed by family members from the three projects. This included 23 families. In most cases the family completed the evaluation as a group at the end of the intervention and agreed on the score given for each question. In the other cases individual family members decided to do their own evaluation.

As can be seen in Figure 14.1, 74 per cent of the family members felt that they were getting along much better at the end of the counselling compared to the beginning. Family members indicated that the problems for which they most wanted help had improved, as indicated in Figure 14.2. Most clients, as illustrated in Figure 14.3, felt that they benefited from the service.

The families responded positively to each of the other questions in the evaluation. For example, most indicated that they no longer had personal or family problems for which they needed further help: 55 per cent of those who responded (17/31) replied 'yes' to this question compared to 22 per cent who replied 'no' (7/31) and 22 per cent who replied that they were uncertain (7/31); 87 per cent (27/31) indicated

On the whole, how are you getting along now compared with when you first began treatment here?

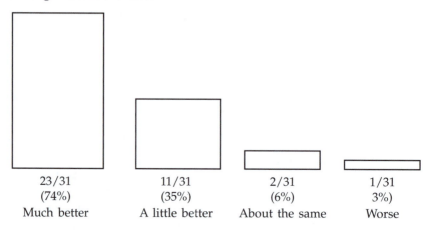

23/31	11/31	2/31	1/31
(74%)	(35%)	(6%)	3%)
Much better	A little better	About the same	Worse

Figure 14.1 General evaluation.

Consider the one problem you most wanted the case worker or counsellor to help you with. How is this problem now compared with how it was when you first started treatment here?

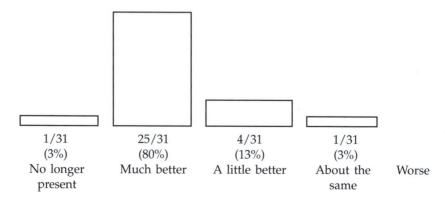

1/31	25/31	4/31	1/31	
(3%)	(80%)	(13%)	(3%)	
No longer present	Much better	A little better	About the same	Worse

Figure 14.2 Focus on the main problem.

that the counselling would help them to handle future problems as they arise with only one person (3%) disagreeing with this statement and 3 (10%) uncertain.

Overall, therefore, most clients believed that they were assisted by the service. Clients were also asked which aspects of the family problem-solving process they found most helpful (see Figure 14.3).

On the whole, how would you rate the extent to which you benefited from the service?

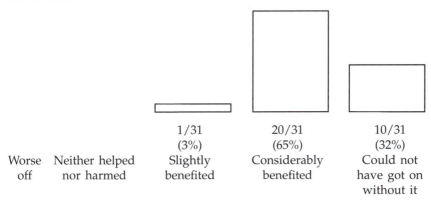

		1/31	20/31	10/31
		(3%)	(65%)	(32%)
Worse off	Neither helped nor harmed	Slightly benefited	Considerably benefited	Could not have got on without it

Figure 14.3 Has the service been beneficial?

One of the criticisms of the family problem-solving approach is that it is too brief to address real problems or underlying issues. However the client questionnaire did not provide strong support for this view: 71 per cent (22/31) stated that the service lasted about the right length of time, 22 per cent (7/31) felt that the service was too short, and one client felt it was too long.

Most clients indicated that they understood what their counsellor was trying to do: 94 per cent (29/31) stated that they understood most or all of the time, with 6 per cent (2/31) indicating that they understood some of the time.

The aspects of the intervention that clients indicated they found most helpful included the counsellors' attempts to help them understand what was happening in their relationship. In response to this question, 87 per cent (27/31) indicated that they found this particularly helpful. The remaining three clients indicated that it was of some help. No clients found it unhelpful.

The clients also believed that the 'counsellor's attempts to help us concentrate on specific problems or goals for us to work on' was very helpful: 80 per cent (25/31) indicated that this was particularly helpful, with the remaining five clients seeing it as helpful.

There was slightly less enthusiasm for working on assignments or tasks at home, with 19 (61 per cent) finding it helpful and 9 (38 per cent) finding it of some help. Two clients found it unhelpful and two indicated that they did not do it.

Clients were slightly more positive about following through at home with solutions worked out in the session: 62 per cent (18/31) found this particularly helpful with 29 per cent (9/31) finding it of some help. Two found it unhelpful and two did not do it.

Workers' views about the model

The workers in the VicSafe study were asked to complete a questionnaire, approximately one year after completing the training course, regarding the relevance and usefulness of the model to their work and the extent to which they were able to help families. Even though only five workers provided evaluation information regarding clients, 19 workers responded to the questionnaire and their responses are outlined below.

The workers completed an average of four sessions per client family. Each worker completed at least two and one as many as nine. The workers involved indicated that they believed the interventions were very successful in terms of achieving the clients' goals as shown in Figure 14.4.

Workers stated that they most often made use of the problem survey and problem exploration stages of the model, with 87 per

How successful do you believe your intervention was with the family or client in terms of achieving the family's or clients goals?

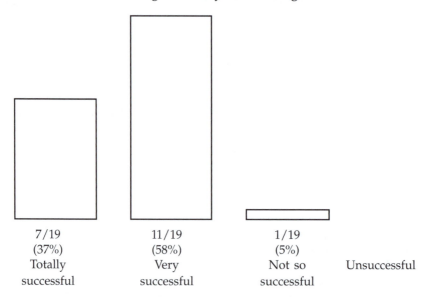

7/19	11/19	1/19	
(37%)	(58%)	(5%)	
Totally	Very	Not so	Unsuccessful
successful	successful	successful	

Figure 14.4 Have goals been achieved?

cent saying that they used those aspects. More than 70 per cent also made use of problem ranking, goal setting and tasks, 60 per cent indicated that they made use of contracts.

It appears, therefore, that despite the difficulty many of these workers had with implementing the model within their agencies, they were able to make use of many aspects of the model and the workers believed that the outcomes were very successful.

Similar responses were gained from 18 students who responded to this survey: 33 per cent (6/18) of the students indicated after the intervention that they believed that the client families had been greatly helped and a further 61 per cent (11/18) indicated that they had been partially helped.

Research support for the model

I am not arguing that the evaluations conducted in the three projects demonstrate the effectiveness of the model. It would be necessary to have an untreated control group and a larger sample to show that the model contributes to reduced recidivism. There may also have been a selection bias in the sample in these evaluations – more satisfied clients may have given consent to be involved in the evaluation and workers may have encouraged clients who appeared to be satisfied with the intervention to be involved in the evaluation.

The evaluations do show, however, that professional human service workers (and students) who have limited experience in working with family groups can learn the model in around 25 hours of training. They also suggest that many families may be willing to remain in this kind of counselling (all but one of the families allocated to the students completed a minimum of six sessions). They also suggest that the families generally found the counselling helpful and that the workers felt that it was helpful for the family members.

I have also argued that the model is likely to be effective because it is based on the principles of effective practice. To quote Andrews and Bonta (2003: 221) following their review of effectiveness of family interventions in corrections, 'behavioural treatment approaches can and do change family interactions along the normative and relationship dimensions and these changes are associated with decreases in delinquent behavior'. A behavioural approach that incorporates each of the effective practice principles, such as collaborative family problem-solving, is likely to work.

Conclusion

In this chapter I have presented the following argument. Families are an important factor in the development of criminality and in the rehabilitation of offenders. Offenders themselves also see family relations as important to them. Family interventions in both youth justice and adult corrections have been shown to be effective in terms of reducing offending. The family interventions that are most effective are those that are consistent with the research about 'what works' in offender rehabilitation. One model that shows potential is a collaborative problem solving-model. This model is consistent with the research about what works and while recidivism studies have not been completed using the model, evaluations from three separate projects suggest that client families in a range of corrections and other settings find it helpful. It is also relatively easily learned as it is a development of skills that workers already have.

References

Andrews, D. and Bonta, J. (2003) *The Psychology of Criminal Conduct*. Cincinnati: Anderson Publishing.

Bonta, J., Rugge, T., Scott, T., Bourgon, G. and Yessine, A. (2008) 'Exploring the black box of community supervision', *Journal of Offender Rehabilitation*, 47 (3): 248–70.

Burke, R. (2005) *An Introduction to Criminological Theory*. Cullompton: Willan Publishing.

Dowden, C. and Andrews, D.A. (2003) 'Does family intervention work for delinquents? Results of a meta-analysis', *Canadian Journal of Criminology and Criminal Justice*, 45 (3): 327–44.

Epstein, N.B. and Bishop, D.S. (1981) 'Problem-centred systems and the family', in A.S. Gurman and P. Kniskern (eds) *Handbook of Family Therapy*. New York: Brunner Mayel.

Farrington, D.P. and Welsh, B.C. (2003) 'Family-based prevention of offending: a meta-analysis', *Australian and New Zealand Journal of Criminology*, 36 (2): 127–51.

Ganem, N.M. and Agnew, R. (2007) 'Parenthood and adult criminal offending: the importance of relationship quality', *Journal of Criminal Justice*, 35 (6): 630–43.

Gavazzi, S.M., Yarcheck, C.M. and Sullivan, J.M. (2008) 'Global risk factors and the prediction of recidivism rates in a sample of first-time misdemeanant offenders', *International Journal of Offender Therapy and Comparative Criminology*, 52 (3): 330–45.

Hayne, D., Petts, R., Maimon, D. and Piquero, A. (2009) 'Exposure to violence in adolescence and precocious role exits', *Journal of Youth and Adolescence*, 38 (3): 269–86.

Latimer, J. (2001) 'A meta-analytic examination of youth delinquency, family treatment, and recidivism', *Canadian Journal of Criminology*, 43 (2): 237–53.

Loeber, R. and Stouthamer-Loeber, M. (1986) 'Family factors as correlators and predictors of juvenile conduct problems and delinquency', in M. Tonry and N. Morris (eds) *Crime and Justice An Annual Review*.

Perlman, H. (1957) *Social Casework: A Problem Solving Process*. Chicago: University of Chicago Press.

Perkins-Dock, R. (2001) 'Family interventions with incarcerated youth: a review of the literature', *International Journal of Offender therapy and Comparative Criminology*, 45 (5): 606–25.

Putkonen, A., Ryynänen, O. and Eronen, M. (2007) 'Transmission of violent offending and crime across three generations', *Social Psychiatry and Psychiatric Epidemiology*, 42 (2): 94–7.

Reid, W. (1985) *Family Problem Solving*. New York: Columbia University Press.

Reid, W. and Epstein, L. (1972) *Task-centred Casework*. New York: Columbia University Press.

Salisbury, E. and Van Voorhis, P. (2009) 'Gendered pathways: a quantitative investigation of women probationers' paths to incarceration', *Criminal Justice and Behavior*, 36 (6): 541–66.

Sexton, T. and Alexander, J. (2002) 'Family-based empirically supported interventions', *The Counseling Psychologist*, 30 (2): 238–61.

Trotter, C. (1994) 'The effective supervision of offenders', PhD thesis, Latrobe University, Melbourne.

Trotter, C. (2006) *Working with Involuntary Clients*. Sydney: Allen and Unwin.

Turner, M.G., Hartman, J.L. and Bishop, D.M. (2007) 'The effects of prenatal problems, family functioning, and neighborhood disadvantage in predicting life-course-persistent offending', *Criminal Justice and Behavior*, 34 (10): 1241–61

Wareham, J., Dembo, R., and Poythress, N.G. (2009) 'A latent class factor approach to identifying subtypes of juvenile diversion youths based on psychopathic features', *Behavioral Sciences and the Law*, 27 (1): 71–95.

Way, I. and Urbaniak, D. (2008) 'Delinquent histories of adolescents adjudicated for criminal sexual conduct', *Journal of Interpersonal Violence*, 23 (9): 1197–1212.

Washington State Institute for Public Policy (2002) *Washington State's Implementation of Functional Family Therapy for Juvenile Offenders: Preliminary Findings*. Online at: www.wsipp.wa.gov/rptfiles/FFTprelim.pdfacc (accessed 13 January 2010).

Woolfenden, S.R., Williams, K. and Peat, J.K. (2002) 'Family and parenting interventions for conduct disorder and delinquency: a meta-analysis of randomized controlled trials', *Archives of Disease in Childhood*, 86 (4): 251–56.

Wright, K.N. and Wright, K.E. (1992) 'Does getting married reduce the likelihood of criminality? A review of the literature', *Federal Probation*, 56 (3): 50–6.

Chapter 15

Collaborating with the community, trained volunteers and faith traditions: building social capacity and making meaning to support desistance

Tom O'Connor and Brad Bogue

Introduction

This chapter tells a story about volunteers, community organisations and faith traditions working alongside probation and parole officers to support men and women in their desistance process. There are dangers in telling this story because everywhere you turn there are concerns and conflicting viewpoints about our topic. Some probation and parole officers are afraid to work with volunteers for reasons of safety; 'volunteers mean well but our clients will manipulate them'. Other officers are wary for reasons of professionalism; 'volunteers want to help but they do not know what they are doing'. Yet, other officers are embracing volunteers and religious groups; 'we could not do our work without them!' Our topic also tends to raise concerns about the separation of religion and state. We realise that different countries, such as France and the US, take very different approaches to the separation of religion and state. The histories of volunteerism and faith group involvement in corrections also differ markedly from country to country. We are confident that a synthesis is possible that reconciles these legitimate concerns and conflicting viewpoints. We open with an account of a faith-informed volunteer programme that we believe has achieved dramatic success.

The COSA story

The story begins in Hamilton, Canada in 1994. Reverend Harry Nigh, the pastor of an inner-city ministry, receives a call from a prison psychologist asking for his help. The prison psychologist is working with a man, let's call him Tim, who is about to be released from prison. Tim is a high profile sex offender. Tim is assessed as having an extremely high risk of recidivism, and he has no support in the community to assist with his re-entry. Tim, however, has identified Pastor Nigh to the prison psychologist as potential support. Tim had built a friendship with the Pastor almost ten years earlier during a prison visitation programme. Because of his notoriety, news of Tim's release has generated a great deal of media response, as well as community outrage, protest and anger. It is obvious to Harry that the fears and response of the community to Tim's release are exacerbating Tim's re-entry needs.

Despite the difficult circumstances, Harry agrees to offer Tim support. Because of the dangerous and serious nature of the case, however, Harry also asks several others from his faith community to help him. Harry also approaches a concerned community member from the local Neighbourhood Watch. The woman from the Neighbourhood Watch group agrees to join the group to ensure that any support given to Tim will be responsible and lead to greater community safety. To make a long story short, Tim and the volunteers went on to develop a network of working relationships, support strategies and friendships that was integral to Tim's successful desistance journey. Tim created a new life for himself and remained crime free for the 12 years of life he had remaining to him.

Around the same time that Tim was released, a friend of Harry's, a prison chaplain called Hugh Kierkegaard, also recruited a group of church-based volunteers to support another high risk releasing sex offender in Toronto. Harry and Hugh began to speak a lot about their experiences and collaborate with the Mennonite community and other friends who had training and experience in restorative justice. This collaboration gave birth to COSA, or Circles of Support and Accountability. COSA is a cooperative movement between community-based organisations, faith-informed volunteers and the Chaplaincy Services Division of Correctional Service Canada (the Federal prison system in Canada).

The Washington State Institute of Public Policy (WSIPP) included an evaluation of COSA in its 2006 meta-analysis of 291 rigorous research studies called 'Evidence Based Adult Corrections Programs:

What Works and What Does Not'. The COSA study (Wilson *et al.* 2005) met the methodological standards for quality research and inclusion in the meta-analysis. The meta-analysis found that the COSA programme had the largest reduction of recidivism (31.6 per cent) and the largest effect size (–.388) among all of the 291 studies (Aos *et al.* 2006).

COSA circles, of four to seven trained volunteers and a core member (the high risk sex offender is called the core member), now operate across Canada and internationally in countries such as England and Wales. To be part of a COSA circle, volunteers must attend a lot of training and the COSA local project coordinator, a paid member of staff who conducts the training, must also feel that each person will make a suitable COSA volunteer (Correctional Service of Canada 2002). Not only are COSA volunteers well trained, but they are professionally supported and they work in conjunction with public institutions such as community agencies, treatment providers, parole and probation officers, police and the courts.

Evaluations of COSA have also found that members of the community are more willing to accept the presence of a high risk and high need sex offender in their community if they know that he or she is involved with a COSA circle (Wilson *et al.* 2007). The Canadian government has recently allocated an additional $8 million of funding to the prison chaplaincy division and its community partners to further expand and develop COSA. COSA, therefore, helps to meet a pressing need in the community to keep people safe and help members of the public address their fears about high risk sex offenders returning to the community.

A new national replication of outcome findings has found that the original COSA findings do not appear to be site specific. Across Canada, offenders in COSA had an 83 per cent reduction in sexual recidivism, a 73 per cent reduction in all types of violent recidivism and an overall reduction of 71 per cent in all types of recidivism as compared to the matched offender control group. The new study concludes that its findings 'provide further evidence for the position that trained and guided community volunteers can and do assist in markedly improving offenders' chances for successful reintegration' (Wilson *et al.* 2009).

What if more community members were to respond as Harry Nigh did to requests for help from probation or parole officers in their local community? What if probation and parole systems were able to work more effectively and efficiently with the Harry Nighs of their community? What if each community had an organised system for training and guiding community volunteers to support and hold accountable the many men and women who need support as they live out their own unique story of desistance?

The integrated model for corrections

Implementing volunteer and community development systems would mean taking seriously the third circle of the integrated model for *Implementing Evidence-based Policy and Practice in Community Corrections* by the Crime and Justice Institute and the US National Institute of Corrections (2009). Put simply, the model posits that there are three interdependent dimensions (see Figure 15.1) to implementing evidence-based policies and practices in community supervision. Each dimension must be given equal value. Agencies that do not work on all three levels fail to become evidence-based.

The first element is to undergo a process of organisational development. This process is necessary before an agency can fully move from traditional to evidence-based forms of supervision. The second component is using evidence-based principles and practices of supervision with fidelity to their own original design. The third is entering into collaboration with community stakeholders. This collaboration enhances internal and external buy-in and creates more holistic system change. The first and second components are internal strategies. The third component is an external strategy and requires correctional agencies to share decision-making with their various partners. But shared decision-making does not come easily or naturally to an organisation that is built on the concept of formal social control and power over others (Crime and Justice Institute 2009).

Why is the third circle so necessary and important? Doing the kind of work we do without the third circle is like asking ourselves to run a marathon on one leg with no prosthesis. The complexity, nuance, and scope of our job – to increase public safety and help lift large numbers of people out of crime – is simply beyond the reach of any internal correctional strategy. Self-enclosed correctional agencies, by definition, can never discover the insights and knowledge necessary to prevent themselves from going around in self-perpetuating circles that remind one of the tragic silent comedy in which the Keystone Kops forever chase but never catch the robbers. We need the external resources of the third circle to bolster the work we currently do. We also need the new possibilities for safety and goodness made

Figure 15.1 The integrated model for implementing evidence-based policy and practices.

available to us through collaboration with external groups. We need to remember that authentic cooperation is the source of legitimate power (Lonergan 1972). Corrections can cooperate with the community and establish interdependent relationships that respect the autonomy, unique role, resources and skill sets of both partners. Doing so will greatly enhance our legitimacy in the eyes of the public and the offenders we serve.

Collaborating with external resources

Large numbers of community correctional agencies are now experimenting with a variety of forms of community engagement. Mentoring is one form of such collaboration that can bring a huge amount of resources to the table. There are many groups, such as veterans, people in recovery, ex-offenders and business people, who might be willing to contribute to their community through mentoring. There is some research to show that carefully structured and well run mentoring programmes for young people at risk can help to bring about social, behavioural and academic change. These youth mentoring programmes work because the mentors are able to develop a trusting relationship with the young person and provide consistent, non-judgemental support and guidance (Sipe 1996,

Tierney *et al.* 2000). We know less about the impact of mentoring with adults, especially adult ex-prisoners. An evaluation of a peer support/mentoring programme called 'Routes Out of Prison' in Scotland sheds a lot of light on the difficulties of working with people coming out of prison who have multiple and complex needs (Schinkel *et al.* 2009). About 40 per cent of the 1,226 men and women (average sign up each year) who signed up for the Routes Out of Prison programme each year in four prisons went on to engage with the programme in the community. The peer mentors (people who had experience with offending, substance abuse or living in areas of multiple deprivation) were able to establish supportive coaching relationships with these men and women and help bridge about 30 per cent of them to employment or training outcomes or connect them with service agencies (Schinkel *et al.* 2009).

There are also encouraging outcome findings from an evaluation of the 'Ready4Work: An Ex-prisoner, Community and Faith Initiative' launched in 2003 by the US Department of Labor and a non-profit, non-partisan community organisation called Public/Private Ventures (Cobbs Fletcher *et al.* 2009: 3). The Ready4Work programme took place in 11 US cities. The programme served approximately 4,500 moderate to high risk, predominantly African-American 18- to 34-year-old men released into the community. The men had served non-violent felony sentences, and most of them had prior criminal histories and incarcerations. Six of the lead agencies in six of the cities were faith-based organisations, three were secular non-profit agencies, one was a mayor's office and one a for-profit entity. Ready4Work services included employment readiness training, job placement and intensive case management, along with referrals for housing, healthcare, drug treatment and other programmes. In addition, participants had the chance to become involved with a one-on-one or group mentoring relationship.

Across the 11 sites, about half of the participants chose the mentoring component. These participants, compared to those who chose not to have a mentor, did better in terms of programme retention, employment and recidivism. Mentored participants spent an average of 9.7 months in the programme compared to 6.6 months for non-mentored participants. Mentored participants were twice as likely to find a job. Comparing those who found a job, people with a mentor were more likely to meet the three-month job retention benchmark for job stability. Finally, mentored participants were 35 per cent less likely to reoffend within one year post-release, regardless of whether they ever became employed. Cobbs Fletcher *et al.* (2009) point out that there was no control group in this evaluation. The study merely compared those who volunteered to work with a mentor to those who did not volunteer. The self-selection or motivation factor could therefore account for the differences in outcomes. Discrepancies in programme quality and structure across the sites may also have played a role in whether or not participants engaged in mentoring. For both of these reasons the findings are not conclusive but they do suggest that mentoring with men and women under community supervision may play an important role in helping them to stay in a programme, find a job, stay employed, and stay out of trouble (Cobbs Fletcher *et al.* 2009: 3–4). An external strategy brings much-needed resources to our table. Engagement with these resources can also help provide the spark and momentum we need to change and improve our own internal practices.

Collaborating with external perspectives

The external strategy allows corrections to interact with and benefit from positive cultural forces as well as new ideas and perspectives from other disciplines. Charles Taylor, the Canadian philosopher, has shown how historical forces and trends in the West, such as the Enlightenment, the establishment of secular democracies, the growth and dominance of rational, instrumental and scientific methods of thinking and the emergence of individualism, have resulted in a broad-based western culture that places a high value on each person's search for authenticity.

> We live in a world where people have a right to choose for themselves their own pattern of life, to decide in conscience what convictions to espouse, to determine the shape of their lives in a whole host of ways that our ancestors couldn't control. And these rights are generally defended by our legal systems. In principle, people are no longer sacrificed to the demands of supposedly sacred orders that transcend them. (Taylor 1991: 2)

Most people today give assent to what Taylor calls the 'ethics of authenticity'. Our culture expects each person to find, express and be faithful to their authentic or true self as they try things out, learn from their mistakes, grow in experience and mature. We highly regard people whom we consider to be authentic in their way of being and expressing themselves in the world.

How does this western story or way of thinking about authenticity play out in corrections? Unfortunately, the recognition that we all can and must continually strive for authenticity seems to have little to do with corrections. Society, in large part, denies this recognition to criminals, inmates, probationers, parolees and ex-offenders. Somehow 'offenders' forfeit what Taylor refers to as 'the moral force of the ideal of authenticity'. In general, on a moral, social and legal level, society tends to forever remain suspicious of inmates and offenders even when they manage to turn their lives around. In the US one out of every 40 voting age adults, or 5.4 million Americans, have permanently lost their right to vote because of a felony conviction. The vast majority of these people are no longer in prison. In several states one in four black men can no longer vote (Manza and Uggen 2006). Looking at the headlines of a Canadian newspaper that covered the release of a COSA core member, we can see how these headlines support values of ostracism, banishment, violence and fear while also denying the possibility of any growth into authenticity for the core member:

- Perv Out Of Jail Today: Police Consider Publishing His New Address
- Pervert A Risk
- Pedophile 'Terrified' To Be Out Of Jail
- A Community Lives In Fear
- Perv's Neighbors In Scary, Ugly Mood
- Neighbors Drive Perv From Home
- Molester, 24-Hour Ultimatum
- Neighbors: We've Done Our Jobs

By contrast, the language used by COSA to express its core values is very different. Notice how the COSA language recognises and seeks to support victims, while the newspaper language pays no attention to those who have been victimised.

- We **affirm** that the community bears a responsibility for the safe restoration and healing of victims as well as the safe re-entry of released sex offenders into the community.

- We **believe** in a loving and reconciling Creator who calls us to be agents in the work of healing.

- We **acknowledge** the ongoing pain and need for healing among victims and survivors of sexual abuse and sexual assault.

- We **seek** to 're-create community' with former offenders in responsible, safe, healthy and life-giving ways.

- We **accept** the challenge of radical hospitality, sharing our lives with one another in community and taking risks in the service of love.

The language of the newspaper is a language of condemnation, hopelessness, separation and violence that seeks to silence and bring an end to a painful story. The COSA language is a language of accountability, service, redemption, collaboration and transformation. The COSA language seeks to foster and keep a story of resilience, healing, the overcoming of betrayal and desistance alive. Ultimately, one language disempowers and creates a dependent person upon whom the criminal justice system acts. The other language empowers and creates agency and interdependent collaboration. Disturbingly, our work takes place in a social context where the disempowering language is generally treated by many in the media and politics as the dominant public language. This is so even though public opinion is much more discriminating and diverse in its attitudes towards crime and punishment (Peter D. Hart Research Associates 2002; Green 2006).

The dominance of this language of condemnation has a profoundly negative effect on every person who works in the field of probation and parole, and on every offender, because it limits our true potentialities and tends to create co-dependency, frustration and failure. The language of condemnation reinforces a Keystone Kops mentality. What is the dominant language within your particular correctional cultures? To what extent is it a language of condemnation or transformation? Speaking for our (the authors) correctional settings we often hear the language of condemnation and seldom the language of transformation.

Alongside the languages of condemnation and transformation we also hear a language of control and punishment through the loss of freedom accompanied by a language of instrumental reasoning which would have us use evidence-based practices and the principles of risk, need and responsivity to increase public safety. We know that such instrumental or programmatic reasoning, when put into practice with fidelity, results in very positive public safety outcomes; on average a 28 per cent reduction in recidivism (Smith *et al.* 2009). We also know that there is another, less dominant, language in our field. This is the language of 'desistance', which differs in tone and substance from the language of instrumental reasoning and effective programming. The language around the desistance process is about personal stories of agency, interdependence, maturation and striving for authenticity.

To be humane and effective we need both our language of instrumental reasoning and our language of desistance. But we also need the community language that comes from external sources such as COSA. The field of corrections has everything to gain by expanding its collaboration with community groups like COSA. Such collaboration enables us to work, think and imagine in the context of different social languages and cultural norms that are more supportive of both our instrumental and desistance languages. It is not by accident that Shadd Maruna advanced our appreciation and understanding of desistance by going out into the community and attending to the true life stories and narratives of career criminals in Liverpool (Maruna 2001). The language of instrumental reasoning and effective programming concerns an internal strategy that is under our control. This language carries its own inherent strengths in terms of creating the conditions for a certain understanding and knowledge, but it also carries its own inherent weaknesses that render it almost incapable of discovering and exploring phenomena such as COSA or desistance. We need a constellation of languages so that we can better imagine, create and support meaning out of the harsh, complex and paradoxical realities of crime, victimisation, suffering, failure, loss of freedom, resilience, recovery, and change that we work with on a daily basis.

A community development approach

Some probation and parole officers are adept at helping their clients to make effective use of community resources. Over the years these officers build up a set of great relationships with the treatment, employment, housing, family, informal social support groups and other resources in the community. John Augustus, the founder of Probation, also knew that creating linkages between his clients and community resources was crucial. Indeed, making effective use of community resources forms one of the five research-supported, core correctional practices for staff (Dowden and Andrews 2004). Today, however, there are so many people under supervision with so many needs, that officers cannot possibly rely solely on an individual approach. We are overwhelmed by our client numbers. So it is better to take a community development rather than an individual offender focus when we consider a collaboration strategy with the community.

Our job is to partner with the community, build up the social capital of the community, and render it more capable of supporting desistance for particular offenders. We have learned how to focus on and strengthen the protective factors for clients. Now we must learn how to focus on and strengthen protective factors in our communities. This means taking an asset-based approach to community development (Kretzman and McKnight 1993). Kretzmann and McKnight show two maps for a single community that bring the value of an asset-based model for community development into sharp relief. The two maps compare the conventional sensationalised media and political perspective that portrays all of the community's needs, deficits and problems (Figure 15.2) with an alternative view that focuses on the positive elements and widespread potential of the community (Figure 15.3).

The point of view represented in Figure 15.2 is realistic. In most communities, where there is a lot of crime, it is easy to point to the presence of high levels of drug abuse, unemployment, truancy, gangs, crime and anti-social attitudes. These are just a few of the negatives that make living in a high crime neighbourhood a risk factor in many

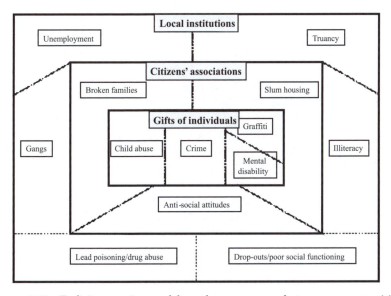

Figure 15.2 Deficit mapping and low dream approach to our communities.

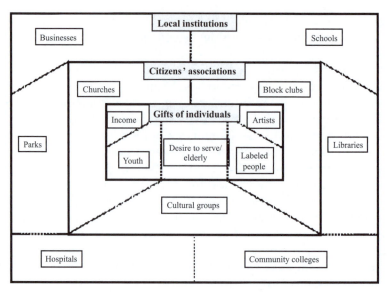

Figure 15.3 Asset mapping and high dream approach to our communities.

of our risk and needs assessments. We call this approach, which always leads with the problems or the bad news, the 'low dream' approach.

But it's also possible to take what we call a 'high dream' approach to our work and lead with what is strong and positive about a situation. The high dream approach, for example, would have us focus first on the many people who have been in prison and made positive and even spectacularly positive contributions to society. Think for a moment of the many people you know personally who have done well after doing time in a prison or under community supervision. Although not quite the same, we can also think of Gandhi, Martin Luther King Jr, Anne Frank, Henry David Thoreau, Malcolm X, St Paul, Aung San Suu Kyi and Nelson Mandela, all of whom were 'inmates'. We have to find more ways of thinking about and imagining what positive psychology calls 'positive deviance' (Cameron 2008) and less about negative deviance. Positive deviance refers to examples of people and organisations who stand out from the normal in the positive direction. A perspective that begins with positive deviance provides an attractive vision that energises our work to bring some good out of the horrors of criminality and prevent further tragedies. We can look at the exact same community, depicted in Figure 15.2, in an entirely more hopeful, realistic and empowering way (Figure 15.3).

Kretzmann and McKnight (1993) point out that even the hardest-hit communities in the poorest neighbourhoods in large cities are filled with resources such as schools, hospitals, libraries, elderly folks with time to give, young people with enthusiasm and energy, businesses, churches, mosques, synagogues, boys' and girls' clubs, AA and NA meetings and a whole variety of other pro-social organisations. What tends to happen, however, in these hard-hit communities is that the linkages and patterns of communication between all of these resources become weakened compared to communities that are thriving. The work of community development, therefore, is to strengthen and increase the linkages between these resources. Parole and probation officers can support the desistance process by strengthening the linkages between the positive resources in their communities and connecting these resources to corrections. When one looks upon a community from a deficit perspective, it's easy to conclude that the community is broken. Thus, the only solution is to pour vast amounts of money and resources into the community from outside the community. The reality, however, is that every community (and offender) has its own internal resources for building itself up, and can do so, especially if it gets the right kind of help. Internally motivated change, supported by external resources, is more likely to succeed than externally motivated change. This is true, both for offenders and communities. This kind of asset-based community development approach shares a great deal in common with a public health model for corrections (US Department of Health and Human Services 2007). Engagement with the 'outside' world is crucial to the development of corrections.

Humanistic, spiritual and religious ways of making meaning

Religious volunteers tend to be very active in corrections in many countries, and there is a growing body of research on the role, impact and future direction of religion in correctional systems (O'Connor and Duncan 2008). The largest group of volunteers who work with prisons, jails and community corrections seem to be related in some way to religious faith traditions. This seems to be so in many countries, such as Canada, England, the US and France. For instance, 1,976 men and women currently volunteer with the Oregon Department of Corrections which has 14 prisons and approximately 14,000 prisoners. Of these volunteers, 75 per cent are 'religious volunteers' who come from a wide variety of faith and spiritual traditions such as Native American, Jewish, Protestant, Catholic, Hindu, Buddhist, Seventh Day

Adventist, Latter Day Saints, Jehovah's Witness, and Earth-Based or pagan such as Wicca. Another 10 per cent of the volunteers in Oregon work in the area of drug and alcohol recovery, primarily from the Alcoholics and Narcotics Anonymous (AA and NA) traditions. These AA and NA volunteers tend to fall into a 'spiritual' category. They are not 'religious' in the sense of belonging to an organised religion. They are generally spiritual, however, because a 'higher power' is a core part of their motivation for volunteering and their way of working. Research on the impact of twelve-step type programmes such as AA and NA has increasingly demonstrated reductions in days of drug/alcohol use. Programme involvement, frequency of interaction with others in the recovery affiliation, as well as the ability of these groups to help people shift social networks, seem to be important causal factors for their success (Moos and Moos 2004b; Tonigan 2001; Moos and Moos 2004a; McGrady *et al.* 2004). The large network of AA and NA groups in almost every community makes these groups natural community partners.

The final 15 per cent of volunteers in Oregon tend to work out of a wide variety of secular contexts and help with education, cultural clubs, recreational activities, life skills development and administrative tasks in the department. Perhaps a good example of this third group, whom we call secular or humanist in their orientation and work, would be many of the people who volunteer in the Inside-Out programme. In 1997 Lori Pompa founded the Inside-Out Prison Exchange Program which is based in Philadelphia at Temple University. Inside-Out trains professors to teach semester-length college-level courses (for example, Introduction to Criminology) inside prisons to about 30 students. Half of the students in the class are incarcerated and half are students from a local university or college. All of the students in the class are expected to participate on an equal level, use only first names, and complete all the course reading and requirements. There are no 'research findings' yet about Inside-Out, but there are many stories about students who undergo a process of change and radical awakening in the course of taking a class. Inside-Out has held nearly 200 classes with over 6,000 students, and trained more than 200 instructors from over 100 colleges and universities in 35 US states and Canada. The Inside-Out programme 'increases opportunities for men and women, inside and outside of prison, to have transformative learning experiences that emphasize collaboration and dialogue, inviting participants to take leadership in addressing crime, justice, and other issues of social concern' (www. insideoutcenter.org/home.html).

As we have seen, a large proportion of volunteers who engage with corrections are from religious or spiritual traditions. This means that we have to address separation of religion and state issues. O'Connor *et al.* (2006) devote a whole paper to the shape of an authentic dialogue between religion and corrections. The authors make one major point about how to have a legally and culturally appropriate engagement between religion and corrections. Our own authenticity, or appropriateness for a government-backed agency such as Connections means that we must engage equally with all of the humanistic, spiritual and religious ways of making meaning that take place among our clients and the communities we partner with. Especially in so far as these ways of making meaning relate to the desistance process.

In his highly acclaimed book *A Secular Age*, Charles Taylor (2007) gives a fascinating account of what it means to live in our modern secular democracies and a secular age. For Taylor, it means that every person has a choice about how they will create a sense of ultimate meaning for their life. Ultimate meaning usually refers to working with questions about the purpose of life, health, justice, suffering, evil and death. The more traditional choice that derives a sense of meaning from a diverse range of religious and spiritual traditions. All of these different religious and spiritual traditions posit a transcendent source or ground of meaning, usually called God or the Divine. But now we live in a secular age, and there is another choice: to make meaning in a way that makes no reference to God or the Divine, but only to human life and the human condition. This purely secular, or humanistic, way of making meaning is new. Never before in history has this choice been available on a broad societal level. Nowadays people take this choice for granted (Taylor 2007).

Historical, philosophical, political and cultural forces have established the right of people to follow any faith tradition of their choice without interference from the state. These developments have also established the right of people 'not to believe', or rather, to put their faith and belief in human life. See, for example, the work of Greg M. Epstein, who is a humanist chaplain at Harvard University and author of *Good Without God: What a Billion Nonreligious People Do Believe* (2009). State officials who work with and serve the public must be prepared to engage equally with all three ways of making ultimate meaning: humanist, spiritual and religious.

For many years professional staff and state employees followed their training and stayed away from questions of religion, spirituality and meaning with their clients. People were fearful of crossing professional and religion/state boundaries, and wanted to respect the autonomy of their clients in matters of faith and religion. The desistance literature, however, has taught us that a particular client's self narrative or way of making meaning and deriving agency in their life is crucial to their desistance process as they mature, develop social bonds and create a new 'redemption' (Maruna 2001). McNeill argues that 'offender management services need to think of themselves less as providers of correctional treatment (that belongs to the expert), and more as supporters of desistance processes (that belong to the desister)' (McNeill 2006: 46) There are three major sources of ultimate meaning that belong to desisters and their communities: humanistic, spiritual and religious. Probation and parole officers who learn how to support all three sources of meaning among their clients can help support desistance.

Probation and parole officers are comfortable asking clients about their education, their drug and alcohol use, their families, their criminal histories, and even their sexual histories and fantasies. Probation and parole officers can also learn to become comfortable asking their clients how they make meaning in life. Adapting the work of Puchalski (1999), we recommend four simple questions as part of the regular process of building rapport with and accessing a client's risk, need, responsivity and protective factors:

1 I wonder if religion or spirituality plays a role in your life or if meaning for you comes more from a human point of view?

2 How important is that way of looking at life for you?

3 Are you part of any community or group of people that shares your views on life?

4 How would you like to bring this part of your life into our work together and your plans for being successful without crime?

Using motivational interviewing approaches and the responsivity principle, officers can discover and support the particular meaning story that is active in each of their clients. One simple way to support this meaning is to help match clients up with the right volunteer and community supports. We know that many of the men and women who are in prison, jails and under community supervision respond in a very positive manner to volunteers from each of the religious, spiritual and humanist milieus. In responsivity terms, different people are open and willing to work with each group of volunteers because they find a match with their own way of being in the world. The more attributes and shared background between the volunteers and the people they support, the stronger the potential for positive social support effects. For example, consider the outreach potential of groups like successful ex-offenders or veterans. There are 12 million veterans in the US alone. Veterans share a number of attributes – majority male, familiar with violence, high prevalence rates of PTSD – with those under community supervision, and so can establish empathic working relationships with them. Many veterans also bring leadership training and experience, skills for recovering from drugs and alcohol, and pro-social commitments to family, work, education and community. With training, these veterans can appropriately apply all of their skills to a correctional and desistance context. No doubt, veterans also have a diverse mix of humanist, spiritual and religious orientations, and additional matching on these variables will increase the potential for forming legitimate working relationships and positive social support effects that promote desistance.

Creating a volunteer and community development system

The financial costs of collaborating with volunteers and community organisations are small, and the return on investment is potentially large. Volunteers donate an estimated 250,000 hours of service each year to the Oregon Department of Corrections (O'Connor and Duncan 2008). This is the equivalent in hours of 121 full-time staff positions, or over $5 million in value if one uses the Independent Sector (2008) figure of $20.25 per volunteer hour to estimate the value of their services. Three full-time volunteer programme staff members in the department recruit, train, card, manage, thank and assist these volunteers to work with every unit in the department. Staff members in each unit supervise the volunteers and guide their work. So volunteers are inexpensive, but they are not free. It takes dedicated time and skill on the part of staff to build a system of training and collaboration with them. This is especially so if we expect volunteers to be effective and safe. Because of their training and natural inclination, professional chaplains, who work out of a variety of humanist, spiritual and religious perspectives, are often excellent at collaborating with community resources and working with and training volunteers (O'Connor et al. 2006). Many prisons currently have professional chaplains on staff, but few probation and parole agencies do. Perhaps it is time for probation and parole agencies to consider hiring dedicated chaplain staff for creating a volunteer and community development system for their agencies.

In a recent paper we outlined a logic model that combined four different sets of skills for probation and parole officers in their work with people under community supervision. We set out a general framework and strategy for community supervision by articulating what four different sets of literatures have taught us about the evidence-based effectiveness of our work (Bogue *et al.* 2008). First, general factor research into the central role of an empathic working relationship between an officer (or any change agent) and their client led us to recommend motivational interviewing approaches for officers as they build rapport and evoke motivation for change with their clients. Second, the contingency management literature shows how important it is for officers to be skilful in using rewards and punishments appropriately to reinforce accountability. Third, the cognitive behavioural treatment literature provides officers with a guide for when and how to refer to cognitive behavioural treatment. This literature also helps officers know how to coach, reinforce and skill train their clients in their new cognitive behaviours such as relapse planning. Fourth, the desistance literature points to the role of officers in supporting social network enhancement for their clients and mobilising community support.

Volunteers have their own sets of skills and unique roles in the correctional process. Volunteers are not miniature probation and parole officers, and we should not try to mould them in this way. However, they are willing and, with training, are able to collaborate with probation and parole officers in a targeted manner that enhances each of the four vital skill sets (above) or approaches to working with offenders. For example, COSA trains its volunteers to support the relapse prevention plans of their core members. AA and NA sponsors are often adept at helping people enhance their social networks. A faith-informed statewide re-entry programme called Home for Good in Oregon trains its volunteers to use motivational interviewing approaches to support moderate and high risk people as they develop pro-social attitudes, values and beliefs and establish a pro-social network of friends and acquaintances (O'Connor *et al.* 2004). Given such volunteer and community development systems, we are more than willing to concur with the findings of Wilson *et al.*, in the 2009 COSA evaluation: there is 'evidence for the position that trained and guided community volunteers can and do assist in markedly improving offenders' chances for successful reintegration'. Corrections can engage and collaborate with the Harry Nighs and their communities in a way that builds social capacity, makes meaning and supports desistance. Such an external strategy will significantly enhance the ability of corrections to move from traditional supervision policies and practices and become fully evidence-based.

References

Aos, S., Miller, M. and Drake, E. (2006) *Evidence-Based Adult Corrections Programs: What Works and What Does Not*. Olympia: Washington State Institute For Public Policy.

Bogue, B., Diebel, J. and O'Connor, T. (2008) 'Combining officer supervision skills: a new model for increasing success in community corrections', *Perspectives: the Journal of the American Probation and Parole Association*, 32: 31–45.

Cameron, K. (2008) *Positive Leadership: Strategies for Extraordinary Performance*. San Francisco: Barrett-Koehler Publishers.

Cobbs Fletcher, R., Sherk, J. and Jucov, L. (2009) *Mentoring Former Prisoners: A Guide for Reentry Programs*. Philadelphia: Public/Private Ventures.

Correctional Service of Canada (2002) *Circles of Support and Accountability: A Guide to Training Potential Volunteers*. Correctional Service of Canada.

Crime and Justice Institute (2009) *Implementing Evidence-Based Policy and Practice in Community Corrections*, 2nd edn. Washington, DC: National Institute of Corrections.

Dowden, C. and Andrews, D.A. (2004) 'The importance of staff practices in delivering effective correctional treatment: a meta-analytic review of core correctional practice', *International Journal of Offender Therapy and Comparative Criminology*, 48: 449–76.

Epstein, G.M. (2009) *Good Without God: What a Billion Nonreligious People Do Believe*. New York: HarperCollins.

Green, D.A. (2006) 'Public opinion versus public judgment about crime: correcting the "comedy of errors"', *British Journal of Criminology*, 46: 131–54.

Independent Sector (2008) *Value of Volunteer Time*. Online at: www.independentsector.org/programs/research/volunteer_time.html (accessed 15 December 2009).

Kretzman, J. and McKnight, J. (1993) *Building Communities from the Inside Out: A Path Toward Finding and Mobilizing a Community's Assets*. Asset-Based Community Development Institute.

Lonergan, B. (1972) *Method in Theology*. Minneapolis: Seabury Press.

Manza, J. and Uggen, C. (2006) *Locked Out: Felon Disenfranchisement and American Democracy*. Oxford University Press.

Maruna, S. (2001) *Making Good: How Ex-Convicts Reform and Rebuild Their Lives*. Washington, DC: Psychological Association.

McGrady, B.S., Epstein, E.E. and Kahier, C.W. (2004) 'Alcoholics Anonymous and relapse prevention as maintenance strategies after conjoint behavioral alcohol treatment for men: 18 month outcomes', *Journal of Consulting and Clinical Psychology*, 72: 155–64.

McNeill, F. (2006) 'A desistance paradigm for offender management', *Criminology and Criminal Justice*, 6: 39–62.

Moos, R.H. and Moos, B.S. (2004a) 'The interplay between help seeking and alcohol-related outcomes: divergent processes for professional treatment and self-help groups', *Drug and Alcohol Dependence*, 75: 155–64.

Moos, R.H. and Moos, B.S. (2004b) 'Long-term influence of duration and frequency of participation in Alcoholics Anonymous on individuals with alcohol use disorder', *Journal of Counsulting and Clinical Psychology*, 72: 81–90.

O'Connor, T.P., Cayton, T., Taylor, S., McKenna, R. and Monroe, N. (2004) 'Home for Good in Oregon: a community, faith, and state re-entry partnership to increase restorative justice', *Corrections Today*.

O'Connor, T.P., Duncan, J. and Quillard, F. (2006) 'Criminology and religion: the shape of an authentic dialogue', *Criminology and Public Policy*, 5: 559–70.

O'Connor, T.P. and Duncan, J.B. (2008) 'Religion and prison programming: the role, impact, and future direction of faith in correctional systems', *Offender Programs Report*, 11: 81–96.

Peter D. Hart Research Associates (2002) *Changing Public Attitudes Toward the Criminal Justice System*. Portland Society Institute.

Puchalski, C. (1999) 'Spirituality and end-of-life care: taking a spiritual history', *Innovations in End-of-Life Care*, 1.

Schinkel, M., Jardine, C., Curran, J., Whyte, B. and Nugent, B. (2009) *Draft Final Report of the Evaluation of the Routes Out of Prison Project*. Edinburgh: Criminal Justice Social Work Development Center for Scotland, University of Edinburgh.

Sipe, C.L. (1996) *A Synthesis of Public/Private Ventures Research: 1988–1995*. Philadelphia: Public/Private Ventures.

Smith, P., Gendreau, P. and Swartz, K. (2009) 'Validating the principles of effective intervention: a systematic review of the contributions of meta-analysis in the field of corrections', *Victims and Offenders*, 4: 148–69.

Taylor, C. (1991) *The Ethics of Authenticity*. Cambridge, MA: Harvard University Press.

Taylor, C. (2007) *A Secular Age*. Cambridge, MA: Harvard University Press.

Tierney, J.P., Grossman, J.B. and Resch, N. (2000) *Making a Difference: An Impact Study of Big Brothers/Big Sisters* (a reissue of 1995 Study). Philadelphia: Public/Private Ventures.

Tonigan, J.S. (2001) 'Benefits of Alcoholics Anonymous attendance: replication of findings between clinical research sites in Project MATCH', *Alcoholism Treatment Quarterly*, 19: 67–77.

US Department of Health and Human Services (2007) *Opening Doors: The HRSA-CDC Corrections Demonstration Project for People Living with HIV/AIDS*. US Department of Health and Human Services.

Wilson, R.J., Cortoni, F. and McWhinnie, A.J. (2009) 'Circles of Support and Accountability: a Canadian national replication of outcome findings', *Sexual Abuse: A Journal of Research and Treatment*, 21: 412–30.

Wilson, R.J., Picheca, J.E. and Prinzo, M. (2005) *Circles of Support and Accountability: An Evaluation of the Pilot Project in South Central Ontario*. Ottawa: Correctional Service of Canada.

Wilson, R.J., Picheca, J.E. and Prinzo, M. (2007) 'Evaluating the effectiveness of professionally facilitated volunteerism in the community-based management of high-risk sexual offenders, Part One: Effects on participants and stakeholders', *Howard Journal*, 46: 289–302.

Part Five

Offenders' compliance with supervision

Chapter 16

Compliance with community penalties: the importance of interactional dynamics

Pamela Ugwudike

Introduction

Compliance with community penalties is a neglected area of empirical and theoretical enquiry. This chapter focuses on the data generated from a study that explored the nature of compliance with community penalties. The study found that interactional processes through which probation officers engage with probationers to manage a range of situational, structural and practical factors may produce (or impede) compliance. Central to these processes is the individualised approach to securing compliance that also facilitates the judicious use of professional discretion.

In many jurisdictions, deterrent enforcement provisions have in recent decades become the primary strategy for ensuring compliance with community penalties. The first National Standards of general application governing the supervision of community penalties in England and Wales were introduced in 1992. The standards signified an attempt to replace discretionary enforcement practices with a more rigid approach to ensuring compliance. Subsequent National Standards have maintained this trend. Invariably, the standards have prescribed an enforcement approach that is primarily deterrence-based (Bottoms 2001). They have also sought to reduce the degree of autonomy available to supervising officers during enforcement.

Although the current National Standards, which came into effect on 30 September 2007, encourage an individualised enforcement approach that can facilitate compliance and avoid unnecessary recourse to enforcement action (MOJ 2007), the Standards also retain the deterrent provisions of the 2002 and the 2005 National Standards that were operative at the time of the study reported in this paper (Home Office 2002; NOMS 2005). Therefore, the standards provide that breach action should normally follow a second unacceptable failure to comply with the requirements of a community order. However, official statistics and the relevant empirical literature provide limited support for this deterrence-based approach to securing compliance (Hough *et al.* 2003; Hearnden and Millie 2003).

Identifying effective compliance strategies

As mentioned earlier, there are limited empirical insights into the processes and the conditions that may be linked to the effective engagement of offenders serving community penalties in England and Wales. The apparent paucity of insights into this subject matter is surprising given the finding that many orders are terminated before completion. According to the latest official statistics, approximately 32 per cent of orders were terminated early for a 'negative reason' (Ministry of Justice 2008: 42). Termination for 'negative reasons' occurs where an order is terminated for non-compliance or where the probationer is convicted of a further offence (Ministry of Justice 2005: 72). Notwithstanding these findings, in the extant empirical literature the subject matter of compliance with community penalties has tended to be peripheral and not central to analysis. However, the few studies that have explored other aspects of supervision practice do provide some insights into the nature of compliance and the possible factors linked to compliance. Collectively, the relevant studies suggest that the form of non-compliance that would typically attract breach action in court is the failure to attend probation appointments ('total absence') (Mair and May 1997; Farrall 2002) rather than the failure to comply with other requirements incorporated in the National Standards such as the requirement to cooperate with the specific directions of the supervising officer. The reluctance to enforce orders as rigidly as prescribed in official guidance has also been observed by studies of probation supervision (Ellis *et al.* 1996) and by studies examining the supervision of community sentences (Vass 1984). There is a tendency to reserve enforcement action for cases involving persistent absenteeism where no notification is provided by the offender (Hedderman 1999). Studies and official audits have also found evidence of widespread professional discretion in enforcement practice and disparities across probation areas (Ellis *et al.* 1996; HMIP 2003).

Other studies reveal the contextual and interactional processes that can affect compliance. For instance, studies show that many probationers expect practical, therapeutic and other support during supervision (Davies 1969; Willis 1981). Perhaps linked to this, probationers tend to offer positive evaluations of their officers and of their supervision experiences and to define their officer's role in welfarist rather than punitive terms (Rex 1999; Ford et al. 1997). Some studies point to specific supervision skills that can be employed to encourage compliance. These skills include collaborative decision-making, empathy, accessibility and also the willingness to listen to the probationer's problems and to discuss possible solutions (see, for example, Mair and May 1997; Rex 1999). Studies also reveal the supervision approaches that are linked to resistance and failure: undue control (Folkard et al 1974); intrusiveness and being judgemental, and patronising or disrespectful approaches (Ford et al. 1997; Rex 1999). Further, meta-analytic studies exploring effective practice skills point to several communication techniques that effectively engage the probationer and effect change (see, generally, Dowden and Andrews 2004; Raynor and Maguire 2006).

Beyond these interpersonal factors, there are structural and other issues that can also impinge on compliance patterns. These include, for example, unemployment or a sporadic employment history, accommodation difficulties, and financial problems (Lawson 1978; Davies 1969; May 1999); peer group influences and adverse family relationships (Davies 1969); substance misuse and a period in the care of social services (McIvor 1992; Mair and May 1997; May 1999); literacy and learning difficulties (May 1999); low levels of self-motivation (Dawson et al. 2005); previous criminal history (Radzinowicz 1958; McIvor 1992) and convictions for specific offences, particularly dishonesty offences such as burglary (McIvor 1992; Mair and May 1997). Other demographic variables like gender and age can also affect compliance; in general, women and older probationers have been found to be more likely to comply (Mair and May 1997).

Given that there is nonetheless a paucity of empirical research directly examining the subject matter of compliance with community penalties, Farrall observes: 'The need for future research on the topic of unauthorised absence from probation supervision cannot be over-stated. Until more is known about why probationers absent themselves … little can be done to minimise such absences' (2002: 275). The study reported in this chapter set out to address this gap in knowledge.

Methodology

Bottoms (2001) provides a useful theoretical standpoint from which one may explore this neglected area of research. Drawing on theories of social order, Bottoms has developed a theoretical framework for understanding the nature of compliance. According to this framework, there are several mechanisms of compliance, namely: constraint-based, habit/routine, normative and instrumental. Constraint-based mechanisms rely on preventive strategies that physically remove the opportunities for non-compliance, while the internalised non-criminogenic dispositions that are acquired during socialisation processes may ensure habit/routine compliance. Normative mechanisms encourage compliance through internalised norms or internalised obligations to comply based on the perceived legitimacy of authority or through the influence of bonds with persons in authority or with others in society (Hirschi 1969; Bottoms 2001; Tyler 1990; 2005). Instrumental mechanisms are underpinned by the classicist notion that the social actor is naturally motivated by considerations of self-interest. As such, instrumental mechanisms seek to secure compliance by ensuring that the projected risks of non-compliance outweigh potential benefits. The current enforcement policy governing the supervision of community penalties is deterrence-based (Bottoms 2001). It relies on the presumption that awareness of the consequences of non-compliance should motivate compliance. Therefore the framework incorporates an instrumental compliance mechanism.

To accomplish its objectives, the study drew on the above theoretical framework and explored the perspectives of probation officers and probationers based in a probation area in Wales, and in addition the perspectives of five probation practitioners based in the Jersey Probation and Aftercare Service. The study aimed to develop insights into the most effective means of encouraging compliance. Data were generated from case records, observations of interactions, in-depth interviews and informal discussions. The approach was designed to allow for the development of a contextualised understanding of compliance which reflects the realities of practice.

The study employed the Grounded Theory methodology and for each item that was conceptualised or coded, the analytic devices that are central to Straussian Grounded Theory methodology were utilised (Strauss and Corbin 1998). These devices help to ensure that each category or conceptualised incident in the data is explored from the widest possible range of perspectives so that each category reflects as closely as possible the meanings intended by the participants. The three devices are: asking questions (interrogating the data); making constant comparisons of the incidents in the data to delineate them; and making theoretical comparisons between emergent categories and the relevant literature. These devices direct the processes of theoretical sampling and the development of emergent categories.

A *caveat* must be included here regarding the generalisability of the study's findings. The probation area in Wales sampled in this study has several distinctive features. For instance, the probation offices in the area cover sparsely populated rural areas that are located within a significant land mass and this poses transportation problems that can affect compliance. Further, it is a small service in terms of both its revenue budget and its staffing levels. The rate of recorded crime in the area is low compared with other areas in England and Wales and there is a significant under-representation of ethnic minorities in the population. However, the characteristics of the officers included in the study are broadly representative of the national average. For instance, the officers' workload, the average length of service reported by the officers and the greater representation of female officers — described as the 'feminisation of the workforce' (Worrall and Hoy 2005; Ministry of Justice 2007) – are consistent with the national population of probation officers.

In terms of the participating probationers, analysis was restricted to the data generated from 25 probationers comprising 15 (60 per cent) male probationers and ten (40 per cent) female probationers. The largest age group of the probationers sampled fell within the 26 and over age range (56 per cent) and the lowest group were those aged below 26 years (44 per cent). Most of the probationers had previous convictions and many were serving their orders for offences of violence linked to substance misuse. Further, most of the probationers sampled were unemployed and had no post-secondary school qualifications. This is consistent with the findings reported by several studies that most probationers suffer significant socio-economic deprivation (Ford *et al.* 1997; Rex 1999). The case records of 15 of the 25 probationers sampled revealed that most (8) were assessed as posing a 'medium' risk of reoffending.

The Criminal Justice Act 2003 introduced a generic community order. The new style order can consist of one or more requirements that may be selected from a menu of 12 requirements. The 12 requirements include the supervision order (which replaced the traditional probation order) and the unpaid work requirement (which replaced the community service order). The new community order was introduced during the study period. Of the group of probationers sampled, 13 (52 per cent) were serving the old-style probation orders (the community rehabilitation order) and four (16 per cent) probationers were serving the old-style community punishment and rehabilitation order. Many probationers – 11 (44 per cent) were serving orders of 12 months' duration and over. For nine (36 per cent) probationers with orders incorporating the unpaid work or community service element, the hours imposed ranged from 50 hours to 200 hours.

The achieved sample differs somewhat from the national population of probation officers and probationers although areas of concordance may exist. This disparity is not surprising given that the sampling method used was theoretical sampling. With this sampling method, sampling proceeds on the basis of the theoretical insights emergent from the data.

Findings: managing contradictions to secure compliance

Several aspects of the study's findings were broadly consistent with the extant empirical literature. For example, reinforcing the existing empirical literature, the probation officers revealed that a narrow definition of compliance prevails in practice; compliance is typically defined in terms of attending routine appointments. Further, breach action is typically reserved for cases involving a persistent failure to attend appointments where the probationer has also failed to contact the officer.

From the three sources of data (the participants' accounts, observations and case records) the study also uncovered key factors that facilitate an understanding of the nature of compliance. Utilising the analytic technique of making theoretical comparisons, the study drew on Pearson's (1975) notion of 'contradictions' and conceptualised its core category as 'managing contradictions'. The concept of 'contradictions' as defined by Pearson represents the constraints that can affect practice. If one extrapolates from Pearson's concept, the contradictions confronting the officers in the present study include practical contradictions that may be posed by childcare, transportation and other potential obstacles to compliance. Similarly, structural contradictions such as the policy provisions that restrict the use of flexible compliance strategies can also affect practice. Thus the study found that compliance is linked to a series of processes through which officers manage several structural, situational and practical contradictions. Based on the respondents' accounts, managing these contradictions appeared to be more relevant to compliance than the objective existence of the deterrent enforcement framework.

Managing practical contradictions: the effort to address obstacles to compliance

To secure compliance, the officers strived to address the contradictions posed by a range of practical problems that impinge on compliance. The study found that addressing these problems could enhance the quality of the relationships between both parties and encourage compliance. This is because the probationers were more likely to evaluate their experiences of supervision and their officers positively where efforts were made to alleviate the problems affecting their ability to successfully complete their orders and where these factors were also taken into account during the enforcement process. Practical problems that could impinge on compliance include childcare issues, accommodation difficulties and the adverse impact of unstructured lifestyles that revolve round substance misuse. As noted above, the area incorporates several offices that are spread across wide geographic areas and this occasionally poses transportation problems. In some cases, probationers were unable to attend appointments because of the financial costs of travelling to the probation offices.

The officers reported that they devised several compliance strategies to manage these practical problems or contradictions and secure compliance. For instance, some officers tended to offer flexible appointments and reminders to facilitate attendance in relevant cases. Officers also made home visits in order to alleviate childcare and transportation difficulties. However, responses to practical problems were variable across the different offices. There appeared to be no structured framework for addressing obstacles to compliance. In some offices, efforts were made to address practical problems. Much tended to depend on the discretion of the individual officers. Some officers attributed full responsibility for complying with the order to the probationers and were therefore reluctant to provide additional assistance in order to facilitate compliance.

I wouldn't normally phone because at the end of the day any order made between the court and the offender is between them. We don't make the order, we stand back and we supervise it. So it's actually the offender's responsibility to comply. (PO14M)

However, most of the officers were more willing to provide a greater degree of support in order to facilitate compliance. According to the officers the main objectives of offering reminders and flexible appointments were to assist the probationers whose lifestyles are chaotic primarily because they are involved in substance misuse and to alleviate childcare and transportation difficulties:

> Travel is a biggie round here as well. I mean people from (...) which must be 20 miles ... 30 miles away, and the bus service is not very regular here. So you will take into account ... People live out in the countryside and if they don't drive, or they are banned from driving you can't force them to. So you know you drive out, home visits ... (PO4M)

The same officer preferred to offer reminders as part of an overall effort to enhance compliance: 'my philosophy [is] I want people to get through the order and that is why ... I phone them up if they miss an appoint to see why' (PO4M).

In one case involving a probationer who was known to be dependent on substances, a home visit to follow up an absence proved to be a life-saving act. The probation officer involved in the case describes the circumstances:

> If he [P1M – her probationer] suddenly disappears that usually raises alarm bells as to what sort of emotional state he's in. So he did it last week where he didn't come in and we went and did a home visit and it turned out he'd actually taken an overdose the previous night. So in those sort of cases we would actually [make a home visit], because there are concerns as to his emotional health ... (PO3F)

Below, the probationer in question (P1M) recalls this incident. To him, the action of the officer represents a manifestation of the caring approach that prevails in current supervision practice.

> I missed the appointment but I mean they actually came down to see whether I was alright. So I was quite – I mean that didn't used to happen in the old days you know? Nobody turn up – and that made me feel like wow! Hang about there is hope here. They do care. I think that's the difference nowadays I think people do care and they show it a lot more. Maybe they cared in the past I don't know but it's shown more now ... (P1M)

In sum, there appeared to be no coherent compliance strategy for alleviating the obstacles to compliance. Individual officers developed their unique approach based on subjective considerations of the appropriateness of each strategy.

Managing relational contradictions: the impact of the quality of interactions

Relational factors, particularly the nature of the relationships between both parties, were also linked to compliance. According to both parties, the effort to develop good working relationships is an essential component of an effective compliance strategy. The quotes below are broadly representative of the officers' views about the importance of developing good working relationships in order to engage the client. The first is from a male probation officer whose professional qualifications are rooted in social work principles. The second quote was made by a female officer who was trained under the new-style training arrangements:

> ... it's about trying to develop a good working relationship with them from the very beginning so that they feel that there's actually some point to them coming here. (PO3M)

> Forget about motivational interviewing, yeah? A lot of it is hot air. At the end of the day you've got to build relationships. That's all it is. (PO17F)

It appears that a 'good working relationship' based on empathy, egalitarianism, honesty and respect was seen as being less likely to antagonise or alienate the probationer and was considered to be the more effective approach to encouraging compliance.

Reinforcing the relevance of good-quality relationships and interactions, most of the probationers interviewed did not cite the deterrent enforcement framework as the main factor that motivates them to comply with their orders. Rather, the therapeutic and practical benefits of interacting with their supervising officer served as incentives that appeared to be more closely linked to compliance. In more general terms, the opportunity to 'talk' to the officer and discuss problems was a significant motivational factor. Below, two probationers describe the factors that motivated them to comply with their order:

> She's [PO8F – my probation officer] brilliant she's good to talk to. She's a good listener … she listens to me well, she's good. It's nice to have someone to talk to. I can talk to my girlfriend and stuff but not about the stuff that's happened. (P13M)

> … I can sit there and tell him almost anything, you know? So he gets a lot off my mind because I can't really speak to my girlfriend about some things my head thinks about and me and my family sort of broke up but and that. (P7M)

Most of the probationers echoed this view. Interactions with the supervising officers could provide the opportunity to discuss problems and possible solutions. The probationers could also benefit from the advocacy and other support provided by the officers. These perceived incentives were cited as key factors that motivated compliance and were more linked to compliance than the deterrent enforcement framework. In addition, based on the probationers' accounts, the factors that could trigger non-compliance were approaches to supervision that were perceived to be disrespectful, dictatorial/or domineering, rooted in a rigid application of rules, lacking in empathy and intrusive.

Managing structural contradictions: individualised responses to non-compliance

To secure compliance, the officers also strived to manage the structural contradictions posed by the policy requirements that govern their work. Of particular relevance here is the impact of the deterrent enforcement framework. Most officers questioned the effectiveness of deterrent enforcement and the quote below from a female officer trained under the current training style for probation officers highlights the perceived ineffectiveness of the deterrent approach and a rigid application of the formal enforcement framework:

> I don't think there's anything to show that [the deterrent framework] is effective, do you see what I mean? I think all that does is just basically mask the problem up. There's only so long that can go on for anyway, everyone is gonna be locked up you know? (PO13F)

To manage the prescriptive enforcement framework and secure compliance, the officers reported that they devised an individualised approach to responding to non-compliance. They saw the individualised approach as being more responsive to the practical problems that can impinge on compliance. The individualised approach is motivated by the need to preserve the quality of the relationships between both parties. A strict application of the formal rules with no consideration of the circumstances of the case could undermine the quality of the relationship between both parties and trigger future non-compliance.

A case study that clearly illustrates the importance of an individualised response to non-compliance is provided here. The case involves a 33-year-old probationer – P2M – who was serving a three-year community rehabilitation order (now the community order with supervision requirement) for theft offences. Describing the circumstances that triggered the decision to deliberately violate his order, the probationer points to the rigid application of rules without due consideration of the specific circumstances of the case: 'it all comes down to the probation officer. You can have any set of rules and regulations but if they're put across by the wrong person they're not gonna do anything' (P2M).

In this case, the probationer believed that the quality of treatment he received was poor because, in his view, the officer failed to take into account the circumstances of non-compliance. Having been denied the opportunity to state his case, the probationer defiantly refused to comply with the order. He failed to attend several appointments and was subsequently breached in court for non-compliance.

More generally, the officers' responses reinforced the importance of an individualised approach rooted in the use of professional discretion, such as: 'I think if people realise that we are not sort of hard-line, straight down the middle they're much more willing to be compliant and engage with us' (PO7F). It follows then that the individualised response to non-compliance was seen by both practitioners and probationers as being less likely to undermine the perceived quality of treatment during enforcement and thus to trigger non-compliance. According to the officers, there are altruistic and pragmatic considerations underpinning the individualised response to non-compliance. Chief among these are the effort to preserve the good working relationships that they develop with their clients, and also the effort to facilitate compliance.

In the third stage of analysis, the emergent theoretical framework indicated that a key factor that is linked to compliance is the individualised response to non-compliance. Although the study originally intended to sample ten officers in Wales, additional officers in Wales and a further five practitioners based in Jersey were recruited into the study. The objective was to explore further the apparent relevance of the individualised approach. The study found that, similar to practices in the Welsh probation area, the officers based in Jersey tend to prioritise a client-centred individualised approach to securing compliance. The key difference is that in the Jersey Probation and Aftercare Service, the client-centred approach appears to be formally endorsed at policy level.

Policy and practice implications: developing an effective compliance strategy

The study highlights the range of practical, structural and relational factors that can affect compliance. These factors are inherently interactional and if not properly managed can affect the quality of interactions between both parties and impinge on compliance, albeit in qualitatively different ways.

Practical factors pertain to the lifestyle and other factors that can affect the probationers' ability to attend appointments. Bottoms' (2001) concept of habit/routine compliance is also relevant here given the finding that chaotic lifestyles may affect compliance. Although the disposition to habitually comply with the law may have been acquired or internalised during socialisation, where substance misuse fuels a chaotic lifestyle it becomes difficult for the probationer to attend routine appointments. The study found that some of the officers adopt several strategies designed to address the obstacles to compliance and encourage compliance in such cases. Examples include scheduling more flexible appointments and offering reminders. Additional obstacles to compliance tend to range from childcare costs to transportation costs. The specific area visited is located in a sparsely populated area that is located within a significant landmass. This topography occasionally poses severe transportation problems, which can in turn affect compliance. Perhaps this and other factors point to the need for a decentralised set of standards that is more attuned to the peculiarities of individual probation areas.

The officers strive to address the practical obstacles to compliance. Importantly, the officers do not discount the potential impact of these obstacles on the ability of the probationers to attend routine appointments. Incorporating a consideration of these factors in decision-making processes, particularly during enforcement decision-making, forms part of the altruistic effort to preserve relationships. Aligned to this is the pragmatic objective of ensuring that more probationers are able to successfully complete their orders.

Relational factors, such as the nature of the relationship between both parties, can also affect compliance. Reinforcing the findings of existing studies, the present study found that good working relationships that facilitate effective communication between both parties, and the collaborative discussion of problems was perceived to be an important aspect of supervision by most of the probationers (see also Rex 1999). Further, the study found that the opportunity to interact with the officer and discuss problems was a more significant motivating factor than the deterrent enforcement framework. From the probationers' accounts, it appeared that discussing problems in order to explore possible solutions tended to produce therapeutic benefits. The therapeutic benefits operated as an important incentive that could motivate instrumental compliance (Bottoms 2001).

Studies have long alluded to the importance of the opportunity to talk with supervising officers in order to discuss problems and possible solutions (Rex 1999). Nevertheless, the impact of the interactions between both parties, which is undoubtedly a crucial aspect of supervision, has been largely ignored (Burnett and McNeill 2005). Ward (2008: 395) points out that the narrow focus on one aspect of practice – the implementation of evidence-based intervention – has led to the marginalisation of 'other approaches more in tune with probation and social work values, despite research evidence of their efficacy'. The present study suggests that key social work principles of practice, including the concern to develop positive relationships during supervision, still apply in practice (see also Annison *et al.* 2008).

The officers also strive to manage the structural problems that may be posed by the potentially prescriptive enforcement standards in order to ensure a degree of compliance. To manage structural contradictions and secure compliance, the officers devise an individualised approach to responding to non-compliance. Again, this approach incorporates an interactional element, given that the approach is motivated in part by the effort to preserve relationships. Further, by taking into account the specific circumstances of each case during enforcement, the individualised approach can enhance the perceived quality of treatment and stimulate normative compliance, which is another form of compliance described by Bottoms (2001). On the other hand, a rigid application of rules can trigger non-compliance. Reinforcing

337

this, legitimacy theorists have conducted large-scale studies that demonstrate the links between the perceived quality of treatment received during interactions with legal authorities and compliance. The perception or belief that one has received unfair treatment may undermine the perceived legitimacy of authority and discourage compliance (see, for example, Tyler 2005; also Robinson and McNeill 2008, and this volume).

One may extend these arguments by examining some of the possible interactive effects of the mechanisms of compliance devised by Bottoms (2001). As Bottoms' theoretical framework, described above, suggests, instrumental mechanisms can encourage compliance through the use of incentives. The therapeutic benefit that may accrue from interactions with the officer was cited by many probationers as an important incentive that can motivate instrumental compliance. It is also quite plausible to contend that the positive relationships the officers strive to develop with the probationers and the accompanying therapeutic benefits can provide fertile ground for cultivating not only instrumental compliance but also normative compliance that is based on a sense of obligation to comply or an attachment to the officer. If one assumes that this is the case, it becomes clear that instrumental mechanisms operating through the use of incentives (for instance, therapeutic benefits) can provide the basis for normative compliance. This may be more probable where instrumental mechanisms are reinforced with the use of flexible enforcement practices that do not undermine the perceived quality of treatment received during enforcement. As noted above, the perception that one has received fair treatment has been identified as an antecedent of perceived legitimacy of authority and compliance.

In sum, normative compliance in its different forms (examples include compliance that is based on a sense of attachment to the officer and compliance that is based on perceived fair treatment and legitimacy) may be more achievable where there is a pre-existing positive relationship even if the relationship originally acted as an incentive and therefore, as an instrumental mechanism of compliance. The latter can eventually produce normative compliance. Alternatively, as Bottoms (2003: 2) observes, poor-quality treatment and undermined perceived legitimacy can indeed 'offset any gains in good behaviour arising from the operation of incentives'. Bottoms (2003: 2) also notes that 'less fairness and a significant legitimacy deficit' can produce non-compliance. The foregoing suggests that an understanding of the potential interactivity between the mechanisms of compliance can contribute to the effort to develop effective compliance strategies. Policy provisions that ignore the importance of mechanisms that can produce normative compliance such as flexible enforcement strategies, and focus instead on the use of instrumental mechanisms in the form of disincentives, may be less productive than strategies that recognise the potential interactivity between the different compliance mechanisms.

Conclusion

The findings of the study reported in this chapter indicate that there is a need to depolarise policy objectives and actual practice. This can be achieved if efforts are made to incorporate within the current policy governing supervision provisions that recognise the importance of maintaining good working relationships during supervision. Aligned to this is the need to grant greater autonomy to the front-line practitioners who interact with probationers and strive to manage the relational, practical and structural contradictions that can affect compliance. One acknowledges that expanding the scope of autonomous decision-making during enforcement can increase the risks of inconsistent and discriminatory practices. Nevertheless, the study suggests that an approach to enforcing compliance that takes into account the relevant circumstances of each case is more closely linked to compliance. By contrast, a rigid application of rules without the exercise of professional discretion can undermine normative compliance that is based on the perception that one has received fair treatment. This may neutralise the potential impact of incentives and produce non-compliance. As Bottoms (2003: 3) rightly observes, knowledge of the 'potentially counterproductive interactions' between the different mechanisms is necessary for developing effective compliance strategies. The present study suggests that instrumental mechanisms in the form of incentives may not produce compliance where the perception that one has received poor-quality treatment undermines the perceived legitimacy of authority and normative compliance.

Policy developments since the study was conducted indicate a shift away from the focus on quantifiable enforcement rates as measures of effective practice, towards a growing recognition of the importance of more qualitative targets that can reflect the processes through which officers secure compliance (HMIP *et al.* 2007; National Audit Office 2008). Further, the current National Standards, published after the study was conducted, acknowledge the need to develop compliance strategies and the need for individualised responses to non-compliance (NOMS 2007). For instance, the standards encourage officers to offer reminders in order to facilitate compliance. Practitioners are encouraged to take into account the circumstances of each case in responding to non-compliance. Several factors may have contributed to this apparent shift away from an avowedly enforcement-oriented approach to securing compliance. For instance, it is possible to contend that this shift may in part be motivated by pragmatic considerations, particularly the concern to reduce the high rates of breach that may have been the product of prescriptive National Standards (HMIP *et al.* 2007).

Certainly, it is clear from this study that deterrence is not an adequate explanatory framework for understanding compliance. Compliance is better understood by exploring the interactions between both parties. To secure compliance, the officers utilise their professional discretion in order to develop an individualised approach that is responsive to the practical, structural and situational factors that affect compliance. Two possible courses of action may be pursued to address the risks associated with the unofficial professional discretion that appears to underpin the individualised approach. One approach may be to curtail discretionary enforcement through rigid monitoring processes. However, studies suggest that this approach can in fact encourage covert practices (Vass 1984). Another possible approach may be to develop less prescriptive National Standards and more flexible compliance policies that are responsive to the range of factors that affect compliance. As mentioned above, recent policy developments indicate that a more flexible approach to encouraging compliance is being advocated. For example, unlike the standards that were operative at the time of the present study, the latest standards permit the greater use of professional discretion during enforcement, although the standards retain the deterrent approach of the previous standards.

Expanding the levels of discretion available to the officers could encourage disparate and possibly discriminatory practices. Nevertheless, the study reported here suggests that an individualised approach that is responsive to the needs of the probationers and involves the judicious use of professional discretion may ensure that more probationers are able to successfully complete their orders.

References

Annison, J., Eadie, T. and Knight, C. (2008) 'People first: probation officer perspectives on probation work', *Probation Journal*, 55 (3): 259–71.

Bottoms, A.E. (2001) 'Compliance and community penalties', in A. Bottoms, L. Gelsthorpe and S. Rex (eds) *Community Penalties: Change and Challenge*. Cullompton: Willan Publishing.

Bottoms, A.E. (2003) Presentation to Cabinet Office Strategic Thinkers Seminar on Future Options for the Correctional Services, 10 June 2003. Online at: www.cabinetoffice.gov.uk/media/cabinetoffice/strategy/assets/ bottomsnotes.pdf (accessed 15 February 2005).

Burnett, R. and McNeill, F. (2005) 'The place of the officer–offender relationship in assisting offenders to desist from crime', *Probation Journal*, 52 (3): 221–42.

Davies, M. (1969) *Probationers in their Social Environment: A Study of Male Probationers aged 17–20, together with an Analysis of those Reconvicted within Twelve Months*. London: HMSO.

Dawson, P., Walmsley, R. K. and Debidin, M. (2005) *A Process Evaluation of the Cognitive Skills Booster Programme Initial Roll-out in 14 Probation Areas and 12 Prisons*, Online Report 41/05. London: Home Office.

Dowden, C. and Andrews, D.A. (2004) 'The importance of staff practice in delivering effective correctional treatment: a meta-analytic review of core correctional practice', *International Journal of Offender Therapy and Comparative Criminology*, 48 (2): 203–14.

Ellis, C., Mortimer, E. and Hedderman, C. (1996) *Enforcing Community Sentences: Supervisors' Perspectives on Ensuring Compliance and Dealing with Breach*. London: Home Office.

Farrall, S. (2002) 'Long-term absence from probation: officers' and probationers' accounts', *Howard Journal of Criminal Justice*, 41 (3): 263–78.

Folkard, M.S. *et al.* (1974) *IMPACT: Intensive Matched Probation and After-Care Treatment. Vol. 1, The Design of the Probation Experiment and an Interim Evaluation*. London: HMSO.

Ford, P., Pritchard, C. and Cox, M. (1997) 'Consumer opinions of the probation service: advice, assistance, befriending and the reduction of crime', *Howard Journal of Criminal Justice*, 36 (1): 42–61.

Hearnden, I. and Millie, A. (2003) *Investigating Links between Probation Enforcement and Reconviction*, Online Report 41. London: Home Office.

Hedderman, C. (1999) *ACOP Enforcement Survey: Stage One*. London: ACOP.

Hirschi, T. (1969) *Causes of Delinquency*. Berkeley, CA: University of California Press.

HMIP (2003) *HMIP Annual Report 2002/2003*. London: HMIP.

HM Inspectorate of Probation, HM Inspectorate of Court Administration and HM Inspectorate of Constabulary (2007) *Thematic Inspection Report: A Summary of Findings on the Enforcement of Community Penalties from Three*

Joint Area Inspections. Online at: http://inspectorates.homeoffice.gov.uk/
hmiprobation/inspect_reports/thematic-inspections1.html/Enforcement_
of_Community_Pe1.pdf?view=Binary (accessed 23 June 09).

Home Office (2002) *National Standards for the Supervision of Offenders in the
Community 2000* (amended 2002). London: Home Office.

Hough, M. Clancy, A. McSweeney, T. and Turnbull, P.J. (2003) *The Impact
of Drug Treatment and Testing Orders on Offending: Two Year Reconviction
Results,* Findings 184. London: Home Office.

Lawson, C. (1978) *The Probation Officer as Prosecutor.* Cambridge: Institute of
Criminology, Cambridge University.

Mair, G. and May, C. (1997) *Offenders on Probation,* Home Office Research
Study 167. London: Home Office.

May, C. (1999) *Explaining Reconviction Following a Community Sentence: The
Role of Social Factors,* Home Office Research Study 192. London: Home
Office.

McIvor, G. (1992) *Sentenced to Serve: Operation and Impact of Community Service
by Offenders.* Aldershot: Avebury.

McIvor, G. (1996) *Working with Offenders.* London: Jessica Kingsley.

Ministry of Justice (2005) *Offender Management Caseload Statistics 2004, England
and Wales.* London: NOMS, Ministry of Justice.

Ministry of Justice (2007) *National Standards for the Management of Offenders:
Standards and Implementation Guidance.* London: Ministry of Justice.

Ministry of Justice (2008) *Offender Management Caseload Statistics 2007,*
Ministry of Justice Statistics Bulletin. London: Ministry of Justice.

National Audit Office (2008) *National Probation Service: The Supervision of
Community Orders in England and Wales: Report by the Comptroller and Audit
General,* HC 203. London: The Stationery Office.

NOMS (2005) *National Standards 2005.* London: National Probation
Office.

NOMS (2007) *National Standards for the Management of Offenders: Standards
and Implementation Guidance.* London: Ministry of Justice.

Pearson, G. (1975) 'Making Social Workers: Bad Promises and Good Omens',
in R. Bailey and M. Brake (eds) *Radical Social Work,* London: Arnold.

Radzinowicz, L. (ed.) (1958) *The Results of Probation: A Report of the Cambridge
Department of Criminal Science.* London: Macmillian.

Raynor, P. and Maguire, M. (2006) 'End-to-end or end in tears? Prospects
for the effectiveness of the national offender management model', in
M. Hough, R. Allen and U. Padel (eds) *Reshaping Probation and Prisons:
The New Offender Management Framework.* London: University of London
Centre for Crime and Justice Studies.

Rex, S. (1999) 'Desistance from offending: experiences of probation', *Howard
Journal,* 38 (4): 366–83.

Robinson, G. and McNeill, F. (2008) 'Exploring the dynamics of compliance
with community penalties', *Theoretical Criminology,* 12: 431.

Strauss, A.L. and Corbin, J.M. (1998) *Basics of Qualitative Research: Techniques
and Procedures for Developing Grounded Theory.* London: Sage.

Tyler, T.R. (1990) *Why People Obey the Law*. New Haven, CT: Yale University Press.

Tyler, T.R. (2005) *Why People Obey the Law*. Princeton, NJ: Princeton University Press.

Vass, A.A. (1984) *Sentenced to Labour: Close Encounters with a Prison Substitute*. St Ives, Cambs: Venus Academia.

Ward, D. (2008) 'What works in probation offender management: evidence for a new direction?', *British Journal of Social Work*, 38: 395–405.

Willis, A. (1981) *Social Welfare and Social Control: A Survey of Young Men on Probation*, Research Bulletin 11. London: Home Office Research Unit.

Worrall, A. and Hoy, C. (2005) *Punishment in the Community: Managing Offenders, Making Choices*, 2nd edn. Cullompton: Willan Publishing.

Chapter 17

Case management in corrections: evidence, issues and challenges[1]

Shelley Turner

Introduction

From its origins in social work, health and employment, case management has been extensively applied to the field of community corrections across Australia, but with virtually no evaluation of its appropriateness to this specific context. Touted as a 'panacea' for solving the complexities of human services delivery, case management has been implemented in correctional contexts as a method of linking treatment and criminal justice systems and providing a framework to support the delivery of rehabilitative interventions. However, while considerable progress has been made to identify 'what works' to reduce recidivism in individual rehabilitative interventions, insufficient attention has been paid to the role of case management. Critics argue that case management is poorly defined, a product of neo-liberal economic politics that promotes cost-efficiency above social care as the primary goal of human services. Moreover, the general ambiguity around the definition of case management has significant implications for the certainty and consistency with which relevant stakeholders can understand, implement, deliver, experience and evaluate case management approaches (Camilleri 2000; Gursansky *et al*. 2003).

This chapter briefly traces the rise of case management approaches in Australian human services and examines issues related generally to the definition, practice and evaluation of case management, before comparing these against the unique context of community corrections. Questions are posed about the application and efficacy of case management models derived from other disciplines to community corrections through a critical discussion of Australian and international research that links the 'what works' literature to case management in community corrections and examines the efficacy of various models. Particular attention is given to exploring the complexities of the role of the community corrections case manager, the continuing rise of inter-agency case management partnerships, and to examining client outcomes from case management approaches in community corrections. Through an examination and evaluation of the literature, it is argued that in the context of community corrections, case management ambiguity has particular and concerning implications for the 'case managed' and that community corrections contexts and populations are characterised by a range of specific issues and needs that should be taken into account when designing, implementing and evaluating case management approaches. Much greater research is required into the efficacy of case management approaches as a supporting framework for rehabilitative interventions in community corrections and to achieving client outcomes. As effective practice with involuntary clients depends to a large degree on effective worker–client relationships (McNeill 2003; Trotter 2006), it is vital to understand how a case management framework supports or hinders case managers and clients to achieve this. In other words, what is it like to be a case manager in community corrections and what is it like to be *case managed*?

Corrections in Australia

The term 'corrections', as used in this chapter, refers to all community and institutionally based services delivered by Australian corrections agencies, while 'community corrections', also known as 'probation and parole' refers specifically and exclusively to services provided by correctional agencies in the community to offenders, who are sentenced by the criminal courts to serve community-based orders, such as probation or community services orders, or who are conditionally released from prison on parole by a parole board. 'Juvenile corrections' and 'juvenile community corrections' refers to similar services and processes, but applies specifically to those provided to juvenile or young offenders. The term 'juvenile justice system' refers to the overarching children's criminal justice system, including legislation, police and courts. Clients of juvenile justice systems, also known as 'juvenile' or 'young' offenders, are children and adolescents as defined by their legal age of criminal culpability and 'adulthood' at the time of committing an offence. As used in this chapter, the terms 'community corrections' and 'corrections' also encompass 'juvenile community corrections' and 'juvenile corrections', unless otherwise made explicit.

The rise of case management

Since their introduction to Australia in the 1970s, notably in the fields of intellectual disability and vocational rehabilitation, case management approaches have been expanded to fields as diverse as aged care, immigration and corrections and have become well established in federal and state government policy and legislation (Gursansky *et al.* 2003; Ozane 1996). Case management approaches emerged and prospered from major developments and shifts in western social and political ideologies, most notably those associated with deinstitutionalisation, the rise of individualism, consumer choice and consumer rights movements, and neo-liberal economic rationalism, including the application of market strategies to areas of traditional government service, such as competitive tendering, decentralisation, privatisation and outsourcing (Austin and McClelland 2000; Gursansky *et al.* 2003; Kennedy *et al.* 2004; Moore 2004; Ozane 1996). Austin and McClelland suggest: 'Examining the evolution of case management is like holding a mirror up to public policy development in the human services over the last several decades' (2000: 4).

The 'buzzword' or 'mantra' of human services, case management has been promoted as a universal remedy for effectively addressing complexities in service delivery and meeting the varying needs and agendas of clients, service providers and funding bodies (Bonta *et al.* 2004; Camilleri 2000; Cudney 2002; Gursansky *et al.* 2003; Moore 2004; Netting 1992). For clients, or 'consumers', case management is purported to provide individualised assessment and treatment and to enhance the choice of service providers and service delivery structure. For service providers, case management professes to be a structured but flexible and efficient process that can increase staff accountability and effectiveness; it also appeals to funding bodies, keen to ensure efficient and effective use of resources to control costs and obtain outcomes. However, critics of case management question these assumptions, with particular concern for the ethical and social justice underpinnings of case management approaches, arguing that it promotes cost-efficiency over client outcomes (Moxley 2003; Netting 1992; Parker 1997). They raise questions about whose interests are best served by case management approaches and what the experiences and outcomes are for those who are 'case managed'.

Defining 'case management'

Case management approaches are presently so widely and commonly used across a range of human services in Australia and other English-speaking countries that some writers suggest the term 'case management' has virtually become 'a euphemism for human service delivery' (Kennedy *et al.* 2001: 29). As a result of such proliferation, case management is a familiar term to all present-day human service workers and one that is generally taken for granted as uniformly defined and collectively understood, which averts attention from the important need for closer examination and analysis of case management to develop good theory and practice (Gursansky *et al.* 2003). Even a cursory examination of the case management literature reveals clear variations in the definition, interpretation and application of case management (Camilleri 2000; Furlong 1996, 1997; Gursansky *et al.* 2003; Holt 2000a, 2000b; McNeill and Whyte 2007). Definitions of the term range from labelling it as a general approach or methodology for work practices, to case management being a profession or specialisation in its own right (Austin and McClelland 2000). There is also disparity and conflict between the concepts of case *management* and case *work*, as well as case *manager* and case *worker*, with the terms sometimes used interchangeably and their definition varying. Nonetheless, while a clear, singular definition of the term 'case management' is elusive, there are a number of features that are generally agreed, in varying degrees, to be common to case management. These include the role of the case manager in 'boundary spanning' or acting as a link between clients and services and providing 'seamless service delivery' through the processes of assessment, planning, coordination, monitoring, reviewing and evaluation (Greene and Vourlekis 1992; Gursansky *et al.* 2003; Moxley 1989; Partridge 2004).

Case management in community corrections

Case management, as it is generally implemented in Australian community corrections contexts, can be described as the overarching framework within which rehabilitative interventions are delivered, reflecting a distinction between the understanding of case work and case management (Day *et al.* 2003; Heseltine and McMahon 2006). For example, the authors of an Australian review of rehabilitation programmes and approaches to reduce juvenile recidivism found that: 'Casework often involves the application of some of the techniques understood to be effective in offender rehabilitation and case management provides the structure in which rehabilitation interventions are offered. Both can have an impact on the success or otherwise of the intervention' (Day *et al.* 2003: 1).

Effective rehabilitative programmes and services are generally agreed to be those that, in order to reduce recidivism, adhere to the 'what works' principles. They are thus characterised by structural and theoretical soundness, assessment of an adult or juvenile offender's risk of recidivism and 'criminogenic' needs, with corresponding levels of service or supervision, and appropriate 'responsivity' of services to individual differences in learning and change styles (Andrews and Bonta 2003; Andrews and Dowden 2006; Andrews *et al.* 1990; Burnett and Roberts 2004; Chui 2003; Latessa 2004; Latessa and Lowenkamp 2005, 2006a, 2006b; Lipsey 1995; Lowenkamp *et al.* 2006; McGuire 1995, 2000; McGuire *et al.* 2002; Ogloff 2002). Consistent with these principles, it follows that effective correctional case management should also incorporate an assessment of risk and needs in order to match supervision levels and define intervention goals, and should provide interventions and services that target criminogenic needs (Bonta *et al.* 2004; Heseltine and McMahon 2006). Moreover, Day *et al.* (2003: 1) argue that, 'a review of case management systems is … of critical importance in terms of integrating effective rehabilitation programs within the entire client management system'.

Evaluating case management outcomes

In broad support of positioning correctional interventions in a community context, there is evidence from the 'what works' literature to suggest that, provided they have been well designed and implemented, services delivered in community rather than custodial settings have better outcomes (Chui 2003; Heseltine and McMahon 2006; McGuire 2000). However, in relation to case management in community corrections, the apparent ambiguity surrounding the definition of case management and the implications this has for effective practice does not appear to bode well for the success of its design and implementation (Hicks 2006; McGuire 2000; Trotter 2006). Yet critical examination of the structures within which rehabilitative interventions take place, such as case management, has largely been neglected, so that compared to areas such as social work and mental health, in the field of community corrections there is a dearth of discussion and reliable outcome studies into the effectiveness of case management approaches (Bonta *et al.* 2004; Camilleri 2000; Heseltine and McMahon 2006; Holloway and Carson 2001; Moore 2004; Partridge 2004; Raynor 2003). Writing about the effectiveness of community correctional case management in reducing reoffending, Heseltine and McMahon (2006: 16) conclude: 'The efficacy of current case management models in community corrections has yet to be empirically explored'.

The inexact definition of case management appears also to be a significant problematic factor in a number of studies that have attempted to analyse and evaluate its various styles and applications and is a particular problem for comparative research (Camilleri 2000; Partridge 2004). For example, it is difficult to compare case management in hospitals or mental health services with case management as it is applied to a corrections or immigration context. This is because a range of terms are used to refer to and describe case management in these settings (such as 'care management' or 'offender management') and the intended purpose and outcomes of case management in these settings vary according to the organisational goals (Birgden and McLachlan 2002; Gursansky *et al.* 2003; McNeill and Whyte 2007). Moreover, as noted by Heseltine and McMahon (2006), in Australia, comparative studies *within* the field of community corrections are hampered by limited understanding of what is occurring in and between constituent jurisdictions, so that the complex challenge of defining case management approaches is mirrored by the equally complex challenge of defining a single, national approach to adult and juvenile community corrections. Nevertheless, there is consensus among researchers that case management is largely defined and shaped by the local and broader contexts in which it occurs; as such, in order to understand and evaluate case management outcomes in community corrections, it is essential to examine the context of community corrections itself (Austin and McClelland 2000; Gursansky *et al.* 2003; Healey 1999; Heseltine and McMahon 2006; Holt 2000a; Ife 1997).

Context of community corrections

There are a number of issues and characteristics inherent to community corrections agencies and populations that are relevant to consider in the design of case management models. First, the role of community corrections is multifaceted. The stated aims of Australian community correctional services, for example, are to ensure 'public safety' through crime prevention and reductions in recidivism, promote offender 'rehabilitation', 'compliance' and opportunities for 'reparation', and provide relevant authorities with 'assessment and advice' (AIC 2004). It is clear that most if not all of these aims are driven by community and wider government expectations of the intended outcomes of correctional services, rather than by client needs or expectations, and this in turn affects the way that case management is designed and implemented in a correctional context. Writing about case management outcomes, Moxley suggests that 'case management programs cannot readily dismiss using those outcomes that powerful external stakeholders value as measures of their performance and effectiveness' (2003: 4). Second, the role of a community corrections worker is equally multifaceted, involving identification of and addressing client criminogenic and other related needs in order to promote rehabilitation, while at the same time ensuring client compliance with court mandates and penalties that have been imposed as punishment for their offences. This is often more simplistically conceptualised as a 'dual role', divided between providing client 'care' and 'control' to simultaneously respond to client 'needs' and their 'deeds'. Heseltine and McMahon argue, 'It is imperative that any model of case management adopted is cognisant of the dual roles of the community corrections officer, as without this, any benefit (in terms of reductions in recidivism) may be lost' (2006: 17).

Third, there are a range of additional issues directly related to the statutory nature of corrections and the associated limitations placed on individual autonomy and available choices for correctional agencies, clients and workers. For example, there are clear difficulties for managers and workers in providing and maintaining consistent levels of service to an unpredictable flow of clients, largely controlled externally by the decisions of police and the judiciary (Moore 2004). To varying degrees, the type of interventions provided by workers and the time-frame within which they are delivered to corrections clients are also limited and defined by these external decision-makers (Moore 2004). However, perhaps the most obvious consideration is that all corrections clients are involuntary, and this in itself challenges the concept of enhanced consumer choice as a benefit of a case management approach with this client group. This is not to say that all involuntary clients are necessarily 'resistant' to intervention, but rather that it is important to acknowledge the coercive, or at least constraining, influence of the criminal justice system in offering clients the possibility of increased or reduced punitive sanctions, depending on their level of compliance with the conditions of a legal mandate (Chui 2006). Workers with involuntary clients, therefore, require particular approaches and skills to build positive worker–client relationships and enhance client motivation for constructive change (Miller and Rollnick 2002; Rooney 1992; Trotter 2006). Trotter (2006) identifies a number of key approaches as effective in producing improved outcomes for involuntary clients, including role clarification, clarification of intervention aims, reinforcing and modelling pro-social values, collaborative problem-solving (based on the client's definition of problems and goals) and an integrated approach that combines them all. In relation to case management, he specifically notes that workers should be 'clear about their particular role as case planner, case manager or problem solver. They should also help the client to understand the role of other workers in the helping process' (Trotter 2006: 73).

These issues are all also relevant to *juvenile* community corrections populations, but some additional factors related to this particular client group should be taken into account when considering effective case management approaches. An obvious but frequently neglected consideration is that clients of juvenile justice systems are children and adolescents and as such have different developmental needs from adults (Day *et al.* 2003, 2004). In society generally, children and adolescents have less in the way of social capital, citizenship rights, independence and individual autonomy than adults, and juvenile correctional clients have less again than either their regular peers or their adult counterparts in correctional systems (O'Connor 1995, 1997; White 1992). Juvenile justice clients are essentially among the most coerced, marginalised and disenfranchised people in our community (Chui 2006) and the concept of case management approaches delivering enhanced consumer choices to these 'case managed' young people appears far removed from the realities of their situations. Adhering to the 'what works' principle of responsivity, it follows that effective practice with juvenile correctional clients must entail the provision of appropriate service responses to the developmental needs of children and adolescents. As Day *et al.* (2004: 4) point out, 'Risk factors, criminogenic needs and responsivity issues are all likely to change over the course of adolescence.' An Australian Institute of Criminology (AIC) review of 'what works' for preventing and reducing offending in young people (aged 12 to 25 years) found that, as for adult offenders, more effective programmes for reducing juvenile recidivism had clear aims and objectives and targeted young people's individual needs and risk factors (Sallybanks 2002). Notably, the report concluded: 'One program does not necessarily "fit all" and a case management approach to dealing with young people may be more appropriate' (Sallybanks 2002: 8).

Community corrections, case management and 'what works'

Heseltine and McMahon declare that 'there is an urgent need to develop further case management practices in community corrections, which are underpinned by the "what works" literature in offender rehabilitation, and have an evaluative component' (2006: 14). In 2000, Holt published a review of research on the subject of case management models in the fields of social work and community health to help develop a clear case management model to aid the delivery of effective practice in probation services (Holt 2000a). He argued that agencies should make a clear distinction between the service coordination or administrative role of a case manager and their role as the 'human link' in the process of supervision (Holt 2000a; Partridge 2004). Informed by the 'what works' literature, Holt (2000a) suggests four key elements to comprise a clear case management model, designed to aid the delivery of effective practice in probation.

1 *Consistency* – a crucial facet to seamless service delivery and prerequisite to increasing client motivation and learning.

2 *Continuity* – of assessment and supervision across time and the entire spectrum of interventions, required to create the sense of a single holistic, supportive and steady relationship for the client.

3 *Consolidation* – of learning, necessary to assist the client to join up fragments of learning to form a whole by using reflective practice and supervision, as well as community integration where a client's strengths can be utilised and confirmed.

4 *Commitment* – required from the case manager to the case plan, the client and the process of supervision, in order to reduce recidivism and promote positive change.

Holt's conclusions were subsequently reviewed and confirmed by McNeill and Whyte (2007) in their examination of the role that case management approaches can play in the reduction of recidivism. However, given the broader context of the criminal justice system to a community corrections setting, McNeill and Whyte (2007) argue that the management of client *compliance* (with the legal order and/or associated case plan) should be included as a fifth feature on Holt's list. Client compliance with the conditions of a legal mandate and possibly those of a case plan may itself be a condition of an offender's probation or parole (Healey 1999). McNeill and Whyte contend that 'through the establishment of effective relationships, the case manager's role in supporting compliance is likely to be particularly crucial to the development of ... normative mechanisms' (2007: 133). 'Normative mechanisms', as defined by Bottoms (2001), are client beliefs, attachments and perceptions of legitimacy about who and what they are complying with, and in order to promote client compliance workers must understand and address these. This goes some way to addressing Heseltine and McMahon's (2006) concern that for any case management model to be effective in reducing reoffending it must be mindful of the dual role of a community corrections worker and also appears to reinforce Trotter's (2006) assertion that role clarification and ensuring client comprehension of the purpose of interventions is important to effective practice.

Case management models and outcomes

An exploratory study, commissioned in 2001 by the UK Home Office, examined and compared models of case management in probation services across England and Wales and identified three main 'models' of probation case management, described as 'generic', 'specialist' and 'hybrid' models (Partridge 2004).

1 *Generic* case management models emphasise the importance of the worker–client relationship over time (Partridge 2004). Case managers supervise caseloads made up of clients with diverse levels of risk and needs and take responsibility for carrying out all the processes, tasks and functions of case management (assessment, coordination, referral, case planning), including additional tasks such as report writing, programme-delivery and supervision; where required they also commission and coordinate client services that are beyond the case manager's capacity to deliver (Partridge 2004).

2 *Specialist* case management models involve the same processes, tasks and functions described for generic approaches, but with the distinction that the case manager is commissioning, rather than delivering services for clients. Case managers work with specific client caseloads (for example, all high risk of recidivism) and are regarded as specialists with skills and training, particular to a context or function (such as assessment or report writing) (Gursansky *et al.* 2003; Partridge 2004). Clients attend separate case management teams that concentrate on different functions (for example, supervision or programme-delivery) and attend a variety of partnership agencies according to their individual needs (such as living skills or substance misuse). As clients move between teams and as their risk/need level is reassessed and reclassified, the responsibility for case management shifts accordingly (Partridge 2004).

3 *Hybrid* case management models involve variations of combinations of components of generic and specialist approaches. They employ a team approach as a mechanism for improving continuity in relationships, the environment and service delivery, and thereby purport to combat some of the impacts on clients of staff shortages, turnover and absences while on leave (Partridge 2004).

The UK Home Office study concluded that while each of the generic, specialist and hybrid probation case management models demonstrated both strengths and weaknesses in terms of outcomes for staff and offenders, generic models provided an overall more coherent supervision experience for offenders (Partridge 2004). Generic models also had the advantage of allowing staff to work with a mixed caseload of clients and have continued contact with the same clients, which meant that consequently staff saw the impact of their work, which boosted their motivation (Partridge 2004). In comparison, while specialist models appeared to particularly benefit senior management by allowing them to closely coordinate service delivery and target resources at certain clients and at major supervision stages, offenders reported the least coherent supervision experience, owing to a large amount of task separation and client movement between different teams (Partridge 2004). Some clients found the split processes of these specialist models confusing and others struggled to engage with multiple service providers (Partridge 2004). These findings appear to support Robinson's assertion that 'offenders are not best served by a system ... in which staff are obliged to engage in a "pass-the-parcel" style of supervision' (Robinson 2005: 307), and correspond with criticisms identified by Trotter (2006) of case management approaches that focus on 'symptoms' rather than the 'person' through 'specialist' agencies and workers. Trotter suggests that 'given the generic nature of the key skills required for work with involuntary clients, outcomes might be improved by maximising continuity of service with individual workers rather than referral to specialised services' (2006: 41).

The rise of specialist case management and client outcomes

Despite these encouraging findings about generic case management models, community corrections services appear to be moving away from generalist towards specialist models. Writing about criminal justice social work in Scotland, McNeill and Whyte (2007: 132) maintain that 'the shift from generic practice (where the caseworker manages and delivers all aspects of the intervention) towards more specialist practice (where case management and programme delivery functions are typically split) has been one of the most significant changes in probation work in the last decade' (2007: 132).

Similarly, community corrections workers in Australia are increasingly expected to 'manage' clients (in particular to 'risk manage'), rather than to provide direct service (Alder 1998; Bechtel 2007; Heseltine and McMahon 2006; Hoge 2001; Trotter 2006). Trotter (2006) notes that the term 'case manager' rather than 'case worker' is currently often used to describe the role of workers with involuntary clients and this can have some bearing on how the work is actually performed, as case *workers* are more inclined to have a direct service or therapeutic role, while case *managers* tend to have a service coordination role. The shift away from generic practice can be linked to an apparent broader philosophical move throughout criminal justice and correctional systems across the UK, USA, Australia and other English-speaking countries, towards a more punitive and risk-based approach to managing offending and offenders, and where the goal of rehabilitation has merit primarily as a way of ensuring community safety and preventing recidivism (Chui and Nellis 2003; McNeill and Whyte 2007).

This appears typical of a 'recipient-centred' case management culture, described by Moxley as frequently 'coercive', where the larger society requires recipients to attain a set of 'prescribed normative outcomes', and where 'recipients' outcomes have much less importance than those that external entities prescribe' (Moxley 2003: 9). Such a culture appears to operate in contrast to the key case management principles identified by Gursansky *et al.* (2003), that case management should be individualised, client-driven and designed around client needs. Similarly, the UK Home Office study (Partridge 2004) recommended that in order to enhance offender engagement, which is important to reducing recidivism, case management approaches in community corrections should acknowledge clients' needs and experiences. However, reflecting a 'recipient-centred culture', the report also found that the development of case management models in community corrections agencies had been:

> ... largely driven by 'supply side' or organisational 'drivers' in terms of targets set centrally and the need to deliver effective practice within the parameters of offender compliance. Consequently, the needs of offenders and their response to different case management structures and processes were rarely taken into account when designing or implementing the models. (Partridge 2004: 46)

This finding supports criticisms made by a number of writers about the way in which case management approaches are applied to human services; they argue that more often than not, despite rhetoric to the contrary, case management approaches are 'agency-centred' rather than 'client-centred' (Austin and McClelland 2000; Furlong 1997). In addition, as noted in the UK Home Office report, this is counter to the 'what works' principle of responsivity, which requires programmes and services to actively respond to identified individual offender learning styles (Partridge 2004).

Inter-agency case management partnerships

In keeping with the shift away from generic practice, and possibly as an attempt to meet the challenge of offender diversion and community integration, many community corrections agencies are involved in contracted or informal 'partnerships' with external voluntary agencies to deliver relevant services (Moore 2003). Government agencies appear to be retaining the responsibility for case planning and management, while progressively handing the responsibility for direct service delivery or case work to community or voluntary organisations (Trotter 2006). Some writers argue that such arrangements are problematic, because community agencies are frequently insufficiently funded to deliver the required services (Cross 1997; Smith *et al.* 1993) and, as case management cannot single-handedly surmount significant shortages of community-based support services (Austin and McClelland 2000), the end result is that clients are more likely to be 'managed' than assisted (Trotter 2006). Moreover, the concept of 'partnership' is one that has a broad range of interpretations (Cross 1997) and when attached to the variety of interpretations of case management, the concept of case management partnerships is decidedly ambiguous. Nonetheless, partnership arrangements between community corrections and voluntary agencies, involving varying degrees of shared case management responsibilities, have in recent years burgeoned and continue to do so, despite inadequate consideration of crucial partnership details, such as the role of community corrections within these arrangements, how the partnerships are established and maintained, and whether or not they 'work' (Altschuler and Armstrong 2002; Camilleri 2000; Chui 2003; Cross 1997; Gibbs 1999; James and Bottomley 1994; Rumgay 2003; Smith *et al.* 1993). Camilleri comments: 'The issue of co-ordination appears to [be] taken-for-granted and not the subject of specific research [and] … this seems ironical given the promise of case management as providing for better co-ordination of services' (2000: 22).

Concerns have also been raised about the impact of a 'contracting culture' on the independence and diversity of voluntary agencies, as such a culture sets principal value on outcomes achieved through economic efficiency (Smith *et al.* 1993). For example, in accordance with Australia's National Competition Policy, many services and programmes traditionally provided by government agencies, including corrections agencies, are now offered up as competitive tenders to the private sector in the form of time-limited and prescribed service contracts (de Carvalho 1996; Parliament of Australia 2003). The cyclical, ongoing process of competitive tendering, the contractual limits on the time and nature of service delivery, and the associated potential staff employment insecurity, have significant implications for the consistency, continuity and commitment with which voluntary agencies can deliver services to correctional clients (Austin and McClelland 2000). This is clearly pertinent to the effective probation case management principles of consistency, continuity and commitment identified by Holt (2000a). In addition, as multiple agencies have to compete for limited government funds through competitive tendering, agencies appear less likely to share information and resources, which can result in fragmentation of the sector through a silo effect and undermine the essence of collaborative partnerships (Austin and McClelland 2000). A recent Australian study into outcome-based contracting in the employment sector found that the pressure and competition for funding resulted in 'creaming' practices, where agencies 'parked' or avoided more complex clients and targeted their resources at 'easy' clients, guaranteed to yield positive 'outcomes' (Hudson *et al.* 2010). Most importantly, the study noted that this disproportionally affected involuntary clients, seen as less likely to have the intrinsic motivation required to achieve the agency's contracted outcomes (Hudson *et al.* 2010).

A primary issue to be considered in partnerships between corrections agencies and non-statutory agencies is that of the compatibility of their aims, philosophy and approaches (Gibbs 1999; James and Bottomley 1994; Smith *et al.* 1993). For example, most non-government community agencies view their clients as 'voluntary', regardless of a client's status with other agencies. This is clearly potentially contradictory and confusing for correctional clients, who by virtue of a court order or mandated case plan are *required* to seek help. Many voluntary agencies do not consider compliance to be a reasonable or ethical objective for clients, nor are they responsible for protecting the public from offenders in the same way as correctional agencies, and therefore they may not operate according to related effective practice principles (Healey 1999; Heseltine and McMahon 2006; James and Bottomley 1994; Smith *et al.* 1993). Such conflicting views between corrections and voluntary agencies can be clearly detrimental to developing a clear and consistent approach with clients (Moxley 2003). Notably, a US Department of Justice report on case management in criminal justice jurisdictions found that most case management arrangements involved 'two case managers, or more likely, a team of case managers – for each client' (Healey 1999: 4) and that their success depended on effectively aligning philosophical perspectives and expectations before delivering interventions, and cooperation and clear communication between workers. It noted that failure to do this could significantly undermine programme performance and client progress (Healey 1999). The findings of this study point to an additional issue of increased stakeholder numbers that are naturally cultivated through partnerships, as case management approaches with large numbers of people have been widely criticised for creating difficulties in case planning, decision-making and the consistent application of effective practice techniques, particularly role clarification, pro-social modelling and problem-solving (Trotter 2006).

Perspectives of the 'case managed'

Kopelman *et al.* suggest that 'directly examin[ing] clients' perceptions of their experiences in a case management program ... can help guide designers and evaluators of case management services' (2006: 189). Through a series of client interviews, the UK Home Office study on case management in probation services identified that:

> ... most offenders did not understand the concept of case management or case managers ... They seemed unaware that they had a case manager who was overseeing and integrating their order. However, most were clear about the distinction between partnership agency staff and probation staff ... [and] most understood what they were trying to achieve during their order ... Offenders were unanimous ... about the importance of working with the same supervising Probation Officer, who they knew and trusted throughout their order. (Partridge 2004: 47)

These findings appear to confirm that case management in community corrections should assist clients to understand workers' roles and the purpose of interventions, but that it is perhaps is more important for workers than for clients to have an understanding of the concept of 'case management' and a 'case manager'. Above all, these findings reiterate and confirm the importance of case management in community corrections facilitating the development of a consistent, continuous and committed worker–client relationship.

An exploratory Australian study, conducted by the Independent Commission Against Corruption (ICAC) in approximately 1993–1994, when case management had only recently been introduced to the New South Wales (NSW) Department of Corrective Services (DCS), involved 77 structured interviews with a random sample of 37 correctional officers and 40 inmates to examine their perspectives on case management in NSW correctional centres (Coulter 1999). While this study focused solely on case management practice in a custodial, rather than community corrections context, the findings are germane in that they appear to support the conclusions reached by Holt (2000), McNeill and Whyte (2007) and Partridge (2004) about what constitutes effective case management in a correctional context. Moreover, this piece of research appears to be the only existing Australian study that directly examines the perspectives of correctional staff and clients on case management and is described as '... an important and rather groundbreaking piece of work, which provides some important insights into the conduct of case management in the New South Wales correctional setting' (Coulter 1999: 26).

The ICAC study concluded that overall, neither officers nor inmates thought that case management was working very well in their correctional centre at the time of the research and that 'case management' meant different things to officers than to inmates (Coulter 1999). Specifically, officers perceived case management to mean better administration and monitoring of inmates, while inmates viewed it a process for working through their difficulties with a specifically appointed officer, who was supportive and trustworthy (Coulter 1999). Notably, the ICAC study found that both inmates and officers emphasised the importance of a mutually positive relationship in order for case management to be effective and felt this was best supported by not changing case officers or case loads, to allow for the development of a consistent and continuous relationship. In particular, the provision of a dedicated officer for inmates to report to was nominated as the 'best thing' about case management by officers and inmates alike and both also recognised the importance of an officer being committed to and having a positive attitude towards both case management and offender rehabilitation for it to 'work' (Coulter 1999). These findings appear to support those of Partridge (2004) that generalist models of case management, which permit staff to have continued contact with clients, not only provide a more coherent supervision experience for offenders, but also function to boost staff motivation, as well as Holt's (2000) assertion that continuity and commitment are key requirement for an effective model of probation case management.

Besides the limited but valuable client insights contained in the UK Home Office and ICAC studies, there is a significant lack of available research and information directly derived from clients themselves about what it is like to be case managed in community corrections (Gibbs 1999; Walker-Buck and Alexander 2006). Notably, a large-scale study conducted between 1993 and 1996 in three English probation counties examined partnerships between the probation service and non-statutory organisations and found that 'the perspective of the user is marginalised, the assumption being that because a user is not part of the decision-making processes of partnership arrangements, their view is not significant enough to make a difference' (Gibbs 1999: 285). This could possibly relate to the 'recipient-centred' (Moxley 2003) case management culture of community corrections, where clients' outcomes are valued less than those predetermined by external entities, such as courts, the police and the public. However, with growing substantiation that client engagement and continuity of worker–client relationships play a vital role in generating desired correctional agency performance measures, and with evidence that 'consumer research' can offer valuable insights to identify strengths, weaknesses and improvement opportunities in service delivery systems, it is clear that regardless of whose outcomes are valued most, greater attention needs to be given to correctional clients' experiences of and outcomes from case management approaches (Kopelman *et al.* 2006; Partridge 2004).

Conclusion

Throughout this chapter, the ostensibly uncritical acceptance of case management approaches in juvenile and adult community corrections, as though they are a cure-all for offenders, has been challenged and it is clear that further research is required into their efficacy (Austin and McClelland 2000; Chui 2003; Day *et al.* 2003; Healey 1999; Heseltine and McMahon 2006; Hicks 2006; Holt 2000a; McNeill and Whyte 2007). While the past few decades have seen a steadily increasing focus in the literature regarding 'what works' to reduce recidivism and effectively rehabilitate offenders, this debate has largely neglected to critically examine the structures within which such rehabilitative interventions take place. From the literature examined in this chapter, it is evident that the issues specific and inherent to a community corrections context and population should be taken into account when designing, implementing and evaluating case management approaches. In addition, there is mounting support for the benefits of employing generic case management models to best support a rehabilitative approach with offenders, as these models assist to enhance the continuity, consistency and commitment of worker–client relationships, which in turn assists to enhance client compliance and reductions in recidivism. However, correctional administrators and agencies appear to currently favour specialist case management models, which provide them with cost and resource efficiencies, but can result in 'symptom-focused' case management or fragmented service delivery and disrupt the development of continuous, consistent and committed worker–client relationships.

It is clear that more research is required into the efficacy of particular case management models to develop a stronger evidence base from which to argue for appropriate models to be applied to correctional settings that support and facilitate rehabilitative interventions and are founded on the 'what works' principles. Given the significance of context to understanding and improving the effectiveness of case management, there is also an apparent need for such research to be localised and specific to particular community corrections contexts (Ogloff 2002). Moreover, the issue of ambiguity in case management also requires attention, as effective practice with involuntary clients entails that workers clarify roles and the purpose of interventions (Trotter 2006). It is vital, therefore, to ensure that expectations of case management approaches are clearly established for all correctional stakeholders, particularly in more complex arrangements such as case management partnerships. Furthermore, as correctional clients shoulder the ultimate responsibility for ensuring their compliance with these expectations, they have the most to lose from case management ambiguity. Thus, rather than continuing to focus solely on workers' and administrators' views on the usefulness of case management approaches, to truly develop good practice it is imperative that future research also directly examines and considers the views of the 'case managed'.

Note

1 The views expressed in this chapter are the author's own views and do not in any way reflect the policy or opinion of the NSW Youth Drug and Alcohol Court Program or NSW Juvenile Justice, Department of Human Services.

References

AIC (2004) *Standard Guidelines for Corrections in Australia – Revised 2004.* Canberra, ACT: Australian Institute of Crimonology.

Alder, C. (ed.) (1998) *Juvenile Crime and Juvenile Justice: Toward 2000 and Beyond*, Research and Public Policy Series 14. Griffith, ACT: Australian Institute of Criminology.

Altschuler, D.M. and Armstrong, T.L. (2002) 'Juvenile corrections and continuity of care in a community context – the evidence and promising directions', *Federal Probation*, 66 (2): 72–7.

Andrews, D.A. and Bonta, J. (2003) *The Psychology of Criminal Conduct*, 3rd edn. Cincinnati: Anderson Publishing.

Andrews, D.A. and Dowden, C. (2006) 'Risk principle of case classification in correctional treatment: a meta-analytic investigation', *International Journal of Comparative and Applied Criminal Justice*, 50 (1): 88–100.

Andrews, D.A., Zinger, I., Hoge, R.D., Bonta, J., Gendreau, P. and Cullen, F.T. (1990) 'Does correctional treatment work? A clinically relevant and psychologically informed meta-analysis', *Criminology*, 28 (3): 369–404.

Austin, C.D. and McClelland, R. (2000) 'Case management in contemporary human services', *Australian Journal of Case Management*, 2 (1): 4–8.

Bechtel, K. (2007) 'Assessing the risk of re-offending for juvenile offenders using the Youth Level of Service/Case Management Inventory (Report)', *Journal of Offender Rehabilitation*, 45 (3): 85.

Birgden, A. and McLachlan, C. (2002, revised 2004) *Reducing Re-offending Framework: Setting the Scene*, Paper No. 1. Melbourne: Department of Justice, Victoria.

Bonta, J., Rugge, T., Sedo, B. and Coles, R. (2004) *Case Management in Manitoba Probation*. Ottawa: Public Safety and Emergency Preparedness Canada.

Bottoms, A. (2001) 'Compliance and community penalties', in A. Bottoms, L. Gelsthorpe and S. Rex (eds) *Community Penalties: Changes and Challenges*. Cullompton: Willan Publishing.

Burnett, R. and Roberts, C. (eds) (2004) *What Works in Probation and Youth Justice: Developing Evidence-based Practice*. Cullompton: Willan Publishing.

Camilleri, P. (2000) 'Researching case management: making it a "fact"?', *Australian Journal of Case Management*, 2 (2): 18–23.

Chui, W.H. (2003) 'What works in reducing reoffending: Principles and programmes', in W.H. Chui and M. Nellis (eds) *Moving Probation Forward: Evidence, Arguments and Practice*. Harlow: Pearson Education.

Chui, W.H. (2006) 'Young offenders', in W.H. Chui and J. Wilson (eds) *Social Work and Human Services Best Practice*. Sydney: Federation Press.

Chui, W.H. and Nellis, M. (eds) (2003) *Moving Probation Forward: Evidence, Arguments and Practice*. Harlow: Pearson Education.

Coulter, J. (1999) *Case Management in New South Wales Correctional Centres*. Sydney, NSW: Independent Commission Against Corruption (ICAC).

Cross, B. (1997) 'Partnership in practice: the experience of two probation services', *Howard Journal of Criminal Justice*, 36 (1): 62–79.

Cudney, A.E. (2002) 'Case management: a serious solution for serious issues', *Journal of Healthcare Management*, 47 (3): 149–52.

Day, A., Howells, K. and Rickwood, D. (2003) *The Victorian Juvenile Justice Rehabilitation Review*. Melbourne: Department of Human Services.

Day, A., Howells, K. and Rickwood, D. (2004) 'Current trends in the rehabilitation of juvenile offenders', *Trends and Issues in Crime and Criminal Justice*, 284.

de Carvalho, D. (1996) *Competitive Care: Understanding the Implications of National Competition Policy and the COAG Agenda for the Community Services Sector*, Discussion Paper 11. Canberra: Australian Catholic Social Welfare Commission.

Furlong, M. (1996) 'The rise and rise of case management', *Arena Magazine*, December 95–January 96: 30–2.

363

Furlong, M. (1997) 'How much care and how much control? Looking critically at case management', *Australian Journal of Primary Health*, 3 (4): 72–89.

Gibbs, A (1999) 'The forgotten voice: probation service users and partnerships', *Howard Journal of Criminal Justice*, 38 (3): 283–99.

Greene, R.R. and Vourlekis, B.S. (eds) (1992) *Social Work Case Management*. Hawthorne, NY: Aldine de Gruyter.

Gursansky, D., Harvey, J. and Kennedy, R. (2003) *Case Management Policy Practice and Professional Business*. Crows Nest, NSW: Allen and Unwin.

Healey, K.M. (1999) *Case Management in the Criminal Justice System*. Washington, DC: National Institute of Justice.

Heseltine, K. and McMahon, E. (2006) 'Case management in community corrections: an effective tool in reducing recidivism?', *Australian Journal of Case Management*, 7 (2): 14–17.

Hicks, S. (2006) 'Case management – care, co-ordination, control or social work?', Monash University.

Hoge, R.P. (2001) 'A case management instrument for use in juvenile justice systems', *Juvenile and Family Court Journal*, 25: 25–32.

Holloway, F. and Carson, J. (2001) 'Review article case management: an update', *International Journal of Social Psychiatry*, 47 (3): 21–31.

Holt, P. (2000a) *Case Management: Context for Supervision, A Review of Research on Models of Case Management: Design Implications for Effective Practice*, Community and Criminal Justice Monograph 2. Leicester: De Montfort University.

Holt, P. (2000b) *Take-Up and Rollout: Contexts and Issues in the Implementation of Effective Practice in the Probation Service*, Community and Criminal Justice Monograph 1. Leicester: De Montfort University.

Hudson, M., Phillips, J., Ray, K., Vegeris, S. and Davidson, R. (2010) *The influence of outcome-based contracting on Provider-led Pathways to Work*, Research Report 638. Norwich: Policy Studies Institute for the Department for Work and Pensions.

Ife, J. (1997) *Rethinking Social Work*. Melbourne: Longman.

James, A.L. and Bottomley, A.K. (1994) 'Probation partnerships revisited', *Howard Journal of Criminal Justice*, 33 (2): 158–68.

Kennedy, R., Gursansky, D. and Harvey, J. (2004) 'Work-based training for case management: assisting agencies to make better decisions', *Australian Journal of Case Management*, 6 (1): 13–19.

Kennedy, R., Harvey, J. and Gursansky, D. (2001) 'The response by Australian universities to case management', *Australian Social Work*, 54 (4): 29–38.

Kopelman, T., Huber, D.L., Kopelman, R., Sarrazin, M.V. and Hall, J.A. (2006) 'Client satisfaction with rural substance abuse case management services', *Care Management Journals*, 7 (4).

Latessa, E.J. (2004) 'From theory to practice: what works in reducing recidivism?' *State of Crime and Justice in Ohio*. Ohio: Office of Criminal Justice Services.

Latessa, E.J. and Lowenkamp, C.T. (2005) 'What are criminogenic needs and why are they important?' *For the Record*, 4th Quarter: 15–16.

Latessa, E.J. and Lowenkamp, C.T. (2006a) 'The risk principle in action: what have we learned from 13,676 offenders and 97 correctional programs?', *Crime and Delinquency*, 51 (1): 1–17.

Latessa, E.J. and Lowenkamp, C.T. (2006b) 'What works in reducing recidivism', *University of St. Thomas Law Journal*, 3 (3): 521–35.

Lipsey, M.W. (1995) 'What do we learn from 400 research studies on the effectiveness of treatment with juvenile delinquents?', in J. McGuire (ed.) *What Works: Reducing Reoffending – Guidelines from Practice and Research.* Chichester: John Wiley.

Lowenkamp, C.T., Pealer, J., Smith, P. and Latessa, E.J. (2006) 'Adhering to the risk and need principles: does it matter for supervision-based programs?', *Federal Probation*, 70 (3).

McGuire, J. (ed.) (1995) *What Works: Reducing Reoffending Guidelines from Research and Practice.* Chichester: John Wiley.

McGuire, J. (2000) 'What works in reducing criminality', in *Reducing Criminality: Partnerships and Best Practice.* Perth.

McGuire, J., Kinderman, P. and Hughes, C. (2002) *Effective Practice in Offending Behaviour Programs: Literature Review.* London: Youth Justice Board for England and Wales.

McNeill, F. (2003) 'Desistance-focused probation practice', in W.H. Chui and M. Nellis (eds) *Moving Probation Forward: Evidence, Arguments and Practice.* Harlow: Pearson Education.

McNeill, F. and Whyte, B. (2007) *Reducing Re-offending Social Work and Community Justice in Scotland.* Cullompton: Willan Publishing.

Miller, W.R. and Rollnick, S. (2002) *Motivational Interviewing: Preparing People for Change*, 2nd edn. New York: Guildford Press.

Moore, E. (2003) 'Case management with juvenile offenders: a framework for statutory supervision', in *Juvenile Justice: From the Lessons of the Past to a Road Map for the Future.* Sydney: Citigate Sebel.

Moore, E. (2004) 'Designing case management systems in juvenile justice contexts', *Australian Journal of Case Management*, 6 (2): 3–9.

Moxley, D. (1989) *Practice of Case Management.* London: Sage.

Moxley, D. (2003) 'Outcomes and alternative cultures of case management', *Australian Journal of Case Management*, 5 (1): 3–11.

Netting, F.E. (1992) 'Case management: service or symptom?', *Social Work*, 37 (2): 160–5.

O'Connor, I. (1995) 'Rights and juvenile justice', in P.A. Swain (ed.), *In the Shadow of the Law: The Legal Context of Social Work Practice.* Sydney: Federation Press.

O'Connor, I. (1997) 'Models of juvenile justice', paper presented to Juvenile Crime and Juvenile Justice: Towards 2000 and Beyond Conference, Australian Mineral Foundation, Adelaide 27 June 1997. Online at: www.aic.gov.au/conferences/juvenile/oconnor.pdf.

Ogloff, J. (2002) 'Offender rehabilitation: from "nothing works" to what next?', *Australian Psychologist*, 37 (3): 245–52.

Ozane, E. (1996) 'Case management applications in Australia', *Journal of Case Management*, 5 (4): 153–7.

Parker, G. (1997) 'Case management: an evidence-based review fails to make its case', *Current Opinion in Psychiatry*, 10 (4): 261–3.

Parliament of Australia (2003) *Australia's National Competition Policy: Its Evolution and Operation*. Online at: www.aph.gov.au/library/intguide/econ/ncp_ebrief.htm (accessed 10 March 2010).

Partridge, S. (2004) *Examining Case Management Models for Community Sentences*. London: Home Office. Online at: www.homeoffice.gov.uk/rds/onlinepubs1.html (accessed 31 May 2007).

Raynor, P. (2003) 'Research in probation: from "nothing works" to "what works"', in W.H. Chui and M. Nellis (eds), *Moving Probation Forward: Evidence, Arguments and Practice*. Harlow: Pearson Education.

Robinson, G. (2005) 'What works in offender management?', *Howard Journal of Criminal Justice*, 44 (3): 307–18.

Rooney, R.H. (1992) *Strategies for Work With Involuntary Clients*. Columbia University Press.

Rumgay, J. (2003) 'Partnerships in the probation service', in W.H. Chui and M. Nellis (eds) *Moving Probation Forward: Evidence, Arguments and Practice*. Harlow: Pearson Education.

Sallybanks, J. (2002) *What Works in Reducing Young People's Involvement in Crime: AIC Report and Literature Review: Review of Current Literature on Youth Crime Prevention*. Canberra: Chief Minister's Department.

Smith, D., Paylor, I. and Mitchell, P. (1993) 'Partnerships between the independent sector and the probation service', *Howard Journal of Criminal Justice*, 32 (1): 25–39.

Trotter, C. (2006) *Working with Involuntary Clients: A Guide to Practice*, 2nd edn. London: Sage.

Walker-Buck, P. and Alexander, L.B. (2006) 'Neglected voices: consumers with serious mental illness speak about intensive case management', *Administration and Policy in Mental Health and Mental Health Services Research*, 33 (4): 470–81.

White, R. (1992) 'Young people, community space and social control', in L. Atkinson and S.-.A Gerull (eds) *National Conference on Juvenile Justice*, 22–24 September, Adelaide.

Chapter 18

The dynamics of compliance with offender supervision

Gwen Robinson and Fergus McNeill

Introduction

A key problem for those who wish to promote community-based penalties as credible alternatives to custody is that such penalties rely to a far greater extent than custodial establishments upon the cooperation or compliance of offenders to make them 'work' (though see Sparks *et al.* 1996). As Bottoms has observed, 'effectiveness and compliance are, in the field of community penalties, topics that are inextricably linked' (2001: 89). It is therefore remarkable that, despite a burgeoning literature on the effectiveness of community penalties – and a common finding of significant problems of attrition in respect of a variety of community-based penalties and specialist programmes (for example, Farrall 2002; Hough *et al.* 2003; Roberts 2004; Raynor 2004) – the topic of offenders' compliance with such penalties has attracted relatively little in the way of empirical or theoretical attention (though see Ugwudike, this volume).

In this chapter we aim to go some way towards remedying the theoretical lacuna in respect of offenders' compliance with community penalties. In doing so we seek to bring together criminological and socio-legal perspectives, drawing in particular on a key theoretical contribution from Tony Bottoms (2001), as well as some recent scholarship on tax regime compliance (Braithwaite 2003). The chapter comprises four main parts. In the first part of the chapter we consider the possible definitions and dimensions of compliance with community supervision and, drawing on Bottoms' (2001) key paper, propose a threefold conceptual framework for thinking about compliance in this context. Second, we review Bottoms' framework for explaining compliance with community penalties and supplement this with reference to recent socio-legal scholarship about private individuals' compliance with tax regimes. We then go on to propose a *dynamic* model of compliance, based on the integration of these two related analyses of compliance. Finally we consider some of the implications of our analysis for the policies and practices of individuals and agencies responsible for the supervision of community penalties.

Definitions and dimensions of compliance

In a key contribution to the scant literature on compliance with community penalties, Bottoms (2001) distinguishes two principal types of compliance. The first of these, 'short-term requirement compliance', refers to compliance with the specific legal requirements of the community penalty. Short-term legal compliance is illustrated by Bottoms with reference to an offender who 'completes [a community sentence] with no breach of the formal requirements of the order: for example, an offender given community service attends regularly at community service work sessions, and works hard and diligently during those sessions' (2001: 88). The second type of compliance Bottoms describes as 'longer-term legal compliance'. This, he explains, is a broader category, which refers to the 'more fundamental issue' of the offender's compliance with the criminal law (2001: 89). Longer-term compliance, then, implies desistance: that is, no further reoffending within a specified time frame.

This is a very useful starting point for thinking about dimensions of compliance with community penalties, and we agree with Bottoms that individuals and organisations supervising offenders subject to community penalties ought to be involved in trying to maximise both. However, in our view, short-term requirement compliance is rather more complex than Bottoms suggests. For one thing, it is worth noting that just what constitutes the 'specific legal requirements of the community penalty' is necessarily context-specific. For example, if we take a cross-jurisdictional comparison of 'probation' in England and Wales and Scotland, we find a key contrast in the treatment of reoffending, which constitutes non-compliance in Scotland but not, since the Criminal Justice Act 1991, in England and Wales.

A further and more important issue for us, however, is that it is possible to think about *degrees* or *dimensions* of short-term requirement compliance. Let us return to Bottoms' example of the offender subject to a community service order. It is clear from this example that to complete the order the offender must attend his work sessions and complete the work assigned. But is it necessary – in terms of short-term requirement compliance – that he 'works hard and diligently' at the assigned task? The offender Bottoms presents is arguably an ideal type: someone who is engaging with the task assigned as opposed to one who is simply 'going through the motions', or meeting the minimum requirements in order to avoid breach. However, we believe that it is possible for an offender to *technically* meet the requirements of an order without necessarily engaging seriously or meaningfully with it.

For this reason we propose a distinction between what we call *formal* and *substantive* compliance (see Figure 18.1). Formal compliance denotes behaviour that technically meets the minimum specified requirements of the order and is a necessary component of short-term requirement compliance. The most obvious example of formal compliance is attending appointments (or work placements) at designated times. Substantive compliance, on the other hand, implies the active engagement and cooperation of the offender with the requirements of his or her order. It is achieved when (for example) the offender subject to community service works hard and diligently; or when the offender on probation shows a genuine desire to tackle his or her problems. This distinction reflects Parker's (2002: 27) differentiation, in the context of corporate compliance systems, between 'legalistic/rule compliance' and 'goal-oriented/substantive' compliance[1].

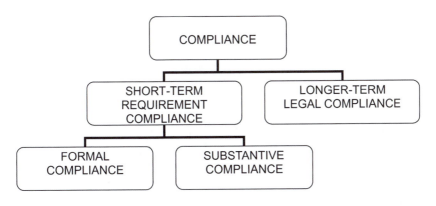

Figure 18.1 A typology of compliance.

A key distinction between formal and substantive dimensions of compliance is that they are sensitive to different methods of measurement. While the former is measurable in quantitative terms (such as proportion of appointments attended, number of work placements completed), the latter is more appropriately measured in qualitative terms, since it denotes the quality (as opposed to the quantity) of engagement. Importantly, it follows that formal compliance is straightforwardly *auditable*, while substantive compliance is not.

Explaining compliance with community penalties

Drawing on theories of social order, Bottoms (2001) presents an outline of what are, in his view, the principal mechanisms underlying compliant behaviour (see Figure 18.2). *Instrumental* or *prudential* compliance is easily understood as arising from rational calculations about the consequences (for the individual) of compliant or non-compliant behaviour. The offender who complies for instrumental/prudential reasons is the 'amoral calculator' described by Kagan and Scholz (1984). For offenders on community supervision, the principal instrumental mechanism at work is the threat of adverse consequences arising from the prosecution of breaches of supervision orders (as in the case of community penalties) or from recall to prison (as in the case of post-release supervision). However, Bottoms (2001) points out that positive incentives can also be deployed – most commonly in the promise of early discharge of supervision requirements as a result of sustained progress and good conduct.

A	**Instrumental/prudential compliance**
	(i) Incentives
	(ii) Disincentives
B	**Constraint-based compliance**
C	**Habitual/routinised compliance**
D	**Normative compliance**
	(i) Acceptance of/belief in norm
	(ii) Attachment leading to compliance
	(iii) Legitimacy

Figure 18.2 Bottoms' fourfold explanatory framework
Source: Adapted from Bottoms (2001: Figure 1).

Bottoms' second category, *constraint-based* compliance, has three sub-types. First, there are certain physical characteristics and limitations of the human body that impose 'natural' constraints on our conduct (for example, we can't burgle a house while asleep). However, offenders can also have additional physical restrictions placed upon them; most obviously when they are sent to prison but also, for example, when they are required to attend (or avoid) certain places at certain times or to abstain from certain behaviours (like drug use). Though these kinds of physical restrictions have not traditionally been a major feature of community penalties – or more accurately of the mechanisms through which such penalties have sought to change and control behaviour – the advent of new technologies such as electronic monitoring and drug testing has very significantly altered the vista of possibilities for community-based constraint (see Nellis, this volume).

The other two sub-types of constraint-based compliance arise as a result of restriction on an offender's access to a possible target of non-compliance (as reflected in the tactics and strategies of situational crime prevention) or as a result of what Bottoms calls 'structural constraint'. This arises where someone is 'cowed into submission by the coercion inherent in a power-based relationship' (2001: 93); here compliance is not properly conceived as being instrumental since no calculation of the consequences is involved.

The absence of rational calculation is also a feature of *habitual* or *routinised* compliance. However, Bottoms (2001) carefully distinguishes between these two mechanisms. *Routine* produces compliance through patterns of being and living that might once have arisen out of rational calculation or normative commitment but have long since become engrained into everyday life. Bottoms provides the example of sending children to school out of routine compliance with the relevant law. However, individuals also develop dispositions or 'habits of mind' that are related to 'settled inclinations to comply with certain laws' (2001: 94). Bottoms suggests that cognitive behavioural programmes that aim to produce altered ways of thinking are seeking to produce new dispositions (or habits) in offenders that, in turn, will be linked to altered behavioural routines. Significantly, he notes that the production of altered dispositions is likely to be central to the production of longer term compliance.

Finally, we turn to Bottoms' discussion of *normative* compliance. Here, Bottoms distinguishes between three sub-types. The first relates to conscious belief or acceptance of a set of norms that, called to mind and actively reflected upon, lead us to behave in a particular way.[2] This is the kind of moral commitment to which a probation officer seeks to appeal when she tries to persuade an offender that he ought not to offend because of the hurt that he will cause a victim. The second sub-type of normative compliance relates not to attachments to particular beliefs but to particular people; as, for example, where an offender decides to give up offending because of the recognition that it is hurting his partner or his children. As Bottoms (2001) notes, this is the type of motivation to comply that is referred to in accounts of desistance that stress the significance of 'social bonds' (Hirschi 1969). The third sub-type of normative compliance – legitimacy – draws explicitly on the theoretical work of British political theorist David Beetham (1991) as well as empirical work on procedural justice by American psychologist Tom Tyler (1990; see also Tyler and Huo 2002; Tyler 2003). For Bottoms, 'legitimacy' is, in common with the second sub-type of normative compliance, fundamentally 'relational', but it is distinct by virtue of its concern with the proper exercise of *formal authority*. Here the probation officer might exercise an influence over the offender's behaviour in and through the recognition that her authority is legitimate and moreover that its exercise is fair and reasonable. Of course, it is possible (indeed perhaps desirable) that these three sub-types might interact, so that a degree of attachment might form between offenders and their supervisors, further underwriting the legitimacy of any attempt to influence offenders' beliefs and thus persuading them to desist and to comply with the law (see Rex 1999; McNeill 2006).

Bottoms' notion of normative compliance is, we think, a particularly interesting one, and the attention paid to offenders' perceptions of the legitimacy of the institutions and individuals responsible for community supervision chimes with recent socio-legal research on the attitudes and behaviours of tax-payers. The ways in which perceptions of legitimacy impact on tax regime compliance is a central concern in a recent paper by Valerie Braithwaite (2003). Braithwaite notes that although authorities may have *legal* legitimacy, this does not guarantee them *psychological* legitimacy in the eyes of regulatees. As regulatees experience, review and evaluate the practices of those regulators to whom they are exposed they develop positions in relation to regulators, their authority and their legitimacy (cf. Tyler 1990). Braithwaite describes five 'motivational postures' (meaning interconnected sets of beliefs and attitudes that are consciously held and openly shared with others) that characterise the ways that tax-payers position themselves in relation to regulators. These divide essentially into postures of *deference* and postures of *defiance* (see Figure 18.3).

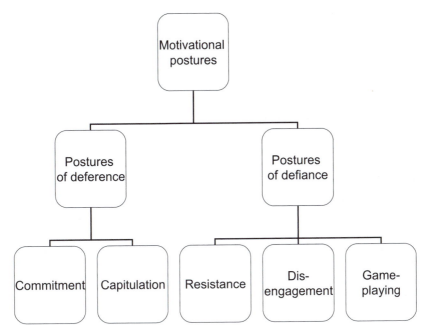

Figure 18.3 Motivational postures of tax-payers.
Source: Braithwaite (2003).

Postures of deference include *commitment* and *capitulation*. The difference between these two postures relates principally to the degree of willingness that rests behind acceptance of the regulator's authority and the decision to comply with its requests; capitulation implies a 'resigned' acceptance of the regulator's authority. In contrast, Braithwaite outlines three postures of defiance: *resistance*, *disengagement* and *game-playing*. Resistance reflects doubts about the regulator's intention to act cooperatively or benignly; this doubt drives vigilance of and resistance to the regulator in the enactment of its functions. Disengagement occurs where similar doubts about the regulator have produced more widespread disenchantment and with it a sense that there is no point in challenging regulatory authority. Finally, game-playing casts the law as 'something to be moulded to suit one's purposes rather than as something to be respected as defining the limits of acceptable activity' (Braithwaite 2003: 19).

Braithwaite (2003) goes on to explore, in an empirical study of tax compliance, the extent to which particular motivational postures are associated with particular forms of compliant and non-compliant behaviour. Unsurprisingly perhaps, the relationships between postures (attitudes) and compliance (behaviours) turn out to be complex; thus, for example, people may dislike and resist authority but still obey it. Braithwaite argues that regulators often make the mistake of expecting consistency between attitudes and behaviour; leading them to confuse non-compliant behaviour with postures of defiance and thus developing an oppositional stance towards defaulting regulatees. She argues that heavy-handed enforcement strategies run the risk of adversely affecting regulatees' attitudes and of turning those who are essentially reasonably well inclined towards the tax system (but have been non-compliant in some respect) into more active (or perhaps committed) resisters. She argues that the withdrawal of consent to the regulator's authority that is provoked by oppressive enforcement critically damages the legitimacy of that authority. This leads her to call for more *responsive regulation*, which works to bring more cooperative motivational postures to the fore (Ayres and Braithwaite 1992). Importantly, responsive regulation works principally through persuasion, but it always holds punishment in reserve for those who will not or cannot be persuaded.

A dynamic model of compliance

One of the insights of Braithwaite's work on 'motivational postures' is that regulatees' attitudes towards compliance – and in turn their 'compliance behaviour' – will not necessarily remain static over time. In particular, these attitudes and behaviours are likely to change or develop in the context of significant interactions between regulatee and regulator (cf. Tyler 1990; Tyler and Huo 2002). If this work is transferable to the community penalties context – and we hypothesise that it is – then it suggests that both the practices of individual probation officers/social workers and the enforcement policies of 'offender management' or 'correctional' agencies are likely to impact significantly on the 'motivational postures' of offenders, for better or worse. In a similar vein, Bottoms' explanatory framework helps us to understand why offenders' compliance behaviour may fluctuate over a period of supervision, thanks to shifts in or changing combinations of 'compliance mechanisms'.

In seeking to understand compliance more fully, then, it is necessary not merely to distinguish between formal, substantive and longer term compliance, but also to explore the likely mechanisms underpinning these levels or dimensions of compliance, as well as the sorts of processes and interactions likely to bring about significant movement between them. The dynamic model of compliance outlined in Figure 18.4 aims to capture the ways in which forms of compliance and their underlying mechanisms might develop in the course of a period of supervision.

Legitimacy deficits ⟵————————————————————⟶ *Legitimacy*

Dimensions of compliance

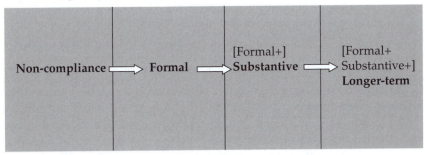

Non-compliance ⟹	Formal ⟹	[Formal+] Substantive ⟹	[Formal+ Substantive+] **Longer-term**

Related motivational postures

Resistance Disengagement Game-playing [Capitulation] [Commitment]	Capitulation [Commitment] [Resistance] [Disengagement] [Game-playing]	Commitment [Capitulation]	Commitment [Capitulation]

Related compliance mechanisms

N/A	Habitual Instrumental Constrained	Normative Habitual [Instrumental]	Normative Habitual [Instrumental]

Figure 18.4 A dynamic model of compliance with community supervision.

This model sets out the dimensions of compliance – formal, substantive and longer-term – we identified earlier, and, for completeness, adds non-compliance (see Figure 18.1). It further suggests that offenders may progress from one dimension of compliance to another, with the arrows indicating the desired progression. We do not, however, mean to imply that all offenders will commence supervision at the same point in relation to the development of compliance, nor that they will progress in a linear manner. Thus, for example, we accept that some offenders might begin an order already committed to longer-term compliance (desistance), while others might begin determined to give it their best shot (substantive compliance) but uncertain about their longer-term prospects. However, to the extent that supervision is primarily concerned with reducing reoffending, where (as perhaps in many cases) an offender begins an order concerned only at best to comply formally, then the task for their supervisor is presumably not just to establish formal compliance but to move beyond it into substantive and (then) longer-term compliance. This task – of moving an offender from merely formal to more substantive compliance with the order – will of course be more challenging where, from the offender's point of view, the order lacks legitimacy. There are many circumstances where such legitimacy deficits might need to be addressed: for example, where orders are imposed irrespective of consent; where the offender regards the community penalty as unduly harsh; where they feel that they have been somehow mistreated or misrepresented at the pre-sentence or sentencing stages of the criminal process; or where they have previous adverse experience of the allocated supervisor or of the agency.

With such initial difficulties in mind, and drawing on Braithwaite's (2003) analysis of motivational postures and Bottoms' (2001) analysis of compliance mechanisms, it seems to us that the hypothesised progression towards longer-term compliance is likely to require and reflect a different mix of postures and mechanisms at different points in the process. Thus, while an offender might initially comply formally for instrumental reasons (perhaps because of the threat of breach or recall), or because of perceived constraints linked to electronic monitoring, or (perhaps) out of an unthinking habit of deference to legal authority, these kinds of mechanisms alone or in concert are unlikely to be able to yield substantive compliance with the spirit of the order, let alone the kinds of changes required to generate longer-term compliance with the law. This is partly because such mechanisms are likely to reflect, at best, capitulation to the authority of the order and of the supervisor. Indeed, instrumental and constraint-based mechanisms might, in some contexts (as reflected in square brackets in Figure 18.4) reflect or signal postures of defiance, such that offenders are more preoccupied with being *seen* to be formally compliant – or 'ticking off a set of boxes' (Parker 2002: 27) – than with complying substantively. Braithwaite's (2003) analysis also suggests the counter-intuitive possibility that non-compliant offenders might, nonetheless, possess underlying postures of deference (capitulation or commitment), but lack the means to actually *behave* compliantly.

If Braithwaite's (2003) analysis can be read across into the context of community supervision, then we might expect that enabling offenders to move beyond postures of defiance seems likely to require a much clearer focus on the deployment or activation of normative mechanisms in order to generate commitment to comply. As we have argued above, following Bottoms (2001), deploying or activating normative mechanisms is likely to require development of offenders' beliefs and attitudes, the generation of positive attachments (or social ties), or an increase in the perceived legitimacy of the regulatory authority (institution and/or individual supervising officer) in the eyes of the offender. Indeed, it might be argued that in order to try to develop offenders' normative beliefs or to support the development of their attachments, a supervisor would *first* need to establish (to use Valerie Braithwaite's term) 'psychological legitimacy'; that is, the moral right to influence another human subject with their consent (cf. Beetham 1991). As Bottoms (2001) suggests, to the extent that supervisors and the agencies within which they operate are concerned with longer-term compliance (or desistance from crime), their best hope arguably rests in encouraging compliance mechanisms that allow for the internalisation of controls implied in commitment (*via* beliefs, attachments and eventually the development of new habits and routines) rather than the imposition of constraints or appeals to threats or rewards. The problem and the costs of constraint-based and instrumental approaches to compliance relate, of course, to their externality; someone or something else needs to keep on constraining, threatening or rewarding. By contrast, the efficiency and effectiveness of internalised controls rests in their (eventual) self-perpetuation (see also Tyler 2006).

Discussion

One of the key points which our analysis brings to the fore is that of the elasticity of the notion of compliance. Compliance – certainly in the context of community penalties – is not easy to define or pin down in any objective sense: rather, it is negotiated or constructed in the context of the specific legal and policy frameworks created in particular jurisdictions. Compliance, in other words, is a dependent variable, and the same can, of course, be said for non-compliance.

Policy-makers, therefore, face decisions about how best to frame or define compliance, and about the relative weight to be accorded to the three dimensions of compliance we have identified: formal, substantive and longer-term. While most would probably agree with Bottoms (2001) that those responsible for managing community penalties ought to be concerned with promoting all of these, it is not entirely surprising that it is the formal dimension of short-term compliance in particular that tends to receive the lion's share of policy attention. This is certainly the case in England and Wales, where the legal requirements of community penalties are set out in legislation and guidance issued by the Ministry of Justice in the form of National Standards (currently Ministry of Justice 2007). While these standards specify the required frequency of contact between offender and supervisor, they are silent on the desired length or quality of that contact.

To an extent, this emphasis on formal compliance makes sense in the community penalties context. For example, it is important that offenders understand what is expected of them, and clear guidelines in respect of frequency of contact are relatively easy to communicate. Second, it is theoretically plausible to suggest that a lack of formal compliance may well be a good indicator of a lack of substantive compliance in at least some cases. Third, where community sentences constitute a form of punishment, they are intended to involve a deprivation of liberty, which is not being realised if the offender fails to keep in touch with his supervising officer as instructed. Finally, as we have already noted, formal compliance is, unlike substantive compliance, amenable to measurement and audit. This becomes important in the context of breaching an offender for non-compliant behaviour: a breach must be proven in court and it is a more straightforward matter to evidence a failure to attend an appointment than a lack of cooperation or engagement on the part of the offender.

However, our 'dynamic' model (see Figure 18.4) indicates that there are problems with policies that privilege formal compliance. First, as Braithwaite's research has shown, formal compliance can mask postures of defiance and, in probation and social work settings, it cannot be read as an indication of low risk. Second, policies that privilege formal compliance create particular problems for the offender who is genuinely motivated to engage with his or her order (the substantive complier) but struggles to keep appointments. Third, such policies can reinforce an image of community supervision as a superficial exercise which principally involves 'turning up' and 'signing in', rather than a meaningful piece of work undertaken in the context of a relationship between offender and supervising officer. This is a dangerous image to convey to offenders, at least some of whom (most notably the 'game-players') will be looking for easy ways to subvert the system and complete their order with the minimum effort and engagement. It is also a dangerous message to convey to those whose motivational posture reflects 'commitment' and who have achieved, or are on their way to achieving, substantive compliance (Kemshall *et al.* 2001; Farrall 2002). Such a message potentially serves to undermine the legitimacy of the supervisory exercise, undo those 'normative' compliance mechanisms that may well be at work, and push the offender toward a less well-disposed motivational posture.

There are also, we think, problems associated with enforcement policies that are overly focused on the formal dimension of compliance and leave little room for practitioners to exercise discretion. On the one hand, clear and consistently applied enforcement policies play an important role in maintaining the legitimacy of community penalties, particularly in the eyes of 'external stakeholders' like sentencers and politicians. However, they arguably place too much emphasis on a model of offenders as 'amoral calculators' (Kagan and Scholz 1984) who act for purely instrumental/prudential reasons. It has been argued that offenders are relatively immune to the deterrent effects of punishment, which is often why they are subject to community penalties in the first place (for example, Hedderman and Hough 2004; Hearnden and Millie 2004) and this seems to have been borne out in England and Wales, where an increasingly 'tough' approach towards enforcement has not had the desired effect of driving up rates of compliance (see Home Office 2005).

We would extend the critique of excessively strict enforcement policies with reference to the wider research literature on regulatory enforcement, which we referred to earlier in the context of our discussion of Valerie Braithwaite's work. This body of research has shown that sanctions that are perceived to be unfair or unreasonable can lead to active resistance towards authority and can reduce the likelihood of future compliance (see Ayres and Braithwaite 1992; Kagan and Scholz 1984; Sherman 1993; Sherman *et al.* 2003; Murphy 2005). In other words, when initial or primary non-compliant behaviour is met with a response that is perceived as unjust, secondary non-compliance may follow. In the context of our model, an inflexible response to formal non-compliance has the potential to jeopardise future substantive compliance. This finding has led to the proposal that if regulators are interested in securing compliance, they should aim to protect their reputation as a legitimate authority (Murphy 2005; cf. Tyler 1990).

Policy-makers in the field of community penalties might therefore learn from scholars in a range of regulatory contexts who have argued that enforcement strategies can be more successful at securing future compliance when they are appropriately 'accommodative' or 'responsive' (see Kagan 1984; Ayres and Braithwaite 1992). While contemporary enforcement policies (certainly in England and Wales) tend towards what the socio-legal literature characterises as a 'sanctioning' or 'deterrence' model which is backward-looking and oriented towards censure and deterring future non-compliance (Hawkins 1984; Reiss 1984), the core motivations of the 'accommodative' or 'responsive' model 'are not to punish an evil, but to repair the harm done and to secure future compliance' (Murphy 2005: 565). For example, in his discussion of regulatory inspectorates and police, Kagan argues for a 'flexible enforcement style – demanding penalties and strict compliance when violations present serious risks, dealing more leniently with less serious violations' (1984: 55). While research conducted in England and Wales has revealed *some* examples of 'responsive regulation' (for example Ellis *et al.* 1996; Hearnden and Millie 2004) in respect of 'ordinary' community penalties,[3] it is perhaps surprising that, in a field otherwise dominated by concern with 'risk thinking' and risk-based calculations (Kemshall 1998; Robinson 2002), enforcement policies have tended towards a 'zero-tolerance' model that leaves little room for the exercise of discretion. We would argue that such discretion could be put to good use in assessing the particular motivational posture underpinning 'non-compliant' behaviour, and weighing up the potential costs and benefits of taking enforcement action against the individual offender on a case-by-case basis.

Notes

1 In this context, Parker argues, substantive compliance denotes a company's engagement with its legal, social, environmental and ethical responsibilities (e.g. creating a more healthy environment, a safer or more equitable workplace), while rule compliance implies 'simplistic obedience to rules' (2002: 27).

2 There is a link here to habitual or routine compliance, where the belief or set of beliefs is implicated in the establishment of dispositions and patterns of behaviour that are no longer the result of active or conscious reflection.

3 It should be noted that the Scottish Drug Court model, as implemented in Glasgow and Fife, does appear to have engaged with ideas associated with 'responsive regulation' (McIvor *et al.* 2006).

References

Ayres, I. and Braithwaite, J. (1992) *Responsive Regulation: Transcending the Deregulation Debate*. Oxford: Oxford University Press.

Beetham, D. (1991) *The Legitimation of Power*. London: Macmillan.

Bottoms, A. (2001) 'Compliance with community penalties', in A. Bottoms, L. Gelsthorpe and Rex, S. (eds) *Community Penalties: Change and Challenges*. Cullompton: Willan Publishing.

Braithwaite, V. (2003) 'Dancing with tax authorities: motivational postures and non-compliant actions', in Braithwaite, V. (ed.) *Taxing Democracy: Understanding Tax Avoidance and Evasion*. Aldershot: Ashgate.

Ellis, T., Hedderman, C. and Mortimer, E. (1996) *Enforcing Community Sentences: Supervisors' Perspectives on Ensuring Compliance and Dealing With Breach*, Home Office Research Study 158. London: Home Office.

Farrall, S. (2002) 'Long-term absences from probation: officers' and probationers' accounts', *Howard Journal*, 41 (3): 263–78.

Hawkins, K. (1984) *Environment and Enforcement*. Oxford: Oxford University Press.

Hearnden, I. and Millie, A. (2004) 'Does tougher enforcement lead to lower reconviction?', *Probation Journal*, 51 (1): 48–58.

Hedderman, C. and Hough, M. (2004) 'Getting tough or being effective: what matters?', in Mair, G. (ed.) *What Matters in Probation*. Cullompton: Willan Publishing.

Hirschi, T. (1969) *Causes of Delinquency*. Berkeley, CA: University of California Press.

Home Office (2005) *Offender Management Caseload Statistics 2004*, Home Office Statistical Bulletin 17/05. London: Home Office.

Hough, M. Clancy, A., McSweeney, T. and Turnbull, P.J. (2003) *The Impact of Drug Treatment and Testing Orders on Offending: Two-year Reconviction Results*, Home Office Research Findings 184. London: Home Office.

Kagan, R.A. (1984) 'On regulatory Inspectorates and Police', in K. Hawkins and J.M. Thomas (eds) *Enforcing Regulation*. Boston: Kluwer-Nijhoff Publishing.

Kagan, R.A. and Scholz, J.T. (1984) 'The "criminology of the corporation" and regulatory enforcement strategies', in K. Hawkins and J.M. Thomas (eds) *Enforcing Regulation*. Boston: Kluwer-Nijhoff Publishing.

Kemshall, H. (1998) *Risk in Probation Practice*. Aldershot: Ashgate.

Kemshall, H., Holt, P., Boswell, G. and Bailey, R. (2001) *The Implementation of Effective Practice in the Northwest Region*. Leicester: De Montfort University.

McIvor, G., Barnsdale, L., Eley, S., Malloch, M., Yates, R. and Brown, A. (2006) *The Operation and Effectiveness of the Scottish Drug Court Pilots*. Edinburgh: Scottish Executive.

McNeill, F. (2006) 'A desistance paradigm for offender management', *Criminology and Criminal Justice*, 6 (1): 39–62.

Ministry of Justice (2007) *National Standards for the Management of Offenders*. London: Ministry of Justice.

Murphy, K. (2005) 'Regulating more effectively: the relationship between procedural justice, legitimacy, and tax non-compliance', *Journal of Law and Society*, 32 (4): 562–89.

Parker, C. (2002) *The Open Corporation*. Cambridge: Cambridge University Press.

Raynor, P. (2004) 'Rehabilitative and reintegrative approaches', in A. Bottoms, S. Rex and G. Robinson (eds) *Alternatives to Prison: Options for an Insecure Society*. Cullompton: Willan Publishing.

Reiss, A.J. (1984) 'Selecting strategies of social control over organisational life', in K. Hawkins and J.M. Thomas (eds) *Enforcing Regulation*. Boston: Kluwer-Nijhoff Publishing.

Rex, S. (1999) 'Desistance from offending: experiences of probation', *Howard Journal*, 38 (4): 366–83.

Roberts, C. (2004) 'Offending behaviour programmes: emerging evidence and implications for practice', in R. Burnett and C. Roberts (eds) *What Works in Probation and Youth Justice*. Cullompton: Willan Publishing.

Robinson, G. (2002) 'Exploring risk management in the probation service: contemporary developments in England and Wales', *Punishment and Society*, 4 (1): 5–25.

Sherman, L.W. (1993) 'Defiance, deterrence and irrelevance: a theory of the criminal sanction', *Journal of Research in Crime and Delinquency*, 30 (4): 445–73.

Sherman, L.W., Strang, H. and Woods, D.J. (2003) 'Captains of restorative justice: experience, legitimacy and recidivism by type of offence', in E. Weitkamp and H. Kerner (eds) *Restorative Justice in Context: International Practice and Directions*. Cullompton: Willan Publishing.

Sparks, R.A., Bottoms, A. and Hay, W. (1996) *Prisons and the Problem of Order*. Oxford: Clarendon Press.

Tyler, T.R. (1990) *Why People Obey the Law.* Princeton: Princeton University Press.

Tyler, T.R. (2003) 'Procedural justice, legitimacy and the effective rule of law', *Crime and Justice*, 30: 283–357.

Tyler, T.R. (2006) 'Restorative justice and procedural justice: dealing with rule breaking', *Journal of Social Issues*, 62 (2): 307–26.

Tyler, T.R. and Huo, Y.J. (2002) *Trust in the Law: Encouraging Public Cooperation with the Police and Courts.* New York: Russell Sage.

Chapter 19

Exploring community service, understanding compliance

Trish McCulloch

Introduction

Introduced in Scotland as pilot projects in 1977 (1973 in England and Wales), Community Service (CS) has since come to occupy a central place in the evolving landscape of community penalties across many jurisdictions. For example, in Scotland in 2007/08, the number of convictions resulting in a CS order was just over 5,600 (approximately one-third of all community sentences). Further, the offence categories with the highest proportion of convictions resulting in a CS order were serious assault, attempted murder, handling an offensive weapon, fraud and fire-raising (Scottish Government 2009: para 8.8). Such statistics attest to the credibility of CS within the Scottish justice system, while also highlighting the considerable demands made of it.

Perhaps in part because of its quickly established and well-reputed position within the often contentious matrix of community penalties, attention to the broader processes, outcomes and potential of CS has, until recently, gone largely unexplored. In recent years this pattern has shifted slightly, triggered in part by the emergence of a small number of studies that suggest that CS may have something to contribute to the project of penality beyond punishment and deterrence. In particular, research has highlighted the reintegrative and rehabilitative potential of CS, resulting in renewed and overdue attention to its legitimate purpose, process and outcomes.

This chapter seeks to contribute to emerging exploratory research in the area of CS, giving particular attention to the dynamics of compliance within it. Amid the many lessons to emerge from recent research, policy and practice attention to the question of 'what works?' in reducing reoffending, the concept of compliance has emerged as critical. In consequence, there now exist a small number of studies that attend to the dynamics of compliance within this context and, more significantly, to the question of *how* workers can aid and influence compliant behaviour (Bottoms 2001; Robinson and McNeill 2008, and this volume).

In this chapter I begin by providing a brief review of the research evidence relating to compliance within community penalties – giving particular attention to research in the area of CS. I will then report on the findings from a small-scale Scottish study which, in exploring worker and offender perspectives on compliance, presents some interesting insights into the dynamics of compliance within CS. Recognising the small scale of the study, and its location within a Scottish context, it is left to the reader to speculate as to the generalisability of the findings discussed. Certainly, the discussion that follows attests to the need for larger-scale and more systematic research in this area. However, it is my impression that the issues raised connect with broader penal trends, questions and issues arising in other jurisdictions – both in relation to the development of CS generally and offender compliance specifically.

Compliance

The concept of compliance exists as both a central and relatively unexplored component of research and critical debate relating to CS. On the one hand, compliance – in the form of successful completion of CS hours – has long been recognised as one of the principal indicators of CS success. Indeed, in early evaluations of the CS pilot projects, the viability of CS was premised largely on the basis that 'orders [were] being made and completed' (Pease *et al.* 1975: 70; see also Duguid 1982). Almost three decades on, and in the context of an expanded vision for CS, compliance and completion of CS continues to be identified as a primary measure of success and effectiveness. As Rex *et al.* discuss in outlining the first output measure for the Community Punishment Pathfinder projects, 'this is a critical measure for community service, not only because of the confidence of the judiciary in such a sentence, but also because for offenders the ability to complete a court-ordered penalty successfully may be significant in influencing other future compliance behaviour, not least re-offending and reconvictions' (2003: 45).

On the other hand, even amid growing awareness of the significance of compliance within community penalties generally (Bottoms 2001; Robinson and McNeill 2008, and this volume) and CS specifically (McIvor 2002; Rex and Gelsthorpe 2002), as yet there exists no published research evidence that attends directly or systematically to the concept of compliance within CS. In light of this fact, this section begins by seeking to (re-)examine the dynamics of compliance as currently understood in relation to community penalties, drawing primarily on Bottoms' (2001) work in this area. Attention is then given to recent CS research, which provides some insight into the compliance dynamic within this area of community penalties.

Understanding compliance

As already noted, the concept of compliance is more than familiar to those involved in the delivery or development of CS. Definitions, however, are notably varied. Typically, compliance has been used to refer to an offender's compliance with the formal requirements of the order, and might, for example, be used to refer to an offender's attendance, performance and/or successful completion of his or her requisite hours. More recently, as Rex *et al.*'s comment highlights, notions of compliance within CS have developed to also encompass *future* compliant behaviour, that is, law-abiding, non-offending or reduced offending behaviour. Despite this elasticity of meaning, compliance is rarely defined within CS policy or practice directives, or in related research discussion.

In the context of this definitional vacuum, Bottoms' (2001) work on compliance within community penalties provides a very helpful introduction to this issue. In deconstructing the notion of compliance, Bottoms exposes the complex and multidimensional nature of compliance within community penalties, while also providing an accessible framework for understanding it. Bottoms begins by distinguishing between two forms of compliance – that of 'short-term requirement compliance' and 'longer-term legal compliance'. The former relates to compliance with the specific legal requirements of a community penalty – the successful completion of a court order. The second relates to an offender's compliance with the criminal law – future law-abiding behaviour or 'non-offending' within a specified time period. Robinson and McNeill (2008, and this volume) build on this definition and propose a further distinction within short-term requirement compliance – between *formal* compliance and *substantive* compliance. Here, formal compliance is used to refer to behaviour that meets the minimum requirements of an order, and in the case of CS might include attending work placements or attending on time. Substantive compliance is used to relate to an offender's active engagement and cooperation within the requirements of the order and might be evidenced, for example, in an offender's positive attitude and engagement with CS tasks. This concept of substantive compliance is particularly relevant to later discussion regarding the relationship between short-term *substantive* compliance and the achievement of longer-term compliance outcomes.

Having established the significance of both short- and long-term compliance for those involved in the supervision of community penalties, Bottoms goes on to map out four variants of, or 'principal mechanisms underpinning', compliant behaviour. Each is shown to be instrumental both to our understanding of compliance and to our capacity to influence compliant behaviour. The compliance mechanisms identified by Bottoms are as outlined in Figure 19.1.

Briefly, *instrumental* or *prudential compliance* relates to the various incentives and disincentives deployed to influence compliance within community penalties – most obviously illustrated in the form of legal

---

A   Instrumental/prudential compliance
        (a)   Incentives
        (b)   Disincentives

B   Normative compliance
        (a)   Acceptance of/belief in norm
        (b)   Attachment leading to compliance
        (c)   Legitimacy

C   Constraint-based compliance

      (1) Physical restrictions or requirements on individual leading to compliance
        (a)   Natural
        (b)   Imposed
      (2) Restrictions on access to target
      (3) Structural constraints

D   Complianced based on habit our routine

Figure 19.1   Four variants of compliant behaviour.
Source: Bottoms (2001).

sanctions to be applied in the event of non-compliance. Normative compliance is divided by Bottoms into three sub-types. The first relates to a conscious or moral belief in the norm in question and might include, for example, an offender's acceptance of his or her sentence as reasonable or fair. The remaining two sub-types relate to the influence of social relationships on compliant behaviour and may include the influence of a partner or family on compliance, or, with regard to legitimacy, the influence of an authority figure – that is, a supervising officer. In light of related research around legitimacy and effective relationships within community penalties (Dowden and Andrews 2004; McIvor 1998), this mechanism is clearly significant and highlights the dynamic and interactional nature of compliance within community penalties. Constraint-based compliance is broadly self-explanatory and relates to the various restrictions and constraints impacting on an individual's compliance as a result of either physical needs (the need for sleep), physical restrictions (prison, or electronic monitoring) and opportunity (or lack thereof). Bottoms' final compliance mechanism – compliance based on habit or routine – relates to compliance that occurs almost unconsciously, either through habit or routine. Interestingly, Bottoms notes that habits or 'dispositions' can, of course, be developed towards longer-term compliance outcomes, again highlighting the dynamic nature of compliant behaviour.

The above framework helpfully illuminates the often simplified dynamic of compliance within CS. Specifically, Bottoms' analysis foregrounds that offender compliance is a dynamic and interactive entity, one that can be (and is) shaped and influenced by multiple and often complex mechanisms – many of which are routinely overlooked in the routine policy and practice of CS. It is no great leap then to suggest that those concerned to influence and support compliance (in both the short and long term) within community penalties need to better understand and explore the mechanisms discussed above in pursuit of more effective targeting of compliance efforts.

Compliance and community service

Noting the dearth of research attention given to CS generally, it is unsurprising to find that research attention to the dynamics of compliance within CS is scant, to say the least. Of the few published research studies that do attend to this issue, none attends in any detailed way to the dynamic or complex nature of compliance as outlined above. Nonetheless, existing findings in this area have much to contribute to our understanding, and at the very least provide a baseline for the development of new knowledge.

McIvor's (1992) seminal study of CS in Scotland was perhaps the first to significantly identify and illuminate a relationship between the quality of offenders' experiences on CS and compliant attitudes and behaviours. McIvor's study found that the offenders who experienced CS as positive and worthwhile were more likely to demonstrate both short- and long-term compliant behaviour (in the form of improved completion rates and reduced recidivism). For the offenders in McIvor's study, a positive experience of CS was associated with engaging in meaningful/rewarding work, the opportunity for contact and exchange with beneficiaries and the opportunity for skills acquisition. Further, in common with probation-based research, offender interviews highlighted the significance of a positive relationship with supervisors (that is, one based on consistency, fairness and mutual respect – features identified as critical in sustaining motivation and commitment to completing CS). Finally, McIvor's study identified a relationship between efforts to help offenders with personal problems and successful completion. As McIvor (2002: 2) writes: 'Schemes that tended to adopt a more problem-focussed, "holistic" approach had better completion rates than would have been predicted.'

A small number of studies have since endorsed McIvor's findings regarding the potential relationship between CS and longer-term compliant behaviour. In an analysis of reconviction rates following community sentences, Lloyd et al. (1995), Raynor and Vanstone (1997) and May (1999) each report findings that indicate that reconviction rates for offenders given CS were slightly lower than those predicted on the basis of individual profiles. Similarly, Killias et al. (2000), in an analysis of the comparative effects of CS and short-term imprisonment, found that offenders sentenced to CS had lower rates of reconviction than those sentenced to prison. Killias et al. also explore the possible mechanisms influencing longer-term compliant behaviour and suggest a relationship between reduced reconviction and an offender's perception and acceptance of their order as fair and legitimate. On the basis of such findings, Rex and Gelsthorpe (2002: 316) speculate: 'could it be … that [as] offenders undergo constructive and reintegrative experiences in undertaking community work … that accepting the sentence as fair in the first place makes them more receptive to these experiences?'

Undoubtedly, the above findings have contributed to the development of a number of UK-wide initiatives aimed at enhancing CS's rehabilitative potential – most notably in the introduction of evidence-based practices within CS supervision. Chris Trotter's (1993) work on pro-social modelling has been particularly influential in this regard, insofar as it is considered to provide an opportune practice framework for the incorporation of features found to be most associated with short- and longer-term compliant behaviour (McIvor 1998, 2002).

The Community Punishment Pathfinder projects provided further opportunity to explore and test out the above findings. Funded under the Crime Reduction programme, the pathfinder projects were established in 2000 with the stated aim of 'develop[ing] the research base to investigate what in CS might be effective in reducing reoffending, focussing on a number of promising approaches' (Rex *et al.* 2003: 311). Accordingly, seven projects were set up across ten probation areas which variously drew upon three identified 'promising approaches': pro-social modelling, skills accreditation and tackling the problems underlying offending behaviour. Noting the scale of the research study, the project aim and the study's identification of compliance as a critical measure of effectiveness, one might expect that this study would have much to contribute to our understanding of compliance within CS. In reality the findings to emerge on this issue are more modest.

Certainly the study provides encouraging data in respect of compliance behaviour in both the short and long term. With regard to formal compliance, 73 per cent of offenders successfully completed their order (in comparison, 71 per cent of community punishment orders and 60 per cent of community service elements of combined orders were successfully completed across England and Wales in 2000; Home Office 2002). Substantive compliance – in the form of cooperation and performance – was also rated highly, with 75 per cent of offenders achieving good or very good cooperation and 81 per cent achieving good or very good performance. The study identifies a number of factors associated with the above outcomes, *all* of which relate to offender circumstances at the point of commencing the order. For example, successful completion of CS was found to be associated with the following factors (as assessed at the point of commencement): age, risk of reconviction, employment or educational status, educational qualifications, stability of accommodation, support from family, partners or friends, sole or shared responsibilities for others and motivation to complete. With regard to cooperation and performance, little association emerged between 'other factors' and performance, though younger offenders, with higher risks of reconviction, were found to perform less well. Though significant, these findings provide little insight into how the *process* of completing CS impacted on short-term and long-term compliance, or indeed of how such processes interact with individual circumstances (for example, age, family ties, employment).

In respect of longer-term compliant behaviour, 61 per cent of the sample who completed Crime Pics II[1] (M&A Research 2009) showed significant reductions in both pro-criminal attitudes and problems. Further, a majority of offenders thought that CS had changed the way they saw things and three-quarters thought that it had made them less likely to offend. Notably, and in common with McIvor's (1992) findings, features that appeared to be most associated within these changes were whether offenders perceived the work to be of value to themselves or beneficiaries. More broadly, the report tentatively concludes that projects focused on pro-social modelling and skills accreditation were among the most promising approaches. Projects focusing on tackling other offending related needs were found to fare less well and 'did not appear to produce positive outcomes overall' (p. vii). Notably, success in this regard was seen to be hampered by an attempt to take on 'too wide a range of initiatives' and/or 'a lack of strong focus' (p. 76) – a finding that is clearly significant in the context of discussion around an expanded role for CS.

The above research evidence has much to contribute to our developing understanding of compliance dynamics within CS. First, there now exists a significant body of evidence that indicates that CS has a legitimate contribution to make to the much coveted outcomes associated with longer-term compliant behaviour. Further, there is now considerable agreement within that research evidence regarding those features or 'mechanisms' of CS that appear to be most promising in supporting compliance. However, the available evidence also attests to the considerable limitations of our knowledge in this area – in large part a reflection of the lack of direct or systematic attention to this outcome within CS. In this respect there is a need for more targeted attention to the issue of compliance (and indeed non-compliance) within CS and to the principal mechanisms that act upon it. Specifically, we need to better understand why offenders do and do not attend CS (formal compliance); what motivates offenders towards substantive compliance and to what extent these short-term outcomes also impact on longer-term compliant behaviour. Further, if we are clear that longer-term compliance (and thus reduced recidivism) is a legitimate objective for CS, there is a need for targeted policy, practice and research attention to what can be done both within and beyond CS to support that outcome.

Acknowledging the above, I turn now to the findings from a small-scale research study which, drawing on staff and offender perspectives, further attests to the complexity and centrality of individual compliance within CS. In common with the empirical studies discussed above, the study reported on did not set out to explore compliance directly. Rather, it was through the process of conducting the research – specifically, discussion with offenders – that the significance and complexity of compliance emerged as a critical factor.

The research study

The research study set out to evaluate the impact of a pro-social modelling (PSM) training programme on the practice of CS supervision within a criminal justice social work team,[2] drawing primarily on staff and offender perspectives. Informed by the above aim, and mindful of the potential limitations of in-service training evaluations (Clarke 2001), Kirkpatrick's (2006) four-level model of evaluation was adopted as an overarching framework, directing evaluation at the following four levels: staff reaction, staff learning, staff behaviour and service outcomes.

The training was delivered to the CS staff team over two consecutive days. The intended outcomes of the training were identified as follows:

1 Provide an improved respectful, caring and enthusiastic delivery of service to clients, with a fair and consistent use of authority.
2 Provide an improved level of support, help and guidance to clients during the course of their order.
3 Provide better pro-social models and reinforcement to clients of their positive behaviour.
4 Improve client attendance and reduce the level of breaches and reviews.

While there was a clear desire that the training would improve the relational skills of staff supervising CS – and in turn formal and substantive compliance – no direct attention was given to the training's longer-term impact in terms of reconviction rates/longer-term compliant behaviour. However, the findings emerging from the study do attend to these issues and suggest that the above processes – applied in the right conditions – may well be associated with compliant behaviour in both the short and long term.

Methodology

From the outset the study was concerned to assess training impact from the perspective of those directly involved in the delivery and receipt of CS (that of staff and offenders). In part, this reflected a realistic appraisal of the resource available in conducting the study. More importantly it reflected a belief that each held a unique vantage point from which to evaluate training impact. In addition, it was hoped that interviewing both groups would permit data triangulation and so provide a more rigorous account. To this end the study employed a multi-method approach to data collection, drawing primarily on qualitative tools. Specifically, the study drew upon the following data sources.

CS staff

Pre-training and post-training questionnaires were sent to all staff attending the training for self-completion and return. Ten of a possible 12 completed questionnaires were returned for each stage. In addition, in-depth, semi-structured interviews were conducted with all 12 staff attending the training. Interviews took place within the agency, were audio-recorded and lasted approximately 45 minutes.

Offenders

Three semi-structured focus groups took place with three CS work teams, involving 25 offenders in total. The decision to interview offenders within a pre-existing group reflected knowledge of the value of group-based interviews in gathering qualitative data – specifically the opportunity for flexibility and participant empowerment – alongside practical concerns to minimise disruption to the CS work-day and maximise offender participation. Focus groups took place within the agency without staff present, were conducted by two researchers and lasted between 60 and 75 minutes.

Agency and national data

Attention was given to relevant agency and national data information systems. This included documentary analysis of national criminal justice social work statistics and agency breach rates for comparative three-month periods before and after the training. At the outset it was hoped that offender perceptions of CS would also be measured by analysis of data from completed Crime-Pics II questionnaires. In the event the agency was not in a position to provide this data.

Data were analysed using thematic content analysis in four stages. Initial analysis began with thematically coding answers to the questionnaires and interview questions. This was followed by identification and coding of additional themes that emerged beyond the answers to the questions. Next, a comparative analysis of staff and offender responses was completed. This led to a progressive refinement of the themes, patterns and relationships.

The research sample

Participation in the study was entirely voluntary. Staff members were invited to participate *via* briefing meetings that took place prior to the training. Of the 12 staff interviewed, three of the participants were female, nine were male. Experience in the job was generally high, though ranged from six months to 12 years.

With regard to offender participants, three CS work teams – comprising two day teams and one evening team – were identified as potential participants. The inclusion of offenders attending an evening team reflected a concern to include the perspective of offenders in employment. The selection of the remaining work teams was based on agency practicalities as to the timing of the groups. Offenders were briefed about the research study and the opportunity for involvement in advance of the groups and again prior to the group starting. Across the three groups, 25 offenders attended and all agreed to participate. 22 of the offenders were male, three were female. The majority of participants had a reasonable amount of CS experience to draw upon (19 of the 25 had been on CS for more than three months) and most were keen to express their views and experience.

Limitations

The methods adopted for the evaluation were limited by the focus of the study and the resources available. Specifically the following factors need to be acknowledged.

- The evaluation was modest in its aim and sought primarily to evaluate training impact on staff learning, behaviour and practice, with attention to service outcomes where feasible.

- The study did not attempt a 'before and after' comparison of staff practice or service outcomes. In part, this reflects the fact that a similar training was delivered to an earlier staff group two years previously; therefore any pre-training measurement would be compromised. In addition, the resource required to create such a measurement was beyond the scope of this study. No comparative control group was identified for like reasons.

- The absence of direct observational data and, in turn, the reliance on participant perspectives requires acknowledgement of the potential for bias in the data gathered.

- The small sample size and the limited information available concerning the larger population of CS staff and offenders must inform speculation about the representativeness of the findings.

Research findings

Staff perspectives

In considering impact on the intended outcomes of the training, staff generally rated training impact highly. Specifically, the data indicated that the training had greatest impact on outcome 1: 'Provide a respectful, caring and enthusiastic delivery of service, with fair and consistent use of authority'; and outcome 3: 'Provide better pro-social models and reinforcement to clients for their positive behaviour'. Responses were most varied in relation to outcome 2: 'Provide an improved level of support, help and guidance to clients through the course of their order', reflecting some variance in views regarding what was meant by support, help and guidance, and the extent to which staff were sufficiently trained or equipped to improve provision in this area. As might be expected, staff members were most reticent in identifying training impact on outcome 4: 'Improve client attendance and reduce the level of breaches and reviews'. Although the majority of respondents considered the quality of worker–offender relationships to be a significant factor affecting attendance and compliance, respondents were quick to assert the often greater influence of other factors on this outcome. Interestingly, 'other factors' highlighted by staff extended beyond offenders' personal and social problems (for example, marital or drug problems) to also encompass significant organisational and socio-political constraints, such as 'poor' or 'boring' placements, staffing levels, public attitudes, external and 'political' pressures, and what some perceived to be the 'numbers game' currently dictating the quality of local CS provision (referred to as the routine prioritising of quantitative outputs over qualitative outputs).

The impact of 'wider factors' was also keenly felt in regard to the broader impact of the training. Staff highlighted various issues that made it difficult to implement the training, including the size of CS teams, the quality of placements available, and the attitudes and/or 'suitability' of offenders. The most frequently cited obstacle – identified by over half of the respondents – was the perceived impact of wider public, professional, political and media attitudes to offenders and/or CS. As one respondent concluded: 'if a pro-social approach is to be truly effective it needs to be implemented at all levels, both within the agency and beyond'.

Offender perspectives

Offender perspectives *broadly* supported staff perspectives, though the findings in this area present a more varied and detailed picture.

First, offenders were quick to endorse the existence of a PSM approach in most supervisors. However, offenders consistently asserted that this was not the case for all. The findings in this area indicate that the PSM training appeared to have no impact on a small but consistent minority of supervisors with whom relationships were described as 'difficult'. Focusing then on their relationship and interaction with 'most' supervisors, the majority of respondents were quick to provide evidence of outcomes 1 and 3 (supporting the findings to emerge from staff interviews). Supporting examples focused on consistency and fairness in the use of authority, the use of praise and encouragement, and, most significantly, the way staff spoke to them. Consistent with wider research findings on the relational element of supervision (McIvor 1992), offenders placed considerable value on being treated respectfully and considered this critical to progress. As one respondent put it: '[they] treat you like a person, not like a criminal'. Another observed: 'Mine is brilliant ... if it wasnae for her I'd have breached ages ago.' For the minority of staff with whom relationships were difficult this was felt to be evidenced in 'the way they speak to you', by the 'lack of give and take' and an unwillingness to 'work alongside' or offer help with work tasks.

Again, in line with the findings to emerge from staff interviews, offender responses were most varied in relation to outcome 2: 'Provide an improved level of support, help and guidance'. Initially, offenders were quick to agree with the above statement. However, further discussion highlighted that for most, responses related to the provision of practical support, help and guidance with CS tasks. When asked to consider the provision of support with wider problems, responses varied. A minority of offenders had experienced help with problems outside of CS and clearly valued this aspect of the role. As one offender noted: 'they've helped me put things into perspective ... problems and things'. Another responded: 'I get loads of help ... with the job and life ... you can actually sit and have a talk to them.'

Where 'help and guidance' did occur it appeared to be largely down to the attitude and motivation of the offender to bring problems into the supervisory relationship, which in turn depended on the quality of that relationship. For most, however, this was deemed to be 'not their job', with some offenders expressing genuine surprise on hearing that fellow offenders had discussed and received help with personal problems from staff. Though many were surprised by the idea that they would discuss or seek help with problems within CS, all agreed that 'other problems' greatly affected motivation, attendance and compliance. The hesitation and uncertainty expressed when discussing this issue is significant and correlates with the uncertainty expressed by staff. In this respect the findings suggest a level of ambiguity – among staff and offenders – regarding the appropriate scope and boundaries of the CS role.

As with staff perspectives, offender responses were most reticent in identifying a relationship between a PSM approach and attendance and compliance within CS (outcome 4). In common with findings from previous studies (McIvor 1998; Rex *et al.* 2003), respondents were clear that the positive attitude and behaviour of staff towards them supported attendance and compliance. Offenders were equally clear that 'negative' attitudes and behaviours on the part of supervisors 'made you think twice' about attending. As one respondent expressed:

'you don't want to come in if it's the supervisor you don't like'. However, staff attitude and approach was not considered as critical to attendance and compliance as 'other' factors. Noting the significance placed by offenders on 'other' factors, attention was also given to factors that offenders considered most critical to compliance within CS; specifically, those factors most likely to aid compliance and those most likely to impede it. The findings to emerge on this issue are, paradoxically, both straightforward and complex.

Offender compliance and the significance of other factors

The most significant 'aid' to compliance identified by offenders was the desire to 'have [their] time back', linked by many to a desire to move forward and 'get on with life'. For most, CS was seen to be 'holding them back' from this process – a finding worth further analysis in the context of Maruna's (2001) work on the significance of offender narratives in supporting desistance.

Other identified 'aids' to compliance included knowledge of consequences – such as 'fear of going to jail' – and relationships with fellow offenders on CS. However, when considered in the light of individual experiences of non-attendance, the above factors appeared to exert limited influence on attendance and compliance decisions; for many of the offenders interviewed (and arguably for the 2,161 offenders reflected in recent breach statistics – Scottish Government 2008), fear of incarceration or a desire to 'have their time back' were not, in themselves, enough when set in the context of individual experience. This message is significant and may suggest that *instrumental* compliance – at least in the form of deterrence or threats – is less influential on individual compliance decisions than is often assumed (see also Ugwudike, this volume). Faced with this anom respondents struggled to explore what they or others could dc help them comply with their order. In part, this was underpinne by a narrative that neither they nor others had much control over the myriad of factors (life problems) affecting compliance. However, there also emerged a sense that participants had not considered what might help with such problems. Certainly, offenders did not consider that others (including CS staff) might assist with this.

When invited to consider more practical aids to compliance, responses were contrastingly clear and forthcoming and related exclusively to the nature of work undertaken. Repeatedly, participants expressed a desire for more 'relevant tasks', 'better jobs' and an end to 'pointless work'. As one respondent summed up:

If you could actually be doing better work rather than sitting there sanding a bit of wood ... you're standing there sanding something and it doesn't need to be sanded, or painting a fence and then coming back and painting it again, it's pointless work that you shouldn't be doing. Fair enough you've got to work 'cos you've done something wrong but when it's work like that ... what's the point of that? It's like they've ran out of things for you to do so they make you do stupid things like that.

Although the experience of engaging in 'pointless' work was familiar to all, some were uneasy expressing this as a problem, suggesting that was 'the point of CS'. As one offender responded: 'It's work and you just come and do it ... basically you know you're gonna get jobs that nobody else is going to do, you're no' here to enjoy yourselves.' This finding resonates with the uncertainty expressed earlier regarding the legitimate scope and purpose of CS. It also suggests that offender conceptions of CS may be very closely associated with their ultimate expectations of it (for example, in relation to change and desistance). Again, in the light of emerging research on the significance of offender narratives (specifically, offenders' attitudes to and expectations of themselves, others and, in turn, of change interventions (see, for example, Maruna 2001)), this finding is significant and suggests that offender perceptions of the purpose or point of CS may well be critical to the outcomes achieved.

Factors considered by offenders to impede compliance focused almost exclusively on practical or operational issues (such as job monotony, the 'cost' of CS, operational frustrations). While discussion occasionally touched on the (greater) significance of wider personal problems, for most such issues were deemed to be beyond the focus of CS and, as such, our discussion. Notwithstanding this reticence, offender discussion did reveal a relationship between non-compliance and a 'lack of motivation' – in particular, an absence 'of things [broader rewards] to motivate you to turn up and complete your hours'. The apparent tension between this view and the view expressed earlier regarding what most helped (that is, the fear of going to jail) was not lost on participants and attests to the complexity of offenders' experience and views on this issue. For example, one offender who very clearly asserted 'you come because you've got to come', later acknowledged that despite being only weeks away from completion, he had recently returned from an eight-week period of unexplained absence. For this individual, and some others, lack of motivation was at least part of the explanation, linked to 'other stuff going on in your life [that] might have nothing to do with CS'. Significantly, for most of the offenders interviewed, such factors were seen to matter a lot more than 'what people here say and do to you'.

Discussion

The above findings present a number of interesting messages regarding the relationship between a PSM approach within CS supervision and offender compliance – few of which are straightforward. In closing I wish to return to three emerging themes, which in the context of an expanding vision for CS seem critical to its future effectiveness.

Revisiting the CS role and task

In exploring compliance within CS the findings reveal a concerning lack of clarity regarding what it is that CS is seeking to achieve. As discussed, emerging evidence regarding the reintegrative and rehabilitative potential of CS has prompted increased speculation and debate regarding the legitimate purpose and focus of CS. On one level, this debate is to be welcomed and accords well with the more complex constructions of CS held by many of the staff interviewed. However, the findings also suggest that the absence of clear and coherent objectives for the service, specifically as they relate to substantive and longer-term compliance outcomes, may in fact impede the successful achievement of these objectives. For example, both staff and offenders described notably diverse supervisory practices in evidence within CS, ranging from pro-social to (unnecessarily) punitive. Significantly, both approaches were seen to be legitimised, and thus rarely questioned, by the at times competing objectives of the service (that is, to punish and to assist). Similar examples can be drawn regarding the nature of work offenders are expected to undertake, the accepted scarcity of local placements and the routine, albeit undesirable, prioritising of quantitative over qualitative outputs. In the context of ongoing debate regarding the intended outcomes for CS, the findings from this study suggest a need to make up our minds regarding what we want CS to achieve. If we are committed to enhancing the effectiveness of CS (as defined by substantive and longer-term compliant behaviour) then there exists a clear rationale for addressing some of the more rudimentary elements of CS that have long been overlooked.

From a different perspective, the findings highlight that offenders appeared to have little if any expectations of CS beyond punishment. Though offenders were keen to point out that the experience of CS was not necessarily punitive – in that many of the supervisors treated and interacted with them positively – this (and other elements of CS) was, for many, beyond what was expected. More disturbingly, offenders appeared to locate the completion of CS within an 'offending' rather than a 'desistance' trajectory, insofar as the process of 'moving forward' or 'getting on with life' (and the priorities associated with that) was seen to commence on completion of the order. In light of Maruna's (2001) work on the significance of individual narratives within the change process, this finding is troubling and would suggest that CS has some work to do if it is to achieve a shift in offender conceptions of CS. Certainly the findings suggest that for the offenders in this study, longer-term compliant behaviour begins *after* CS.

There exists, then, a rationale for revisiting the role and purpose of CS, both locally and nationally. As outlined, there is now a growing body of evidence to suggest that the outcomes of CS can and do extend beyond its more traditionally conceived objectives. However, to date (with the exception of the pathfinder projects), such benefits appear to have been achieved by default rather than design. While, as others have noted (McIvor 1998), there is a need to progress cautiously in this area, the findings from this study suggest that a failure to sensitively incorporate recent developments into official objectives may in fact impede the success of such developments – specifically, realising CS's rehabilitative potential.

The new and emerging context of 'community payback' in Scotland[3] presents both opportunity and challenge in this regard. On the one hand there is opportunity to formally articulate a broader and more constructive vision for CS or 'unpaid work', as envisaged, for example, in the recent report by the Scottish Prisons Commission (2008). Simultaneously, there is a danger that the reparative, reintegrative and rehabilitative ideals of community payback become obscured in misguided efforts to publicly 'package' community payback as punishment first and last.

Getting to grips with support, help and guidance

Noting the range of personal and social problems typically experienced by offenders completing CS (Rex *et al.* 2003), the now well-documented correlation between offenders' problems, compliance and recidivism

(Raynor and Vanstone 1997; McIvor 1998), and the significance offenders in this study placed on 'other stuff going on in your life', a concern to improve the provision of support, help and guidance would seem a particularly legitimate service objective. Indeed, recent research on enhancing the effectiveness of CS has highlighted the potential of a problem-solving approach within practice (McIvor 1998 2002). Additionally, one of the three approaches developed within the Community Punishment Pathfinder projects focused on the use of community service to address the problems underlying offending.

However, the findings from this study suggest considerable ambivalence among staff and offenders regarding the appropriateness and scope of a problem-solving approach within CS. As outlined, while all offenders acknowledged the considerable impact of 'wider' problems on motivation and compliance, most were clearly surprised by the suggestion that they might receive support, help or assistance with such problems within CS. The limited research in this area presents a similarly ambivalent picture. For example, in a paper presented to the Clarke Hall Day Conference, McIvor (1998) discusses the value of 'concrete problem-solving' within CS and advocates the use of a problem-solving approach at the following three levels:

(i)   in the supervisor's approach to the completion of work tasks
(ii) in the development of work tasks which help to alleviate offenders' social problems
(iii) *in actively helping offenders to deal with problems which arise in the course of an order.* (1998: 59, italics added)

In a more recent paper, McIvor's discussion of problem-solving within CS is notably constrained to '*the tasks* that offenders in teams are required to undertake' (2002: 3). Similarly, despite a clear practice focus on this issue within the Community Punishment Pathfinder projects, the findings provide little in the way of direction (Rex *et al.* 2003). Despite encouraging evidence of significant reductions in offenders' 'self-perceived problems', the provisional conclusions of the study suggest that projects prioritising offender-related needs did not appear to produce positive outcomes overall (2003: 76). Significantly, the authors go on to observe that success in this area may have been hampered by implementation problems; in particular, 'a lack of strong focus', a particularly salient observation in light of related findings from the effectiveness literature (which indicate that the provision of help or problem-solving should be focused, clearly targeted, and appropriately resourced (Dowden and Andrews 2004; Raynor and Vanstone 1997)).

In light of the above, perhaps the clearest message to emerge on this issue is the need for further research. Specifically, there is a need to further explore *if* and *how* CS can be effective in assisting offenders with the personal and social problems known to impact on compliance. In the interim, the findings suggest a need for management to clarify the nature and scope of what is currently envisaged in the provision of support, help and guidance within CS, and to effectively communicate that to both staff and offenders. If the provision of support, help and guidance is to extend beyond the completion of CS tasks, then there is a need to better resource and support it (that is, to ensure that staff possess – or have access to – the knowledge, skills and time required to fulfil that role).

The complexity of compliance

Finally, the research findings attest to the considerable complexity of compliance dynamics within CS. Generally, and consistent with existing research data, the findings indicate that the adoption of a pro-social approach within CS supervision certainly *supports* offender attendance, motivation and compliance within CS. However, the findings also signal that staff attitude and approach is only one mechanism among many impacting upon formal, substantive and longer-term compliance.

On one level, the findings endorse existing research messages, with staff highlighting the greater significance of offenders' attitudes and problems, alongside the considerable influence of wider organisational and socio-political constraints. Offenders, again as might be expected, attested to the considerable influence of those they worked alongside, the perceived consequences of non-compliance and, most significantly, the nature of work they were expected to undertake. Despite the familiarity of these messages, each presents a considerable challenge for those concerned to influence and improve offender compliance within CS. For example, despite the fact that the 'nature of work undertaken' has been highlighted as outcome critical in almost every evaluative study of CS to date, these same studies – much like this one – continue to provide ample evidence of offenders engaging in 'pointless work'.

Beyond these familiar messages, offender discussion also highlighted the considerable complexity that surrounds individual attendance, motivation and compliance. The detail emerging from individual accounts suggests that supporting compliance within CS is about much more than what goes on within CS (though this is clearly important). For at least some of the offenders interviewed, there emerged a tentative expression of the need for a more substantive reason, reward or purpose to comply in the longer term.

As is often the case with offender perspectives, there is a common-sense nature to the above finding; there is also a growing body of research evidence to support it (see, for example, Maruna 2001; Ward and Brown 2004; Robinson and McNeill 2008). Nonetheless, offenders' need for a substantive reason to comply perhaps presents one of the greatest challenges to contemporary penal policy and practice. To return to the Scottish context, the new penal discourse currently emerging in Scotland has once again endorsed a commitment to provide offenders with an *opportunity* for change within the context of community penalties – a commitment that, for many (particularly those looking on from other jurisdictions) is to be celebrated and seized. The challenge, however, lies in the perhaps inconvenient truth that offenders – both in this study and others – appear to need more than opportunity for change; they need a reason.

Concluding comments

The above discussion attests to the fact that the professional, political and academic landscape of CS is changing. As efforts to enhance the effectiveness of CS take root we can expect to see the adoption of a number of service initiatives that seek to foster compliant behaviour in both the short and longer term. Unfortunately, to date, such initiatives appear to have been developed and implemented within a policy and practice context where the dynamic of compliance is poorly understood, and where efforts towards compliance routinely sit alongside other mechanisms known to impede that. The above discussion suggests that if we are committed to enhancing the effectiveness of CS there is a need to develop a coherent and holistic strategy capable of achieving effectiveness – one that is clear in its purpose and committed in its practice. Specifically this will require that organisations and their staff better understand and engage with the complexity of compliance within CS, while also acting to ensure that efforts to enhance compliance are not simultaneously compromised by competing service objectives, priorities and practices.

Notes

1 Crime Pics II is a widely used questionnaire for examining and measuring changes in offenders' attitudes to offending. It has been used extensively by prison and probation services across the UK, where it has been frequently used to evaluate the effectiveness of a variety of rehabilitative programmes and other interventions with offenders (M&A Research 2009).

2 In contrast to the rest of the UK, and many other English-speaking countries, responsibility for providing services to the criminal justice system – in the form of assessment, supervision and throughcare of offenders – rests with local authority social work departments. For the last two decades, this has typically been delivered *via* specialist criminal justice social work teams who are tasked to deliver a range of services and schemes, including the provision of reports to the court, probation and community service.

3 The concept of community payback lies at the heart of a recent report by the Scottish Prisons commission (2008) which seeks to respond to Scotland's over-reliance on imprisonment as a means of punishing offenders. One of the report's key recommendations is that 'paying back in the community should become the default position in dealing with less serious offenders' (para 3). Significantly, the report identifies various *forms* of payback, with a clear emphasis on constructive and reparative approaches. Indeed, the report identifies that one of the best ways for offenders to 'pay back' is 'by turning their lives around' (2008: para 3.28).

References

Bottoms, A. (2001) 'Compliance with community penalties', in A. Bottoms, L. Gelsthorpe and S. Rex (eds) *Community Penalties: Change and Challenges*. Cullompton: Willan Publishing.

Clarke, N. (2001) 'The impact of in-service training within social services', *British Journal of Social Work*, 31: 757–74.

Dowden, C. and Andrews, D.A. (2004) 'The importance of staff practice in delivering effective correctional treatment: a meta-analytic review of core correctional practice', *International Journal of Offender Therapy and Comparative Criminology*, 48: 203–14.

Duguid, G. (1982) *Community Service in Scotland: The First Two Years*. Edinburgh: Scottish Office Central Research Unit.

Home Office (2002) *Probation Statistics in England and Wales 2000*. London: Home Office.

Killias, M., Aebi, M. and Ribeaud, D. (2000) 'Does community service rehabilitate better than short-term imprisonment? Results of a controlled experiment', *Howard Journal*, 39 (1): 40–57.

Kirkpatrick, D. (2006) *Evaluating Training Programmes: The Four Levels*, 3rd edn. San Francisco: Berret-Koehler.

Lloyd, C., Mair, G. and Hough, M. (1995) *Explaining Reconviction Rates: A Critical Analysis*, Home Office Research Study 136. London: Home Office.

M&A Research (2009) *M&A Crime Pics II*. Online at: www.crime-pics.co.uk/index.html (accessed 3 March 2010).

Maruna, S. (2001) *Making Good: How Ex-convicts Reform and Rebuild their Lives*. Washington, DC: American Psychological Association.

May, C. (1999) *Explaining Reconviction Following Community Sentences: The Role of Social Factors*, Home Office Research Study 192. London: Home Office.

McIvor, G. (1992) *Sentenced to Serve: The Operation and Impact of Community Service by Offenders*. Aldershot: Avebury.

McIvor, G. (1998) 'Prosocial modelling and legitimacy: lessons from a study of community service', in *Prosocial Modelling and Legitimacy: The Clarke Hall Day Conference*. University of Cambridge Institute of Criminology.

McIvor, G. (2002) *CJSW Briefing: What Works in Community Service?* Criminal Justice Social Work Development Centre.

Pease, K., Durkin, P. and Earnshaw, I. (1977) *Community Service assessed in 1976*, Home Office Research Study. London: Home Office.

Raynor, P. and Vanstone, M. (1997) *Straight Thinking on Probation (STOP): The Mid-Glamorgan Experiment*, Probation Studies Unit Report 4. Oxford: University of Oxford Centre for Criminological Research.

Rex, S. and Gelsthorpe, L. (2002) 'The role of community service in reducing offending: evaluating Pathfinder projects in the UK', *Howard Journal*, 41 (4): 311–25.

Rex, S., Gelsthorpe, L., Roberts, C. and Jordan, P. (2003) *Crime Reduction Programme: An Evaluation of Community Service Pathfinder Projects Final Report 2002*. London: Home Office.

Robinson, G. and McNeill, F. (2008) 'Exploring the dynamics of compliance with community penalties', *Theoretical Criminology*, 12 (4): 431–49.

Scottish Government (2008) *Criminal Justice Social Work Statistics 2007–8*. Edinburgh: Scottish Government.

Scottish Government (2009) *Statistical Bulletin Crime and Justice Series: Criminal Proceedings in Scottish Courts, 2007–08*. Edinburgh: Scottish Government.

Scottish Prisons Commission (2008) *Scotland's Choice: Report of the Prisons Commission*. Edinburgh: Blackwell. Online at: www.scotland.gov.uk/Resource/Doc/230180/0062359.

Trotter, C. (1993) *The Supervision of Offenders: What Works?* Victorian Office of Corrections.

Ward, T. and Brown, M. (2004) 'The Good Lives Model and conceptual issues in offender rehabilitiation', *Psychology, Crime and Law*, 10 (3): 243–57.

Part Six

Offender supervision in its contexts

Chapter 20

The socio-political context of reforms in probation agencies: impact on adoption of evidence-based practices[1]

Faye Taxman, Craig Henderson and Jennifer Lerch

Introduction

Over 6 million Americans are on probation or parole supervision, with another million adults under some type of diversion or specialised programming (Taxman *et al.* 2007). Probation is the most frequently ordered sentence in the United States, with the probation population increasing by 216 per cent from 1982 to 2007 (Pew Foundation 2009). During the recent period of accelerating growth, probation agencies have operated under a goal of monitoring the conditions of release or enforcing a standard of behaviour. Coupled with a spiralling population is the failure rate from probation, with nearly 42 per cent of the offenders failing to complete the period of supervision; this inability of an enforcement-driven probation model to deliver reduced crime and recidivism has led many to question whether probation should emphasise rehabilitation rather than enforcement as its main tenet. Recent attention has been given to the adoption of evidence-based practices (EBPs) that are designed to reduce recidivism, and therefore are better served to improve offender outcomes (Taxman 2002; Byrne 2009). However, to adopt EBPs, probation agencies must confront the often conflicting organisational goals of deterrence (meaning here enforcement through the use of punitive practices and an emphasis on controls such as drug testing, curfews and liberty restrictions) and rehabilitation (meaning here offender change such as involvement in treatment, employment and/or education, programmes and services) that affect the priority placed on different components of the supervision process.

While the stated goals of rehabilitation and punishment are not necessarily incompatible (Clear and Latessa 1993), a need exists to ensure that the goals are clarified in such a manner that promotes the agency's priorities. The often cited conflicting values of rehabilitation and punishment produce varying degrees of organisational support for different programmes and services (Henderson and Taxman 2009). The issues of whether certain programmes and services are offered and the types of offenders that should be provided with access to these services are caught up in this value conflict, and it also filters down to probation staff's views of whether they are perceived by their organisational leaders as being a 'social worker' or an 'enforcer' (Taxman *et al.* 2004).

Research has shown that the community where probation services are provided influences the degree to which an emphasis is placed on the goals of rehabilitation or punishment, which always exist in tension with one another. The political philosophy of the surrounding community (Young *et al.* 2009), the different opinions and perspectives of administrators that lead organisations (Henderson and Taxman 2009; Friedmann *et al.* 2007; Taxman and Kitsantas 2009), and the history of providing different programmes and services all influence the adoption of evidence-based practices. This socio-political environment reflects the norms and values of the community where the probation organisation exists and how external and internal pressures impact the operations of the agency. Internal pressures refer to staff, resources and organisational issues that affect the capacity of the agency to respond, whereas external pressures are the factors outside of the organisation such as the government structure, nature of the community, types of supports in that community, and presence of key stakeholders.

Reforming existing practice usually comes from a desire to improve outcomes, although there can be myriad desired goals. Probation agencies have a long history of conflicting goals, along with a push towards involving offenders in more services and programmes (see Petersilia and Turner 1993). The experiments on intensive supervision of the 1980s focused on increasing the contacts, increasing drug testing, increasing the use of services and other foci depending on the specific goals that probation desires to achieve. A recent surge of interest in reforming probation, with the ultimate goal of reducing recidivism, is part of an ongoing effort to establish community corrections as a respectable punishment scheme that is recognised as legitimate. That is, probation and community corrections can serve to prevent incarceration and to prevent penetration into criminal behaviour by providing the appropriate theoretical framework to assist offenders to desist in their behaviours and to provide opportunities to address criminogenic traits that affect engagement in criminal behaviour. To do so effectively, the current perspective embraces the principles expounded by Canadian researchers (Andrews and Bonta 1998, and this volume) that offer a series of core practices based on providing effective correctional programmes and services that are designed to impact criminal career trajectories and criminogenic factors that affect further involvement in criminal behaviour. Besides a rational empirical strategy that pinpoints the research defining the proven strategies, it is unknown under what circumstances the organisation will be convinced to pursue adopting these EBPs, particularly organisations like probation where the goals vary considerably.

History of reform in probation: what are the main goals?

Over the past several decades, probation in the United States has been confronted with a shifting pendulum regarding the goals of probation supervision. Essentially there have been three large movements in the field that have affected the nuts and bolts of the core business function of supervision. These are enforcement (first generation), accountability (second generation), and the hybrid of accountability and rehabilitation (third generation). Each era of probation reform has emphasised different aspects and components of the supervision process, such as a greater focus on conditions, monitoring, treatment or policies to match needs to services or controls.

Enforcement

This type of supervision falls into the category of monitoring the conditions of release with a watchful eye towards compliance. The emphasis is on providing more conditions to restrict the movement of offenders, and ensuring that the punishment is visible. The monitoring function focuses on compliance, with external controls imposed by formal institutions that place demands on individuals. Since negative behaviour is likely to draw the attention of the criminal justice system, supervision agencies are responsible to respond to the negative behaviour. In this era, little attention was paid to the use of risk instruments to determine the supervision level or identification of the criminogenic needs that affect criminal behavior. Conditions were assigned for punishment purposes. The numerous intensive supervision experiments in the 1990s found that numbers of contacts did not reduce recidivism or technical violations, and often did not result in increased access to services (Taxman 2002; Mackenzie 2000).

Monitoring also translated into more agencies adopting an enforcer model, coupled with law enforcement technologies. Many probation agencies assumed a law enforcement perspective that included arming their staff, with 41 states allowing their parole officers to be armed (38 states allowed probation officers to do the same) (Fuller 2002). For some organisations this raised the profile of the probation staff, including access to benefits afforded those in law enforcement (most notably retirement systems that are usually better than other state employees, and salary enhancements for clothing). It also forced the organisations to participate in law enforcement training, particularly the certification of gun use. And it served to reinforce the commitment to rigorous 'enforcement of conditions' as a form of accountability for the offender.

Accountability through treatment: testing and sanctions

Given the recognition that offenders had criminogenic needs such as substance abuse, correctional programming in the early 1990s began to examine how best to provide treatment services to offenders. The intensive supervision experiments (see Petersilia and Turner 1993), coupled with the evolving 'what works' literature (see Andrews *et al.* 1990; Andrews and Bonta 1998), represented a turning point to combine monitoring with treatment services. Emphasis was placed on accountability, or the offender being responsible for his/her behaviour. The reforms focused on providing evidence or verification that the offender was adhering to the conditions of release through the use of drug testing and treatment sessions. During this era, the focus of the criminal justice system was finding the best avenue to facilitate offender participation in treatment programmes. Drug courts, intensive supervision programmes (ISP), boot camps, and other criminal justice programmes evolved with each incorporating some type of treatment services. Agencies developed different techniques to link offenders with services that generally fell into three categories:

1 *Brokerage* – the parole officer refers the offender to another agency for assessment and/or services without having input into the assessment process and/or the services delivered.
2 *Case management* – The parole officer monitors offenders' participa-

tion in assessment and receiving services. The emphasis is on compliance with the order; and

3 *Dedicated services* – the supervision office offers services on-site where assessment and services are provided at the same location. In some cases these services are paid for by the supervision agency.

Hybrid of accountability and rehabilitation

While the research over the last three decades has many limitations, it does provide guidance to improve criminal justice public policy and supervision practice. The expansion of the 'what works' literature includes a focus not only on programmes, but on expanding the accountability concept to establish systemic efforts in probation organisations to determine the need for services. This EBP model focuses on a cadre of principles that include system reform, quality of treatment programming and services, working alliance between the offender and his/her probation officer, and including community and social networks in the supervision process (see Taxman *et al.* 2004; NIC 2004).

Each of these eras in supervision processes represents where the emphasis of practice has been. It is not the case that all agencies have subscribed to these phases at the same speed or adopted them in identically the same ways. While the third generation is characterised by the adoption of EBPs, agencies have varied greatly, not only in what practices they adopt but also in the manner in which they have implemented these practices into their organisation. This chapter examines how different types of reform strategies correctional agencies may influence the adoption of evidence-based practices.

Methodology

The National Criminal Justice Treatment Practices (NCJTP) survey was administered in 2004–05 and gathered information on the availability and make-up of substance abuse treatment and services in prison, jail and community correctional settings. A component of this survey also captured information on administrative practices in these settings and their use of evidence-based practices (see Taxman *et al.* 2007 for a detailed description of the survey). The study team developed the sampling frame for the community correctional agencies by using a two-stage stratified cluster (Kish 1965). The frame was developed by selecting counties and then surveying all agencies that operate within those 72 jurisdictions. Counties were categorised based on population size (small = less than 250,000 medium = 250,000–750,000; large = more than 750,000), and by region using an eight-category classification to include four regions and the states with the largest prison populations (California, Florida, New York and Texas). This resulted in 24 strata from which counties were drawn, and all counties with a population of 3 million or more were sampled with certainty; the survey was designed to provide national estimates of the experiences of offenders involved in community correctional agencies. The second stage was a census of all probation and parole agencies, prisons/jails and community-based treatment programmes in these counties.

The survey was 32 pages in length and was mailed to administrators (for example, chief probation officers, agency heads, wardens, treatment directors). Surveys were returned from several weeks to several months after mailing. Extensive follow-up efforts were undertaken in order to maximise response rates, and to address any information that was left incomplete on a respondent's submission. The response rate for this survey was 67 per cent (Taxman et al. 2007).

Variables defining evidence-based practices

As discussed by Friedmann, Taxman and Henderson (2007), the operational definition of EBPs followed the Institute of Medicine's (2001) definition: practices that represent the 'integration of best research evidence with clinical expertise and client values'. The items included in the definition of evidence-based practices were a cross-section of research findings on effective interventions, programmatic factors that influence effective outcomes combined, and clinical guidance on effective practice. The first category examined practices that adhere to the Canadian model of risk-need-responsivity, where the focus is on identifying risk and need factors and then ensuring that the types of programmes and services that are offered adhere to the core principles of effective correctional programming. The items on the survey that reflect this criteria are: (1) use of a standardised risk assessment tool; (2) use of substance abuse assessment procedures (such as DSM-IV) and treatment matching (similar to the ASAM or other patient matching criteria); (3) use of therapeutic community, cognitive behavioural or other standardised treatment orientations that have been found to be effective for offender populations (see Andrews and Bonta 1998; NIDA 2000); (4) use of screening tools and clinical strategies to address co-occurring disorders; (5) use of evidence-based family therapies or multi-systemic family interventions; and (6) use of contingency management programmes to provide incentives to encourage compliance with programme conditions.

A third set concerns the delivery of effective programmes and services, including the use of qualified staff, management techniques to assess the overall treatment outcomes to determine the impact of the programme, use of a comprehensive approach to provide treatment and ancillary needs that address dynamic criminogenic needs, and treatment programmes that are of sufficient duration to affect change (at least 90 days). Each component has been identified in the literature as critical to improve outcomes.

Given that many correctional agencies are not direct service providers, the use of techniques to improve the delivery of effective programmes and services is a necessary step. System and service integration requires the coordination of multiple systems (such as housing, mental health, substance abuse, employment, education) to optimise care and to appropriately address criminogenic needs (see Fletcher *et al.* 2009). Besides the nature of the working partnership across systems, the policies and practices that support the use of continuing care or aftercare are needed to expand opportunities for involvement in treatment and to include multiple phases to address multiple criminogenic needs.

Another component is the ability to address the milieu of services – a domain that has a strong research base to demonstrate that it relates to improved client outcomes. Adherence to sound counselling principles, such as establishing a therapeutic alliance and engaging clients in the clinical process is included in the concept. This is often reflected in the use of motivational techniques to engage and retain clients in treatment (for example, motivational interviewing, engagement).

Finally, to improve the responsiveness of the criminal justice system, the following were identified as factors to improve outcomes: the use of drug testing to monitor compliance with treatment conditions; the use of progressive, graduated sanctions to address non-compliance; the use of medications to stabilise the offender to assist with improving retention in substance abuse; the use of detoxification programmes; and the availability of HIV/AIDS testing to assist the offender in addressing risk behaviours that affect his/her social behaviour overall.

Explanatory variables

Attitudes towards rehabilitation and punishment

A 12-item scale was used to measure perceptions of how best to reduce crime (Cullen *et al.* 1993, 2000; Applegate *et al.* 1997). From this 12-item scale, a measure of rehabilitation orientation was created from the rehabilitation subscale (reliability: 0.79). The remaining items created the reference category of punishment orientation using the subscales of punishment, deterrence, incapacitation, just deserts, sanctions for drugs, and sanctions for crime. These items were assessed on a five-item Likert scale, ranging from 1 'strongly disagree', to 5 'strongly agree'.

Organisational needs assessment

These items assessed the organisation's overall functioning as well as its needs (adapted from Lehman *et al.* 2002). This study includes the following two subscales: (1) *staffing needs* (subscale reliability: 0.58); (2) *perceived funding for new programmes* (subscale reliability: 0.63). These items were assessed on a 5-item Likert scale ranging from 1 'strongly disagree', to 5 'strongly agree'.

Organisational structure

The model includes a dichotomous measure of facility type, indicating if the facility is an institution or is community based. Measures of the size of the population served and the size of the facility (based on full-time employees) were also included in the model. The log-transformation of the size of the facility was used.

Data analysis

This study uses the technique of latent class analysis (LCA) to sort individuals into similar groups (latent classes) with respect to a set of observed categorical variables (EBPs) based on an underlying (latent) categorical variable. LCA assumes that individuals' observed responses to a set of categorical items (in this case the presence or absence of EBPs) arise from a mixture of sub-populations (the latent classes). The objective of the analysis is to determine the number and nature of the latent classes through maximising the likelihood of the observed data across a series of models varying in the number of classes the models estimate (Lanza *et al.* 2003).

LCA has several advantages that can be shared with other latent variable modelling approaches including: (a) a maximum likelihood estimation to obtain the estimated probabilities of class membership to account for the probabilistic nature of class assignment (that is all individuals have an estimated probability of belonging in each class); (b) the ability to expand the models to include contextual variables; (c) the capacity to include all available data from participants even if it is incomplete (Schafer and Graham 2002); and (d) a model-based approach to estimating heterogeneity in subscale scores (model-based approaches have the advantage that more rigorous methods can be used in selecting the optimal number of latent classes; see Lubke and Muthén 2005; Nylund *et al.* 2007).

To select the final LCA model requires a number of decisions. First, the model with the optimal number of latent classes must be selected. This decision is typically made on the basis of a convergence of model fit criteria, along with substantive considerations. Non-inferential criteria such as the Bayesian information criterion (BIC) (Schwartz 1978) and entropy (Ramaswamy *et al.*, 1993) are frequently used to guide this decision. In the results reported below, we compared the BIC values across the models with varying numbers of latent classes; the lower BIC values indicate a preferred model. Entropy is a standardised summary measure depicting the classification accuracy of placing participants into classes based on their model-estimated (that is posterior) probabilities of class membership, with higher values indicating better classification. Although we could not use the traditional LRT to guide model selection, there are some inferential alternatives (namely the Lo-Mendell-Rubin Likelihood Ratio Test (L-M-R LRT) and the bootstrap LRT (BLRT)) that are appropriate to use in this context. The L-M-R LRT (Lo *et al.* 2001) compares the improvement in fit between neighbouring class models (comparing c-1 and the c-class models) and provides a statistical test that can be used to determine if there is a significant improvement in fit for the inclusion of one more class. Finally, the BLRT (McLachlan and Peel 2000; Nylund *et al.* 2007) is similar to the L-M-R LRT, but uses bootstrap samples to empirically derive the distribution of the log likelihood difference test comparing c-1 and c-class models.

The first step of the LCA involved selecting the optimal model. This begins with a series of models, starting with a one-class model, with successive models adding one additional class. After selecting the model with the optimal number of latent classes, we included correlates of the latent class variable in the best-fitting model. All of the models presented here were estimated using Mplus, Version 5 (Muthén and Muthén 1998–2008).

Results

Descriptive statistics

Table 20.1 describes the number and percentage of respondents reporting whether an EBP was used in a given facility. It reveals that the more frequently self-reported EBPs included the use of incentives ($n = 283$, 66 per cent), qualified staff ($n = 148^2$, 68 per cent), comprehensive services ($n = 446$, 69 per cent), and standardised substance abuse assessment measures ($n = 379$, 59 per cent). Administrators reported that the following were infrequently used: standardised risk assessment tools ($n = 100$, 23 per cent), specific treatments such as cognitive behavioural treatment or therapeutic communities ($n = 67$, 16 per cent), medications to treat substance abuse problems ($n = 65$, 15 per cent), and detoxification services ($n = 70$, 16 per cent).

Table 20.1 Use of evidence-based practices by respondents.

	n	per cent
Engagement techniques	255	39
Use of standardised substance	379	59
Use of standardised risk assessment tool	100	23
Comprehensive services	446	69
Co-occurring disorders	298	46
Continuing care	230	36
Family involvement	250	39
Systems integration	343	53
Graduated sanctions	138	32
Incentives	283	66
90-day duration	190	44
Drug testing	182	42
Treatment orientation	67	16
Qualified staff	148	68
Assessment of treatment outcomes	126	58
Medications used to treat substance abuse	65	15
Detoxification program	70	16
HIV/AIDS testing	214	50

Note: $n = 647$.

Latent class analysis

Model specification and estimation

As previously reported, LCA was performed using the EBP items reported above from 647 individuals. As shown in Table 20.2, the three-class LPA model provided the best fit to the EBPs. The three-class model had a lower BIC and significant L-M-R LRT and BLRT tests. Average individual posterior assignment probabilities for this solution revealed high values along the diagonal (range: .83 to .95) and low values off the diagonal (range: .02 to .10), both indicating good model classification. A four-class model was also fit, but the BIC was higher, the L-M-R LRT was not significant, and the BLRT did not converge. Taken together, the three-class model provided the best representation of the data.

Evaluating the validity of the three-class model

The face validity of the model is demonstrated by examining the EBP response patterns within each of the latent classes, shown in Table 20.3. The three classes are: non-innovators (n = 172, 27 per cent), clinical (n = 264, 41 per cent), and criminal justice system (n = 211, 32 per cent). The non-innovators class represents those respondents that for the most part reported relatively low use of all EBPs, regardless of their nature.

Clinical innovators reported using EBPs that were clinical in nature more frequently than the other classes, such as using interventions to engage offenders in treatment (69 per cent in clinical innovators as compared to 8 per cent of non-innovators and 24 per cent of criminal justice system innovators). The clinical-oriented innovators also tended to address substance use and co-occurring mental health disorders (74 per cent, 24 per cent, and 26 per cent), and involving families in treatment (83 per cent, 11 per cent and 0 per cent) more often than the other classes. The criminal justice system innovators reported more use of EBPs that basically expanded traditional 'best practices' developed within the criminal justice system. This includes higher proportions using standardised risk assessment tools (41 per cent, 18 per cent, 4 per cent), systems integration (77 per cent, 50 per cent, 29 per cent), and services designed to address offenders' physical and mental health as well as case management needs (86 percent, 59 per cent, and 65 per cent). Figure 20.1 shows the percentage of usage each type of innovator reported for the various EBPs.

Table 20.2 Model fit criteria for one to five-class models.

Model	Loglikelihood	# Parameters	Bayesian information criterion (BIC)	Entropy	L-M-R LRT (p)	Bootstrap LRT (p)	n (per cent) smallest class
Class 1 LCA	−5521.154	18	11,158.809	N/A	N/A	N/A	647 (100)
Class 2 LCA	−5304.573	37	10,848.623	.690	<.001	Not replicated	320 (49)
Class 3 LCA	−5212.724	56	10,787.900	.740	.018	<.001	172 (27)
Class 4 LCA	−5176.230	75	10,837.886	.749	.423	Not replicated	61 (9)
Class 5 LCA	−5139.896	94	10,888.192	.760	.306	Not replicated	35 (5)

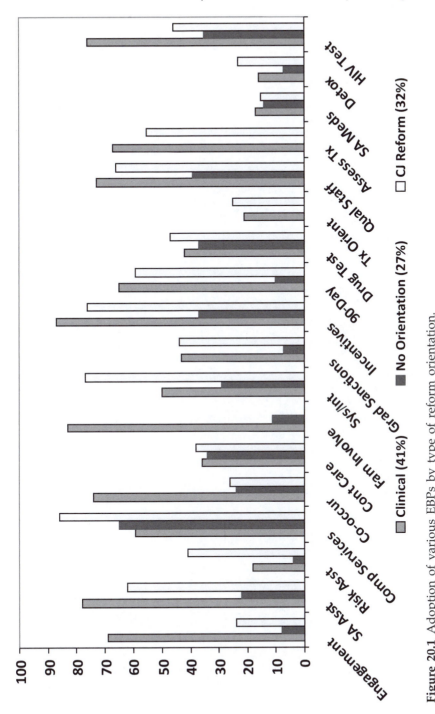

Figure 20.1 Adoption of various EBPs by type of reform orientation.

Table 20.3 Proportion of programmes reporting EBP use and proportions of most likely class membership for three-class model.

	Class 1: Clinical innovators n = 264 (41 per cent)	Class 2: Non-innovators n = 172 (27 per cent)	Class 3: CJ system innovators n = 211 (32 per cent)
Engagement techniques	.69	.08	.24
Use of standardised substance abuse assessment tool	.78	.22	.62
Use of standardised risk assessment tool	.18	.04	.41
Comprehensive services	.59	.65	.86
Co-occurring disorders	.74	.24	.26
Continuing care	.36	.34	.38
Family involvement	.83	.11	.00
Systems integration	.50	.29	.77
Graduated sanctions	.43	.07	.44
Incentives	.87	.37	.76
90-day duration	.65	.10	.59
Drug testing	.42	.37	.47
Treatment orientation	.21	.00	.25
Qualified staff	.73	.39	.66
Assessment of treatment outcome	.67	.00	.55
Medications used to treat substance abuse	.17	.14	.15
Detoxification program	.16	.07	.23
HIV/AIDS testing	.76	.35	.46

Table 20.4 Coefficients, standard errors, and *pseudo* z statistics for correlates of latent class membership.

Class contrast	Coefficient	Standard error	Pseudo z value
Class 1 vs Class 2			
Facility type (institution vs community)	2.13	1.13	1.89*
Size of correctional population	-1.02	0.85	-1.20
Rehabilitation orientation	-0.05	0.51	-0.10
Need for training	-0.64	0.37	-1.73*
Internal support for new programming	<0.01	0.73	<0.01
Size of facility	0.07	0.18	0.37
Class 1 vs Class 3			
Facility type (institution vs community)	0.75	0.47	1.59
Population	-0.05	0.34	-0.14
Rehabilitation orientation	-1.44	0.37	-3.91***
Need for training	-0.80	0.36	-2.21**
Internal support for new programming	-0.76	0.26	-2.93***
Size of facility	-0.01	0.10	-0.13
Class 2 vs Class 3			
Facility type (institution vs community)	-1.39	0.98	-1.42
Population	-.97	0.83	1.18
Rehabilitation orientation	-1.39	0.41	-3.41***
Need for training	-0.16	0.57	-0.29
Internal support for new programming	-0.76	0.72	1.06
Size of facility	-0.08	0.20	-0.40

*p < .05. **p < .01. ***p < .001.
Note: Class 1 = clinical innovators; Class 2 = CJ system innovators; Class 3 = non-innovators.

Correlates of the latent classes using logistic regression results
Table 20.4 depicts associations between latent class membership and the significant predictors of EBP. These associations were tested using the multinomial logistic regression routines included in Mplus. Results indicated that criminal justice innovators were more likely than clinical innovators to be working in a community corrections agency (*pseudo z* = 2.13, *p* = .05), and clinical innovators perceived a marginally higher need for training than criminal justice innovators (*pseudo z* = –1.73, *p* = .08). Relative to the non-innovators, clinical innovators had higher rehabilitation orientations (*pseudo z* = –3.91, *p* < .01), saw a greater need for training (*pseudo z* = –2.21, *p* = .03), and had more internal support for new programming (*pseudo z* = –2.93, *p* < .01). criminal justice innovators also had higher rehabilitation orientations than non-innovators (*pseudo z* = –3.41, *p* < .01).

Discussion

Previous efforts in the early 1990s in the United States demonstrated the demand for correctional agencies to fulfil the public need for being 'tough' on crime through incapacitation policies but also recognising that more emphasis on treatment or rehabilitation goals is important to produce long-term changes in offenders. This study provides evidence that the goal of rehabilitation exists within correctional agency innovators in conjunction with the adoption of evidence-based practices that are in line with traditional criminal justice 'best practices'. This evidence of the coexistence of rehabilitation and punishment oriented goals supports previous studies that examine both correctional and probation staff. Several studies have found correctional staff to view custodial goals as their primary focus, while still including rehabilitation as a goal (Cullen *et al.*, 1989; McIntosh and Saville, 2006; Taxman and Gordon, 2009). In a national survey of state and federal wardens, Cullen *et al.*, (1993) found that wardens prioritised incapacitation as more important than other goals but recognised rehabilitation as the secondary goal. Sluder, Shearer and Potts (1991) found that probation officers were more oriented towards a resource broker and case worker perspective as compared to a law enforcement approach, with older employees and longer job tenure weakly correlated with less support of law enforcement. Ellsworth (1990) found that probation line staff, supervisors and administrators reported goals of rehabilitation and punishment in existence, as well as reporting a preference for both goals.

With this coexistence of goals arises a tension for the system's actors that manifests itself through staff's interactions with the population being served and staff work conditions. McIntosh and Saville (2006) observed that the relationship between the correctional staff and inmates in a Scottish prison was limited by the custodial goals associated with being an officer. In addition, Melnick *et al.* (2009) found that increased support for rehabilitation in correctional settings contributed to increased cynicism and job frustration, along with decreased organisational commitment. The authors conclude that this finding could be the result of discrepancy between the traditional role of corrections 'as custodial institutions' and conflicting values reflecting rehabilitation beliefs (2009: S20). Cullen *et al.* (1985) found that role issues significantly increased job and life stress of surveyed correctional officers. A survey of correctional and treatment staff within a prison illustrated how role-related issues had the largest impact on job stress, and how the stress emanates from a lack of organisational clarity about expectations of the staff (Armstrong and Griffin 2004). Furthermore, the authors noted that role conflict varied by prison security level, with greater problems in minimum security prisons where the goals of punishment and rehabilitation tend to be murky; suggesting that the role conflict comes from the structure of the organisation, since neither security level nor job role explained the role conflict. Similar to this finding, Clear and Latessa (1993) found that differences in orientations towards rehabilitation or control appear to be a product of organisational philosophies more than personal preferences in three intensive supervision programmes.

The third generation of reform, combining accountability with rehabilitation, provides evidence-based practices as a method of addressing these tensions arising from the ambiguous coexistence of punishment and rehabilitative goals. Evidence-based practices provide a structure within which administrators can operationalise goals that support both accountability (maintaining public safety) and rehabilitation (focusing on offender change). Recent research on improving the working alliance between probation officers and supervisees demonstrates how the need for accountability and monitoring (such as drug testing) can be met while still focusing on improving offender outcomes through practices such as enhanced communication (Taxman 1998; Taxman and Ainsworth 2009). When viewed from a third-generation perspective, EBPs provide measurable performance expectations that administrators can use to better shape staff understandings of both organisational goals of accountability and rehabilitation.

Furthermore, being able to solidify the organisational goals and objectives using EBPs provides administrators with an avenue to manoeuvre the socio-political constraints within that they operate. Whether bargaining for resources or being inclusive of other decision-makers' opinions, administrators within these organisations must negotiate support from their internal and external environment to set new goals (Thompson and McEwen 1958). In addition, administrators of these organisations must balance the ambiguity found in public opinion about the proper organisational goals. Research has shown that the public prefers both rehabilitation and punishment to be utilised by probation and correctional staff (Cullen *et al.* 2000). Punitiveness is preferred by the public when factors such as violent crime and child offenders are taken into account, but for the most part they support both goals as a priority for the criminal justice system (Cullen *et al.* 2000). Within the environment of criminal justice actors and the public shared belief of dual goals of rehabilitation and punishment, an opportunity exists for the leaders of these organisations to implement EBPs that monitor and enhance public safety through improving the outcomes of offenders.

This study contributes to a better understanding of the EBPs that correctional innovators have adopted, as well as the importance of different reform orientations to the process of adoption of EBPs. The finding that different reform activities result in varying adoption of EBPs reinforces the importance of a theoretically based framework for reform. If reform activities are going to be successful, then it is important for the underlying orientation to be embraced by administrators at all levels (Young *et al.*, 2009). Similarly, if the end goal is to assist offenders to acquire pro-social skills, then a greater focus on a clinical orientation will foster the structural components to achieve this goal. But the real question is whether the public and criminal justice agencies are interested in (or can be persuaded to become interested in) offender change. This is the question to be answered.

Notes

1 Funding from this study came from Grant U01 DA016213-01 (Action Research to Advance Drug Treatment in the CJS), the Maryland Department of Public Safety and Correctional which has had a 20-year research agreement with Dr Taxman and the National Institute on Drug Abuse R01 DA017729 (Effects of Manualized Treatment on a Seamless System

of Care). The U01 cooperative agreement also received funding from the Center for Substance Abuse Treatment, Bureau of Justice Assistance, Center for Disease Control and Prevention, and National Institute on Alcohol Abuse and Alcoholism. The contents are solely the responsibility of the authors and do not necessarily represent the official views of NIH/NIDA or other federal agencies.

2 Note that the n for the frequencies differs because some of the EBPs were administered to both wardens and treatment directors and some were not.

References

Andrews, D.A. and Bonta, J. (1998) *The Psychology of Criminal Conduct*, 2nd edn. Cincinnati, OH: Anderson.

Andrews, D., Zinger, I., Hoge, R.D., Bonta, J., Gendreau, P. and Cullen, F. (1990) 'Does correctional treatment work?', *Criminology*, 28: 369–404.

Applegate, B.K., Cullen, F.T., and Fisher, B.S. (1997) 'Public support for correctional treatment: The continuing appeal of the rehabilitative ideal', *Prison Journal*, 77: 237–58.

Armstrong, G.S. and Griffin, M.L. (2004) 'Does the job matter? Comparing correlates of stress among treatment and correctional staff in prisons', *Journal of Criminal Justice*, 32 (6): 577–92.

Byrne, J. (1990) 'The future of intensive probation supervision and the new intermediate sanction', *Crime and Delinquency*, 36 (1): 6–41.

Byrne, J. (2009) *Maximum Impact: Targeting Supervision on High-Risk People, Places and Times*. PEW Center, Washington DC. Online at: www.pewcenteronthestates.org/uploadedFiles/Maximum_Impact_web.pdf (accessed 23 October 2009).

Clear, T. R. and Latessa, E. J. (1993) 'Probation officers' roles in intensive supervision: surveillance versus treatment', *Justice Quarterly*, 10: 441–62.

Cullen, F.T., Fisher, B.S. and Brandon K. Applegate (2000) 'Public Opinion about Punishment and Corrections', *Crime and Justice*, 27: 1–79.

Cullen, F.T., Latessa, E.J., Burton, V.S. and Lombardo, L.X. (1993) 'The correctional orientation of prison wardens: is the rehabilitative ideal supported', *Criminology*, 31: 69–92.

Cullen, F.T., Link, B.G., Wolfe, N.T. and Frank, J. (1985) 'The social dimensions of correctional officer stress', *Justice Quarterly*, 2: 505–33.

Cullen, F.T., Lutze, F.E., Link, B.G. and Wolfe, N.T. (1989) 'The correctional orientation of prison guards: do officers support rehabilitation', *Federal Probation*, 53: 33–42.

Ellsworth, T. (1990) 'Identifying the actual and preferred goals of adult probation', *Federal Probation*, 54: 10–15.

Fletcher, B.W., Lehman, W.E., Wexler, H.K., Melnick, G., Taxman, F.S. and Young, D.W. (2009) 'Measuring collaboration and integration activities in criminal justice and drug abuse treatment agencies', *Drug and Alcohol Dependence*, 101 (3): 191–201.

Friedmann, P.D., Taxman, F.S. and Henderson, C.E. (2007) 'Evidence-based treatment practices for drug-involved adults in the criminal justice system', *Journal of Substance Abuse Treament*, 32 (3): 267–77.

Fuller, K. (2002) *Adult and Juvenile Probation and Parole Firearm Survey*. Lexington, KY: American Probation and Parole Association.

Henderson, C. and Taxman, F. (2009) 'Competing values among criminal justice administrators: the importance of substance abuse treatment', *Drug and Alcohol Dependence*, 103 (Suppl. 1): S7–S16.

Institute of Medicine (2001) *Crossing the Quality Chasm: A New Health System for the 21st century*. Washington, DC: National Academy Press.

Kish, L. (1965) *Survey Sampling*. New York: Wiley.

Lanza, S.T., Flaherty, B.P. and Collins, L.M. (2003) 'Latent class and latent transition analysis', in J.A. Schinka and W.F. Velicer (eds) *Handbook of Psychology: Research Methods in Psychology*, Vol. 2. Hoboken, NJ: John Wiley.

Lehman, W.E., Greener, J.M. and Simpson, D.D. (2002) 'Assessing organizational readiness for change', *Journal of Substance Abuse Treatment*, 22: 197–209.

Lo, Y., Mendell, N. and Rubin, D.B. (2001) 'Testing the number of components in a normal mixture', *Biometrika*, 88: 767–78.

Lubke, G. and Muthén, B.O. (2005) 'Investigating population heterogeneity with factor mixture models', *Psychological Methods*, 10: 21–39.

Mackenzie, D.L. (2000) 'Evidence based corrections: identifying what works'. *Crime and Delinquency*, 46: 457–61.

McIntosh, J. and Saville, E. (2006) 'The challenges associated with drug treatment in prison', *Probation Journal*, 53 (3): 230–47.

McLachlan, G. and Peel, P. (2000) *Finite Mixture Models*. New York: Wiley.

Melnick, G., Ulaszek, W.R., Lin, H.J. and Wexler, H.K. (2009) 'When goals diverge: staff consensus and the organizational climate', *Drug and Alcohol Dependence*, 103 (Suppl. 1): S17–S22.

Muthén, L.A. and Muthén, B.O. (1998–2008) *Mplus User's Guide: Version 5*. Los Angeles: Muthén and Muthén.

National Institute of Corrections (2004) *Implementing Evidence-Based Practice in Community Corrections: The Principles of Effective Interventions*. Washington, DC: Community Corrections Division.

National Institute on Drug Abuse (2000) *Principles of Drug Abuse Treatment for Criminal Justice Populations: A Research-based Guide*. (NIH Publication No. 00-4180). Washington, DC: National Institutes of Health, US Department of Health and Human Services, NIH Publication No. 00–4180.

Nylund, K.L., Asparouhov, T. and Muthén, B. (2007) 'Deciding on the number of classes in latent class analysis and growth mixture modeling: a Monte Carlo simulation study', *Structural Equation Modeling*, 14: 535–69.

Petersilia, J. and Turner, S. (1993) 'Intensive probation and parole', in M. Tonry (ed.) *Crime and Justice: An Annual Review of Research*. Chicago: University of Chicago Press.

Pew Foundation (2009) *One in 31: The Long Reach of American Corrections*. Philadelphia: Pew Foundation. Online at: www.pewcenteronthestates.org/report_detail.aspx?id=49382 (accessed 23 October 2009).

Ramaswamy, V., DeSarbo, W., Reibstein, D. and Robinson, W. (1993) 'An empirical pooling approach for estimating marketing mix elasticities with PIMS data', *Marketing Science*, 12: 103–24.

Schafer, J.L. and Graham, J.W. (2002) 'Missing data: our view of the state of the art', *Psychological Methods*, 7: 147–77.

Schwartz, G. (1978) 'Estimating the dimension of a model', *Annals of Statistics*, 6: 461–4.

Sluder, R.D., Shearer, R.A. and Potts, D.W. (1991) 'Probation officers' role perceptions and attitudes toward firearms', *Federal Probation*, 55: 3–11.

Taxman, F.S. (1998) 'Reducing recidivism through a seamless system of care: components of effective treatment, supervision, and transition services in the community', paper presented at the Office of National Drug Control Policy Treatment and Criminal Justice System Conference, Washington, DC.

Taxman, F.S. and Gordon, J. (2009) 'Do fairness and equity matter? An examination of organizational justice among correctional officers in adult prisons', *Criminal Justice and Behavior*, 36: 695–711.

Taxman, F.S. (2002) 'Supervision – exploring the dimensions of effectiveness'. *Federal Probation*, 66 (2): 14–27.

Taxman, F.S and Ainsworth, S. (2009). Correctional milieu: the key to quality outcomes'. *Victims and Offenders*, 1556–4991, 4 (4): 334–40.

Taxman, F.S. and Kitsantas, P. (2009) 'Availability and capacity of substance abuse programs in correctional settings: a classification and regression tree analysis', *Drug and Alcohol Dependence*, 103 (Suppl. 1): S43–S53 (http://doi:10.1016/j.drugalcdep.2009.01.008).

Taxman, F.S., Shepardson, E. and Byrne, J.M. (2004) *Tools of the Trade: A Guide to Incorporating Science into Practice*. Washington, DC: National Institute of Corrections.

Taxman, F.S., Young, D., Wiersma, B., Mitchell, S. and Rhodes, A.G. (2007) 'The national criminal justice treatment practices survey: multilevel survey methods and procedures', *Journal of Substance Abuse Treatment*, 32 (3): 225–38.

Thompson, J.D. and McEwen, W.J. (1958) 'Organizational goals and environment: goal-setting as an interaction process', *American Sociological Review*, 23 (1): 23–31.

Young, D.W., Farrell, J.L., Henderson, C.E. and Taxman, F.S. (2009) 'Filling service gaps: providing intensive treatment services for offenders', *Drug and Alcohol Dependence*, 103 (Suppl. 1): S33–S42.

Chapter 21

Revising the National Outcomes and Standards for criminal justice social work services in Scotland

Tim Chapman

Introduction

This chapter addresses the problem of how a government develops and assures the quality of effective offender supervision throughout its jurisdiction. This is generally accomplished in part by setting the outcomes and standards of practice for supervision. These standards define a framework of practice which if consistently and competently implemented should achieve the outcomes required of supervision services in the criminal justice system. The purpose of such standards is to build and sustain the public's confidence in and support for the supervision of offenders in the community.

The complex process of revising the National Outcomes and Standards for criminal justice social work services in Scotland in 2008 is described. Certain theoretical models were used to balance the interests of the various stakeholders. These are explained. Finally the structure and content of the standards are outlined.

Criminal justice social work in Scotland: history and context[1]

The Scottish probation services were integrated into generic social work departments through the Social Work (Scotland) Act 1968. As a result, offender supervision did not fare well in competition with the demands of child protection. Probation orders declined and the prison population increased. In 1991 the Scottish Office responded to these trends by allocating ring-fenced 100 per cent funding to criminal justice social work services, thus enabling local authorities to establish and fund specialist probation teams. National Objectives and Standards were also introduced in 1991 (Social Work Services Group 1991). They proved critical in supporting the distinct identity and practices of criminal justice social work services in Scotland (Huntingford 1992). 'What works' research and effective practices were integrated into the standards by 1998 (Paterson and Tombs 1998).

Since then Scotland has experienced criminal justice policy trends similar to the rest of the United Kingdom (and many other jurisdictions), resulting in an increased emphasis on public protection through risk management and on reducing reoffending. Nevertheless, practice in Scotland has remained firmly within social work principles and values and there is a strong commitment to social inclusion (Paterson and Tombs 1998; Scottish Office 1998; Justice Department 2001; Robinson and McNeill 2004). Unlike some other jurisdictions, in Scotland neither a national offender management service nor a single correctional administration (combining prisons and probation) has been established. The supervision of offenders, whether on community-based sentences (such as probation), or on release licences (such as parole), continues to be delivered by 32 local authorities.

In 1999 a large measure of government was devolved to a Scottish parliament and this included crime and justice legislation. However, devolution did not solve the problem of how to implement a national approach to offender supervision through 32 fairly independent local authorities. Rather than setting up a national offender management service, Scotland has established eight community justice authorities to implement multi-agency strategic planning. Compliance with standards of practice remains the responsibility of the local authority. They are inspected by the Social Work Inspection Agency.

At the time of writing, legislation establishing a new community sentence structure is being introduced in Scotland. Central to this new structure will be a 'community payback', sentence, which will replace the existing sentences of community service, probation, and the supervised attendance order. The new sentence will:

- Enable the court to impose one or more of a range of requirements on the offender, including unpaid work, supervision, alcohol or drug interventions or a requirement to take part in a programme to address offending behaviour.

- Reserve the sanction of an electronically monitored curfew, as an option to be considered following breach, not at the point of initial imposition of the sentence.

- Provide for an unpaid work and activity requirement as part of the overall sentence lasting from 20 to 300 hours, which must be served within six months (or three months where it is a sentence of 100 hours or less) (instead of 12 months at present) unless the court decides otherwise at the point of sentence.

- Enable Justice of the Peace Courts (the court where the least serious cases are prosecuted) to impose certain requirements including an unpaid work and activity requirement of between 20 and 100 hours.

The revision of the National Outcomes and Standards for criminal justice social work services in Scotland

In 2007 the Scottish Government commissioned a revision of the National Outcomes and Standards for criminal justice social work services in Scotland. Work on this was undertaken between December 2007 and August 2008.[2] The government's thinking on the need for revision was based upon the following factors:

- The focus on level of contact and enforcement in the current standards did not take into account new research and practices in relation to risk management and to reducing reoffending.

- The national standards had not kept pace with the responsibilities and statutory orders that criminal justice social work services now deliver.

- There was now a greater emphasis on public protection, often through coordinated multi-agency strategies.

- There were now higher expectations on performance management and the delivery of 'best value' for public investment.

- Community sentences were being reviewed with a view to reform.

The government required the new national standards to:

- Reflect the most up-to-date research on effective practices.

- Ensure that this research informs not only the level of contact and enforcement but also the purpose, nature and content of contact and its intended outcomes.

- Integrate robust case management, risk and needs assessment and risk management, and interventions based upon 'what works' including accredited programmes.

- Ensure that the standards comply with and reinforce good practices in service planning, delivery and monitoring, performance and information management, effective partnership working and a high priority to public protection.

In addition the standards should reflect the government's policies on criminal justice services, demonstrate concern for victims of crime, be outcome-focused, be shorter and more concise, be user-friendly and be easy to update.

These requirements were clearly the result of considerable reflection on the part of the government and represented a fundamental critique of the current standards. Influenced by research into effective supervision of offenders there was a strong emphasis upon outcomes and a move away from prescribing practice simply in terms of frequency of contact. Effective practice was to be defined in relation to what positive outcomes offenders achieved rather than simply what practitioners did. Consequently the standards would need to support the active participation of offenders in work towards outcomes and this would demand an individualised approach. A focus on measurable outcomes must be based upon evidence-based practice. Such a model of practice entails robust risk and need assessment, integrated planning of tailored interventions and proactive case management. For this to work practitioners and managers would need to rely upon rigorous professional decision-making rather than follow prescribed procedures.

The tasks set by the government were complex, challenging and obviously critically important to perform effectively. They raised serious questions:

- What are the desired outcomes for effective supervision of offenders?

- What if these outcomes seem to conflict? Can public protection and social inclusion be accommodated together in effective supervision?

- Can recent developments in the research into desistance be integrated with the risk, needs and responsivity research?

- Can quality assurance and performance management be implemented effectively alongside individualised professional decision-making?

- Are criminal justice social workers and their managers ready, willing and able to take on greater responsibility for professional decision-making?

Capital as an organising principle for the process of revision

The questions listed above are not simply technical. They are political, intellectual, organisational and social in nature. They cannot be answered through one academic discipline. With this in mind, the concept of different forms of capital was adopted to address these questions. Bourdieu (1986) extends the concept or metaphor of economic capital to other forms such as social and cultural capital. Increasingly resources required to achieve outcomes are conceived as 'capital', that is, political capital, intellectual capital, social capital and so on. Capital is defined as a resource needed to produce the desired outcome. It is a resource that is invested to create added value as opposed to being used as a service or spent to purchase a commodity. Investment requires a calculated commitment in the face of risk. When taking a risk, people need to be confident and to trust the venture in which they are investing (Kanter 2004). The purpose of national standards of practice is essentially to sustain the confidence of a range of stakeholders in the delivery of effective supervision by criminal justice social work services in Scotland.

To construct National Outcomes and Standards to meet the specification of the Scottish government it is necessary to identify and mobilise a range of capitals. The core of offender supervision involves a face-to-face encounter between a practitioner and the individual subject to supervision. A successful encounter is to a large extent dependent upon the investment of each party's 'human capital' (Coleman 1990; McNeill and Whyte 2007). To put it another way, effectiveness is a result of the extent to which both the offender (McMurran 2002; Farrall 2002; McNeill 2009) and the practitioner (Raynor 2004) commit their motivation, energy, time, intelligence, personal qualities, values and capabilities in working collaboratively and consistently towards an outcome. It is clear that standards should be designed to enhance the motivation and skills of both practitioner and offender.

Equally, directing, organising and supervising the human capital of practitioners are key responsibilities of the employing agency. Commitment to quality and capacity to manage performance by an organisation can be defined as its 'organisational capital'. Its importance to the supervision of offenders is expressed in one of the key principles of effective practice: programme integrity or fidelity. The capacity to deliver supervision as planned has been identified as critical to the achievement of positive outcomes (Hollin 1995).

There is now a substantial body of research on the effective supervision of offenders, much of it discussed in this volume. The capacity of an organisation to understand, apply and develop this knowledge to achieve its outcomes represents its 'intellectual capital' (Stewart 1997). National standards should enable criminal justice social work services to become knowledge-based organisations. This involves designing processes (assessment systems, case management, and interventions) on the basis of the most up-to-date knowledge on effectiveness, training and supervising staff, and monitoring and testing the effectiveness of these processes through evaluation. Key to the concept of intellectual capital (Edvinsson and Malone 1997) is the distinction between tacit and explicit knowledge (Nonaka and Takeuchi 1995). Tacit knowledge is carried within the individual based upon what they have learned from experience. In a practitioner this can enhance the explicit research-based knowledge or it can conflict with it and cause a drift from the integrity of a process. It is also important to acknowledge that offenders have tacit knowledge about their lives. They bring their own intellectual capital to the supervision process. Some of this knowledge needs to be challenged through programmed work, as it sustains criminality. Some of it can enhance the process of behavioural change by providing a realistic context for supervision. Standards of practice should respect the intellectual capital that both research and offenders bring to supervision.

The effective supervision of offenders does not take place in isolation but within a network of formal and informal social relationships. This network is often referred to as 'social capital' (Putnam 2000). For the offender these relationships can support efforts to change and create opportunities to desist from offending (Farrall 2002; McNeill 2009). In the form of anti-social associates (such as friends or family) social capital can be a critical risk factor (Andrews and Bonta 1998). Most practitioners recognise that they cannot provide all that is required to supervise an offender effectively. Consequently they use other departments of their local authorities, relevant statutory and voluntary agencies and appropriate resources within the community to support risk management, rehabilitation, reparation and reintegration plans. In Scotland, the Community Justice Authority provides a structure for this form of social capital. Standards of practice should then recognise the importance of social capital to effective supervision of offenders.

Finally, the effective supervision of offenders needs to be supported by adequate funding and this depends upon politicians and policy-makers having confidence in the quality and effectiveness of what is being delivered. This confidence is more likely to be based upon politicians' interpretation of public opinion than on research-based evidence of the effectiveness of supervision. This illustrates the importance of 'political capital', which is accumulated through the pursuit of popular policies and through achieving outcomes valued by the public. For politicians to invest their political capital in and allocate sufficient funds to the supervision of offenders they need to be convinced that national standards will sustain public confidence in criminal justice social work services.

To summarise, unless the revised national outcomes and standards are seen as adding value to an investment of political, social, human, organisational and intellectual capital, they are unlikely to reach their potential to support the delivery of high quality and effective

Table 21.1 Forms of capital and added value

Capital	Added value
Political	The avoidance of scandal or bad news, public protection, value for money.
Social	Social cohesion, community safety.
Human	For offenders, a better life. For practitioners, professional development and satisfaction.
Organisational	Quality of delivery, achievement of outcomes, efficiency, the avoidance of risk, survival.
Intellectual	The application and the development of knowledge.

offender supervision. It is also necessary to recognise that those who have access to such capital may seek different forms of return on their investments (see Table 21.1). The challenge is to accommodate these different interests without corrupting the integrity of offender supervision.

Based upon this conceptual framework, two tasks must be accomplished to achieve a large-scale orientation towards the effective supervision of offenders. First, it is necessary to understand what each of the various forms of capital offers to and requires of national outcomes and standards, and second, to ensure that their requirements are balanced and integrated into a coherent document that makes sense to all parties.

The process of understanding what is required

The first step was to define the intellectual capital underpinning the effective supervision of offenders through a review of the literature.[3] This work was influenced by research into the desistance of offending (Maruna 2001; Farrall 2002) in the belief that desistance is the key desired outcome of supervision. The desistance approach has been strongly supported in the research literature emanating from Scotland (for example, McNeill and Whyte 2007; McCulloch 2005). It followed that the practices and interventions incorporated in the national standards would need to support and to accelerate processes leading to desistance and to avoid hindering them.

National standards of practice must encompass all forms of supervision undertaken by criminal justice social work services in Scotland. Practices with offenders were organised into four categories:

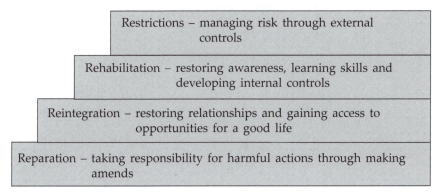

Figure 21.1 Levels of intervention.

reparation, reintegration, rehabilitation and restriction – the four 'Rs' (see Figure 21.1).

The literature review summarised the evidence base for effectiveness of each of these intervention categories. With respect to reparation or making amends in a practical way for harm done to others, research into the effectiveness of restorative justice (Sherman and Strang 2007) and community service (McIvor 1998; Rex and Gelsthorpe 2002) was outlined. These studies demonstrate that offenders 'making good' (Maruna 2001) in ways that make sense to them can reduce reoffending.

Reintegration (or 'resettlement' in the case of ex-prisoners) involves supporting individuals to gain access to accommodation, education, training and employment and enabling offenders to repair personal and social relationships and to become involved in community life. Reparation work can help to overcome the barriers to reintegration. The review reported on the strong empirical evidence for the association of employment and pro-social relationships with desistance (for example, Laub and Sampson 2003).

Some offenders are not ready, willing or able to take advantage of opportunities for reintegration until they have overcome personal or internal barriers to desistance, such as emotional self-regulation, their use of drugs and alcohol, anti-social beliefs and thinking processes that reinforce criminality. Such individuals require rehabilitation programmes. The literature review summarised the extensive range of studies into programmes that proved effective in reducing reoffending. In general the risk, needs and responsivity model was affirmed as at the core of effective rehabilitation (Andrews and Bonta 2003; see also Bonta and Andrews, this volume). The design of the standards also took into consideration that the most successful programmes were those that supplemented group interventions with individual contact, and balanced the focus on cognitive skills, anger management and interpersonal problem-solving, with more applied skills designed to enhance employability (Lipsey et al. 2007). The importance of building relationships and motivation (Trotter 1999; McMurran 2002) were also integrated into the standards so as to encourage programme completion.

Some offenders pose such a risk of serious harm to others that their freedom of movement has to be restricted to protect the public. These restrictions may involve a period in custody where they should be offered opportunities for rehabilitation and reintegration. Others may be permitted to be supervised in the community as long as they submit to restrictions based upon a risk assessment and a risk management plan. Such restrictions are unlikely to achieve desistance from offending on their own (Liebling and Maruna 2006). Indeed, they might prove counter-productive unless they are designed to enable individuals to participate in rehabilitation, reparation and reintegration programmes in the community, where they are likely to be most effective.

Having surveyed the intellectual capital, the next step was to inquire into what political capital might be available to support the new standards. This involved a policy review: parliamentary records of debates on criminal justice, the Scottish government's outcomes for local government, government policy on community penalties (Scottish Government 2007), the government's strategy for offender management (Scottish Executive 2006a), findings from official government inspections, a governmental review of social work (Scottish Executive 2006b), an Association of Directors of Social Work statement on 'The Values and Principles of Social Work Practice in the criminal justice system', a report into social work and reducing reoffending commissioned by the government (McNeill *et al.* 2005), and the national standards from other jurisdictions.

This review led to the following findings on public policy in Scotland:

- The need to contribute to the government's aim for the public to live lives safe from crime, disorder and danger.

- The need to reduce the number of less serious offenders in prison.

- The need for tough community punishments that will protect the public, help offenders to turn their lives around and include some clear payback to the communities that they have harmed.

- The need to improve reparation and rehabilitation, to improve outcomes for persistent offenders, to drive up quality, and to change public attitudes not simply to community disposals but to how they are delivered.

- The requirement that community penalties be of a high quality, effective, immediate, visible, flexible and relevant.

- Practices should include integrated case management, partnerships, standardised risk assessment, evidence-based interventions and tracking for results, a workforce with appropriate skills, sharing information, quality assurance, performance management and outcome measures.

- The need to develop the potential of community service orders.

- The value of working for personal change through direct work, building relationships and an individualised and participative approach.

- Professional autonomy within a clear framework of professional accountability.

- Strong governance and leadership.

It was clear that key policy-makers would expect to see this agenda reflected in the new national outcomes and standards. To meet these aspirations and needs would also require considerable organisational capacity or capital.

A management report was prepared summarising current thinking on organisational development, quality assurance and performance management. Reviewing the literature on knowledge-creating organisations (Nonaka and Takeuchi 1995; Svelby 1997) it was clear that the new standards should enable criminal justice social work services to enhance research-based practice through standardised processes amenable to quantitative measurement ('what works?'), set alongside a knowledge or theory-based practice development focused on outcomes with a higher degree of differentiation in practices ('why and how it works').

The concept of the knowledge organisation emphasises the critical importance of an orientation towards desired outcomes. In practice the supervision of offenders often consists of solving the problems in an offender's life. This activity takes up a great deal of a worker's time and can be mistaken for creating results (Fritz 1989). Problem-solving is taking action to have something go away. Creating results is taking action to have something come into being. Problems can be solved as a means of achieving a goal but their solutions are rarely the goal itself. Problem-solving can encourage a short-term perspective that hinders a strategic approach to sustainable change.

An outcome orientation requires that all processes and activities undertaken in offender supervision should be designed to achieve or support the achievement of the desired outcomes. As worker time and expertise are scarce resources, those processes and activities that do not perform these functions should be eliminated. Furthermore, practitioners and managers need to think systemically and plan strategically so that an activity in one area of practice does not create barriers in other areas.

This systemic and strategic approach depends upon a single point of accountability, in this context a case manager who is responsible for the overall process of supervision and for solving any problems that hinder progress towards planned outcomes. Standards of practice should support the case worker in these responsibilities. Specifically standards should:

- Represent the best, easiest way to achieve outcomes.
- Reflect and sustain current knowledge and expertise.
- Provide a way of measuring performance.
- Provide evidence for the effectiveness of practices.
- Provide a means of both maintaining and improving quality and effectiveness.
- Provide a means for preventing and correcting errors and inconsistencies in practice.
- Identify required competences and training goals.
- Create criteria for performance management and inspections.

The EFQM excellence model (www.efqm.org) was adopted as a structure for the new national outcomes and standards. This model integrates leadership, the deployment of people, policy, strategy, partnerships and resources, the implementation of processes and the achievement of results in a dynamic framework. The fundamental concepts of excellence in this model were considered highly relevant to the project of revising the standards. They include:

- Results orientation
- Customer focus
- Partnership development
- Leadership and constancy of purpose
- People development and involvement
- Management by processes and facts
- Continuous learning, innovation and improvement
- Public responsibility.

Having reviewed the literature on effective practice, policy and management, it was necessary to inquire into human and social capital through consulting criminal justice social workers, managers and stakeholders. Nine regional conferences were conducted to consult criminal justice social work staff throughout Scotland; 316 managers and practitioners participated. In addition to criminal justice social work staff, a wide range of stakeholders (including offenders, police, sentencers, social work inspectors, Scottish government officials, and the voluntary sector) connected to the criminal justice system and to social work were consulted.

The consultations took the form of focus groups or one-to-one interviews and were structured around the following areas:

- Views on the current standards.
- The outcomes of criminal justice social work with offenders.
- How standards can encourage the active participation of offenders in achieving outcomes.
- Views on the 'four Rs' model.
- What standards should say about court reports, assessment, the range of court orders that criminal justice social workers supervise, prison work, the value of one-to-one work, and programmes.
- The role of the case manager.
- Should the standards attempt to define what an effective working relationship between the worker and offender should be?
- How should compliance and enforcement be regulated by standards?
- How can standards influence other organisations to offer services to support the reintegration or resettlement of offenders?
- How detailed do the standards need to be to assure quality of practice and accountability?

Offenders emphasised the need for practical support and rehabilitation programmes specifically for addictions. They were not particularly interested in the detail of content.

Interestingly, there were no significant differences of opinions expressed about the content and structure of the new standards. The most prevalent comment from all parties was that standards provided a clear and readily accessible structure and framework for practice. People wanted new standards to be concise and structured. The combination of general principles and standards supplemented by more specific and detailed guidance on the various court orders was seen as very useful.

Practitioners did not want prescriptive standards that leave no room for flexibility and discretion. Given constraints on resources partnership was considered vital, and something that should be supported by the standards. Responses also made reference to the need for the standards to be reflective of contemporary research into effective practice, particularly in relation to matching assessed risk with intensity of contact and service.

The most prevalent view from the consultations was that levels of offending should be reduced, that the public should be protected and there should be increasing levels of social inclusion (such as improvements in housing and employment) for offenders. Finally, increased levels of public confidence in the management of offenders and meeting more of the needs of the victim were also regarded as being important outcomes. Overall, there was a strong level of agreement that outcomes should be measured in terms of what difference the service makes to the offender, rather than what actions the service has undertaken.

The 'four Rs' model (reparation, reintegration, rehabilitation, and restrictions) was considered a useful framework for the new standards. Those consulted were in strong agreement that there should ideally be a relationship with levels of risk where low risk offenders would be more likely to receive interventions aimed at the levels of reparation and reintegration, and higher risk offenders should be more likely to receive additional interventions based on rehabilitation and restriction.

There was a range of comments that highlighted similarities between the government's notion of 'payback' and reparation where the victim and general public should also perceive value in the work and consequently should have more positive perceptions of supervision. In addition, many groups stressed that acts of reparation should be delivered in a way that is consistent with pro-social modelling (Trotter 1999).

Reintegration was also strongly supported. Comments relating to the value of social capital and enhancing social inclusion were endorsed by all groups. There was strong belief among those consulted that offenders are members of society who should have equal access to resources such as housing, health services, education, training and employment. In addition, the value of relationships with family, friends, peers and support networks were also seen as being necessary for reintegration.

In relation to rehabilitation the aim of promoting change through effective programmes was endorsed, with *caveats* relating to public expectations and the availability of resources. The tailoring of rehabilitation interventions to the levels of risk and needs was supported.

Restrictions were seen as being legitimate in relation to a minority of cases where consideration of public safety is paramount. It was felt that the use of restrictions should relate to the offender's risk level and be limited to those at high risk of serious harm to others. Custody was seen as providing the opportunity for constructive work (such as accessing programmes or education) in addition to having a punishment function. People also emphasised the need for transparent and defensible decisions to be made when restrictions are being imposed.

The use of structured risk and needs assessment tools received considerable support within consultations. There was a clear consensus that the levels of interventions for individual offenders should be based on their assessed level of risk, needs and protective factors. The role of risk assessments in providing a defensible base for decision-making and resource allocation was also commented on by several groups. In relation to assessments for courts, there should be a standard format and timescales. Language should be jargon-free and courts should be given options rather than recommendations.

Those consulted valued one-to-one work and wished it to be endorsed in the new standards and share the levels of rigour expected in group work. For instance, comments from the consultation included recommendations that there should be a clear structure and plans for work; clear objectives with measurable outcomes; adequate levels of training and support. The pro-social modelling approach (Trotter 1999) was specifically mentioned by a number of the groups as having a very valuable role in one-to-one work.

The use of structured, accredited programmes based on cognitive behavioural methods, which addressed the criminogenic needs of offenders and was responsive to their learning styles, was supported by those consulted. Specific concerns were raised by some about the 'contamination' effect of group work and also the need to ensure a high completion rate.

The majority of those consulted were in favour of increased discretion regarding non-compliance and the enforcement of orders particularly on the basis of the risk that the offender posed to the public. However, consultations with representatives from the court maintained that it was for the court to decide upon non-compliance, not the supervising officer.

The offenders who were consulted stressed the importance of the consistent availability of the supervising worker and access to the resources they needed for their rehabilitation and reintegration. They explained that the motivation for change was often fragile and short-lived. So interventions need to be immediate and accessible. In relation to the qualities they regarded as necessary in a good social worker, their answers were consistent with the pro-social modelling approach.

The group strongly endorsed the view that they alone could stop their offending: 'no one else can do it for you'. They indicated that their desistance would be closely linked to their motivation to desist, social support from family and friends, interventions in the areas of mental health and substance use services, and positive ways of coping with loneliness and boredom. They indicated that employment in the form of mundane, low-paid jobs did not encourage desistance. They also said that until they overcame their addictions well-paid jobs might lead them to be tempted to buy drugs.

The process of balancing and integrating capitals

The consultation process and the preparation of literature reviews on effective practices, on policy and on organisational development resulted in a substantial amount of data on intellectual, political, organisational, human and social capital relevant to the task of revising the standards. This knowledge had to be transformed into a concise document that criminal justice social work services staff and their stakeholders could understand, support and use to deliver effective supervision of offenders.

Capital is not evenly or equitably distributed. In any enterprise those who control the most powerful forms of capital tend to dominate. This can be dysfunctional in relation to the achievement of outcomes. For example, effective supervision of offenders can be hindered by:

- An overemphasis on risk management and enforcement, due to powerful political interests reducing the impact of intellectually rigorous rehabilitation programmes.

- An over-zealous managerialist approach (organisational capital) deskilling and reducing the commitment of practitioners (human capital).

- Disregarding the social capital of the offender through too much focus on his or her human capital.

Consequently, in addition to engaging appropriate forms of capital to create and sustain the revised national standards, it was necessary to strive to balance and integrate these capitals so that no one interest or perspective dominated. This was achieved through a steering group representing a range of interests (and forms of capital). The steering group included the Scottish government, the Association of Directors of Social Work, the Risk Management Agency, the voluntary organisations connected to community justice, the community justice areas, the judiciary, and the prison service.

The literature reviews and the report of the consultations were presented to this group. The discussions that followed clarified the group's thinking and priorities so that the drafting of the new standards could begin. The steering group scrutinised every sentence of each draft. Each point or suggestion was listened to with respect and through dialogue a consensus generally emerged. This was a slow, methodical process. Eventually the fourth draft was approved.

Conclusion

The overall aim of the new standards is to gain and sustain the public's confidence in the criminal justice social work services to contribute to the values of:

- *Safety* – by maintaining community safety through protecting the public from serious harm;
- *Justice* – by holding offenders accountable for their actions in order to reduce the risk of reoffending;
- *Social inclusion* – by supporting offenders' efforts to desist from offending through their social inclusion.

Table 21.2 summarises the structure and content of the National Outcomes and Standards.

A separate chapter of the standards document covers each practice (assessment, case management, restrictions, rehabilitation, reintegration, reparation, supporting resources and leadership and management). Each chapter connects the practice with the outcomes and sets out clear and concise expectations in the form of required standards and principles of best practice. The document is concise and much briefer than the previous national standards. The next stage will be to ensure that all staff and stakeholders are aware of

Table 21.2 National Outcomes and Standards: structure and content.

Overall aim	Outcomes	Practice framework and core interventions	Supporting resources	Leadership and management
Public confidence in criminal justice social work services	Public protection and community safety Reduction of reoffending Social inclusion to support disistance from offending	**Assessment** *Case management:* the management of compliance and the active engagement of individuals in processes of change. *Interventions:* 1 restrictions 2 rehabilitation 3 reparation 4 reintegration	Practitioners with the necessary discipline, knowledge and skills to engage and manage offenders towards positive outcomes. A range of resources provided by partnership organisations, the community the families	**Managers' responsibilities** 1 Strategic direction 2 The efficient deployment of finance and resources 3 Managing partnership organisations 4 Managing performance and developing staff 5 Assuring quality 6 Evaluating the outcomes of services

these standards and are prepared for their implementation. The new National Outcomes and Standards document will be supported by guidance on each of criminal justice social work's statutory duties.

The new National Outcomes and Standards for the criminal justice social work services in Scotland have been designed to support the underlying political priorities in Scotland, to apply the most appropriate research-based knowledge to appropriate practices, and to support the supervision of offenders with committed and competent staff, with partnerships and with effective leadership and management. Time and further research will demonstrate whether this integration of political, intellectual, organisational, human and social capitals is successful.

At the time of writing the revised National Outcomes and Standards have not yet been published. The intention is to implement them by the end of 2010.

Notes

1 For an excellent account of criminal justice social work in Scotland see McIvor and McNeill (2007).
2 The team commissioned to conduct the revision consisted of Tim Chapman, a criminal justice consultant, Shadd Maruna, Queens University Belfast, and Mark Penman, an independent forensic psychologist.
3 This literature review was completed by Shadd Maruna.

References

Andrews, D. and Bonta, J. (1998) *The Psychology of Criminal Conduct*, 2nd edn. Cincinnati, OH: Anderson Publishing.
Andrews, D. and Bonta, J. (2003) *The Psychology of Criminal Conduct*, 3rd edn. Cincinnati, OH: Anderson Publishing.
Bourdieu, P. (1986) 'The forms of capital', in J.G. Richardson (ed.) *The Handbook of Theory and Research for the Sociology of Education*. New York: Greenwood.
Coleman, J. (1990) *Equality and Achievement in Education*. Boulder, CO: Westview Press.
Edvinsson, L. and Malone, M.S. (1997) *Intellectual Capital*. London: HarperCollins.
Farrall, S. (2002) *Rethinking What Works with Offenders*. Cullompton: Willan Publishing.
Fritz, R. (1989) *The Path of Least Resistance*. New York: Fawcett-Columbine.
Hollin, C. (1995) 'The meaning and implications of "programme integrity"', in J. McGuire (ed.) *What Works: Reducing Reoffending*. Chichester: Wiley.
Huntingford, T. (1992) 'The introduction of 100% central government funding for social work with offenders', *Local Government Policy Making*, 19: 36–43.
Justice Department (2001) *Criminal Justice Social Work Services: National Priorities for 2001–2002 and Onwards*. Edinburgh: Scottish Executive.
Kanter, R.M. (2004) *Confidence: How Winning Streaks and Losing Streaks Begin and End*. London: Random House.
Laub, J. and Sampson, R. (2003) *Shared Beginnings, Divergent Lives: Delinquent Boys to Age 70*. Cambridge, MA: Harvard University Press.
Liebling, A. and Maruna, S. (eds) (2006) *The Effects of Imprisonment*. Cullompton: Willan Publishing.
Lipsey, M., Landenberger, N. and Wilson, S. (2007) *Effects of Cognitive-Behavioral Programs for Criminal Offenders*. Center for Evaluation Research and Methodology: Vanderbilt Institute for Public Policy Studies.
Maruna, S. (2001) *Making Good*. Washington, DC: American Psychological Association.

McCulloch, P. (2005) 'Probation, social context and desistance: retracing the relationship', *Probation Journal*, 52 (1): 8–22.

McIvor, G. (1998) 'Prosocial modelling and legitimacy: lessons from a study in community service', in *Prosocial Modelling and Legitimacy*, Clarke Hall Day Conference, University of Cambridge Institute of Criminology.

McIvor, G. and McNeill, F. (2007) 'Probation in Scotland: past, present and future', in L. Gelsthorpe and R. Morgan (eds) *Handbook of Probation*. Cullompton: Willan Publishing.

McMurran, M. (ed.) (2002) *Motivating Offenders to Change*. Chichester: Wiley.

McNeill, F. (2009) Towards Effective Practice in Offender Supervision. Glasgow: Scottish Centre for Crime and Justice Research

McNeill, F. and Whyte, B. (2007) *Reducing Offending: Social Work and Community Justice in Scotland*. Cullompton: Willan Publishing.

McNeill, F., Batchelor, S., Burnett, R. and Knox J. (2005) *21st Century Social Work. Reducing Re-offending: Key Practice Skills*. Edinburgh: Scottish Executive.

Nonaka, I. and Takeuchi, H. (1995) *The Knowledge Creating Company: How Japanese Companies Create the Dynamics of Innovation*. New York: Oxford University Press.

Paterson, F. and Tombs, J. (1998) *Social Work and Criminal Justice, Vol. 1: The Policy Context*. Edinburgh: HMSO.

Putnam, R.D. (2000) *Bowling Alone: The Collapse and Revival of American Community*. New York: Simon and Schuster.

Raynor, P. (2004) 'Rehabilitative and reintegrative approaches', in A. Bottoms, S. Rex and G. Robinson (eds) *Alternatives to Prison: Options for an Insecure Society*. Cullompton: Willan Publishing.

Rex, S. and Gelsthorpe, L. (2002) 'The role of community service in reducing offending: evaluating pathfinder projects in the UK', *Howard Journal*, 41 (4): 311–25.

Robinson, G. and McNeill, F. (2004) *Purposes matter: the ends of probation*, in G. Mair (ed.) *What Matters in Probation*. Cullompton: Willan Publishing.

Scottish Executive (2006a) *Reducing Reoffending: National Strategy for Offender Management*. Edinburgh: Scottish Executive.

Scottish Executive (2006b) *Changing Lives: Report of the 21st Century Review Group*. Edinburgh: Scottish Executive.

Scottish Government (2007) *Reforming and Revitalising: Report of the Review of Community Penalties*. Edinburgh: Scottish Government.

Scottish Office (1998) *Community Sentencing: The Tough Option: Review of Criminal Justice Social Work Services*. Edinburgh: Scottish Office Home Department.

Sherman, L. and Strang, H. (2007) *Restorative Justice: The Evidence*. London: Smith Institute.

Social Work Services Group (1991) *National Objectives and Standards for Social Work Services in the Criminal Justice System*. Edinburgh: Social Work Services Group.

Stewart, T.A. (1997) *Intellectual Capital*. New York: Doubleday

Svelby, K.E. (1997) *The New Organizational Wealth: Managing and Measuring Knowledge-Based Assets*. San Francisco: Berrett-Koehler

Trotter, C. (1999) *Working with Involuntary Clients*. London: Sage.

Chapter 22

The purposes of supervision: practitioner and policy perpectives in England and Wales

John Deering

Introduction

This chapter considers the views of probation practitioners about the aims and purposes of supervision and their own practice. Drawing on an empirical study, it argues that this sample of practitioners sees supervision as being about individual change facilitated by a professional relationship based on rapport, empathy and professional discretion and that they try to practise based on these principles. This relationship is seen as holding most hope for positive change in offenders' behaviour and understood as involving far more than a simple management function. I conclude that the everyday practice of probation supervision (at least as represented by this group of practitioners) has not moved as far away from its origins as has sometimes been assumed. While this chapter covers practitioner behaviour in England and Wales, it has implications for the wider corrections debate in terms of the possibility of a gap between government policy and intentions and 'real practice' carried out by practitioners regarding themselves as professionals in the human services. This in turn throws light upon macro level theories of the new penality (for example Feeley and Simon 1992) which see such correctional services practice moving from rehabilitation and reform to one that has largely given up on transformative ambitions to concentrate on offender management and control.

Throughout this chapter, I compare these practitioner accounts with the views of government and the changes in official policy towards the service and its purposes in recent decades. These discourses have emphasised late modern ideas of risk, offender management, public protection and punishment. The chapter concludes by considering the extent of any gap between the views of government and the views of practitioners; a gap that may increase as the National Offender Management Service (NOMS)[1] evolves and moves towards full contestability.

Theoretical and policy context

Theories of late modernity and of the new penality have been well rehearsed and discussed over the past decade or so (see Feeley and Simon 1992; Garland 2001; Kemshall 2003; Rose 2000). Alongside these accounts, mezzo and macro level theories of the rise of risk, the move to the management of offenders, and the managerialism and modernisation of public services (Kemshall 2003; Senior *et al.* 2007; Newburn 2003) have together formed a dominant picture of the aims and practices of the probation service in England and Wales. The service is now said to be based on risk assessment and management and punishment in the community, rather than on rehabilitation and transformation as it has traditionally been regarded, although the aim of rehabilitation has never been abandoned completely (Vanstone 2004; Home Office 2001). Most recently, the aims of probation within NOMS have been declared to be to 'punish, help, change and control' offenders (Straw 2009).

The changes in government intentions and aims for the service have been reflected in attempts to change practitioner behaviour, to the extent that the professional training for probation officers was removed from social work so as to produce practitioners who would focus on the New Labour government's priorities of protecting the public and crime reduction (Straw 1997). *Via* a top-down process of management pressure and audit (Senior *et al.* 2007: 30), practice is generally regarded as having fallen into line behind the desires of government and senior management. Thus practitioners are now said to be 'offender managers', charged with assessing and managing risks, enhancing offenders' motivation to attend accredited programmes, gate-keeping access to services to address certain criminogenic needs and enforcing orders rigorously with a reduced attention to individual needs and circumstances[2]. Where any personal, one-to-one intervention does occur, this is said to be exclusively based in a form of cognitive behaviourism often reduced to the correction of individuals' perceived cognitive deficits.

Against this background, this chapter looks at the attitudes and reported practices of probation practitioners and trainees in four probation areas in 2005–06. The study on which it is based intended to investigate whether or not there could be discerned any difference between the picture of practice described above and what for the purposes of this chapter is called 'real practice'; meaning what occurs between a practitioner and an individual subject to statutory supervision. This is still generally carried out on a one-to-one basis behind closed doors and thus cannot be directly observed or monitored by management; potentially it can therefore allow for a range of different approaches to the supervisory process. Therefore the aim of the study was, and the aim of this chapter is, to attempt to answer the following questions: Do changes represent government and management rhetoric or reality in policy terms? Are they to any extent resisted by practitioners? In what ways? To what extent? What do practitioners describe as their 'practice and belief, values and culture'? What is *actual* practice? How can real practice be revealed, and can baselines be determined to consider questions of change or continuity?

Since the completion of the fieldwork, probation areas and trusts have continued to be audited closely about their enforcement and breach practices, with the attainment of minimum standards being linked to budgets. As Jack Straw (2009: 3) notes, '95% of offenders are being brought back to court for breaching their orders; in 1999 this was a mere 44%'. The government has also sought to encompass its range of aims for the service, those now being to 'punish, help, change and control' offenders, and it is generally argued here that with respect to probation policy discourses, there is much evidence of the kinds of changes that reflect theories of late modernity, new penality, risk and managerialism. In terms of the role of the practitioner, this is also subject to much conjecture as to how it may eventually emerge into the light. Although the NOMS 'Offender Management Model' (NOMS 2006) makes much of a person-centred practice and acknowledges that a meaningful and effective professional relationship is central to successful supervision, the actual plans for the 'offender manager' role outlined in the model have been criticised as possibly resulting in that relationship being a distant one, with the offender manager being no more than a sequencer of interventions, responsible for enforcement but providing little or no 'offending work' (Raynor and Maguire 2006).

The study

As mentioned above, the study was carried out in 2005–06 in four probation areas in England and Wales, and sought to get at 'real practice' as well as the attitudes, values and beliefs of practitioners. Largely a qualitative study, it included interviews with probation officers (POs) as well as probation service officers (PSOs), a formally unqualified grade of practitioners who had come to operate in a manner largely indistinguishable from probation officers with those assessed by management as being of 'lower risk of harm' (but not necessarily of reoffending) in that they had full responsibility for all aspects of supervision, including enforcement.

The sample was a relatively large one of the target population (practitioners engaged in supervision in both high and medium/low risk of harm cases in two probation areas) and included 51 respondents (34 female, 17 male), 35 POs, 11 PSOs and five middle managers. Respondents had a wide range of service in probation (ranging from a few months to more than 30 years) and there were examples of POs trained under three different qualification routes. A questionnaire was also used with 103 trainee POs from four probation areas.

Data were collected through semi-structured interviews with practitioners and some managers, a Likert-scaled attitudinal questionnaire that was designed to reveal attitudes to a range of policy and practice developments, focus groups, and an examination of files and pre-sentence court reports. Use was made of NVivo to facilitate the systematic analysis of interviews *via* the coding of themes identified both deductively from literature and inductively from the initial analysis. This made it possible to analyse sub-samples to consider differences in attitudes, beliefs, values and reported practices. Although the numbers completing the Likert scales were relatively small, chi-square significance testing *via* SPSS was utilised to compare sub-groups (see below). Of particular interest was whether any differences might emerge between responses from qualified POs and unqualified PSOs; between POs qualified under previous social work training arrangements and those more recently trained; between longer serving practitioners and the less experienced.

Results: emerging themes

Perhaps the first point to be emphasised is the overall homogeneity of the data: there were no statistically significant[3] differences in the attitudes and reported practices of any of the sub-groups and this led to a tentative conclusion that practitioners as represented by this sample had a unified approach to practice. This had elements of what might be called 'traditional' probation attitudes and practice, but ones that took cognisance of and had to operate in a very changed overall situation and structure – what Bourdieu (1977) might describe as the individual 'habitus' and the organisational or professional 'field', a phenomenon recently reported upon concerning the practice of pre-sentence reporting in Scotland (McNeill *et al.* 2009).

In coming to such conclusions, it is acknowledged that the difficulty in establishing baselines means that previous practice can only be inferred from theoretical writings and the few existing empirical studies of practice. It is also the case that the results discussed here about actual practice are based on reflections on or accounts of practice, as it was not possible to observe actual supervision sessions. Instead, respondents were asked to describe their practice in real-life examples and emerging ideas and themes from interviews were debated within focus groups as a method of confirming (or disputing) the extent to which they represented reality. Case files and pre-sentence reports (PSRs) were also studied to reveal further insights into practice.

For the purposes of my analysis, I took a baseline of 'traditional' practice that employed a case-work approach with a treatment model. This model involved expert assessment and the employment of a range of interventions aimed at assisting an individual address what were regarded as those problems and attitudes seen as at the root of his or her offending (Vanstone 2004). The aim of this approach was a resolution of these problems and a subsequent reduction in or cessation of offending. This image of practice was contested from time to time. For example in the wake of the 'nothing works' assertions of the 1970s (see Lipton *et al.* 1975) government was said to have lost faith in rehabilitation (see McGuire 2001) and the proponents of the 'non-treatment paradigm' (Bottoms and McWilliams 1979) argued that the service should be collaborative, regarding clients as experts in their own behaviour. In this latter model, rather than offer 'treatment', intervention should try to remove barriers to individuals living non-offending lives. However, it remains unclear how much practitioners were influenced by either 'nothing works' or alternative models for practice and it has been argued that they generally continued to aim to reduce future reoffending offering practical help, advice and advocacy, but also working on attitudes and values (Vanstone 2004). Thus it is not argued here that practice previously employed unconditional social work assistance to offenders that was not rooted in trying to reduce reoffending. Such practice also took account of issues of risk of reoffending and harm and of cooperation with the supervisory process. However, this was considered in terms of 'care and control' (Raynor 1985) rather than the current language of risk.

Overall beliefs about purpose

In *précis*, the findings suggest a belief in the need for an assessment and intervention practice in which individual needs, problems and attitudes should be addressed in a personalised manner. While issues of risk of harm were important, these were seen more as a means to initial assessment; the overarching aim of supervision was behavioural change, not risk management.

The assessment of offenders

The views and practices about assessment discussed here were taken from practitioners involved in the preparation of pre-sentence reports (PSRs). As part of this process, the probation officer is required to complete an OASys assessment which is central to the government's desire to promote 'scientific' assessment of offenders and offending (Home Office 2002). The writing of reports to assist sentencing has a significant history, but to summarise, its origins lie in an initial phase (the Social Enquiry Report) of clinical assessment left entirely to the practitioner and their particular theories and preferences, followed, mainly from the 1990s (and the introduction of the PSR), by an increasing attempt by government and management to influence assessment *via* the development of assessment tools, of which OASys is an example that combines clinical and actuarial methods. Most recently, these have been intended to help deliver offender management and the protection of the public *via* risk of harm assessment (for example, Burnett *et al*. 2007).

The overall conclusion is that respondents believed that individuals' offending could be analysed in terms of causal factors and that it was possible to identify a 'treatment' plan that could be put in place as part of probation supervision. The aim of supervision would be to address relevant problems and criminogenic needs in order to reduce the risk of reoffending. The assessor was generally seen as the expert, but there was also discussion of the importance of using the individual's own insights into their behaviour as part of the assessment and thus some hint of a partnership approach and the influence of a 'desistance' approach (see Farrall 2002). Examples of replies to an open question, *'What do you consider to be the purpose of a pre-sentence assessment?'* included:

> The purpose is for the probation service to assist the court in providing a suitable sentence for that individual, to enable the individual to effectively address both their offending behaviour and their criminogenic needs that are linked. (Female probation officer, three years' experience)

> ... what I explain to the offender is that the reason he is there, is because of the nature of the offence, the magistrates need to know more about your background and the probation service will prepare a detailed report about your offending behaviour, social circumstances, employment, finances, etc., to help us to come up with a proposal ... the magistrates may have a different opinion, but we can look at the proposal we think is the best sentence that would look at, stop you reoffending again in the future. (Female senior probation officer, 15 years' experience)

The aim was clearly to be forward-looking and transformative, with a general anti-custody sentiment being expressed in some proposals to courts. Custody was seen as unlikely to provide the opportunities for change and to reinforce negative aspects of behaviour. There was no apparent appetite for 'punishment' as such, although there did exist an acknowledgement that custody (and punishment) would occur given the nature of certain offences:

> [I'm] trying to keep down tariff, I've never proposed custody, that's not our role, but I would say due to the seriousness I haven't considered a community sentence. (Female probation officer, 14 years' experience)

The question of the protection of the public was, in the majority of PSRs, clearly to be addressed by the reduction of reoffending *via* supervision rather than by incarceration. In terms of intervention, the pre-eminence of cognitive behaviourism and the wider 'what works' agenda was apparent (McGuire 2001), as most proposals for court discussed behavioural change *via* improved thinking skills and changes in attitudes. However, it was also the case that the need for general support and assistance was recognised, and in this way there may have been elements of a 'desistance' approach to practice being expressed, although not expressed directly in these terms (e.g. Maruna *et al.* 2004; Farrall 2002).

There was little to support Feeley and Simon's (1992) notion of the pre-eminence of actuarial assessment and the categorisation of individuals in terms of their risk of harm. Here, something of a contradiction is apparent. Although when asked directly about it, practitioners saw risk of harm assessment as central to practice, when talking more generally about practice, it did seem a little less important than risk of reoffending, as it was here that perhaps the purpose of probation supervision was fundamentally seen as lying. Thus, as with other studies, Feeley and Simon's thesis was seen as providing something of a background and context to practice, but certainly no dominant discourse, nor was the impression of the new penality and risk dominating respondents' thinking and practice, as implied by some theorists (for example, Nash and Ryan 2003). However, practitioners did identify a tendency towards 'up-tariffing' (the categorisation of individuals as 'medium' rather than 'low' risk and 'high' rather than 'medium' risk) by practitioners concerned to 'cover their backs' in a culture of audit and blame. This has also been identified as a by-product of OASys, due to authors being required to formally record their risk assessments (Fitzgibbon 2008).

Finally, with regard to OASys, in general terms respondents were positive about its use but not to the extent of giving a 'ringing endorsement'. It was seen as giving a useful structure to an assessment interview in that it ensured that all issues that might relate to an individual's offending would be investigated. It was also felt by some to be a prompt to their thinking about the extent and significance of particular problems, attitudes or criminogenic needs. However, there was also a feeling expressed that it did little beyond this and that it may have ended up only confirming what the assessor knew already. Thus, some respondents felt that OASys did not lead the process, but rather followed, backed up and confirmed it, which echoes similar findings with a tool in use in some probation areas prior to OASys (Robinson 2002) and in Scotland (McNeill *et al.* 2009). Examples of responses included:

> It is helpful, because you've got it all in sections and specific things you need to cover. (Female Probation Officer, two years' experience)

Nothing new about it, we always asked the same questions, it's just formalising what a good PSR would have covered. (Female Probation Officer, 14 years' experience)

The enforcement of orders and licences

Central to new penality thinking and government policy since the 1990s is enforcement, and more rigid and process-based systems, requiring a return to court after a second unacceptable absence in 12 months (three in the case of licences). These developments were very much current at the time of this fieldwork; in the introduction to the 2000 National Standards the Probation Minister Paul Boateng had stated that the probation service was a 'law enforcement agency' (Home Office 2000). Furthermore, the Criminal Justice Act 2003 was intended to make community sentences 'tougher' in enforcement terms. The effect of these developments was an increase in breach proceedings for non-compliance in England and Wales in the period prior to this fieldwork (Murphy 2004).

While respondents acknowledged the importance of the protection of the public from serious harm, this was seen as being of major importance in a limited number of cases. Enforcement overall was regarded as a general accountability to the courts and the promotion of the engagement of the individual offender in supervision. Replies to the initial open question, *'What is the purpose of enforcement?'* included:

I suppose it's to show to society that we do do something ... to show the government that we are cost effective, that we take things seriously and also the public as well. (Female probation officer, 3 years' experience)

I think the purpose of enforcement is to encourage people to stick to the order so that they can effect the change. (Female probation officer, 26 years' experience)

Practice was seen as needing to be based around practitioner discretion and not about the routine initiation of breach proceedings for unacceptable absences and thus not simply about control (Rose 2000). The issue of individual professional discretion was crucial to this process and might be described as based on the dynamic tension of care and control (Burnett *et al.* 2007, Mair and Canton 2007). Breach was seen as legitimate after an effective withdrawal of consent and was seen as not usually changing or damaging the relationship between the offender and practitioner:

> Given the situation of many people in the real world, strict enforcement is a nonsense, you need to operate judgement, depending on the individual and your assessment of where they are at the time. (Male probation officer, 15 years' experience)

> I do use my judgement, to allow compliance. It keeps them working with you. If they are not working with you, I'm more likely to breach. If they are working with you, I'll be more flexible. (Female probation service officer, three years' experience)

Punishment was acknowledged by a small minority of respondents as being one of the purposes of enforcement, but usually it was seen as a by-product of the main aim of accountability. Overall, respondents were consistent in their views and practices; the only differences emerging were related directly to job role rather than fundamental belief, in that those in the high risk teams were more inclined to breach routinely due to possible implications for the protection of the public.

Views expressed in interview by respondents mainly coincided with data from case files, which revealed a varying degree of discretion in operation, but also a lack of detail about why absences might be regarded as acceptable or otherwise. The following is an extract from notes taken from one section of the file reading:

> One case [from 12] kept all appointments. Ten cases had acceptable absences. The decision to accept these absences rested with the practitioner, mainly without reference to the team manager. Explanations for absences were accepted routinely without any evidence being provided (or apparently requested) and it appeared to be acceptable for individual offenders to telephone beforehand to rearrange appointments. There were five cases where two or more unacceptable absences were recorded but without breach proceedings being commenced. In three cases breach was commenced and concluded.

Overall there was a commitment of respondents to a clinical approach and professional discretion which based decisions about the acceptability of absences in individual circumstances. This was seen as not compromising fair treatment, although the possibility of such a consequence was acknowledged. Implicit in this was the belief that a professional approach would allow differential treatment that was not unfair or discriminatory and was based upon wider considerations of justice (as opposed to a narrow law enforcement approach) and consideration of the ultimate purpose of supervision, the successful engagement of the individual and behavioural change.

Supervision practice

As mentioned above, it has been widely accepted that after the 'nothing works' era and the 'death of rehabilitation', successive governments had begun to exert increasing control over the probation service, with a view to changing practitioner behaviour towards punishment in the community, the protection of the public *via* risk assessment and risk and offender management (see, for example, Newburn 2003; Hudson 2003), although it has been argued that practitioners continued to work to some extent at least in more traditional ways (Vanstone 2004). However, for this sample of practitioners, the fundamental basis of their work was the effective professional relationship, which was made up of rapport, empathy, the setting of boundaries and the maintenance of a professional distance. A further element was pro-social modelling and thus the overall picture described has some parallels with the 'core correctional practices' regarded as essential for effective supervision: the effective use of authority; pro-social modelling, and a genuine and effective working relationship (Dowden and Andrews 2004). Responses to the question 'what is the nature of a professional relationship between you and an individual offender?' included:

> They are aware of responsibilities of being on probation, what I have to do re enforcement, but balanced by my interest in them and what goes on after they leave this office. [It's] definitely more than an enforcement/management relationship. (Male probation officer, 7 years' experience)

> You have to balance the friendliness and stuff. On one extreme, they're not going to tell you anything, but if you're too much the other way then that's when it becomes too difficult to breach and things like that. It's about striking a happy medium, I think. (Female probation service officer, four years' experience)

The purpose of the practitioner role was to engage with individual offenders in a humanistic way that was intended to motivate, encourage and facilitate behavioural change. Thus the ultimate aim was the reduction of reoffending, which appeared synonymous with rehabilitation. It is important to note that while respondents acknowledged that part of their role was 'offender management' it was much more than that: they clearly regarded themselves as having a 'therapeutic' interventionist role that was uniquely theirs and for the majority it was this that had brought them into the probation service. The protection of the public was also a prime aim and this was seen as most likely to be achieved *via* a reduction in reoffending and, in a smaller number of more serious cases, by more law enforcement measures such as the use of recalls to prison and the management of offenders *via* the MAPPA (multi-agency public protection arrangements) process. Examples of responses about purposes were:

> Managing risk, public protection, rehabilitation. These are all linked together – the point of this job is to reduce crime and reoffending and you can't do this without some form of rehabilitation. (Male probation officer, two years' experience)

> My purpose is to help in the rehabilitation of offenders and to stop them reoffending ... It would be good if they could put us out of business ... that should be our aim. (Male probation service officer, one year's experience)

Practitioner values

Discussions of the attitudes of practitioners to changes in government policy within the literature have tended to be theoretical and sometimes speculative, rather than being based on empirical explorations of actual practitioner opinion. For example, Williams (1995) argued for the retention of 'social work' values within the service and it has also been argued that service values should be based upon the notions of restorative justice, community justice and human rights (see Nellis and Gelsthorpe 2003). Stress has also been placed on the quality of personal relationships with supervisees as a vehicle to promote the latter's ability to desist from crime (Raynor 2004; McNeill 2006). The view of the probation service trade union and professional association in England and Wales, Napo, has been that crime has its origins in social injustice, emphasising the need for respect and trust when working with perpetrators and victims; open and fair treatment for all; empowerment of individuals in order to reduce the risk of harm to themselves and others; promotion of equality and anti-discrimination; promotion of the rights of both perpetrators and victims; and building on individuals' strengths as a vehicle for change (Napo 2006: 5).

Empirical studies of professional attitudes and values have been rare, but perhaps indicate the way in which practitioners are influenced by official attempts to redefine the values and purposes of the organisation. One study in the early 1990s (Humphrey and Pease 1992) did not discuss values and attitudes directly, but reported that probation officers defined purpose and effectiveness in terms of diverting from custody. Later in the decade the 'holy trinity' of public protection, rehabilitation (defined as reducing reoffending) and enforcement (Robinson and McNeill 2004: 286) were identified by practitioners as legitimate goals for practice, although they did insist that the former two might be best achieved *via* a good working relationship and attention being paid to the social context of offending.

The views expressed by my respondents are summarised here and reflect a more 'traditional' humanistic approach to working with offenders. Views expressed included a belief in the ability of offenders to change; and that this is facilitated by an empathic professional relationship; the causes of crime were regarded in the main as the result of personal problems and disadvantage; the importance of a non-discriminatory approach; 'disapproval of the behaviour, not the individual'; individualised intervention not aggregate management; professional discretion, not rigid application of rules; a culture opposed to the setting of 'targets' for certain interventions; and a general anti-custody sentiment. Responses to some of these issues included:

I couldn't do the job if I couldn't hold to the fundamental core of respect for the individual and a belief in people's ability to change. (Female probation officer, 14 years' experience)

... they don't want to be leading the lifestyles that they are. I don't believe people are inherently bad and they offend from choice. I think they want to change those factors. (Male probation officer, two years' experience)

I came in to help people, that's what I came in to do. Although it's not the only thing in the job, I still feel that is very much there for me and as soon as I feel I'm not doing that, I'll leave.

463

(Female probation officer, two years' experience)
I keep hold of the fact that it's the behaviour that I dislike, that is unacceptable, not the individual. (Female probation officer, 18 years' experience)

Thus there was little to suggest an adherence to new penality thinking, despite the acknowledgement of the relative importance of risk and enforcement. In the main, practitioners had joined the service to offer constructive 'help' in the broadest sense to try and facilitate personal change, a reduction in personal problems and a reduction in reoffending, which together were seen as 'rehabilitation'. These findings echo those of other studies with probation trainees and recently qualified staff (Annison 2006, Annison *et al.* 2008).

Use of other sources

In order to compare the views of respondents in interview, case files and PSRs were studied and focus groups were held to discuss the emerging themes. In the main these were confirmed, although with some interesting nuances. For example, the focus groups tended to indicate that the model of supervision discussed was an ideal and only possible to be followed with a minority of offenders, although this too may reflect a certain continuity found in an earlier study (Vanstone 1994). The reason for this was increasing workloads, making it harder to give sufficient time to individuals, rather than any more of a 'management' approach to supervision. As a result, some practitioners reported having to 'cherry pick' which of their caseload could be worked with in this manner. In terms of enforcement, files tended to suggest that there was less overtly recorded concern and action over risk management or enforcement than was reported by respondents in interviews.

As mentioned, responses were consistent across sub-groups, with even those concerned with higher risk individuals emphasising the transformative nature of their work, although clearly within a more cautious and risk-aware context. Finally, one interesting issue was how the sub-groups of less and more experienced practitioners described each other: the former tending to see the latter as libertarian and 'unconcerned with enforcement', while the latter saw the former as unnecessarily punitive. However, both groups spoke of their approach and practice in this area in very similar terms.

Discussion: continuity or change?

Given that government has attempted to change the practices of probation practitioners, do the practices and values expressed represent change or continuity (and thus some level of resistance)? Overall, practitioners appeared to operate within a positivist paradigm of 'expert intervention' and there was a persistence of the treatment model based on cognitive behaviourist approaches, plus assistance in the targeting of certain criminogenic needs. In this way, respondents may be seen to have been operating within NOMS policy, but there seems little doubt that while they did not reject wholesale the government's agenda, they came to the job from a rather different angle in that they placed emphasis on different aims and chose where possible to operate in a manner that may be seen to have some elements of continuity to older forms of practice.

Furthermore, there was a rejection of managerialist approaches in terms of the use of targets and rigid enforcement procedures. For example, referrals to accredited programmes were seen as suitable only for the 'right people' and practitioners felt that they should have the freedom to decide whether or not to refer and also when an individual might be ready in motivational terms to commence a programme. This 'targets vs targeting' debate encapsulated the attitude of some practitioners to management, who were seen as removed from professional issues and interested only in a 'tick box' approach. As a result, some described rarely consulting management except to 'cover their backs' in terms of enforcement.

Bearing in mind that direct practice was not observed, and the difficulties of establishing a baseline, practice described by this group appears to represent both change and continuity when compared to practice before the National Probation Service was created in 2001. Change is represented by an increase in more focused work with individuals based largely on cognitive behaviourism, the continued use of accredited programmes, and the more rigid application of enforcement. Continuity is represented by a continuing balance being held between the care and control of individuals (although this is now more likely to be discussed in different terminology around accountability and law enforcement), and the individualised approach to cases, which results in decisions about interventions and enforcement being based on officer assessment of individual factors such as motivation and engagement. The aims of a reduction in problems and hence offending, and an aversion to management and punishment, also represent a continuing thread of practice.

Major issues like risk assessment and management and protection of the public are also newer concerns, but the latter is seen in the main as being achieved by a 'traditional' aim of reducing re-offending.

However, there was clear opposition to more emphasis from government and management for practitioners to become offender managers more and supervisors less. Respondents saw the two roles as indivisible and clearly obtained job satisfaction from building an empathic relationship and working with individual offenders directly on issues that contributed to their offending, which in some cases they defined in wider terms than management appeared to do. No one wished to be a 'technician'; respondents working with offenders assessed as presenting various levels of risk of harm aimed to undertake meaningful work, although those working with the higher risk groups emphasised control elements more than colleagues. The coming of NOMS was regarded negatively and with some anxiety, as it threatened more offender management and possible threats to services *via* contestability.

Conclusion

The last decade or so has seen an almost continuous attempt to change the working practices of the probation service by government, something that seems likely to continue. The whole point of this has been to drive practitioners in those particular directions outlined above, but it is far from clear that, based on this sample of practitioners at least, this has been achieved. In summary, their approach to their work encapsulates the following values, beliefs and practices. Apart from their relationship to government agendas, they also have some implications for late modern theories about probation and criminal justice. There is no wholesale rejection of the government's agenda, but a different emphasis is placed on 'help', discretion and individual factors. Many practitioners reject an offender manager role that precludes a 'real' relationship and an intervention/'therapeutic' role. There is little sense of adherence to rigid enforcement, although enforcement and breach is seen as part of increasing accountability and legitimacy. Risk assessment is seen as vital, but this is intended to facilitate suitable interventions around reduction of reoffending in most cases. Most staff reject target-driven practice. Overall, aspects of the 'new penality' seem to correspond more closely to policy than everyday practice (cf. Kemshall and Maguire 2002; Lynch 1998).

Practitioners clearly accept risk and enforcement agendas, but do not see themselves as 'control workers' (Garland 2001; Rose 2000). Everyday decisions over intervention and enforcement have significant individual impact and may provide a locus for a level of resistance to governmental agendas (Scott 1990; Lipsky 1980; Cheliotis 2006).

However, whatever these data reveal, the context within which practitioners work has changed considerably and shows no sign of remaining fixed in the foreseeable future. In the four years or so since the completion of this fieldwork, there is no doubt that breach rates have increased, although the extent to which this has been affected by practitioners' decisions over unacceptable and acceptable absences needs further investigation. In addition, after a lengthy and difficult gestation, NOMS finally became a statutory body in 2007. At that time the core work of the probation service was protected until mid-2010, and it is simply unknown how far down the road of contestability and the offender manager/supervisor split the service will have to travel.

Overall, it seems likely that it has become harder for practitioners to practice in their preferred manner and may become more so as NOMS moves into an uncertain future, particularly when cuts in budgets forced upon most of the public sector (as a result of the 'credit crunch' and recession that began in 2008) begin to have an impact on recruitment, training, workloads and practices. The consequences of this are simply unknown; at the time of writing (spring 2010) in most areas of England and Wales, directors of offender management have a contract with the existing probation area or trust to provide all the 'usual' services and these local areas have themselves continued to make local partnership arrangements with voluntary and third sector agencies. As such the day-to-day reality of probation governance may have changed little from a practitioner's point of view. The future may be very different and issues of personal and organisational strain may become apparent. Clearly contestability and the role of the offender manager in terms of the relationship they may come to have with offenders are major areas to be decided. In terms of 'real practice', in Bourdieu's terms the conflict between the habitus of the practitioner and the reconfiguration of the field may result in a practice that was not the intention of either government or practitioner and indeed this may already be the case (Bourdieu 1977; McNeill *et al.* 2009). Indeed, following the concept of 'hysteresis', changes in 'real practice' may be lagging behind the major structural changes that have occurred and the consequences may not become apparent for some time (Bourdieu 1990; McNeill *et al.* 2009).

Notes

1 The National Offender Management Service (NOMS) was set up administratively in 2004 and by statute in 2007, after much debate and argument about its final form and functions. It is an agency of the Ministry of Justice (and formerly the Home Office) which has an overarching management function for the work of the probation and prison services. It lets contracts for the full range of duties and activities carried out by these two services. While these remain mainly in the hands of probation and prisons, in time, any current activity could be carried out by a private or voluntary agency under a competitive process of 'contestability'.
2 The latest version of National Standards 2007, issued after the completion of the fieldwork on which this chapter is based, did include the idea of 'compliance' alongside 'enforcement', leaving open the possibility of a more flexible approach to the breach of community sentences
3 Although the numbers completing the Likert scales analysed *via* SPSS were relatively small, chi square significance testing was undertaken, which revealed no statistically significant results between subgroups. In terms of interview data, there was little if any discernible difference in the attitudes and views expressed by sub-groups.

References

Annison, J. (2006) *Career Trajectories of Graduate Trainee Probation Officers.* Plymouth: University of Plymouth.

Annison, J. Eadie, T. and Knight, C. (2008) 'People first: probation officer perspectives on probation work', *Probation Journal*, 55 (3): 259–72.

Bottoms, A. and W. McWilliams (1979) 'A non-treatment paradigm for probation practice', *British Journal of Social Work*, 9: 159–202.

Bourdieu, P. (1977) *Outline of a Theory of Practice.* Cambridge: Cambridge University Press.

Bourdieu, P. (1990) *The Logic of Practice.* Cambridge: Polity Press.

Burnett, R. Baker, and Roberts, C. (2007) 'Assessment, supervision and intervention: fundamental practice in probation', in L. Gelsthorpe and R. Morgan (eds), *Handbook of Probation.* Cullompton: Willan Publishing.

Cheliotis, L. (2006) 'How iron is the iron cage of new penology? The role of human agency in the implementation of criminal justice policy', *Punishment and Society*, 8 (3): 313–40.

Dowden, C. and Andrews, D. (2004) The importance of staff practice in delivering effective correctional treatment: a meta analysis. *International Journal of Offender Therapy and Comparative Criminology*, 48: 203–14.

Farrall, S., (2002) *Rethinking What Works with Offenders.* Cullompton: Willan Publishing.

Feeley, M. and Simon, J. (1992) 'The new penology: notes on the emerging strategy for corrections', *Criminology*, 30 (4): 449–75.

Fitzgibbon, D.W. (2008) 'Fit for purpose? OASys assessments and parole decisions', *Probation Journal*, 55 (1): 55–69.

Garland, D. (2001) *The Culture of Control*. Oxford: Oxford University Press.

Home Office (2000) *National Standards for the Supervision of Offenders in the Community*. London: Home Office.

Home Office (2001) *A New Choreography: An Integrated Strategy for the National Probation Service for England and Wales*. London: Home Office.

Home Office (2002) *Offender Assessment System: OASys*, 2nd edn. London: Home Office.

Hudson, B. (2003) *Understanding Justice*. Buckingham: Open University Press.

Humphrey, C. and Pease, K. (1992) 'Effectiveness measurement in probation: – a view from the troops', *Howard Journal of Criminal Justice*, 31 (1): 31–52.

Kemshall, H. (2003) *Understanding Risk in Criminal Justice*. Maidenhead: Open University Press.

Kemshall, H. and Maguire, M. (2002) 'Public protection, partnership and risk penality: the multi-agency risk management of sexual and violent offenders', in N. Gray, J. Laing and L. Noaks (eds), *Criminal Justice, Mental Health and the Politics of Risk*. London: Cavendish.

Lipsky, M. (1980) *Street-Level Bureaucracy: Dilemmas of the Individual in Public Services*. New York: Russell Sage Foundation.

Lipton, D., Martinson, R. and Wilks, J. (1975) *The Effectiveness of Correctional Treatment*. New York: Praeger.

Lynch, M. (1998) 'Waste managers? The new penology, crime fighting and parole agent identity', *Law and Society Review*, 32 (4): 839–69.

Mair, G. and Canton, R. (2007) 'Sentencing, community penalties and the role of the probation service', in L. Gelsthorpe and R. Morgan (eds), *Handbook of Probation*. Cullompton: Willan Publishing.

Maruna, S. Immarigeon, R. and LeBel, T. (2004) 'Ex-offender reintegration: theory and practice', in S. Maruna and R. Immarigeon (eds), *After Crime and Punishment: Pathways to Offender Reintegration*. Cullompton: Willan Publishing.

McGuire, J. (2001) 'What works in correctional intervention? evidence and practical implications', in G. Bernfeld, D. Farrington and A. Leschied (eds), *Offender Rehabilitation in Practice: Implementing and Evaluating Effective Programs*. Chichester: Wiley.

McNeill, F. (2006) 'A desistance paradigm for offender management', *Criminology and Criminal Justice*, 6 (1): 39–62.

McNeill, F. Burns, N. Halliday, S. Hutton, N. and Tata, C. (2009) 'Risk, responsibility and reconfiguration: penal adaptation and misadaptation', *Punishment and Society*, 11 (4): 419–42.

Murphy, S. (2004) *National Probation Service: Performance Report 12*. London: National Probation Service.

Napo (2006) *Probation Values: Commitment to Best Practice*, London: Napo.

Nash, M. and Ryan, M. (2003) 'Modernising and joining-up government: the case of the prison and probation services', *Contemporary Politics*, 9 (2): 157–169.

Nellis, M. and Gelsthorpe, L. (2003) 'Human rights and the probation values debate', in W.H. Chui and M. Nellis (eds), *Moving Probation Forward*. Harlow: Pearson.

Newburn, T. (2003) *Crime and Criminal Justice Policy*, 2nd edn. Harlow: Longman.

NOMS (2006) *The NOMS Offender Management Model*, 2nd edn. London: NOMS.

Raynor, P. (1985) *Social Work, Justice and Control*. Oxford: Blackwell.

Raynor, P. (2004) 'Rehabilitative and reintegrative approaches', in A. Bottoms, S. Rex and G. Robinson (eds), *Alternatives to Prison: Options for an Insecure Society*. Cullompton: Willan Publishing.

Raynor, P. and Maguire, M. (2006) 'End-to-end or end in tears? Prospects for the effectiveness of the National Offender Management Model', in M. Hough, R. Allen and U. Padel (eds), *Reshaping Probation and Prisons: the New Offender Management Framework*. Bristol: Policy Press.

Robinson, G. (2002) 'Exploring risk management in probation practice: contemporary developments in England and Wales', *Punishment and Society*, 4 (1): 5–25.

Robinson, G. and McNeill, F. (2004) 'Purposes matter: examining the "ends" of probation', in G. Mair (ed.), *What Matters in Probation*. Cullompton: Willan Publishing.

Rose, N. (2000) 'Government and control', *British Journal of Criminology*, 36 (4): 321–39.

Scott, J. (1990) *Domination and the Arts of Resistance: Hidden Transcripts*. London: Yale University Press.

Senior, P., Crowther-Dowey, C. and Long, M. (2007) *Understanding Modernisation in Criminal Justice*. Buckingham: Open University Press.

Straw, J. (1997) *Commons Written Reply*. Hansard.

Straw, J. (2009) *Speech to Trainee Probation Officers*. Probation Study School, University of Portsmouth, 4th February 2009. Online at www.justice.gov.uk/news/speeches-2009 (accessed February 2009).

Vanstone, M. (2004) *Supervising Offenders in the Community: A History of Probation Theory and Practice*. Aldershot: Ashgate.

Vanstone, M. (1994) *A Moral Good Examined: A Survey of Work Undertaken within the Framework of the Standard Probation Order in Mid Glamorgan*. Bridgend: Mid Glamorgan Probation Service.

Williams, B. (1995) *Probation Values*. London: Venture Press.

Chapter 23

Pre-sentence reports in England and Wales: changing discourses of need, risk and quality

Loraine Gelsthorpe, Peter Raynor and Gwen Robinson

'... public protection will always be the Government's first priority ...'

(Home Office 2004: 10)

Introduction

Drawing on probation service social enquiry and pre-sentence reports from different periods of history in England and Wales (from the 1960s up to 2009), this chapter refers to conceptions of offenders' needs and their portrayal in pre-sentence reports as a reflection of the changing contexts of probation practice. We report on pilot work concerning comparative discourse analysis of pre-sentence reports that seeks to make sense of changing representations of offenders against a backdrop of late modern moves towards risk thinking, managerialism and 'populist punitiveness'. Although the contexts for and practices of pre-sentence report writing vary across jurisdictions, since these broader penal trends have influenced policy and practice in many jurisdictions, the evidence from this case study from England and Wales may have resonances in other places. We leave it to those with a greater appreciation of their own jurisdictions to assess how far our findings are pertinent.

A brief history of the development of court reports in England and Wales

Although it is not entirely clear when the first report was 'presented' to the court, Matthew Davenport Hill, a Recorder of Birmingham, instituted in 1841 a register of persons who would report to him on the conduct of certain young offenders. Such reports were sometimes in writing. It is thought that court reports started to become a common feature with the advent of the police court mission in metropolitan police courts from August 1876 onwards (Herbert and Mathieson 1975). The Probation of Offenders' Act 1907 implied that some sort of report should be considered by the court before the making of a probation order – since s.1 of the Act gave permission for some offenders to be placed on probation 'having regard to the character, antecedents, age, health or mental condition of the person charged'. In this sense, the development of reports is closely linked with the development of the probation service from police court missions, which were evangelical and temperance bodies (Nellis 2007; McWilliams 1983). We might even say that the first report writers were in fact 'touting for trade' since their reports involved pleading with the court to give them the opportunity of working with the offender on probation (many of the reports would have been 'stand down' – that is, oral – reports). But we think that after a while there were aspirations for a more impartial and objective approach.

Reports were first used to assist the courts in the making of probation orders, but the Streatfeild Report moved the social inquiry report on from this role somewhat by encouraging the probation officer to express an opinion 'as to the likely effect on the offender's criminal career of a probation order or some other specified form of sentence' (Home Office 1961: para 335). One of the key messages of the Streatfeild Report revolved around a perceived need to promote the principle of individualisation; the recognition of 'the needs of the offender as a person' (Home Office 1961: para 259) and the desire to make punishment fit 'not only the crime but the criminal' (Lord Chancellor's Department 1978: 4). The committee showed themselves to be concerned with all the sentencing aims in the court's mind. They saw this as an approach to be developed if sentencing was to become a constructive tool with which to prevent reoffending and not merely a 'judgment on past events' (Home Office 1961: para 269). To achieve this aim the committee declared: 'Our cardinal principle throughout is that sentences should be based on reliable, comprehensive information relevant to what the court is seeking to do' (Home Office 1961: 84).

Reports in the 1960s and 1970s: a case work approach

The Morison Committee of 1962 added further endorsement to the value of probation officers' reports, regarding the term 'probation report' as unsatisfactory and limiting, and recommended the term 'social enquiry report' (SER) (Home Office 1962).[1] This kind of thinking was reflected in the development and utilisation of rehabilitation in sentencing and probation practice in the 1960s and 1970s in particular, and the idea of social enquiry reports became embedded in courtroom practice from the 1960s onwards. Various Home Office circulars in the 1960s pressed the importance of SERs – and tried to overcome the reluctance of some magistrates to ask for them by emphasising that they were no longer about 'pleas for leniency' from police court missionaries. The message was that 'the true nature of a social inquiry report was that it was a comprehensive and objective document prepared by a professionally trained social worker of the court to assist the court in a more effective sentencing practice' (Herbert and Mathieson, 1975: 11). In other words, it was a key tool for the psychosocial casework approach that probation officers were trained for. Indeed, the 1960s and 1970s were the period when probation work in England and Wales was most dominated by psychosocial casework theory, and seen by its leading thinkers as part of a casework dominated social work profession (see, for example, Foren and Bailey, 1968).

This perspective on reports is rehearsed in research on the role and development of social enquiry reports for the 25-year period after Streatfeild (Bottoms and McWilliams 1986). Notwithstanding various difficulties that had been identified[2] Bottoms and McWilliams essentially argued that report-writing was a social work task. SERs aimed to put offending in its social context and propose community disposals wherever feasible. The probation officer's task was to influence perceptions of blameworthiness and seriousness (Raynor 1980). One might say that the SER was a welfare-based document used to inform justice-based decisions.

Reports in the 1980s: alternatives to custody

Cumulative empirical findings on the impact of penal welfarism and conclusions that penal welfare sanctions, including the probation order, were much less successful in 'treating' offenders than had hitherto been assumed, gathered apace in the 1970s, leading to the conclusion that rehabilitation was not effective. Such a conclusion was epitomised in Robert Martinson's claim in the *Public Interest* that 'With few and isolated exceptions, the rehabilitative efforts that have been reported so far have had no appreciable effect on recidivism' (1974: 25).[3] This was quickly translated into 'nothing works', and combined with a resources crisis that highlighted the costs of imprisonment because of rising crime rates and the practical imperative to keep prison costs within bounds, and an ideological crisis that revolved around a 'neo-classical renaissance' and increasing awareness of the need to pay more attention to offenders' rights, the paternalistic 'coercive caring' of penal-welfarism was increasingly challenged (Gelsthorpe and Morgan 2007). The impact of these various crises was that a new central mission for the probation service as the provider of supervision in the community for those who would otherwise be in prison emerged (Home Office 1984). This was the era of 'alternatives to custody'. If nothing worked, cheaper was better. The new role also suited probation officers who were conscious of the damage prison could do, and were anxious to avoid the amplification of deviancy that they believed could result from excessive or unnecessary intervention in people's lives by correctional systems (Thorpe *et al.* 1980). Risk was sometimes discussed in those days, but usually with reference to risks to the offender's liberty: one of the first actuarial instruments developed in British probation was a 'risk of custody' scale (Bale 1987) used to help identify those at risk of a custodial sentence, and therefore in need of a strong alternative proposal if custody was to be avoided.

Reports in the 1990s: from SERs to PSRs

Despite tough measures introduced to promote 'law and order' in the 1980s, rising crime rates, awareness of the globalisation of crime, and a public sense of crime being 'out of control', led to highly contentious debates about the effectiveness of utilitarian sentencing (Easton and Piper 2005). Influenced by developments elsewhere (particularly the activities of liberal rights lawyers in the USA who were intent upon introducing more rationality and proportionality into sentencing) there was a call for modern retributivism. Protagonist Andrew von Hirsch (1976) maintained that the aim should be to balance fairness and justice rather than maximise utility. He suggested that 'justice' should reflect offenders as moral agents possessing autonomy and that punishment should be in proportion to the seriousness of the crime. At the same time, he argued that penalties should be anchored at a low level; retributivism was not to be based on harsh punishments. Thus emerged the Criminal Justice Act of 1991 in England and Wales, that aimed to base all sentencing on 'desert' and the seriousness of the current offence (proportionality was the key theme). Custody was for cases 'too serious' for community penalties, or used for public protection reasons if offenders were assessed as 'dangerous'.

One significant change here was that the 1991 Act emphasised that probation should be seen as a sentence (and indeed a punishment) in its own right, rather than as an alternative to anything. The 1991 Criminal Justice Act also introduced substantial changes to the reports provided to sentencers. The familiar SER was replaced by the pre-sentence report (PSR) and there was to be a new focus on the circumstances of and reasons for the current offence, and where appropriate, a new concentration on the identification of a 'community sentence' that might help offenders stay out of trouble in the future. Previous patterns of offending were to be covered insofar as they assisted an understanding of the current offence, and the whole report was to be informed by consideration of the seriousness of the offence so that discussion of a possible sentence could concentrate on those outcomes that were 'broadly likely' (Home Office 1992). Despite later revision of section 29 of the Act to increase sentencers' powers to take previous convictions into account in assessing the seriousness of current offences (in the 1993 CJAct), the main principles of pre-sentence reports were not altered. But the Home Secretary issued increasingly prescriptive national standards for the preparation of PSRs. In 1992 those standards laid the expectation that PSRs should address not just mitigating but also aggravating features of the offence, for example. This expectation was toned down when the national standards were revised in 1995, but at this point the expectation was made of a section in the report entitled 'Risk to the public of re-offending'. In writing this, the author of the report was expected to use his or her professional judgement, to consider the nature, seriousness and likelihood of further offences. In even more of a departure from traditional report-writing practices, the author was to address any risk of harm to the public. This was not limited to reports in cases of sexual or violent offences.

The context for recent changes in reports: a culture of risk, populist punitiveness and modern managerialism

The increasing call for criminal justice practitioners to attend to 'risk' perhaps came as no surprise in the context of wider social changes. It is widely accepted that social transformations in society since the 1950s have brought about what David Garland (2001) has depicted as a 'culture of control'. These include economic, technological and 'social' (family and community related) changes. The decline of manufacturing and the rise of the service industry, the emergence of a technologically driven society, increased mobility and changes in the structure of the family all feature here. In similar vein, sociological analyses of late modernity include consideration of changes in the source of 'trust' and the growth of 'ontological insecurity' (Gelsthorpe and Morgan 2007). Jock Young discusses the 'vertigo of late modernity': how insecurities in economic position and status, coupled with feelings of deprivation, can be experienced as a sense of vertigo, tinged with anger and dislike (2007: 12). At risk of simplification, sociologists note that a 'risk society' has emerged in response to the erosion of localised trust that was previously embedded in kinship relations in settled communities. For Ulrich Beck: 'Risk may be defined as a systematic way of dealing with hazards and insecurities induced and introduced by modernization itself. Risks, as opposed to older dangers, are consequences that relate to the threatening force of modernization and its globalization of doubt' (1992: 21).

The argument goes that in an age of anxiety and culture of risk, there is need to work harder to calculate risks in order to deal with life's contingencies. There is a notable pursuit of security (Zedner 2000). Moreover, the 'culture of risk' quickly translates into a 'culture of blame'. The notion of 'risk' is prised away from its moorings within probability calculations and becomes a cultural keyword with much wider reference to debates about social life, accountability, crime, and punishment and so on. This includes debates about the violent and dangerous offender and what should be done with him/her as we move towards a more protectionist society. Indeed, by the close of the twentieth century risk had come to preoccupy much of the probation service's agenda (Robinson 2002). This reflected increased policy, media and public concern with high risk offenders (most notably sex offenders), with the government tapping into perceptions of public opinion and seeking to demonstrate responsiveness to public concerns (reflecting 'populist punitiveness' as described by Bottoms 1995), followed by a raft of legislation to deal more proactively with those deemed to present the highest risk of harm to society. These developments can be placed within a broader penal trend usually referred to as a 'new penology' of risk or actuarial justice (Feeley and Simon 1992). Feeley explains how he 'began exploring new developments in sentencing, parole, career criminals, selective incapacitation, and the like and looking at them through the lens of risk. Actuarial justice was the result' (2006: 219).

Managerialism is another major theme that has contributed to the reshaping of probation practice. The reconstruction of public services in the UK from the 1980s onwards, combined with a modernising government agenda, has led to closer scrutiny and tighter managerial control by the centre of the minutiae of operational policy locally, and contracting out the provision of services to sharpen up the public sector where it has seemed sluggish. This has meant that more or less autonomous probation areas – already subject to national standards – were incorporated into a National Probation Service in 2001, and made subject to further organisational developments as a result of the Carter Report (2003). Early in 2005, a government bill proposed that the Home Secretary be given increased powers to direct probation boards. A general election in May 2005 meant that those particular proposals were swept away, but instead local probation boards were to be substituted by probation trusts (incorporating a wider range of community interests than hitherto and including a 'business mould'), that would have to compete with the voluntary and commercial sectors in making bids to deliver and commission services. The Offender Management Act 2007 confirmed the new governance arrangements and establishes 'competition' and 'contracts' as a foundation for service delivery (Gelsthorpe and Morgan 2007; Senior *et al*. 2007). These new developments may not yet have affected the production of pre-sentence reports, but the managerialist culture (with performance targets and systems analysis) serves to indicate the need for a streamlined production process.

The central role of 'risk measurement'

With a background of a culture of risk and renewed legislative efforts to promote crime reduction, we should note the shift in orientation for the probation service – from welfare to risk-based interventions and bifurcation in the treatment of offenders (high risk and low risk offenders; those who can be re-moralised and socially included and those who cannot, we might say). Risk assessment is also increasingly based on 'criminogenic factors' (those factors most associated with offending) and statistical probabilities rather than predictions (Merrington and Stanley 2007).

Legislative and organisational changes thus ushered in a much more structured approach to risk assessment. From 2001 an Offender Assessment System tool (OASys) was utilised by the National Probation Service and National Offender Management Service (NOMS), as the overarching assessment framework:

[OASys] is a key element of evidence-based practice and a major area of collaboration between the two services [prisons and probation]. It provides a common framework for assessing offenders and matching them to appropriate interventions. This critical tool will help practitioners make sound and defensible decisions about offender risk and enables us to assess the impact of our work with offenders. (NPS 2001: 9–10).

OASys, of course, is the end result of a process that began in the 1980s – with risk of custody prediction scores (Bale 1987) and, in the 1990s, a risk of reconviction predictor developed by the Home Office (OGRS – the Offender Group Reconviction Scale) (see Robinson 2003 for a review of developments in risk assessment technologies in the probation context).

OASys is designed to perform a number of functions, including the assessment of criminogenic needs, risk of reoffending and risk of causing serious harm. The OASys assessment is crucial in informing the allocation of individuals to different 'tiers' of supervision, labelled (1) punish, (2) help, (3) change, (4) control (Burnett et al. 2007). The tiers are not mutually exclusive but layered, so that each involves the interventions of all lower levels as well as those specified at its own level.[4] It is not entirely clear why the Home Office selected the complicated OASys tool rather than the other practical alternatives, especially in light of research that highlights the complexities of the tool (see, for example, Mair 2006: in an article about probation officers' views about OASys entitled 'The worst tax form you've ever seen'. Mair points to their perspectives on OASys as 'too mechanistic' and 'too inflexible', but it is clear that it continues to occupy a central role in thinking about offenders' risks and needs).

Contemporary reports in context

How far are these modern preoccupations with managerialism, populist punitiveness and risk reflected in pre-sentence reports? There are currently three types of pre-sentence report: an oral report (providing specific, concise information, usually on the day it is requested); a fast delivery report (FDR) (to be provided in less complex and serious cases within five working days, although, in practice, often produced on the day), and a standard delivery report (SDR) (to be used in the most serious and complex cases and normally provided within 15 working days). These reports are meant to be viewed as of equal standing, differentiated only by their assessment basis and suitability for use in different circumstances[5]. The CJA 2003 envisaged extensive use of FDRs, and a probation circular (18/2005) provided a framework for deciding that type of PSR would be the most suitable. In broad terms, this involved a cut-off point for FDRs where the OGRS score was under 41, and the necessity of an SDR where the OGRS score was above 41 and where a full risk of harm analysis would be required.

In the early implementation period of FDRs they were considerably underused as a result of their being associated with only low seriousness. As of May 2007, a 'decision tool' to encourage greater use of FDRs was introduced to help court officers to answer two key questions: (1) Is there enough information to enable the court to sentence now? – in that case the court either proceeds to sentence or the court probation officer presents an oral report to supplement court information (previously referred to as 'stand down reports'); (2) Would an FDR assessment secure sufficient information to facilitate safe sentencing? – if the answer is in the positive here the court officer will request an adjournment for an FDR (NPS 2007). A more recent probation instruction (NPS 2009) has directed probation trusts towards greater use of both the FDR and oral reports, with the FDR now being the default position for pre-sentence information. They are to be used across sentencing thresholds, including custody. The FDR is based on risk of serious harm (RoSH) screening, an offender group reconviction score (OGRS), screening for complex offending related problems, for known person status with Children's Services, basic skills deficits, and suitability for accredited programmes, as well as the offender's own assessment. (OASys thus automatically populates part of the pre-sentence template, though the full OASys is reserved for more serious and complex cases for whom there would be an SDR.) Marking a change from the 2005 guidance, in 2009 an OGRS score of under 76 indicates that an FDR is appropriate unless there are counter-indicators relating to RoSH (NPS 2009).

Thus the creation of the National Offender Management Service as a new organisational framework, a changing professional culture (with negation of social work values in the training of probation officers), and replacement of the old adage that the probation officer's role was to 'advise, assist and befriend' with 'assessment, enforcement and breach' (Raynor 2007; Gelsthorpe and Morgan 2007), alongside the focus on risk and risk assessment in pre-sentence reports, are all issues that raise key questions about the changing content and quality of pre-sentence reports. It is to these issues that we now turn.

Quality assurance

At the beginning of the 1990s, Peter Raynor and Loraine Gelsthorpe were commissioned by the Home Office to develop an approach to quality control that could be made available to probation services as the Criminal Justice Act 1991 was being implemented (Gelsthorpe and Raynor 1995; Raynor *et al.* 1995). This was partly to address some of the criticisms of reports that had been identified in the 1980s, and partly to assess the impact of reports on courtroom sentencing.

This is not the place to describe the study in detail, but it is important to say that having developed criteria for the assessment of 'quality' reports (based on 42 variables) and having engaged in various appraisal exercises on a sample of around 150 reports (that is, representing one in 20 reports in five probation areas included in the pilot studies), we arrived at four key findings. First, the 'better' reports were more successful in enabling sentencers to pass community sentences with confidence and to rely correspondingly less on imprisonment. Second, short notice reports (those that were completed on the same day as the court appearance or within seven days) appeared not to affect the overall findings on quality although they tended on average to be less thorough in their discussion of offending behaviour, probably because with some offenders more than one interview was needed to explore this. Third, fewer of the short notice reports used information from sources other than the defendant, the criminal proceedings, and probation records. This tended to exclude information from relatives, partners, employers, or other useful contacts in the community: 38 per cent of same-day reports used such information, compared to 61 per cent of reports prepared over three weeks. Finally, when short notice reports discussed the possibility of a probation order they were less likely to suggest 'packages' involving additional requirements or facilities: these tended to involve third parties and take time to negotiate and set up (22 per cent in short notice reports compared with 47 per cent of reports prepared in more than seven days).

Effectiveness

When the study was commissioned, no one really knew whether reports were impacting on sentencers' decisions: where there was concordance between recommendations and actual sentencing decisions this might simply have indicated accurate guessing on the part of the report writer. We therefore developed a 'quality assurance guide' and compared the outcomes of low and high quality reports

Table 23.1 Quality and impact.

	Quality	
	Below average (*n* 80)	Above average (*n* 70)
Proposing community sentence	43%	62%
Resulting in a community sentence	16%	25%
Community sentence exactly as proposed	13%	18%
Immediate custodial sentences	48%	39%

(see Table 23.1). What we found was that reports did have an impact, and quality mattered too; this needed a much bigger study, of course, but a quality appraisal of reports nevertheless became part of the HM Inspectorate's agenda.

The dominance of risk in PSRs?

Since this research on quality and effectiveness was carried out in the early 1990s, assumptions in England and Wales about the role of probation officers and their reports have changed substantially, and we have outlined a number of those changes in this chapter. The time seems ripe for another look at pre-sentence reports, both to see whether and how they have changed over time, and to test out how far any changes are consistent with the narrative of transformation in the probation service and the criminal justice system that we have presented above. In England and Wales, unlike Scotland (see Tata *et al.* 2008) there has been little systematic research on the style and content of pre-sentence reports on adults since then.[6] As a preliminary exploration of this, we have attempted to test the relevance of some of the ideas we have outlined by carrying out a small pilot study of changes over time in the style and content of pre-sentence reports (formerly social enquiry reports). Six small samples, each consisting of ten reports on adult offenders, were used for this pilot study, drawn from different decades of probation work in England and Wales and prepared in a variety of probation areas. The two most recent samples were collected specially for this study; the earlier samples were drawn at random from material collected in earlier studies by the authors and others, and believed to be reasonably representative of typical practice at the time. We were able to draw on reports spanning nearly half a century of probation service practice, with samples from 1964, 1984–85, 1991, 1998, 2006 and 2009. Considered in relation to the historical development of probation practice as described above (see also Raynor 1997; Vanstone 2004; Gelsthorpe and Morgan 2007; Raynor and Robinson 2009), these include all the main stages in the evolution of probation theory and policy since its emergence as a professionalised universal service in the post-war Welfare State.

Our first sample is drawn from the 1960s, at the height of penal welfarism and probation as psychosocial casework. Our sample from the mid-1980s belongs to the era of 'alternatives to custody'. Our third sample, drawn from the 'quality and effectiveness' study sample collected in 1991 (Gelsthorpe and Raynor 1995), belongs to the period of the 1991 Criminal Justice Act when probation was beginning to be seen as a sentence in its own right rather than an 'alternative' to anything, and when probation officers were starting to be encouraged to think about risk, although without any established methods for doing so.

The 1998 sample moves more clearly into the era of 'risk' and the beginning of 'what works' and evidence-based probation. In fact, this group of reports was collected in one of the early pilot studies of risk assessment in probation (Raynor *et al.* 2000), when the official focus on risk had already been made clear (for example, by HMIP 1995), but various different risk assessment approaches were being tried, and OASys had not yet been developed.[7] Our last two samples, from 2006 and 2009, are drawn from the 'new' National Probation Service established in 2001 and incorporated from 2004 into NOMS, the National Offender Management Service, with OASys used as the official approach to risk and need assessment and a full managerial apparatus of standards, targets, monitoring and league tables in place.

A simple checklist was devised for the pilot study, based partly on the approach used in the 'quality and effectiveness' study of the early 1990s but now focusing not so much on quality as on dominant themes and discourse. In particular, we focus on whether and how the language of 'risk' is explicitly used (see McNeill *et al.* 2009 on this issue in relation to Scotland); on the general (positive or negative) presentation of the offender, and on the nature and content of sentencing proposals.

Table 23.2 Do they mention risk?

Date	1964	1984–85	1991	1998	2006	2009
Risk of further offence	3	1	4	10	10	10
Risk of harm	0	0	2	3	10	10
Risk score	0	0	0	0	0	9

Note: *n* for each year = 10.

Table 23.2 presents our findings in relation to risk. In view of the trends and developments discussed in the first part of this paper, it is no surprise that references to risk become more frequent, to the extent that all reports now contain fairly detailed discussions of risk. Risk of harm, or dangerousness, emerges as a preoccupation later in the time-series than risk of reoffending, which actually features in some reports prepared decades before it became a general policy. However, in the latest samples both kinds of risk are fully represented, and sometimes risk of harm appears the more important of the two.

Table 23.3 focuses on the overall presentation of the offender as a person. What general impression will the report make on the reader who reads it once? This was identified as an important aspect of report-writing by a number of commentators in the 1980s (see, for example, Millichamp *et al.* 1985). *Positive* presentations are those that, on balance, convey a positive or optimistic attitude to the offender and to the possibilities of improvement by mentioning strengths, resources, achievements, prospects, positive behaviour such as cooperation and remorse, while *negative* presentations concentrate on weaknesses, deficits, problems, failures and blameworthiness, sometimes conveying a sense of little real engagement with the offender. Most offenders' situations contain a mixture of negative and positive features, but reports often tend to emphasise one or the other. Some reports present a more mixed picture or leave no clear impression either way, and we have classified these as *neutral*. Of course, these are subjective judgements, but we have found that researchers used to looking at many reports (something that sentencers also have to do) tend to agree in most cases, and we have used two assessors for each of the two most recent samples to produce the reported scores. These are presented in Table 23.3 and show a double movement: presentations during the 'casework' era were mixed; positive presentations dominate during the 'alternative to custody' era, when probation officers were encouraged to promote the use of community penalties and the potential of offenders to benefit from them, but in the two most recent samples almost all the reports are neutral or negative in tone, in roughly equal proportions. A few examples of the language used in the two recent samples of reports may help to illustrate what we mean by the emerging tendency towards more negative presentation:

> The defendant is totally culpable for the offence, that is of a very serious nature ... Based upon the current circumstances of [the defendant's] lifestyle, homelessness, unemployment, lack of stability and generally risk behaviours with misuse of alcohol and cannabis, my assessment is that the risk of re-offending in the future is high.

> [The defendant] demonstrates rigid thinking and a failure to learn from his mistakes ... He displays distorted thinking surrounding his behaviour and uses minimisation of his actions to enable him to justify his offending, in doing so he also displays a disregard for the impact his behaviour has on others.

> The Probation Trust's role is to assess and manage risks and in this instance, the Trust are not in a position to manage the risk [the defendant] presents and are not in a position to engage the defendant in any work, neither would we be able to effect any change.

Table 23.4 concentrates on the proposals in reports, and on how they are presented. In theory we might expect to see substantial changes during the long period represented by our samples. In the case work era, possible sentences might be recommended as the best way to address problems of immaturity or personality development (perhaps 'underlying' rather than 'presenting' problems). In the 1980s one would expect proposals to have been informed by the prevailing ethos of diversion from custody, while the later samples might be

Table 23.3 How the offender is presented.

Date	1964	1984–85	1991	1998	2006	2009
Mainly positive	2	6	4	2	0	1
Mainly negative	3	0	0	2	5	5
Neutral	5	4	6	6	5	4

Table 23.4 Main focus of proposals.

Date	1964	1984–85	1991	1998	2006	2009
Community order proposed	3	10	6	9	7	7
Presented as alternative to custody	1	3	3	2	0	2
Arguments used against custody	0	3	1	1	5	2
Presented mainly as punishment	0	0	4	1	0	4
Presented mainly as reparation	0	0	3	0	0	1
Presented mainly as rehabilitation	3	5	4	4	8	3
Risk management and community protection	0	0	0	1	4	2
Discussion of consent or cooperation	1	9	2	4	5	6

expected to show a clearer focus on risk and its reduction through attention to criminogenic needs. In practice, as Table 23.4 shows, we found a majority of community proposals in every era since the 1980s, together with some continuity in the use of anti-custodial arguments. Consent to a community order and likely cooperation continue to be mentioned in many reports in spite of the abolition of the legal requirement for consent in 1997, and a focus on the rehabilitative purpose of proposals remains fairly strong throughout. However, a punishment-based rationale for proposals is not found before 1991, and arguments based on risk management are mainly a feature of the most recent samples. So it appears from these samples that some new themes and styles of argument have emerged in the 'recommendation' or 'proposal' sections of reports, but they are added to long-term and relatively durable features of the professional culture such as an anti-custodial ethos and an interest in rehabilitation.

Discussion

It is, of course, hazardous to draw firm conclusions from such small samples, and we do not pretend to do so. However, this limited pilot study does suggest some issues or possibilities that deserve to be tested on a larger scale and in a more systematic way.

For example, it seems fairly clear that there has been a shift towards the language of risk, and at the same time a drift towards more negative presentation. The emergence of a discourse around risks and criminogenic needs (or dynamic risk factors) is one of the major components of the evidence-based approach to offender rehabilitation, in that one of the dominant trends for more than a decade has been the RNR or risk-need-responsivity approach derived from the work of Don Andrews and his colleagues in Canada (see Bonta and Andrews, this volume). In this approach, risk assessment is seen to have a number of benefits, including fuller assessment; compliance with the 'risk principle', that concentrates rehabilitative effort on those who need it; the opportunity to demonstrate risk reduction through repeated and quantified assessments; and an assessment process that can promote effective engagement with the offender, if based on dialogue and participation. In addition, the use of risk-need assessment systems promotes rehabilitation by identifying targets for change that will reduce the risk of reoffending if they are addressed. A number of these benefits have been demonstrated empirically in several studies (Andrews and Bonta 2006; Raynor 2007) but that does not mean that they are guaranteed to occur in all circumstances, and the quality of implementation is clearly important. The rapid introduction of risk assessment in British probation was partly driven by a desire to reproduce these positive effects.

On the other hand, critics of risk assessment (such as Hannah-Moffat 2005; Hudson 2003) point to what they believe to be a number of possible dangers, including possible discrimination against minority groups, that needs to be tested in larger samples. Other suggested dangers include over-presentation of negatives and deficits. This is also noted by advocates of the Good Lives Model of rehabilitation (Ward and Maruna 2007; Ward, this volume; Maruna and LeBel, this volume), who argue that RNR models focus too much on deficits and malfunctions, and not enough on offenders' aspirations and strengths. Although this argument sometimes seems exaggerated (for example, there is plenty of evidence of effective work informed by RNR approaches, and it is very difficult to work effectively without optimism and a focus on positive goals), nevertheless it is possible to imagine a process in which information about likely future offending, presented in a negative and objectifying way, could create in sentencers' minds a disposition to impose a more severe sentence on precautionary grounds. Similarly, an approach to assessment that is mechanical, stereotyped, distancing and carried out by an officer who looks at the computer more than at the offender seems unlikely to promote positive engagement or to elicit positive information. In this way the focus on risk, if imposed on practitioners through a managerialist process rather than adopted by them as a natural enhancement to their work, might even be unintentionally contributing to the trend towards increasingly severe sentencing in England and Wales.

Such questions certainly deserve investigation in a larger study. Also worth investigating is the apparent trend towards longer reports (six pages is not unusual, when in the 1980s it was unusual to see more than two) and towards ponderous and rather stereotyped language, often recasting everyday ideas like a moment's impulsiveness or irresponsibility into long diagnostic statements in the jargon of cognitive deficits. The reports are mostly thorough, and the report writers are clearly working hard, but perhaps officers feel that they are expected to write in a certain way. Certainly there is a trend towards prescribed formats and templates, and even the capacity to 'pull through' material generated by the E-OASys software into reports (National Probation Service 2005). Sentencers have often asked for better reports, but it is not clear that this is what they meant. Our next step is to ask them what they want from reports, what they think constitutes a 'good enough' FDR, and what they make of the reports they receive.

Notes

1 Sometimes described as 'social *inquiry* reports'.
2 Drawing on disparate sources (see, for example, Bottoms and Stelman 1988), including our own teaching materials from the 1980s and 1990s, these included the following: (i) over-negative presentation of offenders; (ii) the fact that report writers would sometimes present a catalogue of problems not linked to offending; (iii) a failure to put the offence in context where it was discussed; (iv) prejudicial coverage of background factors outside the defendant's control; (v) the use of jargon and stereotyping and belittling language; (vi) the omission of the offender's perspective on the offence and offending behaviour; (vii) a failure to provide sufficient detail of proposed community-based alternatives to custody; (viii) failure to assess the possible consequences of custody; and (ix) direct or disguised or implied custodial recommendations on 'welfare' grounds (for example, and to paraphrase: 'this young man would obviously benefit from a structured environment and existence ...').
3 See also the full report which followed (Lipton *et al.* 1975) which offered a nuanced and subtle analysis of effectiveness in relation to each type of intervention. For instance, one conclusion was that 'to the degree that casework and individual counselling provided to offenders in the community is directed toward their immediate problems, it may be associated with reductions in recidivism rates. Unless this counselling leads to solution of problems such as housing, finances, jobs or illness which have a high priority for offenders, it is unlikely to have any impact upon future criminal behaviour' (1975: 572). See also Brody (1976).

4 One of the benefits is that this avoids low risk offenders receiving high levels of attention, but one of the problems is that low risk offenders may nevertheless be 'high need' and so they miss out on resources – women included here.

5 Reports do, however, also differ in terms of authorship, with most oral reports prepared by 'assistant' grade staff (probation service officers); FDRs provided by PSOs or qualified probation officers; and SDRs prepared by the latter only.

6 See Phoenix (2009) on pre-sentence reports in relation to young offenders in England and Wales.

7 Interestingly, the 'risk of custody' scales had completely disappeared by this time, in response to the new focus of the 1991 Act. By 1998 'risk' meant either risk of reoffending, or dangerousness (see HMIP 1998).

References

Andrews, D.A. and Bonta, J. (2006) *The Psychology of Criminal Conduct*, 4th edn. Newark: Anderson.

Bale, D. (1987) 'Uses of the risk of custody scale', *Probation Journal*, 34 (4): 127–31.

Beck, U. (1992) *Risk Society: Towards a New Modernity*. London: Sage.

Bottoms, A. (1995) 'The philosophy and politics of punishment and sentencing', in C. Clarkson and R. Morgan (eds) *The Politics of Sentencing Reform*. Oxford: Clarendon Press.

Bottoms, A.E. and McWilliams, W. (1986) 'Social inquiry reports: twenty-five years after the Streatfeild Report', in P. Bean and D. Whynes (eds) *Barbara Wootton, Social Science and Public Policy: Essays in Her Honour*. London: Tavistock Publications.

Bottoms, A.E. and Stelman, A. (1988) *Social Inquiry Reports*. Aldershot: Wildwood House.

Brody, S. R. (1976) *The Effectiveness of Sentencing*, Home Office Research Study 35. London: HMSO.

Burnett, R., Baker, K. and Roberts, C. (2007) 'Assessment, supervision and intervention: fundamental practice in probation', in L. Gelsthorpe and R. Morgan (eds) *Handbook of Probation*. Cullompton: Willan Publishing.

Carter, P. (2003) *Managing Offenders: Reducing Crime*. London: Home Office.

Easton, S. and Piper, C. (2005) *Sentencing and Punishment: The Quest for Justice*. Oxford: Oxford University Press.

Feeley, M, (2006) 'Origins of actuarial justice', in S. Armstrong and L. McAra (eds) *Perspectives on Punishment: The Contours of Control*. Oxford: Oxford University Press.

Feeley, M. and Simon, J. (1992) 'The new penology: notes on the emerging strategy for corrections', *Criminology*, 30 (4): 449–75.

Foren, R. and Bailey, R. (1968) *Authority in Social Casework*. Oxford: Pergamon Press.

Garland, D. (2001) *The Culture of Control*. Oxford: Clarendon Press.

Gelsthorpe, L. and Morgan, R. (eds) (2007) *Handbook of Probation*. Cullompton: Willan Publishing.

Gelsthorpe, L. and Raynor, P. (1995) 'Quality and effectiveness in probation officers' reports to sentencers', *British Journal of Criminology*, 35 (2): 188–200.

Hannah-Moffat, K. (2005) 'Criminogenic needs and the transformative risk subject: hybridizations of risk/need in penality', *Punishment and Society*, 7 (1): 29–51.

Herbert, L. and Mathieson, D. (1975) *Reports for Courts*. London: National Association of Probation Officers.

HMIP (1995) *Dealing with Dangerous People: The Probation Service and Public Protection*. London: Home Office.

HMIP (1998) *Exercising Constant Vigilance: The Role of the Probation Service in Protecting the Public from Sex Offenders*. London: Home Office.

Hirsch A. von (1976) *Doing Justice: The Choice of Punishments. Report of the Committee for the Study of Incarceration*. New York: Hill and Wang.

Home Office and Lord Chancellor's Department (1961) *Report of the Interdepartmental Committee on the Business of the Criminal Courts*. (Streatfeild Report), Cmnd 1289. London: HMSO.

Home Office (1962) *Report of the Departmental Committee on the Probation Service* (Chair: R. P. Morison), Cmd 1650. London: HMSO.

Home Office (1984) *Probation Service in England and Wales: Statement of National Objectives and Priorities*. London: Home Office.

Home Office (1992) *National Standards for the Supervision of Offenders in the Community*. London: Home Office.

Home Office (2004) *Reducing Crime: Changing Lives. The Government Plans for Transforming the Management of Offenders*. London: Home Office.

Hudson, B. (2003) *Justice in the Risk Society*. London: Sage.

Lipton, D., Martinson, R. and Wilks, J. (1975) *The Effectiveness of Correctional Treatment*. New York: Praeger.

Lord Chancellor's Department (1978) *Judicial Studies and Information: Report of a Working Party* (Chair: Lord Justice Bridge). London: HMSO.

Mair, G. (2006) '"The worst tax form you've ever seen"? Probation officers' views about OASys', *Probation Journal*, 53 (1): 7–23.

Martinson, J. (1974) 'What works? Questions and answers about prison reform', *Public Interest*, 35: 22–54.

McNeill, F., Burns, N., Halliday, S., Hutton, N. and Tata, C. (2009) 'Risk, responsibility and reconfiguration', *Punishment and Society*, 11 (4): 419–42.

McWilliams, W. (1983) 'The mission to the English Police Courts 1876–1936', *Howard Journal*, 22: 129–47.

Merrington, S. and Stanley, S. (2007) 'Effectiveness: who counts what?', in L. Gelsthorpe and R. Morgan (eds) *Handbook of Probation*. Cullompton: Willan Publishing.

Millichamp, D., Payne, D. and Thomas, H. (1985) 'A matter of natural justice', *Community Care*, 13 June: 25–7.

Nellis, M. (2007) 'Humanising justice: the English Probation Service', in L. Gelsthorpe and R. Morgan (eds) *Handbook of Probation*. Cullompton: Willan Publishing.

NPS (2001) *A New Choreography: An Integrated Strategy for the National Probation Service for England and Wales – Strategic Framework 2001–2004*. London: Home Office.

NPS (2005) *E-OASys PSR (SDR) Templates*, Probation Circular 89/2005. London: National Probation Directorate.

NPS (2005) *The Criminal Justice Act 2003 – New Sentences and the New Report Framework*, Probation Circular 18/2005. London: National Probation Directorate.

NPS (2007) *Pre-Sentence Report Decision Tool*, Probation Circular 12/2007. London: National Probation Directorate.

NPS (2009) *Determining Pre-Sentence Report Type*, Probation Circular 06/2009. London: National Probation Service.

Phoenix, J. (2009) 'Beyond risk assessment: the return of repressive welfarism', in F. McNeill and M. Barry (eds) *Youth Offending and Youth Justice*. London: Jessica Kingsley.

Raynor, P. (1980) 'Is there any sense in social inquiry reports?', *Probation Journal*, 27: 78–84.

Raynor, P. (1997) 'Evaluating probation: a moving target', in G. Mair (ed.) *Evaluating the Effectiveness of Community Penalties*. Aldershot: Avebury.

Raynor, P. (2007) 'Risk and need assessment in British probation: the contribution of LSI-R', *Psychology, Crime and Law*, 13 (2): 125–38.

Raynor, P. and Robinson, G. (2009) *Rehabilitation, Crime and Justice*, 2nd edn. Basingstoke: Palgrave Macmillan.

Raynor, P., Gelsthorpe, L. and Tisi, A. (1995) 'Quality assurance, pre-sentence reports and the probation service', *British Journal of Social Work*, 25: 477–88.

Raynor, P., Kynch, J., Roberts, C. and Merrington, M. (2000) *Risk and Need Assessment in Probation Services: An Evaluation*, Research Study 211. London: Home Office.

Robinson, G. (2002) 'Exploring risk management in the probation service: contemporary developments in England and Wales', *Punishment and Society*, 4 (1): 5–25.

Robinson, G. (2003) 'Risk and risk assessment', in W.H. Chui and M. Nellis (eds) *Moving Probation Forward: Evidence, Arguments and Practice*. Harlow: Pearson Education.

Senior, P., Crowther-Dowey, C. and Long, M. (2007) *Understanding Modernisation in Criminal Justice*. Cullompton: Willan Publishing.

Tata, C., Burns, N., Halliday, S., Hutton, N. and McNeill, F. (2008) 'Assisting and advising the sentencing decision process', *British Journal of Criminology*, 48 (6): 835–55.

Thorpe, D.H., Smith, D., Green, C.J. and Paley, J. (1980) *Out of Care*. London: Allen and Unwin.

Vanstone, M. (2004) *Supervising Offenders in the Community: A History of Probation Theory and Practice*. Aldershot: Ashgate.

Ward, T. and Maruna, S. (2007) *Rehabilitation*. Abingdon: Routledge.

Young, J. (2007) *The Vertigo of Late Modernity*. London: Sage.

Zedner, L. (2000) 'The pursuit of security', in T. Hope and R. Sparks (eds) *Crime, Risk and Insecurity*. London: Routledge.

Chapter 24

Supervision in historical context: Learning the lessons of (oral) history[1]

Fergus McNeill

Introduction

This collection is principally concerned with the effectiveness of offender supervision. It aims to look beyond questions of the effectiveness of particular intervention programmes or models to examine a much wider range of questions about the moral, political, organisational, professional and inter-personal contexts of offender supervision – and to examine how its associated practices relate to the processes of desistance and reintegration that they exist to support.

In various ways, paying more attention to many of these contextual issues in offender supervision represents an effort not just to advance debates about 'what works?' in offender supervision, but also an admission that it is not necessarily all that easy to describe exactly what offender supervision is, what it means to those involved and how it is experienced by them. Being able to develop a convincing and satisfying answer to questions about the nature and experience of supervision is a necessary prerequisite to answering questions about effectiveness. Before we can understand properly whether something works, we first need to know what that something is. And yet, I wonder how much we really know about how community sanctions are (and have been) constituted and practised and how they are experienced by those subject to them? This problem becomes particularly acute when debates shift from considering the effectiveness of particular interventions to considering the effectiveness of different types of sanctions.

With these questions partly in mind – and to satisfy an enduring curiosity about Scottish probation history – about two years ago I embarked on a small-scale study of oral histories of Scottish probation,[2] along with my colleague Beth Weaver.[3] Our particular interest was in Scottish probation in the 1960s – a period of probation history that seemed to have been forgotten in the aftermath of the organisational restructuring that followed the implementation of the Social Work (Scotland) Act 1968, when probation work was subsumed within generic social work departments. I suspected, on the basis of a few conversations with veterans of 1960s probation, that the 'official' sources of the period tell only a very partial version of what went on in those days (for an account of some of these sources see McNeill 2005; McNeill and Whyte 2007). Though we did not set out to inform debates about the effectiveness of probation, it turns out that the study's findings – or rather its participants – have much to say both about what probation was and about whether, when and how it 'worked'.

Method and analysis

The study involved oral history interviews with 13 former probation practitioners and educators and 12 former probationers with experience of probation in Scotland in the 1960s. This chapter draws principally on the probationers' accounts of supervision. These are the 'user voices' to which other social services are now rightly expected to attend, but somehow when we call them 'offenders', their views and stories are too easily neglected. However, we do so at our peril; these are voices worth listening to.

The 12 probationers comprised 11 men and one woman, ranging in age from 52 to 70. They were recruited through newspaper adverts and then interviewed either at home, at the university or by telephone, depending on their preference. As is common in oral histories, our interviews were loosely structured and ranged in duration from under 20 minutes to over an hour. The process of analysis involved full transcription of all of the interviews and immersion in the data thus generated – using both the audio recordings and the transcripts. As well as searching for recurring themes across the interviews, we also aimed to consider each narrative as a whole – and to look for significant differences in the types of narratives that we collected.

Seven of the participants had been on probation for property offences, two for violence or disorder, one for carrying an offensive

493

weapon and one for truancy. One could not remember even the nature of the offence in question. All of the probationers came from the West of Scotland and most (n = 9) had been on probation as juveniles (the median age at the time of their first probation order was 13.5 years). Academic analyses of the time (Arnott and Duncan 1970) suggest that in the 1960s probation in Scotland was mainly used for juveniles, for first offenders and for minor offences, so there is no reason to think this small sample unrepresentative.

Some brief comment on the nature and status of the evidence thus gleaned is perhaps required in a collection of this nature. Within the discipline of history, debates about the relative merits of different kinds of sources have been very well rehearsed in recent decades. One of the clearest defences of oral testimonies as a source for history is provided by Paul Thompson (1978) in his seminal book *The Voice of the Past*. His chapter on 'Evidence' still deserves to be read, not just by historians but by social scientists and criminologists. Thompson reminds us that both oral and written sources, both official and unofficial accounts, require critical interpretation. In the context of studies of interventions with offenders, for example, we often neglect the vagaries of the 'official' evidence about reoffending. Though too often read uncritically as evidence of change or the lack of it, reconviction data represent the culminations of whole series of social processes (reporting, recording, investigating, detecting, formally processing, prosecuting, sentencing, convicting); all of which are vulnerable to human biases and failures – and perhaps most significantly to discriminatory treatment of disadvantaged groups, both as offenders and as victims (for recent Scottish evidence of this, see McAra and McVie 2005). Thus, even leaving aside more technical problems with reconviction data (Mair 1997), official criminal records are inescapably subjective and socially constructed, for all of their appearance as quantifiable 'facts' in much criminological research.

By way of contrast, oral history at least has the merit of recognising and engaging critically and reflexively with the vulnerabilities of its evidential basis:

> Oral history has no unified subject; it is told from multiple points of view and the impartiality usually claimed for historians is replaced by the partiality of the narrator. 'Partiality' here stands for both 'unfinishedness' and for 'taking sides': oral history can never be told without taking sides, since the 'sides' exist within the telling. (Portelli 1991, in Perks and Thomson 2006: 41)

A number of problems of partiality arose in this project; problems for us as researchers in considering the influence of where we stand and how our identities might have affected the data we gathered and how we analysed and presented it; problems in the self-selecting nature of participation in the study and the unarticulated motivations that doubtless lay behind it; problems in the partialities of individual and collective memories and of their recall; problems in inviting participants to tell the stories of only small parts of their lives, without telling enough about what went before or went after to set these probation stories in context; and problems in the partialities involved in moving from the interview to the transcript, from the transcripts to the analysis, from the analysis to the outputs. All of these methodological challenges and problems have been much debated in the relevant literature (for an excellent overview, see Perks and Thomson 2006). There is too little space here for an account of how such challenges were (inevitably) partially and imperfectly addressed in this project. There is therefore little alternative to simply acknowledging these challenges and allowing the reader to critically assess the relevance and importance of what follows for contemporary policy and practice.

From court to probation

The probationers shared in common many aspects of their social backgrounds that we might summarise as accounts of growing up in tough times and tough places. They related a range of family problems including parental (usually paternal) alcohol use, bereavement and loss, economic hardship, large families, emotionally distant parents and a general lack of oversight occasioned by their parents' hard struggle to make ends meet. In this context, the friendship group, the 'gang' or the 'team', was often very important and sometimes formed the locus of behavioural problems including fighting, theft or other forms of 'mischief'. Many respondents recognised the significance of peer pressure and the associated issues of reputation, status and living up to expectations. With hindsight, they could identify the vulnerabilities that came from the interactions between problems in their environments, their families and among their peers.

Though social enquiry or pre-sentence reports then, as now, were an important feature of probation practice, only three of the 12 probationers recalled any such enquiries. Those that did remembered only basic questioning about their activities, relationships and families. One respondent, however, told a revealing story about being assessed in a remand home. The intelligence he gleaned from other more institutionally experienced boys was that you had to come up with a plausible story about why you were getting into trouble, in order to elicit sympathy rather than condemnation. He opted for the common (but in this case totally untrue) story that his dad was an alcoholic, much to the chagrin of his sister years later:

FM: Ah, I see, aye. So you had to have something – ?

Mark: It's the cause of why you're doing what you're doing.

FM: Yeah, okay, and a drunk father is one good story?

Mark: Aye, like that 'Poor wee Johnny, he was put down as a drunk'. And then my sister found out, she got the report – you see I got the report and I held the report for years and years and then one of my sisters found it – 'What's this? My Da's a drunk?!'

Amusing though Mark found this now, it tells us something interesting perhaps about the pressure to make sense of one's own misdeeds in a way deemed acceptable to or consistent with professional understandings of the times.

Few of the probationers had clear recollections of court. Those that did remember being sentenced spoke mostly of fear and formality – and of the sense of being processed rather than engaged with. If any dialogue with judges was recalled, it was invariably of the admonishing rather than the understanding sort. In somewhat surprising contrast, probation officers clearly made a very significant first impression, for better or worse. Andrew's account was fairly typical:

… my Ma said, 'You better get up quick … there's somebody up to see you.' I remember that vaguely – and running up the stairs and there was this big man, a very imposing man, he looked ginormous, he looked about – he was quite a tall man, he must have been about six foot. And I was really, really overwhelmed by this guy, the suit on, immaculate, speaking with a wee kind of funny accent type thing.

To their young charges, probation officers were intimidating both physically and socially. The officers' mode of dress (dark suits or smart jackets, raincoats and hats) seemed to confirm their higher social positions. Several probationers made clear that they were in no doubt that their probation office was their 'better'.

This social distance between the probationer and the probation officer was clearly something that the probation officer had to bridge in the early stages of supervision if effective communication was to be established. Some officers were skilled at doing so, as Luke and Mary relate:

FM: ... how did he explain how, what the whole thing was going to be about, if you can remember?

Luke: I do remember. He actually explained that it was about helping me change my life and not to get into any sort of further trouble. And his language was very, very acceptable and understandable because he didn't kind of jargonise words, he basically said – 'This is to keep you, helping you to stay out of any more trouble, and I said 'Oh'. He said, 'It's as simple as that'. And there was an immediate bond developed from that point, I knew that this wasn't somebody that was coming into my home and telling me how to live my life. It was somebody that was saying 'I'm here to support you and help you.'

Mary: And it was really good, you know, I was able to tell her about my home life, you know, and how miserable that I felt and she asked me what I wanted to do with my life and, you know, we just hit it off, we just hit it off. And on the occasions, you know, she'd say occasionally to come to Osborne Street and I would go to Osborne Street and she'd take me to tea in town, it was called Miss Cranstoun's. Now, you must remember here I was, a 17-year-old, terrible background, you know, I never had any money and she would take me into this beautiful tearoom, you know, where all these well dressed people were sitting and with the cake stand the waiter coming and you know, I'd be sitting – I was absolutely overawed – overawed with it! And I thought 'Gosh, she's brought me here!', you know, she's brought me here. So then –

FM: Just a bit – what did that convey to you, that she'd brought you there? What did it mean to you?

Mary: I think it said that she liked me and, you know, and she listened to what I was saying and also sitting there and

> looking round as well and I thought, 'I could be here too, I could do this as well,' you know – 'This is what I want to do, this is what I want to do.'

On the other hand, some probationers discerned an underlying lack of care, interest or respect from their officers:

> No, she would never – this woman to me didn't like her job... She didn't like anybody that came in, not just me, you know, because I had never been – I was no' a cheeky person... And so that's the kind of attitude, she was no' just with me, she was like that when I seen her with other people, she'd be quite like a bit of business and head down, didn't look at you kind of thing, you know? (John)

> I think it was a case of he was frustrated with me and I was, you know, I didn't feel as if I was getting any support or respect. You know, there was never any sort of understanding of my problems, my problems were never ever repaired in any way shape or form, it was a case of 'Go to school, full stop'. Don't ask what the underlying problems are, that would be too much to ask, you know. (Bart)

In cases such as these, where the probation officer was seen as being a mere 'pen-pusher' who simply wanted to check up that you were behaving and checking in, the probationer very often 'checked out' – at least in terms of any serious engagement with the order's rehabilitative intent.

On probation: helping, holding and hurting

It is clear from the excerpts that I have already quoted that in many respects the tone was set for probation in its early exchanges – and that this tone depended heavily on not just what messages the probationer officer conveyed but the style in which she or he conveyed them. The basic idea that the probation officer was there to provide help – to 'advise, assist and befriend' as the traditional epithet from the Probation of Offenders Act 1907 put it – was clearly evident for some:

I don't have any doubt the man was trying to help me, guide me, support me – maybe prevent me going to prison, I don't [know] if at the end he could have recommended prison, he maybe, you know – trying to achieve, trying to help me, trying to guide me, trying to support me, trying to advise me, everything ... (Simon)

I think he was genuinely concerned about me. I think he took his job seriously and I think that the options he had, I mean it's not like today's options where they can do all sorts of things with you ... But I think he genuinely liked me even though the big vagabond that I was. (Andrew)

The significance of being liked, being cared for, being seen not just as who you are but as who you might become, was a recurring theme – as is perhaps clearest from Mary's story of her visit to Miss Cranstoun's tearoom. But probation was not just about these kinds of positive help and reinforcement; it also had both 'holding' and 'hurting' dimensions. More often than not the three themes of helping, holding and hurting were intertwined.

By the term 'holding' here I mean not just the support and protection that we can clearly think of as allied to 'helping', but also surveillance and containment. In the former connection, probation often seemed to involve and invoke the notion of quasi-parental guardianship and sometimes (for younger probation officers) fraternal support:

Luke: ... to me he was a tower of strength and partly a source of protection.

FM: Okay – what age was he roughly?

Luke: I thought he would have been – I would probably have said mid-forties.

FM: ... more like a father figure than a big brother or a – ?

Luke: Oh yes, yeah.

Because he would come up to you and give you a cuddle and that – 'Oh, you're doing well, wee man,' and things like that, you know, things like that, you know, it was good – 'Have you been doing what I tell you?' and you'd say, 'Aye ... I done this and done that' – 'Ah, brilliant!' and give you a cuddle and that – 'Stick in, wee man', you know. (Paul, emphasis added)

In many cases, this kind of support and protection seemed to be focused on efforts to merely contain the disruptions and turbulence of adolescence; perhaps a kind of harm minimisation strategy that awaited the normalising and socialising processes of ordinary maturation. Evidently where parents lacked the capacity to fulfil this containing role, probation officers sought to step into the breach.

But sometimes this kind of containment had more overtly constraining and surveillant aspects. These features were brought home to me most clearly by James who articulated a very sharp recollection of the 'geography of supervision'. James had the misfortune of living very near to both the probation office and the police station. His probation officer made it clear that he should be home from school every day within 20 minutes of the lessons ending, just in case the officer might choose to visit. He had to remain at home until after tea, at which point he was allowed out to play, but only in certain nearby streets. The local beat police officer would let the probation officer know if he strayed too far. On Fridays, he was expected to be at the Boys' Guild in the local church. If he failed to show up, the priest would pass the information on. And if his general conduct gave any cause for concern, his mother was more than ready to let the probation officer know. All of this might make a modern-day electronic tag sound easy-going, but what was striking was that despite the irritation caused by all of these impositions and restrictions, James seemed to tolerate them as a burden that was intended to serve his interests, the imposition of which was motivated by care on the probation officer's part.

Others conveyed a similar sense of the probation officer as 'just the all-seeing eye type thing; he knew what was going on' (Andrew), but for some this had a more malign aspect. Thus Peter, who was 26 when the order was imposed and by his own account an occasionally serious offender with a significant alcohol problem, remained highly indignant to this day about alleged police-probation collusion in the breach of his order: 'I'm sure but word was put into the, these probation officers: 'Get him off the fucking streets.' Do you know what I mean?'.

Some support for Peter's suspicions is found in the accounts of the probation officers to whom we spoke, at least in the sense that they made clear that regular flows of information and intelligence between the courts, the police and probation staff were indeed a routine aspect of practice. As Peter's account suggests, in his case the surveillant aspects of probation stretched beyond 'holding' and into 'hurting'.

One of the most common 'pains of probation' (see Durnescu 2009) articulated by the probationers related to the looming threat of and sometimes the actual pains of enforcement action. In Peter's case, these pains were exacerbated by a sense of profound injustice. Peter acknowledged his failure to comply with a probation condition that he must attend Alcoholics Anonymous meetings; he attended one or two meetings but found that they didn't suit him. Despite this, he held down a job, limited his drinking and avoided reoffending. Nonetheless, 18 months into a three-year order, his probation officer lost patience with his persistent refusal to attend AA. With considerable vehemence, Peter related his subsequent arrest and imprisonment as follows:

> I said, 'I've no done fuck all!' He [one of two police officers] said 'I don't know but we've to come for you', he said, 'you go in front of the sheriff at 2 o'clock today'… So I went in front of him, oh, and I said, 'Look – ' and I said – 'He [the probation officer] doesn't agree with some people and I'm one of them', I said, 'I've no done any harm, I've not – I'll need to have a chance of [keeping my] job.' He said, 'You can get a job in three months,' he said, and three months he gave me. That really fucking burst me – do you know what I mean? … Because *it was something for nothing, that was as far as I was concerned, you know.* I was really upset about it, I really was flaming after it. (Peter, emphasis added)

For Matthew, the pains of enforcement action had perhaps deeper roots. Sometime before he reached school age, Matthew and his siblings had been separated from one another and their parents during a brief period of institutional care occasioned by parental illness. The family were reunited and years later, Matthew was getting on well with a young probation officer he regarded as a 'big brother' figure who was trying to steer him away from trouble. However, after several minor further offences, his probation officer suggested that a short custodial remand in relation to one of these new charges might do him some good:

Basically he put in the report that I never – I think I had to be taught a lesson and to this day I still disagree with that because I got remanded in custody to get taught a lesson. *To me, what's all that about? You're supposed to get remanded in custody for reports or for – i.e. 'Lock him up' and that was the story of my life, right through that: 'Lock him up'*... At the end up he passed [me] on to somebody else because he thought I was out of control. Again, I felt rejected. (Matthew, emphasis added)

For Matthew this report recommendation represented another abandonment – with clear echoes of an earlier trauma of which the probation officer was doubtless unaware. Nonetheless, Matthew's sense of betrayal, like Peter's sense of injustice, remains potent and enduring (for more recent evidence of similar reactions to enforcement action, see Digard 2010). Although there are legitimate contemporary concerns about the problems that arise from overly prescriptive and constraining rules on enforcement (see Robinson and McNeill 2008, and this volume; Ugwudike, this volume), both of these cases point to the problems that can arise where practitioner discretion in managing compliance is too excessive or where it is exercised capriciously.

In other cases, even when breach action did not result, the burdens of supervision and the mere threat of further punishment still constituted a 'pain of probation' – especially for adolescents eager to 'spread their wings':

Andrew: Yes, it was a punishment, yes, to me it was, aye.

FM: So – in what sense?

Andrew: In the sense that you were always under the wings, I was always – my parents always threatened me with him .... 'We're going to tell your probation officer,' you know, that type of thing and then that thing you had to be direct, you know, you're a kid and you just want to go out and get about and you had to meet him every week, you know, you had to be there. *It was a burden, aye it was.* I suppose it's like these boys, you know, they've got the time thing, they canny go out at night.

FM: Yeah.

Andrew: Aye, probably, well I felt that way, *I felt restricted so it was like a sentence.* (Emphasis added)

In three cases, the pains of probation extended beyond those legitimated by the courts. In the most troubling interview in the study, Mark described an experience of witnessing sexual abuse by a probation officer. In his account, the officer required boys on probation to attend regular Scout hall meetings, where he put them through intense physical exercise and then insisted they shower before going home:

> So there was just a wee cubicle there, right, and we'd to go in and have the shower and then you'd come out and then he [the probation officer] would rub you down, right? (Mark)

Mark recalled that the boys simply laughed this off and suggested that the probation officer's behaviour was common knowledge in the community – but no one challenged or reported it. That said, when Mark fled the Scout hall during his first visit, his elder brother did intervene, insisting that Mark not be required to attend again and that all further meetings take place in the office with the brother present.

In two other cases, probationers described physical bullying by probation officers. Bart was on probation only for truancy. He had committed no criminal offences prior to the order but in his view the probation experience itself triggered his descent into institutionalisation and delinquency. His description of physical abuse was clear:

Bart: I was actually afraid of him, you know.

FM: How do you mean, physically or – ?

Bart: Well, both physically and, you know, mentally because *he did one day grab me up against a wall in his office by the throat and I can remember his mad eyes blazing* and I can't remember exactly what he was saying to me, you know, but it wasn't nice anyway whatever it was, all because I was still truanting. (Emphasis added)

Probation methods

Interestingly, but perhaps not surprisingly, neither the surveillant nor the punitive aspects of probation featured much in the probation officers' accounts. However, some of them did recognise the deterrent aspect of the probation order's quality as a kind of suspended punishment. Indeed, for some of them it was the order itself that was, in important respects, the probation method. 'Mere' supervision was supposed to bring about change (or at least, as I have already suggested, contain trouble).

Where probationers and probation officers were able to articulate a method (over and above the order) that was being used for supporting change, they tended to stress the role of diversion into constructive and organised youth activities and, for older probationers, into employment. Probationers and officers also shared in common the recollection of probation officers working with or through parents – not perhaps in the sense of engaging in formal 'family work' or addressing family dynamics, but rather in the sense of simply supporting parents in their efforts to contain young people during adolescence, thereby buttressing parental authority.

What was notable in both sets of accounts is how little evidence we found of the considered and consistent use of social casework methods aimed at diagnosing and correcting deviance. This is despite the fact that the official sources and academic texts of the time tend to describe this as the predominant method of practice by the 1960s (McNeill 2005; McNeill and Whyte 2007; Monger 1964; Vanstone 2004). Although it is the subject for another paper, the probation officers' accounts imply that this may have been because probation was learned mainly 'on the job' – from one's peers – rather than through academic engagements in the incipient probation training programme.[4] This kind of professional socialisation may have engendered a conservative practice culture that was slow to adapt to novel ideas and methods.

In discussing their officer's methods, several probationers revealed a degree of realism and perhaps even sympathy for the limited resources at the disposal of the 1960s officer. Set against the context of the tough times and tough places discussed previously, they saw their officers as having no real means of addressing or relieving those broader social pressures:

> I don't think they had any options in they days, I don't think they had any. His method I think was just to try to be friendly and he was patient ... Okay, I got into other things but certainly it helped ... *Really – he didn't have the – I mean in they days, don't forget, a probation officer didn't do anything for you, a probation officer just made sure you were behaving yourself.* (Andrew, emphasis added)

Impacts and imprints

Perhaps despite this perceived lack of methods and resources – and against the grain of the social contexts in which the probationers struggled – there is evidence that probation had some effect. While five of the orders were breached, seven were completed, and two of the probationers reported that probation brought about their complete and permanent desistance from crime. Even among those who breached the orders, or who failed to immediately desist, many spoke of probation decelerating their offending – at least for a while. Typically, like current day probationers, where care had evoked loyalty they spoke of a desire not to let the probation officer down (Rex 1999). Underlying this perhaps lay an appreciation of the probation officer's authenticity – what we might call the moral quality of their work. Though it may be difficult to define this quality clearly – and though the implication of authenticity is that it may not be something that could ever be standardised as a facet of 'effective practice' – the probationers recognised it clearly enough; they knew (or felt they knew) who was well motivated and caring, and who was not.

Looking beyond the immediate impact of the probation orders, there is also some interesting if only suggestive evidence about the longer-term impact of the officers. Of the 12 probationers, it is striking that the subsequent life trajectories of six involved significant professional or volunteer roles as carers of different sorts. Thus, Luke himself became a criminal justice social worker, Paul a member of the Children's Panel,[5] Mary a midwife, Simon a volunteer boxing coach, Andrew a Christian prison visitor and James a welfare rights officer. These involvements in generative activities may well owe something to the probationers' exposure to role models who enabled the probationers to believe in who they might become (see Maruna and LeBel, this volume; McNeill and Maruna 2007; Weaver and McNeill 2010).

Conclusion

So is there anything more here than mere nostalgia for times past and practices lost in the mists of reorganisation and change? I think that there is – indeed, I think that, despite all the methodological limitations acknowledged at the outset, there are two particularly important lessons that can be learned from listening to these voices;

and that there is therefore much to be gained from paying close attention to the life experiences that they convey.

The first lesson for contemporary debates about 'what works?' is that structures and systems are only part of the story of how justice or punishment works out in practice. These voices reveal the extent to which the meanings and natures of sanctions are negotiated between the people involved. Perhaps a key message is that where sanctions aim to elicit change, the skill of the practitioner in bridging the social distance between the punished and the punishers is critical to the process. Equally, the moral quality and the authenticity of the practitioner's performance seem to lie at the heart of the matter (see Liebling 2004); this moral quality profoundly affects the meaning, nature and experience of the sanction. Within this context, the legitimacy of the practitioner – on which his or her influence for good depends – is hard won, easily lost, and almost impossible to recover (see Robinson and McNeill, this volume; McNeill and Robinson, forthcoming).

The second and related lesson concerns not so much the immediate impact of interventions as their lasting 'imprint'. Inviting people to recollect experiences of probation that are over 40 years distant may raise methodological problems, but it also allows for a longer lens picture of the effect of a sanction than most contemporary evaluations (see also Farrall 2003; Farrall and Calverley 2006). Listening to these voices, it occurs to me that, in simple terms, rehabilitative interventions invite and aim to enable people to be or become 'good'; and that this is a long-term project. But how can we expect people whose lives have been far from good to become so unless we allow them to experience 'good'? And might it be that exposing people to 'good' – to fairness, to justice, to respect, to compassion – is both the right thing to do in itself and something that might somehow, sometime, call forth some good in return? Equally, where we return pain for pain, harm for harm, evil for evil, rejection for rejection, what can we really expect to receive in return? Where we interpret lapses and failings in the change process as evidence of the immutability of bad character, do we not ourselves contribute to its confirmation?

In an important way, these voices from the past remind us that our penal values and visions matter. For better or worse, they say something fundamental about who 'the punishers' are, and about what we dare to hope that 'the punished' can become.

Notes

1 This chapter draws heavily on the published version of an annual public lecture: 'Helping, holding, hurting: recalling and reforming punishment', the 6th annual Apex Lecture, at the Signet Library, Parliament Square, Edinburgh, 8 September 2009. I am grateful to Apex for permission to re-use the material here.
2 The study was funded by the British Academy (Award no: SG48403).
3 Lecturer in Social Work, Glasgow School of Social Work.
4 This began in Glasgow in 1962 and many of the probation officers interviewed had experienced it.
5 In Scotland children and young people who come to the attention of the authorities, whether on grounds of care and protection or on grounds of offending behaviour, are dealt with through Children's Hearings. The Hearings involve three lay people sitting as a panel, which considers social work and other advice in determining how best to address the issues raised.

References

Arnott, A. and Duncan, J. (1970) *The Scottish Criminal*. Edinburgh: Edinburgh University Press.

Digard, L. (2010) 'When legitimacy is denied: sex offenders' perceptions and experiences of prison recall', *Probation Journal*, 57 (1): 1–19.

Durnescu, I. (2009) 'Pains of probation: effective practice and human rights', paper presented at the 9th Annual Conference of the European Society of Criminology, University of Ljubljana, 9–12 September.

Farrall, S. (2003) 'J'accuse: probation evaluation-research epistemologies: part 1: the critique', *Criminology and Criminal Justice*, 3: 161–79.

Farrall, S. and Calverley, A. (2006) *Understanding Desistance from Crime: Theoretical Directions in Rehabilitation and Resettlement*. Maidenhead: Open University Press.

Liebling, A. (2004) *Prisons and their Moral Performance: A Study of Values, Quality and Prison Life*. Oxford: Oxford University Press.

Mair, G. (1997) *Evaluating the Effectiveness of Community Penalties*. Aldershot: Avebury.

McAra, L. and McVie, S. (2005) 'The usual suspects? Street life, young people and the Police', *Criminology and Criminal Justice*, 5 (1): 5–36.

McNeill, F. (2005) 'Remembering probation in Scotland', *Probation Journal*, 52 (1): 25–40.

McNeill, F. and Maruna, S. (2007) 'Giving up and giving back: desistance, generativity and social work with offenders', in G. McIvor and P. Raynor (eds) *Developments in Work with Offenders*. London: Routledge.

McNeill, F. and Robinson, G. (forthcoming) 'Liquid legitimacy and community sanctions' in A. Crawford and A. Huckelsby (eds) *Legitimacy and Criminal Justice*. Cullompton: Willan Publishing.

McNeill, F. and Whyte, B. (2007) *Reducing Reoffending: Social Work and Community Justice in Scotland*. Cullompton: Willan Publishing.

Monger, M. (1964) *Casework in Probation*. London: Butterworths.

Perks, R. and Thomson, A. (eds) (2006) *The Oral History Reader*, 2nd edn. London and New York: Routledge.

Rex, S. (1999) 'Desistance from offending: experiences of probation', *Howard Journal*, 36(4): 366–83.

Robinson, G. and McNeill, F. (2008) 'Exploring the dynamics of compliance with community penalties', *Theoretical Criminology*, 12 (4): 431–49.

Thompson, P. (1978) *The Voice of the Past: Oral History*. Oxford: Oxford University Press.

Vanstone, M. (2004) *Supervising Offenders in the Community: A History of Probation Theory and Practice*. Aldershot: Ashgate.

Weaver, B. and McNeill, F. (2010) 'Travelling hopefully: desistance research and probation practice', in F. Cowe, J. Deering and J. Pakes (eds) *What Else Works? Creative Work with Offenders*. Cullompton: Willan Publishing.

Chapter 25

Electronic monitoring: towards integration into offender management?[1]

Mike Nellis

Introduction

In England and Wales, and Scotland, and indeed around the world since the 1990s, electronically monitored (EM) curfews have largely been used for punitive and controlling (rather than rehabilitative) purposes, and as such have become a commonplace feature of community supervision, mostly as a stand-alone sentence, occasionally as a requirement in a multi-component sentencing package and as an early release from prison mechanism (the Home Detention Curfew scheme). They have also been used as a condition of bail and of post-release licences, including parole; as a component of intensive supervision schemes for young offenders; as a means of checking the movements of asylum seekers,[2] and sometimes as an element in the handful of control orders imposed on terrorist suspects (Nellis 2004, 2007; Mair 2005). British governments have remained committed to EM despite the periodic tarnishing of its image in the media, where 'tagging' has come to be seen as a rather lenient penalty compared to the tough 'punishment in the community' that it was officially conceived and projected as in 1989/90, when it was first piloted, and even in 1999 when it first became a nationally available measure. A total of 580,000 offenders have been tagged since then and the scandals that have unfairly come to define its public image relate to only a tiny handful of cases.

The existence of EM was slowly accepted by probation, social work and sentencers in Britain – more so in England and Wales than Scotland – but has rarely been embraced with enthusiasm. With adult offenders only limited attempts were made to integrate EM with other forms of community provision, despite the steady accumulation of international evidence that its stand-alone use had no positive impact on recidivism (Renzema and Mayo-Wilson 2005). Bonta *et al.*'s (2000) much cited Canadian research fitted with this but suggested that EM seemingly added stability to the lives of offenders such that they were better able to complete their structured rehabilitation programmes, and thereby get more benefit from them. Renzema and Mayo-Wilson (2005) themselves suggested that more research be undertaken on the impact of programmes that combined EM with other treatment measures, but what little has been done in Britain has mostly been with young offenders. Padgett *et al.*'s (2006) Florida study showed a crime suppression effect for offenders on community control with EM while the order lasted, but while acknowledging that some offenders were also subject to other measures ignored their possible impact and gave all the credit to EM.

This chapter focuses on recent attempts – both organisational and individual – to integrate EM in a broader offender management strategy in England and Wales, but it is not without international significance. While the particular institutional structures and precise policy frameworks in which EM is embedded do vary between countries, the question of how, and with what, to integrate EM will have to be faced if reduced recidivism *in the longer term* is desired. It is possible, however, that some countries will choose to maintain EM only as a form of stand-alone surveillance, which may reduce crime over the duration of the order, or have other penal effects (freeing up prison places), but will surely fall short of the potential which its American originators saw in it 50 years ago (Gable and Gable 2007).

On parallel tracks: EM and the probation service

For most of its history in Britain, policy on EM and the probation service ran on parallel tracks, reflecting separate policy and administration streams in the Home Office. The Conservative government which introduced EM saw it as something high tariff and distinctively tougher than *mere* probation supervision, while the probation service initially rejected it as alien to its social work-based rehabilitative traditions (Nellis 1991). EM curfew orders, EM bail and EM early release from prison were always intended to be stand-alone measures, forms of control in their own right, whose integration with anything else was not required. The fact that EM was delivered by private sector organisations (initially Premier, Securicor and Reliance) contracted by the Home Office compounded – and indeed helped create – this sense of separate worlds, producing an organisational interface at operational level which there was little incentive or means to bridge (compared, say, to statutory–voluntary partnerships). With EM seen as something quite separate from the forms of supervision for which probation was responsible, there was no requirement for either managers or front-line staff in either the private or public organisations to cooperate for the good of individual offenders.

The question of what it might mean to make EM 'more integrated' arose very soon after national roll-out, with the introduction of the Intensive Supervision and Surveillance Programme (ISSP) for serious and persistent young offenders in May 2000. This was a multi-component sentencing package, intended to reduce offending and lessen the use of custody, containing elements of education and training, offending behaviour work, reparation, an EM curfew, human tracking, and intelligence-led policing, that could be embedded in a supervision order, bail or the post-custody supervision element of a detention and training order. The interim evaluation of the first 41 ISSP schemes indicated that tagging was used in an increasingly standardised way in 72 per cent of cases (augmented by voice verification in 17 per cent of cases), but flagged up the difficulties of integrating EM into the overall supervision programme (Waters *et al.*, 2003)

The Criminal Justice and Court Services Act 2000 introduced two new uses of EM – as a condition in two community penalties (a community rehabilitation order and community punishment and rehabilitation order) and as a condition of a post-release licence or supervision in the community part of a detention and training order (DTO) for young offenders. The most significant finding of the Home Office-funded research into the new uses in three pilot areas was that take-up of them was extremely low (Bottomley *et al.* 2004), due to 'a failure to articulate the policy issues underlying the new legislation' (2004: 47), more so in respect of the community penalties than the post-release licences. Probation officers were overcoming their earlier hostility to EM and sentencers were increasing their use of stand-alone EM-curfews on over-16s (8,164 in 2002 compared to 3,427 in 2000), but it was not clear to either group what the advantages of integrating an EM curfew into community orders would be. Increased inter-agency meetings to discuss the new uses were 'no substitute for clear statements of objectives and procedures' (2004: 48) and probation managers saw no reason to pursue integrated uses of EM when it entailed more work for probation officers in respect of breach, without any new resources.[3] While the absence of official written guidance was sometimes the problem, the researchers also warned against information overload, which made it 'difficult [for practitioners] to separate the relevant and the irrelevant' (2004: 43). Failures of 'recording and communication' (2004: 49) between the courts and the contractors created later confusion between probation and the contractors as to who was responsible for initiating breach action in particular cases. And beyond all these specific policy failings lay the impact of the vast, disorienting changes in administration and governance that the CJ&CS Act 2000 had imposed on the probation service itself (that is, increasing centralisation and a reduction from 55 to 42 local probation areas), amid that taking up new uses of EM was difficult to prioritise.

These reforms were not consolidated before the next round began. The Halliday (2001) review of sentencing proposed blending custody and community supervision into an array of 'seamless sentences'. It argued that the various aims of sentencing, once thought to be in tension with each other – punishment, reduction of crime, rehabilitation, public protection and reparation – could also be blended into coherent sentencing packages. The Criminal Justice Act 2003 gave expression to Halliday, merging hitherto separate community penalties into a single community order with 12 requirements (one of which was an EM curfew), and laying the legislative foundation for a more integrated approach to 'offender management'. It envisaged some quite specific seamless sentences – custody plus and intermittent custody – in which, had they not proved too administratively unwieldy to implement, EM might have figured prominently. The single community order did not itself become operational until April 2005 (and the use of multiple requirements in its early days was far less innovative than had been anticipated (Mair *et al.* 2007)).

By then, the well-publicised case of Peter Williams, a 19-year-old who murdered a woman jeweller in Nottingham while tagged as part of an ISSP, had illustrated the practical difficulty of integrating EM into other forms of community supervision. Arguably, Williams was wrongly assessed as suitable for ISSP (and EM) and certainly placed in boarding accommodation in which he had no incentive to stay, curfewed or not. Premier's monitoring officers and the Youth Offending Team (YOT) each thought the other had more contact with Williams than either had, and at the time of the murder both had lost contact with him, though they were still looking for him (HMIP 2004). In the media, EM (and Serco) bore the brunt of criticism in this case, but the YOT's failure to grasp how much personal support someone as psychologically damaged as Williams actually needed was as much of a failing (Nellis 2006a).

Towards Convergence: EM and NOMS

The National Officer Management Service (NOMS), a 'headquarters' organisation within the Home Office that brought prisons and probation services under a single management umbrella, was created in June 2004. Its immediate origins lay in the White Paper (Home Office 2003) and the subsequent Correctional Services Review (the first Carter report (2003)), which envisioned NOMS – a 'seamless' organisation that would implement Halliday – as the basis of a more coordinated process of 'end to end offender management' than the separate 'silos' of prisons and probation had ever achieved. For the first time (in respect of community supervision), there was to be a strong regional dimension in the creation and coordination of services. In addition, through the mechanism of 'contestability', ten regional offender managers would be able to commission services from the voluntary, private and indeed statutory sectors.

Since 1999, EM had been managed by a small (never more than ten people) Electronic Monitoring Team (EMT) within the Home Office, that commissioned and procured the national contracts and served as a resource for the various organisations – the probation service, the prison service, the courts service, the Youth Justice Board and, from 2004, the Immigration and Detention Services – responsible for implementing particular EM programmes. It also supplied information to parliament, press and public. Its accumulated insights into the ways of the private sector enabled it to negotiate a much more favourable contract in the second round of contracting in 2005, reducing overall costs from £100m to £60m, significantly enhancing 'value for money'. In the new contract, the suppliers were reduced in number from three to two – G4S (formerly Securicor, now merged with Group 4) and Serco (formerly branded as Premier, now without its original US partner, Wackenhut). The EMT was acknowledged by all its English stakeholders to have been very effective at promoting EM, and its expertise was often sought internationally. In 2006, however, it was subject to an internal Home Office review (undertaken by an external consultancy) 'to ensure that [it was] fully prepared and fit for the future development of NOMS' (Avail Consulting 2006: 2). Avail commended much of EMT's work, but judged (not necessarily fairly) that within the team 'EM is not always seen as integral to criminal justice policy' and 'has been isolated from broader sentencing policy' (2006: 19). It concluded that the 'model of delivery is HQ-centric as opposed to regional, doesn't fit with the rest of NOMS' (neglecting that the EMT served other stakeholders as well), and 'does not support placing EM at the heart of the criminal justice system' (2006: 25) – which, strictly speaking, it had never claimed to. It recommended devolving some of EMT's operational functions (not procurement) to the NOMS regions and providing 'additional resources' which 'could be used to support staff in the regions to increase their understanding of EM and raise its profile within the criminal justice system' (2006: 27).[4] The review took place at a time of 'increasing ministerial interest in EM and its uses', born of concern over rising prisoner numbers and a perceived need to 'make alternatives to prison a necessity' (*sic*, 2006: 7): the primary aim of regionalising EM provision was simply about the expansion of its use, rather than any particular concern with its seamless integration with other measures. In the event, Avail's very NOMS-centric report was only one of several internal factors that shaped the future of EMT.

EM and the offender management model

The concept of 'offender management' was intended as a means of constituting and administering 'seamless sentences', but elaborating it in practice proved hard. There were both *systemic* and *individualised* elements to the concept – the former relating to the creation of structures, processes and resources at national, regional and local level, and the latter (borrowing case management approaches from health and social services) to the detailed sentence planning which utilised these resources for the benefit of particular offenders and mapped their 'pathway' though the 'system'. Although the creation of a coherent and viable internal structure for NOMS took longer than the Home Office had anticipated (Nellis and Goodman 2009), an ostensibly well-focused offender management model (NOMS 2005, 2006) was introduced in 2005 to enable prisons and probation services, and their relevant partner agencies 'to turn a succession of unrelated, potentially contradictory experiences into a single coherent one' for each individual offender (Grapes 2007). The OMM was notionally underpinned by an as yet to be developed computerised case recording system called C-NOMIS, and further supported by a pathfinder project (running in 2004–05) in the North West of England, that had shown its principles to be viable and appealing to relevant stakeholders. In essence, the OMM envisaged (mostly) community-based offender managers coordinating interventions from a range of statutory, voluntary and private suppliers before, during and after the sentencing of individual offenders, rather than directly delivering 'interventions' themselves, which would be provided by 'supervisors' and 'keyworkers'.

Interventions were conceptualised as punishment, help, change and control, to be tiered in progressively more intensive combinations, depending on the level of assessed risk – the most intensive would utilise all four elements. There was no clear and consistent sense in the OMM of how EM would fit in, although stand-alone curfews figured as instances of low-tariff punishment, and 'curfews, mobility restriction and surveillance' were characterised as the kind of 'restrictive interventions' that intensive forms of 'control' would entail. 'Networks of relationships' between staff in different organisations, all working with the same offender, were deemed important (NOMS 2005: 37), but, arguably, there was no recognition of how distinctive a 'partner' the private sector EM providers might prove to be, given the history of 'parallel tracks'. It was understood, abstractly at least, that at any given time offenders might also be enmeshed in other, interlocking, case management systems, in child protection, mental health or drug treatment, for example, each with a complex set of protocols governing inter-agency relations and client expectations – and that far from making offender journeys through this labyrinth coherent, an undue prescriptiveness about pathways, and a lack of front-line discretion, may make them onerous and confusing (NOMS 2005: 43, see also Skidmore 2007) .

Towards integration: audit and inspection

Over and above the clear implications of the Avail Consultancy's review for their future relationship with NOMS, the EMT understood from the start that the OMM would affect them, but it was an audit report and an inspection report, and a House of Commons committee's review of the latter, that created a broader and more public debate on what more integrated EM might mean. The National Audit Office's (NAO) report, published in February 2006, focused on the cost-effectiveness of EM as both a court order for adults and as an early release mechanism (the latter use comprises 80 per cent of all tagging). A month after its publication, representatives from the Home Office, the National Offender Management Service and each of the two monitoring companies appeared before the House of Commons Committee of Public Accounts to discuss it. The committee's report, and the evidence on which it was based, appeared in October 2006. The joint inspection by the Probation, Court Administration and Constabulary inspectorates (CJJI 2008) assessed how well EM (again, court orders and early release) was being managed by the agencies involved, concluding, in the words of its title, that it was 'a complicated business'. Between them, these documents cumulatively questioned the continuing viability of using EM as *nothing more* than a stand-alone intervention.[5]

While the NAO rather pointedly did not refer to the implications of the CJA 2003, or to the OMM – its fieldwork began before the latter was published – its first recommendation was to 'improve the coordination between contractors and the criminal justice system' (NAO 2006: 19). Specifically, it recommended better contractor-court communication in respect of enforcement procedures, and greater clarity among prisons, probation and the Home Office itself in respect of authorising offender absences during curfew periods. It also suggested that local Criminal Justice Boards invite contractors 'to attend their meetings' to increase their familiarity with what tagging entailed. The NAO's third recommendation, to 'improve the assessment process for Home Detention Curfew' also required greater and more timely cooperation between prisons and local probation services, and at least until C-NOMIS was operational, more consistent access to criminal records on the police national computer.

The NAO was circumspect on the question of what philosophy underpinned the use of stand-alone EM. It implied, however, that punishment was too limited a purpose, stating tentatively that 'using curfew orders as a community penalty or as a means of early release of convicted offender from prison ... may also help in the rehabilitation of offenders by keeping them with or allowing them to return to their family or other structured environment'. While this says little more than that avoiding the negative effects of imprisonment may be rehabilitative by default, discursively, it represents a subtle departure from the Home Office's emphasis on stand-alone EM as a punishment. Furthermore, the NAO's clear suggestion that more research be undertaken to ascertain EM's potential for reducing recidivism subtly implied that this would inevitably prompt reflection on the stand-alone versus integration issue. Thus, while the NAO did not itself make the case for greater integration of EM with other forms of community supervision, it cautiously opened the door to the argument.

The House of Commons Committee of Public Accounts subsequently interrogated the Home Office and the two contractors about the NAO's findings. Their line of questioning, and their conclusions, openly endorsed the spirit of offender management and their report explicitly recommended in respect of HDC that probation officers should enable offenders to continue with education begun in prison, and in respect of adult curfew orders that they should 'help offenders ... access education, training or work to complement any rehabilitative remedies ordered by the courts' (House of Commons Committee of Public Accounts 2006: 5). In his verbal evidence to the committee Sir David Normington, senior Home Office civil servant, had already indicated that this was a desirable way to go, and explicitly linked EM to rehabilitation: 'In my view, we shall see less of stand-alone Curfew Orders and more of Curfew Orders as part of rehabilitation of the offender and that is where we want to see it go really because the emphasis has to be on trying to rehabilitate these people and stop them offending' (2006: ev4).

This was a clear departure from the 'parallel tracks' tradition, but very much aspirational. The CJJI undertook fieldwork in the period when the OMM was first being implemented and was disappointed 'to find that in almost all cases inspected, offender/case managers tended to view the curfew as a separate punishment, outside their jurisdiction' (CJJI 2008: 33). There was little contact between them and the EM company, only 25 per cent of curfews were integrated into supervision strategies, and only negligible use was made of EM to support rehabilitation. Unlike the NAO report, the CJJI (2008: 7) report actively championed the use of EM for 'crime reductive or rehabilitative purposes', highlighting the handful of 'cases [where] curfews were being used creatively to address patterns of offending behaviour', for example:

An offender/case manager proposed a weekend only curfew in a case where an offender had breached a Sunday work requirement as he had stayed out all night and could not get up in the morning. (2008: 26)

An offender manager became aware of an increasing Risk of Harm to others presented by an offender with deteriorating mental health. Appropriate action was taken to manage the risk, and the EM company was advised that two members of staff should undertake any visits and be aware of the nature of the risk (p30).

Such examples aside, the CJJI mostly observed failure on the part of offender managers to think imaginatively about EM, but acknowledged a legacy of 'parallel tracks' – that with the exception of enforcement there had been little encouragement to probation services to think of EM as a integral part of *their* work. Where information was communicated, some offender managers did use it creatively, in dialogue with offenders about the progress they were making (or not). In addition, echoing Bottomley *et al.* (2004), the CJJI found examples of failure to record and communicate relevant details which undermined coherent offender management. They found examples of lax enforcement (excessive delay in getting offenders to court once breach has been alleged), but also unduly rigid enforcement:

> We found a couple of examples of Home Detention Curfew cases where enforcement was carried out too stringently rather than insufficiently stringently. In these cases offenders were recalled to prison by the Post-Recall Section following the receipt of information from the electronic monitoring company. when a more thoughtful approach, as might have been provided by an offender manager, could well have enabled the offender to complete the licence with an acceptable level of compliance. (CJJI 2008: 10)

In the main, despite steadily improving liaison between the companies and criminal justice agencies, and a clear sense that 'the EM curfew could make a significant contribution to offender management in many cases', the CJJI (2008: 35), still saw 'unrealised potential' in the use of EM. The monitoring companies were deemed to be 'carrying out what they are required to do to an adequate standard' (2008: 11), but in offender management terms, there was still insufficient coordination, a situation that the CJJI aptly characterised as 'meeting the contract but missing the point'. Considering the length of time that EM had been available in England and Wales, this was quite an indictment, and the CJJI admitted, albeit in somewhat euphemistic fashion, that the partitioning of responsibility between private and public sector agencies has indeed been a hard division to bridge: 'it could be that the involvement of the EM companies somehow put curfews in a separate box in the minds of many offender case managers, absolving them of any ownership of responsibility for the management of curfews' (CJJI 2008: 33)

EM has in fact been in 'the separate box' of the private sector from the outset, simply because successive governments had willed it that way. As such, it is hardly surprising that creative, integrated uses of EM have seemingly been sparse (and unpublicised). 'Creative use' was never systematically encouraged by government before the publication of the NAO report, and at local operational level it has been all too easy for staff on both sides of the private/statutory divide (with some honourable exceptions) to work in self-contained ways. However, even as NOMS began to rethink its relationship with EM the inspectorates were tactfully and tentatively warning that the institutional obstacles to greater integration were probably more intractable than had been realised.

Making integration happen?

The roll-out of the offender management strategy took place against the unexpected and momentous splitting of the Ministry of Justice from the Home Office in May 2007, one consequence of that was a more modest, smaller version of NOMS than anticipated (Nellis and Goodman 2009). Managing the rising prison population was affirmed as NOMS's top priority. The second Carter Report (2007), alongside acceptance of a need for many more prison places, reasserted the importance of strengthening community supervision, and in March 2008 £40m of ostensibly new money was allocated to the probation service to facilitate this (with a further £17m promised later). Napo argued that given rising caseloads and increased complexity of work (including the greater liaison with other agencies entailed by offender management) £40m would still be insufficient to cover costs, and that it was less 'new' money and more the rescinding of a proposed cut to the probation service budget. The cancelling in 2008 of C-NOMIS, due to spiralling costs, meant that an ostensibly integral element of offender management – an integrated probation and prison service database – was now missing.

The responsibility for increasing integration of EM with offender management fell to the NOMS National Operations Group (NOG) (into that the EMT had been dissolved in April 2009), the ten NOMS regions, and the 42 local probation areas (and the boards and trusts who managed them). The regions themselves underwent restructuring, with directors of offender management (DOMs) replacing regional offender managers (ROMs) in May 2009. By mid-2008 the regions had appointed EM liaison officers to work with the prisons and probation areas within their boundaries, and with the EM contractors, tasked to boost the use of EM to free up prison places and to promote individualised offender management. NOG also wanted more geographic consistency, because there was by this time a clear (but not easily explained) recognition of significant regional disparities in the use of EM, with the North West using it more than elsewhere, and London underusing it.[6] Dialogue and exhortation have been the main tools of change – including encouraging the simple and time-honoured probation practice of promoting particular sentences in pre-sentence reports – but levers will improve in the future. In 2010 the operational budget for EM (although not for procurement, that will remain at the centre) will be devolved from the EMT to the NOMS regions, so that DOMs will have a clearer sense of the financial limits within that they can promote its use in their region.

Despite the vast scale and pace of the systemic changes taking place in respect of offender management, recent NOMS guidance on court report-writing suggests that plans for the future use of EM with individuals are actually somewhat lacking in ambition. Noting that the CJA 2003 'allows for a community order with a single requirement' (NOMS 2009: 12) (that is true, but hardly in the Act's spirit) the guidance actually distanced the management of stand-alone EM curfews from offender management undertaken 'in a probation area or trust'. The advice on recommending EM curfews to sentencers is as follows:

> ... there will be occasions where a curfew requirement will meet both punitive and public protection purposes of sentencing. The restriction of personal liberty inherent in a curfew requirement should be clearly articulated to the court as well as, where appropriate, the capacity of the curfew requirement to disrupt patterns of offending behaviour. In view of this, it may be an attractive option as a stand-alone requirement in cases where the court's sole purpose of sentencing is punishment ... At higher levels of seriousness the curfew requirement should be considered as a way of adding punitive weight to the sentence, for example where the addition of a curfew requirement to a community order might persuade the court that the imposition of a community order instead of a custodial sentence is appropriate. (NOMS 2009: 16)

This reflects a traditional, established and rather limited conception of EM's potential – the old Home Office view, in fact – and while legitimate and useful as far as it goes, it pulls well back from Sir David Normington's view, expressed to the House of Commons Committee of

Public Accounts in 2006, that 'we shall see less of stand-alone Curfew Orders and more of Curfew Orders as part of rehabilitation of the offender and that is where we want to see it go'. While allowing for the fact that in 'late modern' discourse 'rehabilitation' can encompass 'punishment' (Robinson 2008), there is little aspiration to rehabilitation here. Advice to report writers obviously does not exhaust policy development in this field, but nonetheless there is negligible evidence – to date – that the huge infrastructural changes entailed by NOMS and the OMM are actually generating significant alterations in the way EM is used with individual offenders. Systemically, decision-making about EM policy and strategy is part-devolving from the centre to the regions, but despite earlier rhetoric to the contrary, and the logic of the OMM, it is not clear whether *changes of practice at the individual level* are really desired at all.

In response to the systemic changes, the EM contractors have initiated some internal realignments to facilitate communication in the emerging regional networks, and met with DOMs to discuss regional budgets. Serco designated 30 of its staff as service delivery officers, who maintained the traditional function of enforcement officers (dealing with breaches) but also became key points of contact for external agencies. G4S have relationship managers. Interestingly, a 'showcase' study on G4S's website on good EM practice focuses on a stand-alone order, telling how one particular man, subject to two periods of curfew (that kept him from bad influences in the local pub) rehabilitated himself. No mention is made of other agencies being involved (www.g4s.com.print). In a specific contribution to debates on offender management, Serco has noted that 'where there is interaction between offender and contractor this tends not to be "pastoral, mentoring or coaching" because of contractual obligations [although] where opportunities arise we do try to gently encourage subjects to comply' (Homer 2009: 2. While not precluding integration, Serco is not seeking to enlarge the role of its own monitoring officers:

> If the outcome of this [offender management] strategy is to listen to individuals and offer a 'Samaritan'-type service thereby reducing the prison population, this would be a significant change from the current service we provide. Where too much information is known about the offender then this could adversely affect the service we offer as assumptions and prejudice could influence an inconsistent service. (Homer 2009: 2)

Sentencers have also had to be persuaded of the need to increase the use of EM. Her Majesty's Court Service encouraged the use of bail tagging in September 2005 (BI/241/09/05), pointing out that the new contracts had made it a cheaper resource than hitherto. In May 2006 a letter from the Lord Chief Justice (2006: 2) endorsed this, noting the NAO's expression of full confidence in the reliability of EM technology, although his letter mistakenly gave the impression that a tag 'cannot be removed'. Sentencers had been telling government that they would increase bail, including EM bail, if more accommodation was available, pressure that helped NOMS to create the Bail Accommodation and Support Service. Serco renewed liaison with the London Criminal Justice Board, one outcome of which was a short promotional DVD in which a magistrate was tagged for a week, to see for herself how onerous it was; the experience gave her 'much more confidence in tagging' (Powell 2008: 25).

Since 2005, the probation inspectorate has been undertaking offender management inspections in all 42 criminal justice areas, to monitor progress on the implementation of the OMM. It is not clear that a great deal has been happening in respect of EM, and to get some sense of developments in integrating EM in particular programmes and fields of activity, this chapter concludes with some brief overviews.

Bail and the reduction of remand in custody

The Bail Act 1976 permitted the administrative introduction of new 'bail conditions' whenever new possibilities arose; thus, EM bail did not require new legislation. Once introduced, EM bail was widely used, but not (with adults) restricted to imprisonable offences (meaning that it would not just be used as an alternative to custodial remands). Initially, there was no statutory minimum or maximum curfew period for bail cases, and time spent on EM bail (unlike time remanded in custody) did not come off subsequent custodial sentences. The Act was amended in 2001 to restrict EM bail to defendants charged with imprisonable offences, but in 2006 the Home Office still believed that it was being underused (and that the remand prisoner population was too high), again emphasising in a circular 'that it should be used as an alternative to custody' (Home Office 2006: para 5). The circular emphasised the importance of 'good communication between the agencies' (para 4) involved, and affirmed that there would 'be no objections to tagging defendants accommodated in Approved

Premises' (para 23), but it was essentially relying on exhortation to bring about improvements.

The Criminal Justice and Immigration Act 2008 went beyond circular-style exhortation and introduced a number of alterations (derived from the Carter Report 2007: 28), designed to make EM-bail more credible in the eyes of both courts and defendants. Time served on EM bail became discountable from any subsequent custodial sentence. A minimum daily curfew period of nine hours was set. Significantly, EM bail was now made a specific requirement of the Bail Act, enabling the Ministry of Justice to insist that 'the court must be satisfied that without electronic monitoring the defendant would not be granted bail. This was intended to ensure that tagging was only used where necessary' (Ministry of Justice 2008: 05), although the assumption that *stand-alone* EM will be sufficient to tilt magistrates against a custodial remand – the opposite of the assumption that is made regarding the use of EM in sentencing – is questionable.

NOMS had already created the regionally managed Bail Accommodation and Support Service (BASS) in June 2007 'to allow courts to make greater use of bail and prisons and to make greater use of Home Detention Curfew' by providing a range of accommodation in the community for low risk adult defendants and released prisoners who did not have their own or family homes to go to, so long as they were not sexual, violent offenders, or arsonists (National Probation Service 2008: 1). These were typically three- to five-bedroom houses, not hostels or Approved Premises. ClearSprings Management Ltd was awarded the contract for this.[7] For those on bail (where no offender manager is formally involved), ClearSprings offers a support officer to help with their bail condition, benefits, employment and training and to prepare them to move on; in the first nine months 600 were bailed to them. The need for accommodation in particular geographical areas is ascertained by the ROM/DOM. ClearSprings then liaises with local authorities and police and probation services to find suitable (and perhaps temporary) properties in suitable locations.

BASS was launched with a sense of urgency. Three months in, however, NOMS was still galvanising chairs of probation boards, chief officers and ROMs to 'make the fullest possible use of this service as soon as possible' (National Probation Service 2007b: 2). Five months in, the prison service was doing the same:

So far, BASS has not delivered the number of places that was expected. With population levels remaining high, it is vital that governors ensure the fullest possible use is being made of this service for both HDC and bail. It is important to supply complete and accurate information to avoid delay (Prison Service 2007).

Young offenders and intensive supervision

In 2006, young offenders (aged 10–17) made up 25 per cent of the EM caseload. EM remained a condition in a community rehabilitation order for 16- to 17-year-olds even after the CJA 2003 transmuted that order into a requirement in the single community order for adults. For young offenders under 16, EM could only be combined with a supervision order if a separate curfew order were made. EM could be included in a detention and training order, a 24-month sentence of which the first half was spent in prison and the second half in the community, under the supervision of a local youth offending team – although the custodial part could be shortened still further if HDC was granted. In November 2009 the youth rehabilitation order was introduced for under-18s – the equivalent of the single community order for adults, giving sentences a menu of 18 requirements from which to construct a multi-component disposal. Curfews, curfews with EM and the whole ISSP package figured as separate requirements.

As noted above, ISSP for serious and persistent young offenders provided a pre-OMM opportunity to consider how EM could be integrated into a supervision package. Robin Moore (2005), one of the scheme's evaluators, suggests that practitioners did try to integrate component parts of ISSP into a coherent experience. Tagging was the most common form of surveillance used in ISSP, used in 70 per cent of cases (n = 2,259), popular with sentencers and practitioners, and even some of the youngsters. Nonetheless, more tagged offenders reoffended during the ISSP than a comparable group who were subject to human tracking, leading Moore to speculate that it might have antagonised them. More in-depth research is needed to understand what went on here, and what goes on now on ISSPs.

Research into the Scottish equivalent of ISSPs – Intensive Monitoring and Support Services (ISMS) – was frustratingly inconclusive about the utility of the integral EM curfew (here called a 'movement restriction order') and did not explore how social workers did or did not make use of the fact that a youngster was tagged. One-third of the young offenders subject to it were critical of it, believing that help with education, employment and offending behaviour was more useful to them. The sample (n = 69) was evenly split in judging it to have had a positive or negative impact on their families, while parents themselves tended to be more favourably disposed to it (Khan and Hill 2008). One consequence of the Scottish research (and the resistance of children's panels during the pilots themselves) was that tagging/movement restriction became discretionary with ISMS, rather than compulsory.

Early release and home detention curfew

Early release *via* HDC became available in 1999 to prisoners serving sentences of between three months and four years, largely as a means of managing rising prisoner numbers, although official rhetoric also emphasised its value as a means of structuring – graduating – the release process. The period of early release was increased rapidly from 60, through 90 to 135 days by 2003, each time as a result of pressure on prison places, each time with further restrictions of eligibility – for example, sexual and violent offenders, foreign national prisoners, those serving public protection sentences – to ensure public safety. Completion rates were generally high, but some incidents of serious reoffending while on HDC – a tiny fraction of the 150,000 HDC releases since 1999 – gave critics of early release occasion to question its legitimacy.

The use of HDC peaked at 21,188 in 2002, dropping rather pre-cipitously to 13,666 in 2006. This was probably to be explained by increasing risk aversion on the part of governors, and possibly 'adverse publicity' (Avail Consulting 2006: 7), but the downward trend was accelerated by the introduction of the end of custody licence (ECL) in June 2007, to assist further with managing (reducing) the prison population. ECL targeted almost exactly the same group in the adult prison population as HDC, those serving over four weeks and under four years. It permitted prisoners to be released 18 calendar days ahead of their automatic or conditional release date, subject to standard eligibility restrictions, and licence conditions set by the governor. ECL was attuned to offender management in a number of respects, valuing risk assessment and liaison with outside agencies, including MAPPA, and denying release to prisoners whose supervision licences already required their post-release participation in a community programme, unless offender managers were able to arrange it within the ECL period. Though originally presented as a merely temporary measure by government – and much criticised by opposition parties – ECL quickly became as indispensable as HDC for managing prisoner numbers, pending the building of more prison spaces (Strickland 2008).

For prisoners, ECL was arguably a more attractive alternative form of early release than HDC. They had to wait longer to get it, but the actual period on licence was substantially shorter, and lacked the restriction of the tag. In the first 12 months 31,500 prisoners were released on ECL (of whom 569, 1.4 per cent, reoffended) (Strickland 2008). After a snapshot survey of its members, Napo was quick to condemn the somewhat sudden and indiscriminate use of ECL and the poor quality of risk assessments that led to men convicted of domestic violence returning to their partners' homes and in eight cases committing further offences of assault within days, and then being recalled to prison. In all of the cases submitted (from officers around the country) probation staff took the view that the men were not suitable for release. Many had been turned down for release on the longer home detention curfew scheme because of risk of harm (Napo 2008).

As noted earlier, ClearSprings provides accommodation for people on HDC as well as bail. Between June 2007 and April 2008, 443 prisoners had been released on HDC. Contact sessions with support officers are more limited with bail – one session per week – unless there is a designated offender manager (as there is for a prisoner who has served more than a year), in that case all responsibility falls on them, except for assistance with moving on (National Probation Service 2008: 1/2). Napo has expressed concern about the very limited input from ClearSprings staff, and such cursory contact time barely amounts to 'integrated' offender management (Fletcher 2008).

EM as a licence condition

The purpose of post-release licences is to reduce the risk of re-offending and harm to the public and to aid the process of resettlement, by helping offenders with employment, training, education, accommodation, and reintegration back into family life. There are six standard licence conditions for determinate sentence prisoners, and seven standard licence conditions for indeterminate sentences, that include life sentences and sentences of imprisonment for public protection. Additional licence conditions can be imposed at the request of an offender manager, whose authority now exceeds that of prison governors in this respect, but only in agreement with the Post Release Section of the Ministry of Justice. Typical additional licence conditions include banning contact with past or anticipated victims, creating exclusion zones around (for example) schools, places where victims live or socialise, addresses where the ex-prisoner is at risk of drugs or alcohol, banning the use of certain communication or photographic technology, and EM-curfews. The use of EM in post-release licences – except in respect of HDC – is one of the most under-researched aspects of EM. Offenders on parole licences have had some of the longest experiences of being tagged, but little is known about what this has meant to them, or how – and if – EM is now integrated into the standard procedures of parole supervision.

The use of EM in public protection is similarly unclear, but heir to the same administrative complexity that suffuses its other uses (Nellis 2010). EM can be applied for in a determinate sentence only where the offender has been designated level 3 (high risk) by MAPPA, or has been designated a 'critical public protection case' by the Public Protection Unit. Protocols governing the use of it are written by the Post Release Section. 'It is not envisaged that electronic monitoring will be used routinely for the release licence of lifers or those sentenced to IPP', because in the main they would not be being released at all if they were not already a lower risk than EM would warrant (National Probation Service 2007a: para 22).

Conclusions

This chapter has considered the development of policy in relation to integrating EM into the structures and processes of offender management. It has distinguished between systemic and individualised conceptions of offender management, but it has not discussed practice at the individual level. In the absence of research there is no way of knowing how (or if) either version is being implemented, whether one is more feasible than the other, whether they are even logically related to each other, or whether or not any tagged adult offenders are already having a more integrated experience of supervision than hitherto. That, as we have seen, may not even be the intention of offender management in respect of EM – increased, stand-alone use of it is still the mainstay of NOMS's vision – and while that is a legitimate use it falls short of what creative, individualised, integrated uses of EM might offer. To be fair, it is only since late 2009, in respect of EM, that the systemic elements of the OMM are belatedly being infused into regional NOMS structures, and it may well be that in the minds of senior NOMS managers properly creative understandings of EM's potential have not yet had time to percolate down to the front line of supervision.

What is being missed here is that over the years some probation officers and social workers had already given thought to more creative uses of EM, despite the legacy of 'parallel tracks'. This was never capitalised on, and, consistent with the broader denigration of front-line voices which has accompanied the probation/NOMS reorganisation, may even have been drowned out by information overload from central and regional government. Much could have been done, over the years, if practitioners had had time, and encouragement, to build up 'practice wisdom' about EM's potential – as happened, for example, with the imaginative uses of exclusion zones in the British satellite tracking pilots[8] – without the complex infrastructure of systemic offender management and the blizzard of 'electronic paperwork' hurtling down from 'headquarters'.

Although there is more to be learned about integration from existing and evolving experience in ISSPs and ISMSs, there is still a dearth of detailed British case studies of tagged individuals, and in official studies an over-reliance on brief, decontextualised sound-bites to capture offender experiences. Hucklesby's (2008, 2009) more searching enquiry into EM and desistance and compliance suggests that the experience of an EM curfew may create a moment of reflection in an offender's life, when he pauses to reflect on the direction his life is going in, 'a window of opportunity' that a supervising officer (if there is one) ought surely to exploit and support. Where EM is used to disrupt complex patterns of offending – and there is much to be said about what this actually means – it seems important to have a supervisor who engages with the offender on this, rather than just leaving the disruption to chance, and assuming it happens.

There has been considerable European interest in England and Wales' OMM, but Britain itself could gain useful insights from the experience of those European countries whose own EM programmes blended social support and EM from the start.[9] In Sweden, for example, EM is managed by the probation service and has never been used as a stand-alone measure. In a recent evaluation of a post-prison release scheme, the four-month period of release on EM combined with employment, a monitored ban on the use of alcohol and drugs and provision of relevant services was shown, over a three-year period, to correlate significantly with reduced recidivism: 26 per cent compared to 38 per cent with a near perfectly matched control group (Marklund and Holmberg 2009). The authors suggest that it is EM in combination with structured activities that made the difference, and point up the need for future research that shows more clearly how such integration works.

Measuring the effectiveness of EM depends in part on how the purpose of EM is conceived – as stand-alone surveillance or as a component in an integrated rehabilitation programme, (or both). In addition, in Britain, the division of labour between private and statutory bodies in EM service delivery may place finite limits on how far both systemic and individualised integration can go, and on how much EM can contribute to rehabilitation (Nellis 2006b; Paterson 2007). Neither the NAO nor the CJJI had the authority to question the principle of private sector involvement,[10] but the latter suggested obliquely that the 'complicated business' of contract management and of liaison across the public-private divide was part of the reason why EM still had 'unrealised potential'. That is not to say that good or better practice in community supervision with EM is not possible within prevailing institutional frameworks, but merely to register the fact that if EM was operated from within a public sector probation service the process and detail of offender management would probably look rather different, and be less 'complicated' (if, admittedly, more expensive).

Notes

1 As well as Anthea Hucklesby, I am grateful to a number of people directly involved in the provision of EM at national and regional level who helped with the preparation of this chapter, but who may nonetheless disagree with elements of the account offered here.

2 The experimental use of EM with asylum seekers began in 2004, using EM curfews, voice verification and (at the time of the pilots) satellite tracking, but details of the exact uses, the conclusions drawn and the situation now have never been in the public domain.

3 Bottomley et al. (2004), possibly reflecting the concerns of their respondents, became preoccupied with policy failure to identify who the new uses of EM should be 'targeted' on. In fact the Home Office has rarely thought in terms of targeting EM on specific offence or offender types – the assumption has been that the standardised curfewing of almost any offender to their own home (or other designated place) would have a beneficial restrictive effect, just as many different types of offender can be dealt with on probation, albeit in more tailored and nuanced ways. Stand-alone EM was 'targeted' on offenders at risk of custody in early governmental rhetoric but quickly and unobtrusively slipped down tariff.

4 Avail describes itself as 'a specialist consultancy devoted to the practical application of leading-edge thinking to the modernisation of public services, specifically policing and justice' (company brochure 2009). It describes its work on EM as 'a response to the introduction of new organisational arrangements [in NOMS] for Commissioning and Contestability programmes'. In the long run, Avail Consulting's (2006: 34) report did envisage the *regional commissioning* of EM services, that would entail much time-consuming duplication of work by the private companies. It is not obviously a more efficient means of commissioning than a centrally-based one, and it seriously risks inconsistency of provision between the ten regions.

5 The NAO methodology consisted of reviews of over 700 case files spread across different agencies (including the monitoring companies), focus groups and solo interviews with key staff in these agencies, interviews with 18 curfewees, reviews of performance data and a costing exercise. The inspectorates studied 286 curfew cases across five probation areas and five youth offending teams, drawn from each of the five EM contract areas. In addition they personally interviewed senior and junior staff in all the agencies involved, including central government departments, and telephone interviewed 19 curfewees.

6 The total new starts of all EM penalties in the period January–October 2009 were as follows: North East (3,949); North West (12,076); East Midlands (3,763); Yorkshire and Humberside (7,235); South East (6,411); South West (5,158); West Midlands (4,683); Wales (2,519); London (10,674); Eastern (3,893) (statistics from the Electronic Monitoring Team, December 2009).

7 ClearSprings describes itself as a housing and support service for vulnerable people. It was established in 2000 initially to supply government with accommodation for asylum seekers, before branching out into bail support, eventually displacing the role of approximately 100 probation-run bail hostels (that became hostels for high risk parolees) (Fletcher 2008). ClearSprings lost its contract to Stonham in 2010.

8 The satellite tracking pilots ran in three sites during 2004–06. In the West Midlands drug-using burglars were excluded from all or part of the estates where their burglaries occurred for a period of three months. After one month of total exclusion (and compliance with *all* their supervision requirements), the rules were relaxed to allow them to visit friends or relatives in the zone. The police-probation teams monitoring these offenders found that these 'rewards' were powerful motivators of compliance with the other elements of the intensive supervision. In Manchester a tracked sex offender was forbidden to enter any park in the city. On the software, only three parks actually had electronic exclusion zones 'placed' around them – it would have been too expensive to to cover 200 parks in this way – but the offender was not told this.

9 Sweden, a penally liberal country that rolled out the first European national EM scheme in 1996 (and abandoned plans to open a new prison as a consequence) developed EM within a public sector probation service and the history of EM in that country has been much less contentious than in Britain.

10 Napo constantly questions this, and on the House of Commons Committee of Public Accounts, Labour MP Kitty Usher did take G4S and Serco to task for their seemingly hostile attitude towards trade unions, citing their involvement in labour disputes in several foreign countries (2006: v9). She also invited the Home Office to consider whether such large global corporations were the best sort of organisation to deliver local services in England.

References

Avail Consulting (2006) *Review of Electronic Monitoring Arrangements within NOMS*. London: Avail Consulting.

Bonta, J., Capretta, S.W. and Rooney, J. (2000) 'Can electronic monitoring make a difference? An evaluation of three Canadian Programmes', *Crime and Delinquency*, 46 (2): 61–75.

Bottomley, K., Hucklesby, A. and Mair, G. (2004) 'The new uses of electronic monitoring: findings from the implementation phase in three pilot areas', in K. Bottomley, A. Hucklesby, G. Mair and M. Nellis (eds) *Electronic Monitoring of Offenders: Key Developments*. London: Napo.

Carter, P. (2003) *Managing Offenders, Reducing Crime: A New Approach*. London: Cabinet Office.

Carter, P. (2007) *Securing the Future: Proposals for the Efficient and Sustainable use of Custody in England and Wales*. London: House of Lords.

CJJI (Criminal Justice Joint Inspection) (2008) *A Complicated Business: A Joint Inspection of Electronically Monitored Curfew Requirements, Orders and Licences*. London: HMI Probation, HMI Court Administration and HMI Constabulary.

Fletcher, H. (2008) 'ClearSprings – bail support beds'. *Napo News*, April.

Gable, R.S. and Gable, R.K. (2007) 'Increasing the effectiveness of electronic monitoring', *Perspectives*, 31 (1): 25–29.

Grapes, T. (2007) 'Case management or offender management', in C. Pillay (ed.) *Looking Forward: Developing Effective Practice*, Proceedings from the 34th national trainee probation officers conference. London: Napo.

Halliday, J. (2001) *Making Punishment Work: Report of a Review of the Sentencing Framework for England and Wales*. London: Home Office.

HMIP (2004) Inquiry *into the Supervision of Peter Williams by Nottingham City Youth Offending Team*. London: Her Majesty's Inspectorate of Probation.

Home Office (2003) *Justice for All*. Cm 5563. London: Home Office.

Home Office (2006) *Electronic Monitoring on Bail for Adults – Procedures*, Home Office Circular 025/2006. London: Home Office.

Homer, A. (2009) *Core Principles of Offender Management*. Norwich: Serco

House of Commons Committee of Public Accounts (2006) *The Electronic Monitoring of Adult Offenders*, Sixty-second report of the session 2005-06. London: The Stationery Office.

Hucklesby, A. (2008) 'Vehicles of desistance? The impact of electronically monitored curfew orders', *Criminology and Criminal Justice*, 8: 51–71.

Hucklesby, A. (2009) 'Understanding offenders' compliance: a case study of electronically monitored curfew orders', *Journal of Law and Society*, 36 (2): 248–71.

Khan, F. and Hill, M. (2008) *Evaluation of Includem's Intensive Support Services*. Glasgow: Includem.

Lord Chief Justice (2006) Letter, Bail and 'proceeding in absence'. London: House of Lords.

Mair, G. (2005) 'Electronic monitoring in England and Wales: evidence-based or not?', *Criminal Justice*, 5: 257–77.

Mair, G., Cross, N. and Taylor, S. (2007) *The Use and Impact of the Community Order and the Suspended Sentence Order*. London: Centre for Crime and Justice Studies.

Marklund, F. and Holmberg, S. (2009) 'Effects of early release from prison using electronic tagging in Sweden', *Journal of Experimental Criminology*, 5 (1): 41–61.

Ministry of Justice (2008) *Criminal Justice and Immigration Act 2008 (provisions commencing on 3rd November 2008)*. London. Ministry of Justice.

Moore, R. (2005) 'The use of electronic and human surveillance in a multi-modal programme', *Youth Justice*, 5 (5): 17–32.

Napo (2008) Press release, 'Domestic violence and the end of custody licence – the problem continues', Press Release, 27 June. London: Napo.

National Audit Office (2006) *The Electronic Monitoring of Adult Offenders*. London: The Stationery Office.

National Probation Service (2007a) *Post Release Enforcement – Licence Conditions*, PC 29/2007. London: NOMS.

National Probation Service (2007b) *New Accommodation and Support Service for Bail and HDC*, PC 33/2007. London: NOMS.

National Probation Service (2008) *Accommodation and Support for Bail and HDC*, Briefing, 9 May. London: NOMS.

Nellis, M. (1991) 'The electronic monitoring of offenders in England and Wales: recent developments and future prospects', *British Journal of Criminology*, 31 (2): 165–85.

Nellis, M. (2004) 'The electronic monitoring of offenders in Britain: a critical overview', in K. Bottomley, A. Hucklesby, G. Mair and M. Nellis (eds) *Electronic Monitoring of Offenders: Key Developments*. London: Napo.

Nellis, M. (2006a) 'The limitations of electronic monitoring: the case of Peter Williams', *Prison Service Journal*, 164 (March): 3–12.

Nellis, M. (2006b) 'NOMS, contestability and the process of technocorrectional innovation', in M. Hough, R. Allen and U. Padel (eds) *Reshaping Probation and Prisons: The New Offender Management Framework*. Bristol: Policy Press.

Nellis, M. (2007) 'Electronic monitoring and control orders for terrorist suspects in England and Wales', in T. Abbas (ed.) *Islamic Political Radicalism*. Edinburgh University Press.

Nellis, M. and Goodman, A. (2009) 'Probation and offender management', in A. Hucklesby and A. Wahidin (eds) *Criminal Justice*. Oxford: Oxford University Press.

NOMS (2005) *The NOMS Offender Management Model 1*. London: Ministry of Justice.

NOMS (2006) *The NOMS Offender Management Model 1.1*. London: Ministry of Justice.

NOMS (2009) *Guidance for Court Officers, Report Writers and Offender Managers*. London: Ministry of Justice.

Padgett, K.G., Bales, W.D., and Blomberg, T. (2006) 'Under surveillance: an empirical test of the effectiveness and consequences of electronic monitoring', *Criminology and Public Policy*, 5 (1): 61–91.

Paterson, C. (2007) 'Commercial crime control and the electronic monitoring of offenders in England and Wales', *Social Justice*, 34 (3–4): 98–110.

Powell, Y. (2008) 'Report from Tag-a-Mag Week', *Benchmark*, 26: 24–25.

Prison Service (2007) *Accommodation and Support Services for Bail and Home Detention Curfew*, Prison Service Instruction 49/2007.

Renzema, M. and Mayo-Wilson, E. (2005) 'Can electronic monitoring reduce crime for moderate to high risk offenders?', *Journal of Experimental Criminology*, 2: 215–37.

Robinson, G. (2008) 'Late modern rehabilitation', *Punishment and Society*, 10 (4): 429–46.

Skidmore, D. (2007) 'Offender management as seen by other agencies', in R. Canton and D. Hancock (eds) *Dictionary of Probation and Offender Management*. Cullompton: Willan Publishing.

Strickland, P. (2008) *The End of Custody Licence*. London: House of Commons Library.

Waters, I., Moore, R., Roberts, C., Merrington, S. and Gray, E. (2003) *Intensive Supervision and Surveillance Programmes for Persistent Young Offenders in England and Wales: Interim National Findings*. London: Youth Justice Board.

Chapter 26

Conclusion: where are we now?

Fergus McNeill, Peter Raynor and Chris Trotter

Introduction

This final chapter attempts to provide an overview of what this book tells us about the state of theory, research and practice in offender supervision. In a way it is a summary of what we have learned in the process of working with CREDOS and putting the book together. In this process we have brought together many of the people and materials at the cutting edge of work in this field. There are, unavoidably, some omissions, and new work is being produced all the time: much of the work reported in this volume is new since the most recent similar British compilation (McIvor and Raynor 2007), and the pace of research and innovation shows no sign of slowing down. However, for now this is the most comprehensive available summary, and a good opportunity to assess the general health of this particular corner of social science and societal concern.

Theoretical developments

Our first section covers what are arguably the three most important theoretical orientations in contemporary offender management: Jim Bonta and Don Andrews describe and update the 'risk-needs-responsivity' (RNR) model, originally derived from meta-analysis and now underpinning much of the available evidence on 'what works'; Tony Ward presents the 'Good Lives' strengths-based model, which emphasises a positive approach to helping offenders to achieve their own goals through pro-social means; and Shadd Maruna and Thomas LeBel discuss the 'emerging' desistance-based model, which seeks to align offender management with what criminology tells us about how and why offenders stop offending. These perspectives are perhaps more compatible than they may appear at first sight: for example, it is difficult to see how anybody could work successfully with offenders using the RNR model, as many have demonstrably done, without in practice adopting the optimistic and goal-oriented approach that is claimed as a typical feature of other methods. In some ways the new models represent a shift from *what* works to *how* it works and *why* it works. They also point towards a new research agenda in relation to *who* works and what practitioners actually do: what approaches, skills and attitudes can actually support motivation and desistance? For practical purposes, a key question that now faces us is whether the new paradigms can deliver the clarity of guidance to practitioners that actual improvement requires.

Staff skills and individual supervision

Our second section provides a fairly representative snapshot of where we have reached in the empirical study and assessment of what is working in individual supervision. This is not easy to establish, and the researchers advance patiently some distance behind the theorists, sustained by the possibility of real improvements in effectiveness. Guy Bourgon and his colleagues address the issue of technology transfer, in other words, how workers acquire or develop the skills of effective supervision. They ask the question: do transfer processes result in staff using the new technology as it was intended to be used? They describe a study that involved offering training to Canadian probation officers in effective interventions using the RNR model. The training was supported by feedback, refresher courses and monthly meetings. Audiotapes of probation officer/client interviews were then collected and a detailed coding manual was developed and used to assess the workers' skills. It was found that in comparison to a control group the trained workers made significantly more use of the skills, with the exception of relationship skills.

Peter Raynor and colleagues have also developed an instrument to code interviews between probationers and clients. Their checklist includes many of the skills referred to in the Bourgon *et al.* manual but with some differences in emphasis (less emphasis on cognitive behavioural techniques, for example). Whereas the focus of the

Bourgon chapter is on the effectiveness of the transfer technology, the focus of the Raynor chapter is on the development of the coding instrument and on the extent to which the skills are used by probation officers. They found in their study in the Channel Island of Jersey that the effective practice skills were generally present and could be assessed in the videotaped interviews they examined, but some workers consistently used a higher level of skills than others. Most officers used some relationship skills, and the greater differences were in the use of 'structuring' skills intended to elicit change.

Chris Trotter and Phillipa Evans' chapter also examines interviews between probation officers and their clients. Their study, undertaken in youth justice in NSW in Australia, involved direct observation of interviews, taping of the interviews and follow-up interviews with workers and clients to seek their responses to the interviews. The interviews were then coded with a view to examining the use of effective practice skills, the content of the interviews and an exploratory focus on which aspects of the interviews the workers and clients found to be most effective. The results suggest that while the skills may be present in many interviews they are used in a more informal and conversational manner than might be anticipated from the literature. The study also found a lack of continuity in supervision. Largely due to clients' geographical instability and worker turnover, clients often have more than one supervisor during the period of a probation order.

These studies begin to fill a gap: apart from some work in Canada (Andrews and Kiessling 1980; Bonta *et al.* 2008) there has been very little systematic research on the actual content of one-to-one interviewing, despite the obvious fact that most offender supervision consists mostly of such interviews. The strength of these chapters also lies in the fact that they are being conducted in diverse locations: three locations in Canada; Jersey, a distinctive location because of its highly paid, well-educated staff and its commitment to the 'what works' agenda; and New South Wales where the focus is on young people in a state where almost half the probationers are Aboriginal.

What has been learned from these studies so far? First, that probation officers use at least some of the effective practice skills. Second, that training can make a difference particularly if it involves clinical supervision and follow-up – a finding that is consistent with an earlier study in probation in Australia (Trotter 1996). Third, some staff may find relationship skills more difficult to develop than the more practical skills of problem-solving or structuring an interview. This was so in the Canadian sample, and many workers in the Australian sample also had difficulty with the relationship skill of framing open questions. In Jersey, the reverse seemed to be the case, with good relationship skills found more often than good 'structuring' skills, and this may reflect differences in training. Fourth, the three chapters suggest that coding manuals and checklists may be useful in identifying the extent to which practitioners are likely to be effective.

Each of these studies is still in process and each will involve an examination of the relationships between the various practices by probation officers and outcomes for the offenders, including recidivism rates. CREDOS has provided a forum for collaboration on the development of the coding manuals and checklists and will provide opportunities to compare results from the different studies. The final results are eagerly awaited – and, as this chapter was being prepared for dispatch to the publisher, a report has appeared from the Canadian study that shows that the probation officers who received appropriate training in interviewing skills actually had lower recidivism rates among the offenders they supervised than a randomly allocated control group of officers who did not receive the training (Bonta *et al.* 2010).

Improving supervision

If the quality of supervision is important, what, in addition to training, can help to improve it? Our third section looks at several other possible drivers of improvement. Hazel Kemshall reviews developments in risk and need assessment, and makes a persuasive case for the inclusion of strengths and positive aspects in any assessment: risk assessment on its own can be harnessed to repressive penal practices, while more positive and strength-based approaches to risk management can lead to better rehabilitation and better integration into communities. The uses to which risk assessment is put depend in part on professional cultures and political climate: in some circumstances, but not in all, it will support what we would see as better practice.

Faye Taxman and Judith Sachwald pursue the theme of what facilitates and supports effective practice. An American survey provides impressive empirical support for the view that organisational culture and management style are important determinants of how far an agency will succeed in implementing effective practices with offenders. They show, for example, that knowledge, commitment, belief and the creation of a 'learning culture' in the organisation are more important than budgets or size in determining whether evidence-based practices will be adopted. This is salutary reading for anyone who has observed the poor results of managers or civil servants trying to *impose* effective practice on practitioners.

Pauline Durrance, Nigel Hosking and Nancy Thorburn describe an attempt to give structure and focus to individual supervision through what is, in effect, a one-to-one version of the kind of cognitive behavioural programme more often used in groups. This is not the first attempt to do this but it has clearly now achieved some success, particularly from the point of view of practitioners. It also provides further evidence of the benefits that are flowing from the international agenda in probation, being based on work originally undertaken to support the new probation service in Romania.

Finally in this section, Gill McIvor provides a comprehensive and on the whole encouraging review of the impact of judicial involvement in supervision, developed originally in drug courts but capable of application elsewhere. Positive engagement by sentencers and 'therapeutic jurisprudence' clearly offer some benefits, but they also open up a number of issues that we have hardly begun to explore: what are the implications for the role, training and selection of the judiciary? How does their role differ from that of a case manager, if both are actively involved in supervision?

Significant others

The next section, our fourth, spreads the focus still wider to families and communities. It includes three chapters that focus on working with families and one focusing on involving the wider community in supervision. The theme of these chapters is clear. Families and communities can sometimes be the sites or sources of pressure to offend, but they can also play a vital role in the reduction of offending. Reference is made in the chapters to a body of research that supports this view.

The chapter by Carol Shapiro and Margaret DiZerega points to the importance of including family in assessment processes, and they refer to a project undertaken in Oklahoma Department of Corrections involving staff training in strengths-based family-focused work. In this project, assessment involves asking clients about family members and viewing family members as a resource to both help in the rehabilitation process and assist clients in accessing other resources. The authors also refer to the importance of collaborating with other agencies in working with juvenile and adult offenders and their families.

Bas Vogelvang and Herman van Alphen point to the mixed nature of offenders' family relationships. Families may have a negative influence on some offenders and some entrenched criminal families hamper rather than support the rehabilitation of individual members. Nevertheless for the most part they point to the value of working with families in the rehabilitation process. The authors point to the 'alarming' discrepancy between the incidence of family issues for offenders and the extent of training and interventions that focus on family. They, like Shapiro and DiZerega, point to the importance of assessing for family issues, using eco-maps and identifying supportive families and networks in order to help offenders in the desistance process. Probation officers may not be family therapists; however, they can discuss and support family networks. The authors refer to the concept of a 'wraparound model' of care for offenders, in other words, a holistic model that takes account of family and other community influences and resources. They suggest that family support may be particularly important before release from prison and that family group conferences be used as a method of involving family.

The chapter by Chris Trotter provides a specific outline of how to work with families. Trotter argues, like the other authors, that families are an important factor in the development and continuance of criminal behaviour, and that interventions with families can be effective in reducing reoffending. Trotter argues that the 'what works' principles, such as focusing on medium to high risk offenders, dealing with criminogenic needs and modelling and reinforcing pro-social behaviour, can be applied to work with families. He outlines a collaborative problem-solving model for work with families that has been implemented with some success in several youth justice settings and can be used in the day-to-day supervision of offenders.

Tom O'Connor and Brad Bogue continue the theme of working holistically with offenders and maximising the use of community resources. The authors describe a cooperative programme between COSA (Circles of Support and Accountability), community-based organisations, 'faith-informed' volunteers and chaplaincy services. COSA volunteers work with treatment providers, probation and parole officers, police and courts, and provide a mentoring service to high risk sex offenders. The authors report that the COSA programme has seen considerable reductions in offending of those involved. One of their most telling points relates to the numbers of volunteers in prisons and community corrections who come from religious faith traditions. They point to 2,000 volunteers in the Oregon Department of Corrections, 75 per cent of whom are religious volunteers. These volunteers represent little-studied but valuable resources for offender rehabilitation.

There are synergies with much of the desistance literature in the chapters in this section of the book. While the relevance of assessing risk and dealing with criminogenic needs is acknowledged, the need for a holistic and strengths-based approach to offender rehabilitation is highlighted. In terms of RNR it might be seen as a plea for greater focus on responsivity factors. The argument is for a move beyond one-to-one supervision and group programmes that focus on the offender in isolation from his or her community: a move towards assessing the client's situation from a wide perspective, with a greater focus on working with the client's view of the world, identifying strengths and involving family and community resources. This in turn can help clients to develop more pro-social lifestyles. In particular a degree of alarm is expressed by each of the authors that families are so central to the lives and potential rehabilitation of offenders, yet criminal justice organisations show minimal interest in families, and those involved in the supervision of offenders often lack the motivation and the skills to work with families.

Compliance with supervision

Our fifth section, on compliance with supervision, may at first sight seem to be a return to a focus on the 'small' picture of interaction between supervisors and offenders rather than the 'big' picture of offender management in society. However, the chapters quickly dispel this impression: Pamela Ugwudike shows how compliance is subtly negotiated between supervisors and offenders to achieve a more individualised and flexible approach to enforcement than official policy would permit, and how a punitive and deterrent official approach to enforcement in England and Wales has undermined the ability of practitioners to manage compliance in the way they would wish. Again the legal and judicial context of community sentences is important in understanding what they can achieve. Shelley Turner shows how the adoption of case management as an approach to juvenile supervision in Australia has been driven by a managerial agenda and by the popularity of the case management model in other public services, but does not necessarily meet the needs of offenders or their supervisors.

Gwen Robinson and Fergus McNeill look outside the offender management literature for more theoretical insights into compliance, and find them in a study of why people (generally) pay their taxes. They develop a dynamic model of compliance focusing on how the supervised person's disposition to cooperate can be affected by the nature of the interaction with the supervisor and by the use of flexible and responsive approaches to securing compliance. They also point out the different meanings of compliance, ranging from superficial conformity to an internalised willingness to comply, based on a belief that cooperation is the right thing to do. Perhaps it also helps us to understand some offenders' attitudes to compliance when we consider our own attitudes to paying taxes! In another illustration of how compliance issues in supervision reflect the wider political and regulatory context, Trish McCulloch reports a study of community service in which the contradictory objectives of this kind of sentence (is it primarily for punishment, or for reparation, or to assist the offender by forming a bridge to a better life?) combine to confuse both supervisors and offenders about the best ways to manage compliance. The coherent strategies needed to make supervision work may not sit easily with political representations of offender management.

The contexts of supervision

The final section of the book expands our analytical gaze further still, by seeking to locate offender supervision not just in its professional, political and social contexts, but in some historical context.

Faye Taxman, Craig Henderson and Jennifer Lerch's chapter reports the findings from an extensive survey of correctional administrators in the USA. Its key contribution is to unpick aspects of the nexus of relationships between the contested goals of criminal justice organisations, their varied engagements with different forms of evidence, and the range of dispositions that their professionals evidence. Having outlined a shift in corrections in the USA from an emphasis on enforcement to an emphasis on accountability (for public safety) to a hybrid model combining accountability and rehabilitation, Taxman and her colleagues demonstrate how administrators engage with 'evidence-based practices' in different ways in the service of different goals. Their findings – when set alongside those of other surveys – suggest that US correctional agencies now confront key issues about their goals and identities, as well as about their uses of evidence. Which forms of evidence matter will depend on which goals are to be prioritised – and so the theoretical (or perhaps normative) framework for US correctional work needs to be clarified.

Despite a markedly different approach, Tim Chapman's chapter discusses precisely the same issues. Essentially, Chapman provides a reflective account of the process of working with and for the Scottish government to develop new national objectives and standards for criminal justice social work; in other words, his task was to provide precisely the kind of clarification of goals and methods for which Taxman and her colleagues call. Chapman uses the concept of capital – intellectual, human, social, organisational and political – to organise the story of this particular reform effort. He discusses a careful process of consultation undertaken in pursuit of a consensus around central questions about goals, methods and evidence, and arrives at a *résumé* of the resulting objectives and standards. Both this process and its outcomes should be of interest to those involved in similar services in any jurisdiction.

John Deering's chapter offers yet another different methodological approach but sticks with similar themes concerning probation practitioners' (this time in England and Wales) attitudes, values and beliefs, exploring the extent to which 'real practice' has been transformed in the manner suggested by some recent theories of penal reconfiguration. Analysing findings drawn from an impressive range of mainly qualitative methods, Deering concludes that there is evidence of both continuity and change in 'real practice'. Change is reflected in an increasing focus on cognitive behavioural work, the use of accredited programmes and the more rigid application of enforcement standards. Continuity is represented in the continued insistence on balancing care and control and on taking an individualised approach to cases. That said, he suggests that there is clear opposition to the managerialisation of practice, with probation staff (still) deriving their job satisfaction from building relationships with offenders to work on issues that contributed to their offending. Thus: 'There is no wholesale rejection of the government's agenda, but a different emphasis is placed on "help", discretion and individual factors ... aspects of the "new penality" seem to correspond more closely to policy than everyday practice.'

Further evidence about continuity and change in probation discourses and practices is provided in the pilot study of the historical development of pre-sentence reports in England and Wales reported in the chapter by Loraine Gelsthorpe, Peter Raynor and Gwen

Robinson. Drawing on six small samples of reports from 1964, 1984–85, 1991, 1998, 2006 and 2009, Gelsthorpe and colleagues examine the conceptualisation and portrayal of offenders and their needs contained within the reports. They note a tendency towards greater discussion of risk, a recent shift towards more negative portrayals of offenders, and some changes in the ways in which proposals are crafted. Although measured in their assessment of the limitations of their pilot study, the authors are surely right to conclude that they have established the need for a larger-scale examination of these shifting discursive constructions of offenders, and of their impacts on sentencing.

Developing the historical theme, Fergus McNeill's chapter presents the findings from a recent oral history project examining probationers' experiences of supervision in Scotland in the 1960s. Having noted that this study was not conducted principally to advance debates about 'what works?', and having provided some discussion of the strengths and weaknesses of oral testimony as a form of evidence in such debates, McNeill nonetheless provides an intriguing insight into how the experience of probation was recalled by those subject to it over 40 years ago. The ex-probationers reveal the extent to which the experience and impact of probation was contingent on the qualities of the officer and on his or her capacity to bridge the 'social distance' between offender and practitioner. As well as questioning what probation supervision actually means and what it is, the chapter also raises important questions about the longer-term impacts of interventions and about the role of 'moral performance' in supporting legitimate interventions that can foster change.

In the final substantive chapter in the collection, Mike Nellis turns our attention to one of the potential futures of offender supervision. Nellis provides a detailed and nuanced account of the emergence and significance of electronic monitoring (EM) as a new form of (or contribution to) offender supervision in the UK. Leaving aside debates about the purely punitive or putatively incapacitating uses of EM, Nellis concerns himself with the more interesting and challenging question of whether EM has a useful part to play in an integrated form of offender management that seeks reduced reoffending in the longer term. In other words: can EM support rehabilitation? Nellis' analysis of policy developments in the UK suggests that at least some policy-makers, regulators and practitioners are beginning to reconsider and reconceptualise EM in more rehabilitative terms. However, the legacy of 'parallel tracks' in the development of EM and of rehabilitative interventions is a limited (if encouraging) research base on just how, when and with whom their integration works best.

Conclusion

Finally, we think that this collection offers unambiguous evidence of the range and ambition of current thinking and research on the supervision of offenders. No longer confined to the correctional focus of 'what works', the scope has expanded to question and investigate the purposes of supervision, the legitimacy of supervising agencies, the skills and qualities of practitioners, the impact of politics and policy, the roles of families and communities and many other broader questions. These in turn bring new insights to the pursuit of effective practice. However, the right balance of effort is important: much of this work stands at the intersection of criminology and social work, two disciplines well known for a tendency to generate rather more theory than the kind of empirical findings that can help to shape better practice.

A narrow focus on the pursuit of effective methods without an awareness of context or of their meanings in the lives of supervised offenders runs the risk of repeating the experience of England and Wales, where many promising developments drawn from international research on 'what works' were compromised by an overcentralised and managerialist implementation process and a punitive political climate (Raynor 2007; Whitehead 2007). The opposite risk, perhaps, is that we generate theoretical positions that are attractive and persuasive in themselves, but need much more research and development before they can underpin improved practices. Research of the kind that can produce convincing evidence of positive impacts takes a long time to produce, and so will usually lag behind theoretical developments. There is a further lag before research findings are reflected in practice (if at all), and this reflection is often partial, piecemeal and not a little haphazard – but from the offender's point of view, the service they receive *is* the practice and not the theory. We still need a better understanding of what goes right and wrong in implementation, and why. In the meantime, an important priority is to devise and carry out the research studies that can throw light on the practical implications and potential impact of new forms of practice guided by an improved theoretical rationale.

Many of the chapters in this book show how the study of offender supervision and community penalties is not just a narrow technical interest, but intersects with other fields of social and political science. To take one example, research on compliance with community penalties covers a range from the dynamics of interaction between offenders and their supervisors to how compliance might become desistance, how compliance is affected by the perceived legitimacy of criminal justice agencies, and what kind of practices enhance perceived legitimacy. This in turn raises questions about the policy context, the goals of criminal justice, and the role of the state. Many of us would argue that the state's demand that citizens obey the law has greater legitimacy when the state also aims to guarantee basic necessities and security, so that a crime-free 'good life' can become an achievable goal. For similar reasons, many commentators argue that the provision of rehabilitative services is a state obligation and duty (Carlen 1994; Rotman 1990). Seen in this way, compliance becomes part of a social contract that makes demands on the state and society as well as the offender. Studying the micro system of detailed interaction between offenders and their supervisors leads unavoidably to consideration of the macro systems of policy and social order.

Of course, the realities of working in criminal justice do not always, or often, live up to these high ideals. Regrettably, most of the contributors to this book are working in countries where current policies will increase rather than reduce general levels of punishment and incarceration. The three editors have between us over a century of experience of criminal justice practice and policy, and we know how little weight evidence and sound argument can carry when a politician sees an opportunity for a display of 'toughness'. But it is also clear that the nature and goals of criminal justice systems are good tests of the kind of society we want to be. The Scottish Prisons Commission, when they chose the title *Scotland's Choice* for their report on the use of imprisonment (Scottish Prisons Commission 2008), were making the point that our policy and practice choices in criminal justice are an integral part of what citizenship in a particular society means; like it or not, for better or worse, these choices express who we are. How we treat offenders is a part of how we treat everybody, and each other. As scholars we have a duty to carry out and communicate honest and thorough research; as citizens we want to contribute to social progress and improvement. We hope that this book contributes to building the case that progress is both necessary and possible. The collective experience of the contributors runs not just to hundreds but to thousands of years, and encompasses 11 countries: the breadth and potential of this new research network is astonishing, and marks, we hope, a decisive step forward.

For the future, we hope that CREDOS will generate more international and comparative work: the current volume mainly contains studies carried out in one country with wider implications rather than studies carried out with an international design. We would also hope to see a gradual shift away from the current situation in which almost all the reported research comes from Western anglophone countries. But only four years ago even the current level of international communication in offender supervision research did not exist, until the attractions of Monash University's Italian base in Tuscany brought us together. We hope that this will be the first of many edited collections brought together through CREDOS.

Notes

1 The Offender Assessment System (OASys) was introduced by the Home Office for use in England and Wales from 2001. It is a 'third generation' tool employing both clinical and actuarial measures to provide an assessment of an individual's criminogenic needs, as well as risk of both reoffending and harm. It is seen as essential to offender management and sentence planning.

2 The multi-agency public protection arrangements (MAPPA) were introduced in England and Wales in 2000 under the Criminal Justice and Court Services Act. They involve chief constables and chief officers of probation exercising a duty to implement inter-agency cooperation intended to assess and manage the risks posed by violent and sexual offenders. These procedures were extended under the Criminal Justice Act 2003 to include a wider list of statutory partners.

3 The National Probation Service for England and Wales (NPS) was created in 2001. Prior to this, the service had consisted of 54 semi-autonomous bodies with considerable independence and control over policy and practice locally. One of the reasons behind the setting up of the NPS was to enable central government to exercise control over such policy and practice.

4 From 1 April 2010, the previous 42 probation areas and trusts have become 34 trusts. In due course, under contestability, each may be subject to widespread competition to provide 'probation services' to the director of offender management (DOM). Competition may come from private or voluntary organisations, or even from other trusts. This in turn may lead to a particular trust 'going out of business', should it lose contracts with the DOM.

References

Andrews, D.A. and Kiessling, J.J. (1980) 'Program structure and effective correctional practices: a summary of the CaVic research', in R.R. Ross and P. Gendreau (eds) *Effective Correctional Treatment*. Toronto: Butterworth.

Bonta, J., Rugge, T., Scott, T., Bourgon, G. and Yessine, A. (2008) 'Exploring the black box of offender supervision', *Journal of Offender Reahabilitation*, 47: 248–70.

Carlen, P. (1994) 'Crime, inequality and sentencing', in A. Duff and D. Garland (eds) *A Reader on Punishment*. Oxford: Oxford University Press.

McIvor, G. and Raynor, P. (eds) (2007) *Developments in Work with Offenders*. London: Jessica Kingsley.

Raynor, P. (2007) 'Community penalties: probation, 'what works' and offender management', in M. Maguire, R. Morgan and R. Reiner (eds) *The Oxford Handbook of Criminology*, 4th edn. Oxford: Oxford University Press.

Rotman, E. (1990) *Beyond Punishment: A New View of the Rehabilitation of Offenders*. Westport, CT: Greenwood Press.

Scottish Prisons Commission (2008) *Scotland's Choice*. Edinburgh: Scottish Prisons Commission.

Trotter, C. (1996) 'The impact of different supervision practices in community corrections: cause for optimism', *Australian and New Zealand Journal of Criminology* 29: 1–18.

Whitehead, P. (2007) *Modernising Probation and Criminal Justice*. Crayford: Shaw and Sons.

Index

Aboriginal research officers, use of 135
accountability (probation reform) 412–13
adolescence-limited criminality 73
amoral calculators 370, 379
A Secular Age 315
ASPIRE 158
assessment, family-focused 267–9
ASSET 157
attachment theory 196
authority, effective use of 116–17

Bail Accommodation and Support
    Service (BASS) 523–4
Bail Act 1976 522–3
Bayesian information criterion (BIC) 417
bonding capital 259
bootstrap LRT (BLRT) 417, 420tab
Bottoms' fourfold explanatory
    framework of compliance 370–2,
    386–8
breach 453, 467
    and community penalties 370
    compliance 378, 459
    electronic monitoring 512
    National Standards 326, 330, 340, 459
    offender supervision 431, 502, 505

California Personality Inventory
    Socialisation Scale 131
Cambridge Study in Delinquent
    Development (CSDD) 68

capital, forms of 434–7
Carter Report 477, 513, 519
case management 344–61
    in community corrections 347–8
    context of 349–52
    corrections, meaning of term 345–6
    defining 347
    evaluating outcomes 348–9
    inter-agency partnerships 356–9
    models and outcomes 353–5
    perspectives of the 'case managed'
        359–60
    rise of 346–7
    rise of specialist 355–6
    and 'what works' 352–3
'central eight' risk/needs factors 26
'certificates of good conduct' 79
'certificates of rehabilitation' *see*
    certificates of good conduct
Circles of Support and Accountability
    see COSA
ClearSprings 523, 526
client socialisation *see* role clarification
clinical supervision 94–5, 99, 106–7,
    109–10
C-NOMIS 514, 516, 519
coding of observations 136–7, 138
coercive cycles 74
cognitive behavioural programmes 133–4
Collaboration of Researchers for the
    Effective Development of Offender

Supervision *see* CREDOS
collaboration with community, trained
volunteers and faith traditions 301–18
community development approach
310–13
COSA 302–3, 310
creating a volunteer and community
development system 317–18
external perspectives 307–10
external resources 305–7
humanistic, spiritual and religious
volunteers 313–17
integrated model for corrections
304–5
collaborative family problem-solving
model 286–98
application and evaluation of the
model 292–5
model, description of 287–92
research support 297
worker's views 296–7
community justice centres 221
community orders 219–22, 230–1, 511
Criminal Justice Act 2003 329, 512,
520, 524
Community Payback 222, 401, 405, 431
Community Punishment Pathfinder
project 385, 390, 402
Community Service (CS) 384–404
compliance and 388–92
nature of work within 398–9, 400
see also compliance within
Community Service
compliance 367–80
Bottoms' fourfold explanatory
framework 370–2
definitions and dimensions of 368–71
dynamic model of 374–7, 378
explaining compliance with
community penalties 370–4
compliance with community penalties
(study) 324–40
addressing obstacles to compliance
331–3
developing an effective compliance
strategy 336–9
identifying effective compliance
strategies 326–7
impact of the quality of interactions
333–4

individualised responses to non-
compliance 334–6
managing contradictions to secure
compliance 330–1
methodology 328–30
compliance within Community Service
384–404
complexity of compliance 403–4
help support and guidance 401–3
problem solving approach 402
research study 392–400
revisiting the CS role and task 400–1
understanding 386–8
constraint-based compliance 328, 370tab,
371, 388
contradictions, managing 330–4
practical 331–3
relational 333–4
structural 334–6
core correctional practice skills (CCPs)
115–16, 199
correctional agencies, implementing
evidence-based practises in 172–90
abolishing work unrelated to core
practices 188–9
data drives mid-course adjustments
190
factors affecting likelihood of
implementation 177–9
factors predicting the adoption of in
US 175–7
five step methodology for full usage
of 187–8
goals and objectives 189
handling of competing values by
administrators 179–83
learning culture 189
reform strategies 183–8
vision and mission 188
Correctional Services Review 513
COSA 302–3, 308
court reports, history of in England and
Wales 471–5
reports in the 1960s and 1970s 472–3
reports in the 1980s 473–4
reports in the 1990s 474–5
CREDOS, statement of objectives and
principles 2–4
crime prevention programmes,
effectiveness of family-based 284–5

Criminal Justice Act 1991 474–5, 480
Criminal Justice Act 2003 512
Criminal Justice and Court Services Act
2000 511, 512
Criminal Justice and Immigration Act
2008 523
Criminal Justice and Licensing (Scotland)
Bill 222
criminal justice social work, revising the
National Outcomes and Standards in
Scotland 430–47
aim of the new standards 446
capital as an organising principle for
the process of revision 434–7
history and context 430–2
process of balancing and integrating
capitals 445–6
process of understanding what is
required 437–45
revision of the National Outcomes
and Standards for 432–4
criminogenic needs 20, 26–9
cumulative continuity 74, 75

'death of rehabilitation' 461
dedicated drug courts (DDCs) 220, 225
desistance
'certification' stage of 76
Good Lives Model and 57–61
labelling perspective on 76–8
and reciprocity 261–2
desistance paradigm 65–81
implications of pro-social labelling
perspective for policy 78–80
labelling perspective on desistance 76–8
labelling perspective on persistance
73–6
promise of 66–72
deterrent enforcement framework 325,
331, 333, 334, 337
Dodge, Kenneth 73
drug courts 216–17, 219, 223, 228
Scottish 220
drug treatment and testing orders
(DTTOs) 219–20, 222

ecomaps 247–50 267, 268, 272
EFQM excellence model 441
electronic monitoring (EM) 509–29
bail and the reduction of remand in
custody 522–4
early release and home detention
curfew 525–8
as a licence condition 526–7
making integration happen 519–22
and the offender management model
514–15
and the probation service 510–13
towards convergence, EM and NOMS
513–14
towards integration, audit and
inspection 515–19
young offenders and intensive
supervision 524–5
Electronic Monitoring Team (EMT)
513–14, 520
end of custody licence (ECL) 525–6
enforcement (probation reform) 411–12
'Engaging Communities in Criminal
Justice' 221–2, 226
entropy 417, 420tab
evidence-based practises 172–90, 304–5,
409–26
defining EBP 174
implementing in correctional agencies
172–90
methodology 174–5
results 175–86
reforms in probation agencies
409–26
methodology 413–17
results 418–24
evocative interactions 74
exoneration 272

faith traditions, collaboration with 302–3,
313–17
families and community corrections
241–54
applying a family focused approach
to community supervision 245–7
case studies
multi-agency collaboration 253–4
Oklahoma Department of
Corrections 250
families as context 242
family mapping 247–50
integrating the family-focused
approach at the agency level
250–4

and social networks a a resource for 243–5
families of offenders 282–98
  collaborative family problem-solving 286–98
  and criminality 282–3
  interventions can be effective 284
  principles of effective work with offenders 285–6
  and reoffending 283–4
family dynamics in offender supervision 273–7
  reaching out 273–4
  redefining incongruence 274
  siding 274
  working with responsiveness 277
family-focused supervision 269–72
family group conference 270
family matters in offender supervision 257–77
  applying the framework 267–72
  contextual perspective 261–4
  knowledge base: role of the family in delinquency and desistance 258–64
  offenders and family problems 258–61
  systems framework for offender supervision 264–7
fast delivery report (FDR) 478–9
first-generation risk assessment 24
formal compliance 369–70, 386–7, 390
four Rs model 437–9, 443–4
fourth-generation risk assessment instruments 25, 28, 155, 160
functional family therapy (FFT) 285

general personality and cognitive social learning perspective (GPCSL) 19, 23, 33–4
generic case management models 354–5
Gleuk, Sheldon and Eleanor 68
Good Lives Model (GLM) of offender rehabilitation 41–61, 162–5, 196–7, 486, 534–5
  aetiological assumptions of 52–5
  and desistance 57–61
  five phases of 56–7
  implications of for practice 55–7
  principles, aims and values of 45–52
  ecological selves 50–1

  embodiment, plasticity, cognitive extension 45–7
  goods and risks 50
  nature of intervention 52
  nature of risk 51
  primary human goods 47–9
  values and practical identities 49–50
Good Without God: What a Billion Nonreligious People Do Believe 315
GPCSL perspective *see* general personality and cognitive social learning perspective
GRIPP program 293
Grounded Theory methodology 328

habitual compliance 328, 370tab, 388
Halliday Report 221, 512, 513
Hanson, Damien 158, 159
Home Detention Curfews 516, 523, 524, 545–6
hostile attribution bias 73
human capital 434–5, 441–3
humanistic way of making meaning 314–15
hybrid of accountability and rehabilitation (probation reform) 413
hybrid case management models 354

Inside-Out programme 314
instrumental compliance 328, 370, 387–8
integrated model for corrections 304–5
intellectual capital 435, 437–9
Intensive Monitoring and Support Services (ISMS) 524
Intensive Supervision and Surveillance Programme (ISSP) 511, 524–5
interpersonal skills 118, 119

Jersey Study 113–27
  designing and using the instrument 121–7
  evaluating the methodology 120–1
  methodology of the study 115–19
judicial involvement in offender management 215–34
  arguments against 228–33
  blurring of professional boundaries and competences 229–31
  erosion of due process 232–3

revival of the rehabilitative ideal
and new forms of surveillance
228–9
benefits of 223–7
accommodating diversity 226–7
achieving improved compliance
and outcomes 224–6
enhancing sentence's job
satisfaction 227
improving court processes
223–4
developments in the UK 219–23
emergence of specialist courts
and therapeutic jurisprudence
216–19

Kierkegaard, Hugh 302
'knifing-off' 78

La Bodega de la Familia 243, 245
labelling model for desistance-based
practice 72–80
implications of the pro-social
labelling perspective for policy
78–80
perspective on desistance 76–8
perspective on persistence 73–7
labelling theory 74–5
language of condemnation/
transformation 308–10
latent class analysis 416–17, 419
Level of Service Inventory/Case
Management Inventory 25, 160
licence conditions 526–7
life-course persistent criminality 73
Lo-Mendell-Rubin Liklihood Ratio Test
(L-M-R LRT) 417
longer-term legal compliance 368, 386,
391–2
loyalty, family 263–4

managerialism 477
Maruna's study of offenders 196
mentoring 305–7
merit 263–4
Model Borough 195
Monckton, John, murder of 158
Morison Committee 472–3
motivational interviewing skills 116,
118–19

motivational postures of tax-payers
372–4
multi-agency public protection
arrangements (MAPPA) 156, 462, 525,
546n2
multi-lateral bias 264
multi-systemic therapy (MST) 285

National Criminal Justice Treatment
Practices (NCJTP) survey 174, 413
National Offender Management Service
(NOMS) 159, 513–14
National Outcomes and Standards
see criminal justice social work in
Scotland, revising the National
Outcomes and Standards
National Standards 325–6, 339, 340, 378,
435, 468n2
New Labour 65
new penology 476
'new rehabilitationism' 157
New South Wales juvenile justice study
135–51
client's perspective 149–50
limitations 137–8
methodology 135–7
results 138–49
Nigh, Reverend Harry 302
NOMS case management model 158
NOMS National Operations Group
(NOG) 519–20
NOMS offender management model 161,
199, 453
'non-treatment' paradigm 69
normative compliance 328, 337, 338,
370tab, 371–2, 388
North Liverpool Community Justice
Centre 221, 225, 230
'nothing works' 30, 285, 455, 461, 473

OASys 157, 456, 458–9, 477–8
observation instrument 115–19
observational techniques, of social
research 120–1
Offender Assessment System tool see
OASys
Offender Groups Reconviction Scale
(OGRS) 478, 479
Offender Management Act 2007 477
Offender Management Model 514–15

offender rehabilitation 29–34
  brief history of 29–30
  generality of the RNR model 33–4
  RNR model and 30–3
offender risk assessment 26–9
  need principle 26–8
  responsivity principle 28–9
  risk principle 26
offender supervision
  clarification of term 4–5
  four dimensions of 264–7
offender tiering bands 156, 157, 158
officer behaviour and technology
  transfer measurement 101–3
  assessment of officers 101–2
  assessment of participation 102–3
Olson's circumplex model of family
  functioning 274
Oregon Department of Corrections
  313–14, 317
organisational capital 435

'parallel tracks' 510–13, 515, 517, 518,
  528, 543
persistence, labelling perspective on 73–6
person-environment interactions 73–4
police court missions 472
political capital 436, 439–41
populist punitiveness 471, 475–6, 478
positive deviance approach 312
positive engagement 486, 538
practical reasoning 41
pre-sentence reports (PSRs) 456–9,
  471–87
  central role of risk measurement
    477–81
  context for recent changes 475–7
  dominance of risk 481–5
  history of development of court
    reports 471–5
primary human goods 47–9
Prisoner Rehabilitation Authority (Israel)
  271
proactive interactions 73
probation, history of reform in 411–13
Probation of Offenders' Act 1907 472
problem-solving courts 215–16
problem-solving skills 117, 132, 141–5
progress courts 222
Project Greenlight 93–4

pro-social modelling 116, 117, 118, 162,
  288, 287, 391
  and reinforcement 131–2, 145–6
prudential compliance see instrumental
  compliance
'Pygmalion effects' 76–8
Pygmalion in the Classroom 76

quality, checklist of 114
quality assurance 480–1

Rasch model 177–8, 189
reactive interactions 73
'Ready4Work: An Ex-prisoner,
  Community and Faith Initiative' 306
Red Hook Community Court 221, 224,
  226
Rehabilitation of Offenders Act 1974 79
rehabilitative ideal 228–9
rehabilitation 438, 443
reintegration 438, 444
relational ethics 262, 266–7
relationship skills 133, 146–9
religious volunteers 313–17
reparation 438, 443
restorative justice 165
restrictions 438–9, 444
Rice, Anthony 159
risk assessment
  history of 23–5
  see also risk, needs and strengths
    assessment; risk measurement
risk classifications 157
risk measurement, central role of 477–81
  contemporary reports in context 478–80
  effectiveness 480–1
risk-need instruments see third-
  generation risk assessment
  instruments
risk-need-responsivity model see RNR
  model
risk, needs and strengths assessment
  155–66
  impact on the supervision of
    offenders 158–61
  meshing of risk and needs 156–8
  rediscovering the worker–offender
    relationship 161–2
RNR model 19–36, 201, 486, 534–5
  and offender rehabilitation 30–3

and offender risk assessment 26–9
generality of 33–4
principles 19–23
role clarification 132–3, 139–41, 351, 353, 359
'Routes Out of Prison' 306
routine compliance 370tab, 371

Salford Community Justice Initiative 221, 223–4, 225, 230, 231
Scottish probation, oral histories of 492–506
    from court to probation 495–8
    impacts and imprints 504–5
    method and analysis 493–5
    on probation, helping, holding and hurting 498–503
    probation methods 503–4
'seamless sentences' 512, 514
second-generation risk assessment instruments 24–5
short-term requirement compliance 368–9, 386, 391
skills
    for working with involuntary clients 351
    and strategies in probation supervision 113–27
    and techniques of officers 103–9
social capital 259, 260, 435–6, 441–2
social enquiry report (SER) 473, 475
SOLER test 119
specialist case management models 354
specialist courts, emergence of 216–19
spiritual volunteers 313–17
standard delivery report (SDR) 478–9
staff training 94–5
Strategic Training Initiative in Community Supervision (STICS) 92, 96–110
    clients 97–8
    control group 98
    feedback 100, 103
    implications 109–10
    initial training 98–9
    monthly meetings 99–100, 102–3
    officer behaviour 101–3
    probation officers 96–7
    refresher course 100, 103
    results 103–9

strengths-based approach see Good Lives Model (GLM)
Streatfield Report 472
Structured Supervision Programme (SSP) 193–212
    benefits of 210–12
    content of 197–9
    evaluation of 200–1
    getting offenders onto the programme 202
    history of 194–5
    impact on offenders 207–10
    one to one format 205–6
    reactions to programme content 206–7
    supporting programme delivery 199–200
    take-up of the programme 203–5
    targeting of 201–2
    theoretical approach 195–7
substantive compliance 369–70, 386–7, 390
supervision, purposes of 451–67
    results of the study 455–64
        assessment of offenders 456–9
        enforcement of order and licences 459–61
        overall beliefs about purpose 456
        practitioner values 462–4
        supervision practice 461–2
        use of other sources 464
    the study 454
    theoretical and policy context 452–3
supervision skills 130–51
    application of effective practice principles 134–5
    effective 130–3
    New South Wales juvenile justice study 135–51
support, during probation 498–503

tax payers, behaviours of 372–4
technology transfer 91–110
    challenge of 92–4
    officer behaviour and 101–3
    staff training 94–5
    STICS 96–110
The Risk of Harm Guidance and Training Resource 160
The Voice of the Past 494

therapeutic integrity 134
therapeutic jurisprudence 217–19
third–generation risk assessment
    instruments 25, 28
triangulation 137

version 7C 121, 122, 123–7
VicSafe 292, 296
volunteers, trained 302–3

'what works' 65, 66, 69, 91, 92, 173, 431,
    544

White, Elliot 158, 159
Williams, Peter 512–13
worker-offender relationship 161–2, 333–4
workshop training 94–5
wraparound model 270–1, 539

youth courts 220, 231
Youth Offending Team (YOT) 512–13
youth rehabilitation order 524

Zamble and Quinsey's study of
    ex-prisoners 196